Professional Silverlight 2 for ASP.NET Developers

Introduction xxi

Part I: Silverlight Fundamentals for ASP.NET Developers   1

Chapter 1: Silverlight in a Nutshell 3
Chapter 2: Silverlight Architecture 9
Chapter 3: XAML Condensed 31
Chapter 4: Programming Silverlight 63

Part II: Developing ASP.NET Applications with Silverlight   119

Chapter 5: Creating the User Interface 121
Chapter 6: Silverlight Controls 167
Chapter 7: Styles and Templates 213
Chapter 8: User Interaction 243
Chapter 9: Communicating with the Server. 285
Chapter 10: Working with Data 361
Chapter 11: Creating Custom Controls. 423
Chapter 12: Securing Your Silverlight Application 461
Chapter 13: Audio and Video 481
Chapter 14: Graphics and Animation 515
Chapter 15: Troubleshooting 559
Chapter 16: Performance. 589
Index 621

D1402300

Professional
Silverlight™ 2 for ASP.NET Developers

Professional
Silverlight™ 2 for ASP.NET Developers

Jonathan Swift
Chris Barker
Dan Wahlin
Salvador Alvarez Patuel

Wiley Publishing, Inc.

Professional Silverlight™ 2 for ASP.NET Developers

Published by
Wiley Publishing, Inc.
10475 Crosspoint Boulevard
Indianapolis, IN 46256
www.wiley.com

Copyright © 2009 by Wiley Publishing, Inc., Indianapolis, Indiana

Published simultaneously in Canada

ISBN: 978-0-470-27775-1

Manufactured in the United States of America

10 9 8 7 6 5 4 3 2 1

Library of Congress Cataloging-in-Publication Data is available from the publisher.

No part of this publication may be reproduced, stored in a retrieval system or transmitted in any form or by any means, electronic, mechanical, photocopying, recording, scanning or otherwise, except as permitted under Sections 107 or 108 of the 1976 United States Copyright Act, without either the prior written permission of the Publisher, or authorization through payment of the appropriate per-copy fee to the Copyright Clearance Center, 222 Rosewood Drive, Danvers, MA 01923, (978) 750-8400, fax (978) 646-8600. Requests to the Publisher for permission should be addressed to the Legal Department, Wiley Publishing, Inc., 10475 Crosspoint Blvd., Indianapolis, IN 46256, (317) 572-3447, fax (317) 572-4355, or online at www.wiley.com/go/permissions.

Limit of Liability/Disclaimer of Warranty: The publisher and the author make no representations or warranties with respect to the accuracy or completeness of the contents of this work and specifically disclaim all warranties, including without limitation warranties of fitness for a particular purpose. No warranty may be created or extended by sales or promotional materials. The advice and strategies contained herein may not be suitable for every situation. This work is sold with the understanding that the publisher is not engaged in rendering legal, accounting, or other professional services. If professional assistance is required, the services of a competent professional person should be sought. Neither the publisher nor the author shall be liable for damages arising herefrom. The fact that an organization or Website is referred to in this work as a citation and/or a potential source of further information does not mean that the author or the publisher endorses the information the organization or Website may provide or recommendations it may make. Further, readers should be aware that Internet Websites listed in this work may have changed or disappeared between when this work was written and when it is read.

For general information on our other products and services please contact our Customer Care Department within the United States at (800) 762-2974, outside the United States at (317) 572-3993 or fax (317) 572-4002.

Trademarks: Wiley, the Wiley logo, Wrox, the Wrox logo, Wrox Programmer to Programmer, and related trade dress are trademarks or registered trademarks of John Wiley & Sons, Inc. and/or its affiliates, in the United States and other countries, and may not be used without written permission. Silverlight is a trademark of Microsoft Corporation in the United States and/or other countries. All other trademarks are the property of their respective owners. Wiley Publishing, Inc., is not associated with any product or vendor mentioned in this book.

Wiley also publishes its books in a variety of electronic formats. Some content that appears in print may not be available in electronic books.

To my wife, Fay.
— Jonathan Swift

In memory of Patricia Barker.
— Chris Barker

I thank my wife, Heedy, and two boys, Danny and Jeffery, for their patience, love,
and support while I was working on this book.
— Dan Wahlin

Dedicado a Marta y a mi familia.
— Salvador Alvarez Patuel

About the Authors

Jonathan Swift worked as an Application Development Consultant for Microsoft in the United Kingdom for a number of years and now finds himself managing the team. This means that he spends most of his time traveling around the country helping clients utilize Microsoft developer technologies effectively. Jonathan has been programming for more than 13 years and has worked with numerous technologies, including but not limited to C, C++, Visual Basic, COM, COM+, SQL, ASP, and, of course, all aspects of .NET. As well as programming, Jonathan also spent part of his career working as a Microsoft Trainer, delivering the full suite of Microsoft Official Curriculum courses and specially-designed courses also.

Jonathan tries to keep his blog (`http://blogs.msdn.com/jonathanswift`) up to date, but feels that writing a book is a very good excuse for not doing so. (Other popular excuses including playing the XBox and washing his hair.) When he's not working, Jonathan spends all of his time with his wife and kids, and occasionally gets to exercise his pilot's license at the flying club.

Chris Barker works as an Application Development Consultant for Microsoft in the United Kingdom (`www.microsoft.com/uk/adc`). He spends his days traveling around the country visiting customers and consulting on development practices on the Microsoft platform. More recently, his interest has been captured by RIA development, and as a result, he has delivered several customer workshops on Silverlight. Away from the office, Chris likes to get out and about in his home county of Derbyshire, riding a bike, kicking a football, and sinking a few pints of real ale.

Dan Wahlin (Microsoft Most Valuable Professional for Connected Systems) is a .NET development instructor and architecture consultant at Interface Technical Training (`www.interfacett.com`). Dan founded the XML for ASP.NET Developers web site (`www.xmlforasp.net`), which focuses on using ASP.NET, Silverlight, AJAX, and XML Web Services in Microsoft's .NET platform. He's also on the INETA Speaker's Bureau and speaks at several conferences. Dan has authored/co-authored numerous books over the years on .NET technologies with his latest being *Professional ASP.NET 3.5 AJAX* and *Professional Silverlight 2 for ASP.NET Developers*. Dan also writes for several online technical newsletters, blogs at `http://weblogs.asp.net/dwahlin`, and updates what he's up to from time to time at `www.twitter.com/danwahlin`. When he's not working with technology, he enjoys sports and writing and recording music to relax a little — `http://weblogs.asp.net/dwahlin/archive/tags/Music/default.aspx`.

Salvador Alvarez Patuel has been in the industry for more than 13 years. Currently a senior application development consultant (ADC) at Microsoft, helping customers to architect and build complex solutions using Microsoft technologies in the United Kingdom. Salvador has also been delivering multiple technical sessions around EMEA on Windows Mobile development and has been answering questions on many ask-the-experts events. Before joining Microsoft, he was the main technical architect for real-time engines on popular auctions, TV channels, and the gaming industry. He holds a software engineering degree from his native Argentina and a specialization in artificial intelligence. When Salva is not thinking about ones and zeroes, he enjoys climbing, windsurfing, and recently trying to learn how to play golf.

Credits

Executive Editor
Robert Elliott

Development Editor
Kelly Talbot

Technical Editor
Dave Friedel

Senior Production Editor
Debra Banninger

Copy Editor
Cate Caffrey

Editorial Manager
Mary Beth Wakefield

Production Manager
Tim Tate

Vice President and Executive Group Publisher
Richard Swadley

Vice President and Executive Publisher
Joseph B. Wikert

Project Coordinator, Cover
Lynsey Stanford

Compositor
James D. Kramer, Happenstance Type-O-Rama

Proofreader
Publication Services, Inc.

Indexer
Jack Lewis

Acknowledgments

It turns out that writing a book is a much more challenging affair than you think it's going to be. And I mean by a long way. For the past 18 months since this book was first conceived, there hasn't been a single day go by when I haven't worried about falling behind schedule or not getting finished at all. Remember as a kid when you had some homework to hand in or an exam to revise, and every day leading up to it you knew you should be doing something? Well, that's close to how taking on this book has been, but only close!

This brings me nicely to my first acknowledgement, which is, of course, to my wife, Fay, and our two children, Jonah and Stirling, who've put up with me being a little grumpier (just a little, mind ...) than usual in recent times owing in the whole to the large project that this book has been. Thanks for putting up with me, and I hope you enjoy laughing at my picture on the front cover as much as the readers will!

Secondly, I'd like to thank the other authors in this book, quite literally without whom this book would be, well, about half as long. Chris, for listening to endless late-night and early-morning phone calls — usually from a train so via a poor signal — and helping me correct coding errors, I thank you. Salvador, for stepping in at short notice and lending your Silverlight expertise to this book, as well as endearing it to the female population via your front cover photo, I thank you. And Dan, for getting through your chapters on schedule, providing useful hints and a professional attitude, I thank you also.

Finally, I'd like to say a big thank you to my parents, Linton and Julie, without whose collective genes I wouldn't have become the geek I am today. This coupled with inheriting my father's passion for reading Sci-Fi, of course. Ta very much!

— *Jonathan Swift*

Contributing to this book has been quite a journey, and I am sure that those around me have felt as though they had been writing the book themselves! With that said, I would like to show my gratitude by giving them a mention here. First and foremost, I would like to thank my family — David Barker, Matt Barker, and Marie Barker. In particular, I would like to thank my late mother, Patricia Barker, whose support in my early years is greatly missed.

— *Chris Barker*

I'd like to thank my wife, Heedy, and two boys, Danny and Jeffery, for putting up with the long hours I spend in the office studying new technologies and writing books and articles. I love them and sincerely appreciate their patience with me. I'm extremely lucky to have such a great family.

I'd also like to thank my Mom and Dad, Danny and Elaine, for bringing me up in such a positive, caring environment where succeeding in life was always encouraged. I love both of you and am forever in your debt for the years of service you've given and the many life lessons you've taught me.

— *Dan Wahlin*

Acknowledgments

I would like to dedicate this book to my wife, Marta, for supporting and loving me. She has given me all the strength needed to embark on this adventure. Marta, I really love you. The other big important part of my life is my family — Graciela (ma) and Daniel (pa); my grandparents, Irene, Angel, Coca, and Hugo; my brother Rodrigo; and my sister Macarena. I want to include them in this dedication as they have given me all their support and love no matter how far we are from each other. To them I say: I owe you everything. Los quiero mucho!

I want also to thank my friends Ata, Gei, Maxi, and Horacio for all the good times that we have shared together across the distance. Also to my "local" friends Amit, Andrew, Ralf, Miguele, and Moises and the many more that I am forgetting. Finally, a special mention to my manager Steve Leaback for all his support.

— *Salvador Alvarez Patuel*

Contents

Introduction   **xxi**

Part I: Silverlight Fundamentals for ASP.NET Developers   **1**

Chapter 1: Silverlight in a Nutshell   **3**

Uphill Struggle	**3**
Rich Client or Web Reach?	**4**
Silverlight Steps In	**4**
The Impact of Silverlight on Your Existing ASP.NET Real Estate	**6**
What You Should Still Do in ASP.NET	**6**
The Development Environment Overview	**7**
Summary	**8**

Chapter 2: Silverlight Architecture   **9**

Client/Server Architecture Overview	**9**
Platforms	**10**
The Server	11
The Client	11
Architecture	**12**
Presentation Core	13
.NET Framework	16
Installed Files	23
ASP.NET Integration	**24**
ASP.NET Composite Controls	25
Using ASP.NET Application Services	25
Communicating with ASP.NET from Silverlight	26
Dynamic Generation of XAML from the Server	26
Using the ASP.NET Server Controls for Silverlight	27
Application Life Cycle	**27**
Updating Silverlight	28
Summary	**29**

Contents

Chapter 3: XAML Condensed   **31**

Why All ASP.NET Developers Should Know the Basics   **31**
XAML Syntax and Terminology   **33**
    Namespaces   33
    White Space   34
    Object and Property Elements   36
    Type Converters   37
    Markup Extensions   38
    Attached Properties   40
    Basic Drawing   41
    The Code-Behind   46
    Dynamically Loading XAML   49
    Available Tools   56
Piecing It All Together   **57**
Summary   **61**

Chapter 4: Programming Silverlight   **63**

How a Silverlight Application Is Composed   **63**
    Packaging a Silverlight Application   64
    `System.Windows.Application`   66
    Application Instantiation   69
    A Basic Silverlight Page   72
JavaScript — How Much You Need to Know   **76**
JavaScript — The Basics   **77**
    Object Model   77
    Adding JavaScript to a Page   77
    Variable Usage   78
    Functions   78
    Conditional Statements   79
    Handling Events   80
    DOM Manipulation   80
The Silverlight Object Model   **84**
    `DependencyObject`, `UIElement`, and `FrameworkElement`   84
    Walking the Tree   85
Events, Threading, and Browser Interaction   **90**
    Events   90
    Threading and Asynchrony   95
    Browser Interaction   105
On-Demand XAP Loading   **114**
    `System.Net.WebClient`   114
Summary   **116**

Part II: Developing ASP.NET Applications with Silverlight 119

Chapter 5: Creating the User Interface 121

Expression Suite — A Whirlwind Tour 121
Expression Web 122
Expression Blend 123
Expression Design 129
Expression Media 129
Expression Encoder 130
Expression Studio 130
ASP.NET versus Silverlight Layout 130
Layout Options in ASP.NET 130
Layout Options in Silverlight 131
Full-Screen Support 154
Localization 162
Summary 165

Chapter 6: Silverlight Controls 167

Introduction to Silverlight Controls 168
Defining Controls in XAML 169
Handling Control Events Declaratively 170
Handling Control Events Programmatically 171
User Input Controls 172
The TextBlock Control 173
The TextBox Control 174
The PasswordBox Control 176
The Button Control 176
The HyperlinkButton Control 177
The CheckBox Control 178
The RadioButton Control 179
The RepeatButton Control 180
The Slider Control 182
The Calendar Control 183
The DatePicker Control 186
The ToolTip Control 187
Items Controls 188
The ListBox Control 189
The DataGrid Control 191
The ScrollViewer Control 193
The ComboBox Control 195
The Popup Control 196

Contents

Media Controls   **198**

The `Image` Control   199

The `MediaElement` Control   200

Displaying Download Progress with the `ProgressBar` Control   202

The `MultiScaleImage` Control   203

Silverlight Toolkit Controls   **205**

`AutoCompleteBox` Control   206

`WrapPanel` Control   207

`TreeView` Control   208

`Chart` Control   210

Summary   **212**

Chapter 7: Styles and Templates   **213**

Styles   **213**

Applying Inline Styles   214

Specifying Styles in a Central Location   218

Templating   **224**

`ControlTemplate`   224

`TemplateBinding`   232

Integrating with ASP.NET   **235**

Using the ASP.NET Profile Provider   235

`ImplicitStyleManager`   **239**

Summary   **242**

Chapter 8: User Interaction   **243**

The Silverlight Interaction Context   **243**

Working with `UIElements` Events   244

Interacting with Input Devices   250

Getting the Most from Input Devices   258

Navigation   **266**

Silverlight Navigation in the ASP.NET World   266

Single Plug-in Navigation   267

Multiple Plug-in Navigation   280

Summary   **283**

Chapter 9: Communicating with the Server   **285**

Silverlight Networking and Communication Features   **285**

What Type of Data Can Silverlight Access and Process?   286

Supported Domains and URLs   286

Communication Options 286
Data-Processing Options 288
Cross-Domain Support **289**
Flash Cross-Domain Policy Files 290
Silverlight Cross-Domain Policy Files 291
Creating Services for Silverlight **292**
Creating a WCF Service for Silverlight 292
Creating an ASP.NET Web Service for Silverlight 301
Calling Services with Silverlight **304**
Calling a WCF Service 304
Calling an ASP.NET Web Service 308
Calling REST APIs **310**
Making RESTful Calls in Silverlight 310
Processing XML Data 314
Processing JSON Data 328
Working with Syndication Feeds 332
Using Sockets to Communicate over TCP 337
Using WCF Polling Duplex Services to Communicate over HTTP 347
Summary **359**

Chapter 10: Working with Data **361**

Data Framework **362**
Exploring the Namespaces 363
Is That All? 364
Data-Binding Essentials **365**
Binding 101 366
Binding in Practice 370
Conversions 382
Dependency Properties 384
Performance Considerations 386
Retrieving and Storing Data **387**
Working with Data Repositories 387
Caching 401
Data Controls **401**
Data Templates 402
`DataGrid` 403
Manipulating Data **407**
Traditional Handling 407
LINQ 408
LINQ to XML 412
Validation **416**

Contents

Input Validation   416

Using Dynamic Languages   418

Data-Binding Validation   419

Summary   **420**

Chapter 11: Creating Custom Controls   423

User Controls   **423**

Understanding User Controls   424

Creating User Controls   429

Customizing Current Controls   **435**

Understanding Visual Customization   435

Customizing with Styles   437

Customizing with Skins   440

Putting Everything Together   443

Custom Controls   **447**

What Is a Custom Control?   448

Your First Custom Control   449

Parts Model   454

Summary   **460**

Chapter 12: Securing Your Silverlight Application   461

You're under Attack!   **461**

The Security Model   **463**

Working in a Sandbox   **466**

Cross-Domain Security   **470**

Integrating with ASP.NET Security   **470**

Obfuscation   **478**

Cryptography   **479**

Summary   **479**

Chapter 13: Audio and Video   481

First Steps   **481**

Embedding Audio and Video in Your ASP.NET Application   482

Finer Control   **491**

Controlling Playback   491

Controlling Playback from ASP.NET   500

Timeline Markers   503

`SetSource`   512

Streaming   514

Summary   **514**

Chapter 14: Graphics and Animation   515

Breathing Life into ASP.NET   515
Before Silverlight   516
Silverlight-Enabled Graphics and Animation   516
Graphics in Silverlight   516
The Shape Class   517
Path and Geometry Objects   521
Painting with Brush Objects   526
Transforms   535
Image Handling   540
Image and BitmapImage   540
Advanced Panning and Zooming with Deep Zoom   542
Animating Your User Interface   547
Timeline   547
From/To/By Animations   547
Key Frame Animations   553
Summary   556

Chapter 15: Troubleshooting   559

Is There a Problem?   560
Common Types of Problems   560
Your Toolkit   562
Visual Studio   563
Debugging Your Application   566
HTTP Tracers   570
Red Gate's Reflector   575
Reducing the Likelihood of Problems   576
Unit Testing   576
UI Testing   581
Exception Handling   586
Instrumentation   587
Summary   587

Chapter 16: Performance   589

Performance Bottlenecks   590
Developers versus Designers   590
High Processor Usage   591
Low Frame Rate   591
Unresponsive UI   591

Contents

Instrumentation   **591**

    Monitoring the Frame Rate   592

    Manual Timing   594

Improving Performance   **596**

    Animation   597

    Text   597

    Game Loops   598

    Windowless   600

    Transparent Backgrounds   601

    Opacity and Visibility   602

    Full-Screen Mode   603

    Height and Width   605

    XAML versus Images   606

    Threading   607

    JavaScript versus Managed Code   607

    Element Reuse   611

    Layouts   612

    Working with Data   613

    Reduce Chatty Applications   616

    Runtime Performance   617

Summary   **619**

Index   **621**

Introduction

If you're reading this, then you're about to start programming rich, immersive ASP.NET applications with Silverlight, and you want to make sure you get it right first time. Just buying this book gives you an enormous head start, significantly reducing the learning curve associated with Silverlight 2 development, and saving you and your company both time and money. You're off to the right start.

Our overarching goal in writing this book was to give ASP.NET developers the power to quickly and easily create visually stunning Internet applications, coupled with rich interactivity to fully immerse the user in a new online experience. Silverlight gives you everything you need to do just this, and in serious style!

For the first time ever, the power of the .NET Framework has been unleashed in a plug-in that can be embedded in multiple browsers across multiple operating systems, giving developers tremendous capability and flexibility in rich Internet applications development.

As well as taking you through each feature that ships with Silverlight, this book will make sure you're able to debug, troubleshoot, and performance-tune your Silverlight applications, as well as seamlessly hook into your existing ASP.NET architecture and code base.

It's fair to say that Silverlight is going to change the way that Internet applications are developed and perceived, and this book will help ensure that both you and your applications keep up!

Who This Book Is For

This book is aimed at .NET developers and architects who want to quickly get up to speed with all that Silverlight 2 has to offer.

As well as covering the breadth of features that Silverlight 2 provides, this book makes a point of demonstrating where necessary how the particular feature can be integrated tightly with the ASP.NET host application. An example is in Chapter 7, where the ASP.NET Profile service is utilized directly from within Silverlight to obtain user-specific data.

It's fair to say that although this book is aimed at ASP.NET developers, it covers all of the salient features of Silverlight 2 to the degree that it's a useful programming resource for developers not using ASP.NET also.

If you're fresh to .NET development, however, you might want to check out a beginning .NET book first, to help you overcome the syntax and set-up queries when learning a new language. Otherwise, take a deep breath and dive in!

What This Book Covers

This book covers the full feature set of Silverlight 2, diving into each of the subject areas to give depth and breadth coverage. As well as teaching you about the component parts of the Silverlight API, the book also covers debugging, troubleshooting, and performance-tuning your Silverlight applications, arming you with all the skills and knowledge you'll need to create advanced Silverlight-based applications in record time.

Importantly, this book covers the integration points between ASP.NET and Silverlight, taking you through the different techniques you can use to seamlessly augment your existing or new ASP.NET web sites with the power of Silverlight.

If you want to program in Silverlight and potentially use ASP.NET as the host, then this book covers it all.

How This Book Is Structured

The book is split into two distinct parts. Part I is titled "Silverlight Fundamentals for ASP.NET Developers," and Part II is titled "Developing ASP.NET Applications with Silverlight." Part I is intended to give you grounding in what Silverlight is as a technology and how it fits into the Web-based landscape. The component pieces of a Silverlight application are also laid out at a high level, and any knowledge required before putting an application together is explained.

Part II is written to give you depth of knowledge across the Silverlight feature-set and show you how to leverage the power of both Silverlight and ASP.NET to create compelling applications.

A brief synopsis of each chapter now follows:

❑ **Part I: "Silverlight Fundamentals for ASP.NET Developers"**

❑ **Chapter 1: "Silverlight in a Nutshell"** — This chapter will teach you at a high level what Silverlight is and how it can help you deliver engaging, immersive web applications. Differentiating Silverlight from other Web-based technologies is also covered here, and a description of the required development environment is provided. In short, after reading this chapter, you'll be able to describe Silverlight and explain why you'd want to use it and what gives it the edge over the competition.

❑ **Chapter 2: "Silverlight Architecture"** — Silverlight allows you to rapidly build a well-rounded application with a great user interface, but if you encounter any problems during development, it is going to be important for you to understand the underlying architecture upon which you are developing. This chapter outlines the core features of Silverlight 2 and guides you around the building blocks of this highly flexible framework, paying particular attention throughout to your ASP.NET heritage.

❑ **Chapter 3: "XAML Condensed"** — Quickly getting up to speed with XAML is what this chapter is all about, helping you brush aside the syntax queries and get to grips with the basics of this multi-purpose declarative language. Hooking the XAML files up to .NET code is also shown here, helping you inject dynamic event-driven actions into your Silverlight UI. Finally, one technique for the dynamic creation of XAML is shown in this chapter, followed by a tour of Expression Blend.

❑ **Chapter 4: "Programming Silverlight"** — By the time you get to this chapter, you'll be itching to start coding, and code you will as the feature-agnostic programming constructs that make up a Silverlight application are covered in detail. The composition of a Silverlight application is laid bare and its constituent parts explained at length, as well as detailing the Silverlight application lifetime and how to hook into it. The different options for embedding the Silverlight plug-in within your application are covered, followed by a brief overview of JavaScript and its associated DOM. This then leads onto a discussion of the Silverlight Object Model, explaining how the visual tree is constructed to form the UI. Another technique for dynamically creating XAML and adding it to the visual tree is also shown here. Finally, the Silverlight event model, browser interaction, and threading model are covered for you.

❑ **Part II: "Developing ASP.NET Applications with Silverlight"**

❑ **Chapter 5: "Creating the User Interface"** — You now know how to program Silverlight and how to write XAML. This chapter shows you how to put it all together to start laying out the user interface of your Silverlight application. Each of the layout controls that ship with Silverlight is covered here — `Canvas`, `Grid`, `StackPanel`, and `TabControl` — including information on when to use which one. Information on how to create a scalable UI is also provided in this chapter, followed finally by a section that details how to localize your application, thereby making it available to other languages and cultures.

❑ **Chapter 6: "Silverlight Controls"** — Silverlight 2 provides an assortment of controls that can be used to display and capture data. In this chapter, you'll learn to work with user input controls, items controls, and media controls and see how they can be put to use to build interactive and rich user interfaces. You'll also learn how to use controls such as the `MultiScaleImage` control to work with Silverlight's Deep Zoom technology.

❑ **Chapter 7: "Styles and Templates"** — Altering the look and feel of your application is the crux of this chapter, with the different techniques for applying styling information to the controls that comprise it demonstrated here. As well as this, integrating with the ASP.NET Profile service via WCF is detailed, giving you the ability to personalize your Silverlight application on a per-user basis.

❑ **Chapter 8: "User Interaction"** — What's the point of having a great technology like Silverlight 2 if we can't interact with it? In this chapter, we are going to review the different ways that you can interact with your application, understanding how the `UIElements` work with input devices like the keyboard, mouse, and stylus. We also explore the different ways to navigate around the application and present the different options that we have and in which scenarios each one is preferred.

❑ **Chapter 9: "Communicating with the Server"** — The ability to access data located at distributed sources is key in many Silverlight 2 applications. In this chapter, you'll learn different networking technologies that are available and see how they can be put to use. Several different topics are covered such as creating and calling ASMX and WCF services, calling REST APIs, working with JavaScript Object Notation (JSON) data, pushing data from a server to a client with sockets, and leveraging HTTP Polling Duplex functionality.

❑ **Chapter 10: "Working with Data"** — It is all about data! One of my colleagues always says, "If you are not using data binding in Silverlight 2, you are doing something wrong!" This chapter explains the data framework available within your applications and then dives deep into the inner workings of data binding, showing you the different approaches that you may take. In order to understand how the data is retrieved, we explain the different technologies and techniques to get the most of Silverlight 2 data using the available data controls. Finally, the chapter explains how you can manipulate the data using LINQ and LINQ to XML.

❑ **Chapter 11: "Creating Custom Controls"** — This chapter will take you on a journey in order to discover the different options that you have available to customize the Silverlight 2 controls. We start exploring the user control model that ASP.NET developers are used to, and then we dig into the internals of visual customization. You will be amazed by this powerful new model. Finally, for those who need to push the technology to the limit, the chapter explains how to create a complete custom control from scratch. This is a very dynamic chapter that will present the typical scenarios where these options may be applied.

❑ **Chapter 12: "Securing Your Silverlight Application"** — Whether you're an Enterprise developer or a Silverlight hobbyist, you are going to want to release your application out to the wild at some point. In doing so, you are providing a high level of exposure to your application, and therefore security should not be an afterthought. Thankfully, Silverlight 2 has a security framework built into the run time, which will give you the peace of mind of working within a secure environment. This chapter introduces you to the Silverlight security framework, but also talks you through your security responsibilities as a Silverlight developer.

❑ **Chapter 13: "Audio and Video"** — Embedding high-fidelity audio and video in your Silverlight application is sure to capture your users' imaginations, and this chapter shows you how you can do just this using the Silverlight-provided `MediaElement` control and the ASP.NET Media Server Control. Playback control is demonstrated, as is the more advanced topic of providing synchronization points within your chosen media. This chapter will definitely help you put the WOW factor into your web sites.

❑ **Chapter 14: "Graphics and Animation"** — A detailed tour of the graphics API that ships with Silverlight is first discussed here, including the `Shape`-derived objects that can be rendered to screen and also the `Geometry`-derived objects that can be created and then rendered via a `Path` object. `Brush` objects are covered next, demonstrating the `SolidColorBrush`, `LinearGradientBrush`, `RadialGradientBrush`, `ImageBrush`, and `VideoBrush`, and their usage. Next up is the very cool DeepZoom technology, covering the creation of DeepZoom-enabled images using the DeepZoom Composer and their usage in your Silverlight application via the `MultiScaleImage` control. Finally, the different animation techniques that you can use within your Silverlight application are covered, ranging from the basic From/To/By type to the more advanced Key frame types, including the different transition mechanisms within.

❑ **Chapter 15: "Troubleshooting"** — Writing an application from start to finish without any development issues is still quite some way off. This chapter introduces you to a range of techniques and tools to help you through the hard times when your application isn't behaving as you would expect it to. Besides retrospectively fixing problems within your application, this chapter concludes with the more proactive approach of ensuring that your application hits a known quality bar before you are satisfied that it is ready to be released. Silverlight's testing framework is the flavor of the day here.

❑   **Chapter 16: "Performance"** — Silverlight is an incredibly powerful and flexible framework. Its inherent flexibility often means that there are several ways to achieve your goals.
In choosing an alternative path, you will often find that the penalty is poor performance.
This chapter gives a series of best-practice advice to allow you to make an informed decision when you hit those forks in the road. In addition, you will learn how to instrument
your code in order to simply identify the bottlenecks within your application.

What You Need to Use This Book

To get the most out of this book, it's recommended that you code along with the examples provided, either
by copying the code shown in the chapters or by downloading the samples and running them yourself.

To do this, you're going to need Visual Studio 2008, which is available to download from MSDN, provided you have a subscription. As well as this, you'll also need to download and install the Silverlight
Tools for Visual Studio 2008, which allows you to create Silverlight-based applications within Visual
Studio. This install will also take care of installing the Silverlight run time and SDK for you. You can
download this installer from `www.silverlight.net/getstarted`.

If you want to follow the examples that use Microsoft Expression Blend or the Deep Zoom Composer,
you can also download these from `www.silverlight.net/getstarted`.

As well as these software requirements, you will need a basic working development knowledge of
Microsoft .NET and have experience in Web-based development. A passion for creating rich web applications is advantageous, although not necessary!

Conventions

To help you get the most from the text and keep track of what's happening, we've used a number of
conventions throughout the book.

> **Boxes like this one hold important, not-to-be forgotten information that is directly
> relevant to the surrounding text.**

Notes, tips, hints, tricks, and asides to the current discussion are offset and placed in italics like this.

As for styles in the text:

❑   We show keyboard strokes like this: *Ctrl+A*.

❑   We show URLs and code within the text like so: `persistence.properties`.

❑   We present code in two different ways:

```
We use a monofont type with no highlighting for code examples.
```

```
We use gray highlighting to emphasize code that's particularly important
in the present context.
```

Source Code

As you work through the examples in this book, you may choose either to type in all the code manually or to use the source code files that accompany the book. All of the source code used in this book is available for download at www.wrox.com. Once at the site, simply locate the book's title (either by using the Search box or by using one of the title lists), and click the Download Code link on the book's detail page to obtain all the source code for the book.

> *Because many books have similar titles, you may find it easiest to search by ISBN; this book's ISBN is 978-0-470-27775-1.*

Once you download the code, just decompress it with your favorite compression tool. Alternately, you can go to the main Wrox code download page at www.wrox.com/dynamic/books/download.aspx to see the code available for this book and all other Wrox books.

Errata

We make every effort to ensure that there are no errors in the text or in the code. However, no one is perfect, and mistakes do occur. If you find an error in one of our books, like a spelling mistake or faulty piece of code, we would be very grateful for your feedback. By sending in errata, you may save another reader hours of frustration, and at the same time, you will be helping us provide even higher-quality information.

To find the errata page for this book, go to www.wrox.com and locate the title using the Search box or one of the title lists. Then, on the book details page, click on the Book Errata link. On this page, you can view all errata that has been submitted for this book and posted by Wrox editors. A complete book list including links to each book's errata is also available at www.wrox.com/misc-pages/booklist.shtml.

If you don't spot "your" error on the Book Errata page, go to www.wrox.com/contact/techsupport.shtml and complete the form there to send us the error you have found. We'll check the information and, if appropriate, post a message to the book's errata page and fix the problem in subsequent editions of the book.

p2p.wrox.com

For author and peer discussion, join the P2P forums at p2p.wrox.com. The forums are a Web-based system for you to post messages relating to Wrox books and related technologies and interact with other readers and technology users. The forums offer a subscription feature to e-mail you topics of interest of your choosing when new posts are made to the forums. Wrox authors, editors, other industry experts, and your fellow readers are present on these forums.

At http://p2p.wrox.com you will find several different forums that will help you not only as you read this book, but also as you develop your own applications. To join the forums, just follow these steps:

1. Go to p2p.wrox.com and click the Register link.
2. Read the terms of use and click Agree.

3. Complete the required information to join as well as any optional information you wish to provide and click Submit.

4. You will receive an e-mail with information describing how to verify your account and complete the joining process.

You can read messages in the forums without joining P2P, *but in order to post your own messages, you must join.*

Once you join, you can post new messages and respond to messages other users post. You can read messages at any time on the Web. If you would like to have new messages from a particular forum e-mailed to you, click the "Subscribe to This Forum" icon by the forum name in the forum listing.

For more information about how to use the Wrox P2P, be sure to read the P2P FAQs for answers to questions about how the forum software works as well as many common questions specific to P2P and Wrox books. To read the FAQs, click the FAQ link on any P2P page.

Part I: Silverlight Fundamentals for ASP.NET Developers

Chapter 1: Silverlight in a Nutshell

Chapter 2: Silverlight Architecture

Chapter 3: XAML Condensed

Chapter 4: Programming Silverlight

1

Silverlight in a Nutshell

This chapter is intended to give you a clear overview of Silverlight with the aim of helping you differentiate it from existing technologies and capabilities, as well as help you to understand when to use Silverlight and what to use it for. An overview of the required development environment is also shown toward the end of this chapter. If you are familiar with the general Silverlight principles, you can skip this chapter and move onto the more in-depth architecture chapter coming up next.

Uphill Struggle

As any ASP.NET developer will tell you, delivering a rich and engaging user interface via a browser is always a challenge when compared with doing the same thing in a classic rich-client application. Don't get me wrong — using ASP.NET enables you to create robust, enterprise-ready web applications. These same applications can, if written appropriately, scale to serve enormous numbers of users while providing a good-looking and logical user interface (with the backing of a good design time).

But creating something more than just a functional user interface, creating a user interface that actually excites and drives the user, creating something that leaps out and wows the user, has always been an uphill struggle because a standard web application simply cannot take advantage of the client's processing power to support a rich and powerful user interface (UI).

Trying to develop a rich user interface using only HTML and JavaScript (DHTML) can get you some great results, but managing and writing the amount of script required for truly advanced scenarios is difficult in itself as the cross-platform, cross-browser disconnected environment makes development even more error-prone and challenging. Couple this with managing thousands of lines' worth of supporting JavaScript, and you've got yourself a real headache.

Rich Client or Web Reach?

Because of the difficult nature of producing complex, highly interactive web applications, there has always been the trade-off of "rich versus reach." *Rich* refers to a traditional client application that has full access to the host operating system, API, and processing power and can therefore support an inherently richer user experience. *Reach* refers to web-based applications that are centrally deployed to potentially limitless numbers of users running different operating systems and software, but that cannot take advantage of the clients' full potentials to create a truly rich UI.

So, typically, web application developers have had to contend with finding a happy medium between *rich* and *reach*, delivering an application that can be easily deployed to many thousands or even millions of users but that is ultimately lacking in terms of richness of UI.

Up until now, the main solution to providing richer content via the Web was to use *Macromedia Flash*, a term that encompasses both the Flash Player (a cross-browser plug-in to display Flash content) and the development environment with which to author Flash content. The big drawback with this approach is the time needed to learn to develop in the Flash environment, including learning Flash ActionScript as well as keeping abreast of developments with ASP.NET — no mean feat. In point of fact, it's rare to find a single web developer who is both well-versed in Flash and well-versed in ASP.NET; therefore, when using both technologies, multiple developers are usually required.

Java has also been the tool of choice, as well as Flash, for delivering rich UIs embedded into the browser, but, again, this poses the same issues to an ASP.NET developer that using Flash does — inherently different technologies mixed together to produce the final output, requiring different skill sets and longer development cycles.

Silverlight Steps In

Silverlight 2 is a cross-platform, cross-browser plug-in that supports a stripped-down version of the .NET Framework API for programming Rich Internet Applications (RIA). Silverlight enables you to create visually stunning applications using a development environment and experience akin to that of Windows Presentation Foundation: UIs can be laid out and created using the declarative programming model provided by XAML and then brought to life using the power of the .NET Framework to drive it.

> The term *Rich Internet Application* applies to any web application that has rich, desktop-like functionality. In effect, the web application feels and acts like a fat-client application. In the majority of RIA applications, this richness of functionality is provided via AJAX. However, it also encompasses Java, Flash, and, moving forward, Silverlight-enabled applications.

Some of the high-level features provided in Silverlight 2 include:

❑   **Cross-Platform Support** — Silverlight provides true cross-browser and cross-platform support, running in all popular web browsers (IE, Firefox, Safari, and Opera) and on both Microsoft Windows and Apple Mac OS X platforms. A Silverlight application will run consistently across all these browsers and platforms, leaving you free to concentrate on designing and developing the core of your application without worrying about conversion changes to implement. A third-party implementation named *Moonlight* has also been developed to allow Silverlight to run under GNU/Linux.

❑   **Mobile Support** — Silverlight has initial support for Windows Mobile and Nokia S60 devices.

❑   **Easy Installation** — The Silverlight plug-in is supported by a lightweight download that can install in seconds.

❑   **Streaming Media** — You can stream audio and video, from mobile devices to HDTV video.

❑   **DRM** — Silverlight has support for Digital Rights Management of media files.

❑   **AJAX-Style Updating** — There is no need to refresh the page for changes.

❑   **WPF-Like Graphics** — Access to a powerful graphics system with Windows Presentation Foundation (WPF)-like support

❑   **.NET Framework** — Silverlight is based on a subset of the .NET Framework — therefore a familiar development environment. Silverlight applications can be written in both C# and Visual Basic .NET.

❑   **Rich Control Library** — Silverlight comes with a plethora of UI controls with support for data-binding and automatic layout.

❑   **DLR** — Support for dynamic languages like Ruby and Python has also been included, operating under the Dynamic Language Runtime (DLR).

❑   **LINQ** — Silverlight includes support for language-integrated query, allowing you to program your data access code using a native syntax and strongly typed objects.

❑   **Communications** — Silverlight includes a host of communications options, allowing you full access to any server-based resources you have via XML Web Services, WCF Services, REST, and ADO.NET Data Services.

❑   **JavaScript Extensions** — Silverlight provides extensions to the standard JavaScript language to allow more control over the browser UI and hook-ins to work with the UI elements.

❑   **HTML/Managed Code Bridge** — Silverlight allows interaction between HTML and Managed Code, and vice versa.

If the features above weren't enough, another key selling point for Silverlight is that it's primarily built upon existing technologies and so should feel at least somewhat familiar to anyone who has used .NET, and even more familiar to anyone who has used .NET 3.0 or 3.5. Also, as the native development environment is Visual Studio it shouldn't pose any problems for .NET developers either. This all adds up to an incredibly fast ramp-up time for existing .NET developers once the initial setup and syntax queries have been brushed aside, and therefore a potential lower initial development cost as opposed to that for .NET developers taking on Flash or Java, for instance.

All that is required to run Silverlight in your browser is the Silverlight plug-in, which is a completely free download from Microsoft. If users do not have the plug-in installed and they navigate to a page hosting a Silverlight application, they will be automatically prompted to install it. Because of its small size, on most user connections this will take only seconds to complete.

The Impact of Silverlight on Your Existing ASP.NET Real Estate

Silverlight is all about delivering next-generation media experiences and rich Internet applications (RIAs) via the Web. It allows you to easily add video, animation, and improved interactivity to your web sites, delivering a more intense and consuming experience for your users. Silverlight provides a unified media format that scales from high definition to mobile using WMV and also supports WMA and MP3 for audio. Vector-based graphics are also catered for out-of-the-box, allowing your graphics and animations to scale to any size without losing quality. All this adds up to a much richer, more immersive UI than you can put together with DHTML alone. And to make it even easier to pick up and run with, Silverlight streaming by Windows Media Live provides a free streaming and application hosting solution enabling you to deliver your media-enabled RIAs with ease.

But if you decide to replace large chunks of your current real estate with Silverlight, will it affect the discoverability of your application by search engines? As the user interface of Silverlight applications is defined in text-based XAML, they can still be indexed and searched easily promoting their discoverability via search engines, so this shouldn't be a problem.

If you currently use JavaScript heavily to create a complex UI on the client, Silverlight can be used to replace this with one that not only performs better, but is easier to create and maintain thanks to a XAML-defined UI and type-safe .NET code-behind. And the same code will work cross-browser, cross-platform, saving you the headache of writing custom code for each scenario.

And if your web site relies heavily on advertising, imagine having full ad insertion capabilities at your fingertips, including the ability to deliver broadcast-style video and animated advertisements without loss of motion quality or visual fidelity.

One of the overlooked capabilities that Silverlight can provide you with is a new mechanism for delivering your applications via *Software as a Service* (SaaS). This term basically refers to a web-native application hosted on the Internet for use by paying customers — so they pay for using it, not owning it. As Silverlight helps you develop incredibly rich UIs, it will make it much easier for you to develop and provide applications that can be delivered in this manner, especially with the free hosting offered via Windows Live.

In short, Silverlight will give you the ability to add the wow factor to your ASP.NET applications and give you the ability to add it with relative ease.

What You Should Still Do in ASP.NET

As you're now aware, Silverlight brings a wealth of functionality to the table, but this isn't to say that every ASP.NET application you write from now on should simply be a container for a Silverlight application providing the full site content and experience (well, not yet anyway …). The fact remains that there are some things that you will still need to do in ASP.NET. A few high-level examples are listed below that you can extrapolate to make your own decisions:

❑ **Security Consciousness** — It's worth keeping in mind that Silverlight sits in the browser on the client machine. Therefore, you most certainly wouldn't want to consider automatically moving highly sensitive logic and/or data over to it without good reason. Sensitive operations should be kept and maintained on the server unless a formal threat modeling exercise has shown that this isn't necessary.

❑ **Architectural Awareness** — In keeping with n-tier architecture, you should still leave your database access code (and similar code) in ASP.NET and provide access points for Silverlight. This also promotes abstraction of the databases, which is a good architectural decision.

❑ **Environmental Concerns** — The Silverlight plug-in is not going to be allowed in *all* environments, be they corporate, educational, or private. In situations in which it's against someone's policy, you have no choice but to leave everything in ASP.NET. As well as this, as broad-reaching as Silverlight is, currently it is not supported in every browser on every OS, so you may still need to cater for these exceptions with ASP.NET throughout.

❑ **Ease of Development** — There are some things that are (at the moment) going to be quicker, easier, and more tried and tested to do in ASP.NET. One such example is form creation, including validation for classic data entry. ASP.NET has a proven track record of allowing you to quickly create data entry applications, thanks to the wealth of controls that can be quickly developed against. There would be no perceived improvement in moving the data entry portions of your application into Silverlight at the moment.

The Development Environment Overview

The development environment for Silverlight is very easy to set up. First things first: You're going to need an Integrated Development Environment (IDE) to work with, and that IDE is Visual Studio 2008. To provide the Silverlight project templates, developer runtime, IntelliSense, debugging support, and other development requirements, you will also need to install the Silverlight Tools for Visual Studio 2008. These two items will complete the setup of your development environment, so you're free to use Visual Studio to create and edit Silverlight applications.

Once you have installed all of the above, you can fire up Visual Studio. By selecting File and then New Project, you will have access to the Silverlight project templates as shown in Figure 1-1.

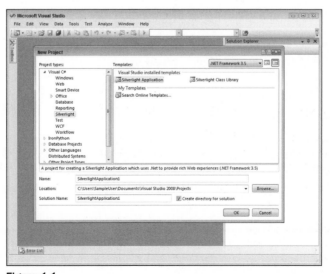

Figure 1-1

From here you can elect to create either a Silverlight application or a Silverlight Class Library (SCL), and then you're on your way. That's all there is to the development environment. In Chapter 3, "XAML Condensed," you take your first steps in actually using this development environment to create a Silverlight application and start learning XAML.

As well as the Visual Studio IDE for Silverlight development, if you fancy yourself to be a bit of a designer as well as a developer, you might want to consider downloading and installing Microsoft Expression Blend, a first-class environment for designers that can be used to work on both WPF and Silverlight applications. Chapters 3 and 5 show how Expression Blend can be used to quickly and easily output XAML that can then be used within your Visual Studio project.

Summary

In this first chapter, you learned at a high level what Silverlight is and how it can help you deliver much more engaging, immersive web applications without the overhead of increased development complexity.

You learned that prior to Silverlight, developing rich, immersive UIs in ASP.NET was challenging for various reasons, primarily arising from the very nature of developing in a disconnected environment with only HTML and JavaScript. This raised the trade-off of "rich versus reach," where you had to make a decision between a graphically rich UI or ease of deployment and uptake, but you couldn't have both.

Silverlight was intended to help solve the problem of "rich versus reach" by allowing you to create visually complex, engaging web applications that can run on a variety of operating systems and browsers. You saw how Silverlight had a simple installation from over the Web and that it provides streaming media support, AJAX-style updating, stunning graphics, and perhaps most importantly, a stripped-down version of the .NET framework to tie it all together.

Because Silverlight was designed to deliver next-generation media experiences and improved interactivity, it supports out-of-the-box the creation of a much more intense and consuming user experience, helping you to give your existing web site the edge over its competitors or to create a brand-new, cutting-edge site.

Importantly, you then learned that using Silverlight doesn't necessarily mean that all of your code, logic, and UI from now on should be moved across from ASP.NET. Four high-level considerations were discussed covering security, architecture, ease of development, and environment that showed what you probably wouldn't want to do in Silverlight and why.

Finally, you took a look at setting up the development environment to allow you to create Silverlight applications. You saw that two main components are required: Visual Studio 2008 and the Silverlight Tools for Visual Studio 2008.

In the next chapter, "Silverlight Architecture," you will take an in-depth look at the components that form the building blocks of Silverlight and the touch points that exist between ASP.NET and Silverlight.

2

Silverlight Architecture

The term *architecture* is used increasingly liberally these days. But how does it apply in the context of Silverlight? *Architecture* in the context of Silverlight refers to the components, or building blocks, of Silverlight itself, but also to how it connects to related technologies, namely, ASP.NET.

This chapter follows the story from client to server and gives you a solid foundation to prepare you for going out there and developing your own Silverlight applications.

There is a pattern to how the material is presented in this chapter: we take a look at one level of the architecture, break it down into elements, describe those elements, and repeat the process until an adequate depth is reached. Once the architecture has been fleshed out, our attention will move to ASP.NET integration and the application life cycle. This approach allows for you to either read through page by page or check back later on to delve into a particular area.

The aim of this chapter is not to get deeply into the code, but rather to explain the concepts. Don't worry, though — there will be plenty of time to get your hands dirty with coding later in the book.

Client/Server Architecture Overview

Figure 2-1 shows where Silverlight fits in the client/server architecture. As the chapter progresses, you will find in-depth discussion of each element of this diagram and the deeper elements of it. Once some context has been established concerning what Silverlight is and what it is composed of, the focus will turn to the integration points between Silverlight and ASP.NET.

> One key point in Figure 2-1 is that although the Silverlight resources are hosted on the web server, they will actually be executed on the client.

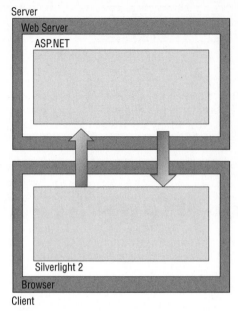

Figure 2-1

There is an intentional abstraction from any particular web server technology in this diagram because one of the great features of Silverlight is that it is server-agnostic. Despite this, the book is aimed at ASP.NET developers, who often host their web applications within IIS.

Although one hosting option on the server has just been briefly discussed, the following section details the support around the platform at both the client and server levels. This includes a comprehensive list of where you can expect to see Silverlight applications being downloaded and executed.

Following the section on the platform, you will take a look inside Silverlight 2 and see how it is composed. Once you have gained a high-level understanding of the Silverlight 2 framework, you will be better positioned to establish what functionality you can harness within your application. This will then serve as a starting point for delving deeper in subsequent chapters.

Platforms

As the software industry has matured, there has been more and more pressure on software vendors to abide by standards to increase their ability to talk to other applications, but more specifically, to increase the reach of their applications and frameworks. This drive has largely come from the development of the Internet and the Web. One of the keys to the success of the Web has been in vendors following standards, namely, in the form of HTML. This meant that a developer could write a web application and be fairly certain that it would run on any browser (on any platform) that could parse HTML. In order for HTML to act as a standard, it continues to be important for vendors to work with a central authority so that any work can be coordinated and kept in-sync. The authority, which fills this gap in the Web space, is the W3C (World Wide Web Consortium).

> **The W3C (World Wide Web Consortium) is an international consortium in which organizations, full-time staff, and the public work together to develop Web standards.**

It is true that the W3C continues to be key to the Web's success, but it is equally true that there is still work to be done by vendors to conform to these standards. For example, there can be instances in which one browser will render an HTML page differently from another vendor's browser. To complicate matters further, some vendors have extended the HTML standard within their browsers to add functionality.

One major limitation of HTML is the richness of the application it can provide in today's world. There have been various technologies over the past few years that have sought to improve this application richness, whether it be AJAX or Flash applications, or even before that, Java and Microsoft's HTML extension, DHTML — each successful to varying degrees. More recently, though, Microsoft has upped its game in this area and introduced Silverlight. With Silverlight comes more than just another technology; it includes an extensible framework in which to build much richer applications. Besides this, however, this framework has been designed in such a way that it reaches out across multiple browsers and platforms. The following two sections detail what these are.

The Server

As Silverlight code is not interpreted or compiled on the server itself, the server platform isn't of particular concern. In other words, if your web server can serve out the resources, then the platform really doesn't matter as far as the client is concerned. Your restriction may come when deciding on a platform for hosting ASP.NET, but even this is more flexible than many people realize, in that you are not restricted only to IIS, but you can also serve off an Apache web server. In fact, you can even serve your ASP.NET applications off Linux courtesy of the Mono project (www.mono-project.com/Main_Page).

The Client

To best illustrate the supported client platform for Silverlight 2, please refer to the following table:

Client Platform	Internet Explorer 6	Internet Explorer 7	FireFox 1.5	FireFox 2.0	Safari
Windows 2000	Yes	n/a	No	No	No
Windows XP SP2+	Yes	Yes	Yes	Yes	No
Windows Server 2003	Yes	Yes	Yes	Yes	No
Windows Vista	n/a	Yes	Yes	Yes	No
Mac OS 10.4.8+ (Intel only)	n/a	n/a	Yes	Yes	Yes

Aside from the PowerPC platform, this list of platforms is expected to be expanded in the future as the Silverlight platform gains momentum and newer operating systems arrive on the scene. One evolving addition is that of the Linux client. Mentioned previously was the Mono project, which is an Open Source community project set up to create a .NET Framework version that could run on the Linux platform.

Early in the development of Silverlight 2, this community (sponsored by Novell) decided to create a Silverlight version that would also run on a Linux client. This project is named *Moonlight*. In a somewhat unprecedented step, Microsoft decided to endorse this project as the official Linux client. However, this will remain a community-supported project.

Now that you know where you can use Silverlight, you are ready to get into the architecture of Silverlight 2.

Architecture

There are several levels at which you can analyze Silverlight's components. Starting at the top level, Silverlight 2 can be thought of logically as being in two parts: the presentation core and the .NET Framework. From its name, you can tell that the presentation core is largely the visual element that provides all of the fundamental rendering ability (and more).

The .NET Framework part allows you to tap into the API from managed code in order to manipulate the presentation core. Of course, it's all well and good having this functionality, but it needs to be hosted somewhere. As Silverlight is targeted to be cross-platform and cross-browser, this hosting is done via a plug-in within the browser. Hosting within a plug-in allows for much richer content in the browser as it allows for an extra level of abstraction from the browser, which enables you to break away from the confines of traditional HTML. This level of abstraction effectively isolates some of the internals of Silverlight from the browser, which makes life easier when producing a run time that is compatible across multiple browsers.

Figure 2-2 will help you to visualize how each of the components sits within Silverlight 2.

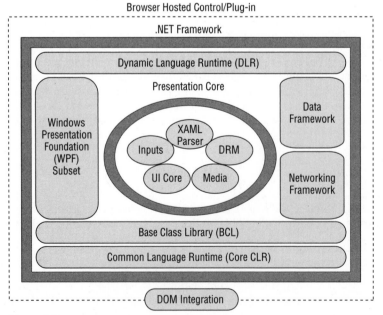

Figure 2-2

This section breaks down the presentation core and the .NET Framework and looks at what they are actually composed of.

Presentation Core

With Silverlight 1.0, you were given the presentation core and a control to host it in. As an end-user you could receive a very rich-looking application. Behind the scenes as a developer, the only API that was exposed to you was an unmanaged interface, which you would typically develop against using JavaScript. Even for a very apt JavaScript developer, it had many shortcomings: historically poor IDE support, error-prone, difficult to debug, inefficient, poor code reusability, and the list goes on.

A managed programming experience was planned for Silverlight from day one, and this is what you get in version 2. The following sections break down the presentation core into its constituent parts, before moving on to the managed programming environment provided by the .NET Framework.

UI Core

The UI Core takes care of the rendering of all the UI elements, as you might expect. This includes rendering images (PNG or JPEG), UI elements (shapes, paths, etc.), and also your animations.

The XAML Parser

Chapter 3 discusses XAML in more detail, but a brief description will be given now in order to explain the function of the XAML parser. XAML, which stands for the "Extensible Application Markup Language," is an XML-based markup that allows you to declare the look and feel of your user interface without the need for code or a designer (although the latter helps!).

In your Silverlight application, you will have one or more XAML files that may define a little, or all, of your presentation to the client. Silverlight needs a way to read and interpret this markup, and it does so via the XAML parser. There is an important word in that last sentence — *interpret*. That is to say, the XAML is not compiled by Silverlight. In .NET Framework 3.0, the Windows Presentation Foundation (WPF) XAML is, in fact, compiled (into an embedded binary resource stored in a format known as *BAML*). With WPF being targeted at the Microsoft platform, it also has the added advantage of being more certain about your machine's hardware, and it can therefore take advantage of your graphics card in its rendering. With Silverlight's XAML parser, you are given the option of software rendering only. As the technology matures, a hardware-rendering ability could be introduced.

Although the XAML Parser does not use your high-end graphics card, it does take advantage of multi-core processors — and as many machines today have at least one dual core processor, some extra horsepower will be given to the Parser.

Another difference between the XAML provided by WPF and that of Silverlight is also worth noting: Silverlight uses a subset of the WPF XAML, and therefore this is all the XAML Parser knows to interpret.

Media

The media component of the core is held within the same unmanaged code library as the rest of the presentation core (further details to come later), but you will be interfacing into this via XAML or .NET via the MediaElement control. The media component has support for a number of codecs. The following is a list of supported formats provided by these codecs:

- Windows Media Video 7, 8, 9 (WMV1, WMV2, WMV3, respectively)

- Windows Media Video Advanced Profile, non VC-1 (WMVA)

- Windows Media Video Advanced Profile, VC1 (WMVC1)

- Windows Media Metafiles (playlists)

- Windows Media Audio 7, 8, 9 (WMA7, WMA8, WMA9, respectively)

- ISO/MPEG Layer-3 in the following configurations:

  - ISO/MPEG Layer-3 compliant data stream input

  - Mono or Stereo channel configurations

  - 8. 11.025, 12, 16, 22.05, 24. 32. 44.1, and 44.8 kHz sampling frequencies

  - 8–320 kilobits per second (kpbs) and variable bit rates

  - However, free format mode (ISO/IEC 11172-3, subclause 2.4.2.3) is *not* supported.

You should read the "Supported Media Formats and Protocols (Silverlight 2)" section of the Silverlight 2 SDK for further details concerning supported and unsupported formats as there are certain details/caveats to be aware of (such as no support for certain playlist features, including Fallback URLs should a reference to a piece of media fail).

In terms of getting the media playing within the application, Silverlight 2 supports progressive downloads (from a web server), streaming media (from a dedicated streaming server), and, of course, having the media stored as a resource within your Silverlight application package. Microsoft has also introduced a service to their "Live" offering, which gives you a lot of free storage in which to host your media for streaming. Further details of the streaming service can be found at `http://dev.live.com/silverlight/`.

Digital Rights Management

The current Web climate has shown a stronger demand from users for richer content and at the forefront of this is the demand for audio and video content as part of the Web experience. Over previous years, the music industry has been fighting the losing battle with music piracy, and as network bandwidth has continued to improve, the concerns have started to be felt by the movie industry. While music and video piracy will no doubt be around for a long time to come, media industries need to take steps to protect their intellectual property, and to do this, they have turned their attention to Digital Rights Management (DRM). DRM has been implemented in various technologies by several vendors over recent years, but the theory remains the same — that is, a media asset should have the ability to be restricted to a predetermined audience for a predetermined amount of time. By having such control over the media, a service provider can introduce charging for content. This model does not have to be the traditional pay-per-view, but could be a subscriber model whereby a service user pays a monthly rental to gain access to an entire media library. Another key piece of this model is that a user who has access to the assets cannot pass on the material to a user who does not.

With Silverlight being core to Microsoft's vision of the next-generation Web experience, therefore, it was imperative to have support not only for media, but for protected media. Microsoft has not been a stranger to DRM technology in the past, as it already has a relatively mature following in the form of Windows Media Digital Rights Management (WMDRM). This technology allows for a piece of media, such as a Windows Media Video (WMV), to be encrypted such that when a user hits the content server to stream or play the video, they are redirected to a Windows Media Licensing Server, which checks to see if the user has the appropriate rights to view the content.

Given that Microsoft has this technology in place already, it may come as a surprise that Silverlight is actually built on a different DRM technology called *PlayReady* — another Microsoft DRM technology. PlayReady has set out to reach different goals from those of WMDRM in that it is designed to be lighter weight and is intended to provide encrypted content that can be played on portable devices. With Silverlight's objective of being lightweight, it had a shared goal with PlayReady DRM, and as a result, Silverlight DRM provides a cross-platform version of a PlayReady client.

Despite Silverlight DRM being built on PlayReady, there is a compatibility story for any existing WMDRM investments — that is, if you have encrypted the content using the WMDRM SDK, this will be playable in Silverlight DRM. However, the caveat is that the license must be supplied by a PlayReady license server, as the license format supplied by a Windows Media license server is not understood by Silverlight DRM. There are also licensing costs associated with developing and deploying the PlayReady content that you should be aware of. You can find more details on the PlayReady web site at `www.microsoft.com/ PlayReady/Licensing/request.mspx`.

For more details on Silverlight DRM and for an architectural overview, please see the article at `www.microsoft.com/silverlight/overview/mediaDetail.aspx?index=4`.

Inputs

It is very pleasing to the eyes to have a load of fancy graphics, but at some point, you are going to want to receive some input from your users. The input component of the presentation core takes care of any physical devices trying to talk to the user interface. These devices can include the keyboard, mouse, and stylus, for example. As you will see on your journey through this book, you can hook up to several events such that when a user performs an action on an input device, you are able to act accordingly within your application. For further information on user input, please see Chapter 8, "User Interaction."

DOM Integration

As mentioned previously, in Silverlight 1.0 you were simply given the presentation core and a control to host it in. The presentation core was, and still is, found within the `AgCore.dll` file, and the plug-in that hosts this library is in a file called `NpCtrl.dll`. Both of these can be found in the Silverlight install folder. The contents of this folder are covered after the section on the .NET Framework.

So, how was it possible to tap into the presentation core from JavaScript? The answer is — by using the methods exposed on the host plug-in. These methods typically expose you to the root control sitting within your XAML. As the UI is built up in a tree-like fashion, once you have access to the root, there is not a lot more work before you can reach every other element or control right down to the leaf level.

The ways in which these methods are exposed depend on the browser hosting technology involved. For example, in Internet Explorer, the plug-in is hosted as an ActiveX control, whereas in the non-Microsoft browsers, it is hosted as a Netscape standards plug-in. Either way, as a developer, you should not for the most part need to worry about these implementation details. After all, it is one of the major features of Silverlight that you do not have to write a browser/platform-specific implementation.

If you wanted to take a look at the `NpCtrl.dll` plug-in in a little more detail, there are two tools that you could use: `OleView.exe` and the Dependency Walker (`depends.exe`). These tools can be found in many Microsoft products, such as some versions of Visual Studio, with the latter being available as part of the Windows Resource Kit and Platform SDK. These tools are discussed in further depth in Chapter 15, "Troubleshooting."

Talking specifically about what ActiveX controls or COM components are is outside the scope of this book, but all you need to know is that OleView will allow you to get a hint at what functionality a control might emit, via something called a *Type Library*. If you have Silverlight installed on your machine and you open up OleView, then you should be able to find the Silverlight control class under the name of AgControl. If you open this up and take a look at the methods exposed by the IAgControl interface, then you will see methods such as Contents and CreateObject. These are accessible via JavaScript as part of the DOM Integration and allow you access to the XAML objects in your Silverlight control instance.

The way this works in non-Microsoft browsers is a little different. ActiveX is not used, but, rather, the Netscape plug-in API — you can now see where the *NP* in NpCtrl.dll comes from. If you use the depends.exe tool, then you can see a list of functions exported by this library. The functions of interest are NP_GetEntryPoints, NP_Initialize, and NP_Shutdown. It is these functions that provide the plug-in capability into the other browsers. If you are interested in the plug-in API, there is further documentation available here: http://developer.mozilla.org/en/docs/Gecko_Plugin_API _Reference:Plug-in_Side_Plug-in_API.

> *Here is a piece of trivia for you. If you have already started to write some Silverlight applications, you may have noticed that a few files and references are prefixed with* Ag. *Why* Ag? *Well, that's because it's the chemical symbol for silver!*

.NET Framework

Silverlight 2 brings a massive advantage over Silverlight 1.0 in that you can use managed code (such as C#) over JavaScript. So, why is managed code called *managed* code? Well, it is because your code is being managed by "something." That "something" is the .NET Framework (or, more specifically, the underlying Common Language Runtime), and as a result, this is a required addition on the client machine. But wait, isn't the .NET Framework (version 3.0) in excess of 50 MB? You do not want to have your users download something of this magnitude the first time they come to access your shiny new web application, as numbers would undoubtedly dwindle. It is for the reasons of bandwidth, client patience, and reach that Microsoft had to look to reduce this package size when bundling it into Silverlight.

This sounds like quite a challenge. How can such a large run time and library be reduced down to something considered quite reasonable? To answer this question, a look is required as to what the .NET Framework is actually made of. The .NET Framework, depending on where you look, can be thought of as being broken up into the following elements:

❑ **Base Class Library (BCL)** — This is a library of classes that provides all the typical coding operations you might require from today's operating systems. These range from assisting you in writing and accessing files (from the System.IO namespace), to holding collections of data, to adding diagnostic support to your application.

❑ **ADO.NET and ASP.NET** — These technologies sit on top of the BCL (although you will sometimes see these in diagrammatic form included within the BCL). They use many of the common features provided by the BCL, but then they offer application-specific functionality such as accessing a data store or providing dynamic content on a web server.

❑ **Common Language Runtime (CLR)** — This is the core of the .NET Framework. It takes care of garbage-collecting resources that have gone out of scope and are no longer in use by the application. It ensures that your code is running securely and as the developer has intended. It ensures that the application code is running in the intended isolated way. It also takes care of many other day-to-day housekeeping tasks that go beyond the scope of this discussion.

❑ **Windows Communication Foundation (WCF), Windows Presentation Foundation (WPF), Windows Workflow Foundation (WF), and CardSpace** — These are the key technologies brought to you in .NET Framework 3.0 over version 2.0:

  ❑ **Windows Communication Foundation (WCF)** — WCF is Microsoft's unified communication platform for building connected applications.

  ❑ **Windows Presentation Foundation (WPF)** — WPF is the graphical framework, which looks to supersede traditional WinForms (Windows Forms applications).

  ❑ **Windows Workflow Foundation (WF)** — WF is a framework for building applications that conform to a particular kind of business or human driven process.

  ❑ **CardSpace** — CardSpace is the technology used to give end-users possession of a digital identity.

Once you have separated these elements of the Framework into blocks like these, you can begin to break down what would be required by Silverlight 2. For instance, all elements of the .NET Framework sit on the CLR, which is really the engine of the .NET Framework. This part of the .NET Framework remains in Silverlight and has become known as the *CoreCLR*.

The CoreCLR is technically the CLR within the Silverlight implementation of the .NET Framework. The CLR remains largely unchanged for Silverlight 2 (when compared to the desktop version of the framework). Bear in mind that you will sometimes see the entire .NET Framework for Silverlight referred to as the CoreCLR.

The next section takes a look at the features that have survived from the desktop implementation of the framework and live on in Silverlight's lightweight incarnation.

What's In and What's Out?

There are several omissions in Silverlight 2's implementation of the framework — some large and obvious, some small and more subtle. It is fairly obvious why some of the blocks have been dropped as they just don't fit into the Silverlight model. A list of some of the absentees can be seen below:

❑ `System.Data` — This namespace no longer exists in Silverlight. This held most of the ADO.NET functionality and was therefore in place to allow for applications to communicate with a database. A database tends to be a centralized resource for many clients, and thus from a Silverlight-application point of view, no direct contact is required — rather, any dealings with such a data store will be done via a web service call.

❑ `System.Deployment.*` — This namespace, brought in for .NET Framework 2.0, added the `ClickOnce` technology, which allowed for an application to be deployed in a seamless way to the client (sometimes referred to as *no-touch deployment*). This overcame problems such as the user not having permissions to run (isolation is taken care of with `ClickOnce`) and allowed for richer applications to be deployed while still maintaining the maintenance benefits of a web application. Silverlight has its own model for providing this functionality and does not use `ClickOnce`.

❑ `System.Runtime.InteropServices.*` — These namespaces provide interoperability between today's managed .NET applications and pre-.NET applications written to the COM standard. This has not been entirely dropped for Silverlight, but, rather, stripped down. This is because parts of the Silverlight core are still written in unmanaged code, and the Silverlight control itself (in Internet Explorer) is an ActiveX control, which is essentially a COM component. So, although you write your Silverlight code in a managed environment, you are occasionally being shielded from an underlying set of unmanaged components. As a Silverlight developer, this is provided seamlessly so that you don't have to worry about it — in fact, owing to the security restrictions in place within Silverlight, you cannot access this functionality directly. The security mechanisms in Silverlight are discussed in more detail in Chapter 12, "Securing Your Silverlight Application."

❑ `System.Runtime.Remoting` — For all intents and purposes, this namespace is no longer accessible in Silverlight. To elaborate, all but one class from the desktop version of the framework has been removed, and the one remaining class is now labeled as `internal (C#)`, or `Friend` if you are a VB.NET developer. Essentially, this means that it is inaccessible to anybody outside of the assembly/file.

❑ `System.Security` — There have been some fairly big changes in the area of Security for Silverlight. Again, please see Chapter 12 for further details.

This is by no means an exhaustive list, and the differences have largely been noted at the namespace level. As you begin working with Silverlight, you will see some more-subtle functionality changes or omissions — for example, the XmlDocument type is no longer available for XML document manipulation, as it has been replaced by the LINQ to XML functionality (XDocument type - see Chapter 10, "Working with Data," for more details). These changes and omissions will not always be to your satisfaction. In the run-up to the Silverlight 2 release, Microsoft was listening to the voices of the community about what to include in the .NET Framework for Silverlight. At the end of the day, however, one of the most important points to realize is that the form factor of the package to install must be as small as possible. If this were to be put in a graph, you would see functionality on one axis and package size on the other. The goal was to try and find the optimum match.

WPF

When the .NET Framework 3.0 was released, there was quite a bit of confusion as to what this actually was. The confusion came from what changed since the .NET Framework 2.0. Well, rather than much changing, this release was about adding several new features, namely, Windows Communication Foundation (WCF), Windows Workflow Foundation (WF), Windows Presentation Foundation (WPF), and Windows CardSpace (as described above).

WPF is the presentation framework that allows you to express your UI either declaratively via XAML or imperatively via code. In Silverlight 2, you are given a lightweight implementation of WPF with which to work. The main reason for this is, again, to lower the download size.

A quick start in XAML is given in Chapter 3.

With XAML comes an accompanying object model, which, in this case, is the subset of WPF. At the heart of any Silverlight application is its controls. The development of these controls is discussed in Chapter 11, but for now, it is worth taking a look at the class hierarchy of Silverlight's Presentation Foundation. This will not be an extensive look at the whole of the object model, but rather the backbone.

To set some context, Figure 2-3 shows a snapshot of the class hierarchy, courtesy of Red Gate's .NET Reflector Tool: www.red-gate.com/products/reflector/.

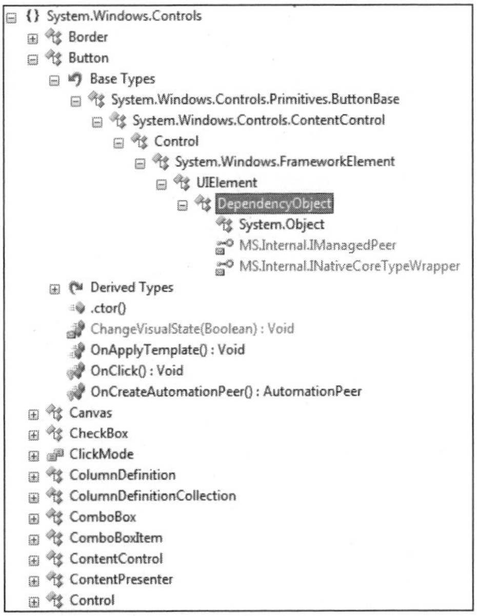

Figure 2-3

Before discussing Figure 2-3, there are a couple of important points to note:

❑　This does not list all of the namespaces and classes involved in the Object Model, but just a slice through the Canvas panel to give an idea of a common class hierarchy in Silverlight 2.

❑　These classes are held within the System.Windows assembly. (See the "Installed Files" section below in this chapter for further details.)

It will make more sense to start with the least functional class in the hierarchy, which, of course, is the root class, and one that should be familiar to every .NET developer, System.Object.

❑　System.Object — This is the base class of every single .NET type. It provides the most generic of functionality.

❑　System.Windows.DependencyObject — The DependencyObject class is central to Silverlight's dependency property system. It allows support in the framework for various services including Attached Properties, Data Binding, Animations, and Styles and Templates. These services are covered in more detail as you progress through the book. All controls within Silverlight will ultimately derive from this class as it provides extra flexibility and decoupling from parent controls. The DependencyObject class will most often be used in conjunction with the Dependency Property class. The DependencyProperty class is used to register properties within your class/control as being available to a dictionary of DependencyObject objects.

❏ `System.Windows.UIElement` — This class is key to hooking up any keyboard and mouse input events and in rendering the element's visual output (which may be subject to any transforms, clipping, etc.). A number of dependency properties are also registered at this level of the hierarchy.

> If you are coming from a WPF development background, you will notice that there is a class missing in this hierarchy — `System.Windows.Media.Visual`. This class provides the ability to control the rendering and clipping of visual elements in WPF. With the cut-down subset of WPF in Silverlight, any remaining `System.Windows .Media.Visual` methods have been moved out into `System.Windows.UIElement`. A good example of this is the `Visual.TransformToVisual(Visual)` method, which now lives in Silverlight as `UIElement.TransformtoVisual(UIElement)`.

❏ `System.Windows.FrameworkElement` — This class adds another layer over its base class, `UIElement`. The key pieces of functionality that this class provides over `UIElement` are regarding layout, data binding, and for allowing the detection of object lifetime events (i.e., when your visual element has been added to the visual tree, etc.). This class also defines the common properties you will see on all controls and panels such as `MinHeight`, `MaxHeight`, `Width`, and so on. When you come to extend Silverlight, you will typically do so lower down the hierarchy, by deriving from the Control and Panel class, in order to save yourself some further work.

> The branch chosen here shows the next class in the hierarchy to be `System.Windows .Controls.Control`. There are obviously a large number of such class hierarchies within Silverlight, but the one chosen here is chosen because it is likely to contain the classes you face on a more regular basis within your Silverlight development. Another common class hierarchy that you will encounter, and which branches at this point of the tree, is the one that demonstrates the various panels that you have at your disposal — in which case, the next class would have been `System.Windows .Controls.Panel`.

❏ `System.Windows.Controls.Control` — The name of this class gives you a good idea of the functionality it provides. You will find it to be the parent of all the Silverlight controls, such as `Button` (the example discussed in this tree), `ListBox`, `DataGrid`, and so on. In fact, this class is relatively small, with its primary objective being to set up the structure of its underlying controls. The key piece of functionality it provides is in setting up the Template property. When you come to develop functionality in your Silverlight application, you will have three options to make with regard to controls: (1) adjust the visual appearance of an existing control; (2) create a composite control (which essentially uses the `UserControl` class, which derives from `Control`); (3) or, you can develop your own control, either by directly deriving from `Control`, or an existing control. These options are explored in more detail in Chapter 7, "Styles and Templates," and Chapter 11, "Creating Custom Controls."

❏ `System.Windows.Controls.ContentControl` — Next in the chain is the `ContentControl`. The purpose of this class, again, is pretty simple, and it can be thought of as a placeholder for any content within a more complex control. In the `Button` scenario being discussed, a button may have several different states, and it may be built up of several more primitive controls — one of those controls is the one that displays the content on the front of the control. More often this is a piece of text such as *Click me*, but the `ContentControl` allows for much more creative content to be placed on the controls that derive from it. The key property that it exposes is the `Content` property, which allows you to set the content to be pretty much anything you like.

❑ `System.Windows.Controls.Primitives.ButtonBase` — This is the level at which things start to get much more concrete, and less abstract. The team developing the control set could have simply had the `Button` class as the next class in the hierarchy, but as with any good control developer, there was a common seat of functionality established across the board. That is, for controls such as `Button`, `HyperlinkButton`, `RepeatButton`, and `ToggleButton` (and who knows what in the future), there was a requirement for them all to change states when clicked with the mouse, or maybe when they were hovered over by the mouse. This is the class that defines and provides an umbrella of functionality for these controls.

❑ `System.Windows.Controls.Button` — Finally, at the leaf of this hierarchy is the `Button` control/class itself. This is the class that implements the functionality and defines a default style for the control. It also defines the various states that the control can be in.

So there you have it, a whistle stop tour of Silverlight's "WPF" hierarchy. It will become increasingly important for you to become familiar with this hierarchy if you are to develop your Silverlight applications in any depth. For example, if you need to extend what is provided out-of-the-box, then you will need to know the most appropriate classes from which to derive. This architecture will fall into place more as you progress through the book and become familiar with the Silverlight 2 SDK.

Networking

While harnessing the processing power of the client provides the ability for a rich user experience, it is highly likely that you will need to communicate with a server from your application at some point. The reasons you have for doing this could reach far and wide, but may include wanting to tap into a news service, pull some data from a database via a web service, or perhaps progressively download some images/resources to improve the user experience. Silverlight 2 takes on all of these challenges and provides you with the supporting tools in the form of classes to achieve these goals.

As web services have matured, there have been various methods developed in order to transport the payload between the client and server, whereby some methods are deemed more suitable than others. For example, if you are working in an Enterprise environment with business-critical applications, you will often want to ensure some kind of reliability that those messages have been delivered correctly, and it may be that you want to declare your intent for doing this within the message header. If you are looking for this type of functionality, you would probably be looking at the WS-* standards, and in the Microsoft world, this is now provided by Windows Communication Foundation (WCF). You can access such web services from your Silverlight application simply by generating a proxy as you would do normally. The approaches you can use to do this are discussed further in this chapter, in the "ASP.NET Integration" section. Something that also comes out of this functionality is the commitment of Silverlight to provide more than just a "mini-games" platform, and also its dedication to providing benefits to real-world business applications.

If you don't need the added complexities of Enterprise Web Services, you can use the simpler cousin, ASP.NET Web Services, whose messages are transported using a SOAP message (without a lot of extras in the SOAP header). If you want to take things even further when transporting data between your client and server, then you can use Plain Old XML (POX), which has none of the complications of a SOAP message.

Another communications protocol that Silverlight supports is the increasingly popular Representational State Transfer (REST) protocol. This has grown in popularity in recent years and is now a supported protocol by many of the industry's big service vendors (e.g., Google, Microsoft Live, etc.). In fact, the Silverlight Streaming Service exposes its services via the REST protocol, which, by the way, can only be used over HTTP.

These days, it's not uncommon for people to receive their news or blog updates via some kind of information feed. Such feeds give the impression that the data is being pushed to the client, rather than the user having to physically browse to a web page. There are a number of applications in the form of gadgets (or widgets, depending on your operating system background) that allow this seamless integration of information into your everyday life (such as the Feed Headlines gadget found in Windows Vista). The common protocols that these syndication services operate by are RSS or ATOM. Once again, Silverlight 2 provides you with the platform on which to consume services that act under these protocols.

There have not been a lot of concrete examples of each of these protocols in this chapter, as these appear in Chapter 9, "Communicating with the Server."

Data

When dealing with data in Silverlight, there is quite an array of classes you can use. These classes allow you to perform various actions, including querying data and reading and writing data; they also act as part of the plumbing for serialization.

Some of these data classes have been around in the .NET Framework for quite some time — you are probably already familiar with classes such as the `XmlReader`, for example. Some other classes have appeared in more recent versions of the .NET Framework.

When the .NET Framework 3.5 was released, a new data query mechanism was shipped in the form of LINQ (language-integrated query). LINQ is a general-purpose data-query language that can be embedded within your .NET code, where it allows for you to query data sources that derive from the `IEnumerable<T>` or `IQueryable<T>` interfaces. This is a very powerful tool, but this power increases when LINQ is extended. One such extension for LINQ that is available within Silverlight is LINQ to XML, which is contained within the `System.Xml` namespace. As Silverlight applications will deal a lot with web services, it is likely they will come into contact with XML, or perhaps you are storing some data as XML locally. Either way, LINQ to XML will provide you with a much more intuitive way of querying that information than the `XmlReader` and `XPath` approaches you may be used to.

> *The LINQ to XML features are implemented by an assembly that comes with the Silverlight SDK, rather than the core runtime functionality. This means that in order to use it as a developer, you will need to reference the assembly installed into the Silverlight SDK folder (by default, this is found in C:\Program Files\Microsoft SDKs\Silverlight\v2.0\Libraries\Client\System.Xml.Linq.dll). Once the assembly has been referenced in your application, it will be downloaded to the client when the user browses to the page hosting your application.*

Dynamic Language Runtime

One of the new features introduced in Silverlight 2 is the Dynamic Language Runtime (DLR).

Dynamic languages are not a new thing. They have been around for years in the guises of Ruby and Python. The new fuss around dynamic languages has come about because of the DLR layer in Silverlight that sits on top of the .NET Framework. This essentially means that you get the best of the dynamic world, while still being able to harness that rich functionality provided to you by the .NET Class Library. So, what is a dynamic language? One of the tenets of a dynamic language is that it uses a dynamic type system. In other words, you don't have to specify what type you are using at design time as it will be inferred at compile time. There have been debates for many years on which approach is best: dynamic languages or static languages (which include C#, VB.NET, etc.). In truth, they are both tools good at doing different jobs. All you need to know for now is that if you are a .NET developer, there is a new tool in town.

Installed Files

To wrap up the architecture section, it is useful to review how this functionality is provided in the context of the Silverlight installation folder. The following list shows the files that get installed in Silverlight 2, along with a brief description of their roles. If you want to dig a little deeper into what these files actually do, you can review Chapter 15, which covers debugging techniques and shows off some of the tools you can use to dig a little deeper.

- ❑ `Silverlight.Configuration.exe` — This provides access to the configuration dialog. Here you can check the version of the run time you have installed, configure the runtime update settings, enable digital rights management (DRM), and delete the application storage for each Silverlight application (or disable application storage).

- ❑ `agcore.dll` — This is a Win32 library (i.e., not a .NET assembly), which provides the core Silverlight functionality as represented by the inner circle of Figure 2-2. This also includes the functionality to allow communication with the browsers object model.

- ❑ `coreclr.dll` — This is another Win32 library, responsible for loading the Silverlight CLR.

- ❑ `dbgshim.dll` — This is one of the debugging dlls and is used by Visual Studio to allow for Silverlight application debugging.

- ❑ `Microsoft.VisualBasic.dll` — This managed assembly contains the Visual Basic run time.

- ❑ `mscordaccore.dll` — This is one of the unmanaged libraries used to debug Silverlight applications.

- ❑ `mscordbi.dll` — This is another one of the unmanaged libraries used to debug Silverlight applications.

- ❑ `mscorlib.dll` — This managed assembly contains the base class library (BCL) for Silverlight.

- ❑ `mscorrc.debug.dll` — This contains resources for the .NET run time.

- ❑ `mscorrc.dll` — This contains resources for the .NET run time.

- ❑ `npctrl.dll` — This is the plug-in that hosts Silverlight within the browser.

- ❑ `npctrlui.dll` — This contains resources used by the browser plug-in.

- ❑ `Silverlight.ConfigurationUI.dll` — This is a resource library used by the executable of the same name.

- ❑ `sos.dll` — This is another one of the unmanaged libraries used to debug Silverlight applications.

- ❑ `System.Core.dll` — This managed assembly contains the core of the run time and includes LINQ support.

❑ `system.dll` — This contains more core support for the managed run time, such as support for generics.

❑ `System.Net` — As is quite obvious from the assembly name, this provides the managed ability for communicating with the outside world, via HTTP, Sockets, and so on.

❑ `System.Runtime.Serialization` — This assembly provides serialization support.

❑ `System.ServiceModel.dll` — This assembly contains the WCF subset supported by Silverlight. Silverlight only supports `basicHttpBinding`.

❑ `System.ServiceModel.Web.dll` — This assembly provides JSON serialization supported. Again, in the fully blown WCF implementation, this contains a larger number of namespaces.

❑ `System.Windows.Browser.dll` — This assembly provides managed access to the browser document object model (DOM). This functionality is often referred to as the *HTML Bridge*.

❑ `System.Windows.dll` — This assembly contains the bulk of the managed API for Silverlight, which largely wraps up the presentation core. It provides access to the Silverlight controls, input elements, and media elements among other functionality.

❑ `System.Xml.dll` — This assembly contains the cut-down XML functionality in Silverlight, such as the `XmlReader` class. You won't find classes like `XmlDocument` in here as these have been dropped in favor of classes such as `XDocument` (found in the `System.Xml.Linq` assembly from the SDK).

❑ `slr.dll.managed_manifest` — This file lists the platform assemblies that are located in the runtime's installation directory. Platform assemblies are not allowed to be packaged up in an XAP file like the assemblies you will develop — this is for security reasons.

ASP.NET Integration

So, you are an ASP.NET developer, and you want to learn Silverlight. It is likely that you are going to be faced with one of two main scenarios: First, you have a nice blank canvas to work on (no pun intended), in that you are starting a new web application from scratch. Second, you have an up-and-running web application, and you want to transform it into a Rich Internet Application (RIA) using Silverlight 2.

One of the first things to realize here is that Silverlight doesn't care if it is being executed as part of an ASP.NET page, an HTML page, or even a PHP page! This is because all it needs is a container on the client that can host the Silverlight plug-in. This may lead you to think that if Silverlight doesn't care about you (as an ASP.NET developer), then why should you care about it? Well, the reason is that although there is no tight coupling between the technologies, there are several *touch points* between the two should you choose to embrace these in your application.

To summarize, the touch points between Silverlight and ASP.NET include:

❑ ASP.NET composite controls

❑ Using ASP.NET Application Services

❑ Communication with ASP.NET from Silverlight

❑ Dynamic generation of XAML from the server

❑ Using the ASP.NET server controls for Silverlight

The following sections provide an overview of each one of these points.

ASP.NET Composite Controls

During your ASP.NET development career, you have likely created a composite control within your web application to encapsulate some common functionality within the site. Composite controls act as a good integration point for Silverlight and allow you to deliver the content to your site with the same encapsulation advantages.

Please note that it is *composite controls* that are referred to here, rather than their cousins, *custom server controls*. Custom server controls can provide an integration point as well if you are comfortable working outside the Visual Studio Designer

All a composite control typically consists of is either server controls or static HTML content. It has previously been discussed that Silverlight will happily execute within an HTML page or an ASP.NET page, and a composite control is no different. This gives scope for various opportunities in which to provide richer content to your users. In other words, you can bundle a Silverlight control up into a composite control and then reuse this throughout your web application. Perhaps you want to gain some advertising revenue from your site, and so you could quite happily host a video that sits inside a user control (or even a web part), and you have the power to position this within your web pages. Of course, another option in this particular example is that you could host the Silverlight control within your Master Page (should you want that amount of reach over your site).

Using ASP.NET Application Services

ASP.NET 2.0 brought with it a number of application services. These services all conformed to a provider model introduced by ASP.NET 2.0 whereby all you needed to know was the type of service you required, rather than worry about the implementation that sat behind the service. This means that you could plug in different implementations behind the scenes; the developer could write against one API, and it wouldn't really matter if the data was being stored in a SQL Server database, an XML file, or another type of data store. The services ASP.NET provides you include the Role, Profile, and Membership providers.

This model was so useful that JavaScript client applications wanted a piece of the action. Therefore, when Microsoft released the ASP.NET AJAX Extensions, there was support added to allow for this. To achieve this in a more seamless way, much of the legwork is hidden away from you in the ASP.NET AJAX Client Library.

To be able to communicate with the server in order to exchange Role or Profile information, the server had to expose these services in a language that the JavaScript clients would understand. This was achieved by tweaking the server application's web.config file so that it made available a JSON (JavaScript Object Notation) proxy for the clients. (There is more on JSON in Chapter 9, "Communicating with the Server.")

So, if a simple JavaScript client can take advantage of these services, you would expect a Silverlight 2 application to be able to do this also, which it can. Examples of how to take advantage of these application services are shown below. (See Chapter 12, "Securing Your Silverlight Application," for a more in-depth look.)

Communicating with ASP.NET from Silverlight

It is all well and good having Silverlight take advantage of the client's processing power, but there will be times when you want to talk back to the server — or, more specifically, ASP.NET. The endpoint being exposed by the server will typically be a web service, and thus there needs to be a way in which Silverlight can communicate along a channel with the web service. This process will seem pretty straightforward to any ASP.NET web developer. You can add a Service Reference through the Visual Studio .NET IDE by right-clicking "References" and selecting "Add Service Reference." This opens a dialog that goes on to create a proxy to that web service, which you can use for the communication. In the desktop framework, you could use a command-line tool called `svcutil.exe` to generate this proxy, although there is no specific version for Silverlight at present.

Dynamic Generation of XAML from the Server

Possibly one of the less-obvious integration points between your Silverlight application and your standard ASP.NET web application is that you have the ability to dynamically generate and manipulate XAML on the server before it is shipped off to the client's machine as part of the application life cycle. The idea behind this is that in the page where you create your Silverlight host, you add in a reference to an ASP.NET page rather than the standard XAML file. All you have to do then is to make your ASP.NET page output some conformant XAML, and at the same time, you can use your ASP.NET page code-behind to manipulate the XAML content.

You may be wondering why you would want to do this on the server rather than the client. After all, by taking advantage of the client's processing power, you are taking some of the load off the server. This is true, but there are times when it works out more efficiently, and other times when more control over the XAML is desired.

Consider, for example, that you wanted to provide a more personalized page to a specific user. He has logged in to your application before and has added some buttons within the application that take him to some favorite content within your site. You have three options here:

❑ Pull down a standard XAML file (as part of your Silverlight application package) as you would normally, check the user via a service call, and call a web service on the server to pull down any customizations for that user.

❑ Check the user when he hits your site for the first time, and provide a separate XAML/XAP Package for that user.

❑ Check the user when he hits your site for the first time, and inject some customizations into a template XAML file.

As this is likely to be a rare request, the last option not only gets you the UI you want in one roundtrip, but also you don't have to store multiple XAML files for different users. The subtle customization differences could be stored in a database, which, of course, your ASP.NET web page has simple, direct access to.

Besides the flexibility this approach offers, it also gives an Enterprise the opportunity to restrict the XAML that is posted out to a client. For the most part, you could provide any restrictions on the client in terms of the functionality that your users could take hold of, but this is a far less secure solution.

Using the ASP.NET Server Controls for Silverlight

Two new ASP.NET server controls that were introduced as part of Visual Studio 2008 are the
`asp:Silverlight` and `asp:Media` controls. These controls are specifically targeted at assisting
you in integrating Silverlight into your application. Their roles are outlined below:

❑   `asp:Silverlight` — This server control allows for a smooth integration of your Silverlight
XAP/XAML files and associated JavaScripts.

❑   `asp:Media` — This control allows you to embed video within your page. It includes support for
adding different skins to the Silverlight media player within the page.

The controls may seem a little familiar to you if you have ever developed with Microsoft's ASP.NET AJAX
Extensions, in that these controls use the same model for including script resources, which can be used
to hook into the respective controls to provide further functionality.

Application Life Cycle

This section concerns exactly what happens the first time you hit that Silverlight application. For the
purposes of this example, assume that you have a freshly installed client machine and that machine is
running Windows Vista. You browse to an application that hosts some Silverlight content. If this content
is hosted within an ASP.NET web page, your page is still going through the same page event life cycle
as it would do at any time. If it is being hosted in a simple HTML page, you are simply asking the web
server to pass you back a static HTML page. The first time you are made aware that this is a Silverlight
application is when you receive a small notification within the page asking you to download the
Silverlight plug-in. This will look something like Figure 2-4.

Figure 2-4

The reason this is being displayed is typically due to some JavaScript files within the web page checking the following criteria: (a) Do you already have the Silverlight plug-in installed? (b) Do you have the
minimum required version of the plug-in installed? You do not have to develop the JavaScript to perform this; the framework for this is provided either by the Silverlight for Visual Studio .NET Tools, or
as part of the Silverlight SDK.

Once you have decided to install the plug-in, you click on the image (as shown in Figure 2-4), and this
does an in-place installation of the latest Silverlight plug-in. You may have to restart your browser at
this point to complete the installation.

Upon restarting the browser and hitting the same page, a different process will be followed. Once again,
if you are using the JavaScript file given to you by the SDK, it will perform the same checks and realize
that you have the appropriate plug-in installed for the page. The code developed by the page creator
will then create an instance of the Silverlight plug-in. (In fact, the page authors could create multiple
instances on the page if they wanted to, but just assume there is one for now.)

As a developer you may want to isolate different areas of Silverlight functionality and have it appear seamlessly within an existing web page. You can do this by hosting multiple plug-ins. Another scenario could be if you are developing a web application within a web part framework, such that more than one of the web parts hosts its own Silverlight plug-in.

Within their plug-in instantiation script, the developer will have specified a number of properties, but most importantly, here is the XAP Package, or XAML page, that she wants to display to the end-user. The Silverlight plug-in will then pull down this package that contains your page resources, along with any other assemblies that may be referenced within the application.

The XAP Package is described in more detail later, but in short, it is a ZIP file containing the various assets that make up your application.

You may be wondering what happens when you hit the page a second time. Does this same process occur again? The answer is probably no. Silverlight uses the Browser cache, which means that the package will not be pulled down every time, but, rather, at set intervals as dictated by the browser.

It was mentioned previously in the chapter that Silverlight is server-agnostic. This means that when you hit a page with Silverlight content, the server side life cycle isn't really that relevant (although it becomes slightly more relevant if you are using dynamic generation of XAML from the server, as discussed previously). The plug-in requests some resources, and all that is needed on the server is a web server that will respond to such requests and download those assemblies/resources to the client. To the user, this is a seamless process, so you are not prompted every time a user resource is going to be downloaded. You may think that this could result in a security hole, but as you will see in Chapter 12, security is very much built into the core of Silverlight so that it plays nicely and isn't allowed to get into any mischief.

Updating Silverlight

The "DOM Integration" section in this chapter talks about the Silverlight plug-in in quite a bit of depth, but there is a key area that it doesn't cover, and that is its role in upgrading the Silverlight run time. When you write your first Silverlight application, if you click your right-button within your browser window, over your Silverlight application region, you'll see the Silverlight Configuration option appear. This validates that you are clicking over the Silverlight Host plug-in within the page. If you actually click on that "Silverlight Configuration" link, you see an About dialog appear, which displays all the usual About information, including the version number of your plug-in. If you look more closely, you can see a tab called *Updates*, which looks like Figure 2-5.

What you are actually seeing here is the execution of the `Silverlight.Configuration.exe` file, which is located within the Silverlight update directory (see the "Installed Files" section for a complete list of files).

This data is stored within the registry in the following key:

```
[HKEY_CURRENT_USER\Software\Microsoft\Silverlight]
"UpdateMode"=dword:00000000
```

The value of the `dword` maps to the option you have selected.

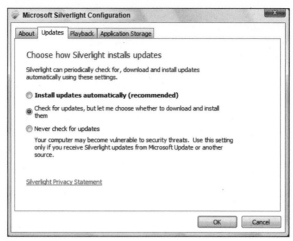

Figure 2-5

Each of these options is fairly self-explanatory, but a brief overview of each is given below:

❑ **"Install updates automatically"** — This will automatically update your Silverlight run time silently in the background. There is not a Windows service constantly running to perform the checks for the latest updates, so these will only be performed while the control is running in your browser. An important point here is that if you are running Windows Vista with User Access Control (UAC) enabled by default, this option will not be available. This is because, for security reasons, the installation requires administrative privileges and therefore a user prompt to install a new version of the plug-in, and thus cannot be done automatically in this situation.

❑ **"Check for updates, but let me choose whether to download and install them"** — This still performs the checks in the same fashion as above, but will prompt you before downloading and installing. As there are two types of updates (feature-oriented and security-oriented), this does give you a little more control over what gets installed. Please note, however, that when you visit a site that is using the latest features, you will not be able to use the application without downloading the latest plug-in/run time.

❑ **"Never check for updates"** — This (not recommended) option will not perform any checks for updates, and therefore you will receive no prompts. The danger here is that you will not be prompted for any security fixes, which could leave your machine vulnerable to attack.

Summary

This chapter has outlined the core elements of Silverlight for you. It has shown that much of the functionality is held within an unmanaged core library, which, in Silverlight 2, is wrapped up in managed (.NET) code. You have seen some of the technical reasons for why Silverlight is structured as it is today, along with how you can tap into its capabilities from your more traditional ASP.NET web applications. Finally, the chapter talked you through what happens under the covers when a user first hits a Silverlight application.

You are now set to use these concepts as a platform on which to learn more in the chapters to follow.

3

XAML Condensed

This chapter takes you through the basics of understanding and writing XAML and shows you how XAML is used to concisely construct the building blocks of a Silverlight user interface. It also discusses why you need to know XAML to a good degree to program effectively in Silverlight. This chapter is not intended to be a XAML language reference or an exhaustive look at every property of every object; it is intended instead to be a whirlwind tour of the 90 percent of XAML that will matter to you as you're developing Silverlight applications.

Throughout the chapter, numerous XAML samples and snippets will be shown to you to explain various concepts that you're free to go ahead and try out. Don't worry if you'd rather just read through to the end of the chapter, though, as there is a full walk-through summarizing the key concepts to cement the knowledge.

Why All ASP.NET Developers Should Know the Basics

Extensible Application Markup Language (XAML, pronounced *zammel*) is an XML-based markup language that is used to instantiate and initialize .NET objects.

XAML first appeared with the introduction of .NET 3.0 and is used not only to construct the user interface in Windows Presentation Foundation and Silverlight, but also to represent workflows in Windows Workflow Foundation and in the XPS (XML Paper Specification). There will no doubt be other technologies that take advantage of XAML moving forward thanks to its general-purpose nature provided inherently by its XML base.

But is it really necessary to learn XAML in order to write Silverlight applications? Can't you just rely on designers and design tools to do the donkey work for you? This particular question has a lot in common with the ASP.NET developer wondering if he or she really needs to bother learning HTML to a good level.

OK, so you can probably get by as an ASP.NET developer without being an HTML expert. Fair enough. But as an ASP.NET developer, everything you do will ultimately result in a stream of plaintext HTML and supporting files being sent to the user's browser for rendering. You may well be interacting with a mainframe to retrieve customer data and dynamically generating graphs on the fly, but in essence, the end goal is to create and send a correctly formatted sequence of plaintext to the browser for parsing and rendering. Nothing more.

And whether you've used the Visual Studio design interface or any other tool to create the HTML for your site (or more likely a colleague in design has provided it for you using her tool of choice), there will undoubtedly be instances when you have to understand at some level what the markup this plaintext creates is trying to achieve. You have to be able to correctly place and format the dynamic data from your mainframe within the static HTML you've been provided with, for example. And you have to be able to work out why your program is producing HTML that "isn't quite right" on occasion.

So, you can most certainly get by as an ASP.NET developer without being an HTML expert, but you do require the basic skills necessary to make sure you're doing your job properly and effectively.

> With XAML, acquiring this basic level of understanding becomes even more important. Drawing comparisons between XAML and other markup languages is a bit misleading, however, the main reason being that unlike other markup languages, XAML directly represents the instantiation of objects from within the .NET libraries. In effect, using XAML is another way to access the .NET API directly, instantiate arbitrary objects, and set their properties and events, albeit declaratively. This means that XAML is at heart a programming language, albeit a declarative one (with flow-control support when mixed with code).

XAML is output by default within Visual Studio and other design tools and will continue to be the default moving forward, for the simple reason that XML and therefore XAML are easier to construct and validate than program code. If you want to become a Silverlight developer, you're simply not going to be able to avoid XAML.

And don't forget: XAML is a general-purpose declarative language; it applies not just to Silverlight and WPF but to other technologies as well. This means that the work you put into learning XAML is transferable to those other technologies and as such multiplies the benefits of learning it.

Because Visual Studio and other design tools output XAML behind the scenes and because designers primarily use XAML to construct the user interface, XAML is in effect the common language that is spoken between the developers and the designers. For communication to take place, both parties need to know what the other is talking about.

Finally, as XAML is just XML, it's hierarchical in nature, which means it's ideally suited for representing the visual tree of a user interface. Trying to do this purely in code would take you longer and prove more difficult.

In short, XAML is at the heart of WPF and therefore Silverlight, and in order to become a Silverlight expert, you need to be able to work with it, understand it, and take advantage of the benefits it brings to the table.

XAML Syntax and Terminology

First things first: Start at the very top of a typical Silverlight XAML file. A XAML file can only have one root element, and in the case of a Silverlight application file, this is a `UserControl` element, shown in the following code.

```
<UserControl x:Class="Chapter03.Page"
    xmlns="http://schemas.microsoft.com/winfx/2006/xaml/presentation"
    xmlns:x="http://schemas.microsoft.com/winfx/2006/xaml"
    Width="400" Height="300">

    <Grid x:Name="LayoutRoot" Background="White">

    </Grid>

</UserControl>
```

In this example, the `Width` and `Height` properties of the `UserControl` are specified, and two namespace declarations are included.

Namespaces

The `xmlns` attribute isn't specific to XAML — it's standard XML and is used to qualify the element it's applied to and the child elements contained within it. Don't bother trying to type these namespace values into your browser to see what's there, as there isn't usually anything there. XML namespace values are nothing more than arbitrary strings to help differentiate between elements with the same name, in much the same way as .NET namespaces are used to fully qualify the types declared within them. At no point will any resolution of the namespace value via a network connection take place.

You will typically see URLs used, though, as they are guaranteed to be unique across companies. (Face it: No company other than Microsoft is going to own the domain name `*.microsoft.com`, are they?)

Of the two namespaces in the example, the first is the default (denoted by the lack of colon and following string) and represents all of the different Silverlight controls you might need in your Silverlight application. Because it's the default, all child elements that are added without a prefix to their names will automatically be scoped to this namespace unless explicitly defined otherwise.

The `:x` immediately following the second `xmlns` (the fact that it's the letter *x* is irrelevant, it could have been *a*, *b*, *c*, or any other string) denotes that in order to qualify a type as belonging to this namespace, its name must be prefixed by `x:`, as in `x:SomeType`. This namespace contains the required language components that are defined in the XAML specification, such as the ability to set an object's name like so:

```
<TextBlock x:Name="myButton" />
```

XAML, unlike other markup languages, is designed to allow for the instantiation and initialization of .NET objects. What happens if you want to instantiate and assign values to a custom type that you've created in XAML or an existing .NET type not scoped within the default namespaces? A special namespace syntax exists to support just this scenario.

Consider the following example:

```
<UserControl x:Class="Chapter03.Page"
    xmlns="http://schemas.microsoft.com/winfx/2006/xaml/presentation"
    xmlns:x="http://schemas.microsoft.com/winfx/2006/xaml"
    xmlns:math="clr-namespace:MyCompany.Math;assembly=MyCompany.Math.dll"
    Width="400" Height="300">

    <Grid x:Name="LayoutRoot" Background="White">
        <TextBox x:Name="MyTextbox" />
        <math:MyObject x:Name="MyCustomObject" />
    </Grid>

</UserControl>
```

Within the `UserControl` declaration, you have the two standard Silverlight namespaces, followed by a custom namespace with a different value syntax:

```
xmlns:math="clr-namespace:MyCompany.Math;assembly=MyCompany.Math.dll"
```

The first thing to note is that the namespace prefix being set for this namespace is `:math`. This means that any type within this namespace you want to use within XAML must be prefixed by `math:` in order to be resolved correctly. The first parameter in the namespace value is `clr-namespace:MyCompany.Math;`, and as the parameter name suggests, it needs to be the value of the fully qualified namespace your types exist within. The next parameter, `assembly=MyCompany.Math.dll`, needs to be the assembly name your type is contained within. The .dll extension is required as it's treated as a URI. With the inclusion of this namespace declaration, you're free to use the types within with ease by using the `<prefix:ClassName>` syntax.

```
<math:MyClassName />
```

This raises an interesting question, however. What if you want to use a type that needs parameters passing into its constructor? The simple answer is, you can't. So be aware that if you're writing a type that you intend to use from XAML, it needs to be written with a default parameterless constructor.

White Space

XAML is XML. As such, XAML is bound by the rules of XML and its white-space handling (handling of space, line feed, and tab characters). When a XAML file is being parsed, the following steps are taken to normalize the white space contained within:

❑ Line-feed characters between East Asian characters are removed.

❑ All white-space characters are converted into spaces.

❑ All consecutive spaces are deleted and replaced with a single space.

❑ A space immediately following the start tag is deleted.

❑ A space immediately before the end tag is deleted.

As you can imagine, in some circumstances, this white-space normalization isn't what you'd want to occur. For instance, you may have defined the following control on your page:

```xml
<UserControl x:Class="Chapter03.Page"
    xmlns="http://schemas.microsoft.com/winfx/2006/xaml/presentation"
    xmlns:x="http://schemas.microsoft.com/winfx/2006/xaml"
    Width="400" Height="300">

    <Grid x:Name="LayoutRoot" Background="White">
        <TextBlock FontSize="72">
            Hello
            World
        </TextBlock>

    </Grid>

</UserControl>
```

When you run this page, the actual output you will get is shown in Figure 3-1.

Figure 3-1

That's not quite what you expected. The white-space normalization routine has replaced the carriage return with a single space. To format the text within the `TextBlock` correctly, you can use the `LineBreak` element, like so:

```xml
<UserControl x:Class="Chapter03.Page"
    xmlns="http://schemas.microsoft.com/winfx/2006/xaml/presentation"
    xmlns:x="http://schemas.microsoft.com/winfx/2006/xaml"
```

```
      Width="400" Height="300">

      <Grid x:Name="LayoutRoot" Background="White">
          <TextBlock FontSize="72">
              Hello
              <LineBreak />
              World
          </TextBlock>

      </Grid>

  </UserControl>
```

This will give you the result you originally wanted. See Figure 3-2.

Figure 3-2

Object and Property Elements

You now know about the two standard namespace declarations in a Silverlight XAML file and why they are there, and also how to include namespaces relating to other types. Now you will look at XAML elements and the supporting syntax in more detail.

An XML element within XAML is known as an *object element* and represents an existing type within a .NET assembly. To assign values to the properties and events contained within the type, standard XML attribute syntax can be used.

XAML is case-sensitive and the object element and property element names must match the type name and type members exactly. Why case-sensitive? XAML is XML, which forces case sensitivity. Another reason is that you can use XAML to instantiate arbitrary objects, so it stands to reason you would need to use the correct case for the type names.

In the following example, the single line of XAML represents the instantiation of the `TextBlock` type, the setting of its `Text` property to the string literal "Hello World," and the assigning of its `Width` and `Height` properties.

```
<TextBlock Text="Hello World" Height="20" Width="100" />
```

This is exactly equivalent to the following C# code:

```
TextBlock tb = new TextBlock();
tb.Text = "Hello World";
tb.Height = 20;
tb.Width = 100;
```

It's instantly apparent that expressing something like this in XAML is cleaner and more concise than doing so in C# code. You might also have spotted a potential issue with the above: What if you need to assign something other than a string literal to the property or event?

If the value you're attempting to set is a primitive type, the XAML loader will attempt a direct conversion to this type from the string literal. In the case of an enumerated type being required, the loader will check for a match against the names contained within the enumerated type. If a match is found, the value fronting the matched name will be returned.

For all other cases, *property element syntax* must be used for values that are too complex to be expressed as a string literal. This entails nesting an element within the object element start and end tags that follows the naming convention `<TypeName.PropertyName>`.

Consider the example of setting the `TextBlock Foreground` color to Blue. If you look in the documentation at the type expected by the `Foreground` property, you can see that it is expecting a type of `System.Windows.Media.Brush`. By using property element syntax, you are able to express this like so:

```
<TextBlock>

    Hello World

    <TextBlock.Foreground>
      <SolidColorBrush Color="Blue" />
    </TextBlock.Foreground>

</TextBlock>
```

Type Converters

Some attributes will allow you to express property element syntax more simply thanks to an object called a *type converter*. A type converter's job is to know how to convert simple string values into an object of the type that is actually needed by the given attribute.

So for the `TextBlock.Foreground` property, if you use simple attribute-based syntax and pass it the string `"Blue"`, a custom type converter kicks in and converts this into the appropriate `System.Windows.Media.SolidColorBrush` type that is expected.

For example:

```
<TextBlock Foreground="Blue" />
```

will take the string `"Blue"` and replace it with a new `SolidColorBrush` set to `Colors.Blue`.

If the property that is exposed to XAML is a primitive type, the XAML loader will attempt to directly convert the given string representation to the correct primitive type.

When it comes to writing your own types that you'd like to be able to expose via XAML, you're free to write your own type converters to allow the consumers of your type to pass simple strings in place of property element syntax where appropriate. Doing this involves inheriting from `TypeConverter` and writing the logic that checks if a value can be converted and how to perform the conversion.

Markup Extensions

Consider property element syntax again. If you set the `Foreground` property of your `TextBlock` to an arbitrary `LinearGradientBrush`, a brand new instance of the `LinearGradientBrush` is always created.

This is because this:

```
<TextBlock>

    Hello World

    <TextBlock.Foreground>
      <LinearGradientBrush>
        <GradientStop Color="Green" Offset="0.5"/>
        <GradientStop Color="Yellow" Offset="1.0"/>
      </LinearGradientBrush>
    </TextBlock.Foreground>

</TextBlock>
```

is the same as doing this:

```
//Construct and initialize our LinearGradientBrush
LinearGradientBrush lgb = new LinearGradientBrush();

GradientStop gs1 = new GradientStop();
gs1.Color = Colors.Green;
gs1.Offset = 0.5;

GradientStop gs2 = new GradientStop();
gs2.Color = Colors.Yellow;
gs2.Offset = 1.0;

lgb.GradientStops.Add(gs1);
lgb.GradientStops.Add(gs2);

//Create our TextBlock and assign our pre-created brush
TextBlock tb = new TextBlock;
tb.Foreground = lgb;
```

Now imagine if the `LinearGradientBrush` was more complex and was needed on 20 `TextBlock` objects on the UI. In code, you would do this:

```
//Construct and Initialize our common LinearGradientBrush
LinearGradientBrush lgb = new LinearGradientBrush();

GradientStop gs1 = new GradientStop();
gs1.Color = Colors.Green;
gs1.Offset = 0.5;

GradientStop gs2 = new GradientStop();
gs2.Color = Colors.Yellow;
gs2.Offset = 1.0;

lgb.GradientStops.Add(gs1);
lgb.GradientStops.Add(gs2);

//Create first TextBlock, assign common brush
TextBlock tb1 = new TextBlock();
tb1.Foreground = lgb;

//Create second TextBlock, assign common brush
TextBlock tb2 = new TextBlock();
tb2.Foreground = lgb;

TextBlock tb3...
```

Can you replicate this behavior in XAML? The answer comes with markup extensions, which allow you to potentially pass an object reference to a property rather than a new instance as would occur via property element syntax. Markup extensions are not used only for this purpose, however, and you'll see them again in areas such as DataBinding and Templates via the `Binding` and `TemplateBinding` objects, respectively.

The following example shows how this can be done:

```
<UserControl x:Class="Chapter03.Page"
    xmlns="http://schemas.microsoft.com/winfx/2006/xaml/presentation"
    xmlns:x="http://schemas.microsoft.com/winfx/2006/xaml"
    Width="400" Height="300">

    <Grid x:Name="LayoutRoot" Background="White">

        <Grid.ColumnDefinitions>
            <ColumnDefinition />
            <ColumnDefinition />
        </Grid.ColumnDefinitions>

        <Grid.Resources>
            <LinearGradientBrush x:Key="SharedBrush">
                <GradientStop Color="Yellow" Offset="0.0" />
                <GradientStop Color="Green" Offset="0.5" />
            </LinearGradientBrush>
        </Grid.Resources>

        <TextBlock Text="Hello"
```

```
                    FontSize="48"
                    Foreground="{StaticResource SharedBrush}"
                    Grid.Column="0" />

        <TextBlock Text="World"
                    FontSize="48"
                    Foreground="{StaticResource SharedBrush}"
                    Grid.Column="1" />

    </Grid>

</UserControl>
```

Note the `Resources` property of the `Grid` object. This gives you the ability to define objects that are going to be needed multiple times in the user interface and store them within this property for subsequent retrieval. To access the objects within this collection, you can use the `StaticResource` markup extension.

A markup extension is always contained within curly braces, and when the XAML parser comes across these curly braces within a property value, it knows to do something other than treat the value as a string literal or string convertible type.

The syntax for looking up a value in the `Resources` property is to enclose the attribute value in curly braces, use the `StaticResource` keyword followed by a space, and then specify the `x:Key` value given to the resource in question.

```
{StaticResource MyResourceXKeyName}
```

Attached Properties

XAML defines an interesting ability that allows certain properties (and events, for that matter) to be specified on types, even if the property definition doesn't actually live within the type that the property is being utilized on. An object can obtain these extra properties when it's added to a container object that defines attached properties. Take adding a `TextBlock` control to a `Canvas`, for example. As well as the standard properties that exist in the `TextBlock` control, three more properties are available and provided by the `Canvas` that contains the `Button`: `Canvas.Top`, `Canvas.Left`, and `Canvas.ZOrder`.

Attached properties are accessed in the form `OwnerName.PropertyName`.

```
<Canvas>

    <TextBlock Canvas.Top="20" Canvas.Left="20" />

</Canvas>
```

It effectively turns the properties in question into global properties that can be set from within any number of different types. This is a technique you'll see commonly used for layout, as in the above example code, as it allows child elements to notify parent elements about significant values. The

`Button` type itself doesn't contain a definition for the properties `Top` and `Left`, but it does need to let its parent know about them so that it can be correctly positioned at layout time.

Basic Drawing

Silverlight 2 ships with the ability to draw three basic shapes as described here. Chapter 14 discusses advanced drawing in more detail, including the more advanced `PolyLine`, `Polygon`, and `Path` shapes.

All these shapes inherit from the base class `Shape`, and as such share many properties including `Height`, `Width`, `Stroke`, and `StrokeThickness`.

Ellipse

The `Ellipse` object allows you to draw an oval or circle on the screen by altering the `Width` and `Height` properties. The following code draws a black circle on a blue background. See Figure 3-3.

```
<UserControl x:Class="Chapter03.Page"
    xmlns="http://schemas.microsoft.com/winfx/2006/xaml/presentation"
    xmlns:x="http://schemas.microsoft.com/winfx/2006/xaml"
    Width="400" Height="300">

    <Grid x:Name="LayoutRoot" Background="LightBlue">

        <Ellipse Width="150"
            Height="150"
            Fill="Black"/>

    </Grid>

</UserControl>
```

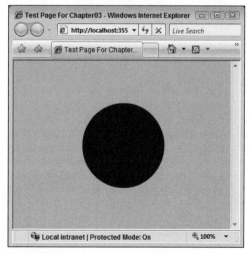

Figure 3-3

You can also alter the color of the border of the ellipse by altering the `Stroke` property and the thickness of this border by altering the `StrokeThickness` property. See Figure 3-4.

```
<UserControl x:Class="Chapter03.Page"
    xmlns="http://schemas.microsoft.com/winfx/2006/xaml/presentation"
    xmlns:x="http://schemas.microsoft.com/winfx/2006/xaml"
    Width="400" Height="300">

    <Grid x:Name="LayoutRoot" Background="LightBlue">

        <Ellipse Width="150"
            Height="150"
            Fill="Black"
            Stroke="Red"
            StrokeThickness="5"/>

    </Grid>

</UserControl>
```

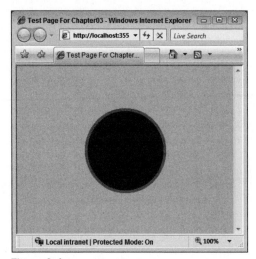

Figure 3-4

Note how the `Fill` property of the ellipse accepts a string value and uses a type converter to convert the string into an object of the right type, which is exactly the same technique as used by the button's `Background` property.

If you wanted to assign something a more advanced color, you could do so using property element syntax. See Figure 3-5.

```
<UserControl x:Class="Chapter03.Page"
    xmlns="http://schemas.microsoft.com/winfx/2006/xaml/presentation"
    xmlns:x="http://schemas.microsoft.com/winfx/2006/xaml"
    Width="400" Height="300">
```

```
        <Grid x:Name="LayoutRoot" Background="LightBlue">

        <Ellipse Width="150"
            Height="150"
            Stroke="Black"
            StrokeThickness="5">

          <Ellipse.Fill>
              <LinearGradientBrush>
                  <GradientStop Color="Green" Offset="0.0" />
                  <GradientStop Color="Yellow" Offset="0.5" />
              </LinearGradientBrush>
          </Ellipse.Fill>

        </Ellipse>

      </Grid>

   </UserControl>
```

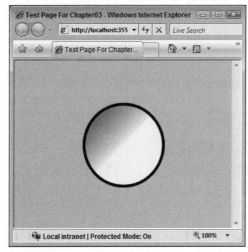

Figure 3-5

Rectangle

Yes, you've guessed it. The `Rectangle` object allows you to describe a rectangle on your display. Like `Ellipse`, it has `Height`, `Width`, `Stroke`, `StrokeThickness`, and `Fill` properties. See Figure 3-6.

```
<UserControl x:Class="Chapter03.Page"
    xmlns="http://schemas.microsoft.com/winfx/2006/xaml/presentation"
    xmlns:x="http://schemas.microsoft.com/winfx/2006/xaml"
    Width="400" Height="300">

    <Grid x:Name="LayoutRoot" Background="LightBlue">

        <Rectangle Height="100"
```

```
            Width="250"
            Fill="Black"
            Stroke="Red"
            StrokeThickness="20" />

    </Grid>

</UserControl>
```

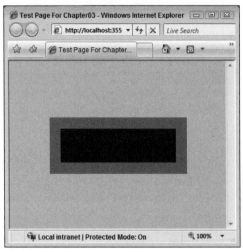

Figure 3-6

And you can apply a more complex brush to the Stroke property, just as you can the Fill property and any other property of a type that expects a brush. See Figure 3-7.

```
<UserControl x:Class="Chapter03.Page"
    xmlns="http://schemas.microsoft.com/winfx/2006/xaml/presentation"
    xmlns:x="http://schemas.microsoft.com/winfx/2006/xaml"
    Width="400" Height="300">

    <Grid x:Name="LayoutRoot" Background="LightBlue">

        <Rectangle Height="100"
            Width="250"
            Fill="Red"
            StrokeThickness="20">

            <Rectangle.Stroke>
                <LinearGradientBrush>
                    <GradientStop Color="Orange" Offset="0.0" />
                    <GradientStop Color="Yellow" Offset="0.5" />
                    <GradientStop Color="Red" Offset="1.0" />
                </LinearGradientBrush>
            </Rectangle.Stroke>
```

```
        </Rectangle>


    </Grid>

</UserControl>
```

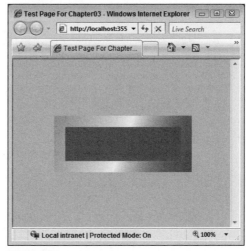

Figure 3-7

Line

The last of the basic shapes you can draw is the Line. You use the X1, X2, Y1, and Y2 properties to control its placement on your display area. The X1 and Y1 properties control the starting point of the Line, and the X2 and Y2 properties control the endpoint.

Although you're free to set the Fill property of a Line object, there really isn't much point. A Line by its very nature has no interior and hence nothing to fill. Instead, you must be sure to set the Stroke and StrokeThickness properties. Without doing so, your line will not be visible on screen. See Figure 3-8.

```
<UserControl x:Class="Chapter03.Page"
    xmlns="http://schemas.microsoft.com/winfx/2006/xaml/presentation"
    xmlns:x="http://schemas.microsoft.com/winfx/2006/xaml"
    Width="400" Height="300">

    <Canvas x:Name="LayoutRoot" Background="LightBlue">

        <Line X1="10" X2="80" Y1="120" Y2="150"
            Stroke="Black"
            StrokeThickness="20"/>

    </Canvas>

</UserControl>
```

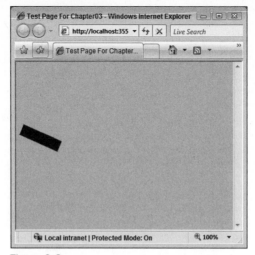

Figure 3-8

The Code-Behind

As you've seen so far, constructing a user interface in XAML is a fairly simple process. You create a .xaml file, make sure there's only one root element, and add the correct namespaces to it, before adding whatever controls are needed to achieve your design.

The next step is turning this no doubt lovely, albeit static UI into a dynamic, event-driven UI. XAML on its own has no concept of flow control, and XAML certainly can't be used to directly handle events. What you need is to borrow the concept of the *code-behind* file from ASP.NET, something you should be intimately familiar with so that the static, purely visual code can jump into life when paired with managed code behind the scenes.

To enable this interaction, you need to put the link in place between your XAML file and the code-behind file. To do this, you use the x:Class attribute in the root element. The x: prefix tells you that this type is contained within the http://schemas.microsoft.com/winfx/2006/xaml namespace. This namespace is the link to the language construct types that can be used in your XAML files. The Class type must be placed in the root element of your XAML file and exists purely to instruct the XAML compiler that your XAML file's event handling and control logic can be found in the class specified. Specifying the class is trivial. You simply need to provide the fully qualified name of the class and the assembly location that the class is contained within.

The following example shows the usage of the x:Class attribute to link a XAML file with a code-behind file whose class is named Chapter03.Page.

```
<UserControl x:Class="Chapter03.Page"
    xmlns="http://schemas.microsoft.com/winfx/2006/xaml/presentation"
    xmlns:x="http://schemas.microsoft.com/winfx/2006/xaml"
    Loaded="UserControl_Loaded"
    Width="400" Height="300">
```

```
    <Grid x:Name="LayoutRoot"
          Background="LightBlue"
          MouseLeftButtonUp="LayoutRoot_MouseLeftButtonUp">


    </Grid>

</UserControl>
```

You'll notice the addition of the `MouseLeftButtonUp` attribute within the `Grid` element. The value of this attribute is a string literal with the same name as the event handling method in the code-behind file. The code within the code behind is listed below:

```
using System;
using System.Collections.Generic;
using System.Linq;
using System.Net;
using System.Windows;
using System.Windows.Controls;
using System.Windows.Documents;
using System.Windows.Input;
using System.Windows.Media;
using System.Windows.Media.Animation;
using System.Windows.Shapes;

namespace Chapter03
{
    public partial class Page : UserControl
    {
        public Page()
        {
            InitializeComponent();
        }


        private void UserControl_Loaded(object sender, RoutedEventArgs e)
        {
            //init code can go in here
        }

        private void LayoutRoot_MouseLeftButtonUp(
                    object sender,
                    MouseButtonEventArgs e)
        {
            Grid grid = sender as Grid;

            LinearGradientBrush lgb = new LinearGradientBrush();

            GradientStop gs1 = new GradientStop();
            gs1.Color = Colors.Green;
            gs1.Offset = 0.5;

            GradientStop gs2 = new GradientStop();
            gs2.Color = Colors.Yellow;
```

```
            gs2.Offset = 1;

            lgb.GradientStops.Add(gs1);
            lgb.GradientStops.Add(gs2);

            grid.Background = lgb;
        }
    }
}
```

The first thing to note in the code is the `partial` keyword against the class definition. The `partial` keyword allows a class definition to span multiple files, typically used to separate designer-generated code from user-written code. When hooking up a code-behind file, the partial class must inherit from the type of class used as the root element of the document. You can, if you choose, omit the derivation code, but the run time will assume it, and for the sake of being explicit, it's best to include it.

Next up you have the first of two handlers that you defined in the XAML file against the `UserControl` and `Grid` elements. `UserControl_Loaded` will be called when — you guessed it — the UserControl is loaded by the run time. When you create a page using Visual Studio, no loaded event is automatically added for you. A constructor, however, is created that takes care of calling `InitializeComponent`. This is where designer-generated code will be placed that is used to construct and initialize the object, assign field-level references to XAML objects, and kick off the initial render for the Silverlight content area.

The `InitializeComponent` code is physically located in an auto-generated file named `[ClassName].g.cs`. This file can be found in the obj directory of your solution following a compilation, as can be seen in Figure 3-9.

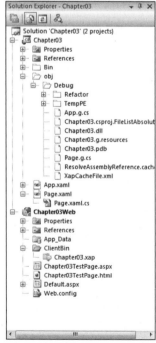

Figure 3-9

The second event handler is one that you have to define yourself, the `LayoutRoot_MouseLeftButtonUp` handler. You'll notice that it follows the standard .NET event-handling signature, with a reference to the raising object passed as the first parameter and event arguments passed as the second. The first parameter, `sender`, is cast to an object of type `Grid` (the type of the element raising this event). A `Linear GradientBrush` is then constructed, and two `GradientStop` objects are added to its `GradientStops` collection. The completed `LinearGradientBrush` is then set as the `Background` property of the `Grid`.

If you compile and run the application, you should see a blue square with yellow text. Upon clicking the Grid with the left mouse button, however, the square will change to a rather sickly green-and-yellow color. See Figure 3-10.

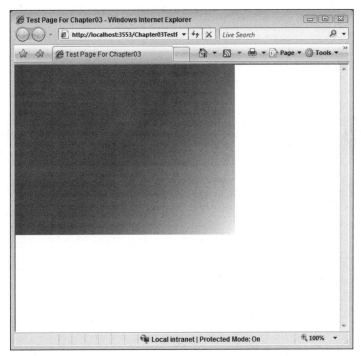

Figure 3-10

Dynamically Loading XAML

As an ASP.NET developer, you're aware that there are many scenarios in which the HTML that makes up your pages can't just be created and edited at design time in Visual Studio (or your tool of preference). For instance, providing different HTML for different users to cater for the individual look and feel of the user interface is not possible at design time only. Runtime decisions have to be made to alter the HTML to be output.

It's almost certainly going to be a requirement in any advanced Silverlight application to allow for requirements such as this — the delivery of XAML whose content and structure aren't completely known until a collection of certain runtime parameters has been completed.

Luckily it's fairly easy to accomplish the dynamic generation of XAML on the server; in fact, it should feel very familiar to you, especially if you've written any AJAX code to return discrete portions of a page.

There are two techniques that can be employed when it comes to dynamically creating XAML: dynamically creating an entire XAML page and referencing it from within the plug-in declaration, and dynamically creating fragments of XAML that can be added to an in-memory Silverlight object tree previously created. You'll look at the first approach in this chapter as it involves no Silverlight coding, and you'll look at the second technique in Chapter 4.

Referencing a Server-Side Page That Dynamically Creates the XAML

The basic premise is this: The ASP.NET Silverlight server control has a `Source` property that is usually set to the location of the Silverlight applications .xap package (more on both the control and .xap files in Chapter 4). However, you're free to set this to the location of any arbitrary XAML file you choose. In point of fact, you're free to set this property to the location of any file providing it returns a valid stream of XAML.

Consider the following declaration for an ASP.NET Silverlight server control in the file LoadDynamicXAML.aspx.

```
<%@ Page Language="C#" AutoEventWireup="true" %>

<%@ Register Assembly="System.Web.Silverlight"
    Namespace="System.Web.UI.SilverlightControls"
    TagPrefix="asp" %>

<!DOCTYPE html PUBLIC "-//W3C//DTD XHTML 1.0 Transitional//EN"
    "http://www.w3.org/TR/xhtml1/DTD/xhtml1-transitional.dtd">

<html xmlns="http://www.w3.org/1999/xhtml" style="height:100%;">
<head runat="server">
    <title>Load Dynamic XAML Example</title>
</head>
<body style="height:100%;margin:0;">
    <form id="form1" runat="server" style="height:100%;">
        <asp:ScriptManager ID="ScriptManager1" runat="server">
        </asp:ScriptManager>
        <div  style="height:100%;">
            <asp:Silverlight ID="Xaml1"
                             runat="server"
                             Source="~/DynamicXAML.ashx"
                             MinimumVersion="2.0.30523"
                             Width="100%"
                             Height="100%" />
        </div>
    </form>
</body>
</html>
```

You can see in this example that the `Source` property hasn't been set to either a valid Silverlight package (.xap file) or, indeed, a static XAML file, but instead an arbitrary ASP.NET generic handler. This handler will be responsible for returning a valid stream of XAML to the caller, in this case the ASP.NET Silverlight server control.

We chose a handler in this instance rather than an .aspx file because a handler is more lightweight and we didn't need the benefit of the full-page life cycle provided inherently by the page object model.

Now, take a look at the contents of the file DynamicXAML.ashx:

```
using System;
using System.Collections;
using System.Data;
using System.Linq;
using System.Web;
using System.Web.Services;
using System.Web.Services.Protocols;
using System.Xml.Linq;

namespace Chapter03Web
{
    /// <summary>
    /// Summary description for $codebehindclassname$
    /// </summary>
    [WebService(Namespace = "http://tempuri.org/")]
    [WebServiceBinding(ConformsTo = WsiProfiles.BasicProfile1_1)]
    public class DynamicXAML : IHttpHandler
    {

        public void ProcessRequest(HttpContext context)
        {
            context.Response.ContentType = "text/xaml";

            context.Response.Write("<Canvas xmlns=" + "\"" +
"http://schemas.microsoft.com/client/2007" + "\" ");
            context.Response.Write("xmlns:x=" + "\"" +
"http://schemas.microsoft.com/winfx/2006/xaml" + "\" ");
            context.Response.Write("Width=" + "\"" + "640" + "\" ");
            context.Response.Write("Height=" + "\"" + "480" + "\"");
            context.Response.Write(">");

            context.Response.Write("<TextBlock Text=" + "\"" +
                                    "Hello, World" + "\" ");
            context.Response.Write("Foreground=" + "\"" + "Blue" + "\" ");
            context.Response.Write("Canvas.Top=" + "\"" + "10" + "\" ");
            context.Response.Write("Canvas.Left=" + "\"" + "10" + "\"" + " />");

            context.Response.Write("</Canvas>");

        }
        public bool IsReusable
        {
            get
            {
                return false;
            }
        }
    }
}
```

Aside from the boilerplate code that is generated for you by the Visual Studio IDE when you create a new generic handler, you can see a series of calls to `context.Response.Write` that send the required XAML to the output stream. Here you're free to use any logic necessary to customize the XAML that is returned, although in this case, for the sake of example, the text *Hello, World* will be displayed in a `Canvas` object. A more realistic scenario might see you querying a database to return specific user preference information.

Take a look at the first line of code within the `ProcessRequest` method — you should notice that the default `ContentType` of `text/plain` has been replaced with `text/xaml`.

So what exactly will this do? Well, the `ContentType` directive helps a browser decide how to display the content. If you navigate using the browser directly to this .ashx page, the browser will render the screen shown in Figure 3-11.

Figure 3-11

Notice that the browser has recognized that the content is not just plaintext and has formatted it nicely as it would XML. Now alter the `ContentType` and set it back to its default of `text/plain` like so:

```
context.Response.ContentType = "text/plain";
```

If you navigate directly to this page now, you will see the screen shown in Figure 3-12.

It's not that different, but having the browser display it as collapsible, color-coded XML in a complicated file is a real bonus. If you're going to use this technique, we can guarantee that you'll spend quite a bit of time navigating directly to the handler or web page responsible for outputting your XAML, trying to work out where you've missed a quote or angle bracket. In addition, it's good practice to be explicit, so you should set the `ContentType` correctly.

Assume that there is a requirement to add *n* lines of text to this file, the content of which is not available until run time, and you want to perform this operation on the server. By stripping out the current hardcoded `<TextBlock>` element and replacing it with a function call, you are able to satisfy this requirement very easily.

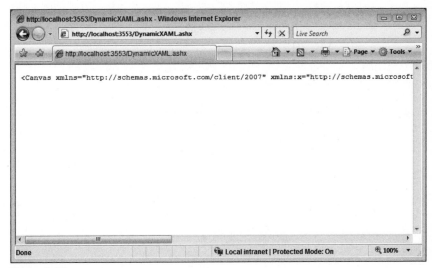

Figure 3-12

Alter DynamicXML.ashx to implement this function:

```csharp
using System;
using System.Collections;
using System.Data;
using System.Linq;
using System.Web;
using System.Web.Services;
using System.Web.Services.Protocols;
using System.Xml.Linq;
using System.Collections.Generic;

namespace Chapter03Web
{
    /// <summary>
    /// Summary description for $codebehindclassname$
    /// </summary>
    [WebService(Namespace = "http://tempuri.org/")]
    [WebServiceBinding(ConformsTo = WsiProfiles.BasicProfile1_1)]
    public class DynamicXAML : IHttpHandler
    {
        public DynamicXAML(): base()
        {
            this.PopulateSimulationData();
        }

        public void ProcessRequest(HttpContext context)
        {
            context.Response.ContentType = "text/xaml";
```

```
            context.Response.Write("<Canvas xmlns=" + "\"" +
                    "http://schemas.microsoft.com/client/2007" + "\" ");
            context.Response.Write("xmlns:x=" + "\"" +
                    "http://schemas.microsoft.com/winfx/2006/xaml" + "\" ");
            context.Response.Write("Width=" + "\"" + "640" + "\" ");
            context.Response.Write("Height=" + "\"" + "480" + "\"");
            context.Response.Write(">");

            this.WriteTextLines(context);

            context.Response.Write("</Canvas>");

        }

        private void WriteTextLines(HttpContext context)
        {
            int canvasTop = 10;
            int canvasLeft = 10;

            foreach (string lineData in this.sampleData)
            {
                context.Response.Write("<TextBlock Text=" + "\"" +
                                                    lineData + "\" ");
                context.Response.Write("Foreground=" + "\"" + "Blue" + "\" ");
                context.Response.Write("Canvas.Top=" + "\"" +
                                    canvasTop.ToString() + "\" ");
                context.Response.Write("Canvas.Left=" + "\"" +
                                    canvasLeft.ToString() + "\"" + " />");

                canvasTop += 20;
            }
        }

        private List<string> sampleData = new List<string>();

        private void PopulateSimulationData()
        {
            sampleData.Add("This is the first line");
            sampleData.Add("This is the second line");
            sampleData.Add("This is the third line");
        }

        public bool IsReusable
        {
            get
            {
                return false;
            }
        }
    }
}
```

The code is very simple. When the handler first loads, a call is made to `PopulateSimulationData()`. This function does nothing more than populate a private member variable of type `List<String>` with some sample data for you to iterate over.

As the handler is being processed, the `WriteTextLines()` method is called. Here, the sample data is iterated over, and the correct XAML markup to be output is appended to the output stream. The `Canvas.Top` and `Canvas.Left` properties are also set for each `TextBlock`, with the `Canvas.Top` property being incremented by 20 each time so the lines of text won't overwrite each other on the `Canvas`.

Browsing directly to the page will give the output shown in Figure 3-13.

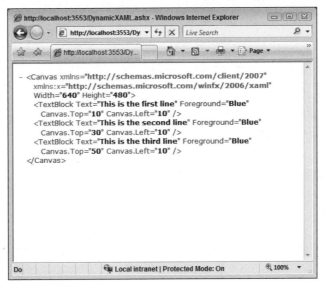

Figure 3-13

Note the dynamically generated XAML to instantiate and populate three `TextBlock` elements. When you access this via a Silverlight-hosted control, you get the correct output, as shown in Figure 3-14.

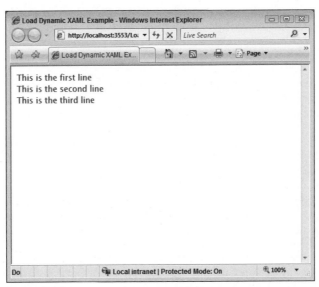

Figure 3-14

Available Tools

There are two integrated development environments that you can use to author Silverlight 2 applications: Microsoft Visual Studio 2008 and Microsoft Expression Blend 2. Throughout the remainder of this book, the focus will be on using Visual Studio 2008 to author your Silverlight applications. This book is aimed at ASP.NET developers first and foremost, and the assumption is that this will be your tool of choice. However, it's worth taking a look at Expression Blend, as there's a very good chance you may use it to construct some advanced UI or animation XAML, or that designers in your team will.

Expression Blend is Microsoft's professional design tool for creating rich user experiences using WPF and Silverlight. Using Expression Blend, a designer can create both Silverlight 1 and 2 applications, construct a compelling user interface using the design-oriented IDE, and then hand the files over to a developer who can open the project within Visual Studio to add the code. Neat. (Of course, a developer is also free to create the application first using Visual Studio with a typical developer's bland and tasteless UI, add all the necessary code, and then ship the files to a designer who can open them directly in Expression Blend to beautify them.)

Expression Blend gives designers a first-class environment for manipulating WPF and Silverlight user interfaces, without the complexity and baggage that come with the full programming support in Visual Studio.

Some of the features within Blend include:

❑ Vector drawing tools, including text and three-dimensional (3D) tools

❑ Real-time animation

❑ 3D and media support

❑ Real-time design and markup views

❑ The ability to import artwork from Expression Design

❑ Interoperability with Visual Studio

To create a rich and compelling WPF or Silverlight UI, you don't have to use Expression Blend, but from a pure design perspective, it certainly makes the job much easier and negates the need for designers to wade through the hefty Visual Studio IDE for creating the UI as they had to do previously.

Enriching your Visual Studio–created XAML file is as easy as right-clicking on the XAML file in Solution Explorer and selecting the "Open in Expression Blend" option. Figure 3-15 shows the IDE in its default state and gives you a good idea about the look and feel of Expression Blend.

So, Expression Blend is a great visual tool for constructing the XAML that comprises your user interface, and it gives designers a much richer design-time experience for accomplishing tasks like animation and media support within your application.

If you need to add code to your WPF or Silverlight application, however, you're going to need to use Visual Studio, as Expression Blend has only the most rudimentary support for code editing (e.g., creating event handler stubs for objects).

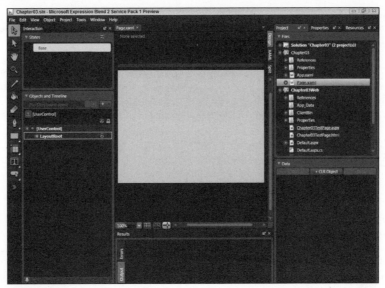

Figure 3-15

Step in Visual Studio 2008. As well as providing native support for working with .NET 3.0 (WPF, WF, and WCF), by downloading and installing the Silverlight tools for Visual Studio, you can also create and edit Silverlight application projects from within the IDE. The support provided by these tools includes:

❏   Project templates for both Visual Basic and C# developers

❏   IntelliSense and code generators for XAML

❏   Debugging of Silverlight applications

❏   Web reference support

❏   Integration with Expression Blend

Although lacking the visual design niceties that are bundled with Expression Blend, Visual Studio comes into its own when it's being used for what it does best — writing code.

Piecing It All Together

You've taken a look at the XAML essentials and stepped through the odd code snippet to boot. Following is a simple example combining everything you've learned so far. If you would rather just step through the code, you can download the code for this chapter from www.wrox.com.

In Chapter 4, more detail is provided about the files that are generated for you, so for now, just take a leap of faith and follow through as best you can.

The first thing you need to do is fire up Visual Studio 2008 and create a new Silverlight Project called *Chapter 03*. Accept the defaults, and the IDE will generate both a Silverlight project and an ASP.NET project to host it in.

Your generated project structure should resemble Figure 3-16 (ignore the LoadDynamicXAML.aspx and DynamicXAML.ashx files in the image, however; these were added for the previous examples), and the XAML code editor should be open on the default Page.xaml that was created.

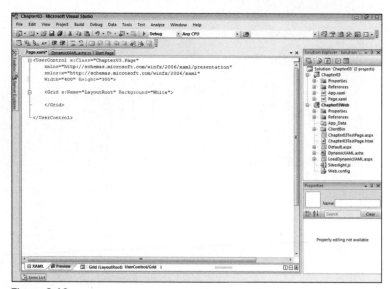

Figure 3-16

To display text in Silverlight, you use the `TextBlock` object. (More information on this and other controls can be found in Chapter 6, "Silverlight Controls.") Add a `TextBlock` element to the page, and set its properties as in the following code:

```
<UserControl x:Class="Chapter03.Page"
    xmlns="http://schemas.microsoft.com/winfx/2006/xaml/presentation"
    xmlns:x="http://schemas.microsoft.com/winfx/2006/xaml"
    Width="400" Height="300">

    <Grid x:Name="LayoutRoot" Background="White">

        <TextBlock Name="textToDisplay"
            Canvas.Left="10"
            Canvas.Top="10"
            Text="This is our Text" />

    </Grid>

</UserControl>
```

If you have Expression Blend installed, try right-clicking on the Page.xaml file in Solution Explorer and selecting "Open in Expression Blend." Expression Blend will open the file, and any changes you now make using Expression Blend can be saved and reloaded in the Visual Studio project. Likewise, changes you make in Visual Studio can be saved and reloaded in Expression Blend.

You're now free to use the design-oriented features of Expression Blend to beautify your page in any way that you see fit. For now, add a simple animation to the TextBlock. If you don't have Expression Blend installed, you can copy the generated XAML that is shown shortly.

By default, the Design Workspace is shown in Expression Blend. You need to open up the Animation Workspace, so from the top-level Windows menu, select Animation Workspace. Your Blend UI should look something like Figure 3-17.

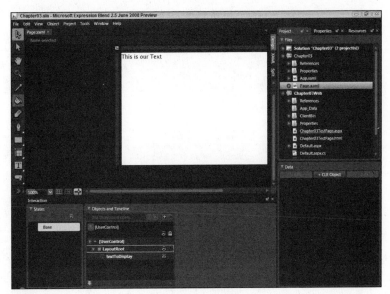

Figure 3-17

You now need to create a new Storyboard and Timeline. In the "Objects and Timeline" panel, you should see a white + button next to some grayed-out text that reads (No Storyboard open). Press this button to open the Storyboard dialog, and then hit the OK button to add a new Storyboard resource. Leave the name as *Storyboard1*. See Figure 3-18.

In the top left of the IDE, you should now see some red text stating that *Timeline recording is on*. Select the TextBlock, and then select one of the second markers in the Timeline at the bottom of the IDE. The second marker you select will be the length of time that this particular timeline will run for. You're going to increase the text size. This will happen gradually over the number of seconds you select here, so something like 10 is appropriate.

Once you've done this, all that remains to do is to select the Properties panel and change the TextBlock text size to something larger. Try 72 (see Figure 3-19), and then save your project and close Expression Blend.

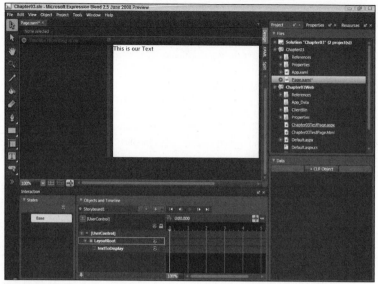

Figure 3-18

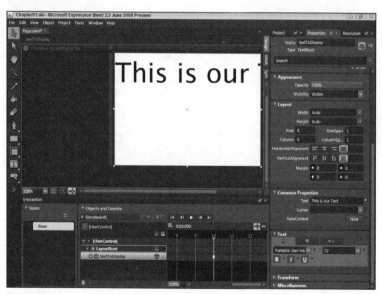

Figure 3-19

When you switch back to Visual Studio, you should be presented with a message box letting you know that Page.xaml has been altered and asking if you would like to reload it. Select Yes, and the XAML should now look like this (again, if you don't have Expression Blend, just copy this code straight into your file):

```
<UserControl x:Class="Chapter03.Page"
    xmlns="http://schemas.microsoft.com/winfx/2006/xaml/presentation"
    xmlns:x="http://schemas.microsoft.com/winfx/2006/xaml"
```

```
        Width="400" Height="300">
    <UserControl.Resources>
            <Storyboard x:Name="Storyboard1">
                <DoubleAnimationUsingKeyFrames BeginTime="00:00:00"
                                        Storyboard.TargetName="textToDisplay"
    Storyboard.TargetProperty=
    "(TextBlock.FontSize)">
                            <SplineDoubleKeyFrame KeyTime="00:00:10" Value="72"/>
                </DoubleAnimationUsingKeyFrames>
            </Storyboard>
    </UserControl.Resources>

    <Grid x:Name="LayoutRoot" Background="White">

        <TextBlock Name="textToDisplay"
            Text="This is our Text" />

    </Grid>

</UserControl>
```

Note the use of *object property syntax* to allow the setting of properties that simply couldn't be specified using string literals. Note also the use of markup extensions to bind a control property to another property.

Chapter 14, "Graphics and Animation," will walk you through the syntax for this animation, so don't concern yourself overly with it for now.

All that remains to be done is for the animation to be started. Switch to the code behind, and add this line of code to the constructor:

```
Storyboard1.Begin();
```

If you hit F5 in Visual Studio, you should be rewarded with the text gradually increasing in size over the time period you specified in the Expression Blend IDE. By now you should be starting to appreciate the new-found ease with which developers and designers can work together, brought about in most part by the ability of both Expression Blend and Visual Studio to work cleanly with the files in question.

Chapter 4 goes over the Silverlight project structure and hosting Silverlight in ASP.NET in more detail.

Summary

In this chapter, you have taken your first in-depth look at XAML. You started off by learning why it's good to know XAML, even if your favorite editor of choice can spit it out for you. You then walked through the building blocks of a XAML file, starting off with the essential namespace declarations before moving on to the syntax governing the elements contained within it.

You learned about object and property syntax, to help specify parameter values that required more than string literals, and you also learned about the Type Conversion process that exists to help with this. You also looked at markup extensions and how they can be used to specify values that already exist in the Resources section of your file.

You then walked through some basic drawing concepts and looked, albeit briefly, at three of the rudimentary shape classes: `Ellipse`, `Rectangle`, and `Line`.

The chapter then showed how you can bring your static XAML file to life by linking it with a code-behind file, a concept close to your ASP.NET hearts, before showing how more ASP.NET techniques can be used to help dynamically generate the XAML itself.

Finally, you looked at the two major IDEs to help you build Silverlight applications — Visual Studio 2008 and Expression Blend 2.

If you have been itching to get coding, Chapter 4 will take you through the ins and outs of programming against the Silverlight API.

Programming Silverlight

In this chapter, you will go through the fundamentals of programming a Silverlight application, looking at the composition of a typical application as well as the feature-agnostic programming constructs that are used when writing all Silverlight 2.0 applications.

You'll start by examining the file and asset structure of a default application as well as the processes involved in actually hosting your Silverlight application within your web site. A discussion on the required level of JavaScript knowledge is provided also, as is a look at the Silverlight object model. Bidirectional communication between the HTML Document Object Model and your Silverlight application is also discussed.

Continuing, various programming features are explained that are used throughout the Silverlight framework. If you are familiar with Windows Presentation Foundation (WPF), you may feel comfortable enough to skim over these as you may well have seen them or something similar before.

Code samples will also be shown that will allow you to download component pieces of your Silverlight application on demand rather than all at once, which is a necessity for producing applications that perform well over the Internet.

How a Silverlight Application Is Composed

A Silverlight application can be made up of many different components, each of which may be needed at different times. Because of this the Silverlight team wanted to make sure that the application model and structure could provide for richer and functionally more complex RIAs. In particular, they wanted to provide the ability to package and deploy an application with its constituent parts, each of which can be described in a manifest file. This file would specify localization and entry point information, among other items of information.

As some of the files that a Silverlight application can work with could be very large (such as audio and video), the Silverlight application should also have the ability to lazy-load resources, which can be referenced both from within its package and from outside.

Packaging a Silverlight Application

When you build a Silverlight application, its constituent parts are packaged together in a simple ZIP archive for deployment. This archive is named *[ProjectName].xap* and is located in the ClientBin directory of the hosting web application.

To examine this in more detail, fire up Visual Studio, and create a new Silverlight application called *Chapter04*. The initial dialog box that will open to take more information regarding your project is shown in Figure 4-1.

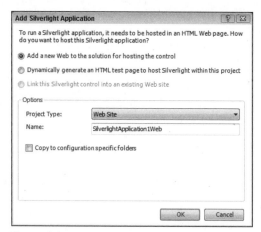

Figure 4-1

There are three options for how the Silverlight project should be created in relation to a project that can be used to host it. The default option is for a new Web to be added to the solution that can host the Silverlight application. When this option is selected, the Project Name and Project Type textboxes are available for entry. *Name* is fairly self-explanatory. *Type* allows you to select whether you want a Web Application Project or a full blown web site to be created. The former will use the ASP.NET development Web server, and the latter will opt for IIS.

The next option down will create a basic HTML test page to host your Silverlight application, and the final option allows you to link your Silverlight control into a preexisting web site.

For this example, the first option is selected, and a Web Application Project will be created to host the Silverlight application, named *Chapter04_Web*.

If you take a look at Solution Explorer, you should have a directory and file structure that resembles Figure 4-2.

Figure 4-2

Before you do anything else, build the entire solution, and you will see that contained within the ClientBin directory in the hosting application is a file called *Chapter04.xap*, as shown in Figure 4-3.

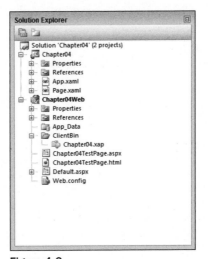

Figure 4-3

As previously mentioned, this file is actually a standard ZIP archive that contains the deployed version of your Silverlight application. In order to inspect the assets within, navigate to the file, rename it from *Chapter04.xap* to *Chapter04.zip*, and simply open it. You will see Chapter04.dll along with other referenced .dlls required for your application to function and a file called *AppManifest.xaml*.

If you open the AppManifest.xaml file, you will see the following markup:

```
<Deployment xmlns="http://schemas.microsoft.com/client/2007/deployment"
            xmlns:x="http://schemas.microsoft.com/winfx/2006/xaml"
            EntryPointAssembly="Chapter04"
            EntryPointType="Chapter04.App"
            RuntimeVersion="2.0.30523.6">
  <Deployment.Parts>
    <AssemblyPart x:Name="Chapter04" Source="Chapter04.dll" />
  </Deployment.Parts>
</Deployment>
```

If you start at the top of this file, the first element you see is the Deployment element. As well as defining the two XAML namespaces, you can see that two attributes are included for specifying both an assembly and class to use as entry points when the application is loaded —
EntryPointAssembly and EntryPointType. The class that is specified in the EntryPointType attribute must inherit from System.Windows.Application and be the fully qualified type name.

Next you will see that the constituent parts of the Silverlight application are defined in the Deployment .Parts element. Only the application assembly itself must be declared in the manifest file. Other assemblies are optional to allow you to lazy-load them yourself if need be. This technique uses the built-in WebClient object and is discussed at the end of this chapter, but realize that for performance reasons, best practice requires that only the files that are needed for the application to run should be specified here. Files containing functionality that is either not required immediately or sometimes unused should be lazy-loaded using the WebClient object.

System.Windows.Application

The System.Windows.Application class is always the starting point for a Silverlight application and as such encapsulates entry point information, application lifetime management, global resources, and the ability to handle unhandled exceptions.

Within the Silverlight file structure, the App.xaml and App.cs files provide you with access to the Application class. For instance, you have the option of handling the application's Startup and Exit handlers, as well as the UnhandledException handler, which are wired up for you by default in the code behind.

```
<Application xmlns="http://schemas.microsoft.com/winfx/2006/xaml/presentation"
             xmlns:x="http://schemas.microsoft.com/winfx/2006/xaml"
             x:Class="Chapter04.App"
             >
    <Application.Resources>

    </Application.Resources>
</Application>
```

The preceding code shows the App.xaml default markup when you create a new project. Below you can see the code behind for this file, with the event handlers pre-wired for you in the constructor:

```
using System;
using System.Collections.Generic;
```

```
using System.Linq;
using System.Net;
using System.Windows;
using System.Windows.Controls;
using System.Windows.Documents;
using System.Windows.Input;
using System.Windows.Media;
using System.Windows.Media.Animation;
using System.Windows.Shapes;

namespace Chapter04
{
    public partial class App : Application
    {

        public App()
        {
            this.Startup += this.Application_Startup;
            this.Exit += this.Application_Exit;
            this.UnhandledException += this.Application_UnhandledException;

            InitializeComponent();
        }

        private void Application_Startup(object sender, StartupEventArgs e)
        {
            this.RootVisual = new Page();
        }

        private void Application_Exit(object sender, EventArgs e)
        {

        }
        private void Application_UnhandledException(object sender,
                            ApplicationUnhandledExceptionEventArgs e)
        {
            // If the app is running outside of the debugger then report the
            // exception using
            // the browser's exception mechanism. On IE this will display it a
            //yellow alert
            // icon in the status bar and Firefox will display a script error.
            if (!System.Diagnostics.Debugger.IsAttached)
            {

                // NOTE: This will allow the application to continue
                //running after an exception has been thrown
                // but not handled.
                // For production applications this error handling should
                //be replaced with something that will
                // report the error to the website and stop the application.
                e.Handled = true;
                Deployment.Current.Dispatcher.BeginInvoke(
                                        delegate { ReportErrorToDOM(e); });
            }
        }
```

```
        }
        private void ReportErrorToDOM(ApplicationUnhandledExceptionEventArgs e)
        {
            try
            {
                string errorMsg = e.ExceptionObject.Message +
                                           e.ExceptionObject.StackTrace;
                errorMsg = errorMsg.Replace('"', '\'').Replace("\r\n", @"\n");

                System.Windows.Browser.HtmlPage.Window.Eval(
    "throw new Error(\"Unhandled Error in Silverlight 2 Application " +
                errorMsg + "\");");
            }
            catch (Exception)
            {
            }
        }
    }
}
```

Notice in the code above how a new instance of the `Page` class is instantiated and given to the `Application.RootVisual` property. This line of code sets the `Page` class as the initial UI to load and display. If you add another page to the Silverlight project that should display first, you should change this line to accept an instance of this new page.

Within the `Startup` event, you can also capture and process any initialization parameters that have been passed to the Silverlight application via the `initParams` property of the containing `<OBJECT>` tag.

Consider the following example, which shows the `initParams` property being set via the `<asp:Silverlight>` element:

```
<%@ Page Language="C#" AutoEventWireup="true" %>

<%@ Register Assembly="System.Web.Silverlight"
    Namespace="System.Web.UI.SilverlightControls"
    TagPrefix="asp" %>

<!DOCTYPE html PUBLIC "-//W3C//DTD XHTML 1.0 Transitional//EN"
    "http://www.w3.org/TR/xhtml11/DTD/xhtml11-transitional.dtd">

<html xmlns="http://www.w3.org/1999/xhtml" style="height:100%;">
<head runat="server">
    <title>Chapter04</title>
</head>
<body style="height:100%;margin:0;">
    <form id="form1" runat="server" style="height:100%;">
        <asp:ScriptManager ID="ScriptManager1" runat="server"></asp:ScriptManager>
        <div  style="height:100%;">
            <asp:Silverlight ID="Xaml1"
                            runat="server"
                            Source="~/ClientBin/Chapter04.xap"
                            MinimumVersion="2.0.30911.0"
                            Width="100%"
```

```
                              Height="100%"
                              InitParameters="Param1=Hello,Param2=World" />
        </div>
    </form>
</body>
</html>
```

Notice how the parameters are specified as name=value pairs within the <asp:Silverlight> element. The following code shows how you can then extract these values at run time from within the Startup event of the Application class:

```
private void Application_Startup(object sender, StartupEventArgs e)
{
    //Assign the root visual object, in this case the Page class
    this.RootVisual = new Page();

    //Extract init params
    string param1 = e.InitParams["Param1"];
    string param2 = e.InitParams["Param2"];
}
```

Application Instantiation

A Silverlight application is embedded within the containing web page using either an <OBJECT> or an <EMBED> tag. You can, of course, write this tag and its parameters manually. However, it's far easier to simply use the <asp:Silverlight> control, which takes care of emitting the relevant HTML and JavaScript on your behalf.

Within this <asp:Silverlight> tag, as well as setting the ID and Runat attributes, you simply set the Source value to the location of the package (or plain XAML file) that contains your Silverlight application, and the rest is taken care of for you. Any JavaScript files that are required by the <asp:Silverlight> control at run time are referenced dynamically with the help of the <asp:ScriptManager> control. (This control is required on the page. If it is omitted, an error message will be raised.)

If for some reason you do still want to write out the plug-in markup manually, you can check out the [ProjectName]TestPage.html file that is added to your project's web host when you create a Silverlight application and associated hosting project. This file contains the bare essential markup for embedding your Silverlight application within a web page. Note also that this file uses the JavaScript file Silverlight.js that is placed in the root of the hosting project automatically for you.

As an ASP.NET developer, it's most likely that you will want to take advantage of the clean model that <asp:Silverlight> provides rather than electing to write the hosting markup and code manually.

Regardless of which method you use, the end result is always that an appropriate <OBJECT> element is included within the page and the relevant parameters are specified, as the following HTML shows:

```
<object data="data:application/x-silverlight,"
        type="application/x-silverlight-2" width="100%" height="100%">
        <param name="source" value="ClientBin/Chapter04.xap"/>
        <param name="onerror" value="onSilverlightError" />
        <param name="background" value="white" />
```

```
                        <param name="minRuntimeVersion" value="2.0.30911.0" />
                        <param name="autoUpgrade" value="true" />
                        <a href="http://go.microsoft.com/fwlink/?LinkID=124807"
                        style="text-decoration: none;">
                                <img src="http://go.microsoft.com/fwlink/?LinkId=108181"
                                alt="Get Microsoft Silverlight" style="border-style: none"/>
                        </a>
                </object>
```

Note the `href` and `image` parameters are specified within the tag. These will be shown if the plug-in is not installed and point to the installation location for the Silverlight run time.

There are certain attributes that should be set when you include the plug-in within your page. These are shown in the following table:

Attribute	Description
id	This is the name that you can use to reference the plug-in from the HTML DOM.
data	This should be set to the Silverlight application MIME type and is used by the Silverlight plug-in to streamline the instantiation process.
type	This should be set to the MIME type of the version of the Silverlight plug-in that is to be loaded.
height	Self-explanatory. Can be set in pixels or as a percentage of the parent container.
width	Self-explanatory. Can be set in pixels or as a percentage of the parent container.

As well as these attributes, as previously mentioned, you will also need to specify the `Source` property, which should point to the location of your Silverlight package.

Note that if you use the `<asp:Silverlight>` control, it will take care of applying the `data` and `type` attributes for you automatically to the underlying `<OBJECT>` tag. Note also that the attributes and events listed in the following tables may be named slightly differently if set via the `<asp:Silverlight>` control, which will ultimately set the properties listed.

There are various other attributes that can be applied against the Silverlight plug-in described in the following table:

Attribute	Description
background	The background color of the Silverlight plug-in
enabledHtmlAccess	Value used to specify whether the plug-in can be accessed from the HTML DOM
initParams	Allows the passing of name=value pairs to aid initialization.
maxFramerate	Integer specifying the desired frame rate. This is the maximum value and can be slower than this as it is dependent on both system load and performance.

Attribute	Description
splashScreenSource	Can be set to an optional XAML splash screen that should be shown while the package is loading.
windowless	Determines whether the plug-in should run in windowed or windowless mode. On a Mac, this property is ignored, and the plug-in always runs windowless.

The Silverlight plug-in also exposes various events that you can wire up to client-side JavaScript handlers if desired. The following table lists these:

Event	Description
onError	Occurs when an error is raised from the Silverlight application instance.
onResize	Fires when the ActualHeight or ActualWidth of the Silverlight plug-in is altered.
onLoad	Fires when the plug-in is instantiated and all content has been loaded (full object tree generated and all XAML parsed).
onSourceDownloadComplete	Fires when the application package specified by the Source property has been downloaded.
onSourceDownloadProgressChanged	Fires when the application package specified by the source property is downloading.

It's worth looking briefly at the steps taken when a Silverlight application is instantiated, to help cement your understanding of the runtime flow and application lifetime:

1. The <OBJECT> tag specifies which version of Silverlight is installed (JavaScript will usually have been used to write out the appropriate tag) and loads the plug-in.

2. The CLR is kicked off, and an AppDomain is created to host the application.

3. The main application assembly along with all other assemblies referenced within the manifest are downloaded and loaded into the AppDomain.

4. The application object itself is now created using the EntryPointType information in the manifest file. The Startup and Exit handlers are wired up, and any user code in the constructor is executed.

5. The Startup event is raised, and the UI is constructed and added to the Application .VisualRoot property.

6. The starting page is loaded, the FrameworkElement.Loaded events fire on the elements within, and the Silverlight plug-in's OnLoad event is then raised.

A Basic Silverlight Page

Turn your attention now to the Page.xaml file that is created for you when you create a new Silverlight application. In keeping with the ASP.NET code-behind model, the presentation of the UI is kept in one file (the .xaml file), and the logic is coded in the .xaml.[vb or cs] file that is referenced in the root element of the .xaml file.

```
<UserControl x:Class="Chapter04.Page"
    xmlns="http://schemas.microsoft.com/winfx/2006/xaml/presentation"
    xmlns:x="http://schemas.microsoft.com/winfx/2006/xaml"
    Width="400" Height="300">

    <Grid x:Name="LayoutRoot" Background="White">

    </Grid>

</UserControl>
```

As previously mentioned, a XAML file can contain only one root element. In this example, the root element is a UserControl element, and the first child within it is an element used for layout, in this case, a Grid control named LayoutRoot.

If you need to create another page in your application, this is done by simply adding another Silverlight UserControl to your project. UserControl separates the component pieces of your application as it allows you to break your application down into more manageable chunks independently from other Silverlight controls. UserControl is also used for composing existing controls together that can possibly be reused later elsewhere.

The code above shows how the code-behind file is referenced using the x:class attribute, specifying the fully qualified class name to link to. You can also provide an assembly parameter in the x:Class value. However, if this is omitted (as in this example), the assembly is assumed to be the one that the project is currently creating.

If you take a look in the code-behind file, you can see that the Page class inherits from UserControl, and a call to InitializeComponent is made in the object constructor.

```
using System;
using System.Collections.Generic;
using System.Linq;
using System.Net;
using System.Windows;
using System.Windows.Controls;
using System.Windows.Documents;
using System.Windows.Input;
using System.Windows.Media;
using System.Windows.Media.Animation;
using System.Windows.Shapes;

namespace Chapter04
{
    public partial class Page : UserControl
    {
        public Page()
```

```
        {
            InitializeComponent();
        }
    }
}
```

The actual `InitializeComponent` code is stored in an auto-generated file. The easiest way to view this code is to simply right-click on the method call and select "Go To Definition." The code in this auto-generated file is responsible for actually parsing the XAML and assigning it to the root layout control specified, in this case, a `Grid` control. This file is placed in the obj/Debug/ directory, which you can see within Visual Studio if you select the "Show All Files" icon in Solution Explorer, as shown in Figure 4-4.

Figure 4-4

Visual Studio uses this file to hide some of the design time complexity from you, for instance, the creation of variables within your class to provide strongly typed access to named elements. Consider the following example XAML:

```xml
<UserControl x:Class="Chapter04.Page"
    xmlns="http://schemas.microsoft.com/winfx/2006/xaml/presentation"
    xmlns:x="http://schemas.microsoft.com/winfx/2006/xaml"
    Width="400" Height="300">

    <Grid x:Name="LayoutRoot" Background="White">

        <Button Width="200" Height="20" Content="Click Me"></Button>

    </Grid>

</UserControl>
```

The Button control that is contained within the root layout element does not have its x:Name property specified. This means that to access it from the code-behind file, you have to manually walk the object tree until you find a Button and work out somehow if this is the Button you want.

Obviously, what is required is to give this element a unique name, which is done via the x:Name attribute. When this property is set, Visual Studio automatically updates the auto-generated file in two important ways: First, it creates an internal Button field named *MyButton*, and then it takes care of assigning the actual instantiated element to this object using the following code within InitializeComponent in the Page.g.cs generated class:

```
#pragma checksum "C:\Users\SampleUser\Documents\Visual Studio 2008\Projects\Chapter
04\Chapter04\Page.xaml"
"{406ea660-64cf-4c82-b6f0-42d48172a799}" "CB261A118F113240BD454ABE5816C799"
//------------------------------------------------------------------------------
// <auto-generated>
//     This code was generated by a tool.
//     Runtime Version:2.0.50727.3053
//
//     Changes to this file may cause incorrect behavior and will be lost if
//     the code is regenerated.
// </auto-generated>
//------------------------------------------------------------------------------

using System;
using System.Windows;
using System.Windows.Automation;
using System.Windows.Automation.Peers;
using System.Windows.Automation.Provider;
using System.Windows.Controls;
using System.Windows.Controls.Primitives;
using System.Windows.Data;
using System.Windows.Documents;
using System.Windows.Ink;
using System.Windows.Input;
using System.Windows.Interop;
using System.Windows.Markup;
using System.Windows.Media;
using System.Windows.Media.Animation;
using System.Windows.Media.Imaging;
using System.Windows.Resources;
using System.Windows.Shapes;
using System.Windows.Threading;


namespace Chapter04 {


    public partial class Page : System.Windows.Controls.UserControl {

        internal System.Windows.Controls.Grid LayoutRoot;

        internal System.Windows.Controls.Button MyButton;

        private bool _contentLoaded;
```

```
        /// <summary>
        /// InitializeComponent
        /// </summary>
        [System.Diagnostics.DebuggerNonUserCodeAttribute()]
        public void InitializeComponent() {
            if (_contentLoaded) {
                return;
            }
            _contentLoaded = true;
            System.Windows.Application.LoadComponent(this, new
    System.Uri("/Chapter04;component/Page.xaml", System.UriKind.Relative));
            this.LayoutRoot = ((System.Windows.Controls.Grid)(this.FindName(
                                    "LayoutRoot")));
            this.MyButton = ((System.Windows.Controls.Button)(this.FindName(
                                    "MyButton")));
        }
    }
}
```

The line to look for here is the very last one, where the FindName method is used to obtain a reference to the element, which is then cast to a Button. This object is then assigned to the member variable MyButton. FindName is provided by FrameworkElement, which UserControl ultimately derives from.

You're also free to handle the events exposed by the UserControl base class yourself, like the Loaded event, for example. The easiest way to wire these events up is to simply add the event in the XAML file and have Visual Studio auto-generate the appropriate code behind to create the instance method and wire it up. Of course, you're free to wire this event up yourself purely in code if you have some decision making that needs to occur first. The following code shows the wiring up in the XAML file:

```
<UserControl x:Class="Chapter04.Page"
    xmlns="http://schemas.microsoft.com/winfx/2006/xaml/presentation"
    xmlns:x="http://schemas.microsoft.com/winfx/2006/xaml"
    Width="400"
    Height="300"
    Loaded="UserControl_Loaded">

    <Grid x:Name="LayoutRoot" Background="White">

        <Button Width="200"
                Height="20"
                Content="Click Me"
                x:Name="MyButton"></Button>

    </Grid>

</UserControl>
```

The following code shows the auto-generated method in the code behind:

```
private void UserControl_Loaded(object sender, RoutedEventArgs e)
{
    MyButton.Content = "New Content";
}
```

You can see that in the Loaded event, the Content property of the Button is simply reassigned. The Loaded event is also provided by the base FrameworkElement class and will be called when the element in question has completed its layout passes, is rendered, and can be interacted with.

So you've seen at a high level the basic structure of a Silverlight application. It's managed and instantiated via the System.Windows.Application class, which, in turn, is accessible via the App.xaml and App.xaml.cs files. You've also seen how pages within a Silverlight application are created by simply adding Silverlight UserControls to the project and using both the XAML and code behind to control the UI and program logic.

There now follows a brief discussion on JavaScript and to what extent knowing this language is a required skill for developing Silverlight applications.

JavaScript — How Much You Need to Know

The primary benefit that Silverlight brings to the table is that it allows you to augment your web site by delivering rich, immersive UIs and content directly within your preexisting web pages. Although you can choose to run your Silverlight application full-screen and have it as the main UI (more on this in Chapter 5, "Creating the User Interface"), user permitting, of course, it's far more likely that it will be used to place additional content within the structure of an existing page. For example, it can be used to deliver high-quality video for an advertisement or to render complex animations that would be difficult and time-consuming to do in DHTML.

In order to interact with and control a typical web page, JavaScript is used to examine, manipulate, and respond to elements and events within the DOM (the tree structure representing the element hierarchy of an HTML page). Using ASP.NET allows you to mostly ignore the JavaScript required to drive typical DOM interaction, as the server-side controls take care of writing this out for you. And the ASP.NET Silverlight and Media controls take away the need for you to include the right .js files and add the right JavaScript method calls to render the <OBJECT> or <EMBED> tag.

But this doesn't change the underlying fact that all these frameworks and tools exist purely to abstract away the underlying technologies. On the whole, of course, this is a very good thing, but it can lead to difficulties in debugging and maintaining the code should (when!) problems arise.

It's also worth noting that, like most abstractions, they help you to code 80 percent of the application much more quickly, but the final 20 percent usually requires either working around the framework in question or bending it to suit your project-specific requirements. This, of course, requires some knowledge of the underlying technologies and components that have been hidden from you in the first place.

Going back to the original point made, which is that a Silverlight application exists within a preexisting page, it's going to be a very common requirement to access and control the Silverlight application from the hosting page itself. With the embedded video example previously mentioned, this might be in the form of playback commands via standard HTML elements (play, pause, stop). Another example is HTML form elements that are used to gather and then inject user-specific data into the Silverlight application on the page. This interaction is handled via JavaScript, and thus rudimentary knowledge of this scripting language is needed. However, you certainly don't need to worry about having to become an expert in it, as the code is pretty simple.

So, much like the discussion in the previous chapter about whether you should learn XAML, you'll probably be able to get by without worrying about learning it, but to be more proficient and code any complex interactions, you're going to need to learn the basics at least.

JavaScript — The Basics

JavaScript, JScript, and ECMAScript are related scripting languages that run interpreted within the browser. As mentioned above, their primary aim is to allow web developers to dynamically alter the elements that make up an HTML page, validate form input, and be able to respond to events that occur throughout the web page's life cycle.

> So what's the difference between JavaScript and JScript and ECMAScript? Well, JavaScript was originally created by Netscape and announced around 1995. The language proved very successful, and this prompted Microsoft to create their own implementation, known as JScript, which first shipped with IE 3.0 in 1996. In 1996, Netscape submitted JavaScript to ECMA International for standardization, and this went through in 1997. ECMAScript is the name of the scripting language standardized by the ECMA. Although JavaScript and JScript provide features that are not included in ECMAScript, they both ultimately aim to be compatible with the base standards it specifies.

A lot of ASP.NET developers out there never have had the need or the inclination to look at JavaScript. If you are like them, the next few sections will give you a whirlwind tour of JavaScript. Feel free to skip this section if you either are already comfortable with JavaScript or really want to try avoiding it as best you can! This is in no way a thorough examination of JavaScript, but is intended to give you enough knowledge to get you started should you wish to learn more.

Object Model

The main object model that is used while programming in JavaScript is the document object model (DOM). This object model allows you to access the elements and members (methods, events, etc.) that compose the web page being developed, both visual and not. This object model is arranged in a hierarchical tree, with one root element representing the window working right down to individual input elements that could appear in a form.

While the DOM is the main object model that is used in JavaScript, alongside this browser-specific object model are the usual programming constructs required to manipulate and react to the DOM, including variable declarations, built-in objects to allow you to work with strings and numbers, date/time handling, …. You get the picture.

Adding JavaScript to a Page

JavaScript functions and statements are written within <script> tags inside a web page. They can also be written in an entirely separate file with a .js extension and then included within the page using the src attribute of the <script> tag (as per the Silverlight .js includes).

```
<script type="text/javascript">
    //…script goes in here
</script>

<script src="test.js" />
```

Variable Usage

To declare a variable in JavaScript, you use the `var` keyword followed by the variable name (case sensitive), making sure it begins with either a letter or an underscore.

```
var myString = "testValue";
var myInt = 42;
var myBool = true;
var myFloat = 3.32;
```

A variable declared within a function is local to the function that it is declared within. Global variables can be placed outside of functions and are available following the point of declaration and up until the page ends.

Functions

Functions are declared using the `function` keyword followed by a parameter list:

```
function SomeFunction(param1, param2)
{
    alert(param1);
    alert(param2);
}
```

This function takes two parameters but doesn't return a value. Note the lack of the `void` instruction before the `function` keyword. Unlike in C#, this is not required in JavaScript. If the function needs to return a value, the return keyword is used from within the function, but no return type needs to be specified, as all variables are variants.

```
function SomeFunction(param1, param2)
{
    alert(param1);
    alert(param2);

    return 0;
}
```

To call a function, simply specify its name followed by any required parameters:

```
var retVal = SomeFunction(1, 2);
```

If the function doesn't return a value, simply omit the variable assignation to the left of the call:

```
SomeFunction(1, 2);
```

Conditional Statements

We won't explain each of these as their usage should be obvious to you as a programmer; the following code demonstrates the main conditional operators:

```
function SomeFunction(param1, param2)
{
    var a = 10;
    var b = 20;

    //if, else and else if
    if (a > 10)
        alert("a is greater than 10");

    if (b == 20)
    {
        alert("b == 20");
        if (a == 10)
        {
            alert("a == 10");
        }
    }

    if (a < 5)
    {
        alert("a < 5");
    }
    else if(a <= 10)
    {
        alert("a <= 10");
    }
    else
    {
        alert("none of the above");
    }

    //switch
    switch (a)
    {
        case 10:
        {
            alert("first branch");
            break;
        }
        case 20:
        {
            alert("second branch");
            break;
        }
        default:
```

```
            {
                alert("neither");
                break;
            }
        }

        //for statement
        for (var i = 0; i < 10; i++)
        {
            alert(i);
        }


        var x = 10;
        //do loop
        do
        {
            alert(x);
            x += 10;
        }
        while (x <= 30);

        //while loop
        while (x < 100)
        {
            x += 10;
            alert(x);
        }
    }
}
```

Handling Events

Each element specified within the DOM has certain events that can be captured and handled (e.g., onclick, onblur, and onfocus). To handle the event, you wire it up in the element declaration and give it the name of the handler.

```
<input type="button" value="AnyTest" onclick="SomeFunction(1,2)" />
```

The body element also allows you to capture and handle the onload and onunload events, onload occurring when the page is first loaded, and onunload firing when the page is unloaded.

```
<body onload="PageLoad();" onunload="PageUnload();">
```

DOM Manipulation

Every element that exists within the DOM is treated as a node in a hierarchical tree structure, with the document node forming the root. Consider a very basic HTML page:

```
<html>
    <head>
        <title>JavaScript Guide</title>
    </head>
```

```
        <body>
            <h1>JavaScript Guide</h1>
            <h2>Sibling node</h2>
        </body>
    </html>
```

You can see here that the <head> node has a single parent (the <html> node) and a single child (the <title> node). The <html> node, though, has two direct children (the <head> and <body> nodes), with the <body> node containing two child nodes (the <h1> element and its sibling the <h2> element). It's easy to see how the document is represented as a tree structure from this example.

In order to gain programmatic access to the different nodes at any level in this tree, JavaScript provides two methods for you to use, document.getElementById and document.getElementsByTagName.

getElementById accepts a single string parameter that corresponds to the id of one of the elements within the document tree. In the following example, the method is used to access the contents of the h2 element using the innerHTML property:

```
<!DOCTYPE HTML PUBLIC "-//W3C//DTD HTML 4.0 Transitional//EN">
<html>
    <head>
        <title>JavaScript Guide</title>
    </head>
    <body>
        <h1>JavaScript Guide</h1>
        <h2 id="subHeading">Sibling node</h2>
        <input type="button" value="click me" onclick="AccessSingleNode()"/>
    </body>
    <script type="text/javascript">
        function AccessSingleNode()
        {
            //using document.getElementById.
            var element = document.getElementById("subHeading");
            alert(element.innerHTML);
        }
    </script>
</html>
```

This is useful when you want to access a single specific element. If you want to access all elements of a particular type, you can use the getElementsByTagName method:

```
<!DOCTYPE HTML PUBLIC "-//W3C//DTD HTML 4.0 Transitional//EN">
<html>
    <head>
        <title>JavaScript Guide</title>
    </head>
    <body>
        <h1>JavaScript Guide</h1>
        <h2 id="subHeading">Sibling node</h2><br />
        <input type="button" value="Access Single Node"
onclick="AccessSingleNode()"/><br />
        <h3>first item</h3><br />
        <h3>second item</h3><br />
```

```
        <h3>third item</h3><br />
        <input type="button" value="Access Multiple Nodes"
    onclick="AccessMultipleNodes()" />
    </body>
    <script type="text/javascript">
        function AccessMultipleNodes()
        {
            var elements = document.getElementsByTagName("h3");
            for (var i = 0;i < elements.length; i++)
            {
                alert(elements[i].innerHTML);
            }
        }

        function AccessSingleNode()
        {
            //using document.getElementById.
            var element = document.getElementById("subHeading");
            alert(element.innerHTML);
        }
    </script>
</html>
```

Note how this method returns an array structure in which each item in the array can be accessed by using [ ] syntax and specifying its ordinal.

Once you have obtained a reference to a node within the DOM, properties exist that allow you to jump to the first child node, the last child node, or the node's parent (firstChild, lastChild, and parentNode). To help navigate the DOM further, nextSibling and previousSibling properties are also provided:

```
<table border="1" id="myTable">
    <tr id="firstRow">
        <td id="firstCell">this</td>
        <td id="secondCell">is</td>
        <td id="thirdCell">a</td>
        <td id="fourthCell">test</td>
    </tr>
</table>
```

Given the table above, the following function shows how navigation can be achieved:

```
function NavigateExample()
{
    var table = document.getElementById("myTable");

    //reference table body, this will be included automatically if
    //not found in the html
    var tableBody = table.firstChild;

    //reference row
    var row = tableBody.firstChild;
```

```
        alert("row id= " + row.id);

        //reference first cell of first row
        var firstCell = row.firstChild;
        alert("firstCell id= " + firstCell.id);

        //reference last cell of first row
        var lastCell = row.lastChild;
        alert("lastCell= " + lastCell.id);

        //reference parent row of first cell
        var parentRow = firstCell.parentNode;
        alert("parentRow= " + parentRow.id);

        //reference second cell of first row
        var secondCell = firstCell.nextSibling;
        alert("secondCell= " + secondCell.id);

        //reference third cell of first row
        var thirdCell = secondCell.nextSibling;
        alert("thirdCell= " + thirdCell.id);
    }
```

As well as being able to access individual nodes in the DOM in this manner, the document object also contains shortcuts to specific collections of elements/nodes. For example, accessing the members of a form can be achieved via a call to document.forms[0], where the number passed in to the [] is the order the form is in the page. (There can be multiple forms in one page.)

```
<form id="myForm" action="">
    FirstName: <input type="text" id="firstName" /><br />
    Surname: <input type="text" id="surname" /><br />
    <input type="button" value="Send Data" onclick="FormTest();" />
</form>
```

Given the form above, you can obtain a reference to it and then access its members like so:

```
//obtain a reference to the form (0 as it's a 0 based collection and this is
//the first and only form
var form = document.forms[0];

//store the value typed into the firstName input box
var firstNameValue = form.firstName.value;

//store the value typed into the surname input box
var surnameValue = form.surname.value;
```

The above sections are only meant to serve as an introduction to JavaScript, delivering some of the general concepts and syntax. To learn more, we recommend that you read *Beginning JavaScript*, 3rd edition, by Jeremy McPeak and Paul Wilton (2007, Wrox Press).

The Silverlight Object Model

As well as the JavaScript DOM, which you use to format and manipulate the hosting page, you also have access to the Silverlight Object Model, which allows you to create and manipulate the objects that collaborate to form the content of a Silverlight application.

The visual elements of a Silverlight application are arranged in a tree-like hierarchy. This is why it is advisable and, indeed, easier to write your markup in XAML, which thanks to its XML roots is inherently hierarchical in format. Although you could compose your UI entirely in code, this would almost certainly take you longer and is not recommended.

DependencyObject, UIElement, *and* FrameworkElement

The three base classes DependencyObject, UIElement, and FrameworkElement are the underlying parents of most of the objects that you will use to construct your Silverlight UI, so it's important to appreciate what each one adds to the mix in the inheritance hierarchy.

```
System.Object
    DependencyObject
        UIElement
            FrameworkElement
                System.Windows.Controls.Border
                System.Windows.Controls.Control
                System.Windows.Controls.Image
                System.Windows.Controls.ItemPresenter
                System.Windows.Controls.MediaElement
                System.Windows.Controls.MultiScaleImage
                System.Windows.Controls.Panel
                System.Windows.Controls.Primitives.Popup
                System.Windows.Controls.TextBlock
                System.Windows.Controls.Glyph
                System.Windows.Shapes.Shape
```

First up at the top of the inheritance tree comes the base class of all things in .NET, System.Object. This is immediately followed by System.Windows.DependencyObject, which provides derived classes with the ability to take advantage of the dependency property system. Dependency properties are used extensively in both WPF and Silverlight and allow the value of object properties to be resolved at run time based on values that exist elsewhere. Good examples of this in action are properties that work in animations, because as their values alter at run time, they trigger other object properties to be recalculated.

Next in the derivation chain comes UIElement, which provides base information for any element that intends to participate in the building of the UI, in particular, the ability to focus and respond to user interaction events from the keyboard and mouse.

Finally, you have the FrameworkElement class, whose job it is to extend UIElement by providing layout abilities, hooks into the different stages of the object's lifetime, and data binding and resource support.

As you can see from the classes that extend FrameworkElement, if you're writing your own control, you're more likely to extend one of these (e.g., System.Windows.Controls.Control) than to extend FrameworkElement itself.

Walking the Tree

As you saw above in this chapter, the root visual object of a Silverlight application is specified via the `Application` object's `RootVisual` property and is set to a `UserControl` instance — the basic building block or visual component of a Silverlight application.

The UI is then built up by progressively adding child elements to this control to form a visual tree that is ultimately rendered by the plug-in. A common programmatic task then, as with any object tree, is to be able to access either an individual element within this tree or to be able to step through the tree one element at a time.

Consider the first task — accessing an individual element by name. If you have provided your XAML elements with an `x:Name` attribute, accessing them programmatically is as easy as simply referencing them in code by their `x:Name` value. You saw above how Visual Studio takes care of the plumbing code required to achieve this, importantly, how the `FrameworkElement.FindName` command is used to return the correct instance.

Now consider walking through the visual object tree from the root downward. This isn't as easy as you might at first think. Unfortunately, not all the container classes share the same programmatic API for walking into their children, which leaves you needing to have prior knowledge of the tree beforehand (somewhat negating the point of walking an object tree) or writing a lot of code to test if the object is of a certain type and if so is using its API for walking its children.

Finally, imagine that you have dynamically added further objects to your object tree, perhaps using the `XamlReader.Load` command. But Visual Studio will not have generated the plumbing code for your elements even if they have their `x:Name` set, and thus you will have to use the `FrameworkElement.FindName` function yourself. Again, this can only be used if your elements have still been assigned an `x:Name` value in the XAML that you opt to load dynamically.

Luckily, the Silverlight team was aware of the inherent difficulties in walking this tree and have (as in WPF) provided the `VisualTreeHelper` class, which takes care of ascertaining for you the child contents of a given control. An example showing its usage follows, starting with some XAML to lay out a basic UI:

```xml
<UserControl x:Class="Chapter04.VisualTreeHelperExample"
    xmlns="http://schemas.microsoft.com/winfx/2006/xaml/presentation"
    xmlns:x="http://schemas.microsoft.com/winfx/2006/xaml"
    Width="400" Height="300">

    <StackPanel x:Name="LayoutRoot" Background="White">

        <Button x:Name="btnWalkTree"
            Content="Walk Tree"
            Click="btnWalkTree_Click"/>

        <Border CornerRadius="10" Background="Yellow">
            <TextBlock x:Name="tbName1"
                Text="Santa Clause"
                HorizontalAlignment="Center"
                VerticalAlignment="Center"
                Margin="3" />
        </Border>
```

```xml
            <Border CornerRadius="10" Background="AliceBlue">
                <TextBlock x:Name="tbName2"
                        Text="Mickey Mouse"
                        HorizontalAlignment="Center"
                        VerticalAlignment="Center"
                        Margin="3" />
            </Border>

            <Border CornerRadius="10" Background="Green">
                <TextBlock x:Name="tbName3"
                        Text="The Tooth Fairy"
                        HorizontalAlignment="Center"
                        VerticalAlignment="Center"
                        Margin="3" />
            </Border>

        </StackPanel>

</UserControl>
```

If you examine this XAML, you will see that it consists of a `StackPanel` object containing five items: a `Button` that is wired up to an event handler, and four `TextBlock` elements contained within individual `Border` elements.

Now, turn your attention to the code-behind file and the `Button` event handler in particular:

```csharp
using System;
using System.Collections.Generic;
using System.Linq;
using System.Net;
using System.Windows;
using System.Windows.Controls;
using System.Windows.Documents;
using System.Windows.Input;
using System.Windows.Media;
using System.Windows.Media.Animation;
using System.Windows.Shapes;

namespace Chapter04
{
    public partial class VisualTreeHelperExample : UserControl
    {
        public VisualTreeHelperExample()
        {
            InitializeComponent();
        }

        private void btnWalkTree_Click(object sender, RoutedEventArgs e)
        {
            //Walk the current visual tree using the VisualTreeHelper
            this.WalkChildren(this);
        }

        private void WalkChildren(DependencyObject depObject)
        {
```

```
                            //grab hold of the name here so it can be inspected
                            string name = String.Empty;
                            FrameworkElement element = depObject as FrameworkElement;
                            if (element != null)
                            {
                                name = element.Name;
                            }

                            int childCount =
                                VisualTreeHelper.GetChildrenCount(element);
                            if (childCount > 0)
                            {
                                for (int i = 0; i < childCount; i++)
                                {
                                    this.WalkChildren(
                                        VisualTreeHelper.GetChild(element, i)
                                        );
                                }
                            }
                        }

                    }
                }
```

In the handler, you can see that a call is made to a method called WalkChildren, passing in the User Control instance, which is the root of the visual tree. Within this method, the VisualTreeHelper .GetChildrenCount and VisualTreeHelper.GetChild methods are used, along with a recursive call to WalkChildren, to allow you to inspect every item in the current visual tree. This works for objects that have been added to the tree dynamically also.

If you compile and run the example, you may be surprised at just how many objects make up a single control such as Button!

Dynamically Loading XAML

In Silverlight, it is possible to dynamically alter the in-memory object tree that forms the user interface. A concrete example will help press this point home. Consider the following XAML and code, from the file DynamicXAML.xaml and .cs in the Chapter 4 folder from this book's web site:

```xml
<UserControl x:Class="Chapter04.DynamicXAML"
    xmlns="http://schemas.microsoft.com/winfx/2006/xaml/presentation"
    xmlns:x="http://schemas.microsoft.com/winfx/2006/xaml"
    Width="400" Height="300">

    <Grid x:Name="LayoutRoot"
        Background="White"
        ShowGridLines="True">

        <Grid.ColumnDefinitions>
            <ColumnDefinition/>
            <ColumnDefinition/>
        </Grid.ColumnDefinitions>

        <Grid.RowDefinitions>
            <RowDefinition/>
```

```
            <RowDefinition/>
        </Grid.RowDefinitions>

        <Button x:Name="btnOK"
                Content="OK"
                Grid.Column="0"
                Grid.Row="0" />

        <Canvas x:Name="dynamicXamlPlaceholder"
                Grid.Column="1"
                Grid.Row="0" />

        <TextBox Text="The Text"
                Grid.Column="1"
                Grid.Row="1"
                Height="20"
                Width="200"/>
    </Grid>

</UserControl>
```

This XAML will result in the UI shown in Figure 4-5.

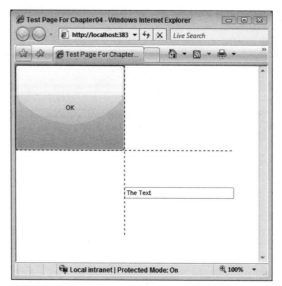

Figure 4-5

Now, consider the case in which you decide to load some XAML dynamically and insert it into the in-memory visual tree created by the XAML you already have.

```
using System;
using System.Collections.Generic;
using System.Linq;
using System.Net;
```

```
using System.Windows;
using System.Windows.Controls;
using System.Windows.Documents;
using System.Windows.Input;
using System.Windows.Media;
using System.Windows.Media.Animation;
using System.Windows.Shapes;

namespace Chapter04
{
    public partial class DynamicXAML : UserControl
    {
        public DynamicXAML()
        {
            InitializeComponent();
        }

        private void UserControl_Loaded(object sender, RoutedEventArgs e)
        {
            this.AddDynamicXaml();
        }

        private void AddDynamicXaml()
        {
            string xaml = "<Button
xmlns='http://schemas.microsoft.com/winfx/2006/xaml/presentation' " +
                        " Content='Test' />";

            object rootNode = XamlReader.Load(xaml);

            Canvas canvas = (Canvas)this.FindName("dynamicXamlPlaceholder");
            canvas.Children.Add((UIElement)rootNode);
        }
    }
}
```

As you can see, there is a private function that is called from the `UserControl.Loaded` event named `AddDynamicXaml`. The first thing that happens within this function is that a valid and well-formed XAML fragment is created as a literal string and stored in a variable. Note that the root element in this XAML needs the `xmlns` declaration to be considered well-formed and valid.

A call is then made to the static `Load` function of the `System.Windows.Markup.XamlReader` class. This function simply takes a string, as in the code sample that represents the XAML to load. The return value is of type `object` and is a reference to the root node of the newly created object tree.

You can see that the code then obtains a reference to the `Canvas` object that is in `Grid` position 1, 0. To obtain this reference, a call is made to the `FindName` method that is provided by the `FrameworkElement` class from which `UserControl` derives. It's then a simple matter of hooking the newly created object tree into the existing tree via a call to the `Canvas` object's `Children.Add` method.

Because the XAML is dynamically loaded, even though the element within it has an `x:Name` specified, the plumbing code to allow programmatic access via a member field simply hasn't been generated. This leaves you needing to rely on the `FindName` method to obtain a reference to it. Figure 4-6 shows the new UI.

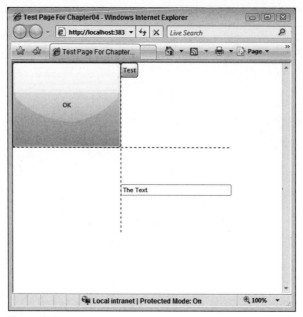

Figure 4-6

Events, Threading, and Browser Interaction

The next three sections take you through the Silverlight object models that allow you to create and respond to events, perform asynchronous as well as synchronous operations, and interact with the hosting browser at run time, starting with Events.

Events

Silverlight is a presentation technology and, like all presentation technologies, relies heavily on user input to drive the flow of the application. Unlike other presentation technologies, however, the Silverlight plug-in itself is embedded within another presentation technology — a web browser. It's worth keeping in mind then that all input events are first and foremost handled by the browser, before being sent on to the Silverlight plug-in to be raised as a Silverlight event.

You've already seen both in Chapter 3 and in this chapter how to wire up events. At its simplest, you edit the XAML to assign a function name to a particular event. Visual Studio can then take care of generating an appropriate handler for you. Or you can wire up an event the old-fashioned way in code.

To ensure you're comfortable with this, take a look at EventsSample.xaml in the Chapter 4 source code.

```
<UserControl x:Class="Chapter04.EventsSample"
    xmlns="http://schemas.microsoft.com/winfx/2006/xaml/presentation"
    xmlns:x="http://schemas.microsoft.com/winfx/2006/xaml"
    Width="400" Height="300">
```

```
<Grid x:Name="LayoutRoot" Background="White">

    <Grid.ColumnDefinitions>
        <ColumnDefinition />
    </Grid.ColumnDefinitions>

    <Grid.RowDefinitions>
        <RowDefinition />
    </Grid.RowDefinitions>

    <TextBox x:Name="txtSomeText"
            Grid.Column="0"
            Grid.Row="0"
            Height="20"
            Width="200"
            GotFocus="txtSomeText_GotFocus"
            LostFocus="txtSomeText_LostFocus"/>

</Grid>

</UserControl>
```

You can see here that there is a TextBox object placed within a Grid control. As well as positioning information, the GotFocus and LostFocus events are given the names of methods to call when their respective events are raised.

In the code behind, you can see that there are two methods matching the names provided here, both of which take two parameters, an object and a RoutedEventsArgs instance.

```csharp
using System;
using System.Collections.Generic;
using System.Linq;
using System.Net;
using System.Windows;
using System.Windows.Controls;
using System.Windows.Documents;
using System.Windows.Input;
using System.Windows.Media;
using System.Windows.Media.Animation;
using System.Windows.Shapes;

namespace Chapter04
{
    public partial class EventsSample : UserControl
    {
        public EventsSample()
        {
            InitializeComponent();

            txtSomeText.MouseEnter += new
MouseEventHandler(txtSomeText_MouseEnter);
        }

        void txtSomeText_MouseEnter(object sender, MouseEventArgs e)
        {
```

```
            txtSomeText.Text = "Mouse entered!";
        }

        private void txtSomeText_GotFocus(object sender, RoutedEventArgs e)
        {
            txtSomeText.Text = "I've got focus!";
        }

        private void txtSomeText_LostFocus(object sender, RoutedEventArgs e)
        {
            txtSomeText.Text = "I've lost focus!";
        }
    }
}
```

Note that not all event handlers share the same parameters. Although all will take an object parameter that holds a reference to the object that raised the event, the actual arguments that are packaged and sent along with the event depend very much on the object raising the event. For instance, the code above also wires up a third event manually, the MouseEnter event. Note that the event arguments passed into this handler are of type MouseEventArgs. This is because they provide more information specific to this type of event — the position of the mouse at the time the event occurred, for example.

If you run this sample, the text in the TextBox will change whenever you click on it and give it focus, if you tab out of it to lose focus, and if you move your mouse over it.

Routed Events

If you've worked with WPF before, you'll most likely be aware of routed events. Note, however, that unlike WPF, Silverlight only supports the bubbling routing strategy, *not* the tunneling one.

This means that certain input events have the ability to bubble up from the element in the visual tree that raised it and progress all the way up to the root element in the visual hierarchy. This can be a useful technique that allows you to handle certain events further up the chain, no matter which descendent element they originate from. A common scenario is a keypress occurring in an element somewhere lower in the hierarchy that has significance to an element further up the chain (*Ctrl+S* for Save, perhaps).

Consider the files EventBubbling.xaml and .cs in the Chapter 4 source code:

```xml
<UserControl x:Class="Chapter04.EventBubbling"
    xmlns="http://schemas.microsoft.com/winfx/2006/xaml/presentation"
    xmlns:x="http://schemas.microsoft.com/winfx/2006/xaml"
    Width="400" Height="300">

    <Grid x:Name="LayoutRoot"
          Background="White"
          KeyDown="LayoutRoot_KeyDown">

        <Grid.ColumnDefinitions>
            <ColumnDefinition />
        </Grid.ColumnDefinitions>
        <Grid.RowDefinitions>
            <RowDefinition />
            <RowDefinition />
        </Grid.RowDefinitions>
```

```xml
            <TextBlock x:Name="tbOutput"
                    Grid.Column="0"
                    Grid.Row="0"
                    FontSize="10"/>

            <StackPanel x:Name="myStackPanel"
                    Grid.Column="0"
                    Grid.Row="1">

                <Button x:Name="myButton">

                    <TextBox x:Name="myTextBox"
                            Height="20"
                            Width="200"
                            KeyDown="myTextBox_KeyDown" />

                </Button>

            </StackPanel>
        </Grid>

</UserControl>
```

This contrived example builds up a visual tree with a Grid at the root, containing a TextBlock and a StackPanel, which contains a Button whose content is set to a TextBox. This example will show you how the TextBox object's KeyDown event is bubbled all the way up the object tree until it hits the root element, Grid. You'll notice that a handler for the KeyDown event is provided both for the TextBox and for the Grid.

The code behind for this XAML shows the two handlers in question:

```csharp
using System;
using System.Collections.Generic;
using System.Linq;
using System.Net;
using System.Windows;
using System.Windows.Controls;
using System.Windows.Documents;
using System.Windows.Input;
using System.Windows.Media;
using System.Windows.Media.Animation;
using System.Windows.Shapes;

namespace Chapter04
{
    public partial class EventBubbling : UserControl
    {
        public EventBubbling()
        {
            InitializeComponent();
        }

        private void myTextBox_KeyDown(object sender, KeyEventArgs e)
        {
```

```
            tbOutput.Text += "\n\nTextBox handled; sender is "
                    + sender.ToString() + ", \nsource is "
                    + e.OriginalSource.ToString() + "\n\n";
        }

        private void LayoutRoot_KeyDown(object sender, KeyEventArgs e)
        {
            tbOutput.Text += "Grid handled; sender is "
                    + sender.ToString() + ", \nsource is "
                    + e.OriginalSource.ToString() + "\n\n";
        }
    }
}
```

Both of the handlers write out three pieces of information to the TextBlock object named tbOutput:
the control that is handling the event, the type of object that the sender parameter is, and also the
value of the Source property, provided via the event arguments.

If you run this example and type something into the TextBox, the output will resemble the following:

```
TextBox handled, sender is System.Windows.Controls.TextBox, source is
    System.Windows.Controls.TextBox

Grid handled, sender is System.Windows.Controls.Grid, source is
    System.Windows.Controls.TextBox
```

Notice how the event indeed bubbles up through the hierarchy and has the opportunity to be handled at
each step along the way. This example handles it in two locations, the child TextBox and the root Grid.

Take a closer look at the output concerning the value of the sender variable and the OriginalSource
property of the event arguments. sender is always of the type that is currently handling the event,
whereas OriginalSource must be used to find out actually which object really first raised the event.

Another interesting property provided by some of the RoutedEventArgs classes is the Handled
property, of type Boolean. You may have come across this property elsewhere, where it is used to prevent the event in question from bubbling any further up the hierarchy. For example, if you altered the
myTextBox_KeyDown handler in the preceding example like so:

```
        private void myTextBox_KeyDown(object sender, KeyEventArgs e)
        {
            tbOutput.Text += "\n\nTextBox handled; sender is "
                    + sender.ToString() + ", \nsource is "
                    + e.OriginalSource.ToString() + "\n\n";

            e.Handled = true;
        }
```

you'd get the following output, proving that the event was "handled" at this stage and prevented from
bubbling further up the object tree:

```
TextBox handled, sender is System.Windows.Controls.TextBox, source is
    System.Windows.Controls.TextBox
```

Threading and Asynchrony

The threading model in Silverlight, similar to both WPF and WinForms, stipulates that only code running on the main UI thread can actually access UI components. This is important and prevents issues arising from multiple threads attempting to access the same UI control at once.

As well as this, if long-running or computationally intensive user code is executed on the UI thread, it would prevent this thread from processing any UI events, effectively freezing the application while the long-running task executes.

Therefore, it is a common pattern in presentation code to keep the UI thread as free as possible, leaving it to do what it does best — handle UI messages and maintain a responsive UI, while delegating any long-running tasks to a separate thread of execution.

As with most programming tasks, there is a multitude of ways to get any one job done, and implementing the aforementioned pattern is no exception. Perhaps the easiest way is the one that is discussed first, taking advantage of the BackgroundWorker class.

BackgroundWorker

To illustrate the issue, take a look at the following example that can be found in NoBackgroundWorker.xaml and .cs in the Chapter 4 downloads. The UI consists of just a TextBox and a Button. When the Button .Click event is raised, a long-running blocking task is simulated via a call to the System.Threading .Thread.Sleep method.

```xml
<UserControl x:Class="Chapter04.NoBackgroundWorker"
    xmlns="http://schemas.microsoft.com/winfx/2006/xaml/presentation"
    xmlns:x="http://schemas.microsoft.com/winfx/2006/xaml"
    Width="400" Height="300">

    <Grid x:Name="LayoutRoot" Background="White">

        <Grid.ColumnDefinitions>
            <ColumnDefinition />
        </Grid.ColumnDefinitions>
        <Grid.RowDefinitions>
            <RowDefinition />
            <RowDefinition />
        </Grid.RowDefinitions>

        <TextBox x:Name="txtEntry"
                Width="200"
                Height="20"
                Grid.Column="0"
                Grid.Row="0" />

        <Button x:Name="btnStartTask"
                Width="100"
                Height="20"
                Grid.Column="0"
                Grid.Row="1"
                Content="Start Task"
```

```
                        Click="btnStartTask_Click" />
        </Grid>

    </UserControl>
```

The code below shows the simulated long-running task in the code behind:

```
using System;
using System.Collections.Generic;
using System.Linq;
using System.Net;
using System.Windows;
using System.Windows.Controls;
using System.Windows.Documents;
using System.Windows.Input;
using System.Windows.Media;
using System.Windows.Media.Animation;
using System.Windows.Shapes;

namespace Chapter04
{
    public partial class NoBackgroundWorker : UserControl
    {
        public NoBackgroundWorker()
        {
            InitializeComponent();
        }

        private void btnStartTask_Click(object sender, RoutedEventArgs e)
        {
            System.Threading.Thread.Sleep(2000);
        }
    }
}
```

Compile and run this example, and then press the button and try typing something in the textbox immediately afterward. You'll notice that because the UI thread is busy (well, it's sat sleeping, but it may as well be busy), it's unable to process even input events, and so the UI appears unresponsive until the UI thread is free again to catch up with its workload. In a scenario like this, what is required is a simple way to offload work to a background worker thread for processing. Silverlight provides just this, the BackgroundWorker class, which you may already be familiar with from prior .NET programming experience.

Essentially, the BackgroundWorker class gives you the ability to specify a handler for its DoWork event. This is the place where the code will run on a background thread. As well as being able to kick work off on this background thread, you are also given the ability to check the status of the work that is running and also to cancel it if need be.

Take a look at the markup and code in UseBackgroundWorker.xaml and .cs:

```
<UserControl x:Class="Chapter04.UseBackgroundWorker"
    xmlns="http://schemas.microsoft.com/winfx/2006/xaml/presentation"
    xmlns:x="http://schemas.microsoft.com/winfx/2006/xaml"
```

```
                   Width="400" Height="300">

        <Grid x:Name="LayoutRoot" Background="White">

            <Grid.ColumnDefinitions>
                <ColumnDefinition />
            </Grid.ColumnDefinitions>
            <Grid.RowDefinitions>
                <RowDefinition Height="50" />
                <RowDefinition Height="50" />
            </Grid.RowDefinitions>

            <StackPanel Grid.Column="0"
                        Grid.Row="0"
                        Orientation="Vertical">

                <TextBox x:Name="txtEntry"
                     Width="200"
                     Height="20" />

                <TextBox x:Name="txtPercentComplete"
                     Width="200"
                     Height="20" />

            </StackPanel>

            <StackPanel Grid.Column="0"
                        Grid.Row="1"
                        Orientation="Horizontal">

                <Button x:Name="btnStartTask"
                    Width="100"
                    Height="20"
                    Content="Start Task"
                    Click="btnStartTask_Click" />

                <Button x:Name="btnCancelTask"
                        Width="100"
                        Height="20"
                        Content="Cancel Task"
                        Click="btnCancelTask_Click" />

            </StackPanel>

        </Grid>

    </UserControl>
```

This XAML will result in a UI containing two texboxes, one for the user to type in (the top one) and the other to report the current progress of the long-running task. As well as this, there are two buttons available, one to actually start the task and the other to allow the user to cancel it.

```
using System;
using System.Collections.Generic;
```

```
using System.Linq;
using System.Net;
using System.Windows;
using System.Windows.Controls;
using System.Windows.Documents;
using System.Windows.Input;
using System.Windows.Media;
using System.Windows.Media.Animation;
using System.Windows.Shapes;
using System.ComponentModel;

namespace Chapter04
{
    public partial class UseBackgroundWorker : UserControl
    {
        private BackgroundWorker backgroundWorker =
            new BackgroundWorker();

        public UseBackgroundWorker()
        {
            InitializeComponent();

            backgroundWorker.DoWork +=
                new DoWorkEventHandler(backgroundWorker_DoWork);

            backgroundWorker.WorkerReportsProgress = true;
            backgroundWorker.WorkerSupportsCancellation = true;

            backgroundWorker.ProgressChanged +=
                new ProgressChangedEventHandler(
                    backgroundWorker_ProgressChanged
                    );

            backgroundWorker.RunWorkerCompleted +=
                new RunWorkerCompletedEventHandler(
                    backgroundWorker_RunWorkerCompleted
                    );

        }

        void backgroundWorker_RunWorkerCompleted(object sender,
                                        RunWorkerCompletedEventArgs e)
        {
            if (e.Error != null)
            {
                txtPercentComplete.Text = e.Error.Message;
            }
            else if (e.Cancelled)
            {
                txtPercentComplete.Text = "Task Cancelled";
            }
            else
            {
                txtPercentComplete.Text = "Task Completed";
            }
```

```csharp
        }

        void backgroundWorker_ProgressChanged(object sender,
                                              ProgressChangedEventArgs e)
        {
            txtPercentComplete.Text = e.ProgressPercentage.ToString() + " %";
        }

        void backgroundWorker_DoWork(object sender, DoWorkEventArgs e)
        {
            const int SECOND = 1000;

            BackgroundWorker backgroundWorker =
                (BackgroundWorker)sender;

            for (int i = 0; i < 20; i++)
            {
                //If user has elected to cancel at this point
                if (backgroundWorker.CancellationPending)
                {
                    e.Cancel = true;
                    return;
                }
                //else continue processing and report our progress
                backgroundWorker.ReportProgress((i + 1) * 5);
                System.Threading.Thread.Sleep(SECOND / 4);
            }
        }

        private void btnStartTask_Click(object sender, RoutedEventArgs e)
        {
            backgroundWorker.RunWorkerAsync();
        }

        private void btnCancelTask_Click(object sender, RoutedEventArgs e)
        {
            backgroundWorker.CancelAsync();
        }

    }
}
```

The first thing to note is the creation of a class-level variable of type `BackgroundWorker` for you to use. Within the class constructor, you can then see that the `DoWork`, `ProgressChanged`, and `RunWorker Completed` events are wired up appropriately. The `ProgressChanged` handler will allow you to update the UI to reflect how far into the work the background task is, and the `RunWorkerCompleted` event provides you with information about the task run, for instance, if it failed or was canceled. Two properties are also set in the constructor, allowing the component to both report its progress and to allow cancellations if instructed.

Now, when the Start button is clicked in the UI, the `BackgroundWorker`, `RunWorkerAsync` method is called, which will result in the `DoWork` event firing. This means that the code within the `background Worker_DoWork` handler will execute, importantly, though, on a background thread that will leave the UI thread free to continue processing messages.

In this example, there is no actual work carried out. To simulate a workload (processing data or such like), a simple loop is used. At each loop iteration, a check is made against the `BackgroundWorker` `.CancellationPending` property to see if the user has requested a cancellation. If this is true, it's up to you as the developer to take appropriate action, namely, to set the `DoWorkEventArgs.Cancel` property to True and exit the method as gracefully as possible.

If this is false, however, processing is continued, and the `BackgroundWorker.ReportProgress` method is called, passing in a figure representing the current task's percentage complete.

Note also the `backgroundWorker_ProgressChanged` event handler. The `ProgressChangedEventArgs` contain the `ProgressPercentage` property, which give you access to the value you've set in the `backgroundWorker_DoWork` handler.

Within the `backgroundWorker_RunWorkerCompleted` handler, the code checks to see if there has been an error or if the task was canceled and reports as appropriate.

If you compile and run this example and click on the Start button, you will notice that as the percentage complete indicator increases, you are still able to type in the textbox and interact with the UI.

`BackgroundWorker` provides a great asbtraction around some of the work that is actually occuring to marshall calls back and forth between the main thread and the background worker thread. The next section goes into a little more detail about how this process actually works.

System.Windows.Threading

The `System.Windows.Threading` namespace within Silverlight provides classes that exist purely to help marshal work between the main UI thread and any background threads that are running. It is quite separate from the `System.Threading` namespace, which provides direct access to `Thread` objects and synchronization primitives that can be created when working with threads. A detailed examination of threads and associated synchronization primitives is beyond the scope of this book, but can be found in the MSDN web site. The key class within `System.Windows.Threading` is the `Dispatcher` class.

System.Windows.Threading.Dispatcher

The `System.Windows.Threading.Dispatcher` object is created and associated with the main thread within a Silverlight application, and its job is to maintain a prioritized queue of work items that are waiting to be run on the thread. This implies, then, that in order to keep the UI responsive, the work items queued in the `Dispatcher` should be small and non-blocking.

If a background thread is used to execute code, this code is not allowed access to the objects created on the UI thread (e.g., a `Button` or `TextBox`). In order for the background code to access objects in the UI thread, it must delegate the work it wants to perform to the `Dispatcher` object of the thread in question.

To do this, `Dispatcher` provides the `BeginInvoke` method, which will add the work item to the queue and return execution immediately to the calling thread.

It will help to look at an example. In the Chapter 4 source code, you will find DispatcherExample.xaml and .cs, which are shown here:

```
<UserControl x:Class="Chapter04.DispatcherExample"
    xmlns="http://schemas.microsoft.com/winfx/2006/xaml/presentation"
    xmlns:x="http://schemas.microsoft.com/winfx/2006/xaml"
```

```
                    Width="400" Height="300">

        <Grid x:Name="LayoutRoot" Background="White">

            <Grid.ColumnDefinitions>
                <ColumnDefinition />
            </Grid.ColumnDefinitions>
            <Grid.RowDefinitions>
                <RowDefinition />
                <RowDefinition />
            </Grid.RowDefinitions>

            <TextBlock x:Name="tbOutput"
                       Width="200"
                       Height="20"
                       Grid.Column="0"
                       Grid.Row="0" />

            <Button x:Name="btnStart"
                    Width="100"
                    Height="20"
                    Grid.Column="0"
                    Grid.Row="1"
                    Content="Start"
                    Click="btnStart_Click" />

        </Grid>

    </UserControl>
```

This XAML defines a basic UI that contains a `TextBlock` and a `Button`. When the `Button` is clicked, a long-running task will execute on a separate thread that needs to update the text block when it completes. As you've already seen, this could be handled easily using the `BackgroundWorker` task. However, you can also use the `Dispatcher` object in the UI thread to do this for you. The following code behind illustrates this concept:

```
using System;
using System.Collections.Generic;
using System.Linq;
using System.Net;
using System.Windows;
using System.Windows.Controls;
using System.Windows.Documents;
using System.Windows.Input;
using System.Windows.Media;
using System.Windows.Media.Animation;
using System.Windows.Shapes;
using System.Threading;

namespace Chapter04
{
    public partial class DispatcherExample : UserControl
    {
        public DispatcherExample()
        {
```

```
        InitializeComponent();
    }

    private void btnStart_Click(object sender, RoutedEventArgs e)
    {
        //manually kick off a long running task
        ThreadStart ts = new ThreadStart(DoLongRunningTask);
        Thread thread = new Thread(ts);
        thread.Start();
    }

    private void DoLongRunningTask()
    {
        const int SECONDS = 1000;
        //close approximation of a long running task :)
        Thread.Sleep(2 * SECONDS);

        //task completes, but needs to access an object on the UI thread.
        Action action = new Action(MarshalToUI);
        this.Dispatcher.BeginInvoke(action);
    }

    private void MarshalToUI()
    {
        tbOutput.Text = "Task completed";
    }

    }
}
```

The btnStart_Click handler takes care of utilizing the Thread and ThreadStart classes from the System.Threading namespace to construct and start a new thread of execution. The method to execute on this new thread is passed as a parameter to the ThreadStart object.

Once this new thread of execution starts, it will simply sleep for 2 seconds, supposedly approximating a real long-running operation. Upon completion, however, there is a need to execute code against the UI thread, so that an object in this thread (in this case a TextBlock) can be programmed against. To do this, the work in question needs to be scheduled with the Dispatcher object of the UI thread, and this is accomplished via the asynchronous BeginInvoke method. This method is overloaded and can either accept an Action delegate (which encapsulates a void method that takes no parameters) or a custom delegate and optional object[] parameters to pass data along with. In this example, the Action delegate points to the MarshalToUI method, which will execute on the UI thread and hence have access to the objects created in this thread.

Although not used in this example, the BeginInvoke method actually returns an object of type System.Windows.Threading.DispatcherOperation. This object gives you the ability to communicate with the delegate in the Dispatcher queue, allowing you to change its priorty or cancel it, for example.

DispatcherTimer

The DispatcherTimer is a high-fidelity timer that runs on the same thread as the Dispatcher object and is reevaluated at the start of every Dispatcher loop. Usage of this object is a simple affair, with the user simply providing the `DispatcherTimer` with a delegate to invoke at a set interval and then calling the `Start` and `Stop` methods as appropriate. The delegate method that is invoked at the set interval allows direct access to objects created on the UI thread, which makes this object very useful, indeed.

DispatcherTimerExample.xaml and .cs in the Chapter04 source demonstrate the use of this object:

```xml
<UserControl x:Class="Chapter04.DispatcherTimerExample"
    xmlns="http://schemas.microsoft.com/winfx/2006/xaml/presentation"
    xmlns:x="http://schemas.microsoft.com/winfx/2006/xaml"
    Width="400" Height="300">

    <Grid x:Name="LayoutRoot" Background="White" ShowGridLines="True">
        <Grid.ColumnDefinitions>
            <ColumnDefinition />
        </Grid.ColumnDefinitions>
        <Grid.RowDefinitions>
            <RowDefinition />
        </Grid.RowDefinitions>

        <StackPanel Grid.Column="0"
                    Grid.Row="0"
                    HorizontalAlignment="Left">

            <TextBlock x:Name="tbElapsedTime"
                    FontSize="10"
                    Text="0"/>

            <Button x:Name="btnStart"
                Content="Start"
                Height="20"
                Width="100"
                Click="btnStart_Click" />

            <Button x:Name="btnStop"
                Content="Stop"
                Height="20"
                Width="100"
                Click="btnStop_Click" />

            <Button x:Name="btnReset"
                Content="Reset"
                Height="20"
                Width="100"
                Click="btnReset_Click" />

        </StackPanel>

    </Grid>

</UserControl>
```

This XAML constructs the basic UI shown in Figure 4-7.

Figure 4-7

There is a `TextBlock` at the top of the screen, which will be used to show a second counter incrementing. The three buttons below it are self explanatory. The code below shows just how easy this timer is to use. First, you need to instantiate and initialize the timer, providing it with a function to call and a set interval to call it at. It's then a simple matter of requesting the timer to stop and start as appropriate.

```
using System;
using System.Collections.Generic;
using System.Linq;
using System.Net;
using System.Windows;
using System.Windows.Controls;
using System.Windows.Documents;
using System.Windows.Input;
using System.Windows.Media;
using System.Windows.Media.Animation;
using System.Windows.Shapes;
using System.Windows.Threading;

namespace Chapter04
{
    public partial class DispatcherTimerExample : UserControl
    {
        DispatcherTimer timer = new DispatcherTimer();

        public DispatcherTimerExample()
        {
            InitializeComponent();

            //init timer, set interval to 1 second and wire up handler
            timer.Interval = new TimeSpan(0, 0, 1);
            timer.Tick += new EventHandler(timer_Tick);
```

```
        }

        void timer_Tick(object sender, EventArgs e)
        {
            //add 1 to the current second counter
            int currentElapsedSeconds = int.Parse(tbElapsedTime.Text);
            currentElapsedSeconds++;
            tbElapsedTime.Text = currentElapsedSeconds.ToString();
        }

        private void btnStart_Click(object sender, RoutedEventArgs e)
        {
            timer.Start();
        }

        private void btnStop_Click(object sender, RoutedEventArgs e)
        {
            timer.Stop();
        }

        private void btnReset_Click(object sender, RoutedEventArgs e)
        {
            tbElapsedTime.Text = "0";
        }

    }
}
```

Browser Interaction

Silverlight allows bidirectional interaction with the hosting HTML page, providing the ability to access the browser document object model (DOM) from within Silverlight and the ability to access selected methods within the Silverlight application from the browser.

Interacting with the Browser from Silverlight

In order to access the DOM of the hosting browser page and potentially manipulate its contents, you're going to utilize some of the functionality contained within the System.Windows.Browser namespace. The three main classes that will allow you to manipulate the DOM are HtmlPage, HtmlDocument, and HtmlElement.

HtmlPage forms the representation of the browser page within which your Silverlight application is hosted and gives you access to items like Cookies and the QueryString as well as the HtmlDocument. HtmlDocument represents the root element of the DOM and is the starting point for your code to traverse the HTML hierarchy. HtmlElement represents an individual element within the hierarchy and allows you to access and manipulate it and its children.

Within the Chapter04 source code for the web application project, you will find DOMFromSL.aspx. This contains the boilerplate code to utilize Silverlight:

```
<%@ Page Language="C#" AutoEventWireup="true" CodeBehind="DOMFromSL.aspx.cs"
Inherits="Chapter04Web.DOMFromSL" %>
```

```
<%@ Register Assembly="System.Web.Silverlight"
             Namespace="System.Web.UI.SilverlightControls"
             TagPrefix="asp" %>

<!DOCTYPE html PUBLIC "-//W3C//DTD XHTML 1.0 Transitional//EN"
"http://www.w3.org/TR/xhtml1/DTD/xhtml1-transitional.dtd">

<html xmlns="http://www.w3.org/1999/xhtml" >
<head id="Head1" runat="server">
    <title>Untitled Page</title>
</head>
<body style="height:100%;margin:0;">
    <form id="form1" runat="server" style="height:100%;">
        <asp:ScriptManager ID="ScriptManager1" runat="server"></asp:ScriptManager>
        <div  style="height:100%;">
            <asp:Silverlight ID="Xaml1"
                             runat="server"
                             Source="~/ClientBin/Chapter04.xap"
                             MinimumVersion="2.0.30911.0"
                             Width="100%"
                             Height="100%" />
        </div>

        <input type="text" id="txtNameInput" value="Enter your name" />
        <input type="button" id="btnGetGreeting" value="Get Greeting" />
        <input type="text" id="txtGreeting" size="100" />

    </form>
</body>
</html>
```

You can see above that there is a form after the Silverlight control that contains three elements, a textbox called txtNameInput, a button called btnGetGreeting, and another textbox called txtGreeting. You're not going to wire these up right away. First off, you're going to see how to go about accessing them from Silverlight and changing their appearance.

In the Silverlight project within the Chapter04 source, you will find DOMFromSL.xaml and .cs. In order to access the HTML DOM, the first thing that you're going to need is an object reference to the calling page itself. You can obtain this reference via a call to the HtmlPage.Document property. You can store this reference in a class-level variable for subsequent access and wire it up in the loaded handler.

```
HtmlDocument htmlDocument;

private void UserControl_Loaded(object sender, RoutedEventArgs e)
{
    this.htmlDocument = HtmlPage.Document;
}
```

When the user clicks on the single button that makes up your Silverlight control, the appearance of the HTML elements is going to be changed. So you need to wire up the Click event of the button to allow you to do this.

Now comes the interesting part, obtaining a reference to the HTML elements from the Silverlight code. To do this, you're going to use the GetElementByID method of the HtmlDocument object. This method takes a single parameter of type string that is the ID assigned to the HTML element and returns an HtmlElement object reference:

```
HtmlElement = HtmlDocument.GetElementByID("elementID");
```

Add the following code to the button-clicked handler to automatically increase the font size of the first textbox and change the background color of the second:

```
private void btnChangeHTML_Click(object sender, RoutedEventArgs e)
{
    //change appearance of HtmlElements in here
    HtmlElement inputName =
        htmlDocument.GetElementById("txtNameInput");

    HtmlElement btnGetGreeting =
        htmlDocument.GetElementById("btnGetGreeting");

    HtmlElement greeting =
        htmlDocument.GetElementById("txtGreeting");

    inputName.SetStyleAttribute("fontSize", "20px");
    greeting.SetStyleAttribute("backgroundColor", "blue");

}
```

Note the use of the SetStyleAttribute method, which takes two parameters, both of type string. The first is the name of the style attribute, and the second is the value to give it. You might at this point notice something a little strange about the names *fontSize* and *backgroundColor*. If you were adding these style attributes to a normal HTML element, you would write the following:

```
<input type="text" style="background-color: Blue; font-size=20px" />
```

So why the difference? Well, if you were to access the background color, font size, or any other property in JavaScript, you would have to use backgroundColor or fontSize rather than the hyphenated versions. This is because hyphens in class member names are not permitted in JavaScript and many other languages. As DOM access from Silverlight is just a wrapper around a bridge to the HTML DOM, the Silverlight team didn't want to do extra work to convert the HTML/CSS property names into the actual names (stripping hyphens, etc.). So these names remain the same as their JavaScript counterparts.

Once you have obtained a reference in this way, you're free to access the element using the methods of the HtmlElement class. These include the ability to manipulate attributes, attach and remove events, and append and remove children.

Therefore, to work with an element in the DOM, you first need to obtain a reference to it. As well as the GetElementByID method to obtain a reference to an individually named element, you can also use the GetElementsByTagName method to return all elements of a specific tag:

```
ScriptObjectCollection HtmlDocument.GetElementsByTagName(string name);
```

Edit the HTML file so that it now contains the following HTML:

```
<form action="">
    <p>
        <input type="text" id="txtNameInput" value="Enter your name" />
        <input type="button" id="btnGetGreeting" value="Get Greeting" />
        <input type="text" id="txtGreeting" size="100" />
    </p>
    <h1>This is the first H1</h1><br />
    <h1>This is the second H1</h1><br />
    <h1>This is the third H1</h1>
</form>
```

You're now going to use the GetElementsByTagName method to return a ScriptObjectCollection containing all the H1 elements in the DOM:

```
private void btnChangeHTML_Click(object sender, RoutedEventArgs e)
{
    //change appearance of HtmlElements in here
    HtmlElement inputName =
        htmlDocument.GetElementById("txtNameInput");

    HtmlElement btnGetGreeting =
        htmlDocument.GetElementById("btnGetGreeting");

    HtmlElement greeting =
        htmlDocument.GetElementById("txtGreeting");

    inputName.SetStyleAttribute("fontSize", "20px");
    greeting.SetStyleAttribute("backgroundColor", "blue");

    ScriptObjectCollection h1Collection =
        htmlDocument.GetElementsByTagName("H1");

    foreach (HtmlElement element in h1Collection)
    {
        element.SetStyleAttribute("backgroundColor", "yellow");
    }
}
```

The code is very straightforward — once you've populated your ScriptObjectCollection, you're able to iterate over it, in this case, using a foreach loop, and then access the individual HtmlElement objects within it at will.

So what about event handling? From a Silverlight application, you're able to handle events raised from the DOM with relative ease. First off, you need to attach a handler to a specific event. You're going to add a handler to the click event of the button btnGetGreeting. Once a reference has been obtained to the element in question, the AttachEvent method is used to specify which event you would like to handle and which handler to use.

```
private void btnChangeHTML_Click(object sender, RoutedEventArgs e)
{
```

```
                //change appearance of HtmlElements in here
                HtmlElement inputName =
                    htmlDocument.GetElementById("txtNameInput");

                HtmlElement btnGetGreeting =
                    htmlDocument.GetElementById("btnGetGreeting");

                HtmlElement greeting =
                    htmlDocument.GetElementById("txtGreeting");

                inputName.SetStyleAttribute("fontSize", "20px");
                greeting.SetStyleAttribute("backgroundColor", "blue");

                ScriptObjectCollection h1Collection =
                    htmlDocument.GetElementsByTagName("H1");

                foreach (HtmlElement element in h1Collection)
                {
                    element.SetStyleAttribute("backgroundColor", "yellow");
                }

                bool success = btnGetGreeting.AttachEvent(
                    "onclick",
                    new EventHandler<HtmlEventArgs>(this.OnGetGreetingClicked));
            }

            //handler that will output a different greeting based on hour value
            public void OnGetGreetingClicked(object sender, HtmlEventArgs e)
            {
                HtmlElement inputName =
                    htmlDocument.GetElementById("txtNameInput");

                string nameValue = inputName.GetProperty("Value").ToString();

                HtmlElement greeting =
                    htmlDocument.GetElementById("txtGreeting");

                DateTime current = DateTime.Now;
                if (current.Hour <= 12)
                    greeting.SetProperty("Value", "Good Morning " + nameValue);
                else if ((current.Hour > 12) && (current.Hour < 18))
                    greeting.SetProperty("Value", "Good Afternoon " + nameValue);
                else
                    greeting.SetProperty("Value", "Good Night " + nameValue);
            }
```

AttachEvent takes two parameters, a string representing the name of the event in the DOM element to handle and an EventHandler. The HtmlEventArgs that are passed in contain lots of information about the mouse, keyboard, and source element and so can be very useful.

As well as this, you can also write code to alter the structure of the DOM itself, appending and removing the elements within it. The following code shows how you can append an element to the final <H1> tag in the DOM. This code assumes that an input button named btnAlterDOM has been added to the HTML page and a handler named OnAlterDOMClicked wired up in the XAML page load method:

```
        private void UserControl_Loaded(object sender, RoutedEventArgs e)
        {
            this.htmlDocument = HtmlPage.Document;

            HtmlElement btnAlterDOM =
                    htmlDocument.GetElementById("btnAlterDOM");

            btnAlterDOM.AttachEvent("onclick", new
                EventHandler<HtmlEventArgs>(this.OnAlterDOMClicked));
        }

        public void OnAlterDOMClicked(object sender, HtmlEventArgs e)
        {
            ScriptObjectCollection h1Collection =
                htmlDocument.GetElementsByTagName("H1");

            HtmlElement element = htmlDocument.CreateElement("input");
            element.SetAttribute("type", "text");
            element.SetProperty("value", "test");

            ((HtmlElement)h1Collection[2]).AppendChild(element);
        }
```

Note how you first create an HtmlElement object using the HtmlDocument.CreateElement method call, passing in the tag name to use for this element. At this point, the newly created HtmlElement is not attached to the DOM. After setting whatever attributes and properties need setting, you then add the element to the DOM using the HtmlElement.AppendChild method.

You can also access methods on objects that have been referenced within the DOM. For instance, you could call the Focus method on an input field or cause the page to navigate to a new URL using the HtmlPage.Navigate method.

```
    HtmlElement inputName = htmlDocument.GetElementByID("txtNameInput");
    inputName.Focus();
```

As you can see, there is rich interaction from Silverlight to the browser, so much so that you could well start delegating carefully selected JavaScript workloads over to Silverlight. (Because switching between JavaScript and managed code incurs overhead, check out Chapter 16, "Performance for more information.") And don't forget, your Silverlight control doesn't have to be visible to take advantage of this functionality. You can easily set its width and height to 0.

As well as interacting with DOM elements, you can also call JavaScript functions from your Silverlight application.

Interacting with Silverlight from the Browser

In order to allow a scripting language in the hosting page to program against your Silverlight class, you first need to register the class in question as a scriptable object. This should be done in one of the initialization steps of your class, so the UserControl_Loaded event is a natural choice.

Take a look at the code in SLFromDOM.aspx within the Chapter04 source directory, which contains the basic code required to host a Silverlight application. A Silverlight page called *SLFromDOM.xaml* can also be found in the Silverlight project.

The first thing you need to do is perform the registering of the class as a `Scriptable` object. This is done via a call to the `HtmlPage.RegisterScriptableObject` method. This method accepts two parameters, a string key and an object reference. For this example, the string key is passed in as *calculator* (this class is going to perform calculations, hence the name), and the object reference is given as the instance of the class you want to expose, referring to the `Calculator` object instance.

```
public SLFromDOM()
{
    InitializeComponent();

    Calculator calculator = new Calculator();

    HtmlPage.RegisterScriptableObject("calculator", calculator);
}
```

Once your Silverlight class has been registered as `Scriptable`, the next step involves obtaining a reference to the Silverlight control that is hosting the `Scriptable` managed object. This is very simple and uses the `OnPluginLoaded` event exposed by the ASP.NET Silverlight control. This event is wired up to a JavaScript event handler, which takes care of assigning a global variable with the Silverlight host instance.

```
var hostingControl = null;
function pluginLoaded(sender)
{
    hostingControl  = sender.get_element();
}
```

Now that you have a reference to the hosting control, you can access its `Content` property, allowing you to gain programmatic access to the underlying object instance that represents the XAML using the string name specified in the registration step, in this case `calculator`:

```
hostingControl.Content.calculator
```

All that remains now is to mark the managed classes' members as `ScriptableMembers` if they should be accessible from JavaScript. Flesh out your class, and add a rudimentary calculation helper class as in the following code sample, or open up SLFromDOM.xaml.cs in the Chapter 4 source directory:

```
using System;
using System.Collections.Generic;
using System.Linq;
using System.Net;
using System.Windows;
using System.Windows.Controls;
using System.Windows.Documents;
using System.Windows.Input;
using System.Windows.Media;
using System.Windows.Media.Animation;
using System.Windows.Shapes;
using System.Windows.Browser;

namespace Chapter04
{
    public partial class SLFromDOM : UserControl
```

```
{
    public SLFromDOM()
    {
        InitializeComponent();

        Calculator calculator = new Calculator();

        HtmlPage.RegisterScriptableObject("calculator", calculator);
    }
}

public class Calculator
{
    //Rudimentary Calculator methods
    [ScriptableMember()]
    public int Add(int op1, int op2)
    {
        return op1 + op2;
    }

    [ScriptableMember()]
    public int Subtract(int op1, int op2)
    {
        return op1 - op2;
    }

    [ScriptableMember()]
    public int Divide(int op1, int op2)
    {
        return op1 / op2;
    }

    [ScriptableMember()]
    public int Multiply(int op1, int op2)
    {
        return op1 * op2;
    }
}
}
```

Switch your attention to the SLFromDOM.aspx file now, where you're going to provide a basic calculator interface that will utilize the managed methods within the `calculator` class. This will be composed of a form containing four sets of two textboxes to take the `op1` and `op2` values and four buttons to execute the method corresponding to each.

```
<form action="">
    <!-- Addition -->
    <input type="text" id="addOp1" /> + 
    <input type="text" id="addOp2" /> = 
    <input type="text" id="addResult" /> 
    <input type="button" id="btnAdd" value="Add" onclick="DoAdd();" /><br />

    <!--Subtraction -->
    <input type="text" id="subOp1" /> - 
```

```
        <input type="text" id="subOp2" /> = 
        <input type="text" id="subResult" /> 
        <input type="button" id="btnSub" value="Subtract" onclick="DoSubtract();"
/><br />

        <!-- Division -->
        <input type="text" id="divOp1" /> / 
        <input type="text" id="divOp2" /> = 
        <input type="text" id="divResult" /> 
        <input type="button" id="btnDiv" value="Divide" onclick="DoDivide();" /><br
/>

        <!-- Multiplication -->
        <input type="text" id="mulOp1" /> * 
        <input type="text" id="mulOp2" /> = 
        <input type="text" id="mulResult" />
        <input type="button" id="btnMul" value="Mutliply" onclick="DoMultiply();"
/><br />
    </form>
```

Notice the four inline calls to JavaScript functions. These functions will be responsible for obtaining a reference to your Silverlight application and calling the necessary functions, passing in appropriate parameters. The functions to do this are shown below. Note the standard DOM calls to access form element contents and the actual call to the Silverlight application:

```
<script type="text/javascript">
        var hostingControl = null;
        function pluginLoaded(sender)
        {
            hostingControl  = sender.get_element();
        }

        function DoAdd()
        {
            var op1 = document.forms[0].elements["addOp1"].value;
            var op2 = document.forms[0].elements["addOp2"].value;
            var result = hostingControl.Content.calculator.Add(
                          parseInt(op1), parseInt(op2));
            document.forms[0].elements["addResult"].value = result;
        }

        function DoSubtract()
        {
            var op1 = document.forms[0].elements["subOp1"].value;
            var op2 = document.forms[0].elements["subOp2"].value;
            var result = hostingControl.Content.calculator.Subtract(
                          parseInt(op1), parseInt(op2));
            document.forms[0].elements["subResult"].value = result;
        }

        function DoDivide()
        {
            var op1 = document.forms[0].elements["divOp1"].value;
            var op2 = document.forms[0].elements["divOp2"].value;
```

```
        var result = hostingControl.Content.calculator.Divide(
                        parseInt(op1), parseInt(op2));
        document.forms[0].elements["divResult"].value = result;
    }

    function DoMultiply()
    {
        var op1 = document.forms[0].elements["mulOp1"].value;
        var op2 = document.forms[0].elements["mulOp2"].value;
        var result = hostingControl.Content.calculator.Multiply(
                        parseInt(op1), parseInt(op2));
        document.forms[0].elements["mulResult"].value = result;
    }
</script>
```

You should now be able to run your code and try out this example. Although basic in structure, it demonstrates the level of interaction that can be achieved between JavaScript and Silverlight.

As well as accessing properties and methods in this way, you can also handle managed events from your JavaScript code. To do this, you must first decorate your managed event with the <ScriptableMember> tag.

On-Demand XAP Loading

In an Internet environment, being able to get your Silverlight application up and running as fast as possible is a must-have goal. Therefore, in the case of a rich and functionally complex Silverlight application, having all the libraries packaged and loaded into a single XAP file will directly violate this goal, as the entire XAP file and all functionality will need to be downloaded before the application can start.

Obviously, if not all this functionality is needed immediately (or even not at all, in most use cases), this would be a tremendous waste of effort and will only annoy your user base as your application takes an age to load and start.

Silverlight provides a way to negate this slow start-up and loading time, however, by allowing you to selectively download and integrate functionality as and when it's required. To accomplish this, the System.Net.WebClient class is used to control the downloading of additional assemblies.

System.Net.WebClient

The WebClient class allows you to programmatically receive data from a resource that is specified via a URI, either as data or as a string. The two methods that you use to accomplish this are OpenReadAsync and DownloadStringAsync.

Assume that you have created a Silverlight library file called MathUtilities.dll and that this library is either not used initially or rarely used by most users. This would make it an ideal candidate for on-demand downloading. After creating the Silverlight library project and adding a reference to it from the original Silverlight application, be sure to click the newly added reference, and in the Properties window, set Copy Local to False. This will prevent the DLL from being packaged within the resulting XAP file and being automatically downloaded when the Silverlight application is loaded by the browser.

The first step is to instantiate a WebClient instance and provide it with a valid URI for the MathUtilities.dll assembly, as well as a callback function to jump into when the DLL has been successfully downloaded. Within the callback, you need to instantiate a new AssemblyPart instance, which represents an assembly that is to be included within the main application package. You simply then call the Load method of this AssemblyPart and give it the assembly that has been loaded — obtained via a call to the Result property of the OpenReadCompletedEventArgs.

```csharp
using System;
using System.Collections.Generic;
using System.Linq;
using System.Net;
using System.Windows;
using System.Windows.Controls;
using System.Windows.Documents;
using System.Windows.Input;
using System.Windows.Media;
using System.Windows.Media.Animation;
using System.Windows.Shapes;
using System.Reflection;

namespace Chapter04
{
    public partial class OnDemandXAP : UserControl
    {
        public OnDemandXAP()
        {
            InitializeComponent();
        }

        private void btnLoadAssembly_Click(object sender, RoutedEventArgs e)
        {
            WebClient webClient = new WebClient();

            webClient.OpenReadCompleted +=
                new OpenReadCompletedEventHandler(webClient_OpenReadCompleted);

            webClient.OpenReadAsync(new Uri("MathUtilities.dll",
                                        UriKind.Relative));
        }

        void webClient_OpenReadCompleted(object sender,
                                        OpenReadCompletedEventArgs e)
        {
            if ((e.Error == null) && (e.Cancelled == false))
            {
                AssemblyPart assemblyPart = new AssemblyPart();
                Assembly assembly = assemblyPart.Load(e.Result);

                //Use types from within loaded assembly
            }
        }
    }
}
```

Summary

You kicked off this chapter by taking a look at what actually constitutes a Silverlight application, both in terms of asset structure and code base. You learned how a Silverlight application is deployed within a XAP file, and how this file really is nothing more than a standard ZIP archive containing assets alongside a deployment manifest. You learned that this deployment manifest can contain localization and entry point information as well as asset listings.

The `Application` class was then discussed. You learned how it controls the lifetime of the application and about the initialization sequence when your Silverlight application is first loaded. You also took a look at some of the events that are raised by the `Application` class and how you can hook up to them via the App.xaml and App.cs files.

The different options for embedding the Silverlight plug-in within a hosting web page were then laid bare — using the `<asp:Silverlight>` control, by far and away the easiest and cleanest choice; manually coding the `<OBJECT>` tag and supporting script; and finally, taking advantage of the JavaScript Helper files that are shipped with the SDK to create the tag on your behalf. The benefits of sticking with the `<asp:Silverlight>` option for this task are obvious.

The next step in writing a Silverlight application is the creation of pages to act as your UI, and you saw how the `UserControl` class is used as the base building block to compose your UI. The code-behind model was explained, including the automatic generation of member variables for XAML elements that are provided with an `x:Name`, a feature that can greatly improve the development experience.

There then followed a brief discussion on the merits of learning JavaScript — how it can help increase your general understanding of Silverlight and that an appreciation for what's happening in the hosting page can increase your ability to find and fix bugs quickly. To get you started, a quick overview of writing JavaScript was provided, covering aspects such as general programming techniques and HTML DOM manipulation.

The Silverlight Object Model was then delved into, and you saw how the visual tree was constructed to form the UI. You also learned how to access the elements in the tree, either by name or by manually walking the nodes. This section concluded by examining the `XamlReader.Load` method and how it can be used to build an object tree dynamically and then append this to the existing in-memory tree.

The next section took you through the Silverlight event model and how routed events are supported but only in bubbling mode. You found that bubbling of certain input events could be useful for helping you support keyboard shortcuts at a level higher than the control they were raised within.

Threading and asynchrony within Silverlight were then discussed, and the different options for executing work on a background thread were demonstrated. Keeping the UI thread free to maintain a responsive UI was stressed, and taking advantage of the `Dispatcher` object to aid in this respect was explained. You also saw how the `DispatcherTimer` object could be used to provide high-fidelity timing to your application.

The ability to communicate bidirectionally between the HTML DOM and the Silverlight Object Model was then explained, and code samples to illustrate communication in each direction were provided. You saw how the `HtmlPage.Document` object provided you with direct access to the HTML DOM from Silverlight and how this DOM could then be manipulated with ease.

Conversely, you saw how the `HtmlPage.RegisterScriptableObject` command is used to expose managed functionality to JavaScript, and how the `ScriptableMember` attribute is then used within a registered class to expose it directly to JavaScript.

Finally, you saw how to improve the starting time and general performance of your application by taking advantage of on-demand loading of XAP files.

The next chapter, "Creating the User Interface," will show you the different options you have when deciding how to lay out your UI, and how the different controls are then added to it. You will also take a quick tour of the Expression suite and see how they can make Silverlight development easier. Localizing a Silverlight application is then discussed.

Part II: Developing ASP.NET Applications with Silverlight

Chapter 5: Creating the User Interface

Chapter 6: Silverlight Controls

Chapter 7: Styles and Templates

Chapter 8: User Interaction

Chapter 9: Communicating with the Server

Chapter 10: Working with Data

Chapter 11: Creating Custom Controls

Chapter 12: Securing Your Silverlight Application

Chapter 13: Audio and Video

Chapter 14: Graphics and Animation

Chapter 15: Troubleshooting

Chapter 16: Performance

Creating the User Interface

In Part I of this book, you looked at some of the building blocks of a Silverlight application, including the components that make up its architecture, how XAML is used to describe the elements of a user interface, and how code behind can be used to turn a static user interface (UI) into a living, breathing page.

In this chapter, you'll start putting the theory you've learned so far into practice.

This chapter will take you through the ins and outs of laying out and creating your user interface within a Silverlight application. You'll get an overview of the Expression Suite of design tools and see how Expression Blend can be used to complement the Visual Studio development environment. You'll also compare and contrast the differing methods of layout between ASP.NET and Silverlight.

You'll then examine each of the main layout controls that are shipped with Silverlight 2 — `Canvas`, `Grid`, `StackPanel`, and `TabControl` — and work out when to use which layout control for various scenarios, as well as how to add standard controls to them.

This chapter also discusses how to create a scalable UI, that is, a UI that allows a user to resize it at will gracefully without it becoming unusable.

Finally, localizing a Silverlight application is looked at, which is certain to be of importance to any ASP.NET developer creating a web site with global reach.

Expression Suite — A Whirlwind Tour

Designers have always had something of a rough deal from Microsoft. The flagship development environment for everything from ATL to web development is Visual Studio, a heavyweight Integrated Development Environment (IDE) packed with features and commands that help increase development speed for innumerable programming projects.

But as good as Visual Studio is at helping programmers, in terms of assisting in design (especially web design), it's always been far behind pure design packages that are finely tuned to the requirements of a designer. And because of its heavyweight nature and code-focused UI, designers have quite rightly been put off using it for *their* purposes. It's simply not the right tool for the job and contains a plethora of menu options and task panes that can be confusing to the untrained user.

Microsoft is aware of this, of course, and has been working hard to rectify the situation by creating a first-class suite of development environments to help designers create graphics, media, web, and Windows applications more quickly and easily.

The result is the Expression Suite of products — dedicated IDEs for tackling the design aspects of Windows applications, web applications, and graphics and media creation and editing. Following are overviews of each of the applications that comprise the Expression Suite; we encourage you to download and try out the applications to see what advantages they provide over Visual Studio (used throughout the remainder of this book) — Expression Blend, in particular.

Expression Web

Expression Web is a feature-rich web design package that allows you to create CSS-based, standards-compliant web sites by default. The ability to create .aspx files as well as standard HTML is included right out-of-the-box and highlights the drive to bring developers and designers closer together within the development environment.

Some of the high-level features included with Expression Web are

❑ **Full Standards Compliance** — W3C XHTML Conformance

❑ **Accessibility Checker** — Expression Web ships with the ability to check the web pages loaded within it for conformance against two industry standards:

    ❑ World Wide Web Consortium (W3C) Web Content Accessibility Guidelines (WCAG)

    ❑ Accessibility guidelines for Section 508 of the U.S. Rehabilitation Act

    The results are then displayed in a dialog box with one line for each violation and further information for correcting the violation available.

❑ **Real-Time Standards Validation** — As you're typing HTML, standards violations are highlighted in real time for you.

❑ **Extensive CSS Support** — Support is provided in terms of design surface, IDE, and rendering.

❑ **CSS Report Tool** — This runs through all the CSS rules on a given page, whether they're in the header section, inline, or in an attached style sheet, and amalgamates them for easy reference in a dialog.

❑ **XML Visualization Tools** — These allow you to create customized views of XML data using simple drag-and-drop techniques.

❑ **XSLT Support**

❑ **Access to ASP.NET Controls** — This provides for tighter integration between designers and developers.

If you actually install and start playing with Expression Web, you'll notice immediately that it's not just a new version of FrontPage (which is good).

Expression Blend

In Chapter 3, you took a quick look at Expression Blend and the high-level features that it makes available to both designers and developers. To build on this, you're now going to see how easy it is to perform common operations using this tool.

After firing up Blend and selecting "New Project" from the File menu, you will be presented with the dialog shown in Figure 5-1.

Figure 5-1

Enter a name for the test application (**TestApp** or something similar will suffice), and select the Language and Location. Make sure you choose the Silverlight .NET template, but take note of the other template application types available to you. Upon confirming your project set-up selections, the IDE will go ahead and create your solution and project files, including the necessary boilerplate files to begin development. Figure 5-2 shows this.

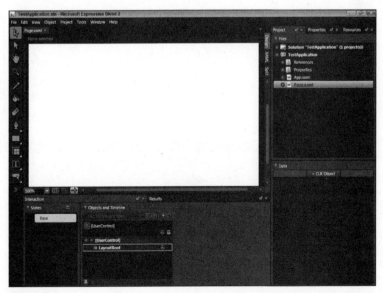

Figure 5-2

The center of the screen contains a design surface for arranging elements using drag-and-drop techniques; you can switch to XAML only or a split view of both Design and XAML using the tabs to the right of this pane. Below the design surface is the Objects and Timeline panel. As you add elements to your UI, the hierarchical view of the objects comprising it will be shown here. From this panel, you also have the ability to design animations that can apply to your UI elements. Add a `Rectangle` to your design surface by double-clicking on the rectangle icon on the far left of the IDE. Figure 5-3 shows the object hierarchy once this is done.

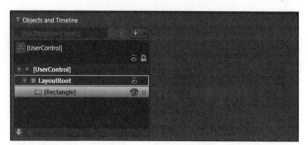

Figure 5-3

The `Rectangle` will be placed with default values of 100 for `Width` and `Height` and a thin black border, as shown in Figure 5-4.

Figure 5-4

If you select the rectangle on the design surface, you are then free to alter its properties either in the Properties window on the right-hand side or by manually editing the XAML that has been generated for you. Figure 5-5 shows the Properties window being used to alter the rectangle's color.

As well as being able to set common properties like color and position easily, further down the Properties window you can alter some of the less frequently used properties, such as the ability to transform the element's position, shape and size (`Translate`, `Rotate`, `Skew`, `Scale`, etc.). Figure 5-6 shows the `Skew` properties being altered in this way. Notice that the design surface and XAML view reflect the property changes made.

Figure 5-5

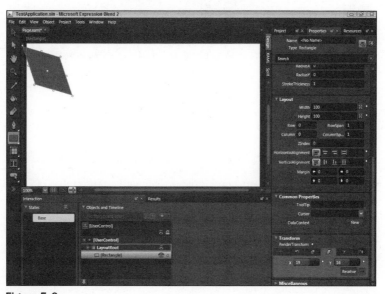

Figure 5-6

Go ahead and double-click on the Text Block icon to add a Text Block to the design surface and also have a go with the Pen tool. This tool helps you create complex `Path` objects on your design surface.

Blend also allows you to quickly apply animations against your UI elements. These options can be accessed by enabling the Animation workspace. Simply select Window and then Active Workspace ➪ Animation Workspace to work with this. By clicking on the plus (+) button next to the Storyboard drop-down list, you can bring up the Create Storyboard Resource dialog, within which you can name the timeline in use, as shown in Figure 5-7.

Figure 5-7

Once this is done, you'll see an animation timeline appear next to the Objects panel, allowing you to easily create and apply animations against your elements. You'll also notice the text "Timeline recording is on" in the upper-left corner of the screen. Simply select an object in the hierarchy, alter its properties, and then move the timeline to set how long this property change should take. In Figure 5-8, the rectangle's position has been changed and the time for this change set to just over 2 seconds.

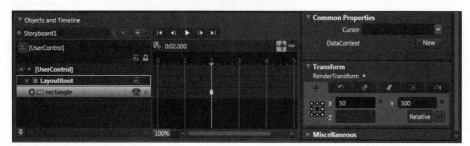

Figure 5-8

Once you're happy with your animations, you can stop timeline recording and you're done; a simple animation against the Rectangle has been defined. Switch to XAML view to see the resulting markup for this.

To add some of the more common controls to the design surface, click on the Asset Library button (the double arrows) at the bottom of the left-hand toolbar. This will open up the Asset Library dialog box, as shown in Figure 5-9.

This dialog (which you'll use often if you work with Blend) gives you access to the full suite of built-in controls, custom controls, and locally specified styles. You're free to select an asset from this dialog and then return to the design surface to draw the chosen asset on it.

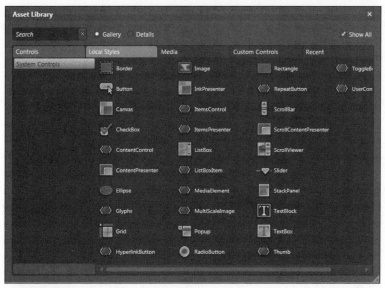

Figure 5-9

When you select an object on the design surface, you can use the Properties pane on the right-hand side to access and alter the range of properties supported by the control in question. Figure 5-10 shows the Properties pane with the Appearance and Layout subsections expanded.

Figure 5-10

As you alter the properties in the pane, the control will be redrawn in real time to show you the effect of the change you have just made. Figure 5-11 shows the effect of changing the `Opacity` property for the Rectangle that was added earlier.

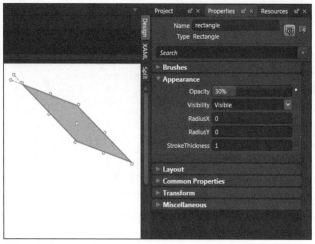

Figure 5-11

Next, a button is added to the design surface, using the Properties window shown in Figure 5-12. The button's text is set to "Click Me," and the font is altered to Webdings.

Figure 5-12

Now, in Silverlight (and WPF for that matter), the objects that comprise the user interface are drawn using vector graphics. This means that scaling to increase or decrease the control's size or skewing or rotating the control about an axis are all completed without having a negative impact on the quality of the control's appearance. Figure 5-13 shows the button created earlier following a few such transformations.

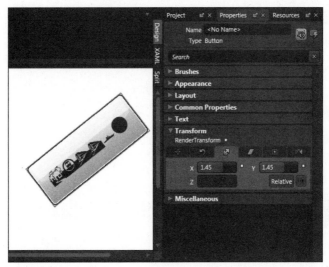

Figure 5-13

Note how the button and its "text" have been smoothly rotated and scaled without a loss in quality.

You've only explored the very basics of Blend in this short section. We encourage you to install Blend and try it out for yourself. The ease with which XAML can be created as compared to other methods (Visual Studio included) is a real bonus.

Expression Design

Expression Design is an advanced graphics and illustration package that allows you to create high-quality assets for both web and Windows applications. Vector-based assets can be created with ease and then transferred in XAML format to either Blend or Visual Studio for inclusion in your projects. As well as the ability to work on both vector- and bitmap-based graphics, both formats can be integrated and worked on in the same document. High-quality effects such as bevel, emboss, and Gaussian blur can be applied to either vector- or bitmap-based assets. Changes can then be made to the effect or the asset, safe in the knowledge that that these effects are nondestructive and editable. In short, if you need to create artwork for your web/Windows applications that can be exported in XAML, Expression Design is the tool for the job.

Expression Media

Expression Media is designed with one main purpose in mind — to make digital asset management easier. Files from more than 100 different media formats can simply be dragged and dropped to import them into the catalog and then searched and annotated, even when the originals are offline. Expression Media comes with advanced batch processing capabilities, allowing you to convert and edit many files at once, as well as keeping track of the changes made via source control functionality. Basic video and image editing is also provided, such as the ability to crop, resize, and adjust levels of brightness. As well as cataloging all of your digital assets, Expression Media comes with the ability to output them in print, via a web gallery or in a slideshow.

Expression Encoder

Expression Encoder is a feature of Expression Media that helps you quickly and easily encode your audio and video digital assets. It includes the ability to create VC-1-encoded content that can be easily displayed via a Silverlight application.

Expression Studio

Expression Studio contains all of the above applications, as well as a copy of Visual Studio Standard Edition.

ASP.NET versus Silverlight Layout

ASP.NET is a programming abstraction that helps developers build complex Enterprise web applications in an object-oriented manner. Since, in reality, ASP.NET does nothing more than wrap the underlying structure of a HTML page, the layout options available within ASP.NET are ultimately derived from the underlying layout options of HTML.

It's useful to quickly recap the layout options available so you can fully appreciate the differences and similarities between the ASP.NET approach and the Silverlight model.

Layout Options in ASP.NET

As ASP.NET is ultimately bound by the constraints of standard web page development, normal HTML layout rules and techniques apply. This means that web pages can be created and arranged using a combination of Cascading Style Sheets (CSS) and Tables. Typically, the layout instructions for CSS-based web pages exist within a separate file (.css). This is what makes CSS so attractive: It enables you to cleanly separate the *structure* of your HTML document from the *presentation* of it.

CSS

Using CSS, a combination of style attributes can be applied against the elements under its control to ordain their placement and appearance — for example, margin settings, width, and height, as well as various positioning strategies, listed below.

As well as being applied against elements such as textboxes and the like, CSS becomes really useful for layout when paired with DIV tags. A DIV tag is used to denote a division/section within an HTML or XHTML document and is used to group related UI elements together. For example, a DIV tag could be used to denote the top navigation bar of a web site, containing various control elements grouped together and positioned as a whole.

Using DIV and CSS should enable you to negate the need for Tables to construct your UI, even if it's complex in nature. We say *should* because it can be a difficult task to author the correct CSS for DIVs while supporting multiple browsers, and so some developers still tend to use Tables. In theory, the advantage gained by separating the structure of your HTML from the presentation should point toward the use of DIVs and CSS.

When using CSS, the following methods of positioning elements can be used:

❑ **Static** — This is the default positioning mode and means that the element will be placed in the position that it is defined in within the normal flow of the document.

❑ **Relative** — Using relative positioning provides you with the ability to set the element's top, bottom, left, or right properties to specify where the element should be moved relative to its default position in the document.

❑ **Absolute** — Absolute positioning allows you to position an element in a set position using the top, bottom, left, and right properties. The important thing to remember about absolute positioning is that the position is applied within the containing element.

❑ **Fixed** — Fixed works in the same way as Absolute, however rather than being positioned with regard to its container, it will be positioned with regard to the browser window.

As well as these, there are other methods to help with layout that operate within the rules above, for example:

HTML Tables

Before CSS was used for layout, HTML tables allowed you to organize the elements of your page in a grid-like manner, splitting the page or a portion of it into rows and columns, sized appropriately to contain your user interface elements. Tables are still commonly used today thanks to their ease of use; the downside is that they limit you to a tighter integration of structure and presentation.

Conclusion

The two broad options you have when creating an ASP.NET web site — CSS and Tables — give you great control and flexibility over the layout of the UI. However, care must be taken if you want to build a UI that can resize gracefully when the browser window is resized or the monitor resolution is changed. Using absolute positioning and hard-coded sizes for elements is a guarantee that your UI will suffer when faced with variable resolutions and screen sizes. Throw in localization and therefore differing text sizes and right-to-left reading, and your problems only get more difficult.

Using relative positioning and variable width element sizes can help alleviate these issues, but it is difficult to get right in a complex UI.

Layout Options in Silverlight

Layout in Silverlight is accomplished with the aid of a selection of element containers, each of which comes with different logic for laying out the elements that are placed within them. Consequently each of these containers, or layout controls, is good for certain scenarios. You'll examine each of the layout controls that ship with Silverlight shortly.

First of all, you need to be aware that within WPF and Silverlight, constructing your user interface by explicitly setting element coordinates is not the recommended approach if you're trying to build a scalable UI. The inability of fixed coordinates to take into account differing resolutions and window sizes, changing content, and even localization means that this approach can be fundamentally flawed. This means that the first layout element available in Silverlight — the `Canvas` control — shouldn't be your first choice when thinking about UI design, certainly for creating a scalable UI anyway (unless you like writing lots of code).

Instead, a technique very similar to relative and flow-based layout is recommended, which means that if you've been building your web sites using relative positioning to take into account resizing of browser windows and the like, you won't be too confused by Silverlight's `Grid` and `StackPanel` controls, which support the automatic reflowing of content within them. If, however, you have always used absolute positioning or are coming at Silverlight from a WinForms background, this may take a little getting used to.

Before you step through the layout options in detail, it's worth looking at two aspects of the layout and rendering system in Silverlight that govern this area — the ability to create resolution-independent displays (planned for a future release) and the layout process in general. You also need to look at the top-level factor controlling the UI of your Silverlight application — the display settings given to the Silverlight plug-in itself.

Resolution-Independent Rendering

The two main factors that affect the size of objects drawn on a monitor are the resolution and the DPI (dots per inch).

The *resolution* refers to the number of pixels that can be displayed, for example, a resolution of $1,024 \times 768$ equates to 1,024 pixels horizontally and 768 pixels vertically. As the resolution of the monitor increases, the size of the objects decreases, and vice versa. This means that although your UI looks great at $1,024 \times 768$, it might be too small to be usable on a monitor set to a much higher resolution, $1,600 \times$, for example.

The *DPI* is used to describe how large a "screen inch" is. For example, if this value is set to 96, 96 pixels will make up 1 screen inch. This value can be higher or lower, of course, and thus a screen inch is usually not equal to a real-world inch. Unlike resolution, when the DPI increases, so do the objects on screen, and vice versa.

To get around the problems presented by differing values in these two areas, Silverlight, like WPF, was *intended* to use device-independent pixels as the primary unit of measurement, rather than hardware pixels. We say "intended" because upon release, this feature didn't make it into Silverlight 2 and will instead be included in a future release. This information is included to make you aware of this functionality for when it is added in. A device-independent pixel is equal to 1/96 of an inch. This value was chosen because 96 is the default setting for DPI on the new Vista platform. Therefore, if you have the DPI set to 96, 1 hardware pixel will be equal to 1 WPF pixel. If you set the DPI to 120, though, WPF will think it needs to increase the size of its device-independent pixel to compensate, and each WPF pixel will be 1.25 hardware pixels in size. If you create a button 96 pixels wide in WPF, it will always be 1 inch wide on screen, no matter the resolution.

Vector Graphics

There are two broad types of computer graphics used today, raster graphics (or bitmap) and vector graphics. Raster graphics are built up pixel-by-pixel in a grid-like manner to eventually form the image, where each pixel can be a different color/shade. The downside with this technique is the inability to scale the image up or down nicely without it turning blocky. The upside is that these images can be very high in quality, even photo-realistic.

Vector graphics, however, can be scaled up or down and maintain their quality because instead of being made up pixel-by-pixel, they are composed of many smaller primitive objects (line, polyline, Bezier curve, etc.), each of which can be described using mathematical statements. The upshot of this is that the image can be scaled to any resolution without turning blocky. The downside is that vector graphics can't currently be used for photo-realistic images and can perform more slowly than bitmaps as many more calculations have to be performed.

Silverlight comes with support for both raster and vector graphics out-of-the-box, so you get the best of both worlds. If you want to make a UI that scales well to multiple resolutions, you would be well advised to create vector graphics for your toolbar images, for example, to prevent blocky/blurry edges when scaled.

To conclude, if you want your image to scale smoothly if the resolution of your application changes, you should use vector graphics, not bitmaps.

The Layout Process

The layout process in Silverlight is essentially the same as that in WPF, using a two-stage "measure-and-arrange" algorithm to calculate the size and position of elements within the top-level parent panel container. Whenever the user interface needs to be drawn (or redrawn), the first operation that takes place is the "measure" operation. This involves the layout system iterating recursively through the child elements that make up the UI, measuring each one in turn and evaluating its desired size. This value is exposed via the `UIElement.DesiredSize` property.

Next, the layout system carries out a second pass, the "arrange" pass, iterating over the elements comprising the UI and finalizing their size and position. In Silverlight, every `FrameworkElement` is actually contained within a bounding box, which turns out to be nothing more than a simple rectangle. Bounding boxes are the objects that are actually laid out and positioned by the layout system during the arrange sweep. Each bounding box is a layout slot within the UI, and the rectangle object defined in this way can be retrieved via a call to the static `LayoutInformation.GetLayoutSlot` method, passing in the `FrameworkElement` object in question. If the element is larger than the layout slot that has been assigned to it, it will be clipped, and so not all of it will be visible. The dimensions of the visible area of an element clipped in this manner can be obtained via a call to the `LayoutInformation.GetLayoutClip` method, again passing in the `FrameworkElement` object in question.

If the element fits within the layout slot, it is positioned within it based on its alignment properties.

Figure 5-14 shows the relationship between a panel and a single child element contained within a layout slot.

You can see that in this example, the `TextBox` is much smaller than the layout slot given to it by the layout system and so is fully visible. However, if the layout system was under pressure for screen real estate and provided a layout slot that was smaller than the `TextBox`, some or all of the `TextBox` would be clipped, and only the layout clip portion of it would be visible, as shown in Figure 5-15.

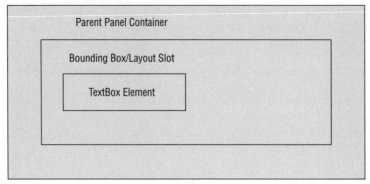

Figure 5-14

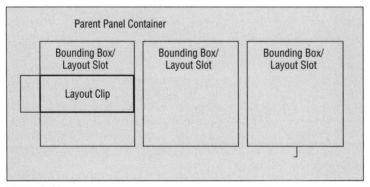

Figure 5-15

Displaying the Silverlight Plug-in Itself

It's all well and good to design and create your Silverlight user interface in isolation, but you need to remember that your UI is constrained at the top level by the placement and sizing instructions applied to the plug-in that will host it, not just the sizes specified against your top-level layout control. Your nice UI won't look quite so nice when you realize that it's twice the size of the area given to the hosting plug-in.

There are various levels where sizing instructions can be placed to constrain your Silverlight application. You'll look at them in order now. First, your Silverlight application is placed into a web page directly within a DIV tag, as shown in the following example:

```
<!DOCTYPE html PUBLIC "-//W3C//DTD XHTML 1.0 Transitional//EN"
    "http://www.w3.org/TR/xhtml1/DTD/xhtml1-transitional.dtd">

<html xmlns="http://www.w3.org/1999/xhtml" style="height:100%;">
<head runat="server">
    <title>Test Page For Chapter05</title>
</head>
<body style="height:100%;margin:0;">
    <form id="form1" runat="server" style="height:100%;">
```

```
<asp:ScriptManager ID="ScriptManager1" runat="server"></asp:ScriptManager>
<div  style="height:100%;">
    <asp:Silverlight ID="Xaml1"
                     runat="server"
                     Source="~/ClientBin/Chapter05.xap"
                     MinimumVersion="2.0.30523"
                     Width="100%"
                     Height="100%" />
    </div>
</form>
</body>
</html>
```

You can see that the DIV tag has its style property set to specify a height of 100 percent, which means the DIV tag will expand vertically to fill whatever space is provided by its parent HTML container. Imagine in this instance if the DIV tag had its width and height properties set to 640 and 480, respectively. If left like this, it wouldn't matter if you set the Canvas control within the contained Silverlight application to be 1,000 pixels by 1,000 pixels, because the remainder will effectively be placed offscreen as it will fall outside the bounds of the containing DIV, as shown in Figure 5-16.

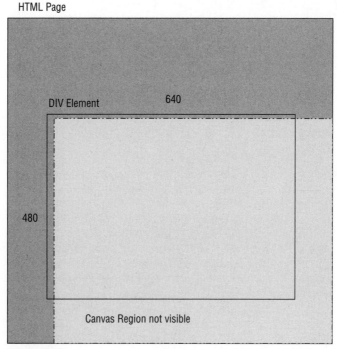

Figure 5-16

The next place in the chain that affects the sizing of your Silverlight application is within the OBJECT tag itself that is output by the ASP.NET Silverlight control. By default, the Width and Height properties of this control are set to 100 percent, which will be propagated to the actual OBJECT tag rendered at run time. If left to 100 percent each, the Silverlight control will expand to fill the entire DIV tag within which it is contained.

Finally, you have the sizing attributes you pass to your top-level layout container; the following `UserControl` is set to a `Height` of 400 and `Width` of 300:

```
<UserControl x:Class="Chapter05.Page"
    xmlns="http://schemas.microsoft.com/winfx/2006/xaml/presentation"
    xmlns:x="http://schemas.microsoft.com/winfx/2006/xaml"
    Width="400" Height="300">
    <Grid x:Name="LayoutRoot" Background="White">

    </Grid>
</UserControl>
```

Be aware of these three different means of altering the size of your Silverlight application when encountering strange behavior. It's very easy to overlook one and waste time debugging the wrong sizing problem.

The Layout Controls

Now that you're comfortable with the Silverlight layout process at a conceptual level, it's time to turn your attention to the controls that enable layout to take place.

In order for an element to be positioned and arranged in your Silverlight user interface, it must be placed within a control that derives from `Panel`. Silverlight provides the `Canvas`, `StackPanel`, `Grid`, and `TabPanel` controls that all inherit from `Panel` and as such allow child elements to be placed and arranged within them.

If you find that none of these controls satisfy your more advanced layout requirements, you can, of course, create your own layout controls and inherit from `Panel` yourself.

Each of these four main layout controls is now discussed, starting with the most basic (and also the most efficient for this reason), `Canvas`.

Canvas

`Canvas` was the first layout control made available in Silverlight 2 and is also the simplest. Support for absolutely positioning child elements using X and Y coordinates is provided by using two `Canvas` attached properties — `Canvas.Left` (which controls the X coordinate) and `Canvas.Top` (which controls the Y coordinate). Positioning of elements within the Z axis of the `Canvas` is provided by the `Canvas.ZIndex` attached property. This allows you to lay elements on top of each other if required.

Using `Canvas` is simple, indeed. You'll now step through a few examples that illustrate just how simple. The examples can be seen in the Chapter 5 source code.

The following XAML shows a `Rectangle` added to a `Canvas` control with the `Canvas.Top` and `Canvas.Left` attached properties both set to 80. This will place the `Rectangle` 80 pixels from the top of the `Canvas` and 80 pixels from the left of the `Canvas`.

```
<UserControl x:Class="Chapter05.CanvasExample"
    xmlns="http://schemas.microsoft.com/winfx/2006/xaml/presentation"
    xmlns:x="http://schemas.microsoft.com/winfx/2006/xaml"
    Width="400" Height="300">
```

```
    <Canvas x:Name="LayoutRoot" Background="White">

        <Rectangle Fill="Blue"
            Canvas.Top="80"
            Canvas.Left="80"
            Width="100"
            Height="50" />

    </Canvas>

</UserControl>
```

The rectangle has been colored blue so that its position is evident, as shown in Figure 5-17.

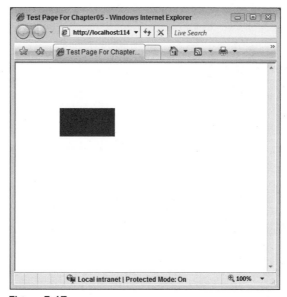

Figure 5-17

If you omit the `Canvas.Top` and `Canvas.Left` properties, they will assume their default values of 0, effectively placing the element in the top-left corner of the `Canvas`.

```
<UserControl x:Class="Chapter05.CanvasExample"
    xmlns="http://schemas.microsoft.com/winfx/2006/xaml/presentation"
    xmlns:x="http://schemas.microsoft.com/winfx/2006/xaml"
    Width="400" Height="300">

    <Canvas x:Name="LayoutRoot" Background="White">

        <Rectangle Fill="Blue"
            Width="100"
            Height="50" />
```

```
                <Rectangle Fill="Green"
                    Width="60"
                    Height="20"
                    Canvas.Top="80" />

        </Canvas>

</UserControl>
```

In the above example, two rectangles are placed within the `Canvas`. The first rectangle will appear in the top-left corner — 0,0 as both the `Canvas.Top` and `Canvas.Left` properties have been omitted. The second rectangle will appear at position 0,80 as the `Canvas.Left` property will default to 0 because of its omission. Figure 5-18 shows the result.

Figure 5-18

Thus, adding elements to the `Canvas` is very easy. Simply set the `Canvas.Left` and `Canvas.Top` properties accordingly. Remember, though, that these properties specify coordinates relative to the containing `Canvas`. This becomes important when you want to nest a `Canvas` within a `Canvas`. Consider the following example:

```
<UserControl x:Class="Chapter05.CanvasExample"
    xmlns="http://schemas.microsoft.com/winfx/2006/xaml/presentation"
    xmlns:x="http://schemas.microsoft.com/winfx/2006/xaml"
    Width="400" Height="300">

    <Canvas x:Name="LayoutRoot" Background="White">

        <Rectangle Fill="Yellow"
            Canvas.Top="30"
```

```
              Canvas.Left="30"
              Height="10"
              Width="40"/>

    <Canvas Background="Green"
       Canvas.Top="100"
       Canvas.Left="30"
       Height="200"
       Width="200" >

          <Ellipse Canvas.Top="10"
             Canvas.Left="10"
             Fill="Blue"
             Height="30"
             Width="30" />

       </Canvas>

    </Canvas>

</UserControl>
```

You can see that a Canvas is free to be placed as a child element within a parent Canvas just as a Rectangle or any other element is. The Canvas.Top and Canvas.Left attached properties in the nested Canvas declaration refer to its position within the parent Canvas. Note, however, that the Canvas.Top and Canvas.Left properties set on the innermost Ellipse are relative not to the outer-most Canvas, but to the Canvas directly containing it, the nested one. Elements placed in a Canvas are always placed relative to the Canvas that directly contains them. Figure 5-19 shows the resulting output.

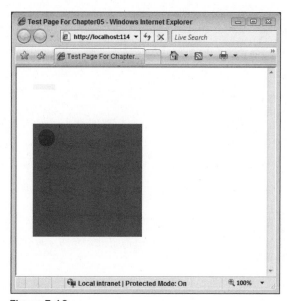

Figure 5-19

You're also free to overlap elements within a Canvas. In the following example, five rectangles have been added to the Canvas, each of which slightly overlaps the previous one. Note that none of the Rectangle objects has its Canvas.ZIndex attached property specified.

```xaml
<UserControl x:Class="Chapter05.CanvasExample"
    xmlns="http://schemas.microsoft.com/winfx/2006/xaml/presentation"
    xmlns:x="http://schemas.microsoft.com/winfx/2006/xaml"
    Width="400" Height="300">

    <Canvas x:Name="LayoutRoot" Background="White">

        <Rectangle Canvas.Left="10"
            Canvas.Top="10"
            Width="100"
            Height="30"
            Fill="Red" />

        <Rectangle Canvas.Left="60"
            Canvas.Top="30"
            Width="100"
            Height="30"
            Fill="Yellow" />

        <Rectangle Canvas.Left="110"
            Canvas.Top="50"
            Width="100"
            Height="30"
            Fill="Green" />

        <Rectangle Canvas.Left="160"
            Canvas.Top="70"
            Width="100"
            Height="30"
            Fill="Blue" />

        <Rectangle Canvas.Left="210"
            Canvas.Top="90"
            Width="100"
            Height="30"
            Fill="Black" />

    </Canvas>

</UserControl>
```

This XAML results in the output shown in Figure 5-20.

Figure 5-20

By default, the order in which elements are added to the Canvas controls the order in which they overlap. In effect, elements will be stacked one on top of the other. If this default behavior is not what you want, you can override it by explicitly setting the Z coordinate yourself via the Canvas.ZIndex attached property.

```
<UserControl x:Class="Chapter05.CanvasExample"
    xmlns="http://schemas.microsoft.com/winfx/2006/xaml/presentation"
    xmlns:x="http://schemas.microsoft.com/winfx/2006/xaml"
    Width="400" Height="300">

    <Canvas x:Name="LayoutRoot" Background="White">

        <Rectangle Canvas.Left="10"
            Canvas.Top="10"
            Width="100"
            Height="30"
            Fill="Red" />

        <Rectangle Canvas.Left="60"
            Canvas.Top="30"
            Width="100"
            Height="30"
            Fill="Yellow" />
```

```
<Rectangle Canvas.Left="110"
    Canvas.Top="50"
    Width="100"
    Height="30"
    Fill="Green"
    Canvas.ZIndex="1" />

<Rectangle Canvas.Left="160"
    Canvas.Top="70"
    Width="100"
    Height="30"
    Fill="Blue" />

<Rectangle Canvas.Left="210"
    Canvas.Top="90"
    Width="100"
    Height="30"
    Fill="Black" />

</Canvas>

</UserControl>
```

The greater the `Canvas.ZIndex` property is compared to that of the other elements, the closer to the foreground that element will be placed. Changing the third `Rectangle` to a value of 1 will place it on top of all the other rectangles that have unspecified values, as can be seen in Figure 5-21.

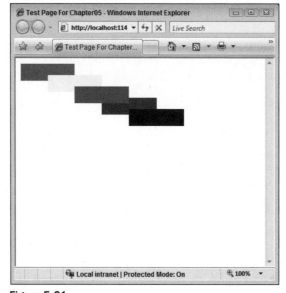

Figure 5-21

There is a final point for you to take in with regard to developing against the Canvas. It's important to remember that although you set the Height and Width properties of the Canvas control, you're ultimately bound by the Height and Width specified by the hosting page itself. Therefore if you set an element to be displayed 200 pixels to the right within your Canvas and if the hosting page sets the Width of your Silverlight control to 100, your element will effectively be placed offscreen and will not be visible. The ASP.NET Silverlight control below explicitly sets the Height and Width to 100:

```
<html xmlns="http://www.w3.org/1999/xhtml" style="height:100%;">
<head runat="server">
    <title>Test Page For Chapter05</title>
</head>
<body style="height:100%;margin:0;">
    <form id="form1" runat="server" style="height:100%;">
        <asp:ScriptManager ID="ScriptManager1" runat="server"></asp:ScriptManager>
        <div  style="height:100%;">
            <asp:Silverlight ID="Xaml1"
                             runat="server"
                             Source="~/ClientBin/Chapter05.xap"
                             MinimumVersion="2.0.30523"
                             Width="100"
                             Height="100" />
        </div>
    </form>
</body>
</html>
```

This results in the following Rectangle being rendered offscreen as its Canvas.Left property is greater than the hosting page's Width setting for the Silverlight control:

```
<UserControl x:Class="Chapter05.CanvasExample"
    xmlns="http://schemas.microsoft.com/winfx/2006/xaml/presentation"
    xmlns:x="http://schemas.microsoft.com/winfx/2006/xaml"
    Width="400" Height="300">

    <Canvas x:Name="LayoutRoot" Background="White">
        <Rectangle Canvas.Top="10"
            Canvas.Left="100"
            Height="20"
            Width="20"
            Fill="Blue" />

    </Canvas>

</UserControl>
```

Grid

The Grid layout object allows you to construct your UI by arranging it within a number of columns and rows. This is similar to the TABLE HTML element you're already familiar with.

Consider the following simple example, which defines a `Grid` that has two columns and two rows:

```xml
<UserControl x:Class="Chapter05.GridExample"
    xmlns="http://schemas.microsoft.com/winfx/2006/xaml/presentation"
    xmlns:x="http://schemas.microsoft.com/winfx/2006/xaml"
    Width="400" Height="300">

    <Grid x:Name="LayoutRoot"
        Background="White"
        ShowGridLines="True">

        <Grid.ColumnDefinitions>
            <ColumnDefinition />
            <ColumnDefinition />
        </Grid.ColumnDefinitions>

        <Grid.RowDefinitions>
            <RowDefinition />
            <RowDefinition />
        </Grid.RowDefinitions>

        <TextBlock Grid.Column="0"
                Grid.Row="0"
                Text="0,0" />

        <TextBlock Grid.Column="0"
                Grid.Row="1"
                Text="0,1" />

        <TextBlock Grid.Column="1"
                Grid.Row="0"
                Text="1,0" />

        <TextBlock Grid.Column="1"
                Grid.Row="1"
                Text="1,1" />

    </Grid>

</UserControl>
```

There are a few things worth calling out in this example. First, the `ShowGridLines` property of the `Grid` object has been set to `True`. This will draw in the lines created by the rows and columns so you can see the effect your changes are making.

Second, notice the syntax for defining the number of `Column` and `Row` objects within the `Grid`. `ColumnDefinition` and `RowDefinition` elements are placed within the `Grid.ColumnDefinitions` and `Grid.RowDefinitions` elements. More on these shortly.

Finally, notice how the four `TextBlock` objects have been placed into their own cells using the `Grid.Column` and `Grid.Row` attached properties.

The output is shown in Figure 5-22.

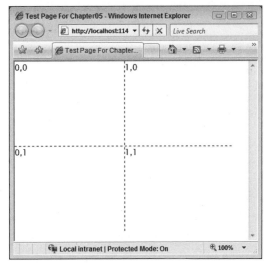

Figure 5-22

At present, since no sizing information has been provided, the default action is for them to be spaced evenly according to the size of their contents. This is most likely not going to suffice, and thus you are given the ability to set the `Column` element's `Width` property and the `Row` element's `Height` property to fine-tune the layout of your `Grid`. Therefore, if you wanted the first `Column` to be 30 pixels wide and the second `Column` to be 70 pixels wide, the following markup could be used:

```
<Grid.ColumnDefinitions>
    <ColumnDefinition Width="30" />
    <ColumnDefinition Width="70" />
</Grid.ColumnDefinitions>
```

The same syntax applies for applying the `Height` property to your `RowDefinition` elements. The following markup will set the first `Row` to be 30 pixels high and the second `Row` to be 70 pixels high:

```
<Grid.RowDefinitions>
    <RowDefinition Height="30" />
    <RowDefinition Height="70" />
</Grid.RowDefinitions>
```

Figure 5-23 shows the result of these changes.

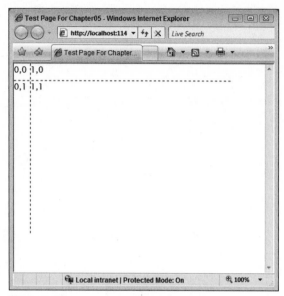

Figure 5-23

In addition to explicitly setting the Width and Height of the Row and Column elements, you can also instruct them to size automatically by specifying Auto. This will size them based purely on the size of the content within them. The markup for this is as follows:

```
<Grid.ColumnDefinitions>
    <ColumnDefinition Width="Auto"/>
    <ColumnDefinition Width="Auto"/>
</Grid.ColumnDefinitions>

<Grid.RowDefinitions>
    <RowDefinition Height="Auto"/>
    <RowDefinition Height="Auto"/>
</Grid.RowDefinitions>
```

Finally and perhaps most usefully, you have the ability to size your Row and Column elements using Star sizing. Star sizing allows you to distribute the space available within your Grid object using weighted proportions. In practice, this means that you can create a Grid that resizes gracefully as the screen size changes around it because the sizes are not fixed/absolute. This also allows the Grid to automatically adjust (within boundaries that you can set) to ranges of content size. An example will help hammer this point home:

```
<UserControl x:Class="Chapter05.GridExample"
    xmlns="http://schemas.microsoft.com/winfx/2006/xaml/presentation"
    xmlns:x="http://schemas.microsoft.com/winfx/2006/xaml"
    Width="400" Height="400">
```

```
<Grid x:Name="LayoutRoot"
      Background="LightBlue"
      ShowGridLines="True">

    <Grid.ColumnDefinitions>
        <ColumnDefinition Width="2*"/>
        <ColumnDefinition Width="*"/>
    </Grid.ColumnDefinitions>

    <Grid.RowDefinitions>
        <RowDefinition Height="2*"/>
        <RowDefinition Height="*"/>
    </Grid.RowDefinitions>

    <TextBlock Grid.Column="0"
               Grid.Row="0"
               Text="0,0" />

    <TextBlock Grid.Column="0"
               Grid.Row="1"
               Text="0,1" />

    <TextBlock Grid.Column="1"
               Grid.Row="0"
               Text="1,0" />

    <TextBlock Grid.Column="1"
               Grid.Row="1"
               Text="1,1" />

</Grid>

</UserControl>
```

In this example, you can see that the values for the Column Width properties have been set to 2* and *, respectively. This means that the first Column will be given two times the available space, and the second Column will receive one times the available space. The same proportions are set against the Row elements, and the resulting output is shown in Figure 5-24.

The benefit of this approach really becomes clear when the Grid is asked to resize and effectively reflow the content within it. In order to achieve this, the plug-in needs to be sized at 100 percent for both Width and Height, and the Width and Height for the container controls within your XAML need to be omitted. These steps ensure that the content will always expand to fill the available space provided to the plug-in.

```
<div style="height:100%;">
    <asp:Silverlight ID="Xaml1"
                     runat="server"
                     Source="~/ClientBin/Chapter05.xap"
                     MinimumVersion="2.0.30523"
                     Width="100%"
                     Height="100%" />
</div>
```

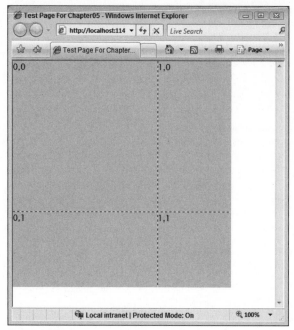

Figure 5-24

By doing this, you can see that as the browser window is resized, the Grid and its contents resize according to the weighted proportions assigned in the Column and Row definitions. Figure 5-25 illustrates this point.

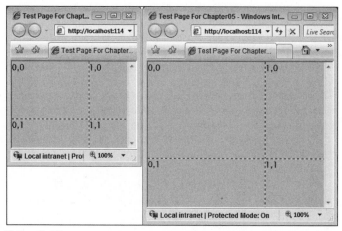

Figure 5-25

You can also fine-tune this behavior further, by specifying maximum and minimum values for both the Column Width and the Row Height — in effect, providing a range within which the Column and Row can resize. The following XAML shows this in action:

```
<Grid.ColumnDefinitions>
    <ColumnDefinition Width="2*"/>
    <ColumnDefinition Width="*" MinWidth="30"/>
</Grid.ColumnDefinitions>

<Grid.RowDefinitions>
    <RowDefinition Height="2*" MaxHeight="400"/>
    <RowDefinition Height="*"/>
</Grid.RowDefinitions>
```

This technique allows you to create a scalable UI that isn't rendered useless when the browser window is resized.

Now turn your attention back to the controls that are placed within the Grid itself. As well as the attached properties to define which Row and Column they should sit within, there are two more properties that allow the control to span multiple Column and Row elements, the Grid.ColumnSpan and Grid.RowSpan attached properties, respectively. These can be set to a number that specifies exactly how many of the rows or columns they are allowed to span. Consider the following example in which the first TextBlock in the previous examples has been set to span two columns:

```
<TextBlock Grid.Column="0"
           Grid.Row="0"
           Grid.ColumnSpan="2"
           Text="This text will span more than one column" />
```

Figure 5-26 shows how this change has affected the UI.

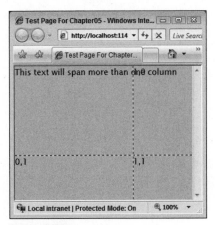

Figure 5-26

StackPanel

The `StackPanel` allows you to do exactly what its name suggests — stack elements, either vertically or horizontally within it (vertical being the default). The elements are positioned relative to the preceding element in the stack, and so you don't have to concern yourself with positioning. The following example shows four elements stacked vertically:

```xml
<UserControl x:Class="Chapter05.StackPanelExample"
    xmlns="http://schemas.microsoft.com/winfx/2006/xaml/presentation"
    xmlns:x="http://schemas.microsoft.com/winfx/2006/xaml">

    <StackPanel x:Name="LayoutRoot" Background="White">
        <TextBlock Text="Item 1" />
        <Button Content="Item 2" />
        <Ellipse Fill="Blue"
                 Height="20"
                 Width="30" />
        <TextBox Text="Item 4" />
    </StackPanel>

</UserControl>
```

Figure 5-27 shows the output of this XAML. To change the items to be stacked horizontally rather than vertically, you can set the `StackPanel.Orientation` property to `Horizontal`.

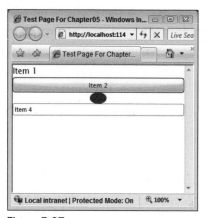

Figure 5-27

```xml
<StackPanel x:Name="LayoutRoot"
            Background="White"
            Orientation="Horizontal">

    <TextBlock Text="Item 1" />
    <Button Content="Item 2" />
    <Ellipse Fill="Blue"
             Height="20"
             Width="30" />
```

```
        <TextBox Text="Item 4" />

    </StackPanel>
```

This will render the UI in Figure 5-28.

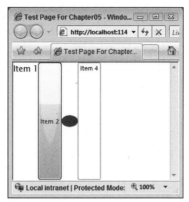

Figure 5-28

Each control that is stacked within the StackPanel can set its own alignment via the Horizontal Alignment and VerticalAlignment properties. These do not affect in any way the stack order or orientation, only how the individual control will be placed within its assigned stack slot.

Margin

Before moving on to the TabControl and associated TabPanel objects, it's worth discussing how the Margin property of individual elements can affect their placement within the layout controls. In order to position an element within a layout container precisely, in addition to the techniques you've already seen, you can also use HorizontalAlignment, VerticalAlignment, and the Margin property provided by the base FrameworkElement class. The Margin property warrants further examination as it's not simply a matter of providing a single value.

Margin accepts a value of type System.Windows.Thickness and is used to specify the amount of space between the object it's set against and the surrounding objects in the layout. By default, this value is set to 0; however, it's rare that your UI will require all the objects being tightly packed in this manner.

There are a variety of ways to specify the Margin size, as you can set it both uniformly for all sides of the element or individually for different Margin sizes on different sides.

The following example illustrates the concept:

```xml
<UserControl x:Class="Chapter05.MarginExample"
    xmlns="http://schemas.microsoft.com/winfx/2006/xaml/presentation"
    xmlns:x="http://schemas.microsoft.com/winfx/2006/xaml"
    Width="400" Height="300">
```

```xml
<StackPanel x:Name="LayoutRoot" Background="LightBlue">

    <!-- Uniform Margin of 30 pixels all the way around -->
    <Button Content="Click Me"
            Margin="30" />

    <!-- Left + Right margin = 20, top + bottom margin = 30 -->
    <TextBox Text="Some Text"
            Margin="20, 30" />

    <!-- left, right, top, bottom values -->
    <TextBlock Text="More Text"
            Margin="10, 10, 5, 5" />

</StackPanel>

</UserControl>
```

The three elements within the StackPanel have each had their Margin property set in different ways. The first element has been given a uniform Margin 30 pixels wide all the way around it. The second element has been given a Margin thickness of 20 to share between the left and right sides, so each receives 10. The top and bottom sides share 30, so each receives 15. Finally, in the third element, each side (left, right, top, and bottom) has had its Margin size set explicitly.

One important point to consider regarding the Margin setting is that it acts additively. If you have two elements next to each other, each with a Margin of 10, the total space between them will be 20.

As you can imagine, combining margin and alignment settings within the layout controls provides you with fine-grained control over the placement of elements within your UI.

TabControl

TabControl allows you to organize a complex UI by breaking it apart into related groups and placing the grouped elements in an arbitrary number of TabItem objects within the containing TabControl.

For each TabItem that you place within the TabControl, you add UI elements via its Content property, and thus you will typically create a layout control directly within the Content property to facilitate the layout of the individual TabItem elements. As you may have inferred from the preceding statement, the TabItem itself is not a layout control. Every TabControl has a single TabPanel object that acts as a layout container. It is this container that actually controls how the TabItems within it will be displayed.

The following C# code sample shows how you can programmatically create a TabControl and populate it with two TabItem controls, each with their Content set to a UI tree with a layout control at the top. (We thought you might be bored with looking at XAML by now.)

```csharp
using System;
using System.Collections.Generic;
using System.Linq;
using System.Net;
using System.Windows;
```

```
using System.Windows.Controls;
using System.Windows.Documents;
using System.Windows.Input;
using System.Windows.Media;
using System.Windows.Media.Animation;
using System.Windows.Shapes;
using System.Windows.Controls.Primitives;

namespace Chapter05
{
    public partial class TabControlExample : UserControl
    {
        public TabControlExample()
        {
            InitializeComponent();

            //instantiate the TabControl
            TabControl tabControl = new TabControl();

            //Add the first tab, and populate it with
            //a Grid containing a TextBlock
            TabItem tab1 = new TabItem();
            tab1.Header = "Tab 1";
            TextBlock textblock1 = new TextBlock();
            textblock1.Text = "Text Block 1";
            Grid grid = new Grid();
            grid.Children.Add(textblock1);
            tab1.Content = grid;

            //Add this TabItem to the TabControl
            tabControl.Items.Add(tab1);

            //Add the second tab, and populate it with
            //a StackPanel containing a Button
            TabItem tab2 = new TabItem();
            tab2.Header = "Tab 2";
            Button button1 = new Button();
            button1.Content = "Click Me!";
            StackPanel stackPanel = new StackPanel();
            stackPanel.Children.Add(button1);
            tab2.Content = stackPanel;

            //Add this TabItem to the TabControl
            tabControl.Items.Add(tab2);

            //Add the TabControl to the UI
            LayoutRoot.Children.Add(tabControl);
        }
    }
}
```

Figure 5-29 shows the resulting UI with the second tab selected.

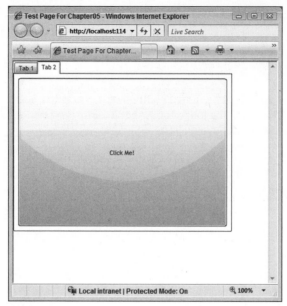

Figure 5-29

Full-Screen Support

There are two display modes that a Silverlight plug-in can support. The Embedded mode is the default mode and is fairly simple to deal with. Full-Screen mode is a little trickier and warrants a more detailed exploration in this section.

Embedded Mode

In Embedded mode, the plug-in is always contained within the hosting browser window. Position and size are dictated by the containing DIV tag. This is the default display mode for a Silverlight application. It is practical for most common scenarios.

Full-Screen Mode

Sometimes displaying your application within the confines of the browser window is not desirable, a couple of good examples being a kiosk application or a game. In these situations, you can switch the display mode to Full-Screen, which will place your application on top of all other applications (browser included) and resize it to the display's current resolution.

Because of the aggressive nature of this feature — it takes over the entire desktop — it cannot simply be activated from anywhere in code. Imagine if an inconsiderate developer forced their Silverlight application to Full-Screen mode in the page loaded event. That would be very frustrating for users navigating to the hosting page of this application.

Instead, it can only be activated in response to specific user-initiated actions: MouseLeftButtonDown, MouseLeftButtonUp, KeyDown, and KeyUp. This prevents a forceful takeover of the desktop by a Silverlight application.

To toggle between Embedded and Full-Screen mode, you need to set the Application.Current.Host .Content.IsFullScreen property to `true` for Full-Screen or `false` for Embedded mode.

The following example shows this behavior in action and also demonstrates some of the nuances of this technique. The source code can be found in the Chapter 5 source code directory.

First off, you should create a XAML page that will be shown in either Embedded or Full-Screen mode. For the purposes of the example, the following XAML file simply creates a button that when clicked toggles between Full-Screen and Embedded mode:

```xml
<UserControl x:Class="Chapter05.FullScreenExample"
    xmlns="http://schemas.microsoft.com/winfx/2006/xaml/presentation"
    xmlns:x="http://schemas.microsoft.com/winfx/2006/xaml">

    <Grid x:Name="LayoutRoot" Background="White">
        <Button Content="Toggle Full Screen Mode"
                Click="Button_Click" />
    </Grid>

</UserControl>
```

Note the event handler that has been wired up on the `Button` object. The following code behind shows how this `Button` handler method toggles between the two modes:

```csharp
using System;
using System.Collections.Generic;
using System.Linq;
using System.Net;
using System.Windows;
using System.Windows.Controls;
using System.Windows.Documents;
using System.Windows.Input;
using System.Windows.Media;
using System.Windows.Media.Animation;
using System.Windows.Shapes;

namespace Chapter05
{
    public partial class FullScreenExample : UserControl
    {
        public FullScreenExample()
        {
            InitializeComponent();
        }

        private void Button_Click(object sender, RoutedEventArgs e)
        {
            Application.Current.Host.Content.IsFullScreen =
                !Application.Current.Host.Content.IsFullScreen;
        }
    }
}
```

When you first run this page, you will see the application hosted within the browser as normal (see Figure 5-30). Try clicking the `Button`, though, and the screen shown in Figure 5-31 will appear.

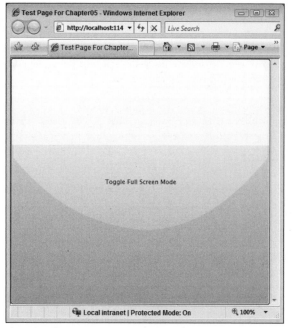

Figure 5-30

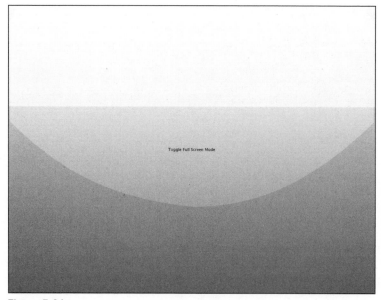

Figure 5-31

Note the "Press Esc to exit full-screen mode" instruction that appears briefly once entering Full-Screen mode. This gives all users the information needed to cancel this behavior if it was unintentional or not required. As well as pressing the *Esc* key to exit Full Screen for both Windows and Macintosh, on Windows, *Alt+F4* can be used to return to Embedded mode.

The application will also automatically revert back to Embedded mode from Full Screen if it loses focus. How can it lose focus when it has taken over the desktop? In a multi-monitor setup, simply selecting another application in a different monitor will do the trick, or using *Alt+Tab* to switch between running applications on Windows, for example.

When in Full-Screen mode, the `Application.Current.Host.Content.ActualWidth` and `Application.Current.Host.Content.ActualHeight` properties can be used to ascertain the true screen size, which is useful for the scaling of your controls if necessary. The `Width` and `Height` properties will not change when entering Full-Screen mode.

To see this in action, a `TextBlock` to show the screen dimensions can be added to your page:

```xml
<Grid x:Name="LayoutRoot" Background="White">
    <Grid.RowDefinitions>
        <RowDefinition />
        <RowDefinition />
    </Grid.RowDefinitions>

    <Button Content="Toggle Full Screen Mode"
            Click="Button_Click"
            Grid.Row="0"/>

    <TextBlock Grid.Row="1"
            x:Name="information" />

</Grid>
```

You can then take advantage of the `Application.Current.Host.Content.FullScreenChanged` event to write out the current screen size to this `TextBlock`:

```csharp
using System;
using System.Collections.Generic;
using System.Linq;
using System.Net;
using System.Windows;
using System.Windows.Controls;
using System.Windows.Documents;
using System.Windows.Input;
using System.Windows.Media;
using System.Windows.Media.Animation;
using System.Windows.Shapes;

namespace Chapter05
{
    public partial class FullScreenExample : UserControl
```

```
    {
        public FullScreenExample()
        {
            InitializeComponent();
            this.DisplayBrowserSize();
            Application.Current.Host.Content.FullScreenChanged +=
                new EventHandler(Content_FullScreenChanged);
        }

        void Content_FullScreenChanged(object sender, EventArgs e)
        {
            this.DisplayBrowserSize();
        }

        private void DisplayBrowserSize()
        {
            information.Text = String.Format("Width: {0}, Height {1},
                            ActualWidth {2}, ActualHeight {3}",
                this.Width,
                this.Height,
                Application.Current.Host.Content.ActualWidth,
                Application.Current.Host.Content.ActualHeight);
        }

        private void Button_Click(object sender, RoutedEventArgs e)
        {
            Application.Current.Host.Content.IsFullScreen =
                !Application.Current.Host.Content.IsFullScreen;
        }
    }
}
```

Note how the `FullScreenChange` event is wired up in the `Page_Loaded` handler. A private method has been added — `DisplayBrowserSize()`, which writes the `UserControl.Height`, `UserControl.Width`, `Application.Current.Host.Content.ActualHeight`, and `Application.Current.Host.Content.ActualWidth` properties to the `TextBlock`-named information in the XAML.

Try running your application now. At first, the `Width` and `Height` standard properties will be correct (possibly NaN if they haven't been explicitly set), and the `ActualWidth` and `ActualHeight` will be correct.

Once switching to Full-Screen mode, however, the `Width` and `Height` remain unchanged, but the `ActualWidth` and `ActualHeight` show the true browser size (see Figure 5-32).

If you have put together a UI that is absolutely sized (say, using a `Canvas`) and want this UI to scale up when entering Full-Screen mode, there is a quick trick you can use to accomplish this. Consider the following UI, a `Button` and a `TextBox` positioned within a `Canvas`:

```
<UserControl x:Class="Chapter05.ScaleUpExample"
    xmlns="http://schemas.microsoft.com/winfx/2006/xaml/presentation"
    xmlns:x="http://schemas.microsoft.com/winfx/2006/xaml"
    Width="400" Height="300">
```

```
<Canvas x:Name="LayoutRoot" Background="White">

    <Button Canvas.Left="20"
            Canvas.Top="20"
            Content="Toggle Full Screen"
            Click="Button_Click" />

    <TextBlock Canvas.Left="20"
               Canvas.Top="60"
               Text="Some Text" />
</Canvas>

</UserControl>
```

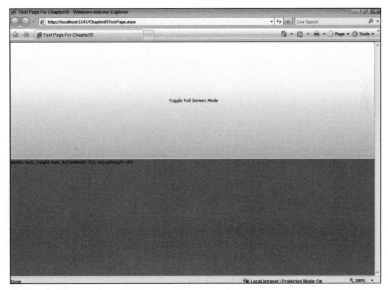

Figure 5-32

Now, when the Button is clicked, the screen is scaled up and Full-Screen mode is entered; however, the Canvas and its contents remain at the same size, which looks odd and leaves plenty of full-screen real estate bare. What is more likely to be needed is for the application to recognize that it's in Full-Screen mode and to scale the UI up accordingly. To do this, you can take advantage of the ScaleTransform class as shown in the following code sample. More on this subject can be found in Chapter 14.

```
using System;
using System.Collections.Generic;
using System.Linq;
using System.Net;
using System.Windows;
using System.Windows.Controls;
using System.Windows.Documents;
using System.Windows.Input;
```

```csharp
using System.Windows.Media;
using System.Windows.Media.Animation;
using System.Windows.Shapes;

namespace Chapter05
{
    public partial class ScaleUpExample : UserControl
    {
        public ScaleUpExample()
        {
            InitializeComponent();
            Application.Current.Host.Content.FullScreenChanged +=
                new EventHandler(Content_FullScreenChanged);
        }

        void Content_FullScreenChanged(object sender, EventArgs e)
        {
            //if full screen, scale UI
            if (Application.Current.Host.Content.IsFullScreen)
            {
                double scaleX =
                    Application.Current.Host.Content.ActualHeight / this.Height;
                double scaleY =
                    Application.Current.Host.Content.ActualWidth / this.Width;

                ScaleTransform transformUI = new ScaleTransform();
                transformUI.ScaleX = scaleY;
                transformUI.ScaleY = scaleX;
                this.RenderTransform = transformUI;
            }
            else
            {
                this.RenderTransform = null;
            }
        }

        private void Button_Click(object sender, RoutedEventArgs e)
        {
            Application.Current.Host.Content.IsFullScreen =
                !Application.Current.Host.Content.IsFullScreen;
        }
    }
}
```

Figures 5-33 and 5-34 show the difference between an unscaled UI in Full-Screen mode and a scaled UI in Full-Screen mode. Note, however, that you only need to do this if you haven't allowed for resizing your UI, via a Grid control, for example.

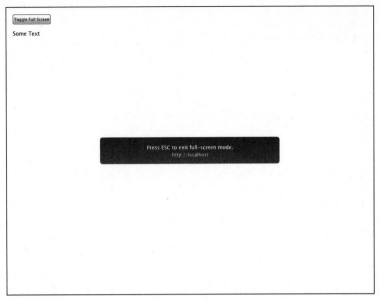

Figure 5-33

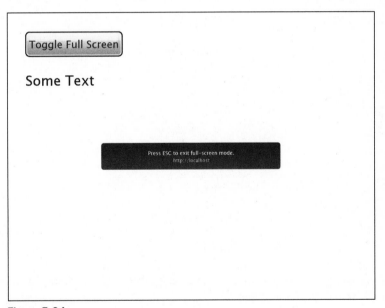

Figure 5-34

Localization

Localization is the act of creating an application that changes its presentation of text at run time based on the current user's locale settings. This means that a German-speaking user would open the application and the text in the application would be written entirely in German, and a French user would view the application in French, and so on.

Localizing your Silverlight application involves creating resource files, one per locale that you want to support, and populating them with all the string content that exists in your application in the appropriate language, with a key to differentiate them. The resource files are named using a special format that includes the locale-specific code of the language resources they contain. For example, the locale code for German is *de*, and therefore the resource file would be named in the format FileName.de.resx. If there may be regional variances in the language (English Great Britain and English U.S.), the formats would be *en-GB* and *en-US*, respectively.

The key thing to take away is that all of the text within your application that would usually be hardcoded is stripped out and isolated into region-specific resource files, ready to be imported and used as needed.

Open the SilverlightLocalizationExample solution in the Chapter 5 source directory. In the Silverlight project, you will notice that two resource files have been created within it, one named *LocalizedStrings.de.resx*, which will be the catch-all German resource container, and one named *LocalizedStrings.resx*, which will be the default fallback resource container, in this example containing the English text. Figure 5-35 shows the project structure in its entirety.

Figure 5-35

If you open up either of these two resource files, you will notice that they each contain two entries with the names *TextBlock1* and *TextBlock2*. These are the unique names that will be used to obtain the associated value against them. Notice how the values are in English in the catch-all fallback file, and that the values should be in German in the German resource file.

If you take a look in Page.XAML, you will see the following markup:

```xml
<UserControl x:Class="SilverlightLocalizationExample.Page"
    xmlns="http://schemas.microsoft.com/winfx/2006/xaml/presentation"
    xmlns:x="http://schemas.microsoft.com/winfx/2006/xaml"
    xmlns:Localized="clr-namespace:SilverlightLocalizationExample.Resources"
    Width="400" Height="300">

    <UserControl.Resources>
        <Localized:LocalizedStrings x:Name="LocalizedStrings" />
    </UserControl.Resources>

    <StackPanel x:Name="LayoutRoot" Background="LightBlue">

        <TextBlock Text="{Binding TextBlock1,
            Source={StaticResource LocalizedStrings}}" />

        <TextBlock Text="{Binding TextBlock2,
            Source={StaticResource LocalizedStrings}}" />

    </StackPanel>

</UserControl>
```

The first item of interest is the new namespace we have specified in the top-level `UserControl` element definition to bring into scope the class that backs the resource file:

```xml
xmlns:Localized="clr-namespace:SilverlightLocalizationExample.Resources"
```

Next, you can see that an instance of the `LocalizedStrings` object has been placed into the `Resources` section of the `UserControl`, ready for subsequent use.

Finally, the two `TextBlock` controls within the `StackPanel` have their `Text` properties bound to the relevant name/value pair in the resource file via the special `StaticResource` binding syntax.

Now, if you open up App.xaml.cs, you will see that some code has been added to the class constructor to manually force the application into German as its `CurrentUICulture`. This is so you can test whether the system is working for German users and you can comment it out to check for English.

```csharp
using System;
using System.Collections.Generic;
using System.Linq;
using System.Net;
using System.Windows;
using System.Windows.Controls;
using System.Windows.Documents;
using System.Windows.Input;
using System.Windows.Media;
using System.Windows.Media.Animation;
using System.Windows.Shapes;
```

```
namespace SilverlightLocalizationExample
{
    public partial class App : Application
    {

        public App()
        {
            System.Threading.Thread.CurrentThread.CurrentUICulture =
                new System.Globalization.CultureInfo("de");

            this.Startup += this.Application_Startup;
            this.Exit += this.Application_Exit;
            this.UnhandledException += this.Application_UnhandledException;

            InitializeComponent();
        }

        private void Application_Startup(object sender, StartupEventArgs e)
        {
            this.RootVisual = new Page();
        }

        private void Application_Exit(object sender, EventArgs e)
        {

        }
        private void Application_UnhandledException(object sender,
ApplicationUnhandledExceptionEventArgs e)
        {
            if (!System.Diagnostics.Debugger.IsAttached)
            {

                e.Handled = true;

                try
                {
                    string errorMsg = e.ExceptionObject.Message +
e.ExceptionObject.StackTrace;
                    errorMsg = errorMsg.Replace('"', '\'').Replace("\r\n", @"\n");

                    System.Windows.Browser.HtmlPage.Window.Eval("throw new
Error(\"Unhandled Error in Silverlight 2 Application " + errorMsg + "\");");
                }
                catch (Exception)
                {
                }
            }
        }
    }
}
```

Compile and run the application — you should be presented with the screen shown in Figure 5-36.

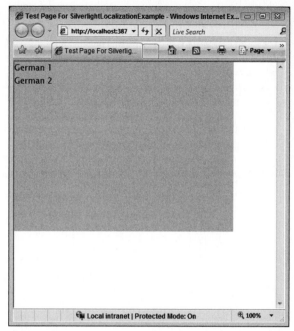

Figure 5-36

Now, comment out the line of code that sets the `CurrentUICulture` to German, and compile and run the application again. Notice how the text is now obtained from the default resource file, which is our English one. In this manner, you can create and add the appropriate resource files to your application and have them automatically picked up and used based on the user's settings.

If you're going to use this technique, take a look in the post-build event for the Silverlight project (it contains code to move the resource DLLs into the correct directory) and also in the csproj file as it contains the `<SupportedCultures>` element. You need to ensure that this element contains a list of all the cultures your Silverlight application is going to support.

Summary

In this chapter, you learned about the capabilities of the new Microsoft Expression Suite of design packages, with the emphasis on Expression Blend. You saw how the close integration between Blend and Visual Studio can help smooth the boundaries between designers and developers and offer for the first time a seamless development experience between the two disciplines.

You also saw how the advanced design time capabilities of Blend enabled you to quickly put together complex UIs without having to manually code by hand a single line of XAML, offering a clear advantage over Visual Studio, which only provides design time support for basic XAML creation.

You then looked at the layout options that are available to you within your Silverlight applications, comparing them to the techniques you're already familiar with in ASP.NET. You saw that the differences are not that great and that building a scalable UI within Silverlight is not a difficult task when using `Grid` or `StackPanel`.

You then walked in detail through each of the layout/container controls that shipped with this first release and explored the reasons for choosing one over the other.

Finally, you looked at the steps involved in localizing your application, allowing your rich, engaging application to interact with multiple languages and cultures.

In the next chapter, you will take a detailed look at each of the controls that ship with Silverlight 2.

6

Silverlight Controls

Today's web and desktop development frameworks provide robust support for capturing and displaying data using built-in controls. ASP.NET is a prime example of such a framework. It offers a rich set of controls capable of capturing end-user input using `TextBox` and `Button` controls, displaying data in multiple formats using `GridView` or `DetailsView` controls, querying databases and parsing XML files using `SqlDataSource` and `XmlDataSource` controls, and even showing advertisements using the `AdRotator` control. It goes without saying that by using controls you can minimize the amount of custom code that has to be written for an application and increase overall productivity.

When Silverlight 1 was released, it provided a solid framework for animating objects and displaying media but included only a minimal set of controls for displaying data. Controls such as `TextBlock` could be used to display text, and `Canvas` could be used to arrange text on a user interface. No controls were available for showing lists of items, capturing user input, or performing more advanced layout functionality, which led to the rise of clever hacks and coding techniques to fill in the holes.

Silverlight 2 provides a robust set of controls that can be used to capture and display data, show media files, provide flexible layout options, display calendars, and even zoom in and out of images. The controls that are available in Silverlight 2 are quite different from controls found in other frameworks such as ASP.NET because they provide extreme flexibility when it comes to the look, feel, and size of controls on a user interface. Silverlight 2 controls can be animated, styled, and transformed in ways that many other application frameworks can only dream of. Imagine a `TextBox` control getting larger or wobbling as a user types in invalid data; or a dynamic grid wherein rows fall in from top to bottom as a search is performed. While that type of functionality may be overkill for applications that you'll build with Silverlight, the sky's the limit when it comes to creative ways of showing and using controls.

This chapter introduces you to many of the controls that are available in Silverlight 2 and shows how they can be defined in XAML and accessed through code. A sampling of controls available in the Silverlight Toolkit are also shown and discussed. Subsequent chapters will discuss different ways that Silverlight controls can be styled, customized, transformed, and even animated.

Introduction to Silverlight Controls

Silverlight 2 provides more than 25 controls that can be grouped into four general categories including user input controls, layout controls (see Chapter 5), items controls, and media controls. Figure 6-1 shows what some of these controls look like in the Visual Studio Toolbox.

Figure 6-1

User input controls include common controls found in many other frameworks such as `TextBox`, `Button`, and `CheckBox`, as well as some nonstandard controls such as `ToggleButton` and `RepeatButton`. Layout controls include `Canvas`, `Border`, `Grid`, and `StackPanel`, and item controls (used to show collections of items) include `DataGrid`, `ListBox`, and `ComboBox`. Finally, media controls include `MediaElement`, `Image`, and `MultiScaleImage`. Additional supporting controls such as `GridViewSplitter` and `ScrollViewer` exist as well.

All of the controls available in Silverlight 2 can be defined declaratively in XAML or dynamically in code like ASP.NET controls. In fact, if you come from an ASP.NET or WPF background, you will find the concept of defining controls in XAML very straightforward. If you're new to the concept of defining controls declaratively, you'll see that it's simple once you know the fundamentals.

Defining Controls in XAML

In Chapter 3, you were provided with an introduction to Extensible Application Markup Language (XAML) and shown how XML elements and attributes could be defined in XAML files. If you're used to defining controls in ASP.NET Web Forms, you'll quickly discover that XAML isn't quite as forgiving with syntax issues. When you're defining controls in XAML, there are three key points to keep in mind. First, XAML is case-sensitive, so it's important that you case your control names and associated attributes properly. Visual Studio allows you to drag and drop controls from the toolbox; thus in many cases, you can avoid manually typing controls into XAML files. Second, attribute values must be quoted. ASP.NET doesn't have this requirement (although you should quote your attributes there as well when defining controls) and is quite forgiving when you don't include quotes around attribute values. Finally, opening tags must always have corresponding closing tags. If you forget to close a tag, you'll have compilation issues.

Short-cut close tags are allowed when a particular control has no content defined. By using short-cut tags where appropriate, you can minimize typing as well as the size of the XAML file. Here's an example of a short-cut close tag for a `TextBlock` control. Notice that no closing `</TextBlock>` tag is required since the control has no content between the start and end tags and only defines attributes.

```
<TextBlock x:Name="tbName" Text="Name: " />
```

With those rules in mind, here's an example of defining a `Grid` control inside a `UserControl` using XAML:

```
<UserControl x:Class="SilverlightApplication1.Page"
    xmlns="http://schemas.microsoft.com/winfx/2006/xaml/presentation"
    xmlns:x="http://schemas.microsoft.com/winfx/2006/xaml"
    Width="400" Height="300">

    <Grid x:Name="LayoutRoot" Background="White">

    </Grid>

</UserControl>
```

Looking at the code, you'll notice that the control defines a `Name` attribute, which is prefixed with the x namespace prefix and sets the `Background` to a value of `White`. The x prefix is defined on the `UserControl` element and points to a unique Uniform Resource Identifier (URI) value of `http://schemas .microsoft.com/winfx/2006/xaml`. You'll use `x:Name` rather than `id` when defining a control name that you may want to access through code. As with ASP.NET controls, all control names within a XAML file must be unique, start with an alphabetic character or underscore, and contain only alphanumeric characters or underscores.

> Silverlight controls that derive from `FrameworkElement` expose a `Name` property that provides a convenient way to set the XAML-defined `x:Name` attribute. You can use `x:Name` or `Name` to define the name of a control in a XAML file.

In addition to the attributes defined on the `Grid` element, you'll see that the beginning `Grid` control element has a matching ending element defined and that the case of both elements matches exactly.

Failure to match up the tags or case controls properly will result in an error when you try to build the application.

Handling Control Events Declaratively

Events are a critical part of the .NET framework and Silverlight. By hooking events to event handlers, you can be notified when a user performs an action such as clicking a button, resizing the user interface, or moving the mouse in or out of an object, plus more. Fortunately, the event syntax used to build ASP.NET applications can also be applied to Silverlight in many cases.

ASP.NET allows events to be hooked to event handlers declaratively or through code. For example, to hook a Button control's Click event to an event handler, the OnClick attribute can be added to the Button control:

```
<asp:Button id="btnSubmit" runat="Server" OnClick="btnSubmit_Click" Text="Go" />
```

The btnSubmit_Click event handler can then be defined in the code file:

```
private void btnSubmit_Click(object sender,EventArgs e)
{
    //Handle event here
}
```

Silverlight provides a similar declarative mechanism for defining control events. Each Silverlight control has a core set of events that are inherited from a base class as well as additional events defined that are specific to the control. For example, Silverlight's Button control exposes several different events such as Loaded, MouseEnter, and MouseLeave that are inherited from UIElement as well as a Click event that is inherited from a base class named ButtonBase.

Hooking a Silverlight control's event to an event handler can be done declaratively in XAML. Here's an example of attaching the Button control's Click event to an event handler:

```
<Button x:Name="btnSubmit" Content="Go" Click="btnSubmit_Click" />
```

Looking at the Click event definition, you'll notice that OnClick isn't used in Silverlight as it is in ASP.NET. Instead, the name of the event is added directly to the XAML element without prefixing it with "On".

As you type an event name on a XAML element, Visual Studio IntelliSense will let you choose to automatically generate a corresponding event handler in the code file. By selecting New Event Handler from the IntelliSense prompt, the event-handler code will be created. Visual Studio also provides support for navigating directly to the event-handler code by right-clicking on the event name in the XAML file and selecting Navigate to Event Handler from the Menu.

Multiple events can be added to a control that's defined in XAML. For instance, to know when a user moves the mouse over a Button control (in cases in which you want to animate the control or perform another action), you can use the MouseEnter event while also handling the Click event. Here's an example of defining the MouseEnter and Click events together on a Button control:

```
<Button x:Name="btnSubmit" Content="Go" Click="btnSubmit_Click"
  MouseEnter="btnSubmit_MouseEnter" />
```

As mentioned above, when you define events in XAML, Visual Studio IntelliSense will show an option to automatically add event handlers in the code file. However, the code that's generated may look a little different from what you're used to seeing when working with ASP.NET pages. The btnSubmit_Click event handler referenced in the XAML for the Button control accepts a different parameter type from the standard EventArgs type used in .NET. It accepts a RoutedEventArgs type for the second parameter, as shown next:

```
private void btnSubmit_Click(object sender, RoutedEventArgs e)
{
    //Handle event
}
```

The Button control's Click event is an example of a routed event (an event typically triggered by the mouse or keyboard that bubbles up to parents), which is why RoutedEventArgs is passed to the event handler instead of EventArgs. Child controls collectively used to create the Button control can raise events — as users interact with them — that are routed up to the Button and handled.

Why does Silverlight substitute EventArgs for RoutedEventArgs, and what's a routed event, anyway? To answer these questions, a brief discussion of control trees is needed. Silverlight relies on control trees behind the scenes to organize and manage parent and child controls. A root control acts as the start of the tree, and child controls are nested under it. The root control's children can also have children of their own, which ultimately creates an object hierarchy or control tree.

Controls defined within a control tree may themselves be composed of other child controls as well. For example, the Button control provided by Silverlight is composed of Grid, Border, and other content controls behind the scenes that when combined render the look and feel of a button. If a user interacts with one of these building block controls using the mouse or keyboard, the event needs to be routed up to the parent Button control so that it can be handled properly. The process of notifying a parent of an action that occurred on a child is referred to as a routed event since mouse or keyboard events triggered by a control are "routed" up the tree so that a parent can be notified when an event occurs. Routed events are similar to event bubbling found in other languages.

An example of a non-routed event is the LayoutUpdated event exposed by Silverlight controls. This event occurs when the layout of objects changes in a Silverlight application owing to properties changing or resizing of the user interface. Because it's not a routed event in Silverlight, the standard EventArgs type is passed to methods that handle the LayoutUpdated event:

```
private void someControl_LayoutUpdated(object sender, EventArgs e)
{
    //Handle event
}
```

Handling Control Events Programmatically

In addition to declaring events declaratively, you can also hook events to event handlers dynamically in code using the C# += operator or the VB.NET AddHandler keyword. This won't come as news to .NET developers since it's the standard way to programmatically work with events. An example of hooking up a Silverlight UserControl's Loaded event and a Button control's Click event to event handlers is shown next:

```
public partial class Page : UserControl
{
    public Page()
    {
        InitializeComponent();
        this.Loaded += new RoutedEventHandler(Page_Loaded);
        this.btnSubmit.Click += new RoutedEventHandler(btnSubmit_Click);
    }

    private void Page_Loaded(object sender, RoutedEventArgs e)
    {
        tbDate.Text = DateTime.Now.ToLongDateString();
    }

    private void btnSubmit_Click(object sender, RoutedEventArgs e)
    {
        //Handle button event here
    }
}
```

As the constructor for the Page class is called, the Loaded and Click events are attached to their respective event handlers. The Loaded event is useful when you'd like to perform a task after all of the controls in a Silverlight application have been loaded and are ready to use. It's similar to the Load event exposed by the ASP.NET Page class. This example locates a TextBlock control named tbDate and assigns the current date to its Text property.

Now that you've seen the general syntax and rules for declaring controls and learned about how events can be wired to event handlers declaratively and programmatically, let's examine some of the different controls available in Silverlight 2. As each control is covered, you'll see different ways it can be used along with key features that it provides. A complete listing of each control's properties, methods, and events will not be shown, however, since the Silverlight SDK provides all of the necessary details, and duplicating them here only adds unnecessary filler pages. Let's start by taking a look at user input controls.

User Input Controls

Silverlight provides several different controls that can be used to collect user input. A list of the controls in this general category include:

❑ TextBlock control

❑ TextBox control

❑ PasswordBox control

❑ Button control

❑ HyperLinkButton control

❑ Checkbox control

❑   RadioButton control

❑   RepeatButton control

❑   Slider control

❑   Calendar control

❑   DatePicker control

❑   ToolTip control

This section discusses each of the controls in this category and shows how they can be defined in XAML.

The TextBlock Control

Label controls are used frequently in development frameworks such as ASP.NET and Windows Forms. Although Silverlight doesn't provide a control named Label, it does provide a TextBlock control that performs the same function as a Label control. You can't use a TextBlock control to capture data, but it's frequently used with other user input controls such as TextBox, which is why it's included in the user input controls category.

The TextBlock control defines a Text property that can be used to define the text value that should be displayed in the user interface. Defining a TextBlock control in XAML is similar to defining a Label control in ASP.NET. Here's a simple example of a TextBlock control:

```
<TextBlock x:Name="tbFirstName" Text="First Name: " />
```

The text to be displayed can also be set as the TextBlock control's content by placing the text between the start and end tags:

```
<TextBlock x:Name="tbFirstName">First Name</TextBlock>
```

In cases in which the text output by the TextBlock may be cut off because of the size of a parent container (such as a Grid row/column) not accommodating the text's size, the control's TextWrapping property can be set to a value of Wrap. Margins can be added around the left, top, right, or bottom of the control by assigning four values to the Margin property separated by commas. If only a single value is defined for Margin, then all margins (left, top, right, and bottom) share the same value. The Margin property is available on all Silverlight controls that derive from the FrameworkElement base class.

An example of using the TextWrapping and Margin properties is shown next:

```
<TextBlock Text="Receive Newsletter?"
 TextWrapping="Wrap" Margin="7,5,0,0" />
```

Font characteristics of a TextBlock can be changed using properties such as FontFamily, FontStyle, and FontSize. The color can be changed using the Foreground property:

```
<TextBlock x:Name="tbFirstName" Text="First Name: " FontFamily="Arial"
 FontSize="14" FontStyle="Bold" Foreground="Maroon" />
```

When you need to format multiple lines of text (in a paragraph, e.g.), you can add multiple TextBlock controls to an interface. However, the TextBlock control also supports Run and LineBreak child elements that can be used to apply custom formatting to specific lines of text. An example of using the `Run` and `LineBreak` elements is shown next. This example adds a margin around the control to give it some space by using the `Margin` property. Ten pixels will be added to the left, top, right, and bottom margins.

```
<TextBlock x:Name="tbStyledText" Margin="10,10,10,10" FontFamily="Arial"
   Width="500" Text="Using the TextBlock with runs…">
   <LineBreak/>
   <Run Foreground="Navy" FontFamily="Verdana" FontSize="34">
      Second Line with Verdana
   </Run>
   <LineBreak/>
   <Run Foreground="Teal" FontFamily="Times New Roman" FontSize="18"
      Text="3rd line with Times New Roman" />
</TextBlock>
```

The output generated using the `Run` and `LineBreak` elements is shown in Figure 6-2.

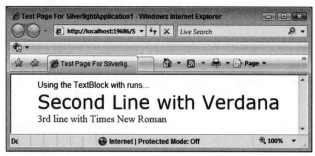

Figure 6-2

The `TextBlock` control extends the `FrameworkElement` class and has several standard events such as `MouseEnter`, `MouseLeave`, and `MouseLeftButtonDown` as a result that can be used to change the appearance of the control as users interact with it.

The `TextBox` Control

Silverlight's `TextBox` control acts much like the `TextBox` control found in ASP.NET. It provides a way to capture unformatted text entered by an end-user while also allowing data that's entered to be filtered or selected using different properties and events. An ASP.NET `TextBox` can be defined in the following manner:

```
<asp:TextBox id="txtName" runat="Server" Font-Names="Arial" />
```

Silverlight `TextBox` controls can be defined in much the same way:

```
<TextBox x:Name="tbName" FontFamily="Arial" Width="100" Height="20" />
```

Figure 6-3 shows an example of a Silverlight `TextBox`. Out-of-the-box, it's not overly impressive and looks like nearly every other textbox you may have encountered before. However, since it's a Silverlight textbox, it's much more flexible and can be animated and transformed.

Phoenix

Figure 6-3

A `TextBox`'s font styles can be set using properties such as `FontFamily`, `FontSize`, and `FontWeight`, and the positioning of a `TextBox` control within a parent container can be set using properties such as `HorizontalAlignment`, `VerticalAlignment`, and `Margin`.

Like the ASP.NET `TextBox` control, the Silverlight version supports different types of textboxes including regular and multi-line. To create a multi-line `TextBox`, set `AcceptsReturn` to `True` and `VerticalScroll BarVisibility` to `Visible` and assign values to the `Height` and `Width` properties as shown next:

```
<TextBox x:Name="tbComments" AcceptsReturn="True"
    VerticalScrollBarVisibility="Visible" FontFamily="Arial"
    Width="300" Height="100" Margin="5" />
```

Figure 6-4 shows an example of a multi-line `TextBox` control.

Figure 6-4

The Silverlight `TextBox` control provides additional features not found in the ASP.NET `TextBox` such as the ability to retrieve text that is selected (highlighted) by a user. Although this same type of task can be done with the ASP.NET `TextBox` using JavaScript on the client side, the Silverlight `TextBox` can access selected text directly through properties such as `SelectedText`, `SelectionLength`, and `SelectionStart`. Text within a `TextBox` can be selected programmatically using the `Select()` method, and focus can be set by calling the `Focus()` method.

An example of selecting all of the text in a `TextBox` named `txtCity` and setting focus to the control when a validation method is called is shown next:

```
private bool Validate()
{
    if (this.txtCity.Text.Length < 3) //Simulate a simple validation rule
    {
        this.txtCity.Select(0, this.txtCity.Text.Length);
        this.txtCity.Focus();
        return false;
    }
    return true;
}
```

This example selects all of the text in the TextBox starting from position 0 to the end of the text. The colors of the selected text can be changed by setting the SelectionForeground and Selection Background properties programmatically or in XAML. An example of changing these properties in XAML is shown next:

```
<TextBox x:Name="txtCity" Text="Phoenix" SelectionForeground="White"
SelectionBackground="Navy" FontFamily="Arial" Width="200" Height="20" Margin="5" />
```

The PasswordBox Control

Silverlight provides a specialized type of textbox called PasswordBox that can be used to capture passwords in a Silverlight application. The PasswordBox control looks like a standard TextBox control but doesn't allow cut, copy, or paste operations to be performed in the textbox. It also stores the data that's entered more securely in memory.

The PasswordBox control provides a PasswordChar property that allows you to control the characters that are displayed in the box as a user types his or her password. The maximum length allowed for the password can also be set using the MaxLength property. An example of defining a PasswordBox control in XAML is shown next:

```
<PasswordBox x:Name="pbPassword" MaxLength="64" PasswordChar="*"
    PasswordChanged="PasswordChangedHandler"
/>
```

Text entered into a PasswordBox control can be accessed through the Password property. The PasswordBox control does not expose the standard Text property found in the TextBox control.

The Button Control

Button controls have been around since user interfaces were first created and haven't changed a lot over the years. Silverlight's Button control is no exception, as shown in Figure 6-5.

Figure 6-5

The Button control acts like the standard Button found in ASP.NET (and many other frameworks) and allows developers to easily know when a user clicks it by exposing a Click event. The Button control derives from a base class named ButtonBase that supplies the core properties, methods, and events for all Button controls in Silverlight.

The Silverlight Button control is different from buttons found in other frameworks because it automatically fills the bounds of its parent container if no height or width values are defined on the control. This can be used to your advantage when a user interface can be resized or displayed in Full-Screen mode since the button will automatically resize itself based on changes in its parent container's size. In cases in which you want the button to stay the same size, you can supply Height and Width property values to constrain a Button control's bounds.

An example of defining a `Button` control in XAML is shown next:

```
<Button x:Name="btnSubmit" Click="btnSubmit_Click" Content="Submit"
 Height="30" Width="75" HorizontalAlignment="Left" VerticalAlignment="Top"
 Margin="7,5,0,0" />
```

Looking through the XAML, you'll see that the button's `x:Name`, `Height`, and `Width` attributes are assigned values, and the button is aligned within its parent container by setting the `Horizontal Alignment`, `VerticalAlignment`, and `Margin` properties. The text content of the button is set using the `Content` attribute. This is different from the way you assign text to an ASP.NET `Button` control and is a result of the Silverlight `Button` being a subset of the `Button` contained in Windows Presentation Foundation (WPF). In addition to the other attributes that are assigned on the `Button` element, the XAML code also defines a `Click` attribute that attaches the control's `Click` event to an event handler.

Earlier in the chapter, you saw that Silverlight events such as the `Button` control's `Click` event pass a `RoutedEventArgs` object to the event handler. Recall that the `Button` control is internally composed of several child controls that route the `Click` event up to the parent `Button` control as a user clicks on them. An example of a click event handler for a button is shown next. Notice that the event handler accepts a `RoutedEventsArgs` parameter as opposed to the standard `EventArgs` parameter found in .NET.

```
private void btnSubmit_Click(object sender, RoutedEventArgs e)
{
    this.tbOutput.Text = "Your data has been submitted";
}
```

The `HyperlinkButton` Control

ASP.NET includes a `LinkButton` control that emulates the behavior of a standard button but looks like a hyperlink. It's used in several controls such as the `GridView` and `DetailsView` controls to select, insert, update, and delete data and can be used in custom scenarios as well.

Silverlight provides a control that's similar to the ASP.NET `LinkButton` called `HyperlinkButton`. `HyperlinkButton` looks like a regular hyperlink, but because it derives from `ButtonBase`, it exposes properties and events found on standard `Button` controls such as `Content` and `Click`. An example of using the `HyperlinkButton` control is shown next:

```
<HyperlinkButton x:Name="hlClear" Content="Clear Text Boxes" Foreground="Navy"
Click="hlClear_Click" Margin="10"/>
```

This code assigns the foreground color of the control to navy blue and hooks the `Click` event to an event handler named `hlClear_Click` that clears text from textboxes:

```
private void hlClear_Click(object sender, RoutedEventArgs e)
{
    this.txtCity.Text = String.Empty;
    this.txtComments.Text = String.Empty;
    this.txtName.Text = String.Empty;
    this.pbPassword.Password = String.Empty;
}
```

HyperlinkButton exposes a NavigateUri and TargetName property that can be used to link to web pages and display them in new windows much as you can do with the standard anchor tag in HTML:

```
<HyperlinkButton x:Name="hlSilverlight" Content="Silverlight.net"
 NavigateUri="http://www.silverlight.net" TargetName="Blank" />
```

The CheckBox Control

Silverlight's CheckBox control derives from a base class named ToggleButton (which, in turn, derives from ButtonBase) that allows different states of a control to be tracked. Although a CheckBox is normally used to track True or False values as in ASP.NET, three states are supported in the Silverlight control including checked, unchecked, and indeterminate. CheckBox provides an IsChecked property (of type Nullable<bool>) that can be used to set the state of the control and determine if it's checked or not as a user interacts with it. In cases in which the control needs to be checked when an application initially loads the IsChecked property can be set to True in the XAML file or programmatically in a code file.

An example of defining a CheckBox in XAML that is automatically checked as the application loads is shown next:

```
<CheckBox x:Name="chkNewsletter" IsChecked="True"
 Content="Check to receive newsletter" Margin="5" />
```

When the user submits the form by pressing a button, the state of the CheckBox control can be determined using the IsChecked property, as shown next:

```
private void btnSubmit_Click(object sender, RoutedEventArgs e)
{
    this.tbOutput.Text = String.Format(
        "Your data has been submitted.  You have{0}chosen to receive the " +
        "newsletter.",
        (this.chkMeeting.IsChecked.HasValue &&
         this.chkMeeting.IsChecked.Value == true)?" ":" not ");
}
```

The CheckBox control derives from ToggleButton, which allows it to track three states rather than only two (the ASP.NET CheckBox can only track two states because of limitations in the various HTML specifications). This is useful when you have On, Off, or unknown values that need to be tracked in a Silverlight application. To allow the CheckBox to track three states, the IsThreeState property must be set to True:

```
<CheckBox x:Name="chkNewsletter" IsThreeState="True"
 Content="Will you attend the annual meeting?" Margin="5" />
```

When IsThreeState is set to True, the first click on a CheckBox will show a checkmark (IsChecked will be True), the second click will put the control in the indeterminate stage and gray-out the background (IsChecked will be null), and the third click will uncheck the control (IsChecked will be False). Figure 6-6 shows an example of the checked, indeterminate, and unchecked stages that a CheckBox control can have when its IsThreeState property is set to True.

Figure 6-6

If you'd like to know when the user toggles between CheckBox states, you can handle the Checked, Indeterminate, and Unchecked events by attaching them to event handlers:

```
<CheckBox x:Name="chkMeeting" IsThreeState="True" Checked="chkMeeting_StateChanged"
    Unchecked="chkMeeting_StateChanged" Indeterminate="chkMeeting_StateChanged"
    Content="Yes" Margin="5" />
```

This example attaches all three events to a single event handler named chkMeeting_StateChanged. The event handler changes the background and foreground colors of the CheckBox as well as the content as a user toggles through the different states:

```
private void chkMeeting_StateChanged(object sender, RoutedEventArgs e)
{
    SolidColorBrush brush = null;
    string text = null;

    if (this.chkMeeting.IsChecked == true)
    {
        brush = new SolidColorBrush(Colors.Green);
        text = "Yes";
    }
    if (this.chkMeeting.IsChecked == null)
    {
        brush  = new SolidColorBrush(Colors.Black);
        text = "Don't Know";

    }
    if (this.chkMeeting.IsChecked == false)
    {
        brush  = new SolidColorBrush(Colors.Red);
        text = "No";
    }
    this.chkMeeting.Background = brush;
    this.chkMeeting.Foreground = brush;
    this.chkMeeting.Content = text;
}
```

The RadioButton *Control*

Radio buttons are another common user input control found in desktop and web applications alike. Silverlight's RadioButton control acts like other radio buttons you've seen before; users can select one item at a time from a list of items. Like Silverlight's CheckBox control, the RadioButton control derives ToggleButton, which gives it the ability to track checked, indeterminate, and unchecked states when the IsThreeState property is set to True.

If you've worked with radio buttons before in ASP.NET, then you'll find that they're very similar in Silverlight. ASP.NET provides two different ways to group radio buttons together. First, a Radio ButtonList control can be used, and individual items can be defined within the list control:

```
<asp:RadioButtonList id="RadioButtonList1" runat="server">
    <asp:ListItem>Male</asp:ListItem>
    <asp:ListItem>Female</asp:ListItem>
</asp:RadioButtonList>
```

Second, individual RadioButton controls can be added into a page and grouped together by assigning the same value to the GroupName property of each control:

```
Gender:
<br />
<asp:RadioButton id="rdoMale" GroupName="Gender" runat="server" Text="Male" />
<asp:RadioButton id="rdoFemale" GroupName="Gender" runat="server" Text="Female" />
```

Silverlight provides similar functionality for RadioButton controls. Controls can be grouped by placing them in a parent container or by setting the GroupName property on each control. The following XAML code shows how RadioButton controls can be grouped inside a parent StackPanel control. The GroupName property doesn't need to be set in this example since the controls are automatically grouped by the parent:

```
<StackPanel Orientation="Horizontal" Grid.Row="2" Grid.Column="1">
    <RadioButton x:Name="rdoMale" Content="Male"  Margin="5" />
    <RadioButton x:Name="rdoFemale" Content="Female"  />
</StackPanel>
```

Radio buttons can also be grouped together so that a user can only select one item at a time by assigning the same value to the GroupName property on each stand-alone control:

```
<RadioButton x:Name="rdoMale" Content="Male"  Margin="5" GroupName="Gender" />
<RadioButton x:Name="rdoFemale" Content="Female" GroupName="Gender"  />
```

The label associated with individual RadioButton controls can be defined using the control's Content property rather than the Text property used in ASP.NET. Figure 6-7 shows how RadioButton controls look in Silverlight.

Figure 6-7

The RepeatButton Control

The RepeatButton control looks like a standard Button (it also inherits from ButtonBase), but acts quite differently under the covers. A standard Button raises a Click event once per mouse click, whereas the RepeatButton raises the Click event over and over on a timed basis when a user holds the mouse button down. Most people use the functionality found in the RepeatButton every day when they click on the top or bottom of a scrollbar or click the + (zoom in) or − (zoom out) buttons in a

Microsoft Office product. By raising the Click event on a timed basis, users can change values quickly without having to physically click the button multiple times.

The RepeatButton control provides Delay and Interval properties that determine how often to raise a Click event. The Delay property controls how long the RepeatButton waits before starting to raise Click events, while the Interval property controls the amount of time between Click events. As events fire, a normal Click event handler can be written to capture the clicks and programmatically scroll a window or increment a value.

In addition to being able to set Delay and Interval values, the RepeatButton also allows you to control how Click events are raised. This is controlled by using the ClickMode property, which accepts one of three values defined in a ClickMode enumeration, as shown in the following table:

Member Name	Description
Release	The Click event will be raised when the RepeatButton is pressed and released (default value).
Press	The Click event will be raised as soon as the RepeatButton is pressed and the mouse pointer is over the control.
Hover	The Click event will be raised when the mouse pointer hovers over the RepeatButton control.

An example of using two RepeatButton controls that have their Delay, Interval, and ClickMode properties set to provide a quick and easy way for a user to increment or decrement a value is shown in the following XAML code:

```
<RepeatButton x:Name="rptBtnDown" Click="RepeatButton_Click" ClickMode="Press"
  Delay="200" Interval="200" Height="20" Width="30" Content=" - "
  Margin="5,0,5,0" />

<TextBlock x:Name="tbYearsOfSchool" Text="12" Margin="5,0,5,0" />

<RepeatButton x:Name="rptBtnUp" Click="RepeatButton_Click" ClickMode="Press"
  Delay="200" Interval="200" Height="20" Width="30" Content=" + "
  Margin="5,0,5,0" />
```

As the Click event is raised [every 200 milliseconds (ms) in this example], the following code updates the tbYearsOfSchool TextBlock control:

```
private void RepeatButton_Click(object sender, RoutedEventArgs e)
{
    int val = int.Parse(tbYearsOfSchool.Text);

    RepeatButton btn = sender as RepeatButton;
    switch (btn.Name)
    {
        case "rptBtnUp":
            val++;
            break;
```

```
        case "rptBtnDown":
            val--;
            break;
    }

    if (val < 0)
        val = 0;
    else if (val > 20)
        val = 20;
    this.tbYearsOfSchool.Text = val.ToString();
}
```

Figure 6-8 shows what the previous XAML code renders when the Silverlight application is run. As the user clicks on the buttons (and holds the mouse button down), the value will automatically increase or decrease depending on which button was clicked.

Figure 6-8

The Slider Control

ASP.NET doesn't have a Slider control built into the framework, but with a little help from the ASP.NET AJAX Toolkit, you can easily add sliders into your web applications. Fortunately, Silverlight does have a built-in Slider control that users can slide up and down to change values. Although Radio Button controls are often used when an application needs to allow users to select a single value from a list of items, a slider can be very effective for picking a value as well. Figure 6-9 shows an example of the default Slider control in Silverlight.

Figure 6-9

The Slider control provides Minimum and Maximum properties to control the range of the Slider as well as a ValueChanged event that is called as the user moves the Slider control's *thumb*. The orientation of the Slider can also be changed by setting the Orientation property to Horizontal (the default) or Vertical.

An example of defining a Slider control in XAML is shown next:

```
<Slider  x:Name="slider" Minimum="0" Maximum="3"
  Margin="5"  Width="150" ValueChanged="slider_ValueChanged" />
```

The Slider in this example allows a value between 0 and 3 to be selected. Changes to the thumb position cause an event handler named slider_ValueChanged to be called when the ValueChanged event fires, which updates the text value of a TextBlock named tbSliderVal. The ValueChanged event passes a RoutedPropertyChangedEventArgs<double> object as shown next:

```
private void slider_ValueChanged(object sender,
    RoutedPropertyChangedEventArgs<double> e)
{
    int rating = (int)Math.Round(e.NewValue);
    this.tbSliderVal.Text = Convert.ToString((Rating)rating);
}
```

This example rounds the value in the event argument parameter's NewValue property using the Math .Round() method (note that the OldValue property can also be accessed in cases in which you need to know the previous value). It then converts the value to a Rating enumeration member and displays the result in a TextBlock. The Rating enumeration is shown next:

```
public enum Rating
{
    Bad,
    Average,
    Good,
    Excellent
}
```

Figure 6-10 shows how the TextBlock control's Text property changes as the user slides the thumb (the Average value displayed in the figure represents the TextBlock). Two TextBlocks containing Bad and Excellent text values, respectively, are also added around the Slider so that the user knows the range of potential values.

Figure 6-10

The Calendar Control

Silverlight provides a built-in Calendar control that provides the ability to add calendars into an application with little to no coding on your part. The Calendar control is similar to the ASP.NET Calendar, although it allows years and months to be selected much more easily.

As a quick refresher, you can define a basic Calendar control in an ASP.NET page using syntax similar to the following:

```
<asp:Calendar ID="calBizWeek" runat="server"></asp:Calendar>
```

A calendar can be added into a Silverlight application in much the same way:

```
<basics:Calendar x:Name="calBizWeek" SelectionMode="SingleRange"
    HorizontalAlignment="Left" />
```

Looking at this code, you may wonder where the basics namespace prefix came from, especially since none of the controls discussed to this point had it. The Calendar control is in the System.Windows .Controls assembly, which isn't referenced by default in Silverlight XAML files since many applications won't need it and can load faster by not including the assembly. If you add the Calendar control into a XAML file, you'll also need to add the namespace and assembly reference to the root element of the file as shown next with the `basics` namespace definition on the `UserControl` element. It's important to note that the line should not wrap and only wraps in the code sample because of space constraints in this page.

```
<UserControl
    xmlns:basics="clr-namespace:System.Windows.Controls;
    assembly=System.Windows.Controls"
    x:Class="UserInputControls.Page"
    xmlns="http://schemas.microsoft.com/winfx/2006/xaml/presentation"
    xmlns:x="http://schemas.microsoft.com/winfx/2006/xaml"
    Background="Black" Width="800" Height="800">

</UserControl>
```

> If you drag the `Calendar` control into the XAML file from the Toolbox, the namespace and assembly reference will automatically be added for you by Visual Studio.

Although `basics` is used for the namespace prefix in this example, you can use any namespace prefix you want as long as the name adheres to standard XML naming conventions.

Once the `Calendar` control has been added into the XAML, there are several different options you can leverage to control how dates are selected by the end-user. The `Calendar` control allows single dates to be selected as well as date ranges. Switching between date selection modes is accomplished by using the `SelectionMode` property, which accepts a `CalendarSelectionMode` enumeration. Members of the `CalendarSelectionModel` enumeration are shown in the following table:

Member Name	Description
MultipleRange	Allows multiple, noncontiguous dates to be selected on the calendar.
None	No selections can be made on the calendar.
SingleDate	Allows a single date to be selected on the calendar.
SingleRange	Allows a contiguous range of dates to be selected on the calendar.

The `Calendar` control's display mode can also be changed to month or year displays by setting the `DisplayMode` property, which accepts one of the following members defined in the `CalendarMode` enumeration:

Member Name	Description
Decade	Shows the calendar in decade mode.
Month	Shows the calendar in month mode.
Year	Shows the calendar in year mode.

Users can change calendar modes as well by clicking the date shown at the top of the calendar. Figure 6-11 shows the default, month, and year modes that are available.

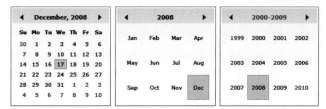

Figure 6-11

When the `Calendar` control loads, it highlights the current date (`DateTime.Today`) if no values are assigned to the `DisplayDate` or `SelectedDate` properties. You can prevent the current day from being highlighted by setting the `IsTodayHighlighted` property to `False`, as shown next:

```
<basics:Calendar x:Name="calBizWeek" IsTodayHighlighted="False" />
```

Dates that are displayed can also be controlled by assigning values to the `DisplayDateStart` and `DisplayDateEnd` properties. Dates not in the start and end range are hidden. A range of selected dates can also be set programmatically through the `Calendar` control's `SelectedDates` property (of type `SelectedDatesCollection`) which exposes an `AddRange()` method. An example of using the `AddRange()` method to highlight business days for the current week is shown next:

```
protected void Page_Loaded(object sender, RoutedEventArgs e)
{
    SetSelectedDateRange(DateTime.Today);
}


//Highlight entire business week
private void SetSelectedDateRange(DateTime date)
{
    this.cal.SelectedDates.AddRange(date, date.AddDays(7));
}
```

When one or more dates selected by a user must be processed by an application you handle the `Calender` control's `SelectedDatesChanged` event. `SelectedDatesChanged` passes a `SelectionChangedEventArgs` object as a parameter, which provides access to dates the user added or removed.

```
protected void Page_Loaded(object sender, RoutedEventArgs e)
{
    this.cal.SelectedDatesChanged +=
      new EventHandler<SelectionChangedEventArgs>(cal_SelectedDatesChanged);
}

void cal_SelectedDatesChanged(object sender, SelectionChangedEventArgs e)
{
    foreach (DateTime dt in e.AddedItems)
    {
        //process date object
    }
}
```

The DatePicker Control

The Calendar control can be useful any time a user needs to select or view dates. However, when a user needs to pick a single date from a calendar or type it directly, Silverlight's DatePicker control can be used. The DatePicker control is composed of a DatePickerTextBox and a Calendar control. A user can press a button on the end of the DatePicker control's textbox to view a calendar and select a date. Figure 6-12 shows the DatePicker control as a user is picking a date from a calendar as well as after the date has been chosen.

Figure 6-12

Like the Calendar control, the DatePicker control is located in the System.Windows.Controls assembly and requires the namespace and assembly to be defined in the XAML file. The example that follows (which was also shown in the Calendar control portion of the chapter) associates the namespace and assembly where the control lives with the basics namespace prefix:

```
<UserControl
    xmlns:basics="clr-namespace:System.Windows.Controls;
    assembly=System.Windows.Controls"
    x:Class="UserInputControls.Page"
    xmlns="http://schemas.microsoft.com/winfx/2006/xaml/presentation"
    xmlns:x="http://schemas.microsoft.com/winfx/2006/xaml"
    Background="Black" Width="800" Height="800">

</UserControl>
```

Once the appropriate namespace and assembly reference have been added, the control can be used in a XAML file:

```
<basics:DatePicker x:Name="dpBirthDate" Width="100" Margin="5" />
```

The DatePicker control has many of the same properties found on the Calendar control such as IsTodayHighlighted, DisplayDateStart, and DisplayDateEnd. It does add an IsDropDownOpen property that can be used to check if the calendar is open as well as a CalendarStyle property that can be used to define the style to apply to the calendar.

DatePicker also adds additional events such as CalendarOpened and CalendarClosed to determine when the user is interacting with the calendar component and DateValidationError, which is raised when a date entered into the textbox isn't valid. Here's an example of handling the DateValidation Error event:

```
private void dpBirthDate_DateValidationError(object sender,
   DatePickerDateValidationErrorEventArgs e)
{
    //Pop-up an alert (or do something better like show a Canvas with a message)
    System.Windows.Browser.HtmlPage.Window.Alert("Invalid date entered: " +
        e.Text);
}
```

The DatePickerDateValidationErrorEventArgs object passed to the event-handler method provides access to an Exception object and the text entered by the end-user, as well as a boolean ThrowException property that can be used to throw the exception. The ThrowException property is set to False by default.

The ToolTip Control

It goes without saying that providing help for users is something every application should do. In reality, very few web-based applications provide help to let users know how to use different parts of an application. HTML controls provide a title attribute that can be used to show how a particular textbox or button can be used, but providing more engaging help isn't built directly into the HTML standard. As a result, many developers write custom JavaScript code to show and hide div elements containing help information.

Silverlight simplifies the process of adding help for users in an application as they interact with different controls. By using the built-in ToolTip control, you can easily shows tips as users mouse over a TextBox, Button, or Calendar, plus much more. Tool tips can be defined directly on a control in cases where simple text should be shown or can be made much more robust and stylish by nesting a ToolTip control inside a control and applying a custom style. Here's an example of defining a tool tip directly on a TextBlock control:

```
<TextBlock Text="Name" ToolTipService.ToolTip="Enter your name" Margin="7,5,0,0" />
```

The ToolTip control relies on a parent ToolTipService object that works behind the scenes to register ToolTips and show help information as the user moves his or her mouse in and out of a control. Figure 6-13 shows what the ToolTip looks like as the user moves the mouse over the TextBlock control.

Figure 6-13

While adding ToolTip help information directly to controls will get the job done in many situations, you can also create enhanced ToolTips that are composed of other Silverlight controls. This is accomplished by nesting the ToolTip control inside the target control as opposed to defining it directly on the control. An example of nesting `ToolTipService` and `ToolTip` controls within a `TextBox` is shown next:

```
<TextBox x:Name="txtName" FontFamily="Arial" Width="200" Height="20" Margin="5">
    <ToolTipService.ToolTip>
        <ToolTip>
            <StackPanel>
                <Border Background="Navy" BorderBrush="Gray" BorderThickness="1">
                    <TextBlock Text="Help" Foreground="White" Margin="2"/>
                </Border>
                <Border Background="Beige" Padding="5" BorderBrush="Gray"
                    BorderThickness="1">
                    <TextBlock Text="Enter your first and last name" />
                </Border>
            </StackPanel>
        </ToolTip>
    </ToolTipService.ToolTip>
</TextBox>
```

This example uses the `StackPanel` and `Border` controls along with `TextBlock` controls to display a more robust tool tip. Figure 6-14 shows what the `ToolTip` looks like as the user interacts with the `TextBox` control.

Figure 6-14

> While you can define a `ToolTip` control directly within a parent control as in the previous example, creating a reusable style is generally preferred. By creating a style, you can define the look and feel for all `ToolTip` controls in one place and even remove the box that Silverlight adds around the `ToolTip` by default. Additional information about creating and applying styles is provided in Chapter 7.

The `ToolTip` control provides properties such as `HorizontalOffset` and `VerticalOffset` to control how the `ToolTip` is displayed as well as an `IsOpen` property that can be used to check if a `ToolTip` is showing. `Open` and `Closed` events can also be used to track if a `ToolTip` is showing or not.

Items Controls

ASP.NET provides several different controls that can be used to display a collection of items such as `GridView`, `Repeater`, `DataList`, and `ListView`. Silverlight also offers several controls that are capable of displaying items in a variety of ways. Controls covered in this section include:

- ❑   `ListBox` control
- ❑   `ItemsControl` control

❑   `DataGrid` control

❑   `ScrollViewer` control

❑   `ScrollBar` control

❑   `ComboBox` control

❑   `Popup` control

This section introduces you to these controls and discusses how they can be used in Silverlight applications. Additional information about how to bind data and define templates for the controls is discussed in following chapters.

The `ListBox` Control

The `ListBox` control provides a flexible way to display a collection of items vertically or horizontally within an application. Like many controls found in ASP.NET, the `ListBox` control relies on templates to determine how items are rendered. You'll typically use the `ListBox` control in data-binding scenarios. This section provides a quick introduction to the control and demonstrates how templates can be used. Later in the book, you'll see how items controls such as the `ListBox` can be bound to a variety of data sources.

Templates provide a way to define how each item in a collection should be rendered. If you have a list of `Customer` objects each with `Name`, `Address`, and `Phone` properties, a template can be created to output the property values in a custom manner. Templates are quite common in ASP.NET, and several different controls support templates such as item templates, alternating item templates, edit item templates, and others. Here's an example of using templates with a `Repeater` control:

```
<asp:Repeater ID="rptCustomers" runat="server">
    <HeaderTemplate>
        <ul>
    </HeaderTemplate>
    <ItemTemplate>
        <%# Eval("Name") %>
        <br />
        <%# Eval("Address") %>
        <br />
        <%# Eval("Phone") %>
    </ItemTemplate>
    <FooterTemplate>
        </ul>
    </FooterTemplate>
</asp:Repeater>
```

Silverlight's `ListBox` control provides a single template named `ItemTemplate` that can be used much like the `Repeater` control's `ItemTemplate` shown in the previous example. However, the `ListBox`'s `ItemTemplate` requires a `DataTemplate` to be placed inside it so that data binding can occur.

> The `ItemTemplate` **property and a few others exposed by the** `ListBox` **control are inherited from a class named** `ItemsControl`. **Although you can use** `ItemsControl` **in place of the** `ListBox`, **the** `ListBox` **control contains additional functionality such as the ability to retrieve the index of an item (inherited from the** `Selector` **class) that a user clicked.**

An example of defining an `ItemTemplate` capable of displaying data from a collection of `Customer` objects is shown next:

```
<ListBox x:Name="lbCustomers" Background="#efefef" Height="150"
  BorderBrush="Black" BorderThickness="1" FontFamily="Arial" Margin="10">
    <ListBox.ItemTemplate>
        <DataTemplate>
            <Grid Width="600">
                <Grid.ColumnDefinitions>
                    <ColumnDefinition Width=".20*" />
                    <ColumnDefinition Width=".20*" />
                    <ColumnDefinition Width=".30*" />
                    <ColumnDefinition Width=".30*" />
                </Grid.ColumnDefinitions>
                <Grid.RowDefinitions>
                    <RowDefinition Height="40" />
                </Grid.RowDefinitions>
                <Image Grid.Column="0" Source="/Images/blue.jpg" Margin="2"
                  VerticalAlignment="top" Height="35" Width="25" />
                <TextBlock Grid.Column="1" Text="{Binding Name}" FontSize="14"
                  Foreground="Navy" />
                <TextBlock Grid.Column="2" Text="{Binding Address}" FontSize="14"
                  Foreground="Red" />
                <TextBlock Grid.Column="3" Text="{Binding Phone}" FontSize="14"
                  Foreground="Green" />
            </Grid>
        </DataTemplate>
    </ListBox.ItemTemplate>
</ListBox>
```

> The data-binding syntax (e.g., `{Binding Name}`) shown in the code sample tells the control which property of the data context object to bind to in the template as each object in the collection is iterated through. Additional details about data binding are provided in Chapter 9.

The `ItemTemplate` shown in this example contains a `DataTemplate`, which, in turn, contains a `Grid` used to arrange an `Image` control and three `TextBlock` controls in the `ListBox`. Each `TextBlock` control is bound to a `Customer` object property. If 50 `Customer` objects are in the collection that is being bound to the `ListBox`, the `ItemTemplate` will be processed 50 times. Figure 6-15 shows an example of what the `ListBox` looks like once it's rendered.

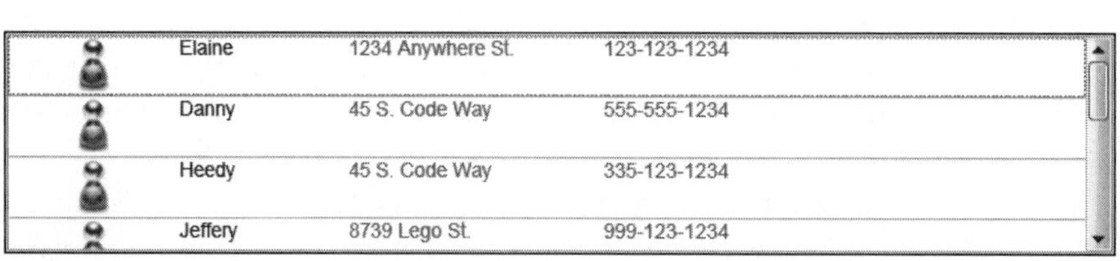

Figure 6-15

All of the data shown in Figure 6-15 is displayed vertically in the `ListBox` control, which is the default orientation. The `ListBox` also supports displaying data horizontally when an application requires that type of format. To display controls horizontally, you can leverage the `ListBox` control's `ItemPanel`, which allows a wrapper control such as a `StackPanel` to be placed around controls output by the `ItemTemplate` to change their orientation. An example of using the `ListBox` control's `ItemPanel` in conjunction with the `ItemTemplate` is shown next:

```
<ListBox x:Name="lbCustomersHorizontal" Background="#efefef" Height="150"
  BorderBrush="Black" BorderThickness="1" FontFamily="Arial" Margin="10">
    <ListBox.ItemTemplate>
        <DataTemplate>
            <StackPanel Margin="10,0,10,0">
                <Image Grid.Column="0" Source="/Images/blue.jpg" Margin="2"
                VerticalAlignment="top" Height="35" Width="25" />
                <TextBlock Text="{Binding Name}" HorizontalAlignment="Center"
                FontSize="14" Foreground="Navy" Margin="5" />
                <TextBlock Text="{Binding Address}" HorizontalAlignment="Center"
                FontSize="14" Foreground="Red" Margin="5" />
                <TextBlock Grid.Column="3" HorizontalAlignment="Center"
                Text="{Binding Phone}" FontSize="14" Margin="5"
                Foreground="Green" />
            </StackPanel>
        </DataTemplate>
    </ListBox.ItemTemplate>
    <ListBox.ItemsPanel>
        <ItemsPanelTemplate>
            <StackPanel Orientation="Horizontal" />
        </ItemsPanelTemplate>
    </ListBox.ItemsPanel>
</ListBox>
```

As each object in the collection is bound, a `StackPanel` control with its `Orientation` property set to `Horizontal` is wrapped around controls defined in the `ItemTemplate`. The result of placing the `StackPanel` around each item is shown in Figure 6-16.

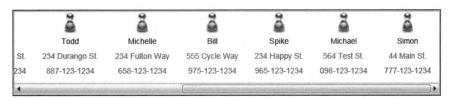

Figure 6-16

As a user selects an item in a `ListBox`, the index can be retrieved using the control's `SelectedIndex` property. Data bound to the selected item can be accessed through the `SelectedItem` property.

The `DataGrid` Control

Grids are popular in desktop and web applications since they provide a simple way to display rows of columnar data. ASP.NET's `GridView` control is arguably one of the most frequently used controls in web applications because of its ability to bind data from a variety of data sources. Silverlight doesn't include a `GridView` control, but *does* provide a `DataGrid` control that can be used to display, filter, sort, and edit columnar data.

The `DataGrid` control is located in the `System.Windows.Controls.Data` assembly, which must be referenced using a namespace prefix before the `DataGrid` can be used. Here's an example of referencing the assembly in the root element of the XAML file and assigning it to a `data` namespace prefix:

```
<UserControl
    xmlns:data="clr-namespace:System.Windows.Controls;
      assembly=System.Windows.Controls.Data"  x:Class="ItemsControls.Page"
    xmlns="http://schemas.microsoft.com/winfx/2006/xaml/presentation"
    xmlns:x="http://schemas.microsoft.com/winfx/2006/xaml"
    FontFamily="Trebuchet MS" FontSize="11"
    Width="800" Height="800">

</UserControl>
```

Once the namespace prefix has been defined, the `DataGrid` control can be added into the XAML file. An example of using a `DataGrid` that auto-generates columns is shown next:

```
<data:DataGrid x:Name="dgCustomers" AutoGenerateColumns="True" />
```

`DataGrid` columns can also be customized much like ASP.NET `GridView` control columns. Several different column types are available including:

- ❑ `DataGridCheckBoxColumn`

- ❑ `DataGridTemplateColumn`

- ❑ `DataGridTextColumn`

To use custom columns, set the `DataGrid` control's `AutoGenerateColumns` to `False` and define the custom columns inside the `DataGrid.Columns` element:

```
<data:DataGrid x:Name="dgCustomers" GridlinesVisibility="All"
   HeadersVisibility="Column" RowBackground="BlanchedAlmond"
   AlternatingRowBackground="White" IsReadOnly="True"
   CanUserResizeColumns="True" Margin="10" HorizontalAlignment="Left"
   AutoGenerateColumns="False" Width="300">
   <data:DataGrid.Columns>
       <data:DataGridTextColumn Header="Name"
          DisplayMemberBinding="{Binding Name}" />
       <data:DataGridTextColumn Header="Address"
          DisplayMemberBinding="{Binding Address}" />
       <data:DataGridTextColumn Header="Phone"
          DisplayMemberBinding="{Binding Phone}" />
   </data:DataGrid.Columns>
</data:DataGrid>
```

This example defines three `DataGridTextColumn` controls that bind to properties of a `Customer` object. It also sets several `DataGrid` properties such as `GridlinesVisibility`, `RowBackground`, `Alternating`

RowBackground, IsReadOnly, and CanUserResizeColumns. Figure 6-17 shows how the columns are rendered once data has been bound to the grid.

Name	Address	Phone
Elaine	1234 Anywhere St.	123-123-1234
Danny	45 S. Code Way	555-555-1234
Heedy	45 S. Code Way	335-123-1234
Jeffery	8739 Lego St.	999-123-1234
Todd	234 Durango St.	887-123-1234
Michelle	234 Fulton Way	658-123-1234
Bill	555 Cycle Way	975-123-1234
Spike	234 Happy St.	965-123-1234
Michael	564 Test St.	098-123-1234
Simon	44 Main St.	777-123-1234

Figure 6-17

Additional details about using the DataGrid control are provided in Chapter 9.

The ScrollViewer Control

The ListBox and DataGrid controls have built-in support for scrolling. There may be times, however, when other controls used in an interface need to have horizontal or vertical scrollbars added. For example, you may have a StackPanel that contains several Border controls inside it that need to have a vertical scrollbar added to fit into a particular area of the screen.

Silverlight's ScrollViewer control provides a way to add scrolling features to controls with minimal effort on your part. By using the control, you can define whether or not horizontal or vertical scrollbars are allowed, set the height of the scrolling area (called the *viewport*), add background colors, and so on. An example of using the ScrollViewer control to add vertical scrolling functionality to child controls contained in a StackPanel is shown next:

```
<ScrollViewer Width="300" Height="175" HorizontalScrollBarVisibility="Disabled"
    VerticalScrollBarVisibility="Visible" HorizontalAlignment="Left">
    <StackPanel Margin="10">
        <Border CornerRadius="10" Background="Navy">
            <TextBlock Text="Walk Dog" Foreground="White"
             Margin="10" FontSize="16" />
        </Border>
        <Border CornerRadius="10" Background="Black">
            <TextBlock Text="Get Gas" Foreground="White"
             Margin="10" FontSize="16" />
        </Border>
        <Border CornerRadius="10" Background="Yellow">
            <TextBlock Text="Buy Groceries" Foreground="Black"
             Margin="10" FontSize="16" />
        </Border>
        <Border CornerRadius="10" Background="Green">
            <TextBlock Text="Sleep" Foreground="White"
             Margin="10" FontSize="16" />
        </Border>
        <Border CornerRadius="10" Background="Gray">
```

```
            <TextBlock Text="Learn Silverlight" Foreground="White"
                Margin="10" FontSize="16" />
        </Border>
    </StackPanel>
</ScrollViewer>
```

This example sets the height and width of the viewport, disables the horizontal scrollbar, enables the vertical scrollbar, and aligns the control to the left. Figure 6-18 shows an example of the ScrollViewer control in action.

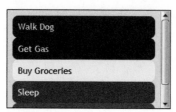

Figure 6-18

The HorizontalScrollBarVisibility and VerticalScrollBarVisibility properties of the ScrollViewer accept one of four values defined in a ScrollBarVisibility enumeration. Each of the enumeration members are described in the following table:

Member Name	Description
Auto	The scrollbar appears when the content can't be fit into the viewport's dimensions. If the content fits into the viewport, then no scrollbar is visible.
Disabled	The scrollbar will not appear even if the content doesn't fit into the viewport's dimensions. The dimension of the parent is applied to the content.
Hidden	The scrollbar is hidden even if the content doesn't fit into the viewport. The content may appear to be clipped when this value is used since the scrollbar is available but hidden from view. Although the mouse cannot be used to scroll, the arrow keys can be used. This is the default value.
Visible	The scrollbar appears even if it's not needed.

Controls such as the ListBox that have scrolling capabilities built in by default can use the Scroll Viewer to enable or disable scrollbars. In cases in which a scrollbar should not be shown (owing to space constraints potentially) but users can still scroll using the arrow keys, the ScrollViewer .HorizontalScrollBarVisibility and ScrollViewer.VerticalScrollBarVisibility attached properties can be defined on the ListBox:

```
<ListBox x:Name="lbCustomersScrollHidden" Background="#efefef" Height="150"
    ScrollViewer.HorizontalScrollBarVisibility="Disabled"
    ScrollViewer.VerticalScrollBarVisibility="Hidden"
    BorderBrush="Black" BorderThickness="1" FontFamily="Arial" Margin="10">
    <ListBox.ItemTemplate>
        <DataTemplate>
```

```
                    <Grid Width="600">
                        <Grid.ColumnDefinitions>
                            <ColumnDefinition Width=".20*" />
                            <ColumnDefinition Width=".20*" />
                            <ColumnDefinition Width=".30*" />
                            <ColumnDefinition Width=".30*" />
                        </Grid.ColumnDefinitions>
                        <Grid.RowDefinitions>
                            <RowDefinition Height="40" />
                        </Grid.RowDefinitions>
                        <Image Grid.Column="0" Source="../../Images/blue.jpg" Margin="2"
                         VerticalAlignment="top" Height="35" Width="25" />
                        <TextBlock Grid.Column="1" Text="{Binding Name}" FontSize="14"
                         Foreground="Navy" />
                        <TextBlock Grid.Column="2" Text="{Binding Address}" FontSize="14"
                         Foreground="Red" />
                        <TextBlock Grid.Column="3" Text="{Binding Phone}" FontSize="14"
                         Foreground="Green" />
                    </Grid>
                </DataTemplate>
            </ListBox.ItemTemplate>
        </ListBox>
```

This example disables the horizontal scrollbar and hides the vertical scrollbar, as shown in Figure 6-19. Because the vertical scrollbar is hidden, users can still navigate through the items with the arrow keys.

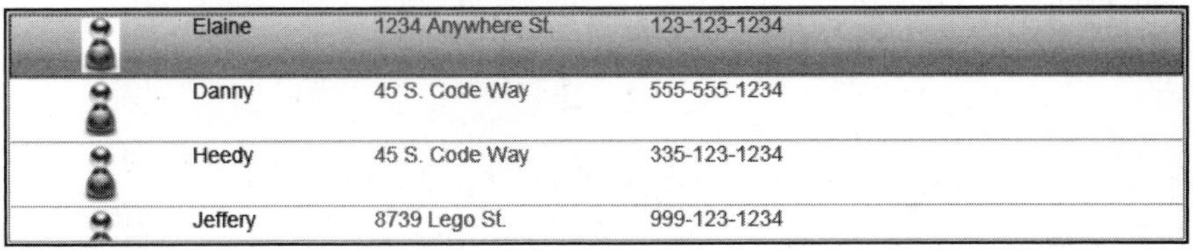

Elaine	1234 Anywhere St.	123-123-1234
Danny	45 S. Code Way	555-555-1234
Heedy	45 S. Code Way	335-123-1234
Jeffery	8739 Lego St.	999-123-1234

Figure 6-19

The COMBOBOX *Control*

ASP.NET provides a DropDownList control that can be used to display items that an end-user can select a single item from. Although Silverlight doesn't expose a DropDownList control, it does provide similar functionality through the ComboBox control. ComboBox items can be added by binding the control to a data source, by hard-coding items into the control using the ComboBoxItem XAML element or by programmatically adding items. An example of displaying states using the ComboBox and ComboBoxItem XAML elements is shown next:

```
<ComboBox x:Name="cbStates" Width="150" Height="20"
  SelectionChanged="cbStates_SelectionChanged">
    <ComboBoxItem Content="Arizona" />
    <ComboBoxItem Content="California" />
    <ComboBoxItem Content="Utah" />
</ComboBox>
```

As a user selects an item in a `ComboBox`, the `SelectionChanged` event is fired. An example of handling this event is shown next:

```
private void cbStates_SelectionChanged(object sender, SelectionChangedEventArgs e)
{
    this.tbState.Text =
        "Selected " + ((ComboBoxItem)this.cbStates.SelectedItem).Content;
}
```

Once the event fires, the selected `ComboBoxItem` can be accessed through the `SelectionChangedEventArg` object's `AddedItems` property or through the `ComboBox` control's `SelectedItem` property. `AddedItems` and `SelectedItem` both return an `Object` type that must be cast to a `ComboBoxItem` type in order to access the item's `Content` property.

The `Popup` *Control*

Showing a list of items is key in many applications, but at some point users will want to see additional details about a `DataGrid` row or `ListBox` item. The `Popup` control allows additional details to be shown for items displayed in `ListBox`, `DataGrid`, or custom controls. Although you can write custom code to show or hide data details, the `Popup` control was designed for that type of task and makes the process simpler. Figure 6-20 shows an example of using the `Popup` control to show additional details about a row in a `DataGrid`.

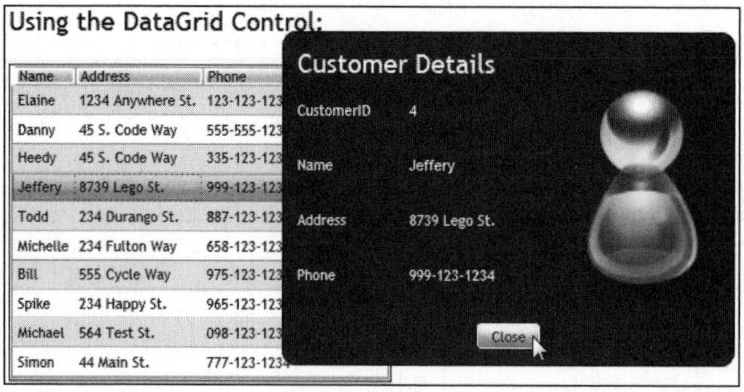

Figure 6-20

Silverlight's `Popup` control can be used in similar ways to ASP.NET's `Panel` control. Both controls allow child controls to be shown dynamically or hidden in an application. The `Popup` control exposes a `Visibility` property (like all controls that derive from `FrameworkElement`), but you'll use its `IsOpen` property to show or hide its contents. An example of using the `Popup` control to display details as a user clicks a row in a `DataGrid` is shown next:

```
<Popup x:Name="popUp">
    <Border CornerRadius="10" Width="350" Height="250" Background="Navy"
    BorderBrush="Black" BorderThickness="2">
        <Grid>
            <Grid.ColumnDefinitions>
```

```
                    <ColumnDefinition Width=".25*" />
                    <ColumnDefinition Width=".35*" />
                    <ColumnDefinition Width=".40*" />
                </Grid.ColumnDefinitions>

                <Grid.RowDefinitions>
                    <RowDefinition />
                    <RowDefinition />
                    <RowDefinition />
                    <RowDefinition />
                    <RowDefinition />
                    <RowDefinition />
                </Grid.RowDefinitions>

                <TextBlock Text="Customer Details" FontSize="20" Foreground="White"
                 Margin="10" Grid.ColumnSpan="3" Grid.Row="0" Grid.Column="0" />

                <Image Source="/Images/blue.png" Grid.RowSpan="4" Grid.Row="1"
                 Grid.Column="2" />

                <TextBlock Text="CustomerID" Margin="10" Foreground="White"
                 Grid.Row="1" Grid.Column="0" />
                <TextBlock Text="{Binding Path=CustomerID}" Margin="10"
                 Foreground="White" Grid.Row="1" Grid.Column="1" />

                <TextBlock Text="Name" Margin="10" Foreground="White" Grid.Row="2"
                 Grid.Column="0" />
                <TextBlock Text="{Binding Path=Name}" Margin="10" Foreground="White"
                 Grid.Row="2" Grid.Column="1"/>

                <TextBlock Text="Address" Margin="10" Foreground="White" Grid.Row="3"
                 Grid.Column="0" />
                <TextBlock Text="{Binding Path=Address}" Margin="10"
                 Foreground="White" Grid.Row="3" Grid.Column="1"/>

                <TextBlock Text="Phone" Margin="10" Foreground="White" Grid.Row="4"
                 Grid.Column="0" />
                <TextBlock Text="{Binding Path=Phone}" Margin="10" Foreground="White"
                 Grid.Row="4" Grid.Column="1"/>

                <Button x:Name="btnPopUpClose" Click="btnPopUpClose_Click" Width="50"
                 Content="Close" Margin="10" Grid.ColumnSpan="3"  Grid.Row="5"
                 Grid.Column="0"/>
            </Grid>
        </Border>
</Popup>
```

A Popup **control can also display controls contained within a Silverlight user control, which is recommended when you'd like more modularity and reuse in your applications. Chapter 11 provides additional details about creating and using user controls. The data binding code shown is discussed in more detail in Chapter 9.**

As a user selects a row in the DataGrid, its SelectionChanged event is fired, which handles calculating where the Popup control should be shown on the screen. Once the calculations are completed, the code sets the control's HorizontalOffset and VerticalOffset properties to the appropriate values and sets its IsOpen property to True to display it:

```
bool gridRowSelected = false;

private void dgCustomers_SelectionChanged(object sender,
  SelectionChangedEventArgs e)
{
    if (gridRowSelected) //Don't show popup when grid first loads
    {
        double x = (this.Width / 2) -
          (((FrameworkElement)this.popUp.Child).Width / 2);
        this.popUp.IsOpen = true;
        this.popUp.HorizontalOffset = x;
        this.popUp.VerticalOffset = -300;
        this.popUp.DataContext = (Customer)this.dgCustomers.SelectedItem;
    }
    else
    {
        gridRowSelected = true;
    }
}

private void btnPopUpClose_Click(object sender, RoutedEventArgs e)
{
    this.popUp.IsOpen = false;
}
```

As the user clicks on the close Button within the Popup control, the btnPopUpClose_Click event is fired, which sets the Popup's IsOpen property to false to close it.

Media Controls

Silverlight provides several controls that can be used to capture and display data. Applications that require more than simply data capture and display can leverage a rich set of media controls that are capable of playing audio and displaying images and video. Controls included in the media controls category include:

- ❑ Image control
- ❑ MediaElement control
- ❑ MultiScaleImage control

This section introduces you to the media controls and gets you started using them. Subsequent chapters provide additional details and dig deeper into their capabilities.

The `Image` Control

The `Image` control included in Silverlight can be used to display images much like the `Image` control found in ASP.NET. Image types supported by the control include JPEG and PNG with indexed color (1-, 4-, or 8-bit) and truecolor (24- or 32-bit) color depths. Gray scale and 64-bit truecolor PNG color depths are not supported.

Images can be retrieved from within Silverlight XAP files or from remote HTTP locations. The location of the image to be displayed by the `Image` control is defined using the `Source` property, which relies on the `BitmapImage` class to handle loading JPEG or PNG images. Here's an example of using the `Image` control to display an image named `blue.png` that's included in a Silverlight project within a folder named Images. The image file has its `Build Action` set to `Content` in the Visual Studio `Properties` window.

```
<Image x:Name="image" Source="/Images/blue.png" Margin="10"
HorizontalAlignment="Left"/>
```

> Because the blue.png file is part of the Silverlight project and marked with a `Build Action` of `Content` in the Visual Studio Properties window, it's included in the XAP file that's placed in the web site's ClientBin folder. The / character preceding the path in the `Source` property instructs the `Image` control to locate the image by starting at the root of the XAP file. If the image file's Build Action was marked as a Resource, it would be embedded in the assembly file as a resource and could be accessed by assigning a value of Images/blue.png to the `Source` property.

Images located on a remote web site can be displayed by assigning an HTTP path to the `Source` property:

```
<Image Source="http://www.xmlforasp.net/images/headerRight.jpg"
Margin="10" HorizontalAlignment="Left"/>
```

In cases in which you want control over whether or not the image fills its parent container, the `Image` control's `Stretch` property can be assigned one of the following `Stretch` enumeration values:

Stretch Value	Description
None	The content does not stretch to fill the parent container's dimensions.
Fill	The content is scaled to fit the output dimensions. Because the content's height and width are scaled independently, the original aspect ratio of the content might not be preserved. That is, the content might be distorted in order to completely fill the output area.
Uniform	The content is scaled to fit the parent container's dimensions. However, the aspect ratio of the content is preserved. This means that if the dimensions of the image don't match the dimensions of the parent control (e.g., the target control is wider), then extra space will show in the dimension that doesn't match. In other words, the image won't try to stretch to fit into the non-matching dimension.
UniformToFill	The content is scaled so that it completely fills the output area but preserves its original aspect ratio. Using this value may result in the image being clipped.

Figure 6-21 shows the effect of changing the Stretch property value on an image.

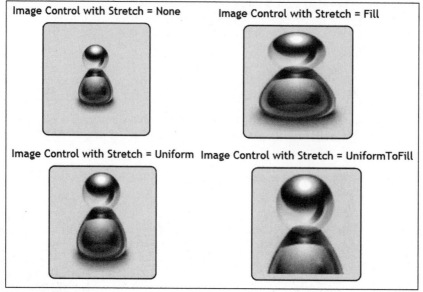

Figure 6-21

The Image control provides a Loaded event that can be used to know when an image has loaded and an ImageFailed event that can be used to know when an image failed to load. An example of handling these events is shown next:

```
private void Image_Loaded(object sender, RoutedEventArgs e)
{
    //Image has loaded.  Perform animation or other action
}

private void Image_ImageFailed(object sender, ExceptionRoutedEventArgs e)
{
    System.Windows.Browser.HtmlPage.Window.Alert("Image failed to load: " +
    e.ErrorException.Message);
}
```

The ExceptionRoutedEventArgs object passed to the Image_ImageFailed event handler contains an ErrorException object that provides access to the error message, stack trace, and inner exception.

The MediaElement Control

Silverlight has provided robust support for different media formats since its initial release, and many sites around the world have leveraged its media capabilities. Applications needing to play various types of audio or video can leverage the built-in media support by adding a MediaElement tag into a XAML file and defining a file source. Different types of audio and video files can be played and interacted with through events exposed by the MediaElement control including WMA, MP3, and WMV files.

The `MediaElement` control supports the following audio formats:

- ❑ WMA 7 — Windows Media Audio 7
- ❑ WMA 8 — Windows Media Audio 8
- ❑ WMA 9 — Windows Media Audio 9
- ❑ WMA 10 — Windows Media Audio 10
- ❑ MP3 — ISO/MPEG Layer-3
- ❑ Input — ISO/MPEG Layer-3 data stream
- ❑ Channel configurations — mono, stereo
- ❑ Sampling frequencies — 8, 11.025, 12, 16, 22.05, 24, 32, 44.1, and 48 kHz
- ❑ Bit rates — 8–320 kbps, variable bit rate
- ❑ Limitations — "Free format mode" (see ISO/IEC 11172-3, sub clause 2.4.2.3) is not supported.

The `MediaElement` control supports the following video formats:

- ❑ WMV1 — Windows Media Video 7
- ❑ WMV2 — Windows Media Video 8
- ❑ WMV3 — Windows Media Video 9
- ❑ WMVA — Windows Media Video Advanced Profile, non-VC-1
- ❑ WMVC1 — Windows Media Video Advanced Profile, VC-1

Several tools are available to convert audio or video files to the formats listed above including Microsoft's Expression Encoder. Expression Encoder makes it easy to add watermarks into video, add leaders or trailers, and add markers that can be used to sync video with other actions that may occur in a Silverlight application.

`MediaElement` provides attributes such as `Source`, `Height`, `Width`, `Stretch`, and more to control what media file is shown and how it's shown. It also provides several different events that can be used to know when the state of a media object has changed such as `BufferingProgressChanged`, `MarkerReached`, and `MediaOpened`. An example of using the `MediaElement` control is shown next:

```
<MediaElement x:Name="mediaElement" Source="/Video/Sandwich_Thief.wmv"
AutoPlay="True" Stretch="None" />
```

> **Although you can assign values to the `Height` and `Width` properties of the `MediaElement` control when using it to display video, it's generally recommended that you let the media fill its container. If you need the media to be smaller, re-encoding it to a different size will lead to a better overall viewing experience.**

This example defines the location of the video file using the `MediaElement` control's `Source` property and automatically starts the video file playing by setting the `AutoPlay` property to `True`.

Audio and video files can also be started, stopped, and paused by calling the `Play()`, `Stop()`, and `Pause()` methods, respectively. An example of calling these methods as an end-user clicks different buttons is shown next:

```csharp
private void MediaButton_Click(object sender, RoutedEventArgs e)
{
    Button btn = (Button)sender;
    switch (btn.Content.ToString())
    {
        case "Play":
            this.mediaElement.Play();
            break;
        case "Pause":
            this.mediaElement.Pause();
            break;
        case "Stop":
            this.mediaElement.Stop();
            break;
    }
}
```

There are many more features available in the `MediaElement` control that are discussed in Chapter 13, "Audio and Video."

Displaying Download Progress with the `ProgressBar` Control

It goes without saying that audio and video files can be large. The speed at which they download can vary greatly depending on the end-user's network connection, network latency, and other factors. Although you can write custom code to handle displaying the progress of a media file being downloaded, Silverlight provides a `ProgressBar` control that can be used to visually notify the user without writing a lot of code. The `ProgressBar` control acts much like the `ProgressBar` found in Windows Forms exposing `Minimum` and `Maximum` properties, as shown next:

```xml
<ProgressBar x:Name="pbBar" Height="20" Width="100"
  Minimum="1" Maximum="100" Margin="10" />
```

The value shown in the `ProgressBar` control can be incremented by changing its `Value` property as shown in the following code. This code handles the `MediaElement` control's `DownloadProgressChanged` event:

```csharp
private void mediaElement_DownloadProgressChanged(object sender, RoutedEventArgs e)
{
    int val = (int)(mediaElement.DownloadProgress * 100);
    if (val > 99)
    {
        this.pbBar.Visibility = Visibility.Collapsed;
        this.tbProgress.Text = "Download Complete!";
        return;
    }
```

```
        this.pbBar.Value = val;
        this.tbProgress.Text = val.ToString() + "%";
    }
```

Figure 6-22 shows how the `ProgressBar` control looks as its `Value` property is incremented.

Figure 6-22

The `MultiScaleImage` *Control*

Zooming in and out of images has always been difficult to achieve on the Web. A handful of technologies can accomplish this task without image pixelation, but web browsers can't do it natively without help from a plug-in. Fortunately, Silverlight provides the `MultiScaleImage` control, which can be used to zoom in and out of images quickly without pixelation. The Hard Rock Café's Memorabilia web site located at `http://memorabilia.hardrock.com` is an excellent example of using the `MultiScaleImage` control for this purpose. Figure 6-23 shows an example of zooming into images displayed on the site.

Figure 6-23

The `MultiScaleImage` controls works by showing different layers of an image from high level (zoomed out) to low level (zoomed in) and only loads the actual pixels that need to be displayed rather than parts of the image that don't fit into the bounds of the viewport. It reads image data from a special file with an .xml extension that can be created using Microsoft's Deep Zoom Composer tool. Images can be arranged in the Deep Zoom Composer and then exported for inclusion into a Silverlight application that uses the `MultiScaleImage` control to display them.

Figure 6-24 shows how the Deep Zoom Composer can be used to arrange images.

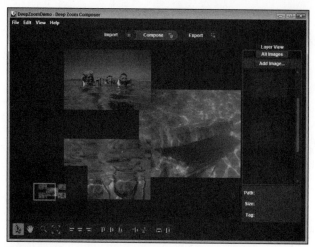

Figure 6-24

Once images have been arranged in the Deep Zoom Composer, they can be exported for use in a Silverlight application. A sample application is created by the tool that you can run immediately after the export process completes. An example of the XAML code created by the tool is shown next:

```xaml
<UserControl x:Class="DeepZoomProject.Page"
    xmlns="http://schemas.microsoft.com/winfx/2006/xaml/presentation"
    xmlns:x="http://schemas.microsoft.com/winfx/2006/xaml"
    Width="1024" Height="768">
    <Grid x:Name="LayoutRoot" Background="#FFFFFFFF">
        <Border BorderThickness="1,1,1,1" Margin="10,10,10,10"
            BorderBrush="#FF9F9F9F">
            <MultiScaleImage x:Name="msi" MinHeight="480" MinWidth="640"
                Height="768" Width="1024"/>
        </Border>
    </Grid>
</UserControl>
```

While this code defines `Height` and `Width` properties on the `MultiScaleImage` control, it doesn't assign the XML source file that contains image information. This is handled in the code file, as shown next:

```
this.msi.Source = new DeepZoomImageTileSource(
  new Uri("GeneratedImages/dzc_output.xml", UriKind.Relative));
this.msi.Loaded += new RoutedEventHandler(msi_Loaded);
```

Additional information about using the Deep Zoom Composer and the `MultiScaleImage` control is provided in Chapter 14, "Graphics and Animation."

Silverlight Toolkit Controls

If you've used ASP.NET AJAX, you've likely used or heard about controls from toolkits such as the ASP.NET AJAX Control Toolkit. Microsoft has also released a Silverlight Toolkit with new controls and functionality that can be used in Silverlight 2 applications. The controls are grouped into "quality bands" with most of the controls fitting into either the "preview" or "stable" bands. This allows Microsoft to develop and release controls more quickly based on feedback from the community. The status of the controls will change over time as bugs are fixed and new features are added, and many controls will eventually be moved into the Release Phase or "mature" band. Additional information about control quality bands can be found at www.codeplex.com/Silverlight/Wiki/View.aspx?title=Quality %20Bands&referringTitle=Home&ANCHOR#Preview.

Controls included in the initial release of the Silverlight Toolkit include the following (note that additional controls will likely be added in the future):

- ❑   AutoCompleteBox
- ❑   ButtonSpinner
- ❑   Chart
- ❑   DockPanel
- ❑   Expander
- ❑   HeaderedItemControl
- ❑   HeaderedContentControl
- ❑   ImplicitStyleManager
- ❑   Label
- ❑   NumericUpDown
- ❑   TreeView
- ❑   ViewBox
- ❑   WrapPanel

The majority of the controls live in the Microsoft.Windows.Controls.dll assembly, which contains several namespaces such as Microsoft.Windows.Controls. Other controls for theming and charting exist as well in separate assemblies. Multiple assemblies were created so that Silverlight 2 applications only download what they need as opposed to downloading larger assemblies containing unused classes and controls.

To get started using the Toolkit controls, you need to reference the appropriate assembly (such as Microsoft.Windows.Controls) provided in the toolkit and then add the controls to your Visual Studio 2008 Toolbox by right-clicking on them and selecting "Choose Items." Select the Silverlight Components tab, browse to the Toolkit assembly, and then check the checkbox next to the controls you'd like to add.

Once the controls are added, you can drag them into a XAML file, which will automatically add the proper namespace onto the `UserControl` root element, as shown next:

```
<UserControl
  xmlns="http://schemas.microsoft.com/client/2007"
  xmlns:x="http://schemas.microsoft.com/winfx/2006/xaml"
  xmlns:controls="clr-namespace:Microsoft.Windows.Controls;
   assembly=Microsoft.Windows.Controls"
  x:Class="…">
</UserControl>
```

In the remainder of the chapter, you'll be introduced to some of the controls found in the Silverlight Toolkit and see how they can be used to enhance Silverlight 2 applications.

AutoCompleteBox *Control*

The `AutoCompleteBox` control acts much like the `AutoCompleteExtender` control found in the ASP.NET AJAX Control Toolkit. It allows data to be displayed under a textbox as users type characters. The XAML code that follows defines an `AutoCompleteBox` control named `acCountries` that displays data after a user types a single character:

```
<controls:AutoCompleteBox x:Name="acCountries"
  MinimumPopulateDelay="200"
  MinimumPrefixLength="1"
  Width="260"
  HorizontalAlignment="Left" />
```

You can bind auto-complete data to the control using the `ItemsSource` property (note that data can be retrieved from any source that Silverlight has access to):

```
private void BindData()
{
    acCountries.ItemsSource = new List<string>() { "USA", "Spain", "Mexico",
      "Canada", "Costa Rica" };
}
```

Figure 6-25 shows what the end-user would see as they type **c** into the textbox.

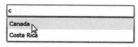

Figure 6-25

The `AutoCompleteBox` control supports filtering auto-complete data using lambdas, exposes a rich set of properties and events, and allows templates to be defined. Figure 6-26 shows an example of applying a custom template to the control's `ItemTemplate` property to display pictures and text as the user types.

Figure 6-26

> The `ItemTemplate` property and the subject of styles and templates are covered in more detail in Chapter 7.

WrapPanel *Control*

The `WrapPanel` control is one of those controls that you'll find yourself using frequently — especially if you need to display a collection of objects in a user interface without resorting to a grid-style layout. Although the standard `StackPanel` provides a way to display controls in a horizontal or vertical manner, any content that exceeds the bounds of the control will be clipped. This presents a problem with images or any other type of data that need to be wrapped rather than clipped. Although there are a few third-party `WrapPanel` controls floating around on the Web, the one available in the Silverlight Toolkit gets the job done quickly and efficiently. Here's an example of using the `WrapPanel` control within an `ItemsControl` (a control that items controls like `ListBox` and `ComboBox` derive from) to define the parent container for images retrieved from Flickr:

```xml
<ItemsControl x:Name="icPhotos" Grid.Row="1" VerticalAlignment="Top">
    <ItemsControl.ItemsPanel>
        <ItemsPanelTemplate>
            <controls:WrapPanel x:Name="wpImages" Margin="10"
                Orientation="Horizontal" VerticalAlignment="Top" />
        </ItemsPanelTemplate>
    </ItemsControl.ItemsPanel>
    <ItemsControl.ItemTemplate>
        <DataTemplate>
            <Rectangle Stroke="LightGray" Tag="{Binding Url}"
                Fill="{Binding
                ImageBrush}" StrokeThickness="2"
                RadiusX="15" RadiusY="15" Margin="15"
                Height="75" Width="75" Loaded="Rectangle_Loaded"
                MouseLeave="Rectangle_MouseLeave"
                MouseEnter="Rectangle_MouseEnter"
                MouseLeftButtonDown="rect_MouseLeftButtonDown">
                <Rectangle.RenderTransform>
                    <TransformGroup>
                        <ScaleTransform ScaleX="1" ScaleY="1" CenterX="37.5"
                            CenterY="37.5" />
                    </TransformGroup>
                </Rectangle.RenderTransform>
            </Rectangle>
        </DataTemplate>
    </ItemsControl.ItemTemplate>
</ItemsControl>
```

> The XAML code shown here provides a sneak peek into the world of Silverlight data binding and custom data templates. Additional information about data binding is provided in Chapter 10.

An example of using the `WrapPanel` control to display a series of images in a "wrapped" manner is shown in Figure 6-27.

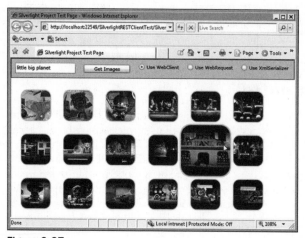

Figure 6-27

TreeView *Control*

The Silverlight Toolkit's `TreeView` control looks and acts much like any standard tree view that you've seen, although it can be styled and customized just about any way you'd like. An example of using the `TreeView` control is shown next:

```
<controls:TreeView Margin="5">
    <controls:TreeViewItem Header="ACME Corporation Employees">
        <controls:TreeViewItem Header="Mike James">
            <controls:TreeViewItem Header="Fred Stel" />
            <controls:TreeViewItem Header="Heedy Taft" />
            <controls:TreeViewItem Header="Seth Johnson" />
            <controls:TreeViewItem Header="Dan Williams" />
            <controls:TreeViewItem Header="Ted Thompson">
                <controls:TreeViewItem Header="Daine Rivers" />
                <controls:TreeViewItem Header="Gillian Pierson" />
            </controls:TreeViewItem>
        </controls:TreeViewItem>
    </controls:TreeViewItem>
</controls:TreeView>
```

If you've ever used the `TreeView` control built into ASP.NET, then the code will look familiar. Figure 6-28 shows what the `TreeView` control looks like once rendered in Silverlight.

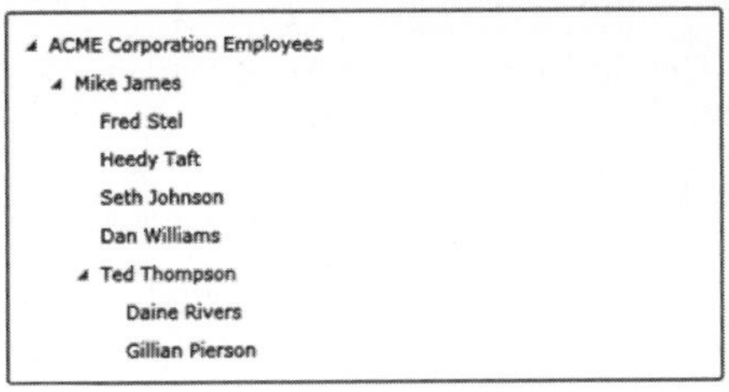

Figure 6-28

The sample code included in the Silverlight Toolkit also provides an example of binding a `TreeView` to an `ObjectCollection` instance (a new object also available in the toolkit) to display a hierarchy. Here's what the `ObjectCollection` looks like. The `Domain`, `Kingdom`, and other related elements are based on custom classes included in the Toolkit samples. They can, of course, be substituted with your own data classes and built up dynamically.

```
<controls:ObjectCollection x:Key="TreeOfLife"
  xmlns="http://schemas.microsoft.com/client/2007">
    <common:Domain Classification="Bacteria">
        <common:Kingdom Classification="Eubacteria" />
    </common:Domain>
    <common:Domain Classification="Archaea">
        <common:Kingdom Classification="Archaebacteria" />
    </common:Domain>
    <common:Domain Classification="Eukarya">
        <common:Kingdom Classification="Protista" />
        <common:Kingdom Classification="Fungi" />
        <common:Kingdom Classification="Plantae" />
        <common:Kingdom Classification="Animalia">
            <common:Phylum Classification="Arthropoda">
                <common:Class Classification="Insecta">
                    <common:Order Classification="Diptera">
                        <common:Family Classification="Drosophilidae">
                            <common:Genus Classification="Drosophila">
                                <common:Species Classification="D. melanogaster" />
                            </common:Genus>
                        </common:Family>
                    </common:Order>
                </common:Class>
            </common:Phylum>
            <common:Phylum Classification="Chordata">
                <common:Class Classification="Mammalia">
                    <common:Order Classification="Primates">
                        <common:Family Classification="Hominidae">
                            <common:Genus Classification="Homo">
                                <common:Species Classification="H. sapiens" />
                            </common:Genus>
                        </common:Family>
                    </common:Order>
                </common:Class>
            </common:Phylum>
            <common:Phylum Classification="Ctenophora" />
```

```
            <common:Phylum Classification="Porifera" />
            <common:Phylum Classification="Placozoa" />
        </common:Kingdom>
      </common:Domain>
  </controls:ObjectCollection>
```

The `TreeView` can be bound to the `TreeOfLife` ObjectCollection using the `TreeView`'s `ItemsSource` property, as shown next (additional information about data binding can be found in Chapter 10, "Working with Data"):

```
<controls:TreeView x:Name="tvTreeOfLife" Margin="5"
   ItemsSource="{StaticResource TreeOfLife}" >
    <controls:TreeView.ItemTemplate>
        <controls:HierarchicalDataTemplate ItemsSource="{Binding Subclasses}">
            <StackPanel>
                <TextBlock Text="{Binding Rank}" FontSize="8" FontStyle="Italic"
                    Foreground="Gray" Margin="0 0 0 -5" />
                <TextBlock Text="{Binding Classification}" />
            </StackPanel>
        </controls:HierarchicalDataTemplate>
    </controls:TreeView.ItemTemplate>
</controls:TreeView>
```

Notice that the `ItemsSource` property is bound to the `TreeOfLife` key defined in the `ObjectCollection` and that each value in the tree view is generated by using a `HierarchicalDataTemplate` that binds to `Rank` and `Classification` properties and displays them using a `StackPanel`. Figure 6-29 shows what the `TreeView` looks like once the different life classifications are rendered:

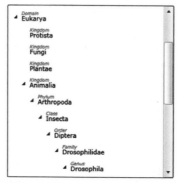

Figure 6-29

Chart *Control*

Charting is an important part of many applications. In the past, developers have relied on custom code, reporting solutions, or third-party controls when they needed to embed different types of charts in applications. The Silverlight Toolkit includes a `Chart` control that can be used to display different types of data. It's located in the `Microsoft.Windows.Controls.DataVisualization` assembly and `Microsoft.Windows.Controls.DataVisualization.Charting` namespace. By using it, you can display line charts, pie charts, and scatter charts and even animate the charts. Here's an example of defining a bar chart that binds to an `ObjectCollection` filled with `PugetSound` objects:

```
<charting:Chart Title="Typical Use">
    <charting:Chart.Series>
        <charting:ColumnSeries
            Title="Population"
            ItemsSource="{Binding PugetSound, Source={StaticResource City}}"
            IndependentValueBinding="{Binding Name}"
            DependentValueBinding="{Binding Population}"/>
    </charting:Chart.Series>
</charting:Chart>
```

The `ObjectCollection` that is bound to the chart is shown next:

```
ObjectCollection pugetSound = new ObjectCollection();
pugetSound.Add(new City { Name = "Bellevue", Population = 112344 });
pugetSound.Add(new City { Name = "Issaquah", Population = 11212 });
pugetSound.Add(new City { Name = "Redmond", Population = 46391 });
pugetSound.Add(new City { Name = "Seattle", Population = 592800 });
```

The output generated by the chart is shown in Figure 6-30.

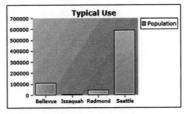

Figure 6-30

An example of defining a pie chart that binds to the same `ObjectCollection` data is shown next:

```
<charting:Chart Title="Typical Use">
    <charting:Chart.Series>
        <charting:PieSeries
            ItemsSource="{Binding PugetSound, Source={StaticResource City}}"
            IndependentValueBinding="{Binding Name}"
            DependentValueBinding="{Binding Population}"/>
    </charting:Chart.Series>
</charting:Chart>
```

Figure 6-31 shows what the pie chart looks like.

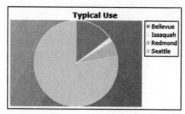

Figure 6-31

There is a lot more that can be done with the Silverlight Toolkit controls discussed in this section, and there are several other controls available that weren't covered. Visit `www.codeplex.com/Silverlight` to download additional documentation and samples. Also, Chapter 7 includes information about the `ImplicitStyleManager` control.

Summary

Silverlight provides a variety of built-in controls that can be used to capture user input, display data items, and play media files. Many of the controls are similar to web controls available in ASP.NET, which should allow you to put them to use more quickly.

The chapter started by showing how controls can be defined in XAML and how events can be hooked to event handlers. It then delved into controls in the user input controls category such as `TextBox`, `Button`, and `Checkbox` and showed how items controls can be used to display collections of data in different ways. Available items controls include `ListBox`, `DataGrid`, and `ComboBox`. Media controls that can be used to show images and play audio and video files were also covered. Available media controls include `Image`, `MediaElement`, and `MultiScaleImage`. Finally, several controls in the Silverlight Toolkit such as `AutoCompleteBox` and `WrapPanel` were discussed.

Several other features can be used with Silverlight controls including styles and templates. In Chapter 7, "Styles and Templates," you'll learn how to create and apply styles and develop custom control templates.

7

Styles and Templates

As you've seen so far, Silverlight comes with a whole host of layout and input controls to build your user interface from. However, all Silverlight applications would look pretty much the same without a sprinkling of individuality, provided through extensive styling and templating support.

In this chapter, you'll start by looking at how different styles can be applied to the elements of your UI inline quickly and easily. In fact, this is something you've already done in the previous chapters. You'll then look at providing some measure of separation between the style definition itself and the controls it's to be applied against, both locally within the page in question and globally across the entire application.

Following this, you'll take a look at the concept of *lookless* controls and how you can completely redefine the *skin* of a control (including the built-in ones) without altering its functionality — a technique called *templating*. This section will also show you how to propagate user-provided values through to the individual elements of your new template, a technique called *template binding*.

Finally, you'll see how it's possible to hook into the ASP.NET Profile Provider to implement personalization in your Silverlight application.

Styles

When you talk about applying a style to an element within an ASP.NET web site and/or a Silverlight application, you are referring to the ability to alter the control's look and feel — altering its size, alignment, and so on. It is hoped that you are either a gifted designer or have the backing of a talented design team.

In order to affect the properties that denote look and feel, you can either set them on a control by control basis (termed *inline*), reapplying the information each and every time, or you can opt to define the styles in a central location and then apply the predefined style information to your controls. This is a model you've seen many times before. In HTML, you can use Style Sheets to store style information that can then be applied against your HTML elements, and you can elect to apply information directly to the HTML elements if need be. In ASP.NET, you have the concept of *themes*, which are defined in skin files and then applied to the server controls. So this model should at least feel familiar. The next sections, "Applying Inline Styles" and "Specifying Styles in a Central Location," will take you through the ins and outs of both approaches.

Applying Inline Styles

The quickest and easiest way to style a control is to directly set the properties on it *inline*, which means within the element definition itself.

You've already seen this technique used probably without thinking about it. Simply setting the `Height` and `Width` properties of a control constitutes altering its style.

The following XAML defines `TextBlock`, `TextBox`, and `Button` elements that comprise a simple login form, arranged within a parent `Canvas`. Notice, however, that only the elements' `x:Name`, `Text/Content`, and `Canvas` attached properties have been set. With regard to style, nothing has been specified, so each control will use its default settings for appearance.

```xaml
<UserControl x:Class="Chapter07.InlineExample"
    xmlns="http://schemas.microsoft.com/winfx/2006/xaml/presentation"
    xmlns:x="http://schemas.microsoft.com/winfx/2006/xaml"
    Width="400" Height="300">

    <Canvas x:Name="LayoutRoot" Background="White">

        <!-- STEP 1, NO STYLE -->
        <TextBlock x:Name="usernameLabel"
                Text="Enter your Username: "
                Canvas.Top="10"
                Canvas.Left="10" />

        <TextBox x:Name="username"
                Canvas.Top="10"
                Canvas.Left="150"/>

        <TextBlock x:Name="passwordLabel"
                Text="Enter your password: "
                Canvas.Top="40"
                Canvas.Left="10"/>

        <TextBox x:Name="password"
                Canvas.Top="40"
                Canvas.Left="150"/>

        <Button x:Name="loginButton"
                Content="Login"
                Canvas.Top="70"
                Canvas.Left="10"/>
        <!-- END STEP 1 -->
    </Canvas>


</UserControl>
```

Figure 7-1 shows the output of this XAML.

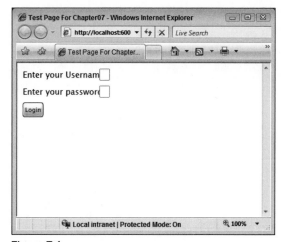

Figure 7-1

Not the best login form in the world, you'll agree. Although the controls are positioned properly, the default width for TextBox is a little too short. So the next step in designing this form is to increase the default width of the TextBox elements to something more appropriate, and also to increase the width of the Button to make it stand out more.

```
<TextBlock x:Name="usernameLabel"
           Text="Enter your Username: "
           Canvas.Top="10"
           Canvas.Left="10" />

<TextBox x:Name="username"
         Canvas.Top="10"
         Canvas.Left="150"
         Width="150" />

<TextBlock x:Name="passwordLabel"
           Text="Enter your password: "
           Canvas.Top="40"
           Canvas.Left="10" />

<TextBox x:Name="password"
         Canvas.Top="40"
         Canvas.Left="150"
         Width="150" />

<Button x:Name="loginButton"
        Content="Login"
        Canvas.Top="70"
        Canvas.Left="10"
        Width="80" />
```

Figure 7-2 shows the form with its new size settings for the TextBox and Button objects. Things are getting better.

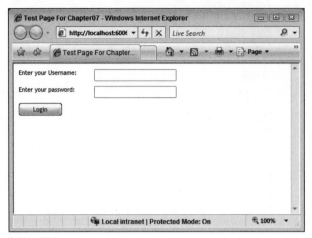

Figure 7-2

Now assume that your company has strict rules on branding, meaning that the text used in this and all other forms must match or closely match the company standard of Times New Roman in size 12. This requirement entails setting both the FontFamily and FontSize properties of each control on your form that will display text content, as shown in the following XAML:

```
<TextBlock x:Name="usernameLabel"
           Text="Enter your Username: "
           Canvas.Top="10"
           Canvas.Left="10"
           FontFamily="Times New Roman"
           FontSize="12"/>

<TextBox x:Name="username"
         Canvas.Top="10"
         Canvas.Left="150"
         Width="150"
         FontFamily="Times New Roman"
         FontSize="12"/>

<TextBlock x:Name="passwordLabel"
           Text="Enter your password: "
           Canvas.Top="40"
           Canvas.Left="10"
           FontFamily="Times New Roman"
           FontSize="12"/>

<TextBox x:Name="password"
         Canvas.Top="40"
         Canvas.Left="150"
         Width="150"
```

```
                    FontFamily="Times New Roman"
                    FontSize="12"/>

        <Button x:Name="loginButton"
                    Content="Login"
                    Canvas.Top="70"
                    Canvas.Left="10"
                    Width="80"
                    FontFamily="Times New Roman"
                    FontSize="12"/>
```

So up to now you've increased the default size of some of the elements and implemented your company's standard font and size. Throw design caution to the wind now — change the label text to be colored green, and add a heading to finish the form off. Your XAML should resemble the following:

```
        <TextBlock x:Name="headingText"
                    Text="Please Login"
                    Canvas.Top="10"
                    Canvas.Left="10"
                    FontFamily="Times New Roman"
                    FontSize="18" />

        <TextBlock x:Name="usernameLabel"
                    Text="Enter your Username: "
                    Canvas.Top="40"
                    Canvas.Left="10"
                    FontFamily="Times New Roman"
                    FontSize="12"
                    Foreground="Green"/>

        <TextBox x:Name="username"
                    Canvas.Top="40"
                    Canvas.Left="150"
                    Width="150"
                    FontFamily="Times New Roman"
                    FontSize="12"/>

        <TextBlock x:Name="passwordLabel"
                    Text="Enter your password: "
                    Canvas.Top="70"
                    Canvas.Left="10"
                    FontFamily="Times New Roman"
                    FontSize="12"
                    Foreground="Green"/>

        <TextBox x:Name="password"
                    Canvas.Top="70"
                    Canvas.Left="150"
                    Width="150"
                    FontFamily="Times New Roman"
                    FontSize="12"/>

        <Button x:Name="loginButton"
                    Content="Login"
```

```
Canvas.Top="100"
Canvas.Left="10"
Width="80"
FontFamily="Times New Roman"
FontSize="12"/>
```

Figure 7-3 shows the final result, which is beautiful, we think you'll agree.

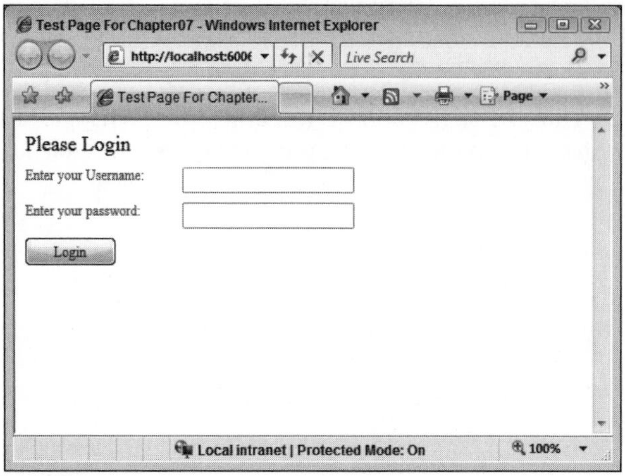

Figure 7-3

Take a moment now to consider some problems with the "inline" approach. Even with this small example, reapplying the same settings to the different controls was a tedious task and in anything much bigger would become time-consuming, not to mention error-prone as complexity really increases.

Also, it's very rare that something doesn't change after it is created, very rare, indeed. For example, more likely than not a company standard will change, which will require you to go through your lovely form and alter style properties to reconform. Not a pleasant thought on a complex form, never mind on a number of them!

Finally, inline styles make it difficult to maintain the same look and feel throughout an entire application, especially when multiple designers and developers are thrown into the mix.

What's needed, then, is the ability to define set styles in a central location that can then be applied to the controls within your application automatically.

Specifying Styles in a Central Location

The ability to define and then reuse set styles is provided by the `Style` object. In order to apply a predefined style to a control or several controls, you first need a way of specifying which controls should take the set style. In Silverlight, you do this by setting the `Style.TargetType` property to the type of element that can use the style and then giving the `Style` object a unique key via the `x:Key` property. `x:Key` can be applied to elements that are defined with a `Resources` section, and thus `Style` objects must be defined in a `Resources` section of your XAML for use.

You learned in Chapter 4 about the `FrameworkElement` class, whose job it is to provide controls further down the derivation chain with layout abilities, object lifetime hooks, and data-binding and resource support. It transpires that every `FrameworkElement`-derived control in Silverlight has a `Style` property that defaults to null. To set this property to one of your predefined styles in XAML, you use the string name provided by the `x:Key` value. Type conversion then takes place to set the actual `Style` object being referenced.

Setters

As well as being able to apply a style to set elements, you also need to be able to define within the style itself what property values it will actually set on the controls that use it. To do this, the `Style` object comes with a `Setter` property that allows you to specify several `Setter` objects. A `Setter` object allows you to specify the name of the property that will be set and the value that should be given to it via the `Property` and `Value` properties, respectively, `FontSize` and `12`, for example. Creating multiple `Setter` objects allows you to predefine any style settings you choose.

The following XAML shows how you could define a `Style` object for `TextBox` elements that sets the `FontFamily`, `FontSize`, and `Width` properties.

```
<Style x:Key="StandardTextBox" TargetType="TextBox">
    <Setter Property="FontFamily"
            Value="Times New Roman" />

    <Setter Property="FontSize"
            Value="12" />

    <Setter Property="Width"
            Value="150" />
</Style>
```

Specifying Styles at the Page Level

Specifying styles at the page level offers numerous advantages over inline styling of your UI elements. First, it aids with style maintenance as it negates the need for style information to be duplicated across multiple changes. Second, it makes it easier to enforce common guidance throughout pages rather than ad hoc styles being applied throughout. Finally, because they're declared only once and then used many times, it reduces the chance of error.

A `Style` object needs to be specified in a `Resources` section of your application. If you have styles that only apply to a single page, you can simply place these in the `Resources` section of the parent container — the `UserControl`. If you want your styles to apply only to the elements within a container further down the hierarchy, you're free to do so, in the `Canvas`, for example. For all of the elements within the page (or other container) that then want to use the style, their `Style` property should be set to the name given to the `Style` in the `x:Key` property.

With this in mind, alter your XAML to include the `TextBox` style definition and application, as shown below:

```
<Canvas.Resources>
    <Style x:Key="StandardTextBox" TargetType="TextBox">
        <Setter Property="FontFamily"
                Value="Times New Roman" />
```

```xml
                        <Setter Property="FontSize"
                                Value="12" />

                        <Setter Property="Width"
                                Value="150" />
            </Style>
</Canvas.Resources>

<TextBlock x:Name="headingText"
           Text="Please Login"
           Canvas.Top="10"
           Canvas.Left="10"
           FontFamily="Times New Roman"
           FontSize="18" />

<TextBlock x:Name="usernameLabel"
           Text="Enter your Username: "
           Canvas.Top="40"
           Canvas.Left="10"
           FontFamily="Times New Roman"
           FontSize="12"
           Foreground="Green"/>

<TextBox x:Name="username"
         Canvas.Top="40"
         Canvas.Left="150"
         Style="{StaticResource StandardTextBox}"/>

<TextBlock x:Name="passwordLabel"
           Text="Enter your password: "
           Canvas.Top="70"
           Canvas.Left="10"
           FontFamily="Times New Roman"
           FontSize="12"
           Foreground="Green"/>

<TextBox x:Name="password"
         Canvas.Top="70"
         Canvas.Left="150"
         Style="{StaticResource StandardTextBox}" />

<Button x:Name="loginButton"
        Content="Login"
        Canvas.Top="100"
        Canvas.Left="10"
        Width="80"
        FontFamily="Times New Roman"
        FontSize="12"/>
```

Note how the Style property is set to {StaticResource StandardTextBox} for the TextBox elements in question. If you compile and run the application, you should still get the same result as before, meaning your new style definition has worked.

Now extract the remaining styles and define them for use as shown below:

```xml
<Canvas.Resources>
    <Style x:Key="StandardTextBox" TargetType="TextBox">
        <Setter Property="FontFamily"
                Value="Times New Roman" />

        <Setter Property="FontSize"
                Value="12" />

        <Setter Property="Width"
                Value="150" />
    </Style>

    <Style x:Key="TextBlockHeader" TargetType="TextBlock">
        <Setter Property="FontFamily"
                Value="Times New Roman" />

        <Setter Property="FontSize"
                Value="18" />
    </Style>

    <Style x:Key="StandardLabel" TargetType="TextBlock">
        <Setter Property="FontFamily"
                Value="Times New Roman" />

        <Setter Property="FontSize"
                Value="12" />

        <Setter Property="Foreground"
                Value="Green" />
    </Style>

    <Style x:Key="StandardButton" TargetType="Button">
        <Setter Property="FontFamily"
                Value="Times New Roman" />

        <Setter Property="FontSize"
                Value="12" />

        <Setter Property="Width"
                Value="80" />
    </Style>
</Canvas.Resources>

<TextBlock x:Name="headingText"
        Text="Please Login"
        Canvas.Top="10"
        Canvas.Left="10"
        Style="{StaticResource TextBlockHeader}"/>

<TextBlock x:Name="usernameLabel"
        Text="Enter your Username: "
        Canvas.Top="40"
```

```
                        Canvas.Left="10"
                        Style="{StaticResource StandardLabel}"/>

        <TextBox x:Name="username"
                 Canvas.Top="40"
                 Canvas.Left="150"
                 Style="{StaticResource StandardTextBox}"/>

        <TextBlock x:Name="passwordLabel"
                   Text="Enter your password: "
                   Canvas.Top="70"
                   Canvas.Left="10"
                   Style="{StaticResource StandardLabel}"/>

        <TextBox x:Name="password"
                 Canvas.Top="70"
                 Canvas.Left="150"
                 Style="{StaticResource StandardTextBox}" />

        <Button x:Name="loginButton"
                Content="Login"
                Canvas.Top="100"
                Canvas.Left="10"
                Style="{StaticResource StandardButton}"/>
```

Notice how it's possible to define more than one `Style` object that targets the same type. This enables you to create multiple styles for objects such as a `TextBox` and then specify exactly which style to use with the `x:Key` value.

Overriding Set Styles

You can now use the `Style` object to predefine your desired styles and apply them to one or many controls. As well as applying a style to a given control, you can also provide inline style information that can potentially clash with information given by the specified `Style` object. When this happens, the values provided "inline" will override those defined in the `Style` object. The `Style` object does *not* change, however, and will continue to apply the properties that don't clash to the elements in question.

This mechanism allows you to take part or most of a `Style`, but then to tweak it for a particular control. The following XAML shows a `TextBlock` overriding the `Foreground` setter with a selection of its own, while still retaining the remaining `FontSize` setter:

```
<Canvas.Resources>
    <Style x:Key="DefaultTextBlock" TargetType="TextBlock">
        <Setter Property="Foreground"
                Value="Green" />

        <Setter Property="FontSize"
                Value="26" />
    </Style>
</Canvas.Resources>

<TextBlock Text="Hello, World!"
           Style="{StaticResource DefaultTextBlock}"
           Foreground="Blue" />
```

To reiterate, overriding part or all of a `Style` setting does not alter the `Style` object in any way, and the other controls that use it will continue to do so.

Specifying Styles at the Application Level

The examples thus far have assumed that you have styles that only need to propagate from either the top-level `UserControl` element or a container within it to their children. In the real world, it's much more likely that you will create styles that should be applied across the entire application, potentially spanning many pages.

To do this, you simply promote your style definitions to the `Resources` section of the `Application` object, within the App.xaml page.

```xml
<Application xmlns="http://schemas.microsoft.com/winfx/2006/xaml/presentation"
            xmlns:x="http://schemas.microsoft.com/winfx/2006/xaml"
            x:Class="Chapter07.App"
            >
    <Application.Resources>
        <Style x:Key="StandardTextBox" TargetType="TextBox">
            <Setter Property="FontFamily"
                    Value="Times New Roman" />

            <Setter Property="FontSize"
                    Value="12" />

            <Setter Property="Width"
                    Value="150" />
        </Style>

        <Style x:Key="TextBlockHeader" TargetType="TextBlock">
            <Setter Property="FontFamily"
                    Value="Times New Roman" />

            <Setter Property="FontSize"
                    Value="18" />
        </Style>

        <Style x:Key="StandardLabel" TargetType="TextBlock">
            <Setter Property="FontFamily"
                    Value="Times New Roman" />

            <Setter Property="FontSize"
                    Value="12" />

            <Setter Property="Foreground"
                    Value="Green" />
        </Style>

        <Style x:Key="StandardButton" TargetType="Button">
            <Setter Property="FontFamily"
                    Value="Times New Roman" />

            <Setter Property="FontSize"
                    Value="12" />
```

```
                    <Setter Property="Width"
                           Value="80" />
            </Style>
        </Application.Resources>
    </Application>
```

Templating

Up to now, you've seen how to implement styles by simply setting control properties with certain values, either directly within the element itself or via predefined `Style` objects. These techniques will normally be used the vast majority of the time and provide a good level of control over the appearance of your Silverlight application. There are some instances, however, where you will need more control than this. For example, say you want to change the actual shape of a control rather than just altering its size or color. You may decide that you would like a star-shaped `Button`, for example. Clearly this would not be possible by simply setting properties on the `Button` class.

ControlTemplate

To enable you to achieve more power over customizing a control's appearance, the `ControlTemplate` class is provided. All objects that inherit from `Control` can have their appearance defined in a `Control Template` (note that all objects that inherit from `FrameworkElement` can have a `Style` set), which is defined in XAML. This definition can then be passed to the `Control.Template` property to be implemented.

"Lookless" Controls

Crucially, this complete separation of visual appearance and behavior from actual implementation allows you to create *lookless* controls. All the functionality can be written and implemented, but the actual appearance and how it behaves visually can be effectively *skinned* and swapped out and replaced as is necessary.

Of course, in order to re-skin a control, you need to have a good idea about how the control expects to interact with its skin. More often than not, code within the control may expect all skins applied to it to have certain elements that it can manipulate. To cater to this expectation, the control developer can create a control contract, which specifies three important pieces of information:

- ❑ A definition of any public properties that can be set to change the visual appearance of the control
- ❑ A definition of all `UIElement` objects that the control expects to have in a skin
- ❑ A definition of `VisualState` objects that control the different states the control can assume in response to user actions

This "contract" of sorts is defined using the `TemplatePart` attribute in the control's code-behind file.

VisualState *Object*

Notice from the preceding list that a control can define several `VisualState` objects. But what exactly are these? A `VisualState` represents the appearance of a control when in a specific state. For example, your `Button` control might be in a "pressed" state, and as such its appearance might need to be changed to reflect this fact (e.g., to look indented).

`VisualState` objects allow you to alter the control's appearance by letting you apply a `Storyboard` to the control when it is in the specified state.

These states themselves are managed and contained within a `VisualStateManager` for each control and a collection of `VisualStateGroup` objects within it. Being able to group the different control states allows you to take into account the fact that some states can be mutually exclusive. For example, a control cannot be focused and unfocused at the same time.

More detail on these objects is given in Chapter 11, "Creating Custom Controls."

Next, you'll see how to use a `ControlTemplate` to re-skin the built-in `Button` object to become star-shaped.

Using Templates

As it turns out, creating a new `ControlTemplate` is done by following the same process as creating a predefined style: You use a `Setter` object to pass your `ControlTemplate` value to the `Template` property. The following XAML uses a `PathGeometry` object to describe a star shape and uses this as the new shape for the `Button`:

```xml
<UserControl x:Class="Chapter07.BasicTemplateExample"
    xmlns="http://schemas.microsoft.com/winfx/2006/xaml/presentation"
    xmlns:x="http://schemas.microsoft.com/winfx/2006/xaml"
    Width="400" Height="300">
    <Grid x:Name="LayoutRoot" Background="White">
        <Grid.Resources>
            <Style TargetType="Button" x:Key="StarButton">
                <Setter Property="Template">
                    <Setter.Value>
                        <ControlTemplate TargetType="Button">
                            <Grid>
                                <Path Fill="Yellow">
                                    <Path.Data>
                                        <PathGeometry>
                                            <PathFigure>
                                                <LineSegment Point="100,100" />
                                                <LineSegment Point="200, 100" />
                                                <LineSegment Point="250, 0" />
                                                <LineSegment Point="300, 100" />
                                                <LineSegment Point="400, 100" />
                                                <LineSegment Point="320, 200" />
                                                <LineSegment Point="400, 300" />
                                                <LineSegment Point="250, 270" />
                                                <LineSegment Point="100, 300" />
                                                <LineSegment Point="180, 200" />
                                                <LineSegment Point="100, 100" />
                                            </PathFigure>
                                        </PathGeometry>
                                    </Path.Data>
                                </Path>
                            </Grid>
                        </ControlTemplate>
                    </Setter.Value>
                </Setter>
            </Style>
```

```
        </Grid.Resources>

        <Button Style="{StaticResource StarButton}" Content="Click Me" />

    </Grid>
</UserControl>
```

Note how a new `Style` object is defined, and the `Setter` object is declared to act on a property named `Template`. The `ControlTemplate` instance is then passed in via the `Setter.Value` element. Figure 7-4 shows the output of this XAML.

Figure 7-4

Behold, our best attempt at a star. It might not win awards, but a star it is, nonetheless. You might notice a few problems with the current implementation of this `StarButton`. First off, the `Content` property that is set to the string "Click Me" hasn't been honored. This text has simply been ignored. Also, there are no effects when the mouse is rolled over the `Button`. Clearly, you have some more work to do.

At this point in time, the "contract" specified by the `Button` class to denote what every skin should have so it can interact with it hasn't been honored. If you look in the documentation for the `Button` class, you will see that it expects certain named elements and "`VisualStates`" (implemented as Storyboards) to exist.

In terms of elements, it expects two:

- ❑   `RootElement` — The root element of the control
- ❑   `FocusVisualElement` — The element with this name will get focus for the control.

The Button class also defines six states that it can be in:

- ❑ Normal State — the default state of the button
- ❑ MouseOver State — The state of the button when the mouse is over it
- ❑ Pressed State — The state of the button when it is pressed
- ❑ Disabled State — The state of the button when it is disabled
- ❑ Focused — The state of the button when it has focus
- ❑ Unfocused — The state of the button when it does not have focus

To implement the required elements, you simply need to name the appropriate elements within your ControlTemplate. For the StarButton example, the Grid container will be named RootElement, and a TextBlock will be added that you will use to display the string content. In addition, the different states that this button should be in need to be implemented via VisualState and Storyboard objects. These VisualState objects should be named as per the state names for the control in question (in the case of the StarButton, these should be Normal, MouseOver, Pressed, Disabled, Focused, and Unfocused).

Generic.xaml

Now, when it comes to altering a control's template, you will generally want to start with the existing definition and make changes to it, rather than starting completely from scratch. These definitions are stored within the control's assembly in a resource named *generic.xaml*. Although you can get at this if you really want to, you might as well just check out the MSDN documentation that lists template requirements for all controls and even the default template itself; you can find the documentation at http://msdn.microsoft.com/en-us/library/cc278069(VS.95).aspx. The default XAML for the Button control that shows you how to go about implementing the different states and named elements for your own template is shown in the following. Don't be frightened by the amount of XAML — work your way through it from top to bottom, and you'll see there isn't actually that much to it.

```
<Style TargetType="Button"
xmlns:vsm="clr-namespace:System.Windows;assembly=System.Windows">
    <Setter Property="IsEnabled" Value="true" />
    <Setter Property="IsTabStop" Value="true" />
    <Setter Property="Background" Value="#FF003255" />
    <Setter Property="Foreground" Value="#FF313131" />
    <Setter Property="MinWidth" Value="5" />
    <Setter Property="MinHeight" Value="5" />
    <Setter Property="Margin" Value="0" />
    <Setter Property="HorizontalContentAlignment" Value="Center" />
    <Setter Property="VerticalContentAlignment" Value="Center" />
    <Setter Property="Cursor" Value="Arrow" />
    <Setter Property="TextAlignment" Value="Left" />
    <Setter Property="TextWrapping" Value="NoWrap" />
    <!-- Cannot currently parse FontFamily type in XAML
      so it's being set in code -->
    <!-- <Setter Property="FontFamily" Value="Trebuchet MS" /> -->
    <Setter Property="FontSize" Value="11" />
    <!-- Cannot currently parse FontWeight type in XAML
      so it's being set in code -->
    <!-- <Setter Property="FontWeight" Value="Bold" /> -->
    <Setter Property="Template">
```

```xml
            <Setter.Value>
                <ControlTemplate TargetType="Button">
                    <Grid>
                        <Grid.Resources>
                            <!-- Visual constants used by the template -->
                            <Color x:Key="LinearBevelLightStartColor">#FCFFFFFF</Color>
                            <Color x:Key="LinearBevelLightEndColor">#F4FFFFFF</Color>
                            <Color x:Key="LinearBevelDarkStartColor">#E0FFFFFF</Color>
                            <Color x:Key="LinearBevelDarkEndColor">#B2FFFFFF</Color>
                            <Color
                            x:Key="MouseOverLinearBevelDarkEndColor">#7FFFFFFF</Color>
                            <Color
                            x:Key="HoverLinearBevelLightStartColor">#FCFFFFFF</Color>
                            <Color
                            x:Key="HoverLinearBevelLightEndColor">#EAFFFFFF</Color>
                            <Color
                            x:Key="HoverLinearBevelDarkStartColor">#D8FFFFFF</Color>
                            <Color
                            x:Key="HoverLinearBevelDarkEndColor">#4CFFFFFF</Color>
                            <Color x:Key="CurvedBevelFillStartColor">#B3FFFFFF</Color>
                            <Color x:Key="CurvedBevelFillEndColor">#3CFFFFFF</Color>
                            <SolidColorBrush x:Key="BorderBrush" Color="#FF000000" />
                            <SolidColorBrush x:Key="AccentBrush" Color="#FFFFFFFF" />
                            <SolidColorBrush x:Key="DisabledBrush" Color="#A5FFFFFF" />
                            <LinearGradientBrush
                    x:Key="FocusedStrokeBrush" StartPoint="0.5,0" EndPoint="0.5,1">
                                <GradientStop Color="#B2FFFFFF" Offset="0" />
                                <GradientStop Color="#51FFFFFF" Offset="1" />
                                <GradientStop Color="#66FFFFFF" Offset="0.325" />
                                <GradientStop Color="#1EFFFFFF" Offset="0.325" />
                            </LinearGradientBrush>
                        </Grid.Resources>
                        <vsm:VisualStateManager.VisualStateGroups>
                            <vsm:VisualStateGroup x:Name="CommonStates">
                                <vsm:VisualStateGroup.Transitions>
                                    <vsm:VisualTransition To="MouseOver"
                                    Duration="0:0:0.2" />
                                    <vsm:VisualTransition To="Pressed"
                                    Duration="0:0:0.1" />
                                </vsm:VisualStateGroup.Transitions>
                                <vsm:VisualState x:Name="Normal" />
                                <vsm:VisualState x:Name="MouseOver">
                                    <Storyboard>
                                        <ColorAnimation
                                        Storyboard.TargetName="LinearBevelDarkEnd"
                                        Storyboard.TargetProperty="Color"
                            To="{StaticResource MouseOverLinearBevelDarkEndColor}"
                                        Duration="0" />
                                    </Storyboard>
                                </vsm:VisualState>
                                <vsm:VisualState x:Name="Pressed">
                                    <Storyboard>
                                        <DoubleAnimation
                                        Storyboard.TargetName="LinearBevelLightEnd"
                                        Storyboard.TargetProperty="Offset" To=".2"
```

```
                                    Duration="0" />
                                <ColorAnimation
                        Storyboard.TargetName="LinearBevelLightStart"
                        Storyboard.TargetProperty="Color"
                        To="{StaticResource HoverLinearBevelLightEndColor}"
                        Duration="0" />
                                <ColorAnimation
                        Storyboard.TargetName="LinearBevelLightEnd"
                         Storyboard.TargetProperty="Color"
                        To="{StaticResource HoverLinearBevelLightEndColor}"
                         Duration="0" />
                                <ColorAnimation
                        Storyboard.TargetName="LinearBevelDarkStart"
                        Storyboard.TargetProperty="Color"
                        To="{StaticResource HoverLinearBevelDarkStartColor}"
                        Duration="0" />
                                <ColorAnimation
                        Storyboard.TargetName="LinearBevelDarkEnd"
                        Storyboard.TargetProperty="Color"
                        To="{StaticResource HoverLinearBevelDarkEndColor}"
                        Duration="0" />
                                <DoubleAnimation
                                Storyboard.TargetName="DownStroke"
                                Storyboard.TargetProperty="Opacity"
                                To="1" Duration="0" />
                        </Storyboard>
                </vsm:VisualState>
                <vsm:VisualState x:Name="Disabled">
                        <Storyboard>
                                <DoubleAnimation
                                Storyboard.TargetName="DisabledVisual"
                                Storyboard.TargetProperty="Opacity"
                                To="1" Duration="0" />
                        </Storyboard>
                </vsm:VisualState>
        </vsm:VisualStateGroup>
        <vsm:VisualStateGroup x:Name="FocusStates">
                <vsm:VisualState x:Name="Focused">
                        <Storyboard>
                                <ObjectAnimationUsingKeyFrames
                                Storyboard.TargetName="FocusVisual"
                                Storyboard.TargetProperty="Visibility"
                                Duration="0">
                                        <DiscreteObjectKeyFrame KeyTime="0">
                                                <DiscreteObjectKeyFrame.Value>
                                                        <Visibility>Visible</Visibility>
                                                </DiscreteObjectKeyFrame.Value>
                                        </DiscreteObjectKeyFrame>
                                </ObjectAnimationUsingKeyFrames>
                        </Storyboard>
                </vsm:VisualState>
                <vsm:VisualState x:Name="Unfocused">
                        <Storyboard>
                                <ObjectAnimationUsingKeyFrames
                                 Storyboard.TargetName="FocusVisual"
```

```xml
                            Storyboard.TargetProperty="Visibility"
                        Duration="0">
                            <DiscreteObjectKeyFrame KeyTime="0">
                                <DiscreteObjectKeyFrame.Value>
                                    <Visibility>Collapsed</Visibility>
                                </DiscreteObjectKeyFrame.Value>
                            </DiscreteObjectKeyFrame>
                        </ObjectAnimationUsingKeyFrames>
                    </Storyboard>
                </vsm:VisualState>
            </vsm:VisualStateGroup>
        </vsm:VisualStateManager.VisualStateGroups>

        <Rectangle x:Name="Background"
RadiusX="4" RadiusY="4" Fill="{TemplateBinding Background}" />
        <Rectangle x:Name="BackgroundGradient"
RadiusX="4" RadiusY="4" StrokeThickness="1"
Stroke="{StaticResource BorderBrush}">
            <Rectangle.Fill>
                <LinearGradientBrush StartPoint="0.7,0"
                                     EndPoint="0.7,1">
                    <GradientStop
                        x:Name="LinearBevelLightStart"
                    Color="{StaticResource LinearBevelLightStartColor}"
                    Offset="0" />
                    <GradientStop x:Name="LinearBevelLightEnd"
                    Color="{StaticResource LinearBevelLightEndColor}"
                    Offset="0.35" />
                    <GradientStop x:Name="LinearBevelDarkStart"
                    Color="{StaticResource LinearBevelDarkStartColor}"
                    Offset="0.35" />
                    <GradientStop x:Name="LinearBevelDarkEnd"
                    Color="{StaticResource LinearBevelDarkEndColor}"
                    Offset="1" />
                </LinearGradientBrush>
            </Rectangle.Fill>
        </Rectangle>
        <Grid x:Name="CurvedBevelScale" Margin="2">
            <Grid.RowDefinitions>
                <RowDefinition Height="7*" />
                <RowDefinition Height="3*" />
            </Grid.RowDefinitions>
            <Path x:Name="CurvedBevel" Stretch="Fill"
              Margin="3,0,3,0"
              Data="F1 M 0,0.02 V 0.15 C 0.15,0.22 0.30,0.25 0.50,
            0.26 C 0.70,0.26 0.85,0.22 1,0.15 V 0.02 L 0.97,0 H 0.02
            L 0,0.02 Z">
                <Path.Fill>
                    <LinearGradientBrush StartPoint="0.5,0"
                                         EndPoint="0.5,1">
                        <GradientStop x:Name="CurvedBevelFillStart"
                        Color="{StaticResource CurvedBevelFillStartColor}"
                        Offset="0" />
                        <GradientStop x:Name="CurvedBevelFillEnd"
                        Color="{StaticResource CurvedBevelFillEndColor}"
```

```
                        Offset="1" />
                </LinearGradientBrush>
            </Path.Fill>
        </Path>
    </Grid>
    <Rectangle x:Name="Accent" RadiusX="3"
               RadiusY="3" Margin="1"
        Stroke="{StaticResource AccentBrush}"
        StrokeThickness="1" />
    <Grid x:Name="FocusVisual" Visibility="Collapsed">
        <Rectangle RadiusX="3" RadiusY="3" Margin="2"
            Stroke="{StaticResource AccentBrush}"
            StrokeThickness="1" />
        <Rectangle RadiusX="3" RadiusY="3"
            Stroke="{TemplateBinding Background}"
            StrokeThickness="2" />
        <Rectangle RadiusX="3" RadiusY="3"
            Stroke="{StaticResource FocusedStrokeBrush}"
            StrokeThickness="2" />
    </Grid>
    <Grid x:Name="DownStroke" Opacity="0">
        <Rectangle Stroke="{TemplateBinding Background}"
            RadiusX="3" RadiusY="3"
            StrokeThickness="1" Opacity="0.05"
            Margin="1,2,1,1" />
        <Rectangle Stroke="{TemplateBinding Background}"
            RadiusX="3" RadiusY="3" StrokeThickness="1"
            Opacity="0.05" Margin="1,1.75,1,1" />
        <Rectangle Stroke="{TemplateBinding Background}"
            RadiusX="3" RadiusY="3"
            StrokeThickness="1" Opacity="0.05"
            Margin="1,1.5,1,1" />
        <Rectangle Stroke="{TemplateBinding Background}"
            RadiusX="3" RadiusY="3" StrokeThickness="1"
            Opacity="0.05" Margin="1,1.25,1,1" />
        <Rectangle Stroke="{TemplateBinding Background}"
            RadiusX="3" RadiusY="3" StrokeThickness="1"
            Opacity="1" Margin="1" />
        <Rectangle RadiusX="4" RadiusY="4"
            StrokeThickness="1"  Margin="1">
            <Rectangle.Stroke>
                <LinearGradientBrush EndPoint="0.5,1"
                                     StartPoint="0.5,0">
                    <GradientStop Color="#A5FFFFFF" Offset="0" />
                    <GradientStop Color="#FFFFFFFF" Offset="1" />
                </LinearGradientBrush>
            </Rectangle.Stroke>
        </Rectangle>
    </Grid>
    <ContentPresenter
      Content="{TemplateBinding Content}"
      ContentTemplate="{TemplateBinding ContentTemplate}"
      HorizontalContentAlignment=
              "{TemplateBinding HorizontalContentAlignment}"
      Padding="{TemplateBinding Padding}"
```

```
                            TextAlignment="{TemplateBinding TextAlignment}"
                            TextDecorations="{TemplateBinding TextDecorations}"
                            TextWrapping="{TemplateBinding TextWrapping}"
                            VerticalContentAlignment=
                                    "{TemplateBinding VerticalContentAlignment}"
                            Margin="4,5,4,4" />
                        <Rectangle x:Name="DisabledVisual" RadiusX="4"
                            RadiusY="4" Fill="{StaticResource DisabledBrush}" Opacity="0"
                            IsHitTestVisible="false" />
                    </Grid>
                </ControlTemplate>
            </Setter.Value>
        </Setter>
    </Style>
```

Notice that this code starts by setting a selection of default values for any button using this template, including Foreground, Background, Margin, and TextAlignment, to name just a few.

Next, within the ControlTemplate itself, you will see the selection of VisualState elements and their associated Storyboards that take care of altering the button's appearance in response to a state change. These are accompanied with a set of predefined colors for use within the different states. More information on managing the visual state of controls is provided in Chapter 11.

Finally, notice within the XAML that defines the actual button and its content a technique called TemplateBinding, which you'll examine next.

TemplateBinding

Looking at the default button template in the previous section, you can see a special syntax called TemplateBinding. This syntax can only be used within the XAML of a ControlTemplate and allows you to bind the value of an arbitrary property in your template directly to a property on the control itself. This technique is what allows you to make sure that when a developer or designer provides Content for your Button, you can propagate this value into your own representation of the Content, for example.

A simple example will demonstrate this concept. Consider again creating your own template for the Button class. Assume that you need an elliptical shape, rather than the standard rectangle. Your XAML will most probably start off looking like this:

```
<UserControl x:Class="Chapter07.TemplateBindingExample"
    xmlns="http://schemas.microsoft.com/winfx/2006/xaml/presentation"
    xmlns:x="http://schemas.microsoft.com/winfx/2006/xaml"
    Width="400" Height="300">

    <Grid x:Name="LayoutRoot" Background="White">

        <Grid.Resources>
            <Style x:Key="NewButton" TargetType="Button">
                <Setter Property="Template">
                    <Setter.Value>
                        <ControlTemplate TargetType="Button">

                            <Grid>
```

```
                                <Ellipse Width="150" Height="100" Fill="Green" />
                                <TextBlock Text="Click"
                                            HorizontalAlignment="Center"
                                            VerticalAlignment="Center" />
                    </Grid>

                </ControlTemplate>
            </Setter.Value>
        </Setter>
    </Style>
</Grid.Resources>

<Button Style="{StaticResource NewButton}" Content="The Content" />
</Grid>

</UserControl>
```

If you run this, you will see the output shown in Figure 7-5.

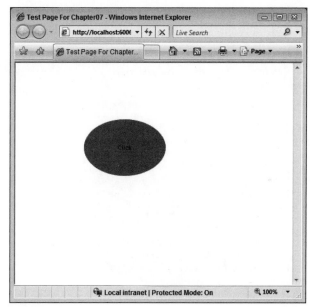

Figure 7-5

Again, the issue here is that the control is not honoring the Content value set by the user of the Button class, in this case, the string "The Content." In order to honor this setting, you need a way of binding the TextBlock in the template to the value the user has provided. This is where TemplateBinding comes in.

The following XAML shows how TemplateBinding can be used to allow the user's settings for Width, Height, and Content to be bound to properties within the custom template. Notice how the TextBlock has been replaced with a ContentPresenter control. As a Button can accept Content that may well not be string-based, this needs to be catered to in the custom template and thus the ContentPresenter can be used to fill this need.

```
<Style x:Key="NewButton" TargetType="Button">
    <Setter Property="Template">
        <Setter.Value>
            <ControlTemplate TargetType="Button">

                <Grid>
                    <Ellipse Width="{TemplateBinding Width}"
                             Height="{TemplateBinding Height}"
                             Fill="Green" />

                    <ContentPresenter Content="{TemplateBinding
Content}"
                                      HorizontalAlignment="Center"
                                      VerticalAlignment="Center" />
                </Grid>

            </ControlTemplate>
        </Setter.Value>
    </Setter>
</Style>
```

If you run this example now, you will see the screen shown in Figure 7-6.

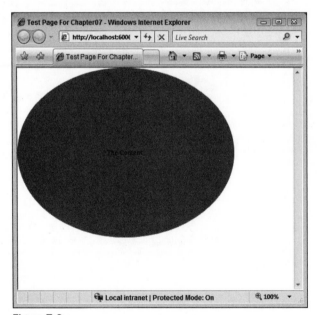

Figure 7-6

As you can see, the Height, Width, and Content values have, indeed, been honored now, thanks to the TemplateBinding functionality.

For more information on templating of controls, see Chapter 11.

Integrating with ASP.NET

You should now have a good working knowledge of styling your Silverlight application, both inline and shared, as well as customizing individual controls via `ControlTemplates`. It's more than likely that your Silverlight application is needed to augment an existing or new ASP.NET application, and because of this, it may need to either share a common "look and feel" or be altered to reflect a user's personalization settings.

Unfortunately, in terms of maintaining a common look and feel, there is no simple way of translating any of your existing CSS or ASP.NET Themes information over to Silverlight other than by hand. If you do need to make sure that textboxes in Silverlight have the same style as their ASP.NET or HTML counterparts, you're going to have to duplicate the style information over to Silverlight and most likely put it in a global location like App.xaml.

This isn't the end of the world. Although you might want to share some style information, it's unlikely that your Silverlight application will need to look exactly like your ASP.NET application (or there would be little point in using it). Providing you add the styling information to a global central location, it's easy to find and maintain.

Using the ASP.NET Profile Provider

If, as is more likely, you'd like your Silverlight application to take into account a user's ASP.NET profile information, you need not worry. Silverlight enables you to hook into ASP.NET's built-in Profile properties system to retrieve information stored on a per-user basis if required.

To do this, it's simply a matter of exposing access to the Profile Provider within your ASP.NET site via ASP.NET Application Services, which shipped as part of the .NET 3.5 release. Don't worry if you haven't exposed these services before — we'll step through the process briefly now (the Chapter 7 source code contains the completed example).

In order to expose the Profile service, you need to start by creating a WCF service to front it. Add a new text file to the web project, and name it something appropriate, finishing with the .svc extension. In this case, the name is *ProfileService.svc*, as highlighted in Figure 7-7.

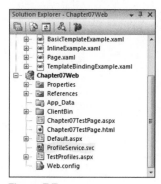

Figure 7-7

Within this .svc file, add the following code to denote the application service you want to work with:

```
<%@ ServiceHost Language="C#"
               Service="System.Web.ApplicationServices.ProfileService" %>
```

And that's it for this file. Save it and close it, and then open the Web.config file, as you're going to need to alter the configuration to actually turn this Profile service on. The config you need to include is shown in the following code:

```
<system.serviceModel>
  <services>
    <service name="System.Web.ApplicationServices.ProfileService"
             behaviorConfiguration="ProfileServiceTypeBehaviors">
      <endpoint contract="System.Web.ApplicationServices.ProfileService"
                binding="basicHttpBinding" bindingConfiguration="userHttp"
                bindingNamespace="http://asp.net/ApplicationServices/v200"/>
    </service>

  </services>
  <bindings>
    <basicHttpBinding>
      <binding name="userHttp">
        <security mode="None"/>
      </binding>
    </basicHttpBinding>
  </bindings>
  <behaviors>
    <serviceBehaviors>
      <behavior name="ProfileServiceTypeBehaviors">
        <serviceMetadata httpGetEnabled="true"/>
      </behavior>
    </serviceBehaviors>
  </behaviors>
  <serviceHostingEnvironment aspNetCompatibilityEnabled="true"/>
</system.serviceModel>

<system.web.extensions>
  <scripting>
    <webServices>
      <profileService enabled="true"
                      readAccessProperties="SampleData1"
                      writeAccessProperties="Sampledata1" />
    </webServices>
  </scripting>
</system.web.extensions>
```

This configuration code sets up a WCF endpoint within the `system.serviceModel` section and then actually switches the Profile Service on from within the `system.web.extensions` section.

That concludes the required steps for exposing the ASP.NET Profile Service and effectively switching it on. Now turn your attention back to the Silverlight project, as you need to add a service reference to it to enable you to consume the profile service. To do this, right-click on the project, and select "Add Service Reference." This will open the dialog shown in Figure 7-8.

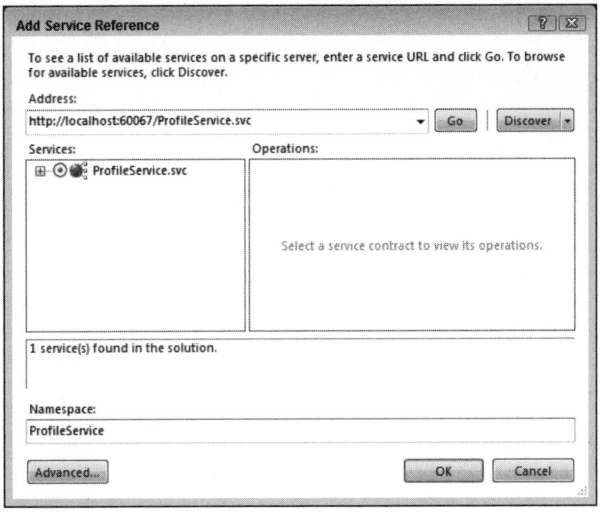

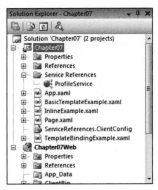

Figure 7-8

Be sure to set the Namespace parameter to something useful rather than the default *ServiceReference1*; in this example, it's been set to ProfileService. Click OK, and leave it to whir for a couple of seconds. Once it's finished, your project structure will contain a new service reference named *ProfileService*, as shown in Figure 7-9.

Figure 7-9

So, you now have a server-side WCF service configured to expose the ASP.NET Profile Service, and you have a proxy on the Silverlight client capable of communicating with it. All that remains is to utilize the proxy to retrieve the information required. In Page.xaml, you will see a very basic UI consisting of a `Grid` with two child elements, a `Button` and a `TextBlock`.

```
<UserControl x:Class="Chapter07.Page"
    xmlns="http://schemas.microsoft.com/winfx/2006/xaml/presentation"
    xmlns:x="http://schemas.microsoft.com/winfx/2006/xaml"
    Width="400" Height="300">
```

```xml
<Grid x:Name="LayoutRoot" Background="White">
    <Grid.ColumnDefinitions>
        <ColumnDefinition />
        <ColumnDefinition />
    </Grid.ColumnDefinitions>

    <Button x:Name="btnGetData"
            Content="Get Data"
            Click="btnGetData_Click"
            Grid.Column="0"/>

    <TextBlock x:Name="tbShowData"
            Text=""
            Grid.Column="1" />
</Grid>

</UserControl>
```

The button has been wired up to an event handler, within which the ProfileService proxy has been used to call the ASP.NET application service, as shown in the following code:

```csharp
using System;
using System.Collections.Generic;
using System.Linq;
using System.Net;
using System.Windows;
using System.Windows.Controls;
using System.Windows.Documents;
using System.Windows.Input;
using System.Windows.Media;
using System.Windows.Media.Animation;
using System.Windows.Shapes;

namespace Chapter07
{
    public partial class Page : UserControl
    {
        public Page()
        {
            InitializeComponent();
        }

        private string _sampleData1 = String.Empty;

        private void btnGetData_Click(object sender,
            RoutedEventArgs e)
        {
            ProfileService.ProfileServiceClient client
                = new Chapter07.ProfileService.ProfileServiceClient();

            client.GetAllPropertiesForCurrentUserAsync(false);

            client.GetAllPropertiesForCurrentUserCompleted +=
                new EventHandler<Chapter07.ProfileService.
                            GetAllPropertiesForCurrentUserCompletedEventArgs>(
```

```
                                         client_GetAllPropertiesForCurrentUserCompleted);
        }

        void client_GetAllPropertiesForCurrentUserCompleted(
            object sender,
            Chapter07.ProfileService.
                           GetAllPropertiesForCurrentUserCompletedEventArgs e)
        {
            this._sampleData1 = e.Result["SampleData1"].ToString();
        }
    }
}
```

In the `Button` event handler, you can see that a new instance of the `ProfileServiceClient` is instantiated and then the `GetAllPropertiesForCurrentUserAsync` method is called, passing in the value `false`. This method returns all the property values stored for the current user, and the `false` parameter allows unauthenticated users to access their properties also.

Next up, the `GetAllPropertiesForCurrentUserCompleted` event is wired up, which will fire when, you've guessed it, the properties for the current user have been retrieved and stored in memory.

Within this handler, you can see that it's extremely simple to interrogate the `GetAllPropertiesFor` `CurrentUserCompletedEventArgs` variable to retrieve the property value you want. Note, in order to actually extract a value, you need to have put one in there first either in ASP.NET or by using the `SetPropertiesForCurrentUserAsync` method on the `ProfileServiceClient` class.

Pretty cool, you'll agree, and if you look back through the steps involved in doing this, both from an ASP.NET and Silverlight perspective, there really isn't much to it.

ImplicitStyleManager

While the default technique of defining and applying styles that you've seen so far works, it certainly can be a pain to add `Style="{StaticResource YourStyleKey}"` to all of the controls needing to pick up a specific style in an application. WPF provides a way to "implicitly" apply styles to controls, but unfortunately this functionality isn't available in Silverlight 2. Enter `ImplicitStyleManager` provided by the Silverlight Toolkit (freely available for download from www.silverlight.net). By using `ImplicitStyleManager`, you can apply styles that target a specific control type without manually adding a `Style` attribute to each control. The class is in the `Microsoft.Windows.Controls.Theming` namespace (`Microsoft.Windows.Controls` assembly). You reference the namespace in the XAML file as shown here:

```
<UserControl x:Class="…"
    xmlns="http://schemas.microsoft.com/winfx/2006/xaml/presentation"
    xmlns:x="http://schemas.microsoft.com/winfx/2006/xaml"
    xmlns:controls=
"clr-namespace:Microsoft.Windows.Controls;
assembly=Microsoft.Windows.Controls"
xmlns:theming="clr-namespace:Microsoft.Windows.Controls.Theming;
assembly=Microsoft.Windows.Controls.Theming"
>
```

Following is an example of using `ImplicitStyleManager` within a control that has styles defined locally within its `Resources` section:

```
<StackPanel>
    <Border BorderBrush="Green" BorderThickness="2" Padding="5"
Margin="5" theming:ImplicitStyleManager.ApplyMode="OneTime">
        <Border.Resources>
            <Style TargetType="Button">
                <Setter Property="Foreground" Value="Green" />
            </Style>
            <Style TargetType="TextBox">
                <Setter Property="FontSize" Value="10.5"/>
                <Setter Property="FontFamily" Value="Trebuchet MS"/>
                <Setter Property="Foreground" Value="#FF00FF00" />
            </Style>
        </Border.Resources>
        <StackPanel>
            <Button Content="Button inside border" />
            <TextBox Text="TextBox inside border"></TextBox>
        </StackPanel>
    </Border>
    <Button Content="Button outside border" />
</StackPanel>
```

This example automatically applies the styles to the appropriate controls (a `Button` and a `TextBox`, in this case). The `theming:ImplicitStyleManager.ApplyMode` attribute makes this possible. Looking at the control definitions in the `StackPanel`, you can see that no `Style` attribute is added. Instead, the styles are "implicitly" applied based on the `Style` element's `TargetType`. Also, it is not necessary to define `x:Key` on the `Style` elements.

`ImplicitStyleManager` can also be used to apply styles defined in a theme file (a XAML file containing a ResourceDictionary section):

```
<Border
    BorderBrush="Green"
    BorderThickness="2"
    Padding="5"
    Margin="5"
    theming:ImplicitStyleManager.ApplyMode="OneTime"
    theming:ImplicitStyleManager.ResourceDictionaryUri="Theming/CustomTheme.xaml">
    <StackPanel>
        <Button Foreground="White" Content="This is a button" Width="200" />
        <CheckBox></CheckBox>
        <TextBox Text="Are you hungry?" />
        <ListBox Height="40">
            <ListBoxItem Content="This is an item" />
            <ListBoxItem Content="This is an item" />
            <ListBoxItem Content="This is an item" />
            <ListBoxItem Content="This is an item" />
```

```
                    <ListBoxItem Content="This is an item" />
                    <ListBoxItem Content="This is an item" />
                    <ListBoxItem Content="This is an item" />
                    <ListBoxItem Content="This is an item" />
                </ListBox>
            </StackPanel>
        </Border>
```

A portion of the CustomTheme.xaml file referenced by the preceding code is shown next:

```
<ResourceDictionary
    xmlns="http://schemas.microsoft.com/winfx/2006/xaml/presentation"
    xmlns:x="http://schemas.microsoft.com/winfx/2006/xaml"
    xmlns:vsm="clr-namespace:System.Windows;assembly=System.Windows"
    xmlns:d="http://schemas.microsoft.com/expression/blend/2008"
    xmlns:mc="http://schemas.openxmlformats.org/markup-compatibility/2006"
    mc:Ignorable="d">

    <Style TargetType="Button">
        <Setter Property="IsEnabled" Value="true"/>
        <Setter Property="IsTabStop" Value="true"/>
        <Setter Property="Background" Value="#FF003255"/>
        <Setter Property="Foreground" Value="#FF313131"/>
        <Setter Property="MinWidth" Value="5"/>
        <Setter Property="MinHeight" Value="5"/>
        <Setter Property="Margin" Value="0"/>
        <Setter Property="HorizontalContentAlignment" Value="Center"/>
        <Setter Property="VerticalContentAlignment" Value="Center"/>
        <Setter Property="Cursor" Value="Arrow"/>
        <Setter Property="FontSize" Value="11"/>
        <Setter Property="Template">
            <Setter.Value>
                <ControlTemplate TargetType="Button">
                    <!-- Template Code -->
                </ControlTemplate>
            </Setter.Value>
        </Setter>
    </Style>


    <!-- Additional Control Styles ->

</ResourceDictionary>
```

You can see that by using the ImplicitStyleManager, you can more easily create different themes that can be applied to controls without having to explicitly declare a Style attribute on each control. This allows for much greater flexibility than is available out-of-the-box in Silverlight 2.

More Silverlight Toolkit controls are discussed in Chapter 6.

Summary

In this chapter, you learned how to change the look and feel of controls in Silverlight. First off, you saw how individual controls could be restyled inline, setting style-related properties directly within the element declaration itself. While this provided a quick and convenient mechanism for adding style information to elements, you saw that in the long run this mechanism causes maintenance issues, because style information is duplicated across different pages and so changes are hard to propagate and common guidance is difficult to enforce.

You then looked at a solution to the problems of extracting style information from individual elements and encapsulating it into `Style` objects. You saw how these `Style` objects allowed you to create named, predefined styles for assigning against the elements that make up your user interface. These objects could then be scoped to the page or container level to improve maintainability locally, or in the Application.Resources section of your App.xaml to provide common styles across an entire application.

Even when using `Style` objects to enforce consistency of design and improve maintainability, you saw that individual elements could be set to override set styles or portions of styles if required.

You then looked at a more advanced styling technique within Silverlight — completely re-skinning a built-in or custom control by replacing its `ControlTemplate`. You saw how this enabled controls to maintain their functionality while having their visual behavior and appearance swapped out as required. All the built-in controls that ship with Silverlight maintain their default appearance in a generic.xaml file that is embedded as a resource in the containing assembly. You learned that although it's possible to get at this, the full specification and listings are available online in the MSDN documentation.

The propagation of user-provided values through to your template elements was covered next, and you saw how to bind the two together using the `TemplateBinding` syntax. In this section, you also took a look at the `ContentPresenter` to bind to values provided for `Content` other than simple strings.

Finally, you saw how it's possible to hook into the ASP.NET Profile Provider via ASP.NET Application Services to make your Silverlight application aware of user settings, in effect personalized for each user of your site. You saw how the process of doing this involved two main steps — exposing the ASP.NET Profile Service and consuming it from within Silverlight — both of which were fairly simple and didn't involve large amounts of code.

In the next chapter, you'll examine the different ways in which your Silverlight application can accept input from the user, and you'll learn about the rich object model supporting this. You'll also look at how you can implement navigation into your application.

8

User Interaction

There is no real point in having an amazing technology like Silverlight if you are not able to interact with it. For this fundamental reason, in this chapter you explore how you can exploit the flexible programming model that Silverlight offers in this area. In order to understand how you can approach the model, you explore the interaction context with the different approaches that you can take in order to interact with the plug-in.

This chapter is divided into two main sections that contribute to the user interaction, bringing a richer user experience into the Silverlight applications. The first section covers the interaction context and describes how you can handle events triggered by the user using different inputs, understanding the functional chain that can take you deeper into the object model available. This understanding will allow you to explore the further functionality that is common in the ASP.NET world, as well as new features that can extend the application behavior. With those basics, you explore the different input devices to understand how they internally work and the special considerations. If you are an experienced ASP.NET developer, you can jump directly into the section, "Getting the Most from Input Devices," where you see how you can get the most from the Ink feature and how to simulate common functionality like drag-and-drop.

In the second section, you explore Silverlight's ability to navigate between user controls, using screen libraries locally as well as remotely, using the current web application as well as using WCF services. The section explains the advantages and the limitations that every ASP.NET developer should know when it comes to designing applications that interact with the plug-in.

The Silverlight Interaction Context

As you are now developing in the Silverlight world, you need to understand the differences and similarities that the model offers. During the previous chapters, you have learned about the architecture and controls that are published from the plug-in. Now you are going to use that knowledge in order to explore the interaction between the application and the ASP.NET world. Silverlight applications run in a sandbox environment, but this does not prevent you from interacting with the external world using familiar ASP.NET techniques. As you have seen before, the object model will publish properties and events that you will be able to interact with using managed code or interpreted unmanaged languages like JavaScript, opening an interesting window when you consider migrating traditional ASP.NET applications into Silverlight. As you will discover, there is not a drastic shift in the programming model from what you are used to. You can see the rich interaction in Figure 8-1.

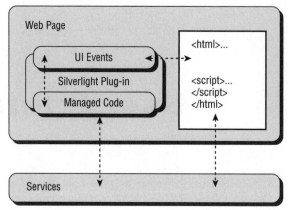

Figure 8-1

The events interaction can be divided into two categories: input events and non-input events. Input events, which are the main focus of this chapter, are primarily handled by the browser and then diverted to the Silverlight application. The second type of events is those raised by the objects instead of the browser. These are commonly used to notify changes in the state. This is a quite common pattern in the .NET programming world.

During this exploration, you are going to find some special behaviors (particularly if you have some WPF experience), like the lack of double-click events, but the idea is to explore the reasons and the work-arounds that will help you deal with these differences.

Working with `UIElements` Events

A Silverlight-based application uses a declarative programming model in which you can define how the user control will behave. If you define the class that is behind the XAML code, you will have a compiled object that includes the managed code behind. But this is not the only story. As you have seen in Silverlight 1.0, you can have XAML code that is not compiled wherein all the functionality relies on the unmanaged code that the ASP.NET application contains. Later in this chapter, you will explore how the users can use interpreted languages like JavaScript.

Handling User Interaction

In order to work with events, you need to use event handlers, which actually will be called when the event is fired. If you have been working with managed code or writing scripts for your web sites, you should be familiar with this concept. The Silverlight model always exposes at least two parameters, the sender and the e parameters. The first parameter provides you with a reference to the object that has raised the event; the second one varies depending on the type of event, but usually provides you with extra information about it (e.g., the X/Y position of a mouse move event). If you are consuming these parameters using managed code, the compiler will check if these exist as it uses a delegate behind the scenes, but this will not be the case in unmanaged code because it is inherently looser.

A *routed event* is a special type of event that can invoke multiple handlers on different listeners. In other words, when your control raises an event, this can "bubble" upward through the element tree (e.g., a button raises the Click event and then is also raised by its parent control), or it can be "tunneled" downward through the element tree, also known as *preview* (i.e., when you click a button, the event is first raised at the container and then is raised by the button). Silverlight supports bubbling routed events but only for a small subset of events, and does not support tunneling events. The other important difference is the use of the Handled parameter. In WPF, you can stop the routing by altering this parameter. This behavior is ignored in Silverlight, but it is recommended that you change the value once an object has handled the event, not only so that developers working on parent elements can query the status of it as an informative parameter but for possible future versions of Silverlight that may introduce this behavior.

In this chapter, you are going to use these events in order to trap the user interaction. Just to review the concepts, you can add a new event handler using XAML if you are linking the control with the x:Class entry in order to include the code behind:

```
<UserControl x:Class="Chapter8.MyControl" ......
<Button x:Name="cmdAccept" Click="Accept_Click"/>
```

In this case, the button named "cmdAccept" will route the Click event to the method published in the code behind, as follows:

```
private void Accept_Click(object sender, RoutedEventArgs e){}
```

If necessary, you can also add the handler using managed code with the same handling model that .NET developers are used to:

```
cmdAccept.Click += cmdAccept_Click;
```

Remember that if you multiply subscribe handlers into events, all of them will be fired, so make sure that you don't add handlers to methods that can be executed multiple times. If you do need to do so, remember to unsubscribe the handler using the operator -=.

So now that you know how to write handlers, it is time to interact with the Silverlight objects. If you are using managed code, you will be familiar with the interaction. You can write code behind that actually fires remote communication, starts background processes, or alters the current objects. You will be delighted to know that this is executing at the client side (unless you are accessing remote services), which will enhance performance. This is one of the areas where you need to shift your mindset when you interact with your plug-in, which is executed locally. In the ASP.NET world, you interact similarly with the objects; the difference is that the code is executed on the server side and then rendered to the client.

Consuming Properties

Now that you understand how the event handlers can be constructed in Silverlight, it is time to start making some noise and see how you can interact with the object properties from managed code. The example that you are going to explore is a simple terms and conditions acceptance, wherein checking the checkbox will enable the Continue button.

Create a quick Silverlight project. Focusing on the main user control, add a checkbox and a button into the grid. Take this opportunity to explore your design abilities working with the power of WPF. After years of working with HTML and ASP.NET controls, you will find the experience quite appealing. You can use tools like Expression Blend 2 to extend the out-of-the-box functionality that comes with Visual Studio 2008. An example of a simple design is shown in Figure 8-2.

Figure 8-2

The first attempt will be the simple one: You are going to use the code behind in order to interact with the traditional properties in the same way that you are used to in the ASP.NET world. The first thing that you need is to reference the handler in the XAML object:

```
<UserControl x:Class="Chapter8.MyControl" …. >

<CheckBox Height="26"
          Margin="25,0,185,14"
          VerticalAlignment="Bottom"
          Content="Accept Terms and Conditions"
          x:Name="chkTerms"
          Checked="ConfirmTerms"/>
```

As this component compiles, the `x:Class` entry is included. (Note that the rest of the properties are omitted for simplicity.) In the code behind, you can add the event handler as previously explained:

```
private void ConfirmTerms(object sender, RoutedEventArgs e)
{
        btnAccept.IsEnabled = true;
}
```

If you are interacting with the properties using a background thread, you will need to interact with the properties using the `Dispatcher` object (explained in Chapter 4) as you cannot change user interface properties from the non-user interface thread. In order to reproduce the example, you should use:

```
this.Dispatcher.BeginInvoke(
    delegate { btnAccept.IsEnabled = true; }
    );
```

You can find this example and the rest of the demos in the code samples for Chapter 8 at www.wrox.com.

Working with Dependency Properties

You can also interact with dependency properties in the same way that you interact with standard properties and attached properties. The advantage of using dependency properties to extend the functionality has been welcomed by the community, as they provide a lightweight model to dynamically extend and interact with XAML objects. This is a new concept introduced by WPF that may look strange at first to the traditional ASP.NET developer; if you don't remember how to use these properties, you can refer to Chapter 10. You can explore how you can transform this simple example and interact with a dependency property.

```
public static readonly DependencyProperty TermsAcceptedProperty =
    DependencyProperty.Register(
    "TermsAccepted", typeof(Boolean),
    typeof(MyControl),
    new PropertyMetadata(new PropertyChangedCallback(Notification))
  );

public bool TermsAccepted
{
        get { return (bool)GetValue(TermsAcceptedProperty); }
        set { SetValue(TermsAcceptedProperty, value);}
}

private void ConfirmTerms(object sender, RoutedEventArgs e)
{
        TermsAccepted = true;
}
```

The example is now changed, and you are interacting with one of the registered dependency properties. Now changing the property will allow you to notify the change to those objects that are bound to the property in a single operation. You can use the methods `GetValue()` and `SetValue()` to alter them as presented in previous chapters. We have also included in the example a notification call-back to execute a special method when the value changes (extending the magic of dependency properties). As you can see, this is an elegant solution that can de-couple the XAML code from the code behind, as you don't refer the objects directly. This model is emphasized throughout the book to help you transition from a strongly coupled model in ASP.NET into the power of Silverlight and the WPF engine.

Interacting with Properties from Scripts

Just as you have explored how easy it is to use the current ASP.NET knowledge in managed code, it is equally important to understand how to interact with objects with programming languages like JavaScript.

Following the previous example, you are going to modify the code to change the `Button` property using JavaScript. The first thing you need to do is publish an object that you want to share between the managed world and the unmanaged one. At first, this may look like a lot of work, but you will quickly realize the potential of it, as it allows you to control and properly define what is callable from HTML. In this scenario, you want to expose only the `IsEnabled` property. Start defining the object that you want to share:

```
public class HtmlBridge
{
```

```
            private Button source;

            public HtmlBridge(Button source)
            {
                    this.source = source;
            }

             [ScriptableMember()]
            public bool IsEnabled
            {
                    set { this.source.IsEnabled = value; }
            }
    }
```

In the code you can appreciate that you are defining a new class called `HtmlBridge` that accepts a
`Button` as parameter (this will be the object to expose). Then you can expose properties and methods
to the unmanaged world using the attribute `[ScriptableMember]`. Now you are ready to link this
new object with your main application.

*It is a pity that common controls like the `Button` control are not decorated with the scriptable attribute
by default, as that would save you from writing the bridging class in certain scenarios.*

```
 public partial class Page : UserControl
{
        public Page()
        {
                InitializeComponent();

                HtmlPage.RegisterScriptableObject("MyApp",
                                        new HtmlBridge(cmdButton));
        }
}
```

The code is registering a new `HtmlBridge` object under the `"MyApp"` key using your button as the source.
This code is now exposing the object to your HTML page. Now that your application is ready to share,
let's see how you consume this interface in your ASP.NET page:

```
<script type="text/javascript">

        var SLCtrl = null;

        function OnLoaded(sender)
        {
                SLCtrl = sender.get_element();
        }

        function OnClick()
        {
                SLCtrl.Content.MyApp.IsEnabled = false;
        }
</script>
```

You are adding two methods. The first one will be executed when the Silverlight plug-in is initialized to obtain the reference to the application. The second one will be executed by the standard ASP.NET button using JavaScript. You can see how the OnClick() method is accessing the scriptable dictionary and executing the property set.

Now you need to add the proper objects that will run these two methods. The first one will be called from your Silverlight plug-in during the OnPluginLoaded event:

```
<asp:ScriptManager ID="ScriptManager1" runat="server"></asp:ScriptManager>

<div  style="height:100%;">
      <asp:Silverlight  ID="Xaml1"
                        runat="server"
                        OnPluginLoaded=" OnLoaded"
                        Source="~/ClientBin/Sl2.xap"
                        Width="100%" Height="100%" />
</div>
```

Now you can add a standard JavaScript call from an HTML button or ASP.NET button depending on your preference:

```
<button id="cmdASPButton" runat="server" onclick="return OnClick()" />
```

You can also use the FindName method to search the Silverlight tree for the specific control name. You can use this technique in order to interact with the plug-in. Note that in this case, JavaScript is not case-sensitive, but XAML objects are, so it is a recommended good practice to stick to the Pascal casing in order to avoid problems in the future.

The AJAX Story in the User Interaction World

This is an interesting area, as you are constantly trying to optimize the performance and the responsiveness of the ASP.NET applications. During the last few years, different technologies came into the environment in order to help with streaming the Web content. As you are aware, the AJAX story is still hot and will continue to serve the Web community as a way of improving the user experience. While Microsoft is investing in the Silverlight stream, it is also constantly working on the ASP.NET side. A great example of this is the AJAX support for ASP.NET. This technology allows you to post back requests that perform partial rendering on the client side, improving the user experience and optimizing the web site performance. Microsoft has released a set of new user controls that require zero code to implement AJAX, making ASP.NET developers' work 10 times less tedious. Silverlight introduces new options to optimize the communication between the server and the client that leaves ASP.NET developers with the dilemma of which direction to go. Migration and integration can be challenging when you start working with Silverlight.

The good news is that Silverlight integrates with the Microsoft AJAX library using the JavaScript model that was presented earlier, therefore reusing the existing infrastructure that your ASP.NET project has, which is a big advantage. Now, if you have a green field scenario, you should start looking into the WCF extensibility that Silverlight supports, as this can use JSON to interact with your AJAX endpoints and other protocols that allow you call other services beyond the server of origin.

Figure 8-3 shows how a XAML button can call your existing methods in order to retrieve information from the server, a very powerful feature that will help with integrating Silverlight components with your current web sites.

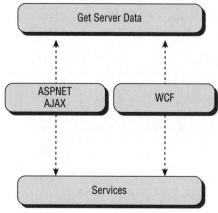

Figure 8-3

Interacting with Input Devices

After the overview regarding how Silverlight uses the event model to address the user interaction and the analogies with ASP.NET, you are now ready to explore the different input devices and how to interact with them.

The Silverlight team has been working hard in order to expand the different interactive scenarios. You need to shift from the traditional point-and-click methodology that you are used to in the ASP.NET world and plan applications for the future. Recent presentations on the Microsoft Surface technologies and Windows 7 user experience are showing that multi-point devices are here to stay. The hardware is also advancing in this area. For the last seven years, manufacturers have been delivering tablet PCs with touch-screen surfaces. What is more, technologies in the gaming industry are contributing with new interaction ideas like motion detectors, which can be applied not only to the entertainment industry, but also to help people with disabilities interact with the devices. But don't get overly excited about the future. Not all of these features are included in the current version of Silverlight, but it *is* designed with these concepts in mind. This will be another shift from the ASP.NET world that will bring new functionality to empower new, brilliant ideas.

The Mouse

In the Silverlight world, the mouse has a more important role than in the ASP.NET world, as it is not merely a simple device that only performs point-and-click operations in order to fire events. You can have a richer interaction with the mouse using the different events that UIElements publishes and the Silverlight functionality that captures the mouse. It has always been a challenge to interact with the mouse beyond the common patterns because of the internals of how Windows handles messages. In the Silverlight world, there is no magic in handling mouse events, but it does provide functionality that makes the capturing a pleasant experience.

Mouse Events

Let's analyze the different events that you can capture using the mouse:

❑ `MouseLeftButtonDown` — This event is fired when the left button of the mouse is held down. It will be fired only once when the action has been triggered.

❑ `MouseLeftButtonUp` — This event is fired when the left button of the mouse is released. The actions of these events can be related to the actions from the `MouseLeftButtonDown`, as they happen one after another.

❑ `MouseMove` — This event is fired when the mouse moves around the control boundaries. Every time that the position changes, it will be fired. It is important to understand that this event is not related to the previous two events (`MouseLeftButtonDown` and `MouseLeftButtonUp`) but is related to the next two events (`MouseEnter` and `MouseLeave`). Why is this important? Because it is a common place for performance-related bugs to occur when developers try to put intensive work into this handler, believing that this event will be fired only when they keep the mouse button pressed (drag mode).

❑ `MouseEnter` — This event is fired when the mouse enters the control boundaries area. This event is fired every time the mouse pointer enters the area and will not be executed again until after a `MouseLeave` event is raised.

❑ `MouseLeave` — This event is fired when the mouse leaves the control boundaries area.

The event handler argument not only includes the sender but also the mouse-specific arguments `MouseEventArgs` and the derived `MouseButtonEventArgs` that will allow you to query the position of the mouse and retrieve stylus information (more on this later in this chapter).

> When you see the `MouseLeftButtonUp` and `MouseLeftButtonDown` arguments, you might wonder what happened to the right-click arguments. Well, there are two different considerations regarding this. The first one takes into account the difficulties of capturing the right-click event when the plug-in is hosted in the browser (as the browser will handle the event before the Silverlight application). The other consideration is regarding cross-device compatibility, as this may run in nonstandard devices in the near future.

Now look at an example applying the concepts reviewed in the previous section, combining them to interact with the XAML objects:

```
<Grid    x:Name="MyGrid"
         Background="White"
         MouseLeftButtonDown="ParentAction"
         MouseEnter="ShowCircle"
         MouseLeave="HideCircle" >

<Ellipse Height="32.889"
         HorizontalAlignment="Stretch"
         Margin="83,53,86,51"
         VerticalAlignment="Stretch"
         Fill="#FF49D131"
         Stroke="#FF000000"
```

```
            x:Name="MyCircle"
            MouseLeftButtonDown="ColorBlue"
            MouseLeftButtonUp="ColorGreen"
            Visibility="Collapsed"/>
</Grid>
```

As you can see in the code, you can mix and match the events within the objects. In this case, the `MouseLeftButtonDown` is handled twice; this will respect the event bubbling and allow you to take action if the children objects have not handled the event. This can be very useful in scenarios wherein you need to protect the application. Be aware that `MouseEnter` and `MouseLeave` will not follow this pattern (routed events) and can only be handled by the control used. The code to control `MyCircle` is the following one:

```csharp
private void ShowCircle(object sender, MouseEventArgs e)
{
        MyCircle.Visibility = Visibility.Visible;
}

private void HideCircle(object sender, MouseEventArgs e)
{
        MyCircle.Visibility = Visibility.Collapsed;
}

private void ColorBlue(object sender, MouseButtonEventArgs e)
{
        MyCircle.Fill = new SolidColorBrush(
                Color.FromArgb(0xFF, 0x00, 0x00, 0xFF));
        e.Handled = true; // Best practice
}

private void ColorGreen(object sender, MouseButtonEventArgs e)
{
        MyCircle.Fill = new SolidColorBrush(
                Color.FromArgb(0xFF, 0x00, 0xFF, 0x00));
        e.Handled = true; // Best practice
}

private void ParentAction(object sender, MouseButtonEventArgs e)
{
        if (!e.Handled) { /* Special action */ }
}
```

Triggering Storyboards

The elegance of the model allows you to access the resources that you may have in the user control in the same way as if you were coding the standard handles. This means that you can create a richer interaction (e.g., such as when the mouse hovers over the objects). The following sample shows a small picture browser where you can highlight the picture that you want to use with your storyboard (see Figure 8-4):

```xml
<UserControl.Resources>
  <Storyboard x:Name="ShowPicture">
```

```
              <DoubleAnimationUsingKeyFrames
              x:Name="MovePicture"
              Storyboard.TargetName="Image2"
            Storyboard.TargetProperty="(UIElement.RenderTransform)"
              BeginTime="00:00:00">
                  <SplineDoubleKeyFrame KeyTime="00:00:00" Value="0"/>
                  <SplineDoubleKeyFrame KeyTime="00:00:01" Value="-68.334"/>
              </DoubleAnimationUsingKeyFrames>
              <.. extra animation details ..>
        </Storyboard>
      </UserControl.Resources>
```

My Photo Picker

Figure 8-4

Some details about the animation have been omitted for simplicity. If you want to explore more, please refer to the Chapter 14. The interesting model that you can apply here when you move the mouse over the picture is to trigger the animation and change the target on the handler as follows:

```
private void Image_MouseEnter(object sender, MouseEventArgs e)
{
        // We stop it if the storyboard is running
        ShowPicture.Stop();

        // We set the new target on the animation
        MovePicture.SetValue(Storyboard.TargetNameProperty,
                                          ((Image)sender).Name);

        // We restart the storyboard
        ShowPicture.Begin();
}
```

As you can see, you are putting all the concepts together regarding how to get the most from the mouse. It really expands the boundaries of the previous experience in ASP.NET with the rich features of WPF. Now let's explore some details of mouse handling.

Getting Relative Positions

If you have been playing with the arguments in the handling method, you probably have been using GetPosition. This method will return the mouse pointer in a Point structure; this contains the X and Y positions that you can use in the event. Note that this call is not asynchronous, which means that if the mouse continues moving, the values will remain the same during the execution of the method. It works like a snapshot of the position when the event was fired.

The position received will be calculated based on what the object passes as a parameter to the method. If you use a null object, the values will be related to the plug-in. If you want to change this behavior, you need to pass the relative object, and the Point structure will be calculated accordingly. You can change the previous example to retrieve the position and maybe alter the animation with that data:

```
Point CurrentPosition = e.GetPosition((Image)sender);
```

> It is tempting to read the last position of the mouse when you leave an object, but the MouseLeave event will not include the position information when you handle this event. Therefore, don't be surprised if the position is null.

Capturing the Mouse

An interesting feature is the ability to capture the mouse beyond the control boundaries. This is a really helpful feature that will allow you to extend the functionality of the MouseMove event. The idea behind it is to retain the event chain from the mouse in the control when the left button is still pressed, only stopping when the user releases the button. This has many implications that you will explore later in this chapter when you see how to get the most out of these devices. In order to capture the mouse, you need to invoke CaptureMouse() as follows:

```
private void Canvas_MouseLeftButtonDown(object sender, MouseButtonEventArgs e)
{
        MyCanvas.CaptureMouse();
}
```

Now that you have the mouse's attention, you can use the MouseMove handler to process the position of the mouse, allowing you, for example, to create a Path that can be used during the dragging until the button is released. If the user releases the button, the mouse capturing will be automatically re-set, but it is considered good practice to call the release method in your code.

```
private void Canvas_MouseLeftButtonUp(object sender, MouseButtonEventArgs e)
{
        MyCanvas.ReleaseMouseCapture();
}
```

Any UIElement object is able to capture and release the mouse. Note that while the mouse is captured, no other element will receive the MouseMove event; this is a common place for bugs to occur.

Using the Mouse Wheel

There is no support for the mouse wheel in Silverlight 2, as you have seen in the events list. This is based on the compatibility model that the plug-in tries to fit. But as using the wheel is a very cool feature when you are zooming pictures, there are many different web sites that explain how to do it and even provide helper classes that support it.

The trick is intercepting the events at the browser level, as the browser supports it. The following example shows how to capture the mouse wheel consuming the event. First, for this example, you transform the rendering of a textbox using the `ScaleTransform` object. The XAML code looks like this:

```
<TextBlock
        HorizontalAlignment="Center"
        VerticalAlignment="Center"
        FontFamily="Verdana"
        FontSize="20"
        Foreground="DarkBlue"
        Text="Use the wheel now!">
        <TextBlock.RenderTransform>
                <ScaleTransform x:Name="MyZoom"/>
        </TextBlock.RenderTransform>
</TextBlock>
```

Now that you have the XAML support, you need to add the event handler. For this, you can use the `HtmlPage` class exposed by the namespace `System.Windows.Browser`. The event will be handled by the custom method that captures the information from the browser regarding the mouse wheel movement.

```
using System.Windows.Browser;
using System.Windows.Controls;
using System;

namespace Chapter8
{
 public partial class Zoom : UserControl
 {
        public Zoom()
        {
                InitializeComponent();
                HtmlPage.Document.AttachEvent("onmousewheel", ChangeZoomLevel);
        }


        private void ChangeZoomLevel(Object sender, HtmlEventArgs args)
        {
                ScriptObject EventData = args.EventObject;

                if (EventData.GetProperty("wheelDelta") != null)
                {
                        double Offset =
                        Convert.ToDouble(EventData.GetProperty("wheelDelta"));

                        MyZoom.ScaleX += (Offset > 0 ? 0.1 : -0.1);
                        MyZoom.ScaleY += (Offset > 0 ? 0.1 : -0.1);
                }
        }
 }
}
```

You need to get the `ScriptObject` in order to retrieve the event information for the wheel movement. This is represented as an offset from the previous position. With this information, you can now alter the scale of the object directly.

> Note that this example has been tested using IE 7. If you are targeting different browsers, you may consider checking the event and property naming specifically for those browsers.

Other Platform Considerations

One thing that the Microsoft team noticed while testing the mouse-handling properties of Silverlight is that during the Safari test, if an unhandled exception is detected in the event handler code, no further events are received at the plug-in. Microsoft is working with other third parties to try to standardize the behavior.

Remember that Silverlight is just a plug-in hosted by a browser, so the application really relies on how the browser interacts with the events. Solid advice is to test your application on different browsers and platforms in order to understand the different behaviors.

The Stylus and Touch Screens

Silverlight 2 supports a new concept in the ASP.NET world, which is the interaction with the stylus/pen and touch screen commonly found in Tablet PCs. The interaction with them is very similar to the mouse interaction, but there are new elements that play an important role in the interaction. If you explore the event arguments, you will find the property `StylusDevice` that will provide information about the points captured by the stylus and the `Inverted` property.

❑   **Inverted** — This is an interesting option. When the user is interacting with a stylus, you can detect if it is inverted and is behaving as an eraser. Note that if you use inputs that cannot be inverted, like a mouse, the value will be always `false`.

These types of inputs are very common in the Ink scenario that you explore later in this chapter, but in the meantime, let's take a look at the output of these devices. If you continue exploring the arguments, you will find `GetStylusPoints(UIElement element)`. This method returns a cloned collection of stylus point locations relative to the reference element passed as an argument. This collection contains all the points since the last mouse event, but if you are using a mouse as an input device, this collection will contain a single point. The content stored in the collection is a number called `StylusPoint`, a dependency property that will return the X and Y positions based on the relative object (as discussed in "The Mouse" section). The stylus point information will be very useful when discussing strokes. In the meantime, is important to understand the significance of the basic objects and how they are filled.

> In Silverlight 1, there was no support for high DPI inputs when using high-resolution monitors. Silverlight 2 takes into consideration the resolution when returning the point values.

The Keyboard

The keyboard is another common input device in the ASP.NET world. There is no big difference in using the keyboard with Silverlight as you deal with the browser. Therefore, you will have some limitations regarding what you can capture as the messages flow depending on the focused object.

Keyboard Events

You have a couple of basic events available in the keyboard world:

❑ `KeyDown` — This event is fired when you press a key in your keyboard while there is focus on the object (sender).

❑ `KeyUp` — This event is fired when the key is released. It should always come after a `KeyDown` event. Again, this is only applicable to focused objects.

As these events need the focus of the object, it is important to highlight that you may have focus on the Silverlight plug-in as well as the individual object, as both of them are considered focused when you work with a `UIElement`.

The event handlers now receive the `KeyEventArgs` object, which exposes specific information about the key (or keys) involved in the event. The first property to explore is the `Key` property. It will return the key in the form of an enumerator. In a globalized world that has different keyboards, it becomes a problem when you try to read the key using the enumerator. For this reason, only portable codes are listed in this enumerator — if the code is not portable, it will return `Unknown`. The same story applies to `PlatformKeyCode`, where only the code is returned.

```
private void KeyPressed_Prank(object sender, KeyEventArgs e)
{
    if (e.Key == Key.Tab)
        ((UIElement)sender).Focus(); // Trust me, this will annoy a user
}
```

Interacting with **TextBox**

There are some controls like `TextBox` that already handle the keyboard input. You can still register an event handler in these controls, and it will be executed. What is internally happening is that the new handler is subscribing to the event handling collection. Note that this will happen in the ASP.NET world, and there is no guarantee regarding the execution order, so do not rely on a particular execution order.

Figure 8-5 shows an example using a `TextBox` and a watermark style *TextBox*, where you can add your own handlers in order to copy the information from one place to another and perform changes to the output.

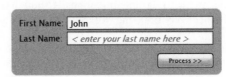

Figure 8-5

Special Considerations

As mentioned before, you have some limitations regarding what you can capture with the event handler when it comes to the keyboard world. As the browser sends these messages, it may capture some of them, like special keys to make the screen full screen or special combinations to control the browser functionality. `Key` and `PlatformKeyCode` do not provide a modifiers list (*modifiers* meaning keys like *Ctrl* or *Alt*). In order to explore them, you must use the static object `Keyboard` and the `Modifiers` property, as the following example shows:

```
private void KeyPressed(object sender, KeyEventArgs e)
{
        if (e.Key == Key.A &&
        ((Keyboard.Modifiers & ModifierKeys.Apple) == ModifierKeys.Apple))
                txtLastName.Text = "You pressed the right keys!";
}
```

As `ModifiersKeys` is a flag enumerator, you can combine each single modifier using binary operations. As you might imagine, being an ASP.NET developer and seeing the Apple entry is an excellent first step in the multi-platform story.

Getting the Most from Input Devices

Now that you have seen the different input devices and the necessary considerations when you use them in the context of Silverlight, it is time to put them into practice. If you have been skipping sections and have some questions regarding the following concepts, please feel free to jump back to them in order to get the full benefit of this section.

There has been a lot of emphasis by the Silverlight team on the user experience and how you can extend what the Web can do for developers and users. One of the most impressive features is the Ink functionality, which we explore next.

Ink

This is one of our favorite features in the user interaction world. The ability to add handwriting and free-hand drawing into your Silverlight application really fulfills the missing features in the web-based application world. As you have seen, the introduction of stylus and touch-screen devices is pushing the software boundaries and introducing new technologies. The need for fast-input devices to complement the screen's content or transform the free input into data is still increasing, and with Silverlight applications, you are on the right track.

An interesting example of how an Ink solution may work very well is in the documents approval process in an organization. Just imagine that you are implementing a workflow system, wherein documents are generated and different people in the company need to review and finally approve them. Today, most of these processes are still manual owing to signing limitations. Although some companies are implementing passwords and certificates in order to continue the workflow, this is not widely accepted in the industry.

If you are trying to solve this problem using ASP.NET skills in conjunction with Silverlight, you can use the Ink features to implement an elegant solution. Let's assume that the application has generated a financial report and the plug-in reads the content and renders it on the screen. See Figure 8-6.

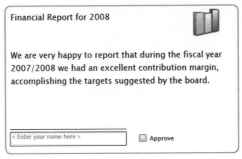

Figure 8-6

The plug-in has rendered the content and presented an option to approve the document that the user can check. Also, for security reasons, you use the text block control to provide a signature space and to inform the users that they need to write their name in the section.

In order to use the handwriting features, you need to have an `InkPresenter` object. You place the object near the signature space and allow the user to directly sign the document using his or her Tablet PC while traveling to an important meeting. The application now looks like Figure 8-7.

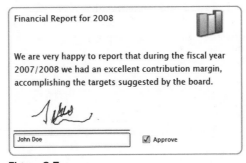

Figure 8-7

The strokes can be retrieved and attached to the document, allowing the distributor to send the final copy with the signatures attached. Perhaps you have recognized the signature model applied, as it is similar to the method commonly used for signing credit card purchases. Now with `InkPresenter`, you have the ability to quickly add this functionality to applications.

Using `InkPresenter`

Now that you have seen a practical example, it is time to start exploring how you can include the presenter in your ASP.NET applications and the implications of it. One of the first things to notice is that `InkPresenter` derives from the `Canvas` class:

```
System.Object
  System.Windows.Controls.Panel
    System.Windows.DependencyObject
      System.Windows.FrameworkElement
        System.Windows.UIElement
          System.Windows.Controls.Canvas
            System.Windows.Controls.InkPresenter
```

The Canvas offers the Background property to display strokes and the Children property to include new UIElements. There is an important thing to remember: The strokes collection is not included in the Children collection and is stored separately in the Strokes dependency property. This is a common question when developers alter the Z order of the Canvas children using Canvas.ZIndex and don't see the strokes reacting.

If you explore the presenter, you will be very familiar with all the properties and methods, as they are inherited from the parent classes; the changes included in the presenter are the Strokes dependency property and an overloaded version of HitTest() to check if the strokes have been hit by the point or rectangle used. The Strokes property is indeed a StrokeCollection object, and as you can imagine, it contains all the strokes that InkPresenter is rendering. This topic relates to the Stylus Points concept explained in the "The Stylus and Touch Screens" section, as a *stroke* is a collection of these points represented in a StylusPointsCollection object. These points can be captured while you are handling the mouse events, specifically the MouseMove event. But since as a developer, you might understand the concepts better if you see code, explore the implementation:

```xml
<InkPresenter    x:Name="MyInk"
                 Background="Transparent"
                 MouseLeftButtonDown="MyInk_MouseLeftButtonDown"
                 MouseMove="MyInk_MouseMove"
                 MouseLeftButtonUp="MyInk_MouseLeftButtonUp"
                 Width="330" Height="260">

    < … Other UIElement children that we want to render … >

</InkPresenter>
```

This is the XAML code to add an InkPresenter in the application. In this case, you are calling it *MyInk*, and you are setting the Background to transparent. Note that you have added the event handlers to support the input devices. Now in the code behind, you add the MouseLeftButtonDown handler to start capturing the stroke:

```csharp
// We need to add the Ink reference
using System.Windows.Ink;

// We use a single stroke object for our active stroke
private Stroke signatureStroke;

private void MyInk_MouseLeftButtonDown(object sender, MouseButtonEventArgs e)
{
        // We capture the mouse to own the MouseMove event
        MyInk.CaptureMouse();

        // We create a new stroke for our signature
        signatureStroke = new Stroke();
```

```
        // Adds this stroke to the collection
        MyInk.Strokes.Add(signatureStroke);

}
```

The first thing that you are doing is capturing the mouse, as has been previously explained; this method will allow you to "hijack" the mouse movement event. You create a new stroke object, which will be used to render the handwritten path. Finally, in order to consider the stroke, you need to add it to the stroke collection in `InkPresenter`. Now it is time to read the user's handwriting:

```
private void MyInk_MouseMove(object sender, MouseEventArgs e)
{
    if (signatureStroke != null)
    {
        // We add the stylus points to my current stroke
        signatureStroke.StylusPoints.AddStylusPoints(
            e.GetStylusPoints(MyInk));
    }
}
```

In this second method, you are querying whether you have an active stroke. Remember that this handler will be called regardless of whether the left button is pressed. You can use other conditions here, but the important consideration is to keep it as lightweight as possible. Once you know that you have an active stroke, you can query the mouse arguments, in this particular case, retrieving the collection of stylus points in reference to the `MyInk` instance. These stylus points are added to the current stroke. Now, in order to finish the task, you need to release it:

```
private void MyInk_MouseLeftButtonUp(object sender, MouseButtonEventArgs e)
{
    // We clear the stroke
    signatureStroke = null;

    // We release the capture
    MyInk.ReleaseMouseCapture();
}
```

The first thing that you are doing is removing the class stroke reference so that further mouse moves are not considered in the stroke. Finally, you release the mouse capture in order to allow other objects to receive the mouse movement events.

When the left mouse click is fired again, a new stroke will be created, and the process is repeated. Straightforward, isn't it?

Playing with the Stroke

In the previous example, you created a new stroke and used it directly in `InkPresenter`. The programming model also offers the ability to change the stroke, creating a richer output if you need it.

You can modify the drawing properties of the stroke in order to modify the output. For example, from the previous example, you can add functionality to correct the text sent by the workflow. See the line marked through the text in Figure 8-8.

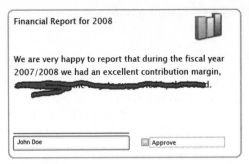

Figure 8-8

In order to implement this type of feature, you need to alter the previous code, altering the `Drawing Attributes` property on the current stroke as follows:

```
private void MyInk_MouseLeftButtonDown(object sender, MouseButtonEventArgs e)
{
        // We capture the mouse to own the MouseMove event
        MyInk.CaptureMouse();

        // We create a new stroke for our signature
        signatureStroke = new Stroke();

        // Defines the attributes
        signatureStroke.DrawingAttributes.Width = 2;
        signatureStroke.DrawingAttributes.Height = 5;
        signatureStroke.DrawingAttributes.Color =
                Color.FromArgb(0xFF, 0xFF, 0, 0);
        signatureStroke.DrawingAttributes.OutlineColor =
                Color.FromArgb(0xFf, 0, 0, 0xFF);

        // Adds this stroke to the collection
        MyInk.Strokes.Add(signatureStroke);

}
```

Eraser Mode

In case the input device has the ability to detect inverted modes or you simply implement the feature using the user interface, you can simulate an eraser. An eraser will be implemented by you in this case, as there is no automatic feature to delete the strokes that you have added in your collection.

Here is where a developer's ability to interpret what needs to be removed comes in handy. As was explained before, the strokes are stored in the stroke collection exposed by `InkPresenter`. Let's implement it in the previous example. For this, you need to add some way of informing the application that it is in "erase mode." If you have an input device with this ability, remember to check the `Inverted` property (don't overlook this feature!). In the document approval application, a checkbox has been added that changes the stylus behavior. Now, when you move the mouse, you need to check in which mode you are and act accordingly:

```
private void MyInk_MouseMove(object sender, MouseEventArgs e)
{
        if (signatureStroke != null)
        {
                // Gets the current points
                StylusPointCollection Points =
                        e.StylusDevice.GetStylusPoints(MyInk);

                // Check if we are in erase mode
                if (chkEraser.IsChecked == true)
                {
                        // Select the strokes affected
                        StrokeCollection ErasedStrokes =
                                MyInk.Strokes.HitTest((Points);

                        if (ErasedStrokes != null)
                        {
                                // Remove the strokes from the collection
                                for (int i = 0; i < ErasedStrokes.Count; i++)
                                {
                                 MyInk.Strokes.Remove(ErasedStrokes[i]);
                                }
                        }
                }
                else
                {
                        // We add the stylus points to my current stroke
                        signatureStroke.StylusPoints.Add (
                                e.StylusDevice.GetStylusPoints(MyInk));
                }
        }
}
```

In the example, you are removing the strokes that are returned by the `HitTest` method. This returns a collection of the strokes intersected. Once you have these strokes, you can directly manipulate them.

> **You may be wondering why you are explicitly using the statement** `"IsChecked == true"`. **The reason is that most of these properties are nullable values, and therefore a Boolean type can store true,** *false*, **or** *null*.

Drag and Drop

Another interesting use of the input devices is the ability to drag and drop objects within the Silverlight plug-in. This is a feature that ASP.NET developers are starting to use in their Web 2.0 applications. Popular web-based e-mail applications are constantly using and sometimes *overusing* this feature. One thing to keep in mind before you jump from your seat and start using the feature is a security limitation that prevents the plug-in from dragging objects from other applications; therefore, you can drag and drop within the Silverlight application only.

Dragging Objects

As you have seen in Chapter 7, you can use a Canvas in order to position the objects using the well-known Top and Left properties (in the canvas context, these are called Canvas.TopProperty and Canvas.LeftProperty). These properties are really useful when you want to start dragging objects around the application. But this is not the only way to drag and move objects around. You can use any other positioning method.

In the example, you are going to simulate dragging an item from a container to other containers. This helps show the different functionality of the drag-and-drop options that you can use in your applications. The application looks like Figure 8-9.

The containers in this case are Border objects to simplify the example, but you can use any other object, for example, a ListBox, in order to add and remove items. The item is another Border object that contains an Image and a TextBlock.

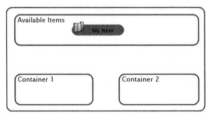

Figure 8-9

The containers in this case are Border objects to simplify the example, but you can use any other object, for example, a ListBox, in order to add and remove items. The item is another Border object that contains an Image and a TextBlock.

In order to implement the drag-and-drop application, you need to use the mouse events concepts of the item, handling the mouse click and the movement to trace the original location and the offset values. With this information, you can alter the Top and Left properties of the canvas.

```
<Border    Height="19"
           HorizontalAlignment="Stretch"
           Margin="0,0,0,0"
           VerticalAlignment="Top"
           RenderTransformOrigin="1,3"
           Background="#FF0798FF"
           BorderBrush="#FF000000"
           CornerRadius="10,10,10,10"
           x:Name="MyItem"
           MouseLeftButtonDown="MyItem_MouseLeftButtonDown"
           MouseLeftButtonUp="MyItem_MouseLeftButtonUp"
           MouseMove="MyItem_MouseMove"
           Canvas.Left="140"
           Canvas.Top="39"
           Width="95">

           <… Contents are placed here …>
</Border>
```

For the event handlers implementation, you define a couple of private objects that can help you track the position and the dragging status, as follows:

```
private bool isDragging;
private Point itemPosition;
```

Now you introduce the implementations, capturing the current position, altering the item position, and releasing the mouse:

```
private void MyItem_MouseLeftButtonDown(object sender, MouseButtonEventArgs e)
{
        // The item captures the mouse events
        MyItem.CaptureMouse();

        // We set up the dragging flag and the current position
        this.isDragging = true;
        this.itemPosition = new Point(
                e.GetPosition(null).X, e.GetPosition(null).Y);
}

private void MyItem_MouseLeftButtonUp(object sender, MouseButtonEventArgs e)
{
        // We remove the flag and the mouse events
        this.isDragging = false;
        MyItem.ReleaseMouseCapture();
}

private void MyItem_MouseMove(object sender, MouseEventArgs e)
{
        if (this.isDragging)
        {
                // Calculates the deltas based on the new position
                double VerticalDelta = e.GetPosition(null).Y -
                        this.itemPosition.Y;
                double HorizontalDelta = e.GetPosition(null).X -
                this.itemPosition.X;

                // Sets the new item position
                MyItem.SetValue(Canvas.TopProperty, VerticalDelta +
                        Convert.ToDouble(MyItem.GetValue(Canvas.TopProperty)));

                MyItem.SetValue(Canvas.LeftProperty, HorizontalDelta +
                        Convert.ToDouble(MyItem.GetValue(Canvas.LeftProperty)));

                // Update position global variables.
                this.itemPosition.Y = e.GetPosition(null).Y;
                this.itemPosition.X = e.GetPosition(null).X;
        }
}
```

You can add special effects when the item is selected, like changing the background color to help the user identify the movement. If you want to play with the example to enhance your knowledge and improve it, a nice challenge would be to "ghost" the item and drag a duplicate item until you release it in the other container. Once released, it should remove the ghosted one. (This is a very common behavior in drag-and-drop applications and is always considered best practice to provide a familiar experience to your users.)

One thing that you may be tempted to do is to use `MouseEnter` and `MouseLeave` on the containers in order to detect when the user is dragging the item over the container objects. The problem is that you have to consider the mouse capture model that will prevent your application from receiving events from other objects. You may also consider moving the mouse capturing to the canvas, but this means that you will need further filtering on the mouse move that will give you some headaches. For this reason, you should analyze the dragging position against the container locations or use the `HitTest` functionality on the `MouseLeftButtonUp`.

> You may notice the lack of drag-and-drop events in Silverlight. That's why you are analyzing different work-arounds. Security limitations prevent the application from using the clipboard to transfer information. Therefore, drag and drop needs to be simulated.

Navigation

If you are looking to create an application using Silverlight that does more than streaming a video, you will need to include several user interaction models. Unless you are a great user interface designer who can fit all the information in a single page and have it still be functional, you will need multiple screens. These screens should help you design an application style component that can be intuitive for the user, delivering a richer experience. You have hundreds of examples of this model, as you have been dealing with wizards, pages, and workflow applications that deal with the navigation object all the time. If you are introducing a Silverlight application in your ASP.NET pages, you want to understand how you can address this challenge.

This section describes different approaches to dealing with the navigation aspect of the user interaction. Silverlight 2 does not have extensive support for multiple screens because this was not one of the main objectives in this version. Therefore, you are going to explore different alternatives that can help you to simulate this behavior. The methods presented here are not exhaustive but can give you an idea of the different approaches that developers are taking in order to meet this challenge. As Silverlight grows and develops, further support will be built into this area.

Silverlight Navigation in the ASP.NET World

For the experienced ASP.NET developer, the navigational model is a commodity, as the HTML technology heavily relies on hyperlinks to transit around web pages. Constant challenges that break this navigational pattern are usually thrown at these developers, and they have been bravely fighting to create amazing work-arounds. During the last 10 years, web developers have been integrating different technologies (such as ActiveX controls, Flash plug-ins, and server side extensions like Web Services) on their pages, which has made the navigation a little more complicated.

Now it is time for a new challenge — Silverlight. Since the beginning of the book, you have been reading that the application runs in a sandboxed plug-in. This means that there is little interaction with the navigation services and components that ASP.NET and the web browser offer. Let's explore some of those challenges and the approach that WPF is taking in the desktop world that may come into the Silverlight world in the future.

Navigation Challenges

One of the first challenges that you have when interacting with ASP.NET is the standard page transition. As each page is treated as an independent entity, the plug-in execution will be lost if you navigate to a new page. The Silverlight application runs independently on the previous page, but as soon as the user leaves that page, the content is disposed. When the user presses the back button on the browser history or another link to return to the previous page, the Silverlight application will be reloaded and restarted, losing the previous state.

Figure 8-10 shows a classic problem in web applications using the page navigation buttons when the page hosts a plug-in. In the case of Silverlight, the sandboxed application model will trigger a completely new initialization, losing the previous state.

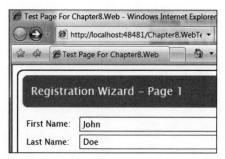

Figure 8-10

During this section, you'll see how you can keep the state on the server side in order to simulate the same patterns that you are used to with the ASP.NET world. What is more interesting is the flexibility of the Silverlight components to expand the limitations that you currently have in the Web environment.

Differences with WPF

If you have previous experience developing applications with XAML and WPF, you may be familiar with the navigational services that the technology provides. These services have been widely accepted as an elegant way to navigate across pages, delivering a seamless experience for developers when they develop applications for the desktop using .NET 3.0 and for the Web using the XBAP model.

Silverlight 2 does not provide the navigation service's objects. Several reasons have been highlighted, but the most compelling is the integration with the browser journal, as some thought needs to be given to this area to figure out the best way to integrate functionality and provide a compelling user and developer experience.

Single Plug-in Navigation

The first approach to navigation that you are going to embark on is using a single Silverlight application in order to simulate the navigation. Although not many applications have been written yet, there is a lot of desire among the early adopters to use this model, as it reduces the deployment complexity and satisfies most user requirements. Having said this, there are some complex scenarios for which a single plug-in will not be enough, and you may need to recur to multiple applications.

As an ASP.NET developer, you are probably thinking about integrating the Silverlight component in your application to complement a specific functionality that can still be sandboxed and is not related with any other web page. If this is the case, using a single plug-in will make your life much easier. If you are planning to integrate it at the web application level, you may consider the following section, in which you explore the use of multiple components.

User Control Transition

One of the most natural ways to navigate across the application is transitioning user controls. This model simulates normal desktop applications, in which the forms are constructed and shown on the screen. The natural difference that you can appreciate is regarding how the screen is hosted, as the form is using the Windows GDI system to render the contents. In the Silverlight world, you don't even have Windows running outside the application.

If you analyze how the application is initialized, you can see that you define the RootVisual property with the first control that you want to render on the screen.

```
public partial class App : Application
{
        public App()
        {
                // Event handling
                this.Startup += this.Application_Startup;
                InitializeComponent();
        }

        private void Application_Startup(object sender,
                StartupEventArgs e)
        {
                // Load the main control
                this.RootVisual = new RemoteContainer();
        }
}
```

Many developers believe that as the root visual property can be set, you can use it as the container reference to change the main screen. The problem is that this property can only be set during this event. The only flexibility that you have at this stage is using the InitParams dictionary in order to read the parameters sent by the HTML initialization and then decide which user control you render:

```
<asp:Silverlight
        ID="MyXamlControl"
        runat="server"
        Source="Chapter8.xap"
        Version="2.0"
        Width="720"
        Height="480"
        InitParameters = "LoadingMode=Remote" >
</asp:Silverlight>
```

Read the initialization parameters using `Application_Startup`:

```
if (e.InitParams != null && e.InitParams.ContainsKey("LoadingMode"))
{
        if (e.InitParams["LoadingMode"].ToUpper() == "REMOTE")
        {
                this.RootVisual = new RemoteContainer();
                return;
        }
}
else
{
        this.RootVisual = new Container();
}
```

With this in mind, you need to look for alternatives for rendering different screens.

An interesting feature in XAML is the ability to have children objects. Most of the components have that ability, and this is an area that you will exploit in order to simulate the navigation. The first thing that you need is to create a container control; this can be a brand-new user control that may contain some objects or just a transparent one that is completely invisible. In this example, you will use a container with a header, so you can quickly identify which control is rendered.

```
<Grid x:Name="LayoutRoot" Background="White">
    <Border Margin="8,8,8,8"
        BorderBrush="#FF00B5FF"
        BorderThickness="1,1,2,2"
        CornerRadius="10,10,10,10">
        <Grid>
                <TextBlock Height="24"
                        Margin="8,8,165,0"
                        VerticalAlignment="Top"
                        Text="This is the header of the local container"
                TextWrapping="Wrap"/>
                <Border Margin="8,42,8,8"
                        BorderBrush="#FF7D7CF0"
                        BorderThickness="1,1,1,1"
                        CornerRadius="10,10,10,10"
                        x:Name="MainContainer">
                        <Grid x:Name="MainContainerGrid"
                                HorizontalAlignment="Left">
                                <!-- here goes the dynamic content-->
                        </Grid>
                </Border>
        </Grid>
    </Border>
</Grid>
```

You are using a couple of borders and grids in order to position the internal screens; the important element in this case is the "MainContainerGrid" that actually will render the dynamic content. The sample looks like Figure 8-11:

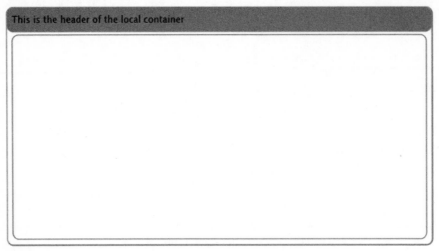

This is the header of the local container

Figure 8-11

The blank space will be filled with the new child that you are going to update dynamically. Now that you have the control, it is time to change the RootVisual property to render the control. You do this changing the App.cs file in the project.

From this point, you need to decide the first screen. There are multiple options regarding how to construct your application architecture, and this will be based on the type of application and how the state is transferred between the screens (in the same way that you do it using Windows Forms). In this example, you have only two screens, and the container will be responsible for coordinating the presentation. For these reasons, the screens will provide events that will be handled by the container in order to decide which is the next action.

The first screen will contain several controls; some of them will capture the first and last name of the user. You are going to send this information to the next screen. The content of the first user control looks like this:

```
<Grid x:Name="LayoutRoot" Background="White">
        <Border Height="56.888" Margin="8,8,8,0" VerticalAlignment="Top"
                Background="#FF0082D0" CornerRadius="10,10,10,10"
                d:LayoutOverrides="Height"/>

        <TextBlock Height="21 " Margin="23,21,35,0" VerticalAlignment="Top"
                FontSize="20" Foreground="#FFFFFFFF" Text="Registration Wizard -
                Page 1" TextWrapping="Wrap" d:LayoutOverrides="Height"/>

        <TextBlock Height="21" HorizontalAlignment="Left" Margin="15,82,0,0"
                VerticalAlignment="Top" Width="97.778" Text="First Name:"
                TextWrapping="Wrap" d:LayoutOverrides="Height"/>
```

```
            < … More controls here … >

            <Button Height="40" HorizontalAlignment="Right" Margin="0,0,19,17"
                    VerticalAlignment="Bottom" Width="145.778" Content="Next"
                    FontSize="14" x:Name="cmdNext" Click="cmdNext_Click"/>
</Grid>
```

You have a single button that will call the `cmdNext_Click` method to handle the event; on the code side, you handle the event firing the action event in order to notify the container:

```
public partial class MyFirstForm : UserControl
{
        /// <summary>
        /// This event is raised when the next button is pressed
        /// </summary>
        public event Action<string> NextButton;

        public MyFirstForm()
        {
                InitializeComponent();
        }

        private void cmdNext_Click(object sender, RoutedEventArgs e)
        {
                if (NextButton != null)
                        NextButton(string.Format("{0} {1}",
                                txtFirstName.Text, txtLastName.Text));
        }
}
```

You can now build the second screen that will present the user's full name and will provide the functionality to go back to the previous screen using the same model. Create a new user control with a `TextBlock` (you use it to render the full name). This time, you will alter the constructor in order to receive the name before rendering.

> As you can see, you are decoupling the screens from the container using the event model. This is a recommended practice that you may use to rapidly extend the application using new screens. Indeed, what is a little more elegant is implementing a common interface, like `IScreen`, so the container does not even know which screen type it is.

With both screens completed, you can now move to the container code. The first thing that you need is to render the initial screen on the grid. Let's handle the user control load event and add the loading method:

```
private void UserControl_Loaded(object sender, RoutedEventArgs e)
{
        LoadFirstPage();
}
```

The LoadFirstPage() method initializes the new user control and assigns the event handler associated with the Next button. The object can now be associated to the grid's children collection:

```
private void LoadFirstPage()
{
        // Initializes the new screen
        MyFirstForm FirstPage = new MyFirstForm();
        FirstPage.NextButton += new Action<string>(FirstPage_NextButton);

        // Adds the new screen
        this.MainContainerGrid.Children.Add(FirstPage);
}
```

If you execute the code, the Silverlight component will render the container and the screen at the same time, as it is shown in Figure 8-12.

Let's go back to the container to add the code for the next button handler. You are going to alter the first method a little as well as remove the current screen from the grid and add the new one, calling the Children.Clear() method. The Previous button on the new screen will take you back to the first screen.

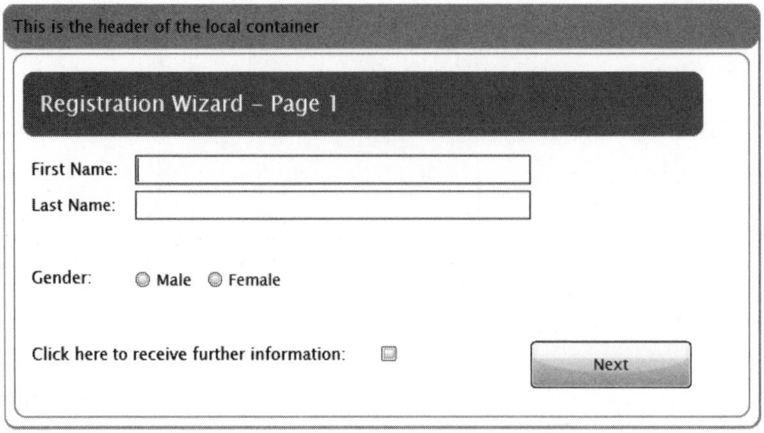

Figure 8-12

```
void FirstPage_NextButton(string fullName)
{
        MySecondForm SecondPage = new MySecondForm(fullName);
        SecondPage.PreviousButton += new Action(SecondPage_PreviousButton);

        // Clears the previous screen
        this.MainContainerGrid.Children.Clear();

        // Adds the new screen
        this.MainContainerGrid.Children.Add(SecondPage);
}
```

```
void SecondPage_PreviousButton()
{
        LoadFirstPage();
}
```

Figure 8-13 shows the result when you execute the application. From the user's point of view, it is still the same application, but internally, you are decoupling each of the screens into individual controls.

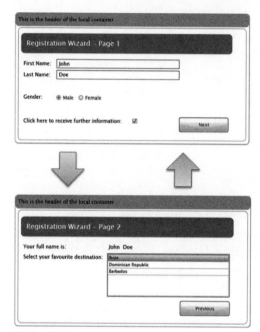

Figure 8-13

The example shown should give you an idea of how to navigate through user controls quickly. At this stage of the book, you may have many different implementation ideas. The important thing to understand is how easily you can manipulate child objects in XAML, not only with grids but with any other container controls. Many developers are starting to build custom controls that handle the navigation container for you; nothing stops you from grabbing the code that you have started in this book and transforming it into a reusable framework.

Adding Effects

Now that you understand how you can simulate navigation in Silverlight 2, you'll add a nice effect to enhance the user experience. In order to do this, you are going to use the animation properties of WPF out-of-the-box because you don't want to reinvent the wheel.

Because of our space limitations, you are only going to see how to add fading into the transition here, but you can expand the effects library using 3D objects to rotate and animate your screens. This is an addition that can be accomplished with your existing ASP.NET knowledge.

Let's build some generic code to fade a screen using the code behind. If you are not sure about using the animation object, please refer to Chapter 14.

```
void FadeScreen(UserControl screen, bool fade)
{
        // Animation duration
        Duration FadingLenght = new Duration(new TimeSpan(0, 0, 3));

        // Type of animation
        DoubleAnimation MainAnimation = new DoubleAnimation();
        MainAnimation.Duration = FadingLenght;
        MainAnimation.To = 0;

        // Main Storyboard
        Storyboard MyFadingStory = new Storyboard();
        MyFadingStory.Duration = MainAnimation.Duration;
        MyFadingStory.Children.Add(MainAnimation);

        // We change the targets
        Storyboard.SetTarget(MainAnimation, screen);
        Storyboard.SetTargetProperty(MainAnimation, "Opacity");

        // We add the resource into the screen
        screen.Resources.Add(MyFadingStory);

        // We trigger the animation
        MyFadingStory.Begin();

}
```

As you can see in the code, you are creating a double type animation in order to decrease a double value based on duration. Then you create the main storyboard that will contain the animation. Remember that you can have multiple animations in the same storyboard. On the next lines, you change the targets, in other words, on which objects the animation will be applied. Finally, you add the resource to the screen so that it is executed.

If you go back to the previous example, you can add the animation to the previous button event handler. See Figure 8-14.

```
void SecondPage_PreviousButton()
{
        // We create the new page
        MyFirstForm FirstPage = new MyFirstForm();
        FirstPage.NextButton += new Action<string>(FirstPage_NextButton);

        // We insert it behind
        this.MainContainerGrid.Children.Insert(0, FirstPage);

        // We fade the current screen
        FadeScreen((UserControl)this.MainContainerGrid.Children[1], true);

}
```

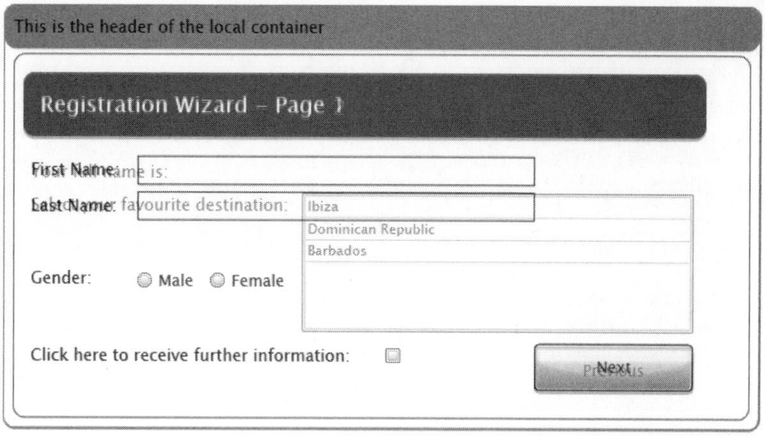

Figure 8-14

Simulating a Modal Screens

If you have developed desktop applications, you should be used to controlling certain functionality using modal screens. This feature has been cloned in the ASP.NET AJAX world with special controls that simulate its behavior. Silverlight comes with very limited, common dialog boxes in order to interact with the local computer, like `System.Windows.Controls.OpenFileDialog`, because of browser and security limitations.

You can easily simulate the behavior using the current navigation knowledge, and you can play with the rendering in order to present a modal style screen to the user like the one presented in Figure 8-15.

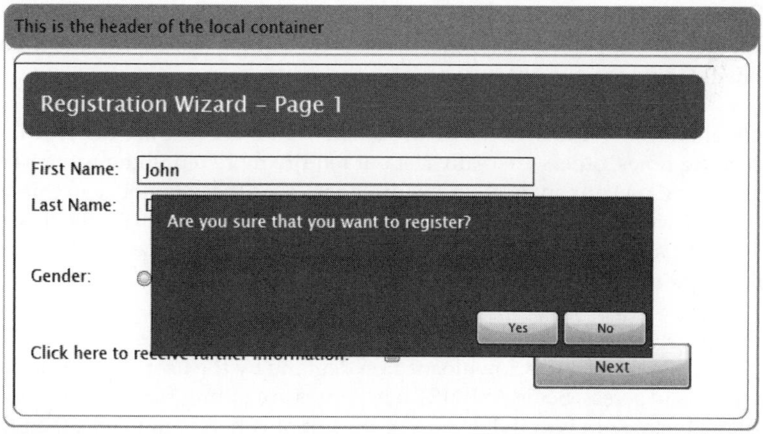

Figure 8-15

You can create a common modal screen that can be reused across your application. For this, you use a new user control, where the size covers the application surface as a background object. This background object should have a solid brush but with the alpha level below 100. This will make it transparent. (If you set no brush, you will be able to use the main screen's controls, breaking the navigation!) When you have the look and feel, just add an event on the dialog box that publishes the `DialogResult` enumerator, so that you can read the output of it.

You can modify the previous example in order to show a dialog screen when you press the Next button:

```
private void cmdNext_Click(object sender, RoutedEventArgs e)
{
        // we show the dialog box
        DialogBox Question = new DialogBox();
        Question.Result += Process_Result;
        MainGrid.Children.Add(Question);
}

void Process_Result(DialogResult result)
{
        // We remove the references
        MainGrid.Children.RemoveAt(MainGrid.Children.Count - 1);

        // we analyze the result
        if (result == DialogResult.Yes)
        {
                if (NextButton != null)
                        NextButton(string.Format("{0} {1}",
                                txtFirstName.Text, txtLastName.Text));
        }
}
```

Screens on Demand

Using a single plug-in control as a container and shifting the different user controls seems to work in most of the scenarios. But what if your screen's library is just too large to be deployed in a single XAP file or your application happens to customize screens based on a workflow return? For this, you will need to consider loading screens on demand from the server.

There are different flavors for this model that you will examine. Some are easier to implement but come with longer loading times; others are really fast but require more plumbing work. The balance is up to you and will be based on your application requirements. One thing to notice in this section is that you are going to use the web site to interact with the Silverlight application with the native web client and WCF services. If you are not familiar with these concepts do not worry as we discuss communication techniques in Chapter 9.

The first option to review is the ability to have multiple screen libraries stored on the server (see Figure 8-16). These libraries can be downloaded on demand by the user depending on the functionality that he or she wants to access. Some ASP.NET developers are opting for a model wherein the ASP.NET page decides how the plug-in is initialized using the initialization parameters, then the application automatically downloads the correct libraries; this can really help reduce the size of the original application.

This option has the advantage of downloading a wide set of objects only one time. Once the assembly is loaded locally, you can create new instances of the screens stored on the library. Let's explore a quick example.

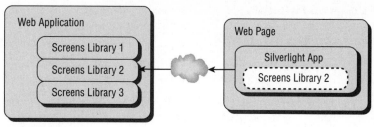

Figure 8-16

The first thing that you need to do is to define the web client object and the storage for the remote assembly:

```
using System.Net;
using System.Reflection;

namespace Chapter8
{
        public partial class RemoteContainer : UserControl
        {
                // Initializes the web client
                private WebClient serverConnection = new WebClient();
                private Assembly remoteScreens;
        }
}
```

Now that you have the objects in place, you need to start the asynchronous remote loading. For this, you use the `WebClient` component and configure the completion handler to finish the load:

```
private void UserControl_Loaded(object sender, RoutedEventArgs e)
{
        // We only can download one item at the time
        if (!this.serverConnection.IsBusy)
        {
                this.serverConnection.OpenReadAsync(
                        new Uri("Chapter8.Screens.dll", UriKind.Relative));

                this.serverConnection.OpenReadCompleted += new
                OpenReadCompletedEventHandler(ServerConnection_
                        OpenReadCompleted);
        }
}
```

You first check if the web client is busy, as it can only handle one request at a time. If the client is available, you start reading the component. This assembly is deployed on the ClientBin folder of the web site.

```
void ServerConnection_OpenReadCompleted
                (object sender, OpenReadCompletedEventArgs e)
{
        // Loads the assembly in our application
        AssemblyPart RemoteAssembly = new AssemblyPart();
```

```
          this.remoteScreens = RemoteAssembly.Load(e.Result);

          // We load the user control
          UserControl RemoteScreen =
                  (UserControl)this.remoteScreens.CreateInstance
                          ("Chapter8.Screens.RemoteScreen");

          // We render the control on our grid
          this.MainContainerGrid.Children.Add(RemoteScreen);
  }
```

With the assembly fully read, you can load the assembly into the application and then create the user control instance that will represent the remote screen.

The second option can be more suitable for a large system in which the screens are completely dynamic and are based on the current application state. For this reason, you may not use a pre-compiled assembly with all the screens. Instead, you can have the objects dynamically generated and exposed through a service to your Silverlight application. Figure 8-17 shows the model.

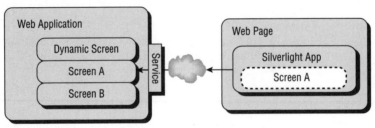

Figure 8-17

For this option, you are going to prepare a WCF service using the basic HTTP binding (you may choose a standard ASMX web service as well). This service will be hosted on the same web application, as for security reasons you should follow this pattern, keeping a single service contract (or interface if you are using standard web services) at the server of origin. The contract or interface that you use will expose a method to request the next screen, returning a user control to the Silverlight application and sending the current screen as a parameter, which contains the result of the current screen. This behavior is very similar to the one that you are used to using in ASP.NET, implementing GET and POST.

With this model, the service can process the next request based on the current screen data. This information can be used by the application or diverted to another internal service within the architecture. The request will be processed, and a new screen will be prepared for the application. Once the screen is ready, you send the results back using the service layer.

```
namespace Chapter8.Web
{
        [ServiceContract]
        public interface IScreens
        {
                [OperationContract]
                string GetScreen(object currentData);
        }
}
```

You define the interface for the service where the GetScreen method receives the current data and returns the XAML string from the generated page. The implementation of the service will use a pre-created XAML file, but you can add functionality here to create the file dynamically.

```
namespace Chapter8.Web
{
        public class Screens : IScreens
        {
                public string GetScreen(object currentData)
                {
                        // We load our XAML file, but this can be replaced with
                        // a dynamic generated screen
                        XmlDocument Doc = new XmlDocument();
                        Doc.Load(AppDomain.CurrentDomain.BaseDirectory +
                                "RemoteScreen.xaml");

                        return Doc.OuterXml;
                }
        }
}
```

To generate the link to your Silverlight application, just right-click on References and click on "Add Service Reference" (or "Add Web Reference" for traditional ASMX web services) to generate the dynamic proxy classes. The next step is to create the service initialization to associate the asynchronous call.

```
public static class Remote
{
        /// <summary>
        /// Event raised when a new screen has been received
        /// </summary>
        public static event Action<UserControl> ScreenReceived;

        /// <summary>
        /// Screen client created with the Add Web reference
        /// </summary>
        private static RemoteScreens.ScreensClient _Server;

        public static void Connect()
        {
                // WCF service initialization
                _Server = new Chapter8.RemoteScreens.ScreensClient();
                _Server.Open();

                // Delegate to address the screen completition
                _Server.GetScreenCompleted += new
                EventHandler<Chapter8.RemoteScreens.GetScreenCompletedEventArgs>
                        (_Server_GetScreenCompleted);
        }

        private static void _Server_GetScreenCompleted(object sender,
                        Chapter8.RemoteScreens.GetScreenCompletedEventArgs e)
        {
                if (e.Error == null)
                {
```

```
                              string XamlPage = e.Result;

                              // Creates the user control from the XAML string
                              UserControl Screen =
                                      (UserControl)XamlReader.Load(XamlPage);

                              if (ScreenReceived != null)
                                      (ScreenReceived(Screen);
                      }
                      else
                      {
                              throw e.Error;
                      }
              }

              public static void GetNextScreen(object currentData)
              {
                      // Calls the WCF service asynchronicly
                      _Server.GetScreenAsync(currentData);
              }
      }
```

The service returns the raw XAML string that needs to be parsed and loaded by the XamlReader class in order to create the user control. With this information, you can pass back the new screen using the ScreenReceived event.

Remember when you started this section that you were planning to find ways to simulate the navigation. Although several options were explored, these are not exhaustive. You can put together the model that fits your application and responds to the user requirements. Future versions of Silverlight might include navigation services that might change these models, but for the time being, these are effective methods.

Multiple Plug-in Navigation

So far you have seen the different ways to render screens using a single plug-in. Although that model may work in most applications, if you need integration with current ASP.NET applications, you might need multiple Silverlight applications somehow linked to each other.

Because each plug-in hosts a single application, you need to link independent applications and transfer the state from one application to the other in order to keep the consistency necessary to support navigation. In this section, you are going to see different alternatives to achieve this behavior, using concepts already learned in this book and other ones that will be complemented with your current ASP.NET knowledge.

Integration with ASP.NET

As soon as the Silverlight application running in the page is posted back to the server, you are likely to lose the current state, as in theory, the application should not be aware of what is going on at the page level. If you are planning to navigate to a new page, it is necessary to use the ASP.NET features in order to transfer that information from one application to the other one.

Luckily, the object model contains a wide range of functions to interact with the browser that will help you to manage that navigation and to trigger some HTML actions from the managed code. If you add the namespace System.Windows.Browser, you can see that a wide range of classes (most importantly, HTMLPage) is available to help you query and control the current web page.

You can see in Figure 8-18 that you can interact with the HTMLPage object in order to post the page back to the server or even navigate to the new screen passing a query string.

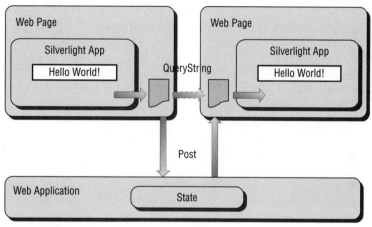

Figure 8-18

Now look at an example of how you can communicate using these methods. For this example, you'll use two different web pages hosting different Silverlight applications. The first application contains a textbox (txtFullName) and a button (cmdPost). You handle the Click event on the button as follows:

```csharp
private void cmdPost_Click(object sender, RoutedEventArgs e)
{
        if (txtFullName.Text.Length > 0)
        {
                // We format the destination using a query string
                string FormatDestination =
                        string.Format(@"SecondPage.aspx?FullName={0}",
                                txtFullName.Text);

                // Sets the new URI with a query string entry
                Uri SourceUri = new Uri(HtmlPage.Document.DocumentUri,
                                                FormatDestination);

                // Navigates to the next page
                HtmlPage.Window.Navigate(SourceUri);
        }
}
```

First, you need to format the destination resource; in this case, you are adding a parameter to the query string list. Once you have the destination formatted, you create a URI based on the current document

URI. Finally, you use the HTML navigation model to swap pages. Now look at how the other application reads the value:

```
private void UserControl_Loaded(object sender, RoutedEventArgs e)
{
        // We read the query string
        Dictionary<string, string> QueryString = (Dictionary<string, string>)
                System.Windows.Browser.HtmlPage.Document.QueryString;

        // We validate it
        if (!QueryString.ContainsKey("FullName"))
        {
                // Alert the user
                HtmlPage.Window.Alert("The request has been corrupted!");

                // Navigate to the first scren
                Uri SourceUri = new Uri(HtmlPage.Document.DocumentUri,
                                        "FirstPage.aspx");

                HtmlPage.Window.Navigate(SourceUri);
        }
        else
        {
                txtFullName.Text = QueryString["FullName"];
        }
}
```

In the example, you can also see how you can integrate further HTML functionality like the alert to inform the user that the new application cannot be initialized.

Using query strings is not the only option; if you explore the different functionality, you can set properties from Silverlight and then post the form using the Submit functionality as follows:

```
HtmlPage.Document.Submit();
```

Using Services

As you can see in Figure 8-19, this behavior is quite similar to the patterns that ASP.NET developers are used to, but in order to expand on the possibilities, you can also use services to transfer information back to the system. This model can be more suitable for full Silverlight deployments, where you need to partition the application in several pages, perhaps because of deployment size requirements or further integration with HTML, like using HTTPHandlers and HTTPModules. You can find all the details about service communication in Chapter 9, "Communicating with the Server."

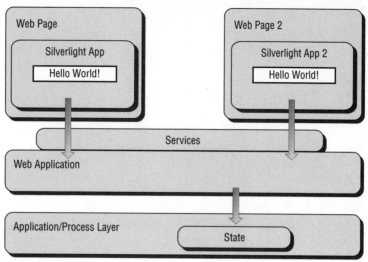

Figure 8-19

Summary

The user interaction architecture really shapes the final user experience, which is the main reason that this chapter is so important. You have seen some best practices used in the community regarding how to solve the common challenges and how to get the most of the current features.

You have been exploring the different input alternatives that a common Silverlight user may use, taking into consideration all the latest devices. A lot of exciting opportunities can still be pursued in this field, and Silverlight definitely is on the right track. One of the great features is the Ink controls, perhaps the real solution to a paperless process in the near future.

As every ASP.NET developer knows, it is hard to create a compelling story using a single web page. The Silverlight world is no different. For that reason, you have seen the different options that you may use in order to navigate around the application, enhancing the content presentation. With time, new practices will be developed as the industry fully adopts the technology, but in the meantime, the content of this chapter can give you the right techniques to start exploring this fascinating world.

9

Communicating with the Server

Integrating data into applications has always been a key part of the development process. The rise of the Internet has resulted in many new options for accessing and storing data since data can live in distributed locations ranging from a database to an XML file to a remote Web Service. The good news is that the techniques used to access distributed/remote data have matured year after year, and we now have many viable methods at our disposal.

In this chapter, you'll see how Silverlight networking and communication features can be used to access distributed data. This includes a discussion of how to create services that Silverlight can call, different ways of handling cross-domain issues, and built-in Silverlight classes that can be used to process data. You'll also see how built-in Silverlight classes can be used to send and receive data from REST services, how RSS and ATOM syndication feeds can be parsed, and how direct socket-to-socket communications can be created and used to push data from a server to a client.

Silverlight Networking and Communication Features

Silverlight provides many built-in networking features that can be used to communicate with local and remote servers to send and receive data. Some of the features can be leveraged visually inside Visual Studio, while others rely on custom code and configuration files. This section provides a high-level look at supported networking features so that you get a feel for the options that are available. Later in the chapter, each feature will be discussed more in-depth so that you can see how to put various networking and communication technologies to use in your Silverlight applications.

What Type of Data Can Silverlight Access and Process?

It goes without saying that there are a lot of different ways in which data can be stored in today's technology-centric world. New techniques are being released on what seems to be a daily basis at times. Fortunately, Silverlight is capable of accessing and processing virtually any type of text-based data in existence including popular formats such as Extensible Markup Language (XML), Simple Object Access Protocol (SOAP), HyperText Markup Language (HTML), and JavaScript Object Notation (JSON), as well as other formats that may be released in the future.

By learning how to work with common data storage formats, you can access data, convert it into a custom object type, and bind the type or collection of types to one or more Silverlight controls. In many cases, you can use built-in Silverlight classes to convert data into custom objects. For example, the `DataContractJsonSerializer` class can be used to serialize/deserialize JSON data, while the `XmlSerializer` class can be used to serialize/deserialize XML data. When you're working with a custom text format such as a fixed-length flat file, you can always resort to creating specialized classes to perform the parsing operation.

Supported Domains and URLs

Silverlight is extremely flexible when it comes to the types of data you can use in an application. However, you can't necessarily access data at any location out-of-the-box. Silverlight restricts the types of URLs that can be called. If a URL begins with `http://` or `https://` you can call it but URLs beginning with `ftp://` or `file://` will be rejected. Calls back to the origin server that initially served up the Silverlight application are fair game, but calls to other servers with different domains (referred to as *cross-domain calls*) may fail with a security exception. A more complete discussion of cross-domain pitfalls and issues is certainly warranted and will be provided later in this chapter.

Communication Options

There are four main options for performing asynchronous calls between a Silverlight application and a data repository, including Web Services, Representational State Transfer (RESTful) calls, sockets, and HTTP polling duplex calls. Web Services provide a way to exchange messages using Simple Object Access Protocol (SOAP) (although some services can work with alternate formats as well), and RESTful calls can exchange a variety of data formats such as XML and JSON, while sockets and HTTP polling duplex calls allow virtually any type of data to be passed between a Silverlight client and a server.

As an ASP.NET developer, you've more than likely heard about the benefits that Web Services offer. After all, Web Services and Service Oriented Architectures (SOAs) have ranked toward the top of the technology buzzword list along with XML and AJAX for years now. If you're new to Web Services, they provide a platform-neutral way to exchange data between disparate systems using an XML format called *SOAP*. Web Services expose a contract defined using Web Service Description Language (WSDL) that a client can use to understand how to communicate with a service. Having a simple XML parser available allows data to be transferred relatively transparently between interested parties without relying on a specific platform, framework, or object model.

Using Visual Studio or a command-line tool, you can create a Silverlight-specific proxy object that can be used to call a Web Service much the same way you'd call a service using a proxy object in ASP.NET. This results in minimal code being written and abstracts the SOAP serialization/deserialization process away from the developer. No XML knowledge is required to call a Web Service using Silverlight, so once the process of creating and using proxy objects is understood, the code is quite straightforward. Standard Web Services can be called whether they're written using ASP.NET, Windows Communication Foundation (WCF), or even using another language such as Java or Python.

Several Web Service alternatives have also become popular on the Web. These alternatives typically focus on more straightforward ways to exchange data and eliminate some of the complexities associated with Web Services. For example, many popular sites such as Flickr, MySpace, Digg, and eBay allow data to be accessed using REST APIs, and some sites exchange data back and forth using Plain Old XML (POX). RESTful calls don't have many of the contract benefits available to Web Service consumers, but they do tend to simplify the overall process of exchanging data. Other sites may rely on JSON rather than XML for data exchange. JSON provides a compact way to serialize and deserialize object graphs into a text-based format easily transported over protocols such as HTTP. It's often used in other technologies as well such as ASP.NET AJAX.

The concept of REST is credited to Roy Fielding, who outlined different network architecture principles that can be used to define and access resources using a Uniform Resource Identifier (URI). To put it another way, REST allows data to be retrieved using simple URLs with actions defined directly in the URL path segments or through defining query string parameters. RESTful calls can be made using built-in Silverlight classes such as `WebClient` and `HttpWebRequest/HttpWebResponse`.

The simplest way to describe REST is through an example. Flickr provides a REST API (in addition to XML-RPC and SOAP APIs) that developers can use to retrieve photos and other information from their web site. An example of what a RESTful call to the Flickr REST API looks like is shown next:

```
http://www.flickr.com/services/rest/?method=flickr.test.echo&format=rest
&foo=bar&api_key=YourKey
```

As with any URL, the previous one and those that follow are subject to change.

Notice that a standard URL is used and that the method or action that the server should perform is added using a query string parameter. Calling this URL results in the following POX response:

```xml
<?xml version="1.0" encoding="utf-8" ?>
<rsp stat="ok">
    <method>flickr.test.echo</method>
    <format>rest</format>
    <foo>bar</foo>
    <api_key>YourKey</api_key>
</rsp>
```

Digg also provides a REST API that allows data to be accessed in a similar manner. If you'd like to retrieve a list of stories from Digg.com, you can make the following RESTful call:

```
http://services.digg.com/stories/topic/microsoft?count=3&
appkey=http://www.smartwebcontrols.com
```

This call results in the following XML response (the response data has been edited for the sake of brevity):

```xml
<?xml version="1.0" encoding="utf-8" ?>
<stories timestamp="1206485104" min_date="1203893100" total="3209"
 offset="0" count="3">
```

```xml
      <story id="5850098"
       link="http://www.downloadsquad.com/2008/03/25/could-windows-
       xp-get-another-stay-of-execution/" submit_date="1206484576"
       diggs="2" comments="0" status="upcoming" media="news"
       href="http://digg.com/microsoft/Could_Windows_XP_get_another…">
          <title>Could Windows XP get another stay of execution?</title>
          <description> Description…</description>
          <user name="spamspanker123"
           icon="http://digg.com/users/spamspanker123/1.png"
           registered="1202407633" profileviews="135" />
          <topic name="Microsoft" short_name="microsoft" />
          <container name="Technology" short_name="technology" />
          <thumbnail originalwidth="200" originalheight="152"
           contentType="image/jpeg"
           src="http://digg.com/microsoft/Could_Windows_XP /t.jpg" width="80"
           height="80" />
      </story>

      <!— More story elements follow —>

  </stories>
```

In addition to calling Web Services and REST APIs, Silverlight also has built-in support for socket-to-socket communication in cases in which a more low-level communication mechanism is needed or you need to get data from a server without constantly polling it. This option opens up the ability to have Silverlight applications talk directly with servers, which can be useful when data such as stock quotes need to be pushed to a client. Web Services, RESTful calls, and sockets will be discussed in more detail throughout this chapter.

Now that you've seen the main options for accessing data using Silverlight, let's take a quick look at options that are available to process data once it's received.

Data-Processing Options

Silverlight has excellent support for parsing and serializing/deserializing data retrieved from distributed servers. Because Silverlight contains a subset of the overall .NET Framework, you have access to powerful features such as language integrated query (LINQ) and reader and writer classes that can be used to parse, process, and map data to CLR objects. Silverlight provides several mechanisms for working with XML data retrieved from a service, RESTful call, or a socket.

Support for working with SOAP services is built directly into Silverlight as mentioned earlier. SOAP messages are typically parsed and mapped to CLR objects (the process of deserialization) using a service proxy object. By using a proxy object, you can avoid writing custom code to process data contained in SOAP messages. In rare cases in which you need to manually call a service and process the raw data yourself, Silverlight provides the classes you need to get the job done.

XML data can be parsed several different ways including using LINQ to XML, the XmlReader class, or the XmlSerializer class. LINQ to XML provides a mechanism for parsing XML data using query syntax, the XmlReader class offers a streaming API that is fast and efficient, and the XmlSerializer class makes it straightforward to map XML data to custom CLR types. XML data can also be generated within Silverlight when you need to send it to a server by using an XmlWriter class.

In cases in which you need to parse XML syndication feeds such as RSS or ATOM, the `XmlReader` and `XmlSerializer` classes can be used, but a simpler strategy is to use the built-in Silverlight syndication classes such as `SyndicationFeed` and `SyndicationItem` that minimize the amount of code you have to write. By learning to use these and other related classes, you can download, parse, and process syndication feeds efficiently and with minimal effort.

Aside from XML data, JSON data can also be serialized or deserialized using a class named `DataContractJsonSerializer`. Open Source JSON reader and writer classes are also available at sites such as `www.codeplex.com/Json`.

These data-processing options provide different alternatives for working with data in a way that is compatible with how you like to build applications. If you're an ASP.NET developer, then you'll more than likely be familiar with many of the available classes.

Cross-Domain Support

Before jumping into the different networking features, it's important to discuss issues that may crop up from making networking calls from a Silverlight application to a server. Calling from one web site domain to another (referred to as *cross-domain calls*) is common in applications that grab data from distributed sources. This is especially true in *mash-up* applications that retrieve data from multiple sites and services. If you've worked with Web technologies like Asynchronous JavaScript and XML (AJAX), then you know that making cross-domain calls from a client browser isn't always as straightforward as it should be.

AJAX uses an `XmlHttpRequest` object that requires all calls to go back to the server that originally served up the AJAX-enabled page to start with. The `XmlHttpRequest` object prevents calls to other Internet domains since different types of security hacks such as cross-site forgery attacks can potentially be used to steal a user's data. Because of this limitation, AJAX applications normally call back to an intermediate service located on the origin server, which, in turn, calls the remote service to retrieve cross-domain data. While this technique works and is used by many sites, it requires extra work and introduces a middleman into the equation (although it does allow different caching techniques to be used that can increase the reliability of data consumed by an application).

Unlike AJAX, Silverlight supports cross-domain calls but can only call back to the same domain (sometimes called the *site of origin*) by default. This means that you can safely call a service hosted at `www.site.com/MyService` from a Silverlight client hosted at `www.site.com` without any additional work on your part. However, the Silverlight client would not be able to call a service located at `www.site.com:9090/MyService` by default since the port is different. Silverlight performs the following checks to see if a server is in the same domain as a Silverlight client:

❑   The protocol is the same.

❑   The domain name is the same.

❑   The port number is the same.

You won't normally have to worry about cross-domain calls if you have full control over the client application and the server application. However, you'll encounter cross-domain problems in situations in which a Silverlight client needs to consume a service exposed by a vendor such as Amazon or Google, or a service hosted in the same domain as the Silverlight client but on a different port or protocol.

You can simulate the behavior of making a cross-domain call by adding a new Web Service project to an existing Silverlight 2 project in Visual Studio. Any attempts to call the service from the Silverlight client will result in a rather confusing error message that states, "The remote server returned an unexpected response: (404) Not Found." At first glance, you may think that the Service Reference is set up incorrectly and that the service's URL needs to be fixed. This isn't the cause of the error in most cases. The error is raised by Silverlight as it realizes that a cross-domain call is being attempted.

Cross-domain calls can be made only if the target server has a special XML cross-domain policy file placed at its root. If Silverlight detects that the file isn't present or that the domain that the call initiated from is denied access, then an exception will be raised. Two types of cross-domain policy files are supported in Silverlight 2: Flash crossdomain.xml files and Silverlight clientaccesspolicy.xml files. Silverlight first checks for the presence of a clientaccesspolicy.xml file on a server when a cross-domain call is initiated. If the file isn't found, it checks for a crossdomain.xml file. Let's take a closer look at both types of cross-domain policy files.

Flash Cross-Domain Policy Files

Cross-domain policy files were first made popular with Flash, which allows data to be aggregated from multiple sites and services. Many of today's popular web sites include a Flash cross-domain policy file named *crossdomain.xml* at their root to allow external Flash applications to talk with them. Silverlight supports a subset of the crossdomain.xml file format. Examples of supported files are shown here:

```
<?xml version="1.0"?>
<cross-domain-policy>
    <allow-http-request-headers-from domain="*" headers"*"/>
</cross-domain-policy>
```

```
<?xml version="1.0"?>
<cross-domain-policy>
    <allow-access-from domain="*" />
</cross-domain-policy>
```

The first example allows any header to be sent from any domain to a server. This is useful when headers such as SOAPAction (used with Web Services) must be allowed. Specific header values can be added to the headers attribute which is more secure than using *. The second example allows access to a server from any domain which works well for RESTful calls. Silverlight only supports a domain attribute value of *.

> *Additional information about crossdomain.xml files can be found at* http://www.adobe.com/devnet/articles/crossdomain_policy_file_spec.html

If you're hosting a service that Flash clients can access, then you'll want to add the crossdomain.xml file into the site root. If only Silverlight clients can access the service, then you can add a file named *clientaccesspolicy.xml* into the site root as discussed next.

> *You may come across crossdomain.xml files that define a Document Type Definition (DTD) at the top of the file that includes a reference to* www.macromedia.com *or* www.adobe.com. *Silverlight 2 doesn't look at the DTD since different versions may be present in the crossdomain.xml file.*

Silverlight Cross-Domain Policy Files

The Flash cross-domain policy file format works well for restricting access to a server by domain, but it doesn't allow specific resources on a server to be locked down. In today's "security comes first" mentality, having more control over what resources can be accessed is a desirable feature. After all, if callers don't need access to every folder on a server, then why give them that level of access in the first place?

To help reduce the attack surface exposed to cross-domain callers, Microsoft released a Silverlight-specific cross-domain policy file called *clientaccesspolicy.xml*. This file provides additional control over which domains can call a server using cross-domain calls, what resources those domains can access, and which HTTP request headers are allowed. An example of a clientaccesspolicy.xml file is shown next:

```xml
<?xml version="1.0" encoding="utf-8"?>
<access-policy>
    <cross-domain-access>
        <policy>
            <allow-from http-request-header="*">
                <domain uri="*"/>
            </allow-from>
            <grant-to>
                <resource path="/Services" include-subpaths="true"/>
            </grant-to>
        </policy>
    </cross-domain-access>
</access-policy>
```

This file allows cross-domain calls made from any domain access to resources located in the Services directory off the server root. The `allow-from` element provides a way to define which domains are allowed access to a service much like Flash's crossdomain.xml file. However, Silverlight's policy file goes a step further by allowing a server to control what resources domains can access using the `grant-to` element as well as which HTTP request headers can be passed using the `http-request-header` attribute. The `http-request-header` attribute accepts a wildcard (*) character as well as non-blacklisted headers. Additional details on current blacklisted headers can be found in the Silverlight SDK or at `http://msdn.microsoft.com`. Multiple request headers can be defined in the `http-request-header` attribute by providing a comma-separated list.

Multiple `policy` elements can be added in cases in which different domains can access different resources:

```xml
<?xml version="1.0" encoding="utf-8"?>
<access-policy>
    <cross-domain-access>
        <policy>
            <allow-from http-request-headers="*">
                <domain uri="*"/>
            </allow-from>
            <grant-to>
                <resource path="/Services" include-subpaths="false"/>
            </grant-to>
        </policy>
        <policy>
            <allow-from http-request-headers="*">
                <domain uri="*.domainName.com"/>
```

```
            </allow-from>
            <grant-to>
                <resource path="/SpecialServices" include-subpaths="true"/>
            </grant-to>
        </policy>
    </cross-domain-access>
</access-policy>
```

This cross-domain policy file allows the domainName.com domain to access the SpecialServices directory as well as subpaths under that directory. In cases in which Silverlight clients can access everything from the root of the server down, the `resource` element's `path` attribute can be given a value of `/`, and the `include-subpaths` attribute can be given a value of `true`.

When Flash or Silverlight clients of a server can access any resource, a simple Flash crosspolicy.xml file placed at the server root will get the job done. When specific resources need to be locked down for Silverlight clients, a clientaccesspolicy.xml file can be placed at the root. If Flash clients won't be calling your server, it's recommended that you use clientaccesspolicy.xml files, since they provide the most robust security owing to their ability to restrict resources and HTTP request headers.

Creating Services for Silverlight

To this point, you've seen that Silverlight is capable of making cross-domain calls to access data located on different servers. This is a great feature if you need to aggregate data from distributed services and display it in your Silverlight application. However, in many cases, an application will access data located on the origin server, so understanding how to create services is an important part of Silverlight development.

In the remainder of this section, you'll see how to create Windows Communication Foundation (WCF) services as well as ASP.NET Web Services that can be consumed by Silverlight. Many books have been written covering WCF and ASP.NET Web Service development features and principles, and this chapter can't do the technologies justice on its own. The goal of the sections that follow is to provide an overview of using the technologies to help jump-start the service development process.

Creating a WCF Service for Silverlight

Let's walk through the process of creating WCF data contracts and service contracts. Once contracts are created, you'll then see how service contracts can be implemented to create a cross-platform service and how a service can be configured to be Silverlight-compatible.

Windows Communication Foundation (WCF) was first released with .NET 3.0 and is an integral part of .NET 3.5. It provides a robust and flexible framework for building different types of services that can be consumed by clients using virtually any language, platform, or object model. WCF is based on key technology standards such as XSD schemas, WSDL, SOAP, and WS-* standards (security, addressing, messaging reliability, etc.) and follows key SOA (Service Oriented Architecture) principles such as loosely coupled contracts, bindings (ways to call a service), and discoverable services. If you're already familiar with building classes and implementing interfaces, then building WCF services will be a natural extension of what you're already doing.

WCF has its own set of ABCs: Address, Binding, and Contract. The Address part represents the location of the physical service, the Binding part represents how you'll *bind* or talk to the service (will it be over HTTP, TCP, or another binding?), and the Contract part defines what operations a service can perform as well as details about those operations such as data types passed back and forth.

To create a WCF service, there are prescribed steps you can walk through to ensure that you adhere to the ABCs. Start by creating a WCF Service Library or WCF Service Application project in Visual Studio. This adds a reference to WCF assemblies such as `System.ServiceModel` that house key classes used by a service. Once the project is created, you can create data contract classes, service interfaces, WCF configuration code, plus more.

The topics that follow provide details on creating WCF services that Silverlight clients can consume. While you can certainly create WCF services by hand or by using Visual Studio's WCF Service Library or WCF Service Application project templates, the Silverlight 2 tools for Visual Studio 2008 also provide a `Silverlight-enabled WCF Service` *item that can be selected to help jump-start the process. Once you've created a web site or ASP.NET Web Application project in Visual Studio, right-click on the project, select Add New Item, and choose* `Silverlight-enabled WCF Service`. *Doing this will add a .svc file into the project along with starter code for the service. WCF configuration code will also be added into web.config.*

Defining a WCF Data Contract

A data contract defines the data that will be passed between a client and a service. Different attributes can be used to define a data contract such as `DataContract` and `DataMember`. The `DataContract` attribute applies to a class, whereas the `DataMember` attribute applies to a field or property. Public properties are recommended over public fields especially when you'll be data-binding classes to Silverlight controls.

An example of creating a simple contract to allow a `Product` object to be exchanged between a service and a client is shown next:

```
namespace Model
{
    [DataContract]
    public partial class Product
    {
        [DataMember]
        public int ProductID { get; set; }

        [DataMember]
        public int CategoryID { get; set; }

        [DataMember]
        public string ModelNumber { get; set; }

        [DataMember]
        public string ModelName { get; set; }

        [DataMember]
        public string ProductImage { get; set; }

        [DataMember(Order=6)]
```

```
            public decimal UnitCost { set; get; }

            [DataMember]
            public string Description { get; set; }
        }
    }
```

Although you can always type this class and its members yourself, LINQ to SQL provides a nice designer surface that can be used to create data contract classes visually and tie them to a database table for simplified O/R mapping. The sample code provided for this chapter uses LINQ to SQL. If you go this route, you'll need to ensure that you change the Serialization Mode to Unidirectional in the LINQ to SQL designer so that the generated classes can be serialized and deserialized when used with WCF services. You can change the Serialization Mode value by right-clicking on the LINQ to SQL design surface and selecting Properties from the menu.

Data entity classes used in services can also be generated using XML schemas (.xsd files) and command-line tools. By doing this, messages exchanged between the client and service will be based on global standards that help to minimize interop issues across different platforms. With .NET you can use the xsd.exe tool with the /classes switch to generate classes from an XSD schema:

```
xsd.exe /classes schemaName.xsd
```

While this will generate the appropriate class and member properties for you, it won't decorate the class with the DataContract attribute and the properties with the DataMember attribute, unfortunately.

WCF's svcutil.exe tool can be used to convert an XSD schema into a class and add the appropriate DataContract and DataMember attributes for you. For example, to automatically generate a data contract class from an existing XSD schema, the following can be run using the Visual Studio command prompt:

```
svcutil.exe /dconly schemaName.xsd
```

The /dconly switch says to create the data contract class from the types defined in the schema. Running this command-line tool will auto-generate a class based on the schema types.

Defining a WCF Service Contract

Once the data contract(s) used by the service is defined, the service contract can be created. Service contracts rely on .NET interfaces and WCF attributes. In its most basic form, a *service contract* defines what operations a service will perform using an interface. Services that implement the contract must, of course, implement all of the members defined in the contract/interface.

The following code demonstrates how to create a service contract and use the ServiceContract and OperationContract attributes to mark the interface as a WCF contract and the methods as WCF operations:

```
[ServiceContract()]
public interface IProductService
{
    [OperationContract]
    Model.Product[] GetProducts();
```

```
    [OperationContract]
    Model.Product GetProduct(int prodID);
}
```

This example defines a service contract named *IProductService* and two operations named `GetProducts` and `GetProduct`. Both operations return the Product data contract discussed earlier.

Creating a WCF Service

Once the service contract has been defined, it must be implemented in order to be useful. When a class implements an interface, it must define all of the members in the interface. The same logic holds true for services that implement service contracts.

WCF Services can be exposed using IIS or can be self-hosted in Console applications, Windows Services, or other types of .NET applications. When hosting services on IIS, the service file will have a .svc file extension rather than the .asmx extension used with standard ASP.NET Web Services. The .svc file contains a `ServiceHost` attribute that points to a code file containing the actual service code:

```
<% @ServiceHost Language=C# Service="ProductService"
        CodeBehind="~/App_Code/Service.cs" %>
```

The code file must implement the appropriate service contract and fulfill all of the contract's requirements in order to compile successfully. An example of implementing the IProductService contract defined earlier on a class named `ProductService` is shown next:

```
public class ProductService : IProductService
{   public Model.Product[] GetProducts()
    {
        return Biz.BAL.GetProducts();
    }

    public Model.Product GetProduct(int prodID)
    {
        return Biz.BAL.GetProduct(prodID);
    }
}
```

The `ProductService` class implements the two methods defined in the `IProductService` class and adds code to call into a business layer. The business layer, in turn, calls a data layer class to communicate with the database. The following code shows the data contract, service contract, service, business layer, and data layer interfaces and classes so that you can see how they related to each other:

```
namespace Model
{

    [DataContract]
    public partial class Product
    {

        [DataMember]
        public int ProductID { get; set; }

        [DataMember]
```

```csharp
        public int CategoryID { get; set; }

        [DataMember]
        public string ModelNumber { get; set; }

        [DataMember]
        public string ModelName { get; set; }

        [DataMember]
        public string ProductImage { get; set; }

        [DataMember(Order=6)]
        public decimal UnitCost { set; get; }

        [DataMember]
        public string Description { get; set; }
    }
}

[ServiceContract(Namespace="http://www.smartwebcontrols.com/samples")]
public interface IProductService
{

    [OperationContract]
    Model.Product[] GetProducts();

    [OperationContract]
    Model.Product GetProduct(int prodID);

}

public class ProductService : IProductService
{
    public Model.Product[] GetProducts()
    {
        return Biz.BAL.GetProducts();
    }

    public Model.Product GetProduct(int prodID)
    {
        return Biz.BAL.GetProduct(prodID);
    }
}

//Business Layer
namespace Biz
{
    public class BAL
    {
        public static Model.Product[] GetProducts()
        {
            return Data.DAL.GetProducts();
```

```
            }

        public static Model.Product GetProduct(int prodID)
        {
            return Data.DAL.GetProduct(prodID);
        }
    }
}

//Data Layer
namespace Data
{
    public class DAL
    {
        static string _ProductImageUrlBase;
        private static string ProductImageUrlBase
        {
            get
            {
                if (_ProductImageUrlBase == null)
                {
                    IncomingWebRequestContext context =
                    WebOperationContext.Current.IncomingRequest;
                    _ProductImageUrlBase =
                      String.Format("http://{0}/ProductImages/thumbs/",
                          context.Headers[HttpRequestHeader.Host]);
                }
                return _ProductImageUrlBase;
            }
        }

        public static Product[] GetProducts()
        {
            using (GolfClubShackDataContext context =
              new GolfClubShackDataContext())
            {
                return (from p in context.Products
                        let imageUrl = ProductImageUrlBase + p.ProductImage
                        select new Product
                        {
                            CategoryID = p.CategoryID,
                            Description = p.Description,
                            ModelName = p.ModelName,
                            ModelNumber = p.ModelNumber,
                            ProductID = p.ProductID,
                            ProductImage = imageUrl,
                            UnitCost = p.UnitCost,
                        }).ToArray<Product>();
            }
        }

        public static Product GetProduct(int prodID)
```

```
        {
            using (GolfClubShackDataContext context =
              new GolfClubShackDataContext())
            {
                return (from p in context.Products
                        where p.ProductID == prodID
                        let imageUrl = ProductImageUrlBase + p.ProductImage
                        select new Product
                        {
                            CategoryID = p.CategoryID,
                            Description = p.Description,
                            ModelName = p.ModelName,
                            ModelNumber = p.ModelNumber,
                            ProductID = p.ProductID,
                            ProductImage = imageUrl,
                            UnitCost = p.UnitCost,
                        }).SingleOrDefault<Product>();
            }
        }
    }
  }
}
```

Configuring a WCF Service

Visual Studio handles adding WCF-specific configuration entries into the web.config file when you initially create a WCF Service web site. The configuration information defines how clients will bind to the service, the contract that the service exposes, and behaviors that the service can perform. A sample WCF system.serviceModel configuration entry added into web.config to support the ProductService class is shown next:

```
<system.serviceModel>
    <services>
        <service name="ProductService" behaviorConfiguration="serviceBehaviors">
            <endpoint contract="IProductService" binding="basicHttpBinding"/>
        </service>
    </services>
    <behaviors>
        <serviceBehaviors>
            <behavior name="serviceBehaviors">
                <serviceDebug includeExceptionDetailInFaults="false"/>
                <serviceMetadata httpGetEnabled="true"/>
            </behavior>
        </serviceBehaviors>
    </behaviors>
</system.serviceModel>
```

Although Visual Studio generates the initial XML configuration code used by a service, you will have to modify the configuration code as you change your interface and service names to ensure that the names defined in your code match up with the names in web.config. This WCF service configuration code references the ProductService using the name attribute, defines what behaviors the service performs using the behaviorConfiguration attribute, and defines the contract IProductService exposed by the service endpoint using the contract attribute. It also defines that clients binding to the service can use standard HTTP bindings. This binding is required for Silverlight clients to call the service successfully.

Bindings such as wsHttpBinding won't work because they allow for message encryption, digital signatures, and so on that Silverlight couldn't support without adding to the downloadable plug-in file size. If you're unable to call a WCF service using Silverlight, one of the first things you'll want to check is that the basicHttpBinding is being used.

Self-Hosted WCF Services and Cross-Domain Policy Files

The WCF service discussed up to this point would be hosted using Internet Information Services (IIS). However, WCF services can be hosted in Windows Services, Console applications, Windows Forms, or other .NET applications without relying on IIS. Silverlight clients trying to hit a self-hosted service from a different domain will encounter security issues unless they're able to retrieve a crossdomain.xml or clientaccesspolicy.xml file as discussed earlier in this chapter.

The solution to this problem is solved by new WCF Web features and attributes available in .NET 3.5 that allow a cross-domain policy file to be retrieved by a Silverlight client even when the WCF service isn't hosted in IIS. This solution was originally created by Microsoft's Carlos Figueira on his blog at http://blogs.msdn.com/carlosfigueira/default.aspx.

By using WCF's WebGetAttribute class (located in the System.ServiceModel.Web), a self-hosted service can serve cross-domain policy files to a Silverlight client much like IIS would serve a static policy file located at its root. Here's an example of using the WCF WebGetAttribute class to allow a service operation to use the Web programming model:

```
[ServiceContract]
public interface ICrossDomainPolicyRetriever
{
    [OperationContract]
    [WebGet(UriTemplate = "/clientaccesspolicy.xml")]
    Stream GetSilverlightPolicy();

    [OperationContract]
    [WebGet(UriTemplate = "/crossdomain.xml")]
    Stream GetFlashPolicy();
}
```

The WebGetAttribute class's UriTemplate property specifies that any calls to /clientaccesspolicy.xml should call the GetSilverlightPolicy method, while calls to /crossdomain.xml should call the GetFlashPolicy method. By using this technique, a self-hosted service can still be used by a Silverlight client in another domain.

A WCF service class that implements the ICrossDomainPolicyRetriever service contract is shown next along with code for the GetSilverlightPolicy and GetFlashPolicy methods:

```
using System;
using System.ServiceModel;
using System.ServiceModel.Web;
using System.IO;
using System.Text;
using System.ServiceModel.Description;


[ServiceContract]
public interface ITest
```

```csharp
{
    [OperationContract]
    string Echo(string text);
}

[ServiceContract]
public interface ICrossDomainPolicyRetriever
{
    [OperationContract]
    [WebGet(UriTemplate = "/clientaccesspolicy.xml")]
    Stream GetSilverlightPolicy();

    [OperationContract]
    [WebGet(UriTemplate = "/crossdomain.xml")]
    Stream GetFlashPolicy();
}

public class SelfHostedService : ITest, ICrossDomainPolicyRetriever
{
    public string Echo(string text) { return text; }

    Stream StringToStream(string result)
    {
        WebOperationContext.Current.OutgoingResponse.ContentType =
            "application/xml";
        return new MemoryStream(Encoding.UTF8.GetBytes(result));
    }

    public Stream GetSilverlightPolicy()
    {
        string result = @"<?xml version=""1.0"" encoding=""utf-8""?>
<access-policy>
    <cross-domain-access>
        <policy>
            <allow-from http-request-headers=""*"">
                <domain uri=""*""/>
            </allow-from>
            <grant-to>
                <resource path=""/"" include-subpaths=""true""/>
            </grant-to>
        </policy>
    </cross-domain-access>
</access-policy>";
        return StringToStream(result);
    }
    public Stream GetFlashPolicy()
    {
        string result = @"<?xml version=""1.0""?>
<cross-domain-policy>
    <allow-http-request-headers-from domain=""*"" headers=""*"" />
</cross-domain-policy>";
        return StringToStream(result);
```

```
    }
    public static void Main()
    {
        string baseAddress = "http://" + Environment.MachineName + ":8000";
        ServiceHost host = new ServiceHost(typeof(SelfHostedService),
          new Uri(baseAddress));
        host.AddServiceEndpoint(typeof(ITest), new BasicHttpBinding(), "basic");
        host.AddServiceEndpoint(typeof(ICrossDomainPolicyRetriever),
          new WebHttpBinding(), "").Behaviors.Add(new WebHttpBehavior());
        ServiceMetadataBehavior smb = new ServiceMetadataBehavior();
        smb.HttpGetEnabled = true;
        host.Description.Behaviors.Add(smb);
        host.Open();
        Console.WriteLine("Host opened");
        Console.Write("Press ENTER to close");
        Console.ReadLine();
        host.Close();
    }
}
```

Creating an ASP.NET Web Service for Silverlight

WCF is a key technology in .NET 3.5 for building services, but it's not the only option that can be used. ASP.NET Web Service functionality is still available when you need to create a Web Service that Silverlight (or other clients) can consume. ASP.NET Web Services (often called *ASMX services* because of the .asmx file extension that is used) don't come with all of the bells and whistles that WCF has, but for Silverlight clients, those typically aren't needed. The following sections will walk you through the process of creating ASMX services.

Creating an ASMX File

Visual Studio has provided support for creating ASP.NET Web Services since .NET first came out in 2002. That support is still available today and makes it easy to get started creating Web Services even if you've never done it before. Two project templates are available in Visual Studio including the ASP.NET Web Service Application template and the ASP.NET Web Service template. Both create an initial .asmx file and associated code-beside file to get you started.

ASP.NET Web Services rely on .NET framework XML and SOAP serialization classes under the covers to convert CLR types to SOAP messages and back. When creating ASP.NET services that Silverlight clients will consume, it's important to use interoperable types that can easily be bound to controls on the client side. For example, DataSets can be returned from ASP.NET Web Services operations but should generally be avoided and replaced with custom data entity classes. These custom classes are normally more lightweight and only contain fields and properties much like the Product class shown earlier in this chapter. By using custom classes, the Web Service Description Language (WSDL) file generated for the service will contain in-depth details about the types being exposed by the service and will be more easily consumed by a variety of clients as a result. Avoiding the use of DataSets with services (ASP.NET Web Services or WCF services) is a good rule of thumb to follow whether you're building services for Silverlight or not.

> Silverlight 2 doesn't include built-in support for DataSets, which is another good
> reason to avoid using them when creating services. Silverlight clients that consume
> services returning DataSet objects will have to write custom code to parse the
> XML data returned from the service.

Defining WebMethods

Once an ASP.NET Web Services project or web site has been created, service operations (methods) can be added directly into the service class and decorated with the WebMethod attribute. This attribute adds Web Services capabilities into the method and allows it to be called through the Web using HTTP and SOAP. Additional attributes such as WebService and WebServiceBinding can also be added to define XML namespaces used in SOAP messages and ensure that the service adheres to the WSI Basic Profile version 1.1 (read more about the WSI Basic Profile at www.ws-i.org/Profiles/BasicProfile-1.1.html).

An example of an ASP.NET Web Service that returns product information is shown next:

```
using System;
using System.Linq;
using System.Web;
using System.Web.Services;
using System.Web.Services.Protocols;
using System.Xml.Linq;

[WebService(Namespace = "http://www.smartwebcontrols.com/samples")]
[WebServiceBinding(ConformsTo = WsiProfiles.BasicProfile1_1)]
public class ProductService : System.Web.Services.WebService
{
    public ProductService()
    {
        //Uncomment the following line if using designed components
        //InitializeComponent();
    }

    [WebMethod]
    public Model.Product[] GetProducts()
    {
        return Biz.BAL.GetProducts();
    }

    [WebMethod]
    public Model.Product GetProduct(int prodID)
    {
        return Biz.BAL.GetProduct(prodID);
    }

}
```

The ProductService class defines GetProducts and GetProduct methods that return a Product array and a Product object, respectively. Both methods are decorated with the WebMethod attribute and use business and data layer classes to retrieve data from the database.

Because both methods return custom `Product` types, the WSDL will be well-defined and easy to consume by clients. Looking at the WSDL generated by the service, you'll see that the custom `Product` type (and array for the `GetProducts` method) is thoroughly defined in the schema, making it easy to consume by any consumer including a Silverlight application.

```xml
<?xml version="1.0" encoding="utf-8"?>
<wsdl:definitions xmlns:soap="http://schemas.xmlsoap.org/wsdl/soap/"
xmlns:tm="http://microsoft.com/wsdl/mime/textMatching/"
xmlns:soapenc="http://schemas.xmlsoap.org/soap/encoding/"
xmlns:mime="http://schemas.xmlsoap.org/wsdl/mime/"
xmlns:tns="http://www.smartwebcontrols.com/samples"
xmlns:s="http://www.w3.org/2001/XMLSchema"
xmlns:soap12="http://schemas.xmlsoap.org/wsdl/soap12/"
xmlns:http="http://schemas.xmlsoap.org/wsdl/http/"
targetNamespace="http://www.smartwebcontrols.com/samples"
xmlns:wsdl="http://schemas.xmlsoap.org/wsdl/">
  <wsdl:types>
    <s:schema elementFormDefault="qualified"
      targetNamespace="http://www.smartwebcontrols.com/samples">
      <s:element name="GetProducts">
        <s:complexType />
      </s:element>
      <s:element name="GetProductsResponse">
        <s:complexType>
          <s:sequence>
            <s:element minOccurs="0" maxOccurs="1" name="GetProductsResult"
              type="tns:ArrayOfProduct" />
          </s:sequence>
        </s:complexType>
      </s:element>
      <s:complexType name="ArrayOfProduct">
        <s:sequence>
          <s:element minOccurs="0" maxOccurs="unbounded" name="Product"
            nillable="true" type="tns:Product" />
        </s:sequence>
      </s:complexType>
      <s:complexType name="Product">
        <s:sequence>
          <s:element minOccurs="1" maxOccurs="1" name="ProductID" type="s:int" />
          <s:element minOccurs="1" maxOccurs="1" name="CategoryID" type="s:int" />
          <s:element minOccurs="0" maxOccurs="1" name="ModelNumber"
              type="s:string"
          />
          <s:element minOccurs="0" maxOccurs="1" name="ModelName"
              type="s:string"
          />
          <s:element minOccurs="0" maxOccurs="1" name="ProductImage"
            type="s:string" />
          <s:element minOccurs="1" maxOccurs="1" name="UnitCost"
              type="s:decimal"
          />
          <s:element minOccurs="0" maxOccurs="1" name="Description"
              type="s:string"
          />
```

```
            </s:sequence>
        </s:complexType>
        <s:element name="GetProduct">
          <s:complexType>
            <s:sequence>
              <s:element minOccurs="1" maxOccurs="1" name="prodID" type="s:int" />
            </s:sequence>
          </s:complexType>
        </s:element>
        <s:element name="GetProductResponse">
          <s:complexType>
            <s:sequence>
              <s:element minOccurs="0" maxOccurs="1" name="GetProductResult"
                type="tns:Product" />
            </s:sequence>
          </s:complexType>
        </s:element>
      </s:schema>
    </wsdl:types>
    <!- Messages,PortTypes, Operations, Binding, Service endpoints defined here ->

</wsdl:definitions>
```

Calling Services with Silverlight

It goes without saying that getting data to and from Silverlight applications is a key feature that many applications will require. Silverlight gaming applications need to transmit high scores to a central server, mash-up applications need to aggregate data from multiple sources, and business applications need to display data and gather user input. All of these applications can tie into one or more services to accomplish these goals.

When Web Services first appeared on the scene, developers had to construct SOAP messages manually and write custom code to communicate with services. Coding against Web Services was error-prone and caused more than one developer to consider (even if briefly) throwing his monitor out the window. Fortunately, tools have matured a lot since those early days and have significantly reduced the amount of code required to communicate between a client and a service. Today's tools abstract away the messaging format and allow developers to call a service using a proxy object that encapsulates all of the complexities associated with calling services. The proxy object handles serializing data from CLR types and also handles deserializing SOAP messages received from a service back into CLR types.

In this section, you'll see how a Silverlight client can access WCF and ASP.NET services and bind data to controls. Later in the chapter, you'll see alternative ways for communicating with different types of services.

Calling a WCF Service

Silverlight applications can integrate with WCF services quickly and with minimal code by using proxy generation capabilities built in to Visual Studio. The proxy that is generated allows asynchronous calls to be made to the service without worrying about relying on custom threading techniques. Instead, you can use a familiar event-driven mechanism to wire up a service call to a callback method, which then binds data to controls on the interface.

Creating a Service Proxy

The process of creating a WCF proxy for a Silverlight application is virtually identical to the process you'd go through to create a WCF proxy for an ASP.NET application. To add a service proxy into a Silverlight project, you can right-click on the project in Solution Explorer and select Add Service Reference from the menu. Figure 9-1 shows an example of the Add Service Reference dialog.

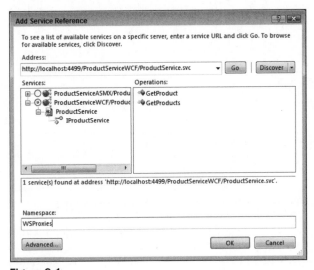

Figure 9-1

> If the service is in a different domain from the Silverlight application, a cross-domain policy file must be defined at the root of the server where the service is hosted.

The path to a service's WSDL file can be typed into the Address textbox, or the Discover button can be clicked to find services in the local solution. In this example, a proxy class will be created that is capable of calling the ProductServiceWCF service once the OK button is clicked. The generated proxy class is wrapped in the WSProxies namespace.

Using a Service Proxy to Make Asynchronous Calls

Once the proxy class has been generated, you can use it in the same way that you'd use any standard .NET class — instantiate the class and access member properties and methods. As you access the methods exposed by the proxy object, you may notice something different compared to ASP.NET Web Service proxy objects you may have used in Web Forms; the Silverlight proxy object doesn't support making synchronous calls. For instance, no GetProducts method appears in IntelliSense as you may expect. You'll instead see a GetProductsAsync method along with a GetProductsCompleted event and a GetProductsCompletedEventArgs class. Why are only asynchronous calls allowed? The short answer is that the Silverlight application is hosted in a browser that is asynchronous by nature. Because synchronous calls can cause the user interface thread to "block" as the call is made, they aren't a good way to call a service in Silverlight, especially since you never know how long the service call will take.

The code that follows demonstrates how a proxy class named `ProductServiceClient` (located in the `WSProxies` namespace) generated using the `Add Service Reference` tool can be used to make an asynchronous call to a WCF service as a button is clicked on a Silverlight interface:

```
private void btnWCFProducts_Click(object sender, RoutedEventArgs e)
{
    //Create proxy and give it the name of the endpoint in the config file
    ProductServiceClient proxy =
      new ProductServiceClient("BasicHttpBinding_IProductService");
    proxy.GetProductsCompleted += new
     EventHandler<GetProductsCompletedEventArgs>(proxy_GetProductsCompleted);
    proxy.GetProductsAsync();
}

void proxy_GetProductsCompleted(object sender,  GetProductsCompletedEventArgs e)
{
    //Bind Product object array to ListBox
    this.lbProducts.ItemsSource = e.Result;
}
```

Once the button's `Click` event is fired, the event handler instantiates the proxy object and wires up `GetProductsCompletedEvent` to an event handler named `proxy_GetProductsCompleted`. The `proxy_GetProductsCompleted` event handler is called after data returns from the Web Service. Once the event handler is wired up, the `GetProductsAsync` method is called, which starts the asynchronous call. When the Web Service call returns, the `GetProductsCompleted` event handler is called, which binds the array of `Product` objects to a `ListBox` control named `lbProducts` defined in a Silverlight user control. The data returned from the service call is encapsulated in the `GetProductsCompletedEventArgs` parameter and accessed through the `Result` property.

The XAML for the user control that data is bound to is shown next, and the output that is generated after the Web Service call returns is shown in Figure 9-2:

```
<UserControl x:Class="SilverlightClient.Page"
    xmlns="http://schemas.microsoft.com/client/2007"
    xmlns:x="http://schemas.microsoft.com/winfx/2006/xaml"
>
    <Grid x:Name="LayoutRoot" Background="White">
        <Grid.RowDefinitions>
            <RowDefinition Height="40" />
            <RowDefinition Height="*" />
        </Grid.RowDefinitions>
        <Grid.ColumnDefinitions>
            <ColumnDefinition />
        </Grid.ColumnDefinitions>

        <!-- Row 0 -->
        <StackPanel Orientation="Horizontal" Grid.Row="0">
            <Button x:Name="btnWCFProducts" Content="Get WCF Products" Margin="10"
             Width="115" Height="20" Click="btnWCFProducts_Click"></Button>
```

```xml
        <Button x:Name="btnASMXProducts" Content="Get ASMX Products"
        Margin="10" Width="115" Height="20"
        Click="btnASMXProducts_Click"></Button>
    </StackPanel>

    <!- Row 1 ->
    <ListBox x:Name="lbProducts" Grid.Row="1" Margin="10">
        <ListBox.ItemTemplate>
            <DataTemplate>
                <StackPanel Orientation="Horizontal">
                    <Image Source="{Binding ProductImage}" Margin="10"
                    Height="100" Width="100" />
                    <TextBlock Text="{Binding ModelName}" />
                </StackPanel>
            </DataTemplate>
        </ListBox.ItemTemplate>
    </ListBox>
</Grid>
</UserControl>
```

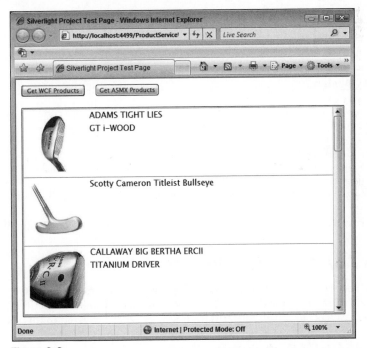

Figure 9-2

Calling the Web Service doesn't require a lot of code, but you may be wondering how the proxy object knew where the service endpoint was located. The answer lies in the Add Service Reference proxy generator tool. While creating the proxy object code, a special client-side configuration file named ServiceReferences.ClientConfig is also created and placed in the Silverlight project by the tool. This file defines how to bind to the WCF service, as shown next:

```
<configuration>
    <system.serviceModel>
        <bindings>
            <basicHttpBinding>
                <binding name="BasicHttpBinding_IProductService"
                 maxBufferSize="65536" maxReceivedMessageSize="65536">
                    <security mode="None" />
                </binding>
            </basicHttpBinding>
        </bindings>
        <client>
            <endpoint
             address="http://localhost:4499/ProductServiceWCF/ProductService.svc"
             binding="basicHttpBinding"
             bindingConfiguration="BasicHttpBinding_IProductService"
             contract="SilverlightClient.WSProxies.IProductService"
             name="BasicHttpBinding_IProductService" />
        </client>
    </system.serviceModel>
</configuration>
```

Looking through the configuration code, you'll notice that the ABCs of the service are defined including the service address, the type of binding, and the contract that should be used. By using the client configuration file, you can avoid hard-coding service endpoints directly into code, which obviously leads to less code and simplified maintenance down the road. The file is packaged up into the Silverlight XAP file when you build the project.

In situations in which you need to define the ABCs of a service through code (as opposed to retrieving them from a configuration file), you can do the following:

```
EndpointAddress addr = new EndpointAddress(
    "http://localhost:4499/ProductServiceWCF/ProductService.svc");
Binding httpBinding = new BasicHttpBinding();
ProductServiceClient proxy = new ProductServiceClient(httpBinding, addr);
```

This code will override any settings found in the ServiceReferences.ClientConfig file.

Calling an ASP.NET Web Service

ASP.NET Web Services can be called from Silverlight applications much like WCF services can. Similar tools and code are used to make this type of call, so a quick overview of the fundamentals of creating and using a proxy object to call an ASP.NET Web Service will be covered in this section.

Creating an ASP.NET Web Service Proxy

Visual Studio's `Add Service Reference` tool discussed in the previous "Calling a WCF Service" section of this chapter can also be used to create a proxy object capable of calling an ASP.NET Web Service. ASP.NET Web Services don't define contracts in the same way that WCF does, but the `Add Service Reference` tool provides a similar visual view of operations supported by the service, as shown in Figure 9-3. The same steps discussed earlier for creating a WCF service proxy apply here.

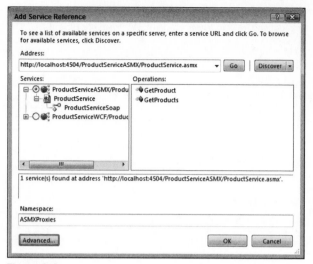

Figure 9-3

Using a Web Service Proxy to Make Asynchronous Calls

After running the Add Service Reference tool to create a proxy, a SOAP client class will be generated that can be used to call an ASP.NET Web Service. As with WCF calls, ASP.NET Web Services calls are made asynchronously. When data from the service returns to the Silverlight application, a callback method is invoked to process the data and bind it to controls.

An example of using a class named ProductServiceSoapClient to call an ASP.NET Web Service asynchronously is shown next. Looking through the code you'll see that it's identical (aside from the proxy type name) to the code used to call a WCF service. This consistency is great because once you learn the pattern for calling services, you can reuse it to call services that are written using different languages and running on different platforms.

```
private void btnASMXProducts_Click(object sender, RoutedEventArgs e)
{
    ProductServiceSoapClient proxy =
      new ProductServiceSoapClient("ProductServiceSoap");
    proxy.GetProductsCompleted +=
      new EventHandler<GetProductsCompletedEventArgs>(proxy_GetProductsCompleted);
    proxy.GetProductsAsync();
}

void proxy_GetProductsCompleted(object sender, GetProductsCompletedEventArgs e)
{
    this.lbProducts.ItemsSource = e.Result;
}
```

After the proxy object is instantiated, an event associated with the service call (GetProductsCompleted in this example) is hooked to a callback method. The call is then started by calling the GetProductsAsync method. Data returned from the service can be accessed through the GetProductsCompletedEventArgs parameter's Result property that is passed to the callback method.

The proxy object relies on a ServiceReference.ClientConfig file to define where the service is physically located. The file is identical to the one generated for WCF proxy objects.

```
<configuration>
    <system.serviceModel>
        <bindings>
            <basicHttpBinding>
                <binding name="ProductServiceSoap" maxBufferSize="65536"
                    maxReceivedMessageSize="65536">
                    <security mode="None" />
                </binding>
            </basicHttpBinding>
        </bindings>
        <client>
            <endpoint
            address="http://localhost:4504/ProductServiceASMX/ProductService.asmx"
            binding="basicHttpBinding" bindingConfiguration="ProductServiceSoap"
            contract="SilverlightClient.ASMXProxies.ProductServiceSoap"
            name="ProductServiceSoap" />
        </client>
    </system.serviceModel>
</configuration>
```

Calling REST APIs

The use of Representational State Transfer (REST) has increased significantly since it was first proposed by Roy Fielding in 2000. REST provides a simpler way to call services and retrieve data while eliminating some of the complexities associated with Web Services. Data services that rely on RESTful calls typically do not provide an official contract such as a WSDL document. As a result, no proxy generation tools are available to generate code for calling a REST API. However, Silverlight provides several classes that can be used to initiate requests and handle responses.

Several different techniques can also be used to process data that is returned from a service. In this section, you'll see how built-in Silverlight classes can be used to call REST services and learn different techniques for processing data returned by REST services.

Making RESTful Calls in Silverlight

At the beginning of the chapter, several popular web sites such as Digg and Flickr were mentioned. These sites and many others allow developers to access data through REST APIs. Some of the REST services return SOAP, some return POX (Plain Old XML), and others return JSON. Silverlight provides several options for making RESTful calls and for processing data that is returned. Requests and responses can be handled using classes such as WebClient, HttpWebRequest, and HttpWebResponse. Let's start out by analyzing the WebClient class and see how it can be used to make asynchronous RESTful calls.

Using the `WebClient` *Class*

Silverlight's `WebClient` class is located in the `System.Net` namespace and acts much like its big brother found in the full version of the .NET Framework. It allows asynchronous requests to be made to Web resources and provides a way to specify a callback method to process response data. It's arguably the easiest way to initiate a request and handle a response in Silverlight since it doesn't require knowledge of stream objects or the process of converting byte arrays into strings. In fact, `WebClient` allows you to access data returned from a REST API as a string.

`WebClient` provides a `DownloadStringAsync` method as well as a `DownloadStringCompleted` event that can be used to initiate asynchronous calls and process response data, as shown in the following code sample:

```
private void StartWebClient()
{
    WebClient restClient = new WebClient();
    restClient.DownloadStringCompleted +=
        new DownloadStringCompletedEventHandler(restClient_DownloadStringCompleted);
    restClient.DownloadStringAsync(CreateRESTUri());
}

private void restClient_DownloadStringCompleted(object sender,
    DownloadStringCompletedEventArgs e)
{
    if (e.Error == null && !e.Cancelled)
    {
        ProcessData(e.Result);
    }
}

private Uri CreateRESTUri()
{
    return new Uri(String.Format("{0}?method={1}&api_key={2}&text={3}&per_page={4}",
        _BaseUri, "flickr.photos.search", _APIKey, this.txtSearchText.Text, 50));
}
```

This example wires the `WebClient`'s `DownloadStringCompleted` event to an event handler named `restClient_DownloadStringCompleted` that kicks off parsing of XML data returned from a call to the Flickr REST API. The data retrieval process is started by calling the `DownloadStringAsync` method, which accepts a URI object as a parameter. Data returned from the RESTful call is accessed through the `DownloadStringCompletedEventArgs` object's `Result` property as a string.

> The `WebClient` class also exposes an `UploadStringAsync` method and `UploadString Completed` event that can be used to upload data to a web site. They work in a similar manner to the `DownloadStringAsync` method and `DownloadStringCompleted` event.

WebClient also provides an OpenReadAsync method and an associated OpenReadCompleted event that can be used to access resources such as font files on a server. This can be useful when server resources used in an application need to be retrieved dynamically. The code that follows shows how the OpenReadAsync method can be used to download a .zip file named ArialFonts.zip from the ClientBin folder on the server and assign a font resource extracted from the file to a TextBlock object named tbDynamicArial. In addition to the WebClient class, you'll notice that the code also relies on a StreamResourceInfo object to access the .zip file contents as well as a font file named ARIALN.TTF within the file.

```csharp
private void Page_Loaded(object sender, RoutedEventArgs e)
{
        WebClient client = new WebClient();
        client.OpenReadCompleted +=
            new OpenReadCompletedEventHandler(client_OpenReadCompleted);
        client.OpenReadAsync(new Uri("ArialFonts.zip",UriKind.Relative));
}

private void  client_OpenReadCompleted(object sender, OpenReadCompletedEventArgs e)
{
    if (e.Error == null && !e.Cancelled)
    {
        StreamResourceInfo zip = new StreamResourceInfo(e.Result,
          "application/zip");
        StreamResourceInfo font = Application.GetResourceStream(zip,
            new Uri("ARIALN.TTF",UriKind.Relative));
        FontSource fSource = new FontSource(font.Stream);
        FontFamily ff = new FontFamily("Arial Narrow");
        UpdateUI(fSource, ff);
    }
}
private void UpdateUI(FontSource fSource, FontFamily ff)
{
    this.tbDynamicArial.FontSource = fSource;
    this.tbDynamicArial.FontFamily = ff;
}
```

Looking through this code, you may wonder if there isn't an easier way to grab a font resource and use it. After all, there's quite a bit of work involved to extract the ARIALN.TTF font from the ArialFonts.zip file and assign it as the FontSource for the TextBlock. Fortunately, a shortcut does exist that can be used directly within XAML. To do this, right-click on the .zip file containing one or more of the fonts used in your application, and select Properties from the menu. In the Properties window, set the Build Action property to Resource to include the .zip file in the .xap that gets generated. Once this is done, you can use the FontFamily attribute to define the .zip file resource to access as well as the font that should be referenced inside the file. Here's an example of referencing the Arial and Arial Black fonts in TextBlock elements. Notice that the file and font are separated with a # character.

```xml
<UserControl x:Class="SilverlightFontClient.Page"
    xmlns="http://schemas.microsoft.com/client/2007"
    xmlns:x="http://schemas.microsoft.com/winfx/2006/xaml"
    Width="600" Height="300">
    <Grid x:Name="LayoutRoot" Background="White">
        <Canvas Margin="10">
            <TextBlock x:Name="tbArial" Canvas.Top="50" Text="Arial Text"
                FontSize="30" FontFamily="ArialFonts.zip#Arial" />
```

```
          <TextBlock x:Name="tbArialBold" Canvas.Top="100" Text="Arial Black"
              FontSize="30" FontFamily="ArialFonts.zip#Arial Black" />
    </Canvas>
  </Grid>
</UserControl>
```

Using the `HttpWebRequest` and `HttpWebResponse` Classes

WebClient isn't the only class available for accessing web resources. Silverlight also provides HttpWeb
Request and HttpWebResponse classes, which can be used to call REST APIs or any web resource
that's accessible, for that matter. These classes are also available in the standard .NET Framework (as is
WebClient), so they're familiar to many ASP.NET developers. An example of using the HttpWebRequest
and HttpWebResponse classes to retrieve data asynchronously from the Flickr REST API is shown next:

```
private void StartWebRequest()
{
    //Add reference to System.Net.dll if it's not already referenced
    HttpWebRequest request = (HttpWebRequest)WebRequest.Create(CreateRESTUri());
    //Start async REST request
    request.BeginGetResponse(new AsyncCallback(GetResponseCallBack),request);
}

private void GetResponseCallBack(IAsyncResult asyncResult)
{
    HttpWebRequest request = (HttpWebRequest)asyncResult.AsyncState;
    HttpWebResponse response =
      (HttpWebResponse)request.EndGetResponse(asyncResult);
    Stream dataStream = response.GetResponseStream();
    StreamReader reader = new StreamReader(dataStream);
    string data = reader.ReadToEnd();
    reader.Close();
    response.Close();
    Dispatcher.BeginInvoke(() => ProcessData(data));
}

private Uri CreateRESTUri()
{
    return new Uri(String.Format("{0}?method={1}&api_key={2}&text={3}&per_page={4}",
        _BaseUri, "flickr.photos.search", _APIKey, this.txtSearchText.Text, 50));
}
```

Looking through the code, you can see that the HttpWebRequest class uses a different asynchronous pattern than WebClient. To use the HttpWebRequest class, you first create an instance by using an abstract
class named WebRequest. WebRequest provides a static Create method that can be used to create a request
to a URL (that is encapsulated in a URI object). Once an HttpWebRequest object is created, it can make an
asynchronous request to the desired resource and get a response by calling the BeginGetResponse
method. BeginGetResponse accepts an AsyncCallback object that points to a callback method as well
as a state object (which is typically the HttpWebRequest object that started the operation).

Once the response is received, the callback method is invoked (GetResponseCallBack in this example),
and data within the IAsyncResult parameter is accessed. The state object (the original HttpWebRequest)
passed when the asynchronous call was first started can be accessed through the AsyncState property
of the IAsyncResult object. The response data can be accessed through an HttpWebResponse object,

which is made available by calling the request object's `EndGetResponse` method. Once the `HttpWebResponse` object is available, its `GetResponseStream` method can be called to access the response data as a stream.

Processing XML Data

To this point, you've seen how Silverlight classes can be used to make RESTful calls and retrieve data from local or remote servers. Accessing data is certainly a step in the right direction, but at some point, you'll need to process the data and bind it to Silverlight controls. This section shows three different ways to process XML data returned from a RESTful call. The available options include using the `XmlReader` class, the `XmlSerializer` class, and using built-in LINQ to XML functionality. Let's start by examining how the `XmlReader` class can be used to parse XML data in a fast, forward-only manner.

Using the `XmlReader` Class

The `XmlReader` class was introduced when .NET 1.0 was first released in 2002. Subsequent releases of the framework have enhanced its functionality and added helper classes such as `XmlReaderSettings` that can be used to supply settings to the reader as it parses XML data. `XmlReader` provides a stream-based API that can parse XML in a forward-only manner. By learning how to use the different methods it exposes, you can parse large amounts of XML data quickly and efficiently.

The `XmlReader` class is abstract, so an instance can't be created using the standard `new` keyword. Instead, call its static `Create` method, which returns an object instance that can be used. The `Create` method has several overloads that can be used to parse XML data contained in streams, objects that derive from `TextReader` and within a Silverlight XAP file. An example of creating an `XmlReader` instance to parse data contained in a `StringReader` object is shown next:

```
String stringData = "<customers><customer id=\"2\" Name=\"John\" /></customers>";
StringReader sReader = new StringReader(stringData);
using (XmlReader reader = XmlReader.Create(sReader))
{
    //Parse XML data
}
```

Once an `XmlReader` instance is created, it can be used to parse XML data by calling its `Read` method. Each call to `Read` advances the reader to the next XML token in the stream starting at the top of the document and moving down to the bottom. As content is found during the parsing process, different methods such as `ReadContentAsDecimal` and `ReadContentAsDateTime` can be called to convert data into different CLR types. XML attribute nodes can be accessed using methods such as `GetAttribute`, `MoveToAttribute`, and `MoveToNextAttribute`.

The best way to learn how to use the `XmlReader` class is by example, so let's examine how an XML document retrieved from the Flickr REST service can be parsed. The following XML document contains photo information returned from Flickr that can be used to construct URLs and retrieve images from their servers:

```
<?xml version="1.0" encoding="utf-8" ?>
<rsp stat="ok">
  <photos page="1" pages="31875" perpage="100" total="3187432">
    <photo id="2375848757" owner="13128942@N05" secret="8b08b4c89c" server="2201"
```

```
        farm="3" title="Dogs ready to go" ispublic="1" isfriend="0" isfamily="0" />
      <photo id="2376686792" owner="25029759@N04" secret="a2f3ac27db" server="3218"
       farm="4" title="Inseparable" ispublic="1" isfriend="0" isfamily="0" />
      <photo id="2376683204" owner="22160786@N08" secret="7e60b3903a" server="2410"
       farm="3" title="rjk dog 003" ispublic="1" isfriend="0" isfamily="0" />
      <photo id="2375847463" owner="63299638@N00" secret="62fd3effd2" server="2014"
       farm="3" title="Hudson &amp; Kobe" ispublic="1" isfriend="0" isfamily="0" />
    </photos>
  </rsp>
```

As XML data is parsed, its values can be assigned to string objects, but it's generally better to parse an XML document and map the data to a custom object's properties. Mapping the XML data to custom object properties allows the data to be accessed in a strongly typed manner within an application and allows the data to be bound to various Silverlight controls. The data associated with each <photo> element in the previous XML document can be mapped to properties of the Photo class shown next:

```
namespace SilverlightRESTClient.Model
{
    public class Photo
    {
        public string ID { get; set; }
        public string Owner { get; set; }
        public string Secret { get; set; }
        public string Title { get; set; }
        public bool IsPublic { get; set; }
        public bool IsFriend { get; set; }
        public bool IsFamily { get; set; }
        public string Url { get; set; }
        public string Server { get; set; }
        public ImageBrush ImageBrush { get; set; }
        public string Farm { get; set; }
    }
}
```

Mapping XML data to an instance of a Photo object is accomplished by calling the XmlReader object's Read method. As mentioned earlier, calling Read moves to the next XML token in the stream. Read isn't the only method that can be used to move through an XML document, though. You can also use methods like ReadToDescendant or ReadToFollowing to move the reader to a specific element. This is useful when you'd like to skip a group of elements that aren't relevant to an application.

As photo elements are found during the parsing process, their attributes (id, server, farm, etc.) can be iterated through, parsed, and assigned to a Photo object's respective properties. An example of performing this type of XML-to-object mapping is shown next:

```
private List<Model.Photo> XmlReaderParseData(string data)
{
    StringReader sReader = new StringReader(data);

    XmlReaderSettings settings = new XmlReaderSettings();
    settings.IgnoreComments = true;
    settings.IgnoreProcessingInstructions = true;
    settings.IgnoreWhitespace = true;
```

```
    using (XmlReader reader = XmlReader.Create(sReader,settings))
    {
        List<Model.Photo> photos = new List<Model.Photo>();
        while (reader.Read())
        {
            if (reader.Name == "photo")
            {
                Model.Photo photo = new Model.Photo();
                while (reader.MoveToNextAttribute())
                {
                    string val = reader.Value;
                    switch (reader.Name.ToLower())
                    {
                        case "farm":
                            photo.Farm = val;
                            break;
                        case "id":
                            photo.ID = val;
                            break;
                        case "isfamily":
                            photo.IsFamily = ConvertBoolean(val);
                            break;
                        case "isfriend":
                            photo.IsFriend = ConvertBoolean(val);
                            break;
                        case "ispublic":
                            photo.IsPublic = ConvertBoolean(val);
                            break;
                        case "owner":
                            photo.Owner = val;
                            break;
                        case "secret":
                            photo.Secret = val;
                            break;
                        case "server":
                            photo.Server = val;
                            break;
                        case "title":
                            photo.Title = val;
                            break;
                    } //end switch
                } //attribute while loop
                reader.MoveToElement();
                photo.Url = CreatePhotoUrl(photo);
                ImageBrush brush = new ImageBrush();
                BitmapImage bm = new BitmapImage(new Uri(photo.Url));
                brush.ImageSource = bm;
                photo.ImageBrush = brush;
                photos.Add(photo);
            } //photo
        } //reader while loop
        return photos;
    } //using
}
```

```
private bool ConvertBoolean(string val)
{
    return (val == "0") ? false : true;
}


private string CreatePhotoUrl(Model.Photo photo)
{
    //http://farm{farm-id}.static.flickr.com/{server-id}/{id}_{secret}_{size}.jpg
    //farm-id: 1
    //server-id: 2
    //photo-id: 1418878
    //secret: 1e92283336
    //size: m, s, t, b

    return String.Format(_BasePhotoUrl, photo.Farm, photo.Server,
                                 photo.ID, photo.Secret, "s");
}
```

The code starts by loading data retrieved from the Flickr REST service into a `StringReader` object. An `XmlReaderSettings` class is then created to instruct the `XmlReader` to ignore comments and processing instructions that may be found in the XML document. The `XmlReaderSettings` object is passed to the `Create` method used to create an `XmlReader` instance along with the `StringReader` object. Once the `XmlReader` object is created, the parsing process begins.

As each `photo` element is parsed in the XML stream, a new `Photo` object is created to store the element's data. The code then iterates through all of the `photo` element's attributes using the `MoveToNextAttribute` method. Each attribute name is checked and mapped to the `Photo` object's appropriate property using a `switch` statement.

Once all of the attributes have been iterated through, a URL is constructed to retrieve the Flickr image by calling the custom `CreatePhotoUrl` method. The URL is then fed into a `BitmapImage` object used as the source for an `ImageBrush`. The `ImageBrush` can be bound to different Silverlight controls to show the image in the Silverlight interface. As each `Photo` object is created, it's added to a `List<Photo>` collection object that's returned from the `XmlReaderParseData` method and bound to the Silverlight `ItemsControl` control shown next. Notice that the `ImageBrush` object from each photo is bound to the `Fill` property of a `Rectangle` object.

```xml
<ItemsControl x:Name="icPhotos" Grid.Row="1">
    <ItemsControl.ItemsPanel>
        <ItemsPanelTemplate>
            <wp:WrapPanel x:Name="wpImages" Margin="10"
                Orientation="Horizontal"
                VerticalAlignment="Top" />
        </ItemsPanelTemplate>
    </ItemsControl.ItemsPanel>
    <ItemsControl.ItemTemplate>
        <DataTemplate>
            <Rectangle Stroke="LightGray" Tag="{Binding Url}"
                Fill="{Binding ImageBrush}" StrokeThickness="2"
                RadiusX="15" RadiusY="15" Margin="15"
                Height="75" Width="75" Loaded="Rectangle_Loaded"
                MouseLeave="Rectangle_MouseLeave"
                MouseEnter="Rectangle_MouseEnter"
```

```
                  MouseLeftButtonDown="rect_MouseLeftButtonDown">
               <Rectangle.RenderTransform>
                  <TransformGroup>
                     <ScaleTransform ScaleX="1" ScaleY="1" CenterX="37.5"
                        CenterY="37.5" />
                  </TransformGroup>
               </Rectangle.RenderTransform>
            </Rectangle>
         </DataTemplate>
      </ItemsControl.ItemTemplate>
   </ItemsControl>
```

Figure 9-4 shows an example of the output after the Photo objects have been bound to the ItemsControl control.

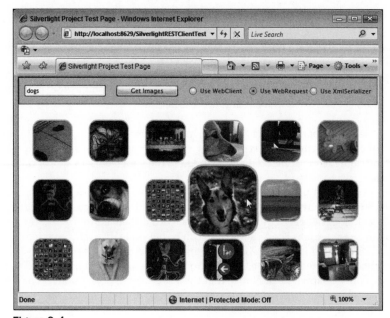

Figure 9-4

The XmlReader class provides an extremely efficient API for parsing XML but does require some work to parse data in an XML document. In cases in which you don't need that type of fine-grained control over the XML parsing process, the XmlSerializer class is another option that's available to use in Silverlight.

Using the XmlSerializer Class

You've seen how the XmlReader class can parse XML data node by node in a forward-only manner. While it can be used to map XML data to CLR objects, there's another option available that's designed to simplify the process of mapping XML data to objects. Silverlight provides an XmlSerializer class (located in the System.Xml.Serialization namespace) that can act as the middleman between an XML document and an object. It's capable of deserializing XML data into objects and serializing objects into XML with only a few lines of code. There's some initial set-up work required for the `XmlSerializer` to perform its magic, but by using built-in .NET Framework tools, you can minimize the amount of time it takes to get the serialization process up and running.

`XmlSerializer` uses the `XmlReader` class and other helper classes under the covers to parse XML data and map it to object properties. However, you'll need to create the custom classes used to store the data. Creating custom classes can be done by hand or by using a .NET Framework command-line tool named `xsd.exe`. The `xsd.exe` tool is commonly used for generating strongly typed `DataSets` from XSD schemas, but can also be used to generate classes from schemata as well. The easiest way to access the `xsd.exe` tool is through the `Visual Studio Command Prompt` that's added to your system when you install Visual Studio.

Before using the `xsd.exe` tool, you need to create an XSD schema that describes the XML format that will be deserialized to objects. The easiest way to do this is by using Visual Studio's `Create Schema` tool. Load the XML data retrieved from a RESTful call into Visual Studio, and select XML ➪ Create Schema from the menu. An XSD schema will automatically be generated that describes the XML document's format. You'll more than likely need to change some of the schema data types it creates since it can only guess at what they should be.

Here's an example of an XSD schema document named Photos.xsd created from Flickr XML data using Visual Studio:

```xml
<?xml version="1.0" encoding="utf-8"?>
<xs:schema attributeFormDefault="unqualified" elementFormDefault="qualified"
    xmlns:xs="http://www.w3.org/2001/XMLSchema">
  <xs:element name="rsp">
    <xs:complexType>
      <xs:sequence>
        <xs:element name="photos">
          <xs:complexType>
            <xs:sequence>
              <xs:element maxOccurs="unbounded" name="photo">
                <xs:complexType>
                  <xs:attribute name="id" type="xs:string" />
                  <xs:attribute name="owner" type="xs:string"/>
                  <xs:attribute name="secret" type="xs:string" />
                  <xs:attribute name="server" type="xs:string"  />
                  <xs:attribute name="farm" type="xs:string" />
                  <xs:attribute name="title" type="xs:string" />
                  <xs:attribute name="ispublic" type="xs:string" />
                  <xs:attribute name="isfriend" type="xs:string" />
                  <xs:attribute name="isfamily" type="xs:string" />
                </xs:complexType>
              </xs:element>
            </xs:sequence>
            <xs:attribute name="page" type="xs:int" />
            <xs:attribute name="pages" type="xs:int" />
            <xs:attribute name="perpage" type="xs:int" />
            <xs:attribute name="total" type="xs:int" />
          </xs:complexType>
        </xs:element>
      </xs:sequence>
```

```
        <xs:attribute name="stat" type="xs:string" />
    </xs:complexType>
  </xs:element>
</xs:schema>
```

To convert the schema into equivalent CLR objects and save you the trouble of typing all of the classes and associated properties, the xsd.exe tool can be used with the following command-line arguments:

```
xsd.exe /classes /namespace:SilverlightRESTClient.Model
/enableDataBinding Photos.xsd
```

The classes generated by running the xsd.exe command are placed in the SilverlightRESTClient .Model namespace and have built-in support for data binding and property change notifications. They rely on System.Xml.Serialization attributes such as XmlElement and XmlAttribute to ensure that XML data is mapped to properties correctly. The classes will use the same casing as schema element and attribute definitions by default, which may not match standard .NET code-naming and casing conventions. However, you can always modify the code after it's been generated.

> The first time you try to compile classes generated by xsd.exe in a Silverlight project, you'll get a compiler error. After ensuring that all of the proper assemblies are referenced in your Silverlight project, delete any attributes such as System.SerializableAttribute and System.ComponentModel .DesignerCategoryAttribute that the compiler complains about from the generated code. Since Silverlight only contains a subset of the standard .NET Framework, some of the attributes can't be used.

> Normally, touching code generated by a tool is not recommended. However, in this case, the tool is being used to generate starter code and save you time. If you don't like this approach, you can always resort to writing the classes yourself, although you'll have to ensure that XmlElement and XmlAttribute attributes are applied properly to class and property definitions so that the XmlSerializer knows how to map the XML data.

An example of a class named rsp (the root element of the schema) that's generated using xsd.exe is shown next:

```
namespace SilverlightRESTClient.Model {
    using System.Xml.Serialization;

    /// <remarks/>
    [System.CodeDom.Compiler.GeneratedCodeAttribute("xsd", "2.0.50727.1432")]
    [System.Diagnostics.DebuggerStepThroughAttribute()]
    [System.Xml.Serialization.XmlTypeAttribute(AnonymousType=true)]
    [System.Xml.Serialization.XmlRootAttribute(Namespace="", IsNullable=false)]
    public partial class rsp : object, System.ComponentModel.INotifyPropertyChanged
    {

        private rspPhotos photosField;
```

```
                private string statField;

                public rspPhotos photos {
                    get {
                        return this.photosField;
                    }
                    set {
                        this.photosField = value;
                        this.RaisePropertyChanged("photos");
                    }
                }

                [System.Xml.Serialization.XmlAttributeAttribute()]
                public string stat {
                    get {
                        return this.statField;
                    }
                    set {
                        this.statField = value;
                        this.RaisePropertyChanged("stat");
                    }
                }

                public event System.ComponentModel.PropertyChangedEventHandler
                  PropertyChanged;

                protected void RaisePropertyChanged(string propertyName) {
                    System.ComponentModel.PropertyChangedEventHandler propertyChanged =
                    this.PropertyChanged;
                    if ((propertyChanged != null)) {
                        propertyChanged(this,
                        new System.ComponentModel.PropertyChangedEventArgs(propertyName));
                    }
                }
            }
        }
```

Photo data retrieved from Flickr can be deserialized to an rspPhotosPhoto type that's also generated using xsd.exe from the schema shown earlier. Here's what the rspPhotosPhoto class looks like:

```
public partial class rspPhotosPhoto : object,
  System.ComponentModel.INotifyPropertyChanged {

private string idField;
private string ownerField;
private string secretField;
private string serverField;
private string farmField;
private string titleField;
private string ispublicField;
private string isfriendField;
private string isfamilyField;

/// <remarks/>
[System.Xml.Serialization.XmlAttributeAttribute()]
```

```csharp
public string id {
    get {
        return this.idField;
    }
    set {
        this.idField = value;
        this.RaisePropertyChanged("id");
    }
}

/// <remarks/>
[System.Xml.Serialization.XmlAttributeAttribute()]
public string owner {
    get {
        return this.ownerField;
    }
    set {
        this.ownerField = value;
        this.RaisePropertyChanged("owner");
    }
}

/// <remarks/>
[System.Xml.Serialization.XmlAttributeAttribute()]
public string secret {
    get {
        return this.secretField;
    }
    set {
        this.secretField = value;
        this.RaisePropertyChanged("secret");
    }
}

/// <remarks/>
[System.Xml.Serialization.XmlAttributeAttribute()]
public string server {
    get {
        return this.serverField;
    }
    set {
        this.serverField = value;
        this.RaisePropertyChanged("server");
    }
}

/// <remarks/>
[System.Xml.Serialization.XmlAttributeAttribute()]
public string farm {
    get {
        return this.farmField;
    }
    set {
        this.farmField = value;
        this.RaisePropertyChanged("farm");
```

```
        }
    }

    /// <remarks/>
    [System.Xml.Serialization.XmlAttributeAttribute()]
    public string title {
        get {
            return this.titleField;
        }
        set {
            this.titleField = value;
            this.RaisePropertyChanged("title");
        }
    }

    /// <remarks/>
    [System.Xml.Serialization.XmlAttributeAttribute()]
    public string ispublic {
        get {
            return this.ispublicField;
        }
        set {
            this.ispublicField = value;
            this.RaisePropertyChanged("ispublic");
        }
    }

    /// <remarks/>
    [System.Xml.Serialization.XmlAttributeAttribute()]
    public string isfriend {
        get {
            return this.isfriendField;
        }
        set {
            this.isfriendField = value;
            this.RaisePropertyChanged("isfriend");
        }
    }

    /// <remarks/>
    [System.Xml.Serialization.XmlAttributeAttribute()]
    public string isfamily {
        get {
            return this.isfamilyField;
        }
        set {
            this.isfamilyField = value;
            this.RaisePropertyChanged("isfamily");
        }
    }

    public event System.ComponentModel.PropertyChangedEventHandler PropertyChanged;

    protected void RaisePropertyChanged(string propertyName) {
        System.ComponentModel.PropertyChangedEventHandler propertyChanged =
```

```
                    this.PropertyChanged;
            if ((propertyChanged != null)) {
                propertyChanged(this,
                    new System.ComponentModel.PropertyChangedEventArgs(propertyName));
            }
        }
    }
```

After the custom classes are created, the XmlSerializer class can be used to deserialize XML data into object instances. The XmlSerializer's constructor accepts a Type object representing the type that XML data should be deserialized to. Passing the object type to the constructor causes code generation magic to happen behind the scenes that handles parsing the XML and mapping it to the proper object type. To fill the target object type with data, the Deserialize method is called. An example of deserializing data to the rsp type shown earlier is as follows:

```
XmlSerializer xs = new XmlSerializer(typeof(Model.rsp));
Model.rsp rsp = (Model.rsp)xs.Deserialize(dataStream);
```

A more complete example of retrieving Flickr XML data using HttpWebRequest and HttpWebResponse, deserializing it, and binding it to Silverlight controls is shown next:

```
private void StartXmlSerializerRequest()
{
    //Add reference to System.Net.dll if it's not already referenced
    HttpWebRequest request = (HttpWebRequest)WebRequest.Create(CreateRESTUri());
    //Start async REST request
    request.BeginGetResponse(new AsyncCallback(GetXmlSerializerResponseCallBack),
        request);
}

private void GetXmlSerializerResponseCallBack(IAsyncResult asyncResult)
{
    HttpWebRequest request = (HttpWebRequest)asyncResult.AsyncState;
    using (HttpWebResponse response =
        (HttpWebResponse)request.EndGetResponse(asyncResult))
    {
        Stream dataStream = response.GetResponseStream();
        //rspPhotosPhoto class generated from XSD schema based on
        //Flickr POX. Used xsd.exe
        //After xsd.exe generates code you will need to remove a few
        //attributes to compile the project
        XmlSerializer xs = new XmlSerializer(typeof(Model.rsp));
        Model.rsp rsp = (Model.rsp)xs.Deserialize(dataStream);
        //Process data on GUI thread
        Dispatcher.BeginInvoke(() => ProcessRspObject(rsp));
    }
}

private void ProcessRspObject(Model.rsp rsp)
{
    //Assign Url to each photo object as well as ImageBrush to paint photo
    if (rsp != null && rsp.photos.photo != null)
    {
        foreach (Model.rspPhotosPhoto photo in rsp.photos.photo)
```

```
            {
                photo.Url = this.CreateXmlSerializerPhotoUrl(photo);
                ImageBrush brush = new ImageBrush();
                brush.ImageSource = new BitmapImage(new Uri(photo.Url));
                brush.Stretch = Stretch.Uniform;
                photo.ImageBrush = brush;
            }
            DisplayXmlSerializerPhotos(rsp.photos);
        }
        else
        {
            ShowAlert("Unable to proces photo data.");
        }
    }

    private string CreateXmlSerializerPhotoUrl(Model.rspPhotosPhoto photo)
    {
        return String.Format(_BasePhotoUrl, photo.farm, photo.server,
                                    photo.id, photo.secret, "s");
    }

    //Bind photos to ItemsControl control defined in XAML
    private void DisplayXmlSerializerPhotos(Model.rspPhotos photos)
    {
        if (photos != null && photos.photo.Length > 0)
        {
            this.icPhotos.ItemsSource = photos.photo;
        }
        else
        {
            ShowAlert("No photos found.");
        }
    }
```

The XmlSerializer class provides another option for converting XML data into objects without writing a lot of custom code. Using the XmlReader and XmlSerializer classes, you can parse any type of XML data returned from a service. However, there's another option available that provides extreme flexibility while minimizing the amount of code that you have to write. It's called LINQ to SQL and is covered next.

Using LINQ to XML

.NET 3.5 provides an important new technology called *language integrated query* (LINQ) that provides a way to query objects, data sources, and even XML within an application using SQL-like syntax. LINQ is a powerful technology that's also available to use in Silverlight applications. You can use LINQ when you'd like to sort, filter, or group objects. Although a complete discussion of LINQ can't be covered in a single chapter, this portion of the chapter will examine how LINQ to XML functionality can be used in Silverlight to parse XML data returned from a REST service (or any other service for that matter) and map data to custom objects.

LINQ to XML relies on an object named XDocument to parse XML data and load it into memory so that LINQ queries can be performed. To use the XDocument class and related classes with LINQ, you'll need to reference the System.Linq.Xml assembly and import the System.Linq.Xml namespace. The XDocument class provides the following methods that can be used to parse XML and load it into memory so that it can be accessed using LINQ:

- ❏ `Load` — Used to load XML data from a `URI`, `XmlReader` or `TextReader`.
- ❏ `Parse` — Loads XML data from a string variable.
- ❏ `ReadFrom` — Loads XML data from an `XmlReader` object.

Let's examine different ways that LINQ to XML can be used to query the following XML document named *Photos.xml*:

```xml
<?xml version="1.0" encoding="utf-8" ?>
<rsp stat="ok">
  <photos page="1" pages="31875" perpage="100" total="3187432">
    <photo id="2375848757" owner="13128942@N05" secret="8b08b4c89c" server="2201"
    farm="3" title="Dogs ready to go" ispublic="1" isfriend="0" isfamily="0" />
    <photo id="2376686792" owner="25029759@N04" secret="a2f3ac27db" server="3218"
    farm="4" title="Inseparable" ispublic="1" isfriend="0" isfamily="0" />
    <photo id="2376683204" owner="22160786@N08" secret="7e60b3903a" server="2410"
    farm="3" title="rjk dog 003" ispublic="1" isfriend="0" isfamily="0" />
    <photo id="2375847463" owner="63299638@N00" secret="62fd3effd2" server="2014"
    farm="3" title="Hudson &amp; Kobe" ispublic="1" isfriend="0" isfamily="0" />
    <photo id="2376687094" owner="22160786@N08" secret="25c5c4fd23" server="2318"
    farm="3" title="rjk dog 008" ispublic="1" isfriend="0" isfamily="0" />
  </photos>
</rsp>
```

To access all `title` attributes in the XML document, you'll first need to load the document into memory using the `XDocument` class:

```
XDocument doc = XDocument.Load("Photos.xml");
```

Once the XML document has been loaded, the following LINQ to XML query can be executed to retrieve `title` attribute data. The query starts by accessing all descendant `photo` elements using the `XDocument` class's `Descendants` method and then selects each `title` attribute value using the `Attribute` method.

```
IEnumerable<string> titles = from photo in doc.Descendants("photo")
                                  select photo.Attribute("title").Value;
```

Unwanted nodes in the XML document can also be filtered out using a LINQ `where` clause. Here's a LINQ to XML example that locates all `title` attribute values with a length greater than 15 characters:

```
IEnumerable<string> titles = from photo in doc.Descendants("photo")
                             where photo.Attribute("title").Value.Length > 15
                             select photo.Attribute("title").Value;
```

LINQ to XML is also quite useful when you'd like to parse an XML document and map values to a custom object such as the `Photo` object shown next (this same object was used in earlier examples in the chapter):

```
public class Photo
{
    public string ID { get; set; }
```

```
        public string Owner { get; set; }
        public string Secret { get; set; }
        public string Title { get; set; }
        public bool IsPublic { get; set; }
        public bool IsFriend { get; set; }
        public bool IsFamily { get; set; }
        public string Url { get; set; }
        public string Server { get; set; }
        public ImageBrush ImageBrush { get; set; }
        public string Farm { get; set; }
    }
```

To extract all attribute values from each photo element in the Photos.xml file shown earlier and project the values to the Photo class, the following code can be used:

```
private void StartLINQtoXMLRequest()
{
    WebClient client = new WebClient();
    client.DownloadStringCompleted +=
     new DownloadStringCompletedEventHandler(client_DownloadStringCompleted);
    client.DownloadStringAsync(this.CreateRESTUri());
}

private void client_DownloadStringCompleted(object sender,
   DownloadStringCompletedEventArgs e)
{
    ProcessWithLinqToXml(e.Result));
}

private void ProcessWithLinqToXml(string xmlData)
{
    XDocument doc = XDocument.Parse(xmlData);
    List<Model.Photo> photos = (from photo in doc.Descendants("photo")
                                select new Model.Photo
                                {
                                    Farm = photo.Attribute("farm").Value,
                                    ID = photo.Attribute("id").Value,
                                    IsFamily =
                                            ConvertBoolean(
                                            photo.Attribute("isfamily").Value),
                                    IsFriend =
                                            ConvertBoolean(
                                            photo.Attribute("isfriend").Value),
                                    IsPublic =
                                            this.ConvertBoolean(
                                            photo.Attribute("ispublic").Value),
                                    Owner = photo.Attribute("owner").Value,
                                    Secret = photo.Attribute("secret").Value,
                                    Server = photo.Attribute("server").Value,
                                    Title = photo.Attribute("title").Value,
                                }).ToList<Model.Photo>();
    if (photos != null)
    {
        foreach (Model.Photo photo in photos)
```

```
        {
            photo.Url = this.CreatePhotoUrl(photo);
            ImageBrush brush = new ImageBrush();
            brush.ImageSource = new BitmapImage(new Uri(photo.Url));
            brush.Stretch = Stretch.Uniform;
            photo.ImageBrush = brush;
        }
        this.DisplayPhotos(photos);
    }
    else
    {
        ShowAlert("Unable to proces photo data.");
    }
}

private bool ConvertBoolean(string val)
{
    return (val == "0") ? false : true;
}

private Uri CreateRESTUri()
{
    return new Uri(String.Format("{0}?method={1}&api_key={2}&text={3}&per_page={4}",
    _BaseUri, "flickr.photos.search", _APIKey, this.txtSearchText.Text, 50));
}
```

The LINQ to SQL query parses each `photo` element attribute and maps the value to the appropriate property in the `Photo` class. The collection of `Photo` objects is then returned as a `List<Photo>` by calling the `ToList<T>` method. Although the `XDocument` class does load the XML document being parsed into memory as opposed to streaming the data like the `XmlReader` class, the `XDocument` class combined with LINQ to SQL query capabilities provides a flexible way to map XML data to objects with a minimal amount of code.

Processing JSON Data

Silverlight provides excellent support for parsing XML data returned from Web Services, REST APIs, or other types of services. Because many services return XML data, you'll find that classes such as `XmlReader`, `XmlSerializer`, or `XDocument` are used frequently in Silverlight applications. However, XML data isn't the only type of data that can be returned from services. Services may also support JavaScript Object Notation (JSON), which provides a compact way to exchange data between clients and services. JSON was originally designed to be used with the JavaScript language, but there may be cases in which you'll need to work with it in Silverlight using a language such as C# or VB.NET. In those cases, you can use Silverlight's `DataContractJsonSerializer` class, which supports serializing CLR objects to JSON and deserializing JSON messages to CLR objects.

The `DataContractJsonSerializer` class is located in the `System.Runtime.Serialization.Json` namespace. To use it, you'll need to reference the `System.ServiceModel.Web` assembly in your Silverlight project. `DataContractJsonSerializer` looks and acts much like the `XmlSerializer` class discussed in this chapter and provides methods such as `ReadObject` for deserialization and `WriteObject` for serialization. The `ReadObject` method accepts a stream of data containing the JSON data to deserialize, and the

`WriteObject` method accepts the stream to serialize JSON data to as well as the source object. Signatures for both methods are shown next:

```
public Object ReadObject(
  Stream stream
)

public void WriteObject(
  Stream stream,
  Object graph
)
```

JSON Fundamentals

Several REST APIs including the one provided by Flickr allow data to be returned as JSON. JSON delimits objects by using brackets and separates property names from values using a colon character. An example of using JSON to pass photo data from Flickr to a client is shown next:

```
{
  "id":"555242564", "owner":"555371@N00", "secret":"555afd69d",
  "server":"2226", "farm":3, "title":"Camp Chihuahua: Class In Session",
  "ispublic":1, "isfriend":0, "isfamily":0
}
```

This JSON fragment specifies where photo data starts and ends using { and } characters, separates property names and values using a colon, and separates properties using a comma. An array of photo object data can be defined using square bracket characters as shown next:

```
{
  "photo":
  [
    {
      "id":"2386242564", "owner":"3911171@N00", "secret":"555afd69d",
      "server":"2226", "farm":3, "title":"Camp Chihuahua: Class In Session",
      "ispublic":1, "isfriend":0, "isfamily":0
    },
    {
      "id":"2386239664", "owner":"25111971@N02", "secret":"555cced92",
      "server":"3229", "farm":4, "title":"kid and dog",
      "ispublic":1, "isfriend":0, "isfamily":0
    }
  ]
}
```

Objects can also define sub-objects by adding nested brackets as shown in the following JSON message:

```
{
  "photos":
  {
    "page":1, "pages":32047, "perpage":100, "total":"3204603",
    "photo":
    {
```

```
[
    {
        "id":"2386242564", "owner":"3911171@N00", "secret":"555afd69d",
        "server":"2226", "farm":3, "title":"Camp Chihuahua: Class In Session",
        "ispublic":1, "isfriend":0, "isfamily":0
    },

    {

        "id":"2386239664", "owner":"25111971@N02", "secret":"555cced92",
        "server":"3229", "farm":4, "title":"kid and dog", "ispublic":1,
        "isfriend":0, "isfamily":0
    }
    ]
    }
  },
  "stat":"ok"}
}
```

Using the `DataContractJsonSerializer` Class

A complete understanding of the JSON messaging format isn't required to use the `DataContractJson Serializer` class because it handles the process of serializing and deserializing data for you. However, you'll need to know enough to create matching CLR classes that JSON data can be deserialized to within a Silverlight application. Classes that map to the previous JSON message example are shown next:

```
public class FlickrResponse
{
    public string stat { get; set; }
    public photos photos { get; set; }
}

public class photos
{
    public int page { get; set; }
    public int pages { get; set; }
    public int perpage { get; set; }
    public int total { get; set; }
    public photo[] photo { get; set; }
}

public class photo
{
    public string id { get; set; }
    public string owner { get; set; }
    public string secret { get; set; }
    public string title { get; set; }
    public int ispublic { get; set; }
    public int isfriend { get; set; }
    public int isfamily { get; set; }
    public string server { get; set; }
    public string farm { get; set; }
```

```
                //Custome properties used for data binding
                public string Url { get; set; }
                public ImageBrush ImageBrush { get; set; }
        }
```

Notice that the properties defined in each class match the case of the properties contained in the JSON message. This casing even applies to the names of child classes such as photos and photo. This is essential for proper deserialization of JSON messages! Failure to match the case between JSON messages and CLR objects can result in data being lost.

To deserialize a JSON message, you can call the DataContractJsonSerializer class's ReadObject method and pass it a stream containing JSON data. An example of retrieving data from the Flickr REST service and deserializing it is shown next. Data is retrieved using the HttpWebRequest and HttpWeb Response objects. The code to deserialize the JSON data is located in the GetJSONResponseCallBack method. Notice that the type of CLR object that the JSON data should be deserialized to is passed to the DataContractJsonSerializer class's constructor.

```
        private Uri CreateJSONUri()
        {
            return new Uri(String.Format("{0}?method={1}&api_key={2}&text={3}" +
                "&per_page={4}&format=json&nojsoncallback=1",
                _BaseUri, "flickr.photos.search", _APIKey, this.txtSearchText.Text, 50));
        }


        private void StartJsonRequest()
        {
            //Add reference to System.Net.dll if it's not already referenced
            HttpWebRequest request = (HttpWebRequest)WebRequest.Create(CreateJSONUri());
            //Start async REST request
            request.BeginGetResponse(new AsyncCallback(GetJSONResponseCallBack), request);
        }


        private void GetJSONResponseCallBack(IAsyncResult asyncResult)
        {
            JSON.FlickrResponse res = null;
            HttpWebRequest request = (HttpWebRequest)asyncResult.AsyncState;
            using (HttpWebResponse response =
              (HttpWebResponse)request.EndGetResponse(asyncResult))
            {
                Stream dataStream = response.GetResponseStream();
                //Deserialize JSON message into custom objects
                DataContractJsonSerializer jsonSerializer =
                  new DataContractJsonSerializer(typeof(JSON.FlickrResponse));
                jsonObj = (JSON.FlickrResponse)jsonSerializer.ReadObject(dataStream);
                Dispatcher.BeginInvoke(() => ProcessJsonObject(jsonObj));
            }
        }


        private void ProcessJsonObject(JSON.FlickrResponse jsonObj)
        {
            //Assign Url to each photo object as well as ImageBrush to paint photo
            if (jsonObj != null && jsonObj.photos.photo != null)
```

```
        {
            foreach (JSON.photo photo in jsonObj.photos.photo)
            {
                photo.Url = this.CreateJSONPhotoUrl(photo);
                ImageBrush brush = new ImageBrush();
                brush.ImageSource = new BitmapImage(new Uri(photo.Url));
                brush.Stretch = Stretch.Uniform;
                photo.ImageBrush = brush;
            }
            DisplayJSONPhotos(jsonObj.photos.photo);
        }
        else
        {
            ShowAlert("Unable to proces photo data.");
        }
    }

    private string CreateJSONPhotoUrl(JSON.photo photo)
    {
        //http://farm{farm-id}.static.flickr.com/{server-id}/{id}_{secret}_{size}.jpg
        //farm-id: 1
        //server-id: 2
        //photo-id: 1418878
        //secret: 1e92283336
        //size: m, s, t, b

        return String.Format(_BasePhotoUrl, photo.farm, photo.server, photo.id,
                                            photo.secret, "s");
    }

    private void DisplayJSONPhotos(JSON.photo[] photos)
    {
        if (photos != null && photos.Length > 0)
        {
            this.icPhotos.ItemsSource = photos;
        }
        else
        {
            ShowAlert("No photos found.");
        }
    }
```

Working with Syndication Feeds

Really Simple Syndication (RSS) and Atom Syndication Format (ATOM) are XML formats used by companies and blogs around the world to syndicate feeds that can be accessed and subscribed to by clients. If you're looking for sports scores, world news, technology news, or information about hundreds of other topics, there's probably an RSS or ATOM syndication feed available that you can use. While the different XML techniques discussed in this chapter can be used to retrieve and parse RSS or ATOM data, Silverlight provides a set of classes designed specifically for working with syndication feeds. By using these specialized classes, you can access syndication feed data directly in a strongly typed manner. Before discussing Silverlight's syndication feed classes, let's examine what syndication feeds look like and how they can be used to exchange data between publishers and subscribers.

RSS and ATOM Syndication Feeds

RSS and ATOM both rely on a simple metadata format to exchange data between publishers and subscribers. RSS describes data using `item` elements, while ATOM uses `entry` elements. RSS is available in several different versions ranging from .91 to 2.0, although RSS 2.0 is the predominant version used on today's web sites and blogs. ATOM was created to fill in some of the perceived holes in RSS 2.0 and is currently at version 1.0. ATOM adds features that aren't found in RSS 2.0 such as the ability to describe the type of content contained in a feed (e.g., text, binary, or HTML) and better support for internationalization of specific feed entries through inclusion of the `xml:lang` attribute. An overview of the RSS and ATOM formats is provided next.

RSS uses XML markup to describe item titles, links, publishers, publication dates, categories, and more. Individual `item` elements can contain a variety of child elements such as `title`, `link`, `pubDate`, `description`, and `category`. An example of an RSS feed document with multiple items is shown next:

```xml
<?xml version="1.0" encoding="utf-8" ?>
<rss version="2.0" xmlns:dc="http://purl.org/dc/elements/1.1/"
  xmlns:slash="http://purl.org/rss/1.0/modules/slash/"
  xmlns:wfw="http://wellformedweb.org/CommentAPI/">
  <channel>
    <title>Dan Wahlin&amp;#39;s WebLog</title>
    <link>http://weblogs.asp.net/dwahlin/default.aspx</link>
    <description>Silverlight, ASP.NET, AJAX, XML, and Web Services
      Exploration
    </description>
    <dc:language>en</dc:language>
    <generator>Community Server</generator>
    <item>
      <title>Video: Silverlight Rehab</title>
      <link>http://weblogs.asp.net/dwahlin/archive/2008/04/01/
        video-silverlight-rehab.aspx       </link>
      <pubDate>Wed, 02 Apr Year 05:34:00 GMT</pubDate>
      <guid isPermaLink="false">c06e2b9d-981a-45b4-a55f-ab0d8bbfdc1c:6059689</guid>
      <dc:creator>dwahlin</dc:creator>
      <description>
        …Ommited for the sake of brevity
      </description>
      <category
    domain="http://weblogs.asp.net/dwahlin/archive/tags/Silverlight/default.aspx">
        Silverlight
      </category>
    </item>
    <item>
      <title>Interesting 3rd Party Controls and Demo Applications for ASP.NET and
        Silverlight
      </title>
      <link>http://weblogs.asp.net/dwahlin/archive/2008/03/27/interesting-3rd-part-
        controls-and-demo-applications-for-asp-net-and-silverlight.aspx</link>
      <pubDate>Fri, 28 Mar Year 06:38:00 GMT</pubDate>
      <guid isPermaLink="false">c06e2b9d-981a-45b4-a55f-ab0d8bbfdc1c:6039815</guid>
      <dc:creator>dwahlin</dc:creator>
      <description>
        …Omitted for the sake of brevity
```

```
      </description>
      <category
       domain="http://weblogs.asp.net/dwahlin/archive/tags/
            Silverlight/default.aspx">
       Silverlight
      </category>
     </item>
    </channel>
  </rss>
```

ATOM can also be used to describe items, although it uses `entry` elements instead of `item` elements. The content of an `entry` is described using a `type` attribute so that a client can know how to handle the data. An example of an ATOM feed document is shown next:

```
<?xml version="1.0" encoding="UTF-8" ?>
<feed xmlns="http://www.w3.org/2005/Atom" xml:lang="en">
  <title type="html">Dan Wahlin&amp;#39;s WebLog</title>
  <subtitle type="html">ASP.NET, AJAX, XML, and Web Services Exploration</subtitle>
  <id>http://weblogs.asp.net/dwahlin/atom.aspx</id>
  <link rel="alternate" type="text/html"
    href="http://weblogs.asp.net/dwahlin/default.aspx" />
  <link rel="self" type="application/atom+xml"
    href="http://weblogs.asp.net/dwahlin/atom.aspx" />
  <generator uri="http://communityserver.org" version="3.0.20510.895">
    Community Server
  </generator>
  <updated> 200X-04-04T06:41:08Z</updated>
  <entry>
    <title>Using Silverlight 2 ItemsControl Templates</title>
    <link rel="alternate" type="text/html"
      href="http://weblogs.asp.net/dwahlin/archive/200X/04/03/using-silverlight-2-
      itemscontrol-templates.aspx" />
    <id>http://weblogs.asp.net/dwahlin/archive/200X/04/03/using-silverlight-2-
        itemscontrol-templates.aspx</id>
    <published>200X-04-04T06:41:08Z</published>
    <updated>200X-04-04T06:41:08Z</updated>
    <content type="html">
      ...Ommitted for brevity
    </content>
    <author>
      <name>dwahlin</name>
      <uri>http://weblogs.asp.net/members/dwahlin.aspx</uri>
    </author>
    <category term="Silverlight"
      scheme="http://weblogs.asp.net/dwahlin/archive/tags/Silverlight/
      default.aspx" />
  </entry>
  <entry>
    <title>Video: Silverlight Rehab</title>
    <link rel="alternate" type="text/html"
      href="http://weblogs.asp.net/dwahlin/archive/200X/04/01/video-silverlight-
      rehab.aspx" />
    <id>http://weblogs.asp.net/dwahlin/archive/200X/04/01/
        video-silverlight-rehab.aspx</id>
```

```
      <published>200X-04-02T05:34:00Z</published>
      <updated>200X-04-02T05:34:00Z</updated>
      <content type="html">
        ...Ommitted for brevity
      </content>
      <author>
        <name>dwahlin</name>
        <uri>http://weblogs.asp.net/members/dwahlin.aspx</uri>
      </author>
      <category term="Silverlight"
        scheme="http://weblogs.asp.net/dwahlin/archive/tags/Silverlight/
        default.aspx" />
    </entry>
</feed>
```

Using Syndication Feed Classes

Silverlight provides classes such as SyndicationFeed and SyndicationItem that can be used to parse and iterate through RSS and ATOM syndication feeds. These specialized classes reside in the System.ServiceModel.Syndication.dll assembly and System.ServiceModel.Syndication namespace. You'll typically use the SyndicationFeed class to start the process of parsing an RSS 2.0 or ATOM 1.0 feed.

> **If the syndication feed is in a different domain from the Silverlight application, a cross-domain policy file must be defined at the root of the server where the feed is hosted.**

The SyndicationFeed class provides a Load method that accepts an XmlReader object instance containing syndication feed data. The XmlReader can stream data received from objects such as WebClient or HttpWebResponse. An example of using the SyndicationFeed class's Load method to parse data retrieved using HttpWebRequest and HttpWebRequest objects follows:

```
private void StartSyndicationFeedRequest()
{
    HttpWebRequest request = (HttpWebRequest)HttpWebRequest.Create(
      new Uri(this.txtUrl.Text));
    AsyncCallback callback = new AsyncCallback(FeedResponseCallback);
    request.BeginGetResponse(callback, request);
}

private void FeedResponseCallback (IAsyncResult asyncResult)
{
    XmlReader reader = null;
    HttpWebResponse response = null;
    try
    {
        HttpWebRequest request = (HttpWebRequest)asyncResult.AsyncState;
        response = (HttpWebResponse)request.EndGetResponse(asyncResult);
        Stream dataStream = response.GetResponseStream();
        reader = XmlReader.Create(dataStream);
        //Load Syndication Feed
        SyndicationFeed feed = SyndicationFeed.Load(reader);
```

```
                Dispatcher.BeginInvoke(() => BindItems(feed));
        }
        finally
        {
            reader.Close();
            response.Close();
        }
    }

    private void BindItems(SyndicationFeed feed)
    {
        this.lbRssItems.ItemsSource = feed.Items;
    }
```

After feed data has been loaded into memory using the `Load` method, the `SyndicationFeed` class's `Items` property can be called to access the items or entries depending on the feed type. `Items` is of type `IEnumerable<SyndicationItem>`, so it can be bound to various Silverlight controls. The `SyndicationFeed` class also allows new items to be created by calling methods like `CreateItem` and `CreateCategory`, and it can save items using methods like `SaveAsAtom10` and `SaveAsRss20`.

The `SyndicationItem` class provides several properties that can be used to access an item's title, link, author, publication date, text content, category, and so on. It also provides methods that can be used to create feed items such as `CreateCategory`, `CreatePerson`, and `CreateLink`. An example of using the `SyndicationItem` class to display details about syndication feed items is shown next:

```
    private void ShowFeedItem(SyndicationItem item)
    {
        string content = null;
        if (this.gridContent.Visibility == Visibility.Visible) return;
        this.gridContent.Visibility = Visibility.Visible;
        HtmlCleaner cleaner = new HtmlCleaner();
        this.tbTitle.Text = (string)cleaner.Convert(item.Title.Text, null, null,
            System.Globalization.CultureInfo.InvariantCulture);

        //RSS 2.0
        if (item.Summary != null)
        {
            content = (string)cleaner.Convert(item.Summary.Text, null, null,
                System.Globalization.CultureInfo.InvariantCulture);
        }

        //ATOM 2.0
        if (item.Content != null && item.Content.Type.ToLower() == "html")
        {
            TextSyndicationContent textContent =
                item.Content as TextSyndicationContent;
            content = (string)cleaner.Convert(textContent.Text, null, null,
                System.Globalization.CultureInfo.InvariantCulture);
        }
        this.tbContent.Text = content;
        this.hlLink.NavigateUri = item.Links[0].Uri;
        this.tbPubDateRun.Text = item.PublishDate.ToString("d");
    }
```

Syndication feed item content is accessed differently depending on whether the feed follows the RSS 2.0 or ATOM 1.0 formats. To access RSS 2.0 content, you use the `SyndicationItem` class's `Summary` property. The code example feeds the `Summary` property's `Text` content through an HTML cleaning method to remove HTML characters so they're not displayed in the Silverlight application. ATOM 1.0 content can be accessed using the `SyndicationItem` class's `Content` property, which returns a `SyndicationContent` object. The code example verifies that the content isn't `null` and checks the type of the content using the `Type` property to ensure that it's HTML. It then casts the `SyndicationContent` object to a `TextSyndicationContent` object so that the text can be retrieved and cleaned. Figure 9-5 shows the output generated from calling the `ShowFeedItem` method in the previous code sample.

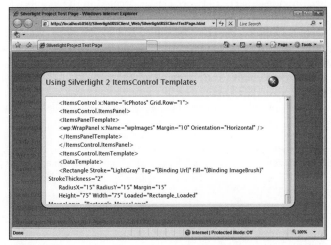

Figure 9-5

The syndication feed classes available in Silverlight provide a way to access data without resorting to custom XML parsing or serialization code. By using classes such as `SyndicationFeed` and `SyndicationItem`, you can read feed content with a minimal amount of code and effort.

Using Sockets to Communicate over TCP

The ability to communicate between a browser and a server over HTTP has always been a key feature of web-based applications. After all, without the request/response mechanism, the Web would cease to exist as we know it today. However, with all of their benefits, web applications do have the inherent limitation of having to initiate contact with a server to check for data changes (think of a sporting event application that allows a client to display scores as they change on the server). The server can't initiate contact to notify the client when data changes, so clients must consistently make calls to check for changes. This process can lead to unnecessary traffic being sent over the wire.

ASP.NET AJAX relies heavily on this type of client-to-server interaction to see if data has changed and even provides a `Timer` control to simplify the process of calling a server on a timed basis. While controls such as `Timer` get the job done, having a way for the server to push data to the client as it changes is certainly preferable and more efficient for some applications. Silverlight's support for network sockets makes this type of *push* activity a reality.

A network socket is comprised of an IP address and a port that together can be used to send messages between clients and servers using protocols such as TCP and UDP. Applications that use sockets to communicate typically have a server that listens for messages (exposing a local IP address and port) sent using a protocol such as TCP. Remote clients connect to the server's IP address and port. Once a client connection is accepted by a server, communication between the two parties can begin and go in either direction. The process of creating a server that can listen for client connections made using sockets is discussed next.

Using Sockets on a Server

The .NET Framework provides a set of network classes located in the `System.Net.Sockets` namespace that can be used to listen for client connections made to sockets. Using classes like `Socket`, `TcpListener`, and `TcpClient`, a server can be created that's capable of pushing data to a connected client. The `TcpListener` and `Socket` classes provide a means to listen for and accept client connections. Once a connection is made, the client stream can be accessed using the `TcpClient` class. Both the `TcpListener` and `Socket` classes can accept connections synchronously or asynchronously.

An example of using the `TcpListener` class to listen for and handle client connections asynchronously is shown next:

```
TcpListener _Listener = null;
static ManualResetEvent _TcpClientConnected = new ManualResetEvent(false);

public void StartSocketServer()
{
    try
    {
        //Allowed port range 4502-4534
        _Listener = new TcpListener(IPAddress.Any, 4530);
        _Listener.Start();
        Console.WriteLine("Server listening…");
        while (true)
        {
            _TcpClientConnected.Reset();


            Console.WriteLine("Waiting for client connection…");
            _Listener.BeginAcceptTcpClient(new AsyncCallback(OnBeginAccept),null);


            _TcpClientConnected.WaitOne(); //Block until client connects
        }
    }
    catch (Exception exp)
    {
        LogError(exp);
    }
}
```

This example creates a new instance of a `TcpListener` object capable of listening on port 4530 using any IP address. Once the `TcpListener` object is created, its `Start` method is called to start listening for client connections. As connections come into the server, they're handled asynchronously by wiring the

BeginAcceptTcpClient method to a callback method named OnBeginAccept that processes the connection and accesses the client stream.

> **Port 4530 is used because Silverlight can only communicate with a server using ports 4502 through 4534.**

Here's what the OnBeginAccept callback method looks like:

```
private void OnBeginAccept(IAsyncResult ar)
{
    _TcpClientConnected.Set(); //Allow waiting thread to proceed
    TcpListener listener = _Listener;

    //Accept connection and access TcpClient object
    TcpClient client = listener.EndAcceptTcpClient(ar);
    if (client.Connected)
    {
        Console.WriteLine("Client connected…");

        //Access client stream
        StreamWriter writer = new StreamWriter(client.GetStream());
        writer.AutoFlush = true;

        Console.WriteLine("Sending initial team data…");

        //Create XML message that will be sent to client upon connecting
        writer.WriteLine(GetTeamData());

        //Start timer that sends data to Silverlight client
        //on a random basis to update team scores
    }
}

private string GetTeamData()
{
    StringWriter sw = new StringWriter();
    using (XmlWriter writer = XmlWriter.Create(sw))
    {
        writer.WriteStartElement("Teams");
        foreach (string key in _Teams.Keys)
        {
            writer.WriteStartElement("Team");
            writer.WriteAttributeString("Name", key);
            Dictionary<Guid, string> players = _Teams[key];
            foreach (Guid playerKey in players.Keys)
            {
                writer.WriteStartElement("Player");
                writer.WriteAttributeString("ID", playerKey.ToString());
                writer.WriteAttributeString("Name", players[playerKey]);
                writer.WriteEndElement();
            }
            writer.WriteEndElement();
```

```
        }
        writer.WriteEndElement();
    }
    return sw.ToString();
}
```

When the OnBeginAccept method is called, the listener's EndAcceptTcpClient method is called to accept the connection and reference a TcpClient object that represents the calling client. Once the connection is made, the client's data stream is accessed and passed to a StreamWriter instance that is used to send team data returned from the GetTeamData method down to the client. Score data is then sent to the client on a timed basis. Additional details about the server application can be found in the code download for this chapter.

Using Sockets in a Silverlight Client

Silverlight applications can connect directly to remote servers using socket classes available in the System.Net and System.Net.Sockets namespaces. Once connected, data can be pushed from the server to one or more clients without the need for client polling. Several classes — such as DnsEndPoint, Socket, and SocketAsyncEventArgs — can be used to connect to a remote server.

The DnsEndPoint class is used to define the IP address of the target server as well as the port, while the Socket class defines the type of connection and actively connects a client to a server. The SocketAsync EventArgs class is used to define asynchronous callbacks and pass any desired user state (referred to as the UserToken) between method calls. An example of using these classes in a Silverlight application is shown next:

```
void Page_Loaded(object sender, RoutedEventArgs e)
{
    DnsEndPoint endPoint =
        new DnsEndPoint(Application.Current.Host.Source.DnsSafeHost, 4530);
    Socket socket = new Socket(AddressFamily.InterNetwork,
        SocketType.Stream, ProtocolType.Tcp);

    SocketAsyncEventArgs args = new SocketAsyncEventArgs();
    args.UserToken = socket;
    args.RemoteEndPoint = endPoint;
    args.Completed +=
        new EventHandler<SocketAsyncEventArgs>(OnSocketConnectCompleted);
    socket.ConnectAsync(args);
}

private void OnSocketConnectCompleted(object sender, SocketAsyncEventArgs e)
{
    byte[] response = new byte[1024];
    e.SetBuffer(response, 0, response.Length);
    e.Completed -=
        new EventHandler<SocketAsyncEventArgs>(
        OnSocketConnectCompleted);
    e.Completed +=
        new EventHandler<SocketAsyncEventArgs>(OnSocketReceive);
    Socket socket = (Socket)e.UserToken;
    socket.ReceiveAsync(e);
}
```

After `DnsEndPoint` and `Socket` objects are created, the asynchronous callback method to call once the client is connected to the server is defined using the `SocketAsyncEventArgs` object's `Completed` event. After the event argument values are set, the `Socket` object's `ConnectAsync` method is called to connect to the server.

When the server accepts the connection, the `OnSocketConnectCompleted` method is called, which serves the purpose of defining a response buffer and hooking the `Completed` event to a different callback method named `OnSocketReceive` that processes XML messages sent from the server. The `Socket` object that initiated the connection is passed between the callback methods using the `SocketAsyncEventArgs` object's `UserToken` class, which is designed to hold any state that needs to be passed as asynchronous calls are made.

As XML message data is received from the server, the `OnSocketReceive` callback method is called, which deserializes the data into CLR objects and updates the user interface. The code for the `OnSocketReceive` method is shown next:

```
private void OnSocketReceive(object sender, SocketAsyncEventArgs e)
{
    StringReader sr = null;
    try
    {
        string data = Encoding.UTF8.GetString(e.Buffer, e.Offset,
          e.BytesTransferred);
        sr = new StringReader(data);
        //Get initial team data
        if (_Teams == null && data.Contains("Teams"))
        {
            XmlSerializer xs = new XmlSerializer(typeof(Teams));
            _Teams = (Teams)xs.Deserialize(sr);
            this.Dispatcher.BeginInvoke(UpdateBoard);
        }

        //Get updated score data
        if (data.Contains("ScoreData"))
        {
            XmlSerializer xs = new XmlSerializer(typeof(ScoreData));
            ScoreData scoreData = (ScoreData)xs.Deserialize(sr);
            ScoreDataHandler handler = new ScoreDataHandler(UpdateScoreData);
            this.Dispatcher.BeginInvoke(handler, new object[] { scoreData });
        }
    }
    catch { }
    finally
    {
        if (sr != null) sr.Close();
    }
    //Prepare to receive more data
    Socket socket = (Socket)e.UserToken;
    socket.ReceiveAsync(e);
}
```

Objects created during the deserialization process are rerouted from the asynchronous call thread back to the Silverlight user interface thread using the `Dispatcher` class's `BeginInvoke` method. This model of routing data between threads is common in Windows Forms and WPF applications. The `UpdateBoard` and `UpdateScoreData` methods used to modify the user interface are shown next:

```csharp
private void UpdateBoard()
{
    this.tbTeam1Score.Text = "0";
    this.tbTeam2Score.Text = "0";
    this.lbActions.Items.Clear();
    if (_Teams != null && _Teams.Team != null)
    {
        for (int i = 0; i < 2; i++)
        {
            TeamsTeam team = _Teams.Team[i];
            if (i == 0)
            {
                this.tbTeam1.Text = team.Name;
            }
            else
            {
                this.tbTeam2.Text = team.Name;
            }
        }
    }
}

private void UpdateScoreData(ScoreData scoreData)
{
    //Update Score
    this.tbTeam1Score.Text = scoreData.Team1Score.ToString();
    this.tbTeam2Score.Text = scoreData.Team2Score.ToString();

    //Update ball visibility
    if (scoreData.Action != ActionsEnum.Foul)
    {
        if (tbTeam1.Text == scoreData.TeamOnOffense)
        {
            AnimateBall(this.BB1, this.BB2);
        }
        else //Team 2
        {
            AnimateBall(this.BB2, this.BB1);
        }
    }
    if (this.lbActions.Items.Count > 11) this.lbActions.Items.Clear();
    this.lbActions.Items.Add(scoreData.LastAction);
    if (this.lbActions.Visibility == Visibility.Collapsed)
      this.lbActions.Visibility = Visibility.Visible;
}

private void AnimateBall(Image onBall, Image offBall)
{
    //Animate basketballs
    this.FadeIn.Stop();
    Storyboard.SetTarget(this.FadeInAnimation, onBall);
```

```
        Storyboard.SetTarget(this.FadeOutAnimation, offBall);
        this.FadeIn.Begin();
    }
```

Figure 9-6 shows an example of what the Silverlight client application looks like after several messages have been received from the server and processed by the UpdateScoreData method.

Figure 9-6

Creating a Silverlight 2 Client-Access-Policy Socket Server

Silverlight 2 checks for a client access policy before accessing sockets located on the site of origin or cross-domain servers. The following code shows an example of a client access policy for sockets:

```xml
<?xml version="1.0" encoding ="utf-8"?>
<access-policy>
  <cross-domain-access>
    <policy>
      <allow-from>
        <domain uri="*" />
      </allow-from>
      <grant-to>
        <socket-resource  port="4530" protocol="tcp" />
      </grant-to>
    </policy>
  </cross-domain-access>
</access-policy>
```

This XML code allows Silverlight to access a TCP socket on port 4530. A range of ports can be specified in the port attribute if needed (e.g., 4530–4534). Before Silverlight tries to call a server with a socket, it makes a call to the target server on port 943 to check the client access policy and see if the server allows socket connections. This helps minimize various types of hacker attacks. If a client access policy is available on the server and the policy allows access to the port the client is trying to call, processing of the socket code continues and Silverlight tries to connect. If not, the client will be unable to connect because of access being denied by Silverlight.

The following code shows an example of creating a client-access-policy socket server that Silverlight can connect to on port 943:

```
using System;
using System.Collections.Generic;
using System.Text;
using System.Net;
using System.Net.Sockets;
using System.IO;
using System.Threading;
using System.Reflection;
using System.Configuration;

namespace PolicySocketServices
{
    class PolicySocketServer
    {
        TcpListener _Listener = null;
        TcpClient _Client = null;
        static ManualResetEvent _TcpClientConnected = new ManualResetEvent(false);
        const string _PolicyRequestString = "<policy-file-request/>";
        int _ReceivedLength = 0;
        byte[] _Policy = null;
        byte[] _ReceiveBuffer = null;

        private void InitializeData()
        {
            string policyFile = ConfigurationManager.AppSettings["PolicyFilePath"];
            using (FileStream fs = new FileStream(policyFile, FileMode.Open))
            {
                _Policy = new byte[fs.Length];
                fs.Read(_Policy, 0, _Policy.Length);
            }
            _ReceiveBuffer = new byte[_PolicyRequestString.Length];
        }

        public void StartSocketServer()
        {
            InitializeData();

            try
            {
                //Using TcpListener which is a wrapper around a Socket
                //Allowed port is 943 for Silverlight sockets policy data
                _Listener = new TcpListener(IPAddress.Any, 943);
                _Listener.Start();
                Console.WriteLine("Policy server listening...");
                while (true)
                {
                    _TcpClientConnected.Reset();
```

```
                Console.WriteLine("Waiting for client connection…");
                _Listener.BeginAcceptTcpClient(
                    new AsyncCallback(OnBeginAccept), null);
                _TcpClientConnected.WaitOne(); //Block until client connects
            }
        }
        catch (Exception exp)
        {
            LogError(exp);
        }
    }

    private void OnBeginAccept(IAsyncResult ar)
    {
        _Client = _Listener.EndAcceptTcpClient(ar);
        _Client.Client.BeginReceive(_ReceiveBuffer, 0, _
            PolicyRequestString.Length, SocketFlags.None,
            new AsyncCallback(OnReceiveComplete), null);
    }

    private void OnReceiveComplete(IAsyncResult ar)
    {
        try
        {
            _ReceivedLength += _Client.Client.EndReceive(ar);
            //See if there's more data that we need to grab
            if (_ReceivedLength < _PolicyRequestString.Length)
            {
                //Need to grab more data so receive remaining data
                _Client.Client.BeginReceive(_ReceiveBuffer, _ReceivedLength,
                    _PolicyRequestString.Length - _ReceivedLength,
                    SocketFlags.None, new AsyncCallback(OnReceiveComplete),
                        null);
                return;
            }

            //Check that <policy-file-request/> was sent from client
            string request =
                System.Text.Encoding.UTF8.GetString(
                ReceiveBuffer, 0, _ReceivedLength);
            if (StringComparer.InvariantCultureIgnoreCase.Compare(request, _
            PolicyRequestString) != 0)
            {
                //Data received isn't valid so close
                _Client.Client.Close();
                return;
            }
            //Valid request received….send policy data
            _Client.Client.BeginSend(_Policy, 0, _Policy.Length,
                SocketFlags.None,
                new AsyncCallback(OnSendComplete), null);
        }
        catch (Exception exp)
        {
```

```
                    _Client.Client.Close();
                    LogError(exp);
                }
                _ReceivedLength = 0;
                _TcpClientConnected.Set(); //Allow waiting thread to proceed
            }

            private void OnSendComplete(IAsyncResult ar)
            {
                try
                {
                    _Client.Client.EndSendFile(ar);
                }
                catch (Exception exp)
                {
                    LogError(exp);
                }
                finally
                {
                    //Close client socket
                    _Client.Client.Close();
                }
            }

            private void LogError(Exception exp)
            {
                string appFullPath = Assembly.GetCallingAssembly().Location;
                string logPath = appFullPath.Substring(0,
                  appFullPath.LastIndexOf("\\")) + ".log";
                StreamWriter writer = new StreamWriter(logPath, true);
                try
                {
                    writer.WriteLine(logPath,
                        String.Format("Error in PolicySocketServer: "
                        + "{0} \r\n StackTrace: {1}", exp.Message, exp.StackTrace));
                }
                catch { }
                finally
                {
                    writer.Close();
                }
            }
        }
    }
```

Looking through the code, you'll see that it uses the `TcpListener` class to listen for incoming client connections. Once a client connects, the code checks the request for the following value:

```
<policy-file-request/>
```

Silverlight automatically sends this text to the policy file socket once it connects. If the request contains the proper value, the code writes the contents of the client access policy back to the client stream (see the `OnReceiveComplete` method). Once the policy file is received, Silverlight parses it, checks that it allows access to the desired port, and then accepts or rejects the socket call that the application is trying to make.

> *The information in the sections "Creating a Silverlight 2 Client-Access-Policy Socket Server" and "Using WCF Polling Duplex Services to Communicate over HTTP" is taken from Dan Wahlin's articles and is provided courtesy of Dr. Dobb's Journal.*

Using WCF Polling Duplex Services to Communicate over HTTP

In the previous sections, you saw how data can be pulled from Web Services and RESTful services and even pushed from servers to Silverlight clients using sockets. Silverlight 2 provides another way to push data from a server to a client using WCF and HTTP. WCF's support for duplex service contracts makes this possible and opens up unique opportunities for pumping data to Silverlight applications.

Many of the WCF services that are created follow the simple request/response mechanism to exchange data that works well for many applications. In addition to standard HTTP bindings, WCF also supports several others, including a polling duplex binding made specifically for Silverlight that allows a service to push data down to a client as the data changes. This type of binding isn't as "pure" as the push model available with sockets because the Silverlight client does poll the server to check for any queued messages, but it provides an efficient way to push data to a client without being restricted to a specific port range. Once a communication channel is opened, messages can be sent in either direction. The Silverlight SDK states the following about how communication works between a Silverlight client and a duplex service:

> *The Silverlight client periodically polls the service on the network layer and checks for any new messages that the service wants to send on the callback channel. The service queues all messages sent on the client callback channel and delivers them to the client when the client polls the service.*

Creating Contracts

When creating a WCF duplex service for Silverlight, the server creates a standard interface with operations. However, because the server must communicate with the client, it also defines a client callback interface. An example of defining a server interface named IGameStreamService that includes a single service operation follows:

```
[ServiceContract(Namespace = "Silverlight",
 CallbackContract = typeof(IGameStreamClient))]
public interface IGameStreamService
{
    [OperationContract(IsOneWay = true)]
    void GetGameData(Message receivedMessage);
}
```

This interface is a little different from the standard WCF interfaces you may have seen or created. First, it includes a CallbackContract property that points to the client interface. Second, the GetGameData operation is defined as a one-way operation. Client calls are not immediately returned as a result of setting IsOneWay to true and are pushed to the client instead. The following code shows the

`IGameStreamClient` interface assigned to the `CallbackContract`. It allows a message to be sent back to the client by calling the `ReceiveGameData` method.

```
[ServiceContract]
public interface IGameStreamClient
{
    [OperationContract(IsOneWay = true)]
    void ReceiveGameData(Message returnMessage);
}
```

Looking at the `ReceiveGameData` operation, you can see that a polling duplex service communicates with a Silverlight client using WCF `Message` types. This provides complete control over the data sent between the client and the service and allows communication between the two to be loosely coupled. The downside of this is that messages must be manually serialized/deserialized by the client and service since the WSDL type information uses the `xs:any` element. Here's what the service's WSDL types section looks like when a service uses the `Message` type as a parameter for an operation. Looking through the schema, you'll notice the inclusion of the `xs:any` element.

```xml
<xs:schema elementFormDefault="qualified"
  targetNamespace="http://schemas.microsoft.com/Message"
  xmlns:xs="http://www.w3.org/2001/XMLSchema"
  xmlns:tns="http://schemas.microsoft.com/Message">
<xs:complexType name="MessageBody">
  <xs:sequence>
    <xs:any minOccurs="0" maxOccurs="unbounded" namespace="##any"/>
  </xs:sequence>
</xs:complexType>
</xs:schema>
```

Creating the Service

Once the server and client contracts are defined, a service class can be created that implements the `IGameStreamService` interface. The following code creates a service that simulates a basketball game similar to the one demonstrated using sockets with Silverlight and sends game updates to a Silverlight client on a timed basis:

```csharp
using System;
using System.ServiceModel;
using System.ServiceModel.Channels;
using System.Threading;

namespace WCFPushService
{
    public class GameStreamService : IGameStreamService
    {
        IGameStreamClient _Client;
        Game _Game = null;
        Timer _Timer = null;
        Random _Random = new Random();

        public GameStreamService()
        {
```

```
            _Game = new Game();
        }

        public void GetGameData(Message receivedMessage)
        {

            //Get client callback channel
            _Client =
                OperationContext.Current.GetCallbackChannel<IGameStreamClient>();

            SendData(_Game.GetTeamData());
            //Start timer which when fired sends updated score information
            _Timer = new Timer(new TimerCallback(_Timer_Elapsed), null, 5000,
                Timeout.Infinite);
        }

        private void _Timer_Elapsed(object data)
        {
            SendData(_Game.GetScoreData());
            int interval = _Random.Next(3000, 7000);
            _Timer.Change(interval, Timeout.Infinite);
        }

        private void SendData(object data)
        {
            Message gameDataMsg = Message.CreateMessage(
                MessageVersion.Soap11,
                "Silverlight/IGameStreamService/ReceiveGameData", data);

            //Send data to the client
            _Client.ReceiveGameData(gameDataMsg);
        }
    }
}
```

The service first creates an instance of a Game class in the constructor, which handles simulating a basketball game and creating new data that can be sent to the client. Once the client calls the service's GetGameData operation (a one-way operation), access to the client's callback interface is retrieved by going through the OperationContext object and calling the GetCallbackChannel method. The teams involved in the game are then created on the server and pushed to the client by calling the SendData method. This method calls the Game object's GetTeamData method. Although not shown here (but included in the book's downloadable sample code), the GetTeamData method generates an XML message and returns it as a string. The SendData method then creates a WCF Message object, defines that SOAP 1.1 will be used (required for this type of communication), and defines the proper action to be used to send the XML data to the client. The client's ReceiveGameData operation is then called, and the message is ultimately sent to the client.

Once the client receives the team data, the server will start sending simulated score data on a random basis. When the Timer object created in the initial call to GetGameData fires, the _Timer_Elapsed method is called, which gets updated score information and pushes it to the Silverlight client by calling the SendData method.

Creating the Service Factory

Once the service class is created, a service factory can be created along with a service host. The factory is responsible for creating the appropriate host, while the host defines the service endpoint. An example of creating service factory and host classes is shown in the following code:

```
using System;
using System.ServiceModel;
using System.ServiceModel.Activation;
using System.ServiceModel.Channels;
using System.ServiceModel.Configuration;

namespace WCFPushService
{
    public class PollingDuplexServiceHostFactory : ServiceHostFactoryBase
    {
        public override ServiceHostBase CreateServiceHost(string constructorString,
            Uri[] baseAddresses)
        {
            return new PollingDuplexServiceHost(baseAddresses);
        }
    }

    class PollingDuplexServiceHost : ServiceHost
    {
        public PollingDuplexServiceHost(params System.Uri[] addresses)
        {
            base.InitializeDescription(typeof(GameStreamService),
                new UriSchemeKeyedCollection(addresses));
        }

        protected override void InitializeRuntime()
        {
            // Define the binding and set time-outs
            PollingDuplexBindingElement bindingElement =
                new PollingDuplexBindingElement()
            {
                ServerPollTimeout = TimeSpan.FromSeconds(10),
                InactivityTimeout = TimeSpan.FromMinutes(1)
            };

            // Add an endpoint for the given service contract
            this.AddServiceEndpoint(
                typeof(IGameStreamService),
                new CustomBinding(
                    bindingElement,
                    new TextMessageEncodingBindingElement(
                        MessageVersion.Soap11,
                        System.Text.Encoding.UTF8),
                    new HttpTransportBindingElement()),
                    "");

            base.InitializeRuntime();
        }
    }
}
```

The service factory class (`PollingDuplexServiceHostFactory`) creates a new instance of the service host class (`PollingDuplexServiceHost`) within the `CreateServiceHost` method. The service host class then overrides the `InitializeRuntime` method and creates a `PollingDuplexBindingElement` instance that defines the server polling and inactivity time-outs. The Silverlight SDK states the following about the `PollingDuplexBindingElement` class's `ServerPollTimeout` and `InactivityTimeout` properties:

> The `ServerPollTimeout` property determines the length of time that the service holds a poll from the client before returning. The `InactivityTimeout` property determines the length of time that can elapse without any message exchange with the client before the service closes its session.

The `PollingDuplexBindingElement` class is located in an assembly named `System.ServiceModel`.`PollingDuplex.dll`, which is part of the Silverlight SDK. You'll need to reference the assembly in your WCF project as well as the `System.ServiceModel.Channels` namespace to use the `PollingDuplexBindingElement` class. Once the binding element is created, a call is made to the host object's `AddServiceEndPoint` method, which references the `PollingDuplexBindingElement` object and the server's `IGameStreamService` interface to create a custom binding that uses HTTP under the covers for message exchange.

Once the factory and service classes are created, the factory can be referenced in the service's .svc file in the following manner:

```
<%@ ServiceHost Language="C#"
        Factory="WCFPushService.PollingDuplexServiceHostFactory" %>
```

Looking through all of the code, you can see that there's definitely some initial set-up work required to get a Silverlight callable WCF HTTP polling duplex service created. Because the client has to poll the service to check for queued messages, you may wonder what the benefit is over writing a manual polling Silverlight client that calls a WCF service. Microsoft's Scott Guthrie gave me additional details about the HTTP polling duplex process that helps answer this question:

> The duplex support does use polling in the background to implement notifications — although the way it does it is different than manual polling. It initiates a network request, and then the request is effectively "put to sleep" waiting for the server to respond (it doesn't come back immediately). The server then keeps the connection open but not active until it has something to send back (or the connection times out after 90 seconds — at which point the duplex client will connect again and wait). This way you are avoiding hitting the server repeatedly — but still get an immediate response when there is data to send.

When the client polls in the background, it sends the following message to the server:

```
<s:Envelope xmlns:s="http://schemas.xmlsoap.org/soap/envelope/">
    <s:Body>
        <wsmc:MakeConnection
            xmlns:wsmc="http://docs.oasis-open.org/ws-rx/wsmc/200702">
            <wsmc:Address>
                http://docs.oasis-open.org/ws-rx/wsmc/200702/
                    anoynmous?id=7f64eefe-9328-4168-8175-1d4b82bef9c3
            </wsmc:Address>
        </wsmc:MakeConnection>
    </s:Body>
</s:Envelope>
```

The server responds with a message similar to the following each time an update to the score occurs:

```
<s:Envelope xmlns:s="http://schemas.xmlsoap.org/soap/envelope/">
  <s:Header>
    <netdx:Duplex xmlns:netdx="http://schemas.microsoft.com/2008/04/netduplex">
      <netdx:Address>
        http://docs.oasis-open.org/ws-rx/wsmc/200702/anonymous?
        id=70379401-a551-494e-abe6-2a0c056b1026
      </netdx:Address>
        <netdx:SessionId>7bbdbba3-8eaf-4735-a343-8deba1f0859b</netdx:SessionId>
    </netdx:Duplex>
  </s:Header>
  <s:Body>
    <string xmlns="http://schemas.microsoft.com/2003/10/Serialization/">
      &lt;?xml version="1.0" encoding="utf-16"?&gt;&#xD;
      &lt;ScoreData xmlns:xsi="http://www.w3.org/2001/XMLSchema-instance"
      xmlns:xsd="http://www.w3.org/2001/XMLSchema"&gt;&#xD;
      &lt;Action&gt;Turnover&lt;/Action&gt;&#xD;
      &lt;Team1Score&gt;4&lt;/Team1Score&gt;&#xD;
      &lt;Team2Score&gt;2&lt;/Team2Score&gt;&#xD;
      &lt;LastAction&gt;Code Warriors: J. Doe turned it
      over&lt;/LastAction&gt;&#xD;
      &lt;LastActionPlayerID&gt;755d8a43-6222-4d85-b48f-
      ad9d23b1898b&lt;/LastActionPlayerID&gt;&#xD;
      &lt;LastActionPoints&gt;0&lt;/LastActionPoints&gt;&#xD;
      &lt;TeamOnOffense&gt;Bug Slayers&lt;/TeamOnOffense&gt;&#xD;
      &lt;/ScoreData&gt;
    </string>
  </s:Body>
</s:Envelope>
```

Creating a Silverlight Duplex Polling Receiver Class

Calling and receiving data in Silverlight requires a fair amount of code to be written. Before showing the code to interact with a polling duplex service, it's important to understand the general steps involved. Here's a synopsis of what you need to do to send and receive data in a Silverlight client:

1. Reference assemblies and namespaces.

   1a. Reference `System.ServiceModel.dll` and `System.ServiceModel .PollingDuplex.dll` in your Silverlight project.

   1b. Import the `System.ServiceModel` and `System.ServiceModel.Channels` namespaces.

2. Create a factory object.

   2a. Create a `PollingDuplexHttpBinding` object instance, and set the `ReceiveTimeout` and `InactivityTimeout` properties (open and close time-out values can also be set).

   2b. Use the `PollingDuplexHttpBinding` object to build a channel factory.

   2c. Open the channel factory, and define an asynchronous callback method that is called when the open completes.

3. Create a channel object.

3a.   Use the factory class to create a channel that points to the service's HTTP endpoint.

3b.   Open the channel, and define an asynchronous callback method that is called when the open completes.

3c.   Define a callback method that is called when the channel closes.

4.   Send/receive messages.

4a.   Create a `Message` object, and send it asynchronously to the service using the channel object. Define an asynchronous callback method that is called when the send completes.

4b.   Start a message receive loop to listen for messages pushed from the service, and define a callback method that is called when a message is received.

4c.   Process data pushed by the server, and dispatch it to the Silverlight user interface for display.

Now that you've seen the fundamental steps, take a look at the code that makes this process work. The following code shows a class named `PushDataReceiver` that encapsulates the factory and channel classes and handles all of the asynchronous operations that occur. The class allows an object of type `IProcessor` to be passed into it along with a service URL, service action, and initial data to send to the service (if any). The `IProcessor` object represents the actual Silverlight `Page` class used to update data on the user interface in this case. As data is received, the Page class's `ProcessData` method will be called.

```
using System;
using System.Net;
using System.ServiceModel;
using System.ServiceModel.Channels;
using System.Threading;
using System.IO;
using System.Xml.Serialization;

namespace SilverlightPushClient
{
    public interface IProcessor
    {
        void ProcessData(object receivedData);
    }

    public class PushDataReceiver
    {
        SynchronizationContext _UiThread = null;
        public IProcessor Client { get; set; }
        public string ServiceUrl { get; set; }
        public string Action { get; set; }
        public string ActionData { get; set; }

        public PushDataReceiver(IProcessor client, string url, string action,
          string actionData)
        {
            Client = client;
            ServiceUrl = url;
            Action = action;
            ActionData = actionData;
```

```
            _UiThread = SynchronizationContext.Current;
        }

        public void Start()
        {
            // Instantiate the binding and set the time-outs
            PollingDuplexHttpBinding binding = new PollingDuplexHttpBinding()
            {
                ReceiveTimeout = TimeSpan.FromSeconds(10),
                InactivityTimeout = TimeSpan.FromMinutes(1)
            };

            // Instantiate and open channel factory from binding
            IChannelFactory<IDuplexSessionChannel> factory =
                binding.BuildChannelFactory<IDuplexSessionChannel>(
                    new BindingParameterCollection());

            IAsyncResult factoryOpenResult =
                factory.BeginOpen(new AsyncCallback(OnOpenCompleteFactory),
                    factory);
            if (factoryOpenResult.CompletedSynchronously)
            {
                CompleteOpenFactory(factoryOpenResult);
            }
        }

        void OnOpenCompleteFactory(IAsyncResult result)
        {
            if (result.CompletedSynchronously)
                return;
            else
                CompleteOpenFactory(result);
        }

        void CompleteOpenFactory(IAsyncResult result)
        {
            IChannelFactory<IDuplexSessionChannel> factory =
                (IChannelFactory<IDuplexSessionChannel>)result.AsyncState;

            factory.EndOpen(result);

            // Factory is now open. Create and open a channel from channel factory.
            IDuplexSessionChannel channel =
                factory.CreateChannel(new EndpointAddress(ServiceUrl));

            IAsyncResult channelOpenResult =
                channel.BeginOpen(new AsyncCallback(OnOpenCompleteChannel),
                    channel);
            if (channelOpenResult.CompletedSynchronously)
            {
                CompleteOpenChannel(channelOpenResult);
            }
        }

        void OnOpenCompleteChannel(IAsyncResult result)
```

```
{
    if (result.CompletedSynchronously)
        return;
    else
        CompleteOpenChannel(result);
}

void CompleteOpenChannel(IAsyncResult result)
{
    IDuplexSessionChannel channel =
     (IDuplexSessionChannel)result.AsyncState;

    channel.EndOpen(result);

    // Channel is now open. Send message
    Message message =
        Message.CreateMessage(channel.GetProperty<MessageVersion>(),
         Action , ActionData);
    IAsyncResult resultChannel =
        channel.BeginSend(message, new AsyncCallback(OnSend), channel);
    if (resultChannel.CompletedSynchronously)
    {
        CompleteOnSend(resultChannel);
    }

    //Start listening for callbacks from the service
    ReceiveLoop(channel);
}

void OnSend(IAsyncResult result)
{
    if (result.CompletedSynchronously)
        return;
    else
        CompleteOnSend(result);
}

void CompleteOnSend(IAsyncResult result)
{
    IDuplexSessionChannel channel =
     (IDuplexSessionChannel)result.AsyncState;
    channel.EndSend(result);
}

void ReceiveLoop(IDuplexSessionChannel channel)
{
    // Start listening for callbacks.
    IAsyncResult result = channel.BeginReceive(new
     AsyncCallback(OnReceiveComplete), channel);
    if (result.CompletedSynchronously) CompleteReceive(result);
}

void OnReceiveComplete(IAsyncResult result)
{
    if (result.CompletedSynchronously)
```

```
                        return;
                else
                    CompleteReceive(result);
        }

        void CompleteReceive(IAsyncResult result)
        {
            //A callback was received so process data
            IDuplexSessionChannel channel =
             (IDuplexSessionChannel)result.AsyncState;

            try
            {
                Message receivedMessage = channel.EndReceive(result);

                // Show the service response in the UI.
                if (receivedMessage != null)
                {
                    string text = receivedMessage.GetBody<string>();
                    _UiThread.Post(Client.ProcessData, text);
                }

                ReceiveLoop(channel);
            }
            catch (CommunicationObjectFaultedException exp)
            {
                _UiThread.Post(delegate(object msg)
                  {
                    System.Windows.Browser.HtmlPage.Window.Alert(msg.ToString());
                  }, exp.Message);
            }
        }

        void OnCloseChannel(IAsyncResult result)
        {
            if (result.CompletedSynchronously)
                return;
            else
                CompleteCloseChannel(result);
        }

        void CompleteCloseChannel(IAsyncResult result)
        {
            IDuplexSessionChannel channel =
             (IDuplexSessionChannel)result.AsyncState;
            channel.EndClose(result);
        }
    }
}
```

When the PushDataReceiver class's Start method is called by Silverlight, it creates a channel factory instance that is used to create a channel instance. The CompleteOpenChannel callback method shown previously then sends an initial message to the service endpoint and encapsulates the data to be sent in a WCF `Message` object. The message data is then sent along with the proper service action to call on the server. After the initial message is sent, a receive loop is started (see the `ReceiveLoop` method), which listens for any messages sent from the server to the client and processes them accordingly. Once a message is received, the `CompleteReceive` method is called, and the message data is routed back to the Silverlight `Page` class for display.

Processing Data Using the `XmlSerializer` Class

The `PushDataReceiver` class shown earlier dispatches data received from the server back to the Silverlight `Page` class for processing. Data sent from the server is in XML format, and multiple techniques can be used to process it in Silverlight ranging from the `XmlReader` class to LINQ to XML functionality to the `XmlSerializer` class. Each of these techniques was covered earlier in the chapter.

The example shown here relies on the `XmlSerializer` class to process the data because it provides a simple way to map XML data to CLR types with a minimal amount of code. Although you can create the CLR classes that XML data maps to by hand, creating an XSD schema and using .NET's `xsd.exe` tool to generate code from the schema works quite well. As a quick review, the `xsd.exe` tool provides a simple way to generate C# or VB.NET code from an XSD schema and ensures that the XML data will be successfully mapped to the appropriate CLR types' properties. The following is an example of using the tool:

```
xsd.exe /c /namespace:SomeNamespace Teams.xsd
```

One of the XSD schemata used to generate C# code with `xsd.exe` is shown in the following code:

```xml
<?xml version="1.0" encoding="utf-16"?>
<xs:schema attributeFormDefault="unqualified" elementFormDefault="qualified"
  xmlns:xs="http://www.w3.org/2001/XMLSchema">
  <xs:element name="Teams">
    <xs:complexType>
      <xs:sequence>
        <xs:element maxOccurs="unbounded" name="Team">
          <xs:complexType>
            <xs:sequence>
              <xs:element maxOccurs="unbounded" name="Player">
                <xs:complexType>
                  <xs:attribute name="ID" type="xs:string" use="required" />
                  <xs:attribute name="Name" type="xs:string" use="required" />
                </xs:complexType>
              </xs:element>
            </xs:sequence>
            <xs:attribute name="Name" type="xs:string" use="required" />
          </xs:complexType>
        </xs:element>
      </xs:sequence>
    </xs:complexType>
  </xs:element>
</xs:schema>
```

> If you use the xsd.exe tool to generate classes that will be used in a Silverlight client, you'll have to remove a few lines that don't compile from the auto-generated code. The xsd.exe tool generates code designed to run on the full version of the .NET Framework, but with a few minor modifications you can also use the code with Silverlight. Simply remove the namespaces and attributes that the compiler says are invalid from the auto-generated code.

Once data is received by the Silverlight client from the WCF polling duplex service, it's processed by a method named ProcessData (the method called by the PushDataReceiver class) in the sample application. ProcessData uses the XmlSerializer class to deserialize XML data into custom Teams and ScoreData objects. The Teams and ScoreData classes were generated from XSD schemata using the xsd.exe tool mentioned earlier.

```csharp
public void ProcessData(object receivedData)
{
    StringReader sr = null;
    try
    {
        string data = (string)receivedData;
        sr = new StringReader(data);
        //Get initial team data
        if (_Teams == null && data.Contains("Teams"))
        {
            XmlSerializer xs = new XmlSerializer(typeof(Teams));
            _Teams = (Teams)xs.Deserialize(sr);
            UpdateBoard();
        }

        //Get updated score data
        if (data.Contains("ScoreData"))
        {
            XmlSerializer xs = new XmlSerializer(typeof(ScoreData));
            ScoreData scoreData = (ScoreData)xs.Deserialize(sr);
            //ScoreDataHandler handler = new ScoreDataHandler(UpdateScoreData);
            //this.Dispatcher.BeginInvoke(handler, new object[] { scoreData });
            UpdateScoreData(scoreData);
        }
    }
    catch { }
    finally
    {
        if (sr != null) sr.Close();
    }
}
```

As team and score data is pushed from the server to the client, the data is updated on the Silverlight interface, as shown in Figure 9-7.

Figure 9-7

Summary

Silverlight provides several different options for requesting, receiving, and processing data from remote services and web sites. In this chapter, you've seen how Silverlight can be used to call WCF and ASP.NET Web Services using a proxy object and how classes like `WebClient` and `HttpWebRequest` can be used to request data from REST services. By using these classes along with related helper classes, you can retrieve data from services that have the proper cross-domain policy files in place.

The chapter also covered different strategies for converting XML and JSON data into CLR objects. By using classes like `XmlReader`, you can have complete control over how XML data is mapped to objects. In cases in which XML data matches up with custom classes, you can use the `XmlSerializer` class to deserialize XML data into objects with little effort and code. LINQ to XML functionality can also be used to parse XML data in a more flexible manner. In addition to XML parsing options, the `DataContract JsonSerializer` class can be used to deserialize JSON messages into CLR objects.

The final sections of the chapter discussed how syndication feed classes can be used to parse RSS and ATOM feeds and how sockets and HTTP polling duplex techniques can be used to push data from a service to a client. By learning to use the different networking and parsing classes available in Silverlight, you'll be able to integrate data from a variety of locations into your applications.

10

Working with Data

As you start to dig deeper into the Silverlight architecture, you can see that an important part of the model is the data framework. This area is one of the most used in the ASP.NET development world as well as during server and smart-client development. ADO.NET has been a great asset for developers as it really transformed the data access programming model, adding feature-rich components and data types that have helped to reduce development and testing time. Because the data framework is a subset of the full .NET implementation, you will need to understand what is possible and which work-arounds you can use to achieve your objectives when using Silverlight.

This chapter presents different alternatives for manipulating data from the servers into your Silverlight applications, and considerations and best practices for storing and caching the results as well as the Data Services (Astoria project) that will really help to extend the line of business applications into new paradigms like Silverlight.

After you learn about retrieving and storing data from the different repositories, you'll explore the different ways to bind the data to your XAML objects, in order to keep a clean separation between the model and the views. This chapter covers the different controls and techniques needed to present and interact with data, including the use of dependency properties.

As the Silverlight team is committed to the new ideas concerning query languages, this chapter also introduces the LINQ implementation to the Silverlight world, with multiple examples that can help you understand the best implementations of this feature.

Finally, you'll review the different alternatives for validating data. As you can see, this will be a very interesting chapter that you may revisit in the future, as handling data is a fundamental part of your Silverlight dream.

Data Framework

To really understand how the data is manipulated in Silverlight, this section analyzes the different namespaces and assemblies that make the data framework. The main idea is to help you visualize the data context that Silverlight includes in order to compare it with the data techniques that you have already mastered with ASP.NET.

Silverlight differs from other technologies in that it does not use the DataSet functionality: it does not include the System.Data and the subset of namespaces that include client functionality for SQL Server, Oracle, or other ODBC resources. The main reason behind this difference is the context where you execute the application: there is no local database, and the information that you are going to consume will come mainly from services or actually be deployed with the XAP package.

In Figure 10-1, we can see how a traditional ASP.NET application uses the data framework on the server side with no interaction on the client side. In contrast, in the Silverlight world, a partial support for the data framework on the client side expands the functionality without affecting the server-side functionality. ASP.NET uses server-based data support, while Silverlight uses server and client support.

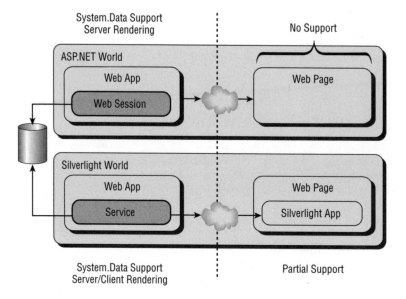

Figure 10-1

In the ASP.NET world, data-retrieval operations can have access to the full *System.Data* namespace and all the subset namespaces, as the rendering happens on the server. The browser just displays the information retrieved; this provides a clear division between where things happen in a Web environment. Silverlight runs at the client side, which means that the role of the server may change, as it will provide the data in a different format in order to be rendered by the client application. This reliance on the client results in format, manipulation, and presentation limitations. On the server side in many scenarios, the client does the processing and rendering, and you can trick the model to retrieve data, process it at the server level, and then send the formatted XAML to be rendered by the Silverlight application. Separating these two worlds really expands what is currently possible in ASP.NET development.

> It is true that you can also play with data using JavaScript and other languages in the ASP.NET world, but this chapter focuses on the Silverlight and .NET libraries that are not available in the unmanaged world.

Exploring the Namespaces

When one of the authors, Salvador, was a little kid he used to be really intrigued by how things worked. If you are reading this book, I am pretty sure that you have also opened radios or computers just to see how things are put together. To see just how Silverlight is put together, this section explores the different namespaces that are included in the Silverlight package and makes some comparisons with the full .NET implementation, so in the future when you are unsure about the supportability, you can come to this section and review the assemblies included.

XML Namespaces

Silverlight data is primarily modeled and handled using XML. Love it or hate, it is the model to follow to get the most from the current application. Previous chapters used XML to show examples, but in this one, we are going to dive into what is included and what is not, as well as the new additions that are exclusive for Silverlight.

The System.XML namespace has not been fully ported; therefore, to simplify our understanding, let's review what has changed and what has been added — you can assume that the types and objects *not* included in this section were *not* ported to Silverlight. Don't worry if you don't understand all the concepts in this section. The full XML data support with lots of examples is described later in this chapter. But if you are already familiar with XML, you may find this briefing very useful.

The main objects that you use with this namespace are XmlReader and XmlWriter, which along with the settings objects used for the instance creator make up the core of this namespace. XmlResolver and XmlConvert help you manipulate the data; and there is support for XMLSchema and XML Serialization. If you have read the communications techniques in Chapter 9, you have already explored the serialization features.

Keep in mind the following changes in functionality:

❏ XmlResolver — Used to resolve XML resources using an URI. Silverlight offers a new method called SupportsType for returning other types in addition to the Stream supported by the full implementation of .NET.

❏ XmlReaderSettings — This object supports XMLReader. In Silverlight 2, the ProhibitDTD property has been removed, and instead Silverlight uses DtdProcessing exposing the enumerations Prohibit, Ignore, and Parse, with a default value of DtdProcessing.Prohibit. This property has the ability to ignore DOCTYPE using the Ignore enumerator.

❏ Xml.Linq — Silverlight has added several new members to work with the Linq to XML version that is shipped with Silverlight — for example, most of the Save() commands have been changed to use streams instead of file paths.

The following objects have been included in the Silverlight implementation to support the specific functionality:

❑ `XmlPreloadedResolver` — Situated on the `Resolver` namespace, this type is used when calls to the network are not desired, and instead the cache is used. The current implementation includes XHTML 1.0 and RSS 0.91 DTDs.

❑ `XmlXapResolver` — This resolver is the most common one in Silverlight as it helps to resolve the resources in the application's XAP package.

Serialization Namespaces

An interesting area that we want to highlight regarding serialization is the support for data contract serialization that is used to deserialize instances of classes that use the `DataContract` attribute, mostly used when interacting with services.

Data Controls Namespaces

Beyond the assemblies and namespaces that Silverlight provides to handle data, there are also data presentation offerings that you can use to render the information and perform automatic binding; therefore, it is important that you are aware of them.

Some people have argued that Silverlight controls are very simple or not good enough for a serious application. In reality, many Microsoft partners are already developing controls that can provide a very rich experience for Silverlight 2. Microsoft's business is not to provide the full range of controls to solve all business problems. They are merely offering a technology that allows developers to be creative when expanding on the basic controls.

Having said that, in this particular chapter, we are going to emphasize the two main controls — the first one is the `DataGrid` control, and the other one is the `ListBox`.

LINQ Namespaces

Finally but not least important, Silverlight provides a wide support of LINQ functionality under this namespace. `System.Linq` includes the base classes for the integrated query language that will allow you to query objects using LINQ in your Silverlight applications.

LINQ is also implemented in order to query XML under `System.Xml.Linq`. You may find references on the Web to *XLINQ*. Most of the functionality has been ported from the full .NET implementation except for the following features:

❑ **Extensions** — This bridge class that supports the DOM (XML Document object model) and the Schema features of System.Xml have not been included.

❑ **XSLT (Extensible Stylesheet Language Transformation)** — The extensible style-sheet language transformation features have not been ported to Silverlight.

Is That All?

After reading the previous section, you may be wondering what you can do with Silverlight with so few options. The reality is that the namespaces listed are just the plumbing that comes out-of-the-box in the

Silverlight plug-in. If you don't like XML, you can use your common .NET data structures and types to receive and render information. The main idea here is to highlight what is already included in Silverlight as you may be already familiar with these namespaces.

Remember that you can create custom data containers that your Silverlight application understands just by extending them using your custom DLLs. Many different helper classes can be found by browsing around the community and visiting Open Source repositories like www.codeplex.com, www.codeproject.com, and many others. Figure 10-2 shows how the Silverlight application uses custom formats.

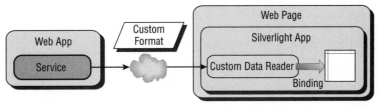

Figure 10-2

One of the main design objectives in Silverlight was to be as lightweight as possible; this means that the team included only the essential plumbing that can be easily ported to other platforms. XML being an open standard that many developers and platforms support, it was a natural option. Beyond this, in order to explore the richness of Silverlight, we are going to review some other ideas, not only interacting with databases and files, but also with local resources and storage.

At this stage of the book, we have exposed you to different technologies and features that we are going to put together in order to help you build a real extension for your line of business application or just the coolest Silverlight application ever made, because at the end, it is not all about boring applications!

Data-Binding Essentials

To understand how to work with data, it is interesting to learn and review how Silverlight works with data binding. Data-binding technology provides you with the ability to display and interact with data, completely separating the view from the model; this means that developers and designers can work separately without worrying about breaking the interaction between the screen and the application.

Data binding has been around for long time — to be honest, after working so many years in this industry, we have seen mixed reactions to this technique. Some developers have used and overused this model, and some others still link the data and the user interface controls using code, as they usually prefer to have more control over the presentation. The main problem with the previous binding models was that the code was still coupled with the interface, breaking the separation model. Many patterns have been developed to solve this issue, like the Model View Controller (MVC) or Model View Presenter (MVP), but some architects and developers still see a lot of rework needed to implement them.

Windows Presentation Foundation has been designed with this separation in mind, and that's why Microsoft is releasing different development environment packages, like Visual Studio for developers and the Expression Suite for designers. The idea is that each group develops independently, just agreeing on the target property names, and if they change, it is still easy for designers or integrators to modify these properties.

This does not mean that using data binding is the only way to link data to the user interface controls. You can still call the controls by name, but be aware that you are coupling the items. As you are learning a new technology, now maybe is a good time to drop some old bad habits and start exploring the power of data binding!

Binding 101

At this stage of the chapter you may have an initial understanding about how binding fits in the big picture. Next, we dig deeper into the binding world of Silverlight, understanding what it is, how it is implemented, and how to get the most out of it.

Simply put, *data binding* is the connection between the user interface and the business objects that allows data to flow between one section and the other one. Figure 10-3 shows a graphical representation of the concept of binding.

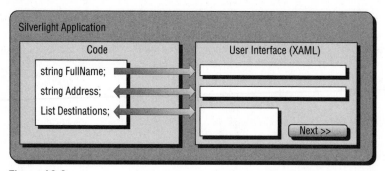

Figure 10-3

In Figure 10-3, different types of arrows indicate how the data flow works. This can be independently assigned if needed, but just to continue illustrating the binding, check out how the XAML is modified in order to link the objects:

> **All the source code presented in this chapter can be found in the samples for Chapter 10 published on the Wrox web site.**

```
<TextBox Height="19"
        Margin="82,47,8,0"
        VerticalAlignment="Top"
        FontFamily="Verdana"
        FontSize="12"
        FontStyle="Italic"
        Foreground="#FFF94806"
        Text="{Binding FullName}"
        TextWrapping="Wrap"
        d:LayoutOverrides="Height"
        x:Name="txtFullName"/>
```

Notice how the `Text` property is modified in order to bind it to the `FullName` property (this is the path by default). Now if you alter the code behind as follows:

```
public class BindingSimpleModel
{
        public string FullName
        {
                get { return fullName; }
                set { this.fullName = value; }
        }
}

private BindingSimpleModel model = new BindingSimpleModel();

private void InitBindings()
{
        // we set the name using our model
        model.FullName = "John Doe";

        // we define the context
        txtFullName.DataContext = model;
}
```

when the code is executed, the `Text` property of the XAML control `TextBox` is changed based on the contents set in the code. In this case, we are using a structure that contains the property `FullName`, setting the value and then defining the binding context to our target control. This has helped us introduce the `DataContext` property; this functionality allows the elements to get information about the data source that is used in the binding operation. What is more, the `DataContext` property is actually a bindable property that facilitates scenarios when the binding context is bound to a parent context. This means that if you assign the `DataContext` in the grid, this can be used by all its children `UIElements`.

When you run the code, the `"txtFullName"` textbox will display *John Doe* on the screen.

To completely decouple the code, you can also set the context using XAML code, as you can bind properties beyond the code behind, using other XAML objects:

```
<Grid.DataContext>

        <!--You can define your data context here, for example a binding - ->
        <Binding/>

</Grid.DataContext>
```

Later in this chapter, we are going to exploit these concepts in real examples, but if you were just browsing the book to find a quick way to bind your objects, you have something to start with. Now, if you want to explore the different options and customize how the bindings work, you should keep reading, as we are going to dig into the architecture and inner workings of the binding model.

Architecture

Now that you have seen the basic binding in action, exploring behind the bindings can provide a deeper understanding of each part. The first thing that we are going to explore is the different parts involved in a binding, as the binding is defined independently and then assigned to a user interface object. In the previous simple example we used the default binding that is created with the " {Binding} " statement in the XAML code, a simple but effective way to use it, but this can be configured and customized to enhance the experience. Figure 10-4 shows the binding architecture.

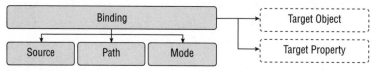

Figure 10-4

Let's review each of these components to get the full binding picture:

❑ **Binding** — This is the parent object that is responsible for defining the binding, performing all the plumbing and notifications based on the parameters set.

❑ **Source** — This property defines where the content is located; for example, in the previous sample code, the source was the `BindingSimpleModel` structure instance. (Note that although we have used a CLR object, the source can be a static resource.) As we have seen, you can use the `DataContext` to get or set the source.

❑ **Path** — The path is the property name from the source; in the previous example, it was the `FullName` property. Because the source may contain many other properties, it is important to define which one we are going to use.

❑ **Mode** — The mode will define how the binding will work. In the Silverlight world, this can be `OneWay`, `OneTime`, or `TwoWay`. This represents how the data will flow between the source and the target. These options are explained in detail later in this section.

❑ **Target Object** — Once the binding object is created, you need a target object to create the destination link. This object will usually be a `UIElement` that will present the information. Remember that a single binding object can have more than one target, as they are independent.

❑ **Target Property** — This is the property that will present the data in the target object. Note that the target property must be a dependency property, but you don't have to worry too much about this constraint as most of the properties on the `UIElements` are already dependency properties. In the example, the target property was the `Text` property in the `TextBox` object.

As you can see, these properties are not very difficult to learn. The complexity comes when we introduce the different ways to achieve the same objectives. The reason behind all these different methods is to support the flexibility that WPF and Silverlight offer you, being able to define the bindings in the code behind, using XAML code, or a mix of both.

Data Flow

When you construct the architecture of the data flow between the source and the target, you may want to customize how the data is transferred from point to point. Figure 10-3 above shows arrows going in multiple directions. The direction of the flow is defined by the binding mode. The Silverlight implementation of WPF supports only three of the four models that are supported in the full .NET implementation: `OneWay`, `TwoWay`, and `OneTime`. The missing one is the `OneWayToSource`, which inverts the `OneWay`; however, you can still simulate this functionality using the `TwoWay` mode.

❑ OneWay — In this binding mode, the data flows from the source property into the dependency property of the target object only. This means that any change in the Model will be translated to the View, but changes in the user interface control will not be propagated back to the source. For example, if you are binding the back color of a control, there is no need to transfer the changes back, as the user may not be able to do so.

```
Binding CustomBinding = new Binding();
CustomBinding.Mode = BindingMode.OneWay;
```

❑ TwoWay — Using this mode, the source and the target are constantly in sync. This means that if you change the property value of the source object, this will be transferred to the target dependency property at the same time. If the user changes the content of the user interface control or any other custom code, the changes will be sent back to the source property. This is an excellent scenario when the application wants to capture values from a form.

```
Binding CustomBinding = new Binding();
CustomBinding.Mode = BindingMode.TwoWay;
```

❑ OneTime — This is the simplest and easiest to configure. The one-time binding will send the data from the source to the target dependency property only once, when the data context or binding is initialized. There is no tracking from either side, making this choice faster than the other ones as it implements less overhead.

```
Binding CustomBinding = new Binding();
CustomBinding.Mode = BindingMode.OneTime;
```

You may ask now how the OneWay and TwoWay models actually track back the changes made to their properties. The reality is that you will need to implement the INotifyPropertyChanged interface in the source object, as the dependency property will subscribe to the PropertyChanged event. It is important to highlight that the implementation has to be done manually, as you may alter when this event is triggered.

```
public class BindingSimpleModel : INotifyPropertyChanged
{
        public event PropertyChangedEventHandler PropertyChanged;

        private string fullName;

        public string FullName
        {
                get
                {
                   return fullName;
                }
                set
                {
                        this.fullName = value;

                        // Notifies the change
                        OnPropertyChanged("FullName");
                }
        }
```

```
/// <summary>
/// Notifies when a property is changed
/// </summary>
/// <param name="property">property name</param>
private void OnPropertyChanged(string property)
{
        if (PropertyChanged != null)
        {
                PropertyChanged(this,
                        new PropertyChangedEventArgs(property));
        }
}
}
```

Note that we are using the explicit property name. Internally, this is accessing the *Path* of the binding using `PropertyPath`. The target to the property source flows automatically. If you have previous experience with WPF and have been using the `UpdateSourceTrigger` property to change the flow behavior, you should be aware that the `UpdateSourceTrigger` property is not supported in Silverlight 2.

```
<TextBox Height="19"
        Margin="82,47,8,0"
        VerticalAlignment="Top"
        FontFamily="Verdana"
        FontSize="12"
        FontStyle="Italic"
        Foreground="#FFF94806"
        Text="{Binding Path=FullName, Mode=TwoWay}"
        TextWrapping="Wrap"
        d:LayoutOverrides="Height"
        x:Name="txtFullName"/>
```

You can see in the above code snippet that you can define the binding mode also using XAML.

> Remember, if your source object does not implement the `INotifyPropertyChanged`, it will behave as a `OneTime` binding, no matter which mode you have selected.

Binding in Practice

To explore the different ways to define and control bindings, we are going to use the flight reservation example. The form is very simple: It has a textbox to enter the full name, a box for selecting select a destination, and a checkbox to verify whether the passenger needs a Visa. The sample looks like Figure 10-5.

In order to understand the different ways in which we can set up the binding process, we are going to mix and match different techniques in the example. You may choose which is the best option for your specific project, but the idea is to show you as many examples as possible, so you can refer to this chapter the next time that you need to remember the syntax.

For the different models that we are going to explain, we are going to use the same binding pattern, which will help us to use all the different modes. Once we dominate the basic binding modes, we are going to expand the binding options when we jump into complex bindings. The illustration in Figure 10-6 shows the data flow.

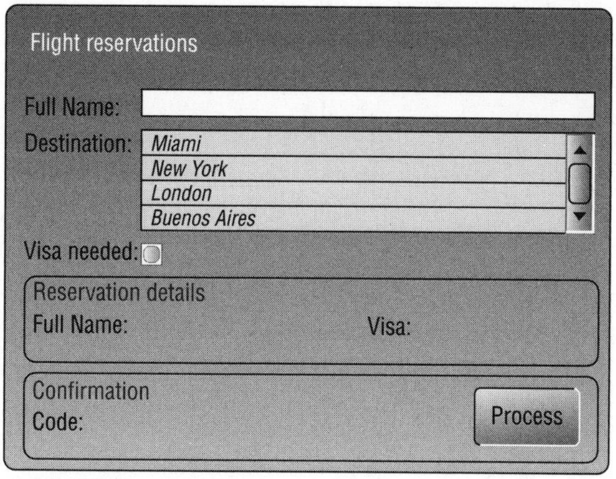

Figure 10-5

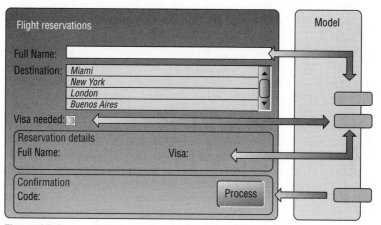

Figure 10-6

The full name will originally flow *from* the model *to* the user interface, but when the name is changed, it will be copied to the full name field in the reservation panel through the source objects. The same thing will happen with the Visa option. Finally, when the "Process" button is clicked, the application will generate a new reservation code at the model level, which will flow to the user interface.

> In Silverlight 2, you cannot bind a `UIElement` with another `UIElement` directly; you need to use a CLR object source as a bridge between them for this.

We are going to use an extended version of the model that we presented earlier in this chapter, in order to include the other parameters. The model looks like this:

```
public class BindingModel : INotifyPropertyChanged
{
        public event PropertyChangedEventHandler PropertyChanged;

        private string fullName;
        private bool visaRequired;
        private string code;

        public bool VisaRequired
        {
                get { return this.visaRequired; }
                set
                {
                        this.visaRequired = value;

                        OnPropertyChanged("VisaRequired");
                }
        }

        public string Code
        {
                get { return this.code; }
                set
                {
                        this.code = value;
                        OnPropertyChanged("Code");
                }
        }

        public string FullName
        {
                Get       {return this.fullName;}
                set
                {
                        this.fullName = value;
                        OnPropertyChanged("FullName");
                }
        }

        private void OnPropertyChanged(string property)
        {
                if (PropertyChanged != null)
                {
                        PropertyChanged(this,
                                new PropertyChangedEventArgs(property));
                }
        }
}
```

Note that in many examples in the Internet, the event is raised before changing the value, which is not correct. Always set the value first and notify the property change after in order to reflect the changes.

Code-behind Binding

Code-behind binding represents a model in which everything is set from the managed code rather than the XAML code. This gives you the maximum flexibility beyond what the designers do with the XAML code. The only important piece of information here is the name of the UIElement control and the type. With that information, you are ready to prepare the data binding.

Before viewing the full source code, let's explore how to create a binding using the code behind. The first thing that you need is a Binding object; you create an instance, and then you set the properties you explored in the architecture section:

```
Binding MyBinding = new Binding();

// The model will be the object that contains the properties, in this case is the
// model instance
FullNameBinding.Source = model;

// We define the path, in other words, the name of the property
FullNameBinding.Path = new PropertyPath("FullName");

// Finally we set up the data flow mode
FullNameBinding.Mode = BindingMode.TwoWay;

// Once we have the binding, we can associate the same binding to one or multiple
// targets as well as the property target.
txtFullName.SetBinding(TextBox.TextProperty, FullNameBinding);
```

The SetBinding method assigns the binding to the target object. This method will need the dependency property to be set as target property and the binding that contains the source information.

```
public partial class BindingCodeBehind : UserControl
{
        // This is just a structure that contains the FullName property
        private BindingModel model = new BindingModel();

        private void InitFullNameBinding()
        {
                Binding FullNameBinding = new Binding();

                // Full name (two way binding)
                FullNameBinding.Source = model;
                FullNameBinding.Path = new PropertyPath("FullName");
                FullNameBinding.Mode = BindingMode.TwoWay;
```

```
                    // we manually set the binding
                    txtFullName.SetBinding(TextBox.TextProperty, FullNameBinding);

                    // Confirmation binding
                    Binding DuplicateFullNameBinding = new Binding();

                    // The source copies the content
                    DuplicateFullNameBinding.Mode = BindingMode.OneWay;
                    DuplicateFullNameBinding.Source = model;
                    DuplicateFullNameBinding.Path = new PropertyPath("FullName");

                    lblReservationDetails.SetBinding(TextBlock.TextProperty,
                                DuplicateFullNameBinding);
            }

            private void InitVisaBinding()
            {
                    // we initialize the binding with the path
                    Binding VisaBinding = new Binding("VisaRequired");

                    // visa name (one way binding)
                    VisaBinding.Source = model;
                    VisaBinding.Mode = BindingMode.TwoWay;

                    // we re-use the binding
                    lblResVidaDetails.SetBinding(TextBlock.TextProperty, VisaBinding);
                    chkVisa.SetBinding(CheckBox.IsCheckedProperty, VisaBinding);
            }

            private void InitCodeBinding()
            {
                    // we initialize the binding with the path
                    Binding CodeBinding = new Binding("Code");

                    // visa name (one way binding)
                    CodeBinding.Source = model;
                    CodeBinding.Mode = BindingMode.OneWay;

                    // we manually set the binding
                    lblConDetails.SetBinding(TextBlock.TextProperty, CodeBinding);
            }

            public BindingCodeBehind()
            {
                    InitializeComponent();

                    // Initializes the bindings
                    InitFullNameBinding();
                    InitVisaBinding();
                    InitCodeBinding();
            }
```

```
            private void cmdProcess_Click(object sender, RoutedEventArgs e)
            {
                    Random Rnd = new Random();
                    model.Code = Rnd.Next(1000, 9999).ToString();
            }
    }
```

You can see in the example how the binding works from the model in two directions as well as copying the contents to another UIElement; this is also known as *bridging*. Further on, the Visa binding is reused in two different controls. The output of the checkbox is just rendering Boolean values, but later in this chapter, you are going to see how you can add conversion during the binding operation.

As you can see, all the bindings have been set up without touching the XAML code; the only thing that you need to know is the control name. This is something that you need to consider when you work with designers.

Using DataContext

The first example in this chapter used the DataContext property to set the binding source. Now we are going to exploit all the advantages of it. DataContext allows you to use inheritance in order to use the same binding source; this means that a single binding source can be consumed by children objects without specifying it. You can change the previous example to add the data context to the grid level as follows:

```
    private void InitContext()
    {
            MainGrid.DataContext = model;
    }

    private void InitVisaBinding()
    {
            // we initialize the binding with the path
            Binding VisaBinding = new Binding("VisaRequired");

            // visa name (one way binding)
            VisaBinding.Mode = BindingMode.TwoWay;

            // we re-use the binding
            lblResVidaDetails.SetBinding(TextBlock.TextProperty, VisaBinding);
            chkVisa.SetBinding(CheckBox.IsCheckedProperty, VisaBinding);
    }
```

The MainGrid object in this example is the grid that groups all the objects; this means that it is the parent element for our target objects. Note that we are not specifying the source property on the binding. Right now, this may not look very useful; it will make more sense when we use it on the XAML and mixed examples.

XAML Binding

This section uses the same example but with XAML code. The first thing that you need to address is how to reference the model object from the XAML environment. For this, you need to add a new namespace to the user control. You can do this using the xmlns command. In this example, the namespace entry is called "MySource".

Once you have the namespace, you can start referencing objects from the XAML code. As the markup extensions in Silverlight only allow you to refer to `StaticResources`, you need to add them to the user control resource list. (Note that this resource can reside in another object if you need it to.) With the reference, you can associate a key and also fill the properties with initialization values. In this case, we are initializing it using the `"Hello from XAML!"` entry.

```
<UserControl
    x:Class="Chapter10.Controls.BindingFromXAML"
    xmlns="http://schemas.microsoft.com/winfx/2006/xaml/presentation"
    xmlns:x="http://schemas.microsoft.com/winfx/2006/xaml"
    Width="400" Height="300"
    xmlns:d="http://schemas.microsoft.com/expression/blend/2008"
    xmlns:mc="http://schemas.openxmlformats.org/markup-compatibility/2006"
    mc:Ignorable="d"
    xmlns:MySource="clr-namespace:Chapter10.Controls">

<UserControl.Resources>
        <MySource:BindingModel x:Key="Model" FullName="Hello from XAML!" />
</UserControl.Resources>

<Grid x:Name="LayoutRoot">

        <!--- … Design entries removed for simplicity … -->

        <!-- Full Name-->
        <TextBox Height="19"
                Margin="82,47,8,0"
                VerticalAlignment="Top"
                FontFamily="Verdana"
                FontSize="12"
                FontStyle="Italic"
                Foreground="#FFF94806"
                TextWrapping="Wrap"
                Text="{Binding Source={StaticResource Model},
                                        Path=FullName, Mode=TwoWay}"
                d:LayoutOverrides="Height"
                x:Name="txtFullName"/>


        <!-- Visa checkbox -->
        <CheckBox HorizontalAlignment="Left"
                Margin="82,139,0,121"
                x:Name="chkVisa"
                Width="21.778"
                Content="CheckBox"
                d:LayoutOverrides="Width"
                IsChecked="{Binding Source={StaticResource Model},
                                        Path=VisaRequired, Mode=TwoWay}"/>
```

```
        <!-- Processing Button -->
        <Button Height="35.111" HorizontalAlignment="Right" Margin="0,0,
                x:Name="cmdProcess" VerticalAlignment="Bottom" Width="66.667
                Content="Process" Click="cmdProcess_Click"/>

        <!-- Reservation labels -->
        <TextBlock Height="19.555"
                HorizontalAlignment="Stretch"
                Margin="85,0,157,78"
                VerticalAlignment="Bottom"
                FontSize="12"
                Text="{Binding Source={StaticResource Model},
                                        Path=FullName, Mode=OneWay}"
                TextWrapping="Wrap"
                x:Name="lblReservationDetails"
                d:LayoutOverrides="Height"/>

        <TextBlock Height="19.555"
                HorizontalAlignment="Right"
                Margin="0,0,19,78"
                VerticalAlignment="Bottom"
                FontSize="12"
                Text="{Binding Source={StaticResource Model},
                                        Path=VisaRequired, Mode=OneWay}"
                TextWrapping="Wrap"
                x:Name="lblResVidaDetails"
                d:LayoutOverrides="Width, Height"
                Width="94.073"/>

        <!-- Confirmation labels -->
        <TextBlock Height="19.555" HorizontalAlignment="Stretch"
                Margin="82,0,99,19" VerticalAlignment="Bottom" FontSize="12"
                Text="" TextWrapping="Wrap" x:Name="lblConDetails"
                d:LayoutOverrides="Height" />
    </Grid>
</UserControl>
```

When it is time to bind the target properties, you just include the "{Binding}" entry, and you will be able to set the initialization properties. The main difference here is concerning the source — as this is residing at the resource level, you will need to access it as a normal resource. The other parameters should be familiar to you. The *Path* is defined in order to reference the source property, and the *Mode* to specify the data flow direction.

> In Silverlight 2, it is important to define the resources before calling the StaticResource command, as this will not work if the resource is after the calling method. This is reminiscent of the old C times, when all the definitions should be defined before calling them.

ext? You can still define the `DataContext` using the XAML code in the same
ode behind. You can alter the XAML code and set the parent object with a data
ble to remove the source parameter from the bindings.

```
>
    Source ="{StaticResource Model}"/>
xt>
```

Mixing

Now that you fully understand how to declare the bindings using managed code and XAML code, you
can experiment mixing the techniques in the same application. Because the previous examples are not
exclusive, you can define the binding paths using XAML and define the `DataContext` using the code
behind. Indeed, it is quite common to find this type of implementation.

Remember that you can define a binding with partial information; this will not trigger an error as the
binding engine will be responsible for locating the missing parameters. The main reason for this is that
you should be able to inherit information from parent elements.

The other big reason why this is common is because many architects and developers prefer to handle
the instances of the source object at the managed-code level, populating and validating it before performing the binding. If the source contains all the parameters for the presentation controls, just define
the context at the parent level. This reduces the overhead of assigning the source to each binding, as it
reflects only once to load the content.

> As you may know, binding may use .NET reflection in order to discover the object
> structure. This topic is discussed further in the performance considerations section.

```
XAML Code:

        Text="{Binding Path=FullName, Mode=TwoWay}"

Managed Code:

        private void InitContext()
        {
                MainGrid.DataContext = model;
        }
```

Complex Bindings

So far we have been discussing bindings with a single object; if we have a property called `FullName`, it
will contain a single string that can be easily bound to the target property. In certain scenarios, this is
not enough, and you will need to look into more complex bindings that contain data collections.

In this example, we are going to change the binding model by incorporating the list of destinations
with a two-way binding and a one-way binding to the reservation details. The data flow looks like
Figure 10-7.

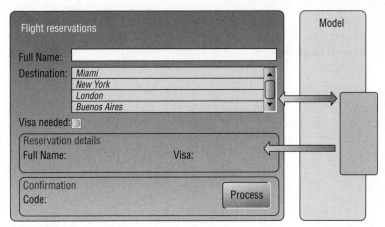

Figure 10-7

With a new collection to bind to the application, you need to review the model structure in order to include the list. But because the binding will be in two-way mode on each single item of the collection, you need to find a way to notify changes per item, rather than per collection. You can do this manually, creating a custom item for your collection and implementing `INotifyPropertyChanged` to the entry and `INotifyCollectionChanged` for the collection. The other option is to use the `ObservableCollection`, which has a built-in implementation of the collection notification.

```csharp
/// <summary>
/// Destination item
/// </summary>
public class Destination : INotifyPropertyChanged
{
        public event PropertyChangedEventHandler PropertyChanged;

        private string name;

        public string Name
        {
                get { return name; }
                set
                {
                        name = value;
                        OnPropertyChanged("Name");
                }
        }

        public override string ToString()
        {
                return name;
        }

        public Destination() {}

        public Destination(string destination)
        {
```

```
                        Name = destination;
            }

        private void OnPropertyChanged(string property)
        {
                if (PropertyChanged != null)
                {
                        PropertyChanged(this,
                                new PropertyChangedEventArgs(property));
                }
        }
    }

    /// <summary>
    /// Destinations collection
    /// </summary>
    public class Destinations : ObservableCollection<Destination>
    {
        public Destinations() : base()
        {
                Add(new Destination("Miami"));
                Add(new Destination("New York"));
                Add(new Destination("London"));
                Add(new Destination("Buenos Aires"));
        }
    }
}
```

If you are planning to use your own collection and implement the `INotifyCollectionChanged`, it is recommended to use a `List<T>` object as a base class, or at least implement the interface as it provides the minimal functionality required for the binding. Since you are manually controlling the collection, remember to call this event every time an item is changed (add/update/remove), or you just can customize this behavior as well, limiting the notifications.

With the model in place, now you can alter the sample to implement this collection binding. This example uses a *ListBox*. The binding description can be in managed code or in XAML. Here we use a bit of both worlds:

```
<Grid.Resources>
        <DataTemplate x:Key="Salva">
                <StackPanel>
                        <TextBlock FontFamily="Verdana" FontSize="11"
                                FontStyle="Italic" Text="{Binding Path=Name}"/>
                </StackPanel>
        </DataTemplate>
</Grid.Resources>

<ListBox        Height="62.668"
                Margin="82,72,8,0"
                x:Name="lstDestinations"
                VerticalAlignment="Top"
                d:LayoutOverrides="Height"
                ItemsSource="{Binding }"
                ItemTemplate="{StaticResource Salva}"
                Background="#FFFFFFFF"/>
```

Don't worry about the `DataTemplate`. We will review it when we explain how to work with data controls, but just picture it as a way to define a template that you can use in each item. If you check the `ListBox`, the example is specifying the binding in the `ItemSource` property and the item template to a local resource. The target object has the binding; now each item should fetch the path of the individual item. That's why there is another binding in the `Text` property.

Finally, you need to set the source. The following example uses the `DataContext` in the code behind in order to set the current collection:

```
private void InitBindings()
{
        // Associates the destinations list
        lstDestinations.DataContext = this.destinations;
}
```

> You can use as a source any object that implements `IEnumerable`. **This applies to all collection style** `UIElements`, **like the** `ItemsControl`, **the** `ListBox`, **and the** `DataGrid`.

On most occasions, you need to get the selected item from the list bound to your model. In WPF, you can bind the selected item to your label, but in this case, you have to do it using the `TwoWay` mode. Here are some changes to the example that will allow you to do that:

```
Changes to the model:

private Destination currentDestination;

public Destination CurrentDestination
{
        get { return this.currentDestination; }
        set
        {
                this.currentDestination = value;
                OnPropertyChanged("CurrentDestination");
        }
}

Changes to the XAML control:

private void InitBindings()
{
        // Associates the destinations list
        lstDestinations.DataContext = this.destinations;

        Binding SelectionBinding = new Binding();
        SelectionBinding.Source = model;
        SelectionBinding.Path = new PropertyPath("CurrentDestination");
        SelectionBinding.Mode = BindingMode.TwoWay;

        lstDestinations.SetBinding(ListBox.SelectedItemProperty,
```

```
                                                   SelectionBinding);
        lblReservationDetails.SetBinding(TextBlock.TextProperty,
                                               SelectionBinding);
    }
```

Conversions

Sometimes you will want the data to flow freely from the model to the user interface, but on most occasions, you will want to modify how it is presented. This is one of the main reasons why the team decided to port the conversion feature into Silverlight 2. The implementation is extremely easy and very flexible; indeed, the community is actively using it because the results are quite predictable.

The basic flow of the conversion process works as illustrated in Figure 10-8.

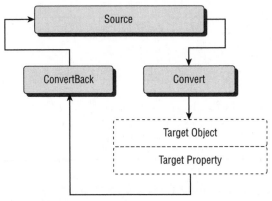

Figure 10-8

As you can see, two different methods are exposed by the IValueConverter interface, and you need to implement them in order to create a binding conversion. When the data flows from the source property into the target property, the Convert() method will be invoked. In the case of TwoWay binding, the ConvertBack() method will be executed. This allows you to completely transform what the user sees and what the system stores.

To create a simple converter for the Visa requirement checkbox in order to avoid showing True or False, the code looks like this:

```
public class BindingConversion : IValueConverter
{
        public object Convert(object value, Type targetType, object parameter,
                                  System.Globalization.CultureInfo culture)
        {
            bool CurrentValue = (bool) value;

            if (CurrentValue)
                    return "Required";
            else
                    return "Not Required";
```

```
        }

        public object ConvertBack(object value, Type targetType, object parameter,
                                    System.Globalization.CultureInfo culture)
        {
            return value;
        }
    }
```

This example does not consider the conversion back to the source because the checkbox is a True/False response, and the `TextBlock` is Read Only (`OneWay`). Now, you need to associate the converter to the binding; using the code behind, you can change the example as follows:

```
private void InitVisaBinding()
{
        // we initialize the binding with the path
        Binding VisaBinding = new Binding("VisaRequired");

        // visa name (one way binding)
        VisaBinding.Source = model;
        VisaBinding.Mode = BindingMode.OneWay;
        VisaBinding.Converter = new BindingConversion();

        // We bind the text block
        lblResVidaDetails.SetBinding(TextBlock.TextProperty, VisaBinding);

        // we need to use another binding that does not use the converter
        VisaBinding = new Binding("VisaRequired");

        // visa name (two way binding)
        VisaBinding.Source = model;
        VisaBinding.Mode = BindingMode.TwoWay;

        chkVisa.SetBinding(CheckBox.IsCheckedProperty, VisaBinding);
}
```

You can do the same if you need to modify the binding using your XAML code as you are going to see in the next code block, but before that, let me explain another interesting feature. As you may have noticed, the interface receives several parameters. Let's explore them so that you can make the most of the conversion:

❑   `value` — This is the simplest parameter, and you are going to receive the raw value from the source or the target. You can manipulate it at this stage.

❑   `targetType` — This is the target that the destination is expecting to receive. You can analyze it or cast the result if necessary.

❑   `parameter` — You can use this optional parameter to send information to the conversion process. This is a free parameter that you can initialize in the binding. The XAML code block will show the implementation. The binding parameter is `ConverterParameter`.

❑   `culture` — You can specify the culture that you want to use if you don't want the default one. The binding parameter is `ConverterCulture`.

The following code shows how you can reference the conversion object and send extra parameters using XAML code:

```
<UserControl.Resources>
        <source:BindingConversion x:Name="Conversion"/>
</UserControl.Resources>

        <CheckBox
                HorizontalAlignment="Left"
                Margin="82,139,0,121"
                x:Name="chkVisa"
                Width="21.778"
                Content="CheckBox"
                d:LayoutOverrides="Width"
                IsChecked="{Binding Path=VisaRequired, Mode=TwoWay,
                                    Converter={StaticResource Converter},
                                    ConverterParam=100}"/>
```

In this example, the parameter 100 will be sent to the converter instance. You can alter the conversion output based on this (these) value(s). If you run the example now, the application will render "Required" or "Not Required," when the user clicks the Visa checkbox.

Dependency Properties

One of the most celebrated features in WPF is the inclusion of a new property system that allows the application to interact with dependency properties. Silverlight 2 has included this feature, and it is widely used across the controls. Most of the properties are implemented as dependency properties. But if you are not familiar with them, you may be asking yourself what exactly that means.

In the traditional CLR object, you can define properties; this is a concept that is widely understood and is one of the basics of object-oriented programming. .NET languages rely heavily on traditional properties in order to interact with the objects and the base class library. But they have some limitations; for example, they are quite difficult to program dynamically. This means that you should know the type and name before using it, which can be limiting in some scenarios. Many developers have ended up using reflection in order to use the properties by name, but this adds a performance overhead to the application.

Changing the whole model is not possible; therefore, you need a way to extend the properties to incorporate a more robust modeling alternative. The answer to this was to create a new property system that contains a global property management. These properties can contain any type and can be set at run time, as they can be accessed using strings (property bag model).

But it is not just that dependency properties can be implemented to provide self-contained validation or to implement callbacks to notify changes to other dependency properties. The properties system is the DependencyProperty object, responsible for managing all the dependencies. For each individual property, the base class is the DependencyObject.

Let's see how you can declare a dependency property:

```
public partial class BindingDependencyProperty : UserControl
{
        public static readonly DependencyProperty FullNameProperty =
```

```
                DependencyProperty.Register("FullName",
                typeof(string),
                typeof(BindingDependencyProperty),
                null);

        public string FullName
        {
                get { return (string)GetValue(FullNameProperty); }
                set { SetValue(FullNameProperty, value); }
        }
}
```

The static `Register` method is necessary to include the property in the bag. Internally, it is adding the dependency property into a dictionary, where the key is the name (string) of the property; this is usually called a *Dependency Property Identifier*. You must also specify its type and the owner's type — in this case, the class. It is considered good practice to name your dependency property using the format <your property name>Property; for example, if you want to register "Age," you will have to use the name *AgeProperty*. Silverlight 2 doesn't impose the restriction, but it is good to use it.

As you have noticed, the dependency property can be accessed by a normal property wrapper. For this, you need to use the CLR functions `GetValue` and `SetValue`. These helper methods read and write the information from the property service directly for you.

The dependency property can be declared in order to notify other objects about the changes, which may be useful to simulate the lack of `ElementName` binding in Silverlight 2. The following example shows how you can implement a callback notification:

```
public static readonly DependencyProperty OtherProperty =
                DependencyProperty.Register("Other",
                typeof(string),
                typeof(BindingDependencyProperty), null
                );

public static readonly DependencyProperty FullNameProperty =
                DependencyProperty.Register("FullName",
                typeof(string),
                typeof(BindingDependencyProperty),
                new PropertyMetadata(new PropertyChangedCallback(Notify))
                );

private static void Notify(DependencyObject sender,
                                    DependencyPropertyChangedEventArgs e)
{
        // We can access both values
        Debug.WriteLine("Previous Value: " + e.OldValue);
        Debug.WriteLine("New Value: " + e.NewValue);

        // we can refer to the same or other dependency property for any object
        sender.SetValue(BindingDependencyProperty.OtherProperty, e.OldValue);
}
```

Now, binding a dependency property takes the same syntax that you have used all along in this chapter; in this case, as the dependency properties are registered to the code behind the XAML user control, you can use the this command:

```
private void InitBinding()
{
        Binding MyBinding = new Binding();

        MyBinding.Source = this;
        MyBinding.Path = new PropertyPath("FullName");
        MyBinding.Mode = BindingMode.TwoWay;

        txtFullName.SetBinding(TextBox.TextProperty, MyBinding);
}
```

Performance Considerations

This section analyzes the different performance considerations that you must understand when determining which type of object you are going to use as a source, because the binding process can take different routes for resolving objects.

For this you need to understand that during run time, the binding properties need to be found, addressed, and updated. Similar to the way things work in ASP.NET, CLR objects can be reflected to enumerate properties and methods. Data binding in Silverlight works in a very similar way to how it works in WPF, and heavily relies on reflection to run. As you may or may not know, reflecting an object is a very expensive operation in .NET; for this reason, you need to think carefully about how you design them to reduce the overhead.

The most expensive model is one in which you use a simple CLR object that does not notify you about changes — a very common scenario for the OneTime mode. In this scenario, the resolution will use reflection to discover the metadata and to provide access to it.

There is another way to retrieve the information, and it is used for objects that implement INotify PropertyChanged. This is a common model if you want to have bindings with a OneWay or TwoWay mode. In this case, reflection will still be used, but it will directly query the source type, reducing the overhead. These solutions are still using reflection, as we are still using a CLR object property. Recall in the previous section when we introduced the dependency properties and the reasons for supporting them in Silverlight 2.

The most efficient way to bind properties is using dependency properties in the source object. However, using dependency properties is not the only way. In some scenarios, dependency properties are not the best option. A good example is when you need to consume structures that are widely used in the application, but converting them to dependency properties would add extra overhead. However, if you can use them, the binding will not use reflection in order to get the information; the data-binding engine will directly resolve the property reference (as this can be accessed by name). Figure 10-9 summarizes the techniques showing the performance gain.

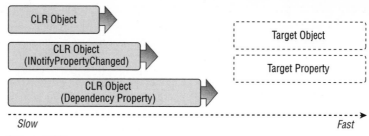

Figure 10-9

Another area of concern is when you bind a large CLR object as a source. There is a big difference in performance when you bind a large object as opposed to a small object with only a few properties. This means that if you are planning to use a single object with hundreds of properties, try to consider using multiple small objects with fewer properties. Some early tests show the results reflected in the following table. (Note that the results may vary from environment to environment.)

Source Type	Binding Time + Rendering Time (milliseconds)
1 CLR object with 500 properties	675 ms
500 CLR objects with one property	166 ms

As you can see, the difference is significant, even considering the binding-time overhead for 500 objects.

Test, test, and then test again. Each implementation is completely different. Usage scenarios influence how the application behaves, but the idea of this section is to explain the internal cost and provide some point of reference on which you can base your understanding and enhance your designs.

Retrieving and Storing Data

Data is one of the essential parts of your Silverlight application and is the life force of data binding. This section is dedicated to the different techniques of retrieving and storing data that will be manipulated later. To understand this section, be sure to review Chapter 9, which explains the internals of server communication. In this section, you learn how to retrieve data from different locations and implement some best practices for storing the information as efficiently as possible.

Everybody loves new technology, and for this reason, this section explores some concepts and ideas that are being developed by Microsoft for retrieving data from services. This project is called *Astoria* (now renamed *ADO.NET Data Services*). You are going to spend some time with it as well, so you can have the full picture when selecting the best method.

Working with Data Repositories

Silverlight 2 allows you to access data from different places, but as in a sandboxed application, there are some limitations. We are going to present some techniques to access and store data in your application.

There are two groups of repositories you can play with — local ones and remote ones. You saw some of them in detail in other chapters. Here we give you a quick overview of how to get and save your data. Also check the Chapter 10 demos for accessing data if you want to copy and paste some of this code.

One important thing to remember at this stage is that Silverlight does not have access to the local filesystem for security reasons. There were some discussions about adding a SaveFile dialog box in order to allow the user to save files whenever he or she wants, but there were some security concerns about this that will need to be resolved. For example, you can create a malicious application that when you try to save a file writes until your disk space runs out! You may think that is a little radical, but as a web developer, you well know that some people will try to damage others. With this snapshot of the risk that you may be exposed to, you may understand why there is no filesystem access in Silverlight 2.

Local Data

The "local data" category includes all the data that is not retrieved from a different machine, or at least has been loaded in the current application. Figure 10-10 shows you the different alternatives regarding accessing local data. As you know, the XAP package (where your Silverlight application is grouped and compressed) that you deploy with your application can contain content files (as you can rename the XAP file to ZIP, and you can explore the content). We can access this content in different ways and store it in our temporary space. Let's start with the resources.

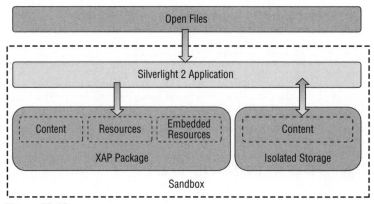

Figure 10-10

Using Local Resources

The resources are automatically included in the XAP package when you develop your Silverlight application. You can play with them by changing the property Build Action, from Content, to resource, to embedded resource. These options are available because different resources need to be accessed using different techniques.

❑ **Content** — The content files will remain separate from the assembly; this behavior is exactly the same that you are used to with ASP.NET, as you can add files to be deployed on the server for external access (or update). If you rename the XAP to ZIP, you can see that your content files are there. The advantage of them is that they can be loaded on demand (ideally for large files); the other big advantage is that different assemblies can share the same content file.

❑ **Resources** — You can opt to embed the file in your assembly and treat it as an internal resource. This is very common when you develop a Windows Forms application; images are embedded in the form so it can quickly access them. The advantage is the access speed, but you are paying in memory storage as the resources are loaded with the assembly.

❑ **Localizable Resources** — The type is described as embedded resources, but actually these are RESX (traditional resource) files. These types of files are usually used to store strings and localizable information, as the localization system of Silverlight can load the correct language if it is included.

❑ **XAML Resources** — As we have seen before, we can define the control resources in order to reuse the XAML specifications of a user control or specific control. These resources are stored using keys; therefore, you can access them like a dictionary. These types of resources are also called *Silverlight resources* (instead of application resources). These are not covered in this chapter, but you can find information on these in Chapter 7, where we explain styles and templates.

Here you explore how you can open data that is stored as Content. As with everything in Silverlight, you can do this using the code behind or using the managed code. An important thing to understand is that all the content that is stored in the XAP package can be accessed through a relative URI, meaning that depending on where you store the Content file, you have to alter the URI address.

We can start seeing how we can access the relative URIs using the code behind in the example below:

```
using System.Windows.Media.Imaging;

public partial class AccessingResources : UserControl
{
        public AccessingResources()
        {
                InitializeComponent();

                LoadImage();
        }

        private void LoadImage()
        {
                // We define the image location in our project
                Uri ImageLocation = new Uri("/Controls/Accessing/SLLogo.jpg",
                                                        UriKind.Relative);

                // We load the image
                BitmapImage ContentImage = new BitmapImage(ImageLocation);

                // We assign the image to our image control
                imgLogo.Source = ContentImage;
        }
}
```

Note that this includes the full path of the image; otherwise, it will raise a "Not Found" exception. Now, if you want to do this on the XAML code, it is much simpler:

```
<Image  x:Name="imgLogo"
        Height="54.304"
```

```
              HorizontalAlignment="Left"
              Margin="8,0,0,8"
              VerticalAlignment="Bottom"
              Width="62.855"
              Source="/Controls/Accessing/SLLogo.jpg"
    />
```

If you change the image file to be a resource, you just need to change the URI address, as now it should look into the assembly folder rather than the content located on the XAP file. For this, you will need to change the method as follows:

```
private void LoadResourceImage()
{
        // We define the image location in our project
        Uri ImageLocation = new
                    Uri("/Chapter10;component/Controls/Accessing/SLLogo.jpg",
                        UriKind.Relative);

        // We load the image
        BitmapImage ResourceImage = new BitmapImage(ImageLocation);

        // We assign the image to our image control
        imgLogo.Source = ResourceImage;
}
```

Again, the XAML code needs to be changed in order to include the assembly reference:

```
<Image    x:Name="imgLogo"
          Height="54.304"
          HorizontalAlignment="Left"
          Margin="8,0,0,8"
          VerticalAlignment="Bottom"
          Width="62.855"
          Source="/Chapter10;component/Controls/Accessing/SLLogo.jpg"
    />
```

One common question in loading local content files is how you can load text, as opening files requires streams. For this, you will have to use the `Application` object as follows:

```
Stream YourStream = Application.GetResourceStream("/Text.txt").Stream;
```

Then you can use the `StreamReader` to get the content of it.

Note that we are building URIs to access resources — these must be explicit. Wildcards like "~" used in ASP.NET will not work in this context.

When you use localizable resources, your application will load the correct one depending on the language; for example, in this demo, there is a resource file called *MyResources.resx*, which is the default resource file that will be loaded if no specific language is defined. But if you add MyResources.resx.es, it will load that one when the language is Spanish. Note that the resource files should contain the same keys. Accessing them is extremely easy, but let's first see how you can add a resource file in your project, as is shown in Figure 10-11.

Figure 10-11

When you create your resource files in Silverlight, you must change the Access Modifier to Internal or Public in order to be able to directly access the resource file using your code. You can do this by opening the resource file using Visual Studio's embedded Resource Editor and changing the combo box, as shown in Figure 10-12.

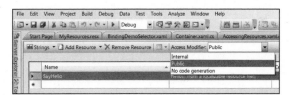

Figure 10-12

Once you have completed these steps, you can access the resource files directly from your code without worrying about changing the filenames when the language changes.

```
private void LoadLocalizedResources()
{
        lblString.Text = MyResources.SayHello;
}
```

Using Isolated Storage

The Silverlight application cannot access the local filesystem for security reasons; therefore, if your application needs to store and retrieve information on the local deployment, it must use isolated storage.

This section covers only using isolated storage to manipulate files and the configuration you use to bind to your controls. If you want to learn more about isolated storage, refer to Chapter 12.

Let's imagine that you need to retrieve data from your site of origin or another Web Service that you want to persist on the local deployment. You can use this storage to save this information; the application will be able to access it again (unless the user cleans the files, so please always check if the information exists). Note that the information does not roam but stays on that machine; therefore, your application needs to consider the relevant instruments to allow this roaming.

By default, you only have 100 kilobytes on the isolated storage. You should try to design your application to store no more than this; it is true that you can query for more space using the command `TryIncrease QuotaTo`, but it will prompt the user, and he or she may say "No."

We are going to reuse the reservations example; in this case, the full name will be loaded from the isolated storage when the user clicks on the Process button. Let's check how you load the information:

```
private void LoadFromStorage()
{
        IsolatedStorageFile MyApplicationFile = null;

        try
        {
                // Gets the reference to the isolated storage for this file
                // (you can have get it from the domain as well)
                MyApplicationFile =
                        IsolatedStorageFile.GetUserStoreForApplication();

                // Check if the folder exists, otherwise it creates one
                if (!MyApplicationFile.DirectoryExists("Reservation"))
                {
                        MyApplicationFile.CreateDirectory("Reservation");
                }

                string FileLocation = System.IO.Path.Combine("Reservation",
                                        "Current.txt");

                // Check if the file exists, if so we load the text
                if (MyApplicationFile.FileExists(FileLocation))
                {
                        // We get the stream from the isolated storage
                        using (IsolatedStorageFileStream IsolatedStream =
                                MyApplicationFile.OpenFile(FileLocation,
                                        FileMode.Open))
                        {
                                // We open a stream reader with the current
                                // one
```

```
                        StreamReader Reader = new
                                StreamReader(IsolatedStream);

                        // Reads the string and sets the dependency
                        // property
                        FullName = Reader.ReadToEnd();
                        Reader.Close();
                }
            }
        }
        catch (Exception ex)
        {
            // Do something :)
        }
        finally
        {
            // Remember to dispose
            if (MyApplicationFile != null)
                MyApplicationFile.Dispose();
        }
    }
```

Note that the sample uses the binding property FullName; therefore, this two-way mode will send the information back to your property ready to be saved, as is shown in Figure 10-13.

```
private void cmdSave_Click(object sender, RoutedEventArgs e)
{
    IsolatedStorageFile MyApplicationFile = null;

    try
    {
        // Gets the reference to the isolated storage for this file
        // (you can have get it from the domain as well)
        MyApplicationFile =
            IsolatedStorageFile.GetUserStoreForApplication();

        // Check if the folder exists, otherwise it creates one
        if (MyApplicationFile.DirectoryExists("Reservation"))
        {
            string FileLocation =
                System.IO.Path.Combine("Reservation",
                    "Current.txt");

            // We get the stream from the isolated storage
            using (IsolatedStorageFileStream IsolatedStream =
                MyApplicationFile.OpenFile(FileLocation,
                    FileMode.OpenOrCreate))
            {
                // We open a stream reader with the current
                // one
                StreamWriter Writer = new
                    StreamWriter(IsolatedStream);
```

```
                                    // Saves the current value on the file
                                    Writer.Write(FullName);
                                    Writer.Close();
                        }
                }
        }
        catch (Exception ex)
        {
                // Do something :)
        }
        finally
        {
                // Remember to dispose
                if (MyApplicationFile != null)
                        MyApplicationFile.Dispose();
        }
}
```

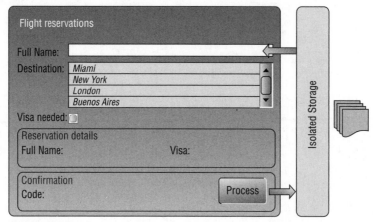

Figure 10-13

Interacting outside the Sandbox

Silverlight 2 not only allows you to interact with data using the local storage but also with the hosting computer. Of course, security restrictions exist, but the team included the "Open File" dialog box that you can use to query the current user for a file to be consumed and processed by the application.

In this section you are going to use it to load data sent by the current user. But not only that, you'll see how you can give files back to the user using a nice work-around:

```
private void cmdLoad_Click(object sender, RoutedEventArgs e)
{
        // We prepare the file dialog with the customization
        // properties
        OpenFileDialog FileDialog = new OpenFileDialog();
```

```
            FileDialog.EnableMultipleSelection = false;
            FileDialog.Filter = string.Format("{0} (*.txt)|*.txt | {1} (*.*) | *.*",
                    MyResources.TextFiles, MyResources.AllFiles);
            FileDialog.FilterIndex = 1;

            // Check the dialog response
            if (FileDialog.ShowDialog() == DialogResult.OK)
            {
                    FileInfo SelectedFile = FileDialog.File;

                    // We open the file stream
                    using (StreamReader Reader = SelectedFile.OpenText())
                    {
                            // We link it to our binding
                            FullName = Reader.ReadToEnd();
                    }
            }
    }
}
```

The sample now has a button to load the full name from an external file, and you assign it to your target property. As the binding is two way, the user interface will be automatically changed. Note that because you are reading an external file, it is a good idea to add a converter that also validates the content; otherwise, you will create a security problem that may crash your application or even corrupt your servers.

While we were playing with Silverlight 2, trying to get it as functional as possible, we found that we were not able to provide files to our users because of security restrictions. Therefore, we created the different techniques that are used in this book. Remember that nothing stops you from sending information back to the server of origin, and the user is able to access it through the ASP.NET web site. With this information in mind, you could generate content in your Silverlight 2 application based on the user input (and even the external data that the user may provide), and send it back to the server, using a Web Service, for example.

The service on the server side can generate a file and store it in a specific location that the user will be able to access. This location information can be sent back to the application and presented as a link. The user can then click on the link to download the file. This process is represented in a graphical model in Figure 10-14.

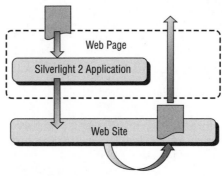

Figure 10-14

As you can see, you should not get frustrated with the technology limitations; you just need to be creative using all the techniques learned in this book and using your current knowledge of ASP.NET. Always remember that you are running a web site!

If you want to know more about this process you can check Chapter 12 where we present the security implications of this interaction.

Remote Data

Loading time is something that is always in the mind of a software designer, and for this reason, Silverlight offers you the ability to pack content and resources in the same package in order to have them ready to use when they are needed. But this is not always the best alternative. At times you may need data that the user will query on demand. For this, you need to store the information on the server or back in your main application if you are planning to use Silverlight as a line-of-business application extension.

Using Site-of-Origin Resources

In the local section, you have been exploring how you can access data using content files, resources files, and localizable resources. But in some cases, these files may not be included in the package. The files will be stored back on the server, where the page has been loaded.

The good thing is that for Silverlight, you can use the same syntax as content files to download content files automatically. The application will first look into the XAP package, and if the requested resource is not there, it will go directly to the site of origin in order to locate it. Once the content is downloaded, it will remain accessible for the rest of the instance.

If you want to configure content to behave in this way, remember to change the build action to "None" and then make sure that you deploy the file with your XAP file on the web server (so it can be located by your application). This will work for either code behind or XAML code — just use the same syntax as Content files:

```
<Image  x:Name="imgLogo"
        Height="54.304"
        HorizontalAlignment="Left"
        Margin="8,0,0,8"
        VerticalAlignment="Bottom"
        Width="62.855"
        Source="/SLLogo.jpg"
/>
```

The logo will be loaded from the server if it is not found in the XAP container.

Consuming Remote Data

In Chapter 9, you saw how you can connect to different types of services using the network stack that Silverlight 2 offers; in this case, you are going to put it into practice to retrieve the reservation information from the server, using WCF. For this, the example needs a couple of extra buttons, one to consume direct data and the other one to retrieve it from a database, as shown in Figure 10-15.

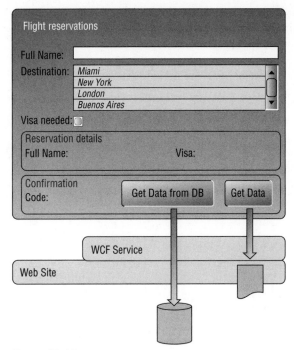

Figure 10-15

To start consuming data from the service, you need to define a Web Service using WCF. This example uses the same service with two different methods — the first one, GetReservation, will process the request locally using a DataContract; and the second one, GetReservationFromDatabase, will retrieve information from an external database. The interface looks as follows:

```
[ServiceContract]
public interface IDataService
{
        [OperationContract].
        Reservation GetReservation();

        [OperationContract]
        Reservation GetReservationFromDatabase();
}


[DataContract]
public class Reservation
{
        private string fullName;

        [DataMember]
        public string FullName
```

```
        {
                get { return this.fullName; }
                set { this.fullName = value; }
        }
    }
```

The implementation of `GetReservation` will just create a new object and return it when the method finishes:

```
public Reservation GetReservation()
{
        Reservation NewReservation = new Reservation();
        NewReservation.FullName = "John Doe from Server";

        return NewReservation;
}
```

If you haven't done that, you must create a client proxy object using the "Add Service Reference" (you can find this option by right-clicking on your Silverlight project in Visual Studio). Once you have created the client proxy, you will be able to call the remote procedure. You use the full name binding as usual to get the information presented on the user interface. Now when you click "Get Data," you invoke the web method asynchronously.

```
private void cmdLoad_Click(object sender, RoutedEventArgs e)
{
        BasicHttpBinding Binding = new BasicHttpBinding();

        EndpointAddress RemoteService = new EndpointAddress(new
                Uri("http://localhost:20136/Chapter10.Web/DataService.svc"));

        RemoteDataService.DataServiceClient NewClient = new
                Chapter10.RemoteDataService.DataServiceClient(
                        Binding,
                        RemoteService);

        NewClient.GetReservationCompleted += new
                EventHandler<GetReservationCompletedEventArgs>
                        (NewClient_GetReservationCompleted);

        NewClient.GetReservationAsync();

}

void NewClient_GetReservationCompleted(object sender,
                                                GetReservationCompletedEventArgs e)
{
        FullName = e.Result.FullName;
}
```

The automatic binding will work because your proxy has inferred the object type from the discovery process.

Now you can modify the other method in order to go to the database. As you can imagine at this point, this works exactly in the same way as ASP.NET: You will have a connection to your database in your web application, perform a query (or execute a stored procedure), read the results, and format them for your application. A simple implementation is shown here just in case you are not familiar with it:

```
public Reservation GetReservationFromDatabase()
{
        // Establish the connection
        SqlConnection NewConnection = new SqlConnection();
        NewConnection.ConnectionString =
                "Server=YourServer;Database=YourDatabase;Trusted_Connection=yes;";

        // Perform your query
        SqlCommand QueryCommand = new SqlCommand(
                "SELECT FullName FROM Reservation");

        // Associate the scalar
        Reservation NewReservation = new Reservation();
        NewReservation.FullName = QueryCommand.ExecuteScalar().ToString();

        NewConnection.Close();

        return NewReservation;
}
```

When querying the database, you cannot send the `DataSet` object back to Silverlight because it does not understand it. Therefore, you will need to transform your results into a proper structure as shown in the example or send the information using an XML string, as you are going to see in the section below, "Manipulating Data," which shows how to deal with XML in your Silverlight 2 applications.

Another interesting area is the use of REST for transforming DataContracts into XML directly, as this is supported by Silverlight and heavily used in ADO.NET Data Services.

As you have seen in this section, once you reach the server, the functionality is very similar to the ASP.NET programming model, except you need to send the information back to the client (in this case, your application) in a package that can be decrypted. Nothing stops you from creating your own parser and serializer and optimizing the package size to improve the user experience.

ADO.NET Data Services

Visual Studio 2008 SP1 introduced several enhancements to the development environment; it wasn't only a patch to fix bugs, it was another way to introduce different projects that have been under research for several years. One of these enhancements was the introduction of ADO.NET Data Services (formerly known as *Astoria).*

If you are not familiar with it, ADO.NET Data Services is a technology that brings together two other technologies that .NET supports as well. The first one is ADO.NET Entity Framework (also supplied with the service pack), and the other one is the ability of WCF to publish RESTful POX services. This means that you can create logical entities based on your physical database and use Data Services to expose them with REST to your Silverlight application.

With this technology, you will be able to manipulate the entity model using normal HTTP verbs back to your server; for example, you can query your service, which exposes the entity called *Cars*, and filter it based on the miles-per-gallon parameter as follows:

```
http://localhost:8182/YouService.svc/Cars[MPG>5]
```

In order to consume the services, you will need to set up a Data Services model. For this you need to place an entity model on your web server, which you can do by adding a new item called the *ADO.NET Entity Data Model*. You can create a new model or inherit one using your current database. The application is all Wizard style and therefore straightforward. Once you have your data objects defined, it is time to add the service. For this you can add another item called the *ADO.NET Data Service*. This will generate a new svc file for your web data. The data source class needs to consume the entity model that you have created. When the service is up and running, you can jump into the Silverlight world.

To consume the Data Services, you need to add a reference to the extension, and the assembly name is `System.Data.Services.Client`. The first thing that you need to do is add the web data context as follows:

```
DataServiceContext MyDataContext = new  DataServiceContext (
                                    "http://localhost:8182/YourService.svc");
```

The data context is telling the library where to look for a Data Services implementation. You need to create the internal structure that will contain the results from the query; in this case, it is just the car model and miles per gallon.

```
public class Car
{
        private string model;
        private int mpg;

        public string Model
        {
                get { return this.model;}
                set { this.model = value;}
        }

        public int MPG
        {
                get { return this.mpg;}
                set { this.mpg = value;}
        }
}
```

Finally, you need to build the query that will allow you to retrieve the content from the service. The content will be automatically mapped to the internal structure that you have just created:

```
DataServiceQuery<Car> MyCars =
        MyDataContext.CreateQuery<Car>("/Cars?$orderby=mpg");
```

The full utilization of REST will allow you to use other methods like POST in order to add a new car into the database. If you are not familiar with this technology, check the ADO.NET Data Services web site (http://msdn.microsoft.com/en-us/data/bb931106.aspx).

Caching

This section discusses the caching techniques possible with Silverlight. You may already know what kind of caching you are able to perform, but here's a recap of some of these ideas and some examples of how to put them into practice.

The first scenario involves caching the XAP application per se. If you have worked with Flash, you may know that the browser will automatically cache the package (unless configured not to do so), but what if you don't want to cache the XAP file? Well, in this case, you can use an old trick — adding a random number at the end of the request that will retrieve your application, thereby fooling the browser to avoid caching it. The other alternative that you can try is setting the HTTP content expiration for the XAP file in order to download only newer XAP files. For this you will need to configure your IIS on your web server.

The other scenario is caching data. You have been exploring the different ways that your application can store information using isolated storage. This is a common pattern that you can reuse to cache information as the isolated data will remain in storage until the user clears it. Remember that you can use storage on the domain level in order to share cached information of different applications running on the same domain.

What about using the ASP.NET caching system? You can still use it in order to store initialization parameters for the Silverlight control using the cache mode VaryByParam, sending cached information to the Silverlight application. This case also applies if you are interacting with JavaScript and your web page already has cached information.

Data Controls

In this section, you will see how to put together the data that you have retrieved and the binding techniques covered previously.

Now it is time to introduce the presentation controls that are mainly designed to present collection of data in a consistent manner. These controls are quite familiar for the ASP.NET developer and users, as they reproduce the models that popularized applications like Excel and Outlook during the 1990s.

Silverlight 2 comes with a rich set of controls that you can use for your applications, but in this instance, we are going to focus mainly on the DataGrid. There are already a lot of companies producing controls for Silverlight that will provide richer functionality. But if you are using Silverlight out-of-the-box, you mainly find these controls very useful and visually rich. This richness is driven by DataTemplates.

Data Templates

As you have seen in the complex binding project, you can create an item template for your list box using `DataTemplate`. The templates allow you to design the content of each item in a graphical way, allowing you to customize how each list box item or whichever control that inherits from `ItemsControl` will look like.

Let's see how you can define a template for your list box with another example, in this case an application that lists your contacts, allowing the user to start a chat conversation, as shown in Figure 10-16.

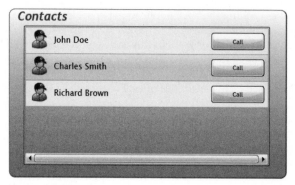

Figure 10-16

Each item in the list has a custom presentation. The `ItemsControl` object allows you to define an item template. What you usually do is first design a new control using a nice XAML designer, then, if you want to use the data template, you just copy and paste the XAML code and you are done. Here is some sample code:

```xml
<ListBox x:Name ="lstContacts" Margin="23,38,27,30" Width="450">
        <ListBox.ItemTemplate>
                <DataTemplate>
                    <Grid x:Name="MyTemplate"
                         Background="#227FBCF0" Height="45.778" Width="445">

                        <Image HorizontalAlignment="Left" Margin="8,4,0,8 "
                         Width="48" Source="/Controls/DataControls/Man.png"/>

                        <TextBlock Margin="51,11,169,13 "
                        TextWrapping="Wrap" x:Name="lblName"
                        FontFamily="Portable User Interface"
                        FontSize="14" Foreground="#FF000000"
                        Text="{Binding FullName}"/>

                        <Button HorizontalAlignment="Right" Margin="0,8,8,8"
                        VerticalAlignment="Stretch" Width="96.444"
                        Content="Call" d:LayoutOverrides="Width"
                        x:Name="cmdCall"/>
                    </Grid>
```

```
                        </DataTemplate>
                </ListBox.ItemTemplate>
        </ListBox>
```

In the example you can appreciate how easy it is to define a template for your list box. Note that you can still do data binding inside the template, and this follows the same pattern that you learned in the complex binding example.

You can also use normal resources as a data template; this will complement what you reviewed in the resource section — just move the data template content into the resource area and add an identification key:

```
<UserControl.Resources>
        <DataTemplate x:Key="MyDataTemplate">
                <Grid x:Name="MyTemplate"
                        Background="#227FBCF0"
                        Height="45.778" Width="445">

                        <!--- All the content goes here -- >

                </Grid>
        </DataTemplate>
</UserControl.Resources>

<ListBox x:Name="lstContacts"
        Margin="23,38,27,30"
        Width="450"
        ItemTemplate="{StaticResource MyDataTemplate}"/>
```

DataGrid

So far you have seen the common data controls used to display data. Now is the time to introduce the `DataGrid` control. This control provides a flexible way to display your data based in rows and columns; these columns have different types based on the built-in templates that come with the data grid, but as you can imagine, you can customize this behavior as well.

In this section, you are going to explore how you can use the data grid control and how you can bind information with it based on the automatic columns. Once you have learned the basics, you are going to explore how you can customize the behavior and presentation overriding the built-in functionality.

The first thing that you need to do in order to get the data grid working is to add the correct namespace, as the data grid is located in `System.Windows.Controls.Data`. For this you need to modify your user control header as follows:

```
xmlns:Data="clr-namespace:System.Windows.Controls;
                assembly=System.Windows.Controls.Data" >
```

Now you can use the `Data` namespace in order to work with your data grid and all its elements. But before you start defining your data grid, you need to configure the data binding. As you have seen in the previous bindings, you will need to configure the `ItemSource` dependency property with an `IEnumerable` object — in this case, you are going to use the contacts model that was used in the data template. The model has the full name, which is a string; the Boolean property IsPrivate to define the contact privacy; and finally, an image field that contains a picture of the contact. You are going to use an observable collection to create a double binding structure. The model looks like Figure 10-17.

Figure 10-17

The first feature presented is automatic column generation. By default, the grid contains automatic columns for strings and numbers (using the DataGridTextBoxColumn) and Boolean values using a checkbox-style column (using the DataGridCheckBoxColumn). The only thing that the data grid needs is the source. In this case, you already have the source and therefore you can define it. Let's check how you do this and what the result will be:

```
<UserControl x:Class="Chapter10.Controls.DataGridSample"
    xmlns="http://schemas.microsoft.com/winfx/2006/xaml/presentation"
    xmlns:x="http://schemas.microsoft.com/winfx/2006/xaml"
    FontFamily="Trebuchet MS" FontSize="11"
    Width="500" Height="300"
    xmlns:Data=
"clr-namespace:System.Windows.Controls;assembly=System.Windows.Controls.Data">

    <Grid x:Name="LayoutRoot" Background="White">
        <StackPanel Margin="10,10,10,10">
            <Data:DataGrid x:Name="MainGrid"
                           Height="120" Width="400"
                           Margin="10,5,0,10" AutoGenerateColumns="True">
            </Data:DataGrid>
        </StackPanel>
    </Grid>
</UserControl>
```

You need to supply the item source by creating an instance of your collection and assigning it to the object:

```
MainGrid.ItemsSource = new Contacts();
```

The data grid will automatically read the format of the item and will try to render using the default columns because you are using the `AutoGenerateColumns` dependency property. If you run the example, you will get the result shown in Figure 10-18.

Figure 10-18

Note that because the picture property is an image, this is not rendered because the grid does not know how to do it.

As the model implements an observable collection and the property changed interface, you can change the value of the cell and the changes will be reflected back to the model — the magic of two-way binding fully in action!

If you change the auto-generated parameter to `False`, you will be able to define the columns that you need; in this case, you use the first two columns that come out-of-the-box, and the third one will be a picture. Now is when you start to put everything together as we are going to use binding and a data template to achieve this. The code now changes like this:

```
<Data:DataGrid x:Name="CustomizedGrid" Height="120" Width="400" Margin="10,5,0,10"
AutoGenerateColumns="False" ItemsSource="" RowBackground="AliceBlue">

       <Data:DataGrid.Columns>
              <Data:DataGridTextColumn
                     Header="Full Name"
                     Width="120"
                     Binding="{Binding FullName}"
                     FontSize="14" />
              <Data:DataGridCheckBoxColumn
                     Header="Private"
                     Width="60"
                     Binding="{Binding IsPrivate}"/>
              <Data:DataGridTemplateColumn
                     Header="Picture"
                     Width="60">
                     <Data:DataGridTemplateColumn.CellTemplate>
                            <DataTemplate>
                                   <Image  Width="32" Height="32"
                                          Stretch="Uniform"
                                          Source="{Binding Picture}"/>
                            </DataTemplate>
                     </Data:DataGridTemplateColumn.CellTemplate>
              </Data:DataGridTemplateColumn>
       </Data:DataGrid.Columns>
</Data:DataGrid>
```

Note how you define the column template using the data template that contains an image control. You can still use resources in this example if you need to because it behaves as a normal template. If you run this, you will get Figure 10-19.

Figure 10-19

The flexibility does not finish there; you can add extra detail to the current selection. This may help in scenarios in which showing all the information is impractical. What you can do is to present the minimum information for the user in the main row and use the row detail to present extra information when the user selects it. In this example, you are going to add an extra field called *Address* and display it only if the user selects that row. For this you need to change the XAML code as follows:

```
<Data:DataGrid x:Name="CustomizedGrid" Height="220" Width="400" Margin="10,5,0,10"
AutoGenerateColumns="False" ItemsSource="" RowBackground="AliceBlue"
RowDetailsVisibilityMode="VisibleWhenSelected">

        <Data:DataGrid.RowDetailsTemplate>
            <DataTemplate>
                <StackPanel Orientation="Horizontal">
                    <TextBlock FontSize="14" Text="Address: "
                            Foreground="Blue"/>
                    <TextBlock FontSize="14" Text="{Binding Address}"
                            Foreground="Blue"/>
                </StackPanel>
            </DataTemplate>
        </Data:DataGrid.RowDetailsTemplate>

        <Data:DataGrid.Columns>
                        <Data:DataGridTextColumn
                            Header="Full Name"
                            Width="120"
                            Binding="{Binding FullName}"
                            FontSize="14" />

            <- - Other columns her - - >

        </Data:DataGrid.Columns>
</Data:DataGrid>
```

In the example now, you have `RowDetailsVisibilityMode` set to define the behavior of the extra details. In order to use this dependency property, you will need to add `RowDetailTemplate`, which, as you can imagine, is another data template.

Now when we run the example, you can see how the selected item changes when the user clicks on it. Figure 10-20 shows the results.

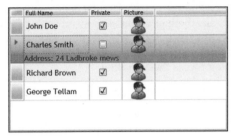

Figure 10-20

As you can see, the data grid is still the powerhorse of data presentation. Now with the features that WPF and Silverlight bring together you will have plenty of room for extending the functionality of the common standard controls.

Manipulating Data

Silverlight 2 consumes data like any other application, with certain limitations that you have been exploring in this chapter. One thing that is still missing is handling and manipulating the data that you retrieve from your repository (local or remote). So far the examples have been binding directly from one point to the other one, but in certain scenarios, you will need to retrieve data, keep it cached in memory or isolated storage, and manipulate it depending on what the user selects.

If you think about how data can be received from the repositories, you end up with structures or objects that represent the data or just XML strings. Silverlight 2 provides you with different techniques that can help you to manipulate these objects before binding or presenting the results.

You need now to plan how you are going to discover this functionality. You need to follow the data pattern from when you read it until you present it, and during this journey, you are going to learn how you can manipulate it. For this, you are going to explore the direct handling and the introduction of LINQ into the Silverlight world.

Traditional Handling

Before the LINQ days, you used to handle and manipulate data all the time. Each element was transformed and linked manually, with plenty of code complexity. As an ASP.NET developer, you have been manipulating objects and `DataSets` in order to retrieve and present data. Most of the applications used to query directly into the database with the selected query and linked the results to grids or other user interface controls. If you haven't used data binding, you have been doing a lot of plumbing!

We'll divide the traditional handling problem into two areas: the first one is using ad hoc queries in order to retrieve information. Using this common pattern, you end up querying the server many times just to change the presentation or to alter the filters. With the introduction of `DataSet`, you have been able to manipulate the content without going back to the data source (as the `DataSet` handles most of these actions locally and commits them at a later stage), and some developers have started to use it to avoid round-trips to the database server. But as we are in the ASP.NET world, this happens on the server side most of the time, whereupon you can save the round-trip to the database server, but you still need to go back to the web server to process these results.

The second problem area is format diversification. The data may be stored not only in the database but also in files, other web sites, Web Services, and other applications. The introduction of WCF has really helped us to consume information from different locations with minimum disruption to the application architecture. If you want to query a database, you have to use one format; if you have a file that has to be converted in a collection, you will need another format. This creates a natural overhead for developers and architects that prevents them from efficiently manipulating data without going back to the sources.

The traditional handling presents many other types of overhead that in the end increase the project risk and add complexity to the system. This has been widely understood in the computer science community, and universal query languages have been proposed for years. Luckily for us, the technology is here.

LINQ

The .NET team understood the problems of traditional data handling when they were designing .NET 3.5 and added LINQ support. This has been welcomed by the community, but many people still believe that the switch will take years because of the steep learning curve and migration costs. Putting aside the length of time it takes to make the change, the Silverlight team made the right decision to join the adventure and added support for LINQ.

> If you are completely new to the technology, you can read this section to understand LINQ basics and how it is implemented in Silverlight. If you want to explore the technology further and learn about the different LINQ providers, we suggest you buy a specialized book about it and explore the full potential of LINQ.

So, what is LINQ? *Language-integrated query (LINQ)* is a programming model that uses queries to manipulate any kind of data independently from the data source format. This means that you can use the same query language to query data from SQL Server, a data set, a collection, XML, Entities, and so on. There are event providers for Amazon. Just to visualize what LINQ is, look at the following little code example. It uses the traditional observable collection for manipulation; this time it is all about customers.

```
public class Customers : ObservableCollection<Customer>
{
        public Customers()
             : base()
        {
                Add(new Customer("John Doe", "USA", 100f));
                Add(new Customer("Richard Gene", "UK", 170f));
                Add(new Customer("Carlos Torres", "Argentina", 50f));
                Add(new Customer("Paul Richy", "USA", 130f));
```

```
                    Add(new Customer("Miguel Fuentes", "Spain", 430f));
                    Add(new Customer("Yu Ming", "China", 180f));
                    Add(new Customer("Carl Stevens", "UK", 10f));
            }
    }

    private Customers customers = new Customers();

    private void SimpleLinq()
    {
            var Results = from c in customers
                        where c.Country == "UK"
                        select c.FullName;

            foreach (string item in Results)
            {
                    Debug.WriteLine(item);
            }
    }
```

The customer constructor accepts three parameters — the full name, the country, and the balance. With this information, we can create an instance and query it with the full power of IntelliSense. You may find the language familiar except for the difference that language structure is inverted to the traditional SQL. The reality is that the ANSI SQL language wasn't designed with discovery in mind (think about when it was created!), and therefore, a more efficient way to write queries is to first define what you want to query. This gives you IntelliSense, where you can filter the content and then finally build what you want. The result of this query may not be known because the structure can be dynamic, which is why we use the var data type. But the compiler infers the type and provides IntelliSense when you manipulate the object at a later stage. As you can expect, after running this code, you will get only the two UK entries.

Now, one important thing about the Silverlight LINQ implementation is that it supports only LINQ to objects and LINQ to XML (more on this later) out-of-the-box. There is no point in supporting LINQ to DataSet because there is no ADO.NET support in the Silverlight application!

The compiler is actually creating lambda expression trees in order to execute this code. The code generated is:

```
IEnumerable<string> Results = this.customers.Where<Customer>(delegate (Customer c)
            {
                    return (c.Country == "UK");
            }
        ).Select<Customer, string>(delegate (Customer c)
            {
                    return c.FullName;
            }
        );
```

As you can see, it is using extension methods in order to build the tree, with delegates to execute the functionality. You can create your code using lambda expressions as well if you feel more comfortable with the syntax; there is no execution penalty. Another important point is that the query is actually executed when it is accessed. This means that the execution of the tree will be done when you reach the foreach statement.

Now that you have the basics, let's see how you can manipulate a collection and bind the results using different queries.

As Figure 10-21 shows, a collection is going to contain all the data, but you can present different subsets on demand by binding the correct result set. The following code enhances the example by adding some extra conditions and returning the full content:

```
private void SimpleLinq()
{
        // We select full name and balance from customers in argentina and UK
        var Results = from c in customers
                        where c.Country == "UK" || c.Country == "Argentina"
                        select c;

        // We assign the binding source
        MainGrid.ItemsSource = Results;
}
```

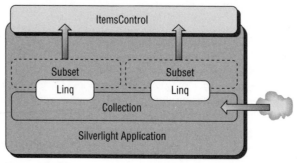

Figure 10-21

MainGrid is a DataGrid with automatic columns. If you execute this code, it will return all the customers who live in the United Kingdom and Argentina. As you are selecting c, it will render all the columns from the collection. With this type of functionality, you can have a grid that shows different results based on what the customer selects.

What is even more interesting is the ability to use common query functionality like joins and ordering. For this, you will need another collection; in this case, we have quickly created another list with addresses and added an index. You can alter the query expression in order to incorporate more functionality.

```
private void cmdJoinList_Click(object sender, RoutedEventArgs e)
{
        Random Rnd = new Random();

        // We select information based on balance
```

```
            var Results = from c in customers
                          join d in details on c.Details equals d.Id
                          where c.Balance > Rnd.Next(10, 200)
                          orderby c.Balance descending
                          select c;

            // We assign the binding source
            MainGrid.ItemsSource = Results;
    }
```

In this example, you may be asking yourself why we don't show the address information. There is a limitation in Silverlight 2 that the binding does not support anonymous types; this means that you cannot create a new structure using this model. But what if you want to do so? Let's explore how you can do it.

For this, you will need to create another structure that will contain the partial results, transform it, and finally bind it. We hope that this will be solved in future versions of Silverlight. But for now, here is the code example:

```
    private struct PartialResults
    {
            public string FullName { get; set; }
            public string Country { get; set; }
            public float Balance { get; set; }
            public string Address { get; set; }
    }

    private void cmdJoinList_Click(object sender, RoutedEventArgs e)
    {
            Random Rnd = new Random();

            List<PartialResults> MyList = new List<PartialResults>();

            // We select the full results
            IEnumerable<PartialResults> Results = from c in customers
                                    join d in details on c.Details equals d.Id
                                    where c.Balance > Rnd.Next(10, 200)
                                    orderby c.Balance descending
                                    select new PartialResults { FullName = c.FullName,
                                            Country = c.Country,
                                            Balance = c.Balance,
                                            Address = d.Address };

            // We assign the binding source
            MainGrid.ItemsSource = Results;
    }
```

The code now has changed to create a named type rather than the anonymous one; this is an elegant way to get around the binding issue. If you execute the code, you are going to have the results shown in Figure 10-22. The list renders the partial list with all the columns because automatic columns were used in the data grid.

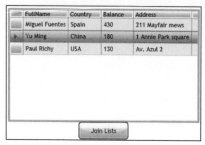

Figure 10-22

The Silverlight LINQ implementation matches nearly 99 percent of the features that you can find in the System.Core assembly introduced in .NET 3.5. Therefore, you can continue exploring the power of LINQ with objects and apply the knowledge in your Silverlight applications.

Beyond the current implementations, if you are familiar with LINQ you should know that the full .NET implementation and ASP.NET world include other flavors. In the world of Silverlight, there is another implementation, LINQ to XML.

LINQ to XML

Silverlight 2 relies heavily on XML when data is retrieved using RESTful services. XML plays a fundamental role in today's applications, and if you have been working with ASP.NET, we are very sure that you are familiar with its potential. Having said this, there is a big piece missing in the Silverlight data presentation story: When you retrieve data in XML format, there is no native XML-binding provided. This is a feature that WPF developers have been enjoying for years, and they are quite surprised to find out that it is not supported. There are some rumors about including this feature in future versions of Silverlight.

Beyond the missing binding, you can still manipulate XML data using LINQ as it is supported in this case. We have started to see the potential for manipulating objects in the LINQ to object section, and now we'll explore how you can query XML data using the same query language.

This example uses a sample XML data file that contains customer names and extra attributes. The XML content looks like this:

```
<?xml version="1.0" encoding="utf-8" ?>
<Customers>
        <Customer      FullName="John Doe"
                       Country ="USA"
                       Id ="0"
                       Address="23 Batch Campus"/>
        <Customer      FullName="Michael King"
                       Country ="UK"
                       Id ="1"
                       Address="1 Battersea park"/>
        <Customer      FullName="Roger Batman"
                       Country ="UK"
                       Id ="2"
```

```
                                 Address="99 Columbia road"/>
              <Customer         FullName="Jose Cuello"
                                 Country ="Mexico"
                                 Id="3"
                                 Address="12 Esperanza"/>
              <Customer         FullName="Gregory Torres"
                                 Country ="Mexico"
                                 Id="5"
                                 Address ="Madagasgar 8"/>
       </Customers>
```

Now that you have the XML content, let's explore how you can perform a simple query operation using LINQ to XML. This will help you understand the introduction of the XDocument object, which is the heart of LINQ to XML and helps you process, manipulate, and validate XML.

```
private void LoadXML()
{
        XDocument XMLSource = XDocument.Load(
                    "Chapter10;component/Controls/Manipulating/Data.xml");

        IEnumerable<string> Results =  from c in XMLSource.Descendants("Customer")
                                       where c.Attribute("Country").Value == "UK"
                                       select c.Attribute("FullName").Value;

        foreach (string name in Results)
        {
                Debug.WriteLine(name);
        }
}
```

When you execute this code, you will get two entries in your enumerable object, "Michael King" and "Roger Batman." You can see the similarities with LINQ to objects when it comes to the query language, but you can also appreciate that the way that you access the content and the elements is different.

The LINQ to XML API introduces the X objects, which help the system build a proper content tree. The parent is XDocument. XElement, XNode, XAttributes, and other intermediate objects help describe and manipulate the contents of the XML structure. That is the main reason why you are loading the XDocument object with the contents. This example uses an XML file as a resource and then uses the object to query and filter specific items in it.

XNamespace provides the ability to create XML on the fly and use LINQ to query the results; this will start to demonstrate the power of it as our Silverlight application is based on XAML, which uses the XML format. The following code shows how to create dynamic content:

```
private void CreateContent()
{
        XDocument CustomXML = new XDocument(
                new XDeclaration("1.0", "UTF-16", "yes"),
                new XElement("Cars",
                        new XElement("Car",
                                new XAttribute("Id", "100"),
                                new XElement("Owner",
```

```
                                    new XAttribute("Name", "Salvador"),
                                    new XAttribute("Country", "Argentina")))),
                    new XElement("Car",
                            new XAttribute("Id", "103"),
                            new XElement("Owner",
                                    new XAttribute("Name", "John"),
                                    new XAttribute("Country", "England")))));

    var Results = from cars in CustomXML.Descendants("Car")
                    where Convert.ToInt16(cars.Attribute("Id").Value) == 100
                    select cars.Element("Owner").Attribute("Name").Value;

    foreach (var entry in Results)
    {
            Debug.WriteLine(entry.ToString());
    }
}
```

The example shows how to create the content and then how to query not only based on attributes, but also how you can manipulate the elements.

Dynamic XAML with LINQ

Now you may wonder how you can integrate LINQ into object creation, because you can have a template XML content file in your application and create elements based on a query. The result can be XAML that you can inject into your application if necessary! This is starting to unleash the power of LINQ to XML and the XML namespace in Silverlight.

```
private void GenerateXAMLContent()
{
        XDocument XMLSource = XDocument.Load(
                    "Chapter10;component/Controls/Manipulating/Data.xml");

        // Default namespace
        XNamespace xmlns =
                "http://schemas.microsoft.com/winfx/2006/xaml/presentation";

        // Dynamic XAML
        XElement MyTextBlock = new XElement(xmlns + "Border",
                new XAttribute("Margin", "8,8,8,8"),
                new XAttribute("BorderBrush", "#FF005CA9"),
                new XAttribute("BorderThickness", "2,2,2,2"),
                new XAttribute("CornerRadius", "10,10,10,10"),
                        new XElement(xmlns + "StackPanel",
                            new XAttribute("Orientation", "Vertical"),
                            from customers in XMLSource.Descendants("Customer")
                            where customers.Attribute("Country").Value == "UK"
                            select new XElement(xmlns + "TextBlock",
                                    new XAttribute("Width", "40"),
                                    new XAttribute("FontSize", "12"),
                                    new XAttribute("Text",
                                    customers.Attribute("FullName").Value))));
```

```
                     // Parse and load the XAML
                     UIElement MyElement = (UIElement)XamlReader.Load(MyTextBlock.ToString());

                     // Alter the current UI
                     MainGrid.Children.Add(MyElement);

        }
```

The first thing you need to consider is adding the default namespace to the dynamic XAML (otherwise, it won't parse). With that information, you can create a new XElement using the technique explained in the previous example. In this case, you use XAML objects and their attributes. Upon the dynamic XAML generation features, the important piece of information here is the introduction of LINQ within the element construction. The example is querying the original XML content and creating a TextBlock on the fly based on the query result! This is really showing the potential of LINQ to XML within Silverlight.

Binding from XML

A feature that directly binds XML with the UIElements is missing. In this section, you are going to look at a work-around that you can use when you are manipulating XML content. This example uses the same XML example used in the beginning of this section.

By using the Select statement with LINQ, you can create return types dynamically. With this feature, you can transform the result of your query expression into a bindable object as shown here:

```
    public struct PartialResults
    {
            public string FullName { get; set; }
            public string Country { get; set; }
            public string Address { get; set; }
    }

    private void LoadGrid()
    {
            XDocument XMLSource = XDocument.Load(
                            "Chapter10;component/Controls/Manipulating/Data.xml");

            IEnumerable<PartialResults> Results = from c in
                                    XMLSource.Descendants("Customer")
                                    where c.Attribute("Country").Value == "UK"
                                    select new PartialResults
                                    {
                                        FullName = c.Attribute("FullName").Value,
                                        Country = c.Attribute("Country").Value,
                                        Address = c.Attribute("Address").Value
                                    };

            MyDataGrid.ItemsSource = Results;
    }
```

You can bind your structure to the data grid without restrictions; this means that you can have your full model object ready to support the results from the query. When you execute this code, you will have the full application running, including the dynamic XAML as introduced before. Figure 10-23 shows the results.

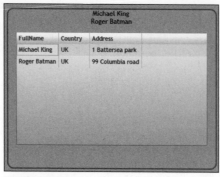

Figure 10-23

Validation

Validating user input in a form has evolved over the years. No one knows better than developers of ASP.NET how the technology and tools in this area have changed how we interact with users. The bugs and hacks that some malicious users have exploited over the years have really contributed to the evolution of these validation tools. The techniques may come from client-side validation or rely on the server to perform validation; this decision was a key factor when developers thought about round-trips to the server and responsiveness requirements.

Silverlight applications also require some kind of architectural decision because the application will run on the client side as much as it can and perform server callbacks only when necessary. The only difference that you are facing in the Silverlight world is that you don't have such a good support system for validation.

WPF developers are already familiar with the data validation and binding validation provided with the technology. Silverlight support is only a subset and does not provide support for the IDataErrorInfo interface. What does this mean? Well, you have to come out with a different approach when it is time to validate user input.

Input Validation

In this section, you'll explore how you can validate user's input using the current available objects that come with Silverlight 2. For this, you need to change your mindset for a moment and think in the same way that Windows Forms developers think when they validate input. Because the application is running on the desktop and you have access to the event model, you can trap the user interaction and provide automatic feedback if necessary.

You can categorize the validation process in different stages and mix and match them according to your requirements:

❑ **Inline** — This technique is commonly used in the ASP.NET development environment because it really helps to warn the user about possible problems with the form. This model will present the results of the first validation as soon as the user presses a key or loses focus on the control.

The ASP.NET validation control helps greatly in this area because it can perform logical checks and present the error messages without going back to the server if necessary. This type of validation is also present in Silverlight except you lack controls to do it, but nothing stops you from trapping the event and presenting an error message like this:

```
<StackPanel Orientation="Horizontal"
        VerticalAlignment="Center" HorizontalAlignment="Center">
        <TextBlock Text="Percentage (0-100): " FontSize="14"/>
        <TextBox x:Name="txtPercentage" Width="100" FontSize="14"
                    LostFocus="txtPercentage_Validation">
            <ToolTipService.ToolTip>
                    <TextBlock Text="Please enter a value between 0 and 100"/>
            </ToolTipService.ToolTip>
        </TextBox>
</StackPanel>

private void txtPercentage_Validation(object sender, RoutedEventArgs e)
{
        int Result;

        if (int.TryParse(txtPercentage.Text, out Result))
        {
                if (Result >= 0 && Result <= 100)
                {
                        txtPercentage.Background = new
                                        SolidColorBrush(Colors.White);
                        txtPercentage.Foreground = new
                                        SolidColorBrush(Colors.Black);
                        ToolTipService.SetToolTip(txtPercentage, "Please enter a
                                        value between 0 and 100");
                        return;
                }
        }

        txtPercentage.Background = new SolidColorBrush(Colors.Red);
        txtPercentage.Foreground = new SolidColorBrush(Colors.White);
        ToolTipService.SetToolTip(txtPercentage, "Value must be between 0 and
                                        100");
}
```

You can see that old-school normal validation is still applied in Silverlight without the need to go back to the server. Remember that the ToolTip can contain as much content as you want, as it is seen in Figure 10-24; therefore, nothing stops you from adding a graphic or changing the font style of the error ToolTip.

Figure 10-24

❑ **Form-Based** — The second classic option is Form validation. This is performed when the Form is submitted to the system. In the ASP.NET world, this is usually performed on the server side, but in the Silverlight world, you can validate the input without going back to the server. Remember that you have the full power of .NET to validate the user input, so you can decide what to do before round-tripping back to the server. This type of validation can make more sense in the Web environment, but in the Silverlight world, it may be better to stay with inline validation to keep the nice user experience that you are already providing with ASP.NET.

With this in mind, nothing stops the community from releasing new validation controls in the same way that they are present in the ASP.NET world, as you can create custom controls and distribute them with your Silverlight applications. Check out `www.codeplex.com` for some examples.

Using Dynamic Languages

In some scenarios, the validation may be dynamic, or the logic is simply located in resources produced by external applications. The result can be a file with any allowed dynamic language that will interact with your Silverlight application and perform the validation using that code.

This model may fit integration stories, where the web application controls all the validation using JavaScript, for example, and you want to extend that validation logic (including round-trips to the server) using the code. For this, you will need to interact with the dynamic language engine that works perfectly with Silverlight 2.

> **You can download the latest DLR SDK from the codeplex web site,** `www.codeplex.com`.

Let's see an example of how this can be achieved. This code uses a `TextBox` that will trigger if the validation focus is lost:

```
private ScriptScope scope;
private ScriptSource source;

public InputValidation()
{
        InitializeComponent();

        InitializeValidation();
}

private void InitializeValidation()
{
        // We initialize the runtime
        ScriptRuntime MyRuntime = JScript.CreateRuntime();

        // We select the language, in this case javascript
        ScriptEngine JSEngine = MyRuntime.GetEngine("js");

        // We create the execution scope
        scope = JSEngine.CreateScope();

        // We set the local variables, in this case the textbox
```

```
                    scope.SetVariable("MyTextBlock", txtDLR);

            // We define the code to execute, this can be an
            // external file
            source = JSEngine.CreateScriptSourceFromString("if (MyTextBlock.Text !=
                        'DLR') MyTextBlock.Text = 'Here goes DLR';}",
                            SourceCodeKind.SingleStatement);
    }

    private void txtDLR_Validation(object sender, RoutedEventArgs e)
    {
            // Executes the dynamic validation
            source.Execute(scope);
    }
```

As you can see, you use the DLR engine to define the execution scope based on the language chosen. In that scope, you define a local variable that will reference the targeted `TextBox`, named "MyTextBlock". With that scope defined, you can execute the code that you want. This example shows a hard-coded entry, but you may use an external file or stream. When the textbox loses focus, it executes the event handler that calls the JavaScript function. You can see the power of DLR for code integration in just a few lines of code. To explore more about the features of dynamic languages, please don't forget to check Chapter 17, where DLR functionality is explored.

Data-Binding Validation

Data binding does not provide a validation pipeline as it does in WPF, which means that once again, it is up to you to implement the validation. The problem with data binding is that the "evil" input may land in the source object and corrupt your data structure. For this reason, you need to take special actions to avoid the situation.

In this particular case, you may not want the corrupted value in your source object; therefore, you can do some tricks in order to avoid getting into that situation. Do you remember the conversion model for data binding that was introduced at the beginning of this chapter? Well, you know now that this object is executed before sending the values from one place to the other. It seems like a good place to introduce some data manipulation if the validation criteria are not met.

```
    public class Conversion : IValueConverter
    {
            public event Action ValidationError;

            public object Convert(object value, Type targetType, object parameter,
                                    System.Globalization.CultureInfo culture)
            {
                return value;
            }

            public object ConvertBack(object value, Type targetType, object parameter,
                                    System.Globalization.CultureInfo culture)
            {
                return Validate(value);
            }
```

```
        private object Validate(object value)
        {
                if (value.ToString() == "Binding")
                {
                        return value;
                }
                else
                {
                        if (ValidationError != null)
                                ValidationError();

                        return string.Empty;
                }
        }

private void InitializeBinding()
{
        Binding NewBinding = new Binding();
        Conversion NewConversion = new Conversion();
        NewConversion.ValidationError += new
                                        Action(NewConversion_ValidationError);

        NewBinding.Mode = BindingMode.TwoWay;
        NewBinding.Path = new PropertyPath("Field");
        NewBinding.Source = new Model();
        NewBinding.Converter = NewConversion;

        txtBinding.SetBinding(TextBox.TextProperty, NewBinding);
}

private void NewConversion_ValidationError()
{
        txtBinding.Background = new SolidColorBrush(Colors.Red);
}
```

As you can see in the example, you can intercept the value from the converter and apply the validation logic. If the validation fails, you can reset the source target value in order to avoid data corruption. In this example, events are provided to handle the validation error and inform the user.

You can be as creative as necessary regarding how to validate information in Silverlight 2 because of the current limitations. But as you can appreciate at this time, the run time is pretty small, and only the essential functionality can be included. Validation is not hard, as you have the full potential of .NET in your hands.

Summary

You have reached the end of this long chapter; if you have been reading from the beginning, you should have a good idea of what it is like to work with data in the Silverlight world. You have been through a journey. You started by increasing your understanding of the namespaces included and scoping the data possibilities. It is important to understand that there is no support for traditional ADO.NET, but you do have access to ADO.NET Data Services (Astoria) released in the .NET 3.5 SP1.

Learning the basics of binding is essential, as WPF and Silverlight heavily rely on this technology in order to properly separate the model from the presentation. Our recommendation is to use binding, as it is considered best practice and will save you coding time. You have not only reviewed what data binding is, but also learned how to perform collection binding using the observable collection supplied in the libraries.

You learned how you can retrieve data; this complements Chapter 9, "Communicating with the Server," regarding the different local storages like resources, content, and isolated storage. Silverlight 2 also includes remote access to data using Web Services and RESTful interfaces, which really extends the boundaries of your application.

The power of LINQ has been revealed, using LINQ to objects and LINQ to XML. We are confident that you will exploit these features in conjunction with data binding in order to retrieve data and perform query operations on the fly, using a familiar language in the ASP.NET world. The Silverlight team has invested in this technology because Microsoft firmly believes that it is the future of query manipulation.

Finally, understanding the validation limitations and the work-arounds using traditional .NET forms validation can give you the tools to protect your application from incorrect input. This should give you an idea of how you can leverage current ASP.NET knowledge into the Silverlight 2 world.

11

Creating Custom Controls

When you are developing user interfaces for your web applications, you usually consider two important aspects of presentation controls. The first one involves the internal functionality that the control will have and how it will interact with your application. We call this control logic. The other one is how the control looks; users are quite demanding about how the user interface presents the information, and this is an important selling point for nontechnical users. Indeed, we are moving away from developers designing the user interface in order to introduce a more intuitive approach, usually delivered by user-experience designers. In the Silverlight world, you should stick to the same rules, but as you learned in Chapter 6, a limited number of controls are available out-of-the-box. So, how can you extend the presentation options?

This chapter reviews the different ways that you can choose when you need to create your custom controls. In the ASP.NET world, you also have the ability to do this, but if you went beyond a user control and jumped into custom controls, you probably suffered a lot because of the complexity.

To learn about custom controls, we are going to take you on a journey. The first thing that you need to understand is what type of customization you need for your project, as you will find different alternatives that may confuse you. For this reason, we are going to analyze each of these options and provide possible implementation scenarios.

Finally, we will cover how Silverlight 2, with a little help from WPF, brings you a rich set of options from the traditional user controls and visual customization to a fully templatable control.

User Controls

The first custom control that we want to introduce is the user control. If you have been working with ASP.NET, you may be familiar with this concept. In theory Silverlight and ASP.NET handle user controls the same way. A *user control* is a container that groups several controls that are then exposed to the application as a single entity; this means that you can reuse the grouped controls of the different XAML containers. Indeed, you may ask yourself if this is the same behavior encountered in a normal XAML page. You would be completely right — if you check the XAML code of your Silverlight page, you will find that it starts with the following tag:

```
<UserControl x:Class="Chapter11.Controls.UserControlDemo"
    xmlns="http://schemas.microsoft.com/winfx/2006/xaml/presentation"
    xmlns:x="http://schemas.microsoft.com/winfx/2006/xaml"
    FontFamily="Trebuchet MS" FontSize="11"
    Width="400" Height="300"/>
```

> **All the source code presented in this chapter can be found on the Wrox web site:**
> www.wrox.com.

You can create a user control at will if you need to do so, using the Visual Studio project explorer or external tools like Blend. You are going to explore how to do this and how to alter the user control definition in order to make it visible to the parser. But before you dive into the details, let's see what a user control is and how you can decide if you need one.

Understanding User Controls

A user control is a very efficient way to group controls that you need to keep together. Not only are the controls grouped visually, but the logic behind them is also grouped. This means that you can reuse it in your application, fitting it nicely into the object-oriented model, where you have a control that is completely autonomous from the rest of the application.

In the web development world, we tend to group controls that usually are deployed together in order to achieve an objective. This means that if you want to add a section in your web page that allows the user to search content on the web site, you will likely include a label with the word *Search*, a textbox that allows the user to enter the content that he or she wants to find, and finally, a button that triggers the search. Now, when the user enters the words in the textbox and clicks the Search button, the search executes by reading the parameters from that grouped control.

In the ASP.NET world, you create an *ASCX* file, commonly known as a web user control, and you can start designing it. This example uses an asp:label, asp:TextBox and an asp:Button:

```
<%@ Control Language="C#"
  AutoEventWireup="true" CodeBehind="WebUserControl1.ascx.cs"
Inherits="Chapter11.WebDemo.WebUserControl1" %>

<asp:Label ID="lblSearchText" runat="server">Search: </asp:Label>
<asp:TextBox ID="txtSearchContent" runat="server"></asp:TextBox>
 
<asp:Button ID="cmdSearch" runat="server" Text="Search !" />
```

Now you can reuse the search user control in your web page, but for this, you need to make the page aware of the location of the control. In the ASP.NET page, you would register the control in the page header as follows:

```
<%@ Page Language="C#" AutoEventWireup="true" CodeBehind="Default.aspx.cs"
Inherits="Chapter11.WebDemo._Default" %>
```

```
<%@ Register  TagPrefix ="MyControl" Src ="~/WebUserControl1.ascx" TagName =
"Search" %>

<!DOCTYPE html PUBLIC "-//W3C//DTD XHTML 1.0 Transitional//EN"
"http://www.w3.org/TR/xhtml1/DTD/xhtml1-transitional.dtd">

<html xmlns="http://www.w3.org/1999/xhtml" >
<head runat="server">
    <title>My Test Page</title>
</head>
<body>
    <form id="form1" runat="server">
    <div>
        <MyControl:Search ID = "NewControl" Visible = "true"
                                           runat = "server"></MyControl:Search>
    </div>
    </form>
</body>
</html>
```

The control will be rendered on the page, but if you want to reuse the functionality in another page or even on the same page, you just include another extra reference. What is more, if you need to fix a bug in the user control, you just modify the user control code logic, and once compiled, that will be reflected in all the pages that use the control.

If you think about it for a minute, you will immediately see the benefits of a user control, as it provides the logic and functionality encapsulation pattern, making your deployments more elegant. Can you do this manually? Yes, of course, but you may easily lose track of where the code has been implemented, leading to bugs and inconsistencies in the application. And what does that mean? It means that you risk losing some credibility as a developer, and you don't want that to happen!

If you browse some web sites around the Net, you will quickly realize that user controls are used everywhere. Figure 11-1 shows stars and dotted lines where the user controls have been used; this means that, for example, the browsing control may be used in other pages without rewriting the functionality.

Figure 11-1

425

We presented how we create user controls in the ASP.NET world. Here we show you how to provide the same functionality in Silverlight, as with the direct comparison you may find it easier to understand. The concepts behind what is a user control are exactly the same. The Silverlight team introduced the same model that ASP.NET and Windows Forms developers have used.

Here is the same example presented on the web page in the Silverlight application. The first thing that you need is a user control, which as you have seen, is just a piece of XAML:

```
<UserControl
 xmlns="http://schemas.microsoft.com/winfx/2006/xaml/presentation"
 xmlns:x="http://schemas.microsoft.com/winfx/2006/xaml"
 xmlns:d="http://schemas.microsoft.com/expression/blend/2008"
 mc:Ignorable="d"
 x:Class="Chapter11.SearchControl"
 d:DesignWidth="640" d:DesignHeight="480" Width="300" Height="50">

<Grid x:Name="LayoutRoot" Background="White" >
        <Button HorizontalAlignment="Right" Margin="0,8,8,8"
                VerticalAlignment="Stretch" Width="88.667" Content="Search"/>
        <TextBlock HorizontalAlignment="Left" Margin="14,13,0,17 " Width="54.889"
                Text="Search:" TextWrapping="Wrap" d:LayoutOverrides="Width"/>
        <TextBox Margin="82,13,107,13" Text="" TextWrapping="Wrap" FontSize="14"/>
</Grid>
</UserControl>
```

Now, in order to present the user control in your page, you need to tell the main user control where to discover the recently created one; otherwise, you will receive parser errors as experienced in ASP.NET. Here's how you modify your main page:

```
<UserControl x:Class="Chapter11.Controls.UserControlDemo"
    xmlns="http://schemas.microsoft.com/winfx/2006/xaml/presentation"
    xmlns:x="http://schemas.microsoft.com/winfx/2006/xaml"
    FontFamily="Trebuchet MS" FontSize="11"
    xmlns:Custom ="clr-namespace:Chapter11.Controls.Custom"
    Width="400" Height="300">
    <Grid x:Name="LayoutRoot" Background="White">
        <Custom:SearchControl></Custom:SearchControl>
    </Grid>
</UserControl>
```

The registration that you use in ASP.NET has been replaced with a namespace declaration; in this case, the name "Custom" is the same as "TagPrefix". Finally, with the namespace included, you can insert the user control directly in your grid in order to render it.

The same concept applies to the code behind; the control logic will travel with the user control complementing the encapsulation story. You may have noticed that you are making a differentiation between the logic behind it and the visual representation. The reason will become much clearer as you read this chapter because we are going to play with different parts of the controls to demonstrate when to use one control or another one. If you need to picture how the user control fits this model, review Figure 11-2.

The user control has a single piece of logic behind it that manages the visual events, but the user control is just a container that may include other controls and even other user controls. Each of these controls is not losing its own logic, because the model is repeated on each level. What you control on the logic side is the interaction of these controls. This means that if you include the search user control on your page (another user control), the search control will execute all its internal logic no matter what the main user control is doing.

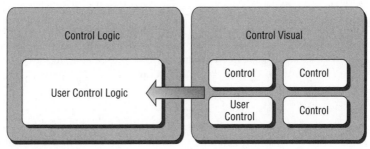

Figure 11-2

Deployment

The user control will be shipped with your Silverlight application; no extra work is required if you include it as another XAML page in your project. But don't be fooled by that behavior — the user control does not need to be part of your current Silverlight assembly, as it may come from another project.

Some developers and software houses may have a collection of user controls already grouped in a different assembly. This may help them to manage the common functionality for multiple applications easily. If you want to reuse those controls in your application, you can just add the DLL where these controls are contained and access them within your project. The assembly will be included in the XAP Package and deployed when the application is downloaded.

This leads to two new points: The first one is regarding how you register the controls in your main user control; now you need to specify the assembly as well, and you can do this by altering the registration as follows:

```
xmlns:CustomExternal =
"clr-namespace:Chapter11.ExternalControls;assembly=Chapter11.Common"
```

The assembly entry specifies the assembly name and where the controls are located.

The second point that we want to highlight is the overuse of common assemblies. Remember that if you are looking for loading performance, having a massive set of DLLs with many controls that your application may not use may affect download time. This suggests that you are grouping too many objects in a single assembly; it is considered best practice to group them based on usage, and if you need to have multiple controls that cover the same area, for example, security, create extended namespaces, for example:

❑ **YourCompany.Common.Security.dll** — Basic controls commonly used across all the applications

❑ **YourCompany.Common.Security.Certificates.dll** — Special controls that some applications may use

Remember that, as shown in previous chapters, you can retrieve assemblies on demand from the server side. This means that you may leave them until the user selects a function that may need it. This can save you some loading time as well.

Scenarios

Now that you understand what a user control is, this section presents guidelines and some possible scenarios where you may choose to use user controls. This list of possibilities is not exhaustive and should be treated as a guideline.

The first question that you should ask yourself is regarding the encapsulation. If you are planning to deliver controls that work together in order to achieve a specific task, you are in the user control area. Remember that once the controls have been grouped, you cannot use them independently beyond the boundaries of the user control. You should keep this in mind when designing how the control will interact with the rest of the application.

> **Developers have been known to break the encapsulation pattern exposing the individual controls of the user controls to the external application. This is considered bad practice and should be avoided.**

The other area to consider is reusability; if the control is very specific and not likely to be used in any other application, you may achieve your objective without using a user control. Having said this, one approach is to decompose your application in functional layers, as each section of your application is there for a reason. With this in mind, you can group the areas in user controls, as this helps you to separate the functionality properly and reduces the temptation to introduce cross-calls that usually break object-oriented patterns.

With encapsulation and reusability in mind, you can separate the two models: One will target independent functionality that can be shared across multiple phases of your applications. Some examples can be the search functionality or a postcode finder. These user controls will perform specific functionality without disrupting the common application state machine, but the output helps the user achieve the objective of the current application state. The other model can be expressed as an object-oriented helper, where the user controls don't know anything about the other ones, but the combination of them makes the application. The user controls can communicate between each other using an interface and streaming events when they need to change the state. This model is usually supported by a coordinator object. Figure 11-3 represents it graphically.

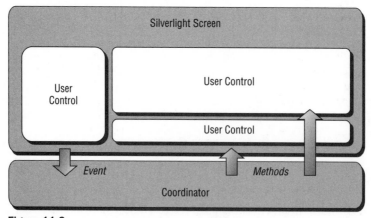

Figure 11-3

Creating User Controls

This section presents how to create a user control step-by-step using the most common tools. For this we are going to create an application that displays a Contacts List. As we have seen in the scenarios section, each entry of the Contacts List will have a custom presentation with multiple controls; this means that this is a perfect scenario for a user control. The final output of our application will look like Figure 11-4.

Figure 11-4

Each entry in our Contacts List will contain multiple controls that will handle a set of particular functions, like "show more details," "send an SMS," or "write an e-mail." Each of these user controls is self-contained, and you just repeat the rendering in each instance of the contact list.

If you need the full source code, just download the code sample for Chapter 11 from wrox.com.

Adding the User Control

The first thing that you need to do is add the user control to your project. Working completely independently from the container is considered the best practice. This means that your contact entry can be used in other parts of your application.

You can add a user control using Visual Studio or Expression Blend. We show you both procedures. In Visual Studio, just right-click on your project, and select Add?New Item. A dialog box will appear with the different types of items that you can include in your application.

Select "Silverlight User Control" and name the control **ContactControl.xaml**. Figure 11-5 shows you the selection screen.

Figure 11-5

Remember to use consistent naming conventions; in this case, we like to use the suffix *Control* for all our user controls. It is up to you to select the naming convention, but once you select one, try to keep it. Your code will look more professional.

The dialog box creates another XAML file in your project; if you open it, it will look like your main Silverlight page (remember that it is also a user control). Visual Studio will also create the code-behind file.

You can do exactly the same using Expression Blend — just right-click on the project and add a new item; your user control screen will appear. Note that in Blend you have the option to not include the code-behind file. What is more, in Blend you have the ability to create a user control from your main page design; this can make your life easier when you are including controls in your main page, and you suddenly decide that a set of controls should be separated. Figure 11-6 shows the New Item dialog box and the user control screen.

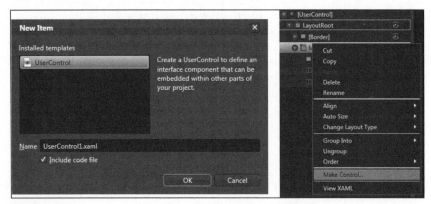

Figure 11-6

Customizing the User Control

Having the user control allows you to start designing it in the same way that you design a normal XAML page. Don't worry about the code behind yet; just focus on the visuals. Add the image control, the TextBlocks, a checkbox, and two buttons. Include proper names as your logic will need them in order to operate the group controls. By default, all the controls will be created as "private," meaning that your container will not have direct access to the individual controls, only your code behind. Don't be tempted to make them "public" so that you can manipulate them from outside. You may break the functionality by using this not-very-elegant solution. Instead, use the properties to access the user control functionality rather than the individual controls.

If you have added a new user control in your Silverlight project, just modify the default code; the example below may help you introduce the changes:

```xml
<UserControl x:Class="Chapter11.Controls.Custom.ContactControl"
    xmlns="http://schemas.microsoft.com/winfx/2006/xaml/presentation"
    xmlns:x="http://schemas.microsoft.com/winfx/2006/xaml"
    FontFamily="Trebuchet MS" FontSize="11"
    Width="400" Height="100"
    xmlns:d="http://schemas.microsoft.com/expression/blend/2008"
    xmlns:mc="http://schemas.openxmlformats.org/markup-compatibility/2006"
    mc:Ignorable="d"
    Loaded="UserControl_Loaded">

<Grid x:Name="LayoutRoot">
        <!-- Main Container -->
        <Border Margin="0,0,0,0" BorderThickness="1,1,1,1"
                        CornerRadius="10,10,10,10">
                <Border.Background>
                        <LinearGradientBrush EndPoint="0.5,1" StartPoint="0.5,0">
                                <GradientStop Color="#FF5CE8E8" Offset="0.007"/>
                                <GradientStop Color="#FF0569B0" Offset="1"/>
                        </LinearGradientBrush>
                </Border.Background>
                <Grid>
                        <Image HorizontalAlignment="Left" Margin="11,6,0,8"
                                Width="96.535" Stretch="Uniform"
                                d:LayoutOverrides="Width" x:Name="imgPicture"/>
                        <TextBlock Height="25.111" Margin="85,8,73,0"
                                VerticalAlignment="Top" FontFamily="Verdana"
                                FontSize="16" FontWeight="Normal"
                                TextWrapping="Wrap" x:Name="lblName"/>
                        <TextBlock Height="25.111" Margin="85,33,73,39"
                                VerticalAlignment="Stretch" FontFamily="Verdana"
                                FontSize="14" FontWeight="Normal"
                                TextWrapping="Wrap" d:LayoutOverrides="Height"
                                x:Name="lblPhone"/>
                        <TextBlock Height="25.111" Margin="85,0,73,14"
                                VerticalAlignment="Bottom" FontFamily="Verdana"
                                FontSize="14" FontWeight="Normal"
                                TextWrapping="Wrap" d:LayoutOverrides="Height"
                                x:Name="lblEmail"/>
                        <Button HorizontalAlignment="Right" Margin="0,14,8,0"
                                VerticalAlignment="Top" Width="115.667"
```

```
                                        Content="Send SMS" x:Name="cmdSMS"
                                        d:LayoutOverrides="Width, Height" Height="21.111"/>
                            <Button HorizontalAlignment="Right" Margin="0,41,8,35"
                                        VerticalAlignment="Stretch" Width="115.667"
                                        Content="Send Email" Height="21.111"
                                        d:LayoutOverrides="Width, Height"
                                        x:Name="cmdEmail"/>
                            <CheckBox Height="21.111" HorizontalAlignment="Right"
                                        Margin="0,0,8,8" VerticalAlignment="Bottom"
                                        Width="108.815" Content="More Details"
                                        d:LayoutOverrides="Width, Height"
                                        x:Name="chkMoreDetails"
                                        Checked="chkMoreDetails_Checked"
                                        Unchecked="chkMoreDetails_Unchecked"/>
                </Grid>
            </Border>
        </Grid>
    </UserControl>
```

This code added a couple of events: The first one will be executed when the user control is loaded because you are going to bind your external properties with your internal controls. The other one is for the checkbox because you are going to show extra information when the checkbox is clicked.

To expose properties to the XAML designer, you need to publish them as dependency properties; these properties will be bound to the internal controls in your user control. Modify the code behind of your user control to expose them like this:

```
public partial class ContactControl : UserControl
{
        public static readonly DependencyProperty PictureProperty =
        DependencyProperty.Register("Picture",
        typeof(string), typeof(ContactControl),null);

        public static readonly DependencyProperty ContactNameProperty =
        DependencyProperty.Register("ContactName",
        typeof(string), typeof(ContactControl), null);

        public static readonly DependencyProperty ContactPhoneProperty =
        DependencyProperty.Register("ContactPhone",
        typeof(string), typeof(ContactControl), null);

        public static readonly DependencyProperty ContactEmailProperty =
        DependencyProperty.Register("ContactEmail",
        typeof(string), typeof(ContactControl), null);

        public static readonly DependencyProperty ContactAddressProperty =
        DependencyProperty.Register("ContactAddress",
        typeof(string), typeof(ContactControl), null);


        public string Picture
        {
                get { return (string)GetValue(PictureProperty); }
                set { SetValue(PictureProperty, value); }
```

```
        }

        public string ContactName
        {
                get { return (string)GetValue(ContactNameProperty); }
                set { SetValue(ContactNameProperty, value); }
        }

        public string ContactPhone
        {
                get { return (string)GetValue(ContactPhoneProperty); }
                set { SetValue(ContactPhoneProperty, value); }
        }

        public string ContactEmail
        {
                get { return (string)GetValue(ContactEmailProperty); }
                set { SetValue(ContactEmailProperty, value); }
        }

        public string ContactAddress
        {
                get { return (string)GetValue(ContactAddressProperty); }
                set { SetValue(ContactAddressProperty, value); }
        }
}
```

With this code you can now alter your container to add the user control to the main screen. As you have seen before, you need first to register the namespace for your user control, as shown in the following code. Registration provides access to the new dependency properties exposed by your control.

The following code shows how the container should look:

```
<UserControl x:Class="Chapter11.Controls.UserControlDemo"
    xmlns="http://schemas.microsoft.com/winfx/2006/xaml/presentation"
    xmlns:x="http://schemas.microsoft.com/winfx/2006/xaml"
    FontFamily="Trebuchet MS" FontSize="11"
    xmlns:Custom ="clr-namespace:Chapter11.Controls.Custom"
    Width="400" Height="500">

  <Grid x:Name="LayoutRoot" Background="White">
      <StackPanel Orientation="Vertical">
              <Custom:ContactControl x:Name="First" Picture="Marta.png"
                      ContactEmail="Email1@Temp.com" ContactName="Marta
                      Ballesteros" ContactPhone="555-123-1234" ContactAddress="23
                      John Street" ></Custom:ContactControl>
              <Custom:ContactControl Picture="Daniel.png"
                      ContactEmail="MyEmail@Domain.com" ContactName="Daniel
                      Alvarez" ContactPhone="555-321-4321"
                      ContactAddress="Penbridge 11"></Custom:ContactControl>
              <Custom:ContactControl Picture="Graciela.png"
                      ContactEmail="GEmail@NoPlace.co.at" ContactName="Graciela
                      Patuel" ContactPhone="555-444-5353" ContactAddress="100 Roe
                      Alley"></Custom:ContactControl>
```

```
            </StackPanel>
        </Grid>
    </UserControl>
```

Within your own user control, you can add as much functionality as you want. In order to show you the potential, the following code adds animations that present the extra information when the user checks the "More Details" checkbox. One animation shows the details, and another hides them. You trigger them using the event handlers for the checkbox like this:

```
<UserControl.Resources>
        <Storyboard x:Name="MoreDetailsTransition">
            <DoubleAnimationUsingKeyFrames BeginTime="00:00:00"
                Storyboard.TargetName="MoreDetails"
                Storyboard.TargetProperty="(UIElement.RenderTransform).
                (TransformGroup.Children)[3].(TranslateTransform.Y)">
                <SplineDoubleKeyFrame KeyTime="00:00:00" Value="0"/>
                <SplineDoubleKeyFrame KeyTime="00:00:00.5000000" Value="-
96.593"/>
            </DoubleAnimationUsingKeyFrames>
            <DoubleAnimationUsingKeyFrames BeginTime="00:00:00"
                Storyboard.TargetName="MoreDetails"
                Storyboard.TargetProperty="(UIElement.Opacity)">
                <SplineDoubleKeyFrame KeyTime="00:00:00" Value="0"/>
                <SplineDoubleKeyFrame KeyTime="00:00:00.5000000"
                Value="1"/>
            </DoubleAnimationUsingKeyFrames>
        </Storyboard>

        <!-- Reverse storyboard supressed for simplicity ->

< Code Behind >

private void chkMoreDetails_Checked(object sender, RoutedEventArgs e)
{
        MoreDetailsTransition.Begin();
}

private void chkMoreDetails_Unchecked(object sender, RoutedEventArgs e)
{
        MoreDetailsRemove.Begin();
}
```

The result is a completely independent user control that contains the functionality for each contact adding its own special functionality, no matter what the container looks like. Running the project will present a user control similar to the one shown in Figure 11-7.

Figure 11-7

Customizing Current Controls

Some developers are unaware that their toolbox provides the ability to customize the look and feel of the current controls. Even more, the toolbox provides much more powerful customization tools than those in the traditional Windows Forms controls environment. This is a feature that you as a web developer have been using with styles and CSS files, allowing you to change how your web site and controls look depending on customer or user preferences. Silverlight and WPF allow you to do the same.

If you have never customized a control, let me explain exactly what that means. Let's suppose that you have your Windows Forms application and you want to change how a button looks. The first approach that you can take is to alter the button's public properties. Changing classic properties like background and foreground colors can make your button look a little different, but you are limited by the designer's constraints. What if you want to go further? In the traditional model, you may end up overriding the OnPaint method to alter how the button is rendered or even creating a completely new custom control using the internals of GDI+ to get the correct look and feel. This has been quite hard to do for application developers. Web developers have had some freedom in how the controls look, as they can apply styles that alter the rendering, generating richer user interfaces.

Understanding Visual Customization

In this section, you'll review how you can alter the visual side of a control without creating a new one. This is another way of creating custom controls without changing their logic. Remember the model that Silverlight implements: The visuals are separated from the logic. Figure 11-8 shows that now you work on the visual customization rather than on the logic. In the user control section, you saw that you organize the controls with different controls, and then you create new control logic.

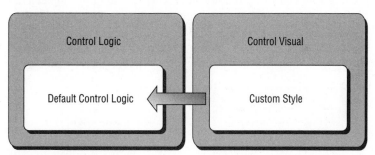

Figure 11-8

In this case, you touch only the visuals, which can be very useful if you want to alter the look and feel, but you are happy with the behavior. What is more, you can change a template at run time to make your Silverlight application match your customized web site. As you are changing the visuals on your control, all the functionality remains the same, as you can see in Figure 11-9. You can transform the current default button with a completely new look and feel.

Figure 11-9

You can make such changes using two techniques: The first one is styling your control, where minor property changes will create a new look and feel. The second method is through skinning, in which the control will apply a completely new template.

The different visual alternatives can be stored at the application level or at the user control level, indeed, in any form of resource storing methodology. Because UIElements has style and template dependency properties, you can change them at run time. What is more, you can even bind them if necessary! We are starting to unveil the customization potential using all the concepts exposed in this book.

Before jumping into creating a completely customized control, let's analyze some of the scenarios in which customizing the current controls may be the answer, reducing the risk and effort of the implementation.

Scenarios

With Silverlight, you can easily customize how your controls look without changing the functionality. With control templating, you can change any control just by changing the XAML code; you can wrap these resources in different assemblies if you want to in order to reuse the templates in multiple applications.

A good scenario for using style customization is when you need to provide a normalized user interface, where the designers designate the use of specially designed buttons to provide consistency. They can change some properties, but by default, the button will look like the one designed by the lead designer.

Another excellent scenario requiring this technique is when you want to customize your application per instance. This means that you can allow the user to change the look and feel, choosing different templates, but leaving your code behind untouched. There are multiple implementations in which the requirements push your development in a multi-tenant environment, where your application needs to look different based on the customer who uses your system. Silverlight and control customization via styles and skinning allow you to do this. Figure 11-10 presents two different screens using the same managed code (logic) and the same services.

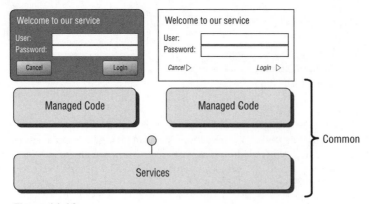

Figure 11-10

You are going to explore how you do this in the section, "Putting Everything Together," as you are combining the power of styles and of skinning.

The "wow" factor

I personally love to customize controls; seriously, when I was working in a different company previously, I had customized buttons, panels, lists, you name it — no matter if it was Windows Forms or the Web. As architects, you also need to think about the user experience, and on many occasions, the "wow" factor should be there in order to succeed. Redesigning how a control looked was difficult, time-consuming, and error-prone. I found myself working on completely new buttons when what I really wanted was just a different look and feel.

When I first discovered WPF, things started to change. I was amazed with the architecture that allowed me to customize the visuals without touching the logic! That reduced the time that I had to spend testing and making sure that the button worked, giving me more time to focus on the look and feel. What is more, this new model helped me reduce the project risk.

Customizing with Styles

The first type of customization that you are going to explore is styling. Defining the style of a control can help lead designers define how a control should look by default; that is, when the control is used, it will automatically look like the original design. This can save plenty of time when you need to deliver hundred of screens.

You can define the style once and apply it to multiple controls without any problems. You can store the style in the application level or only in the user control, because you need to store it as a resource. When you apply a style to a control, the look and feel changes automatically, but this does not stop the designer from changing the properties again. Remember that the local changes take precedence over the global styles.

You can create a `Style` object as a resource. To do so, you need to define the `TargetType` of the style; this helps the parser understand the dependency properties that are available in that control and prevent some common errors. You can set any dependency property using the `Setter` object as shown here:

```
<UserControl.Resources>
    <Style TargetType="Border" x:Key="BorderStyle">
        <Setter Property="Background" Value="#FF1090B5"/>
        <Setter Property="CornerRadius" Value="20,20,20,20"/>
    </Style>
</UserControl.Resources>
```

As you can see, you can only change the current dependency properties that the control exposes. This is a limitation that you will override when you jump into fully customized controls in the next section. This means that customizing with styles is quite basic, but it may do the job if you want normalization and rapid control design.

Now that you have the resource ready, let's see how you can change the look and feel of the control. In the previous example, the `Border` type is being customized; therefore, you can customize your current border implementation as follows:

```
<Border Margin="32,91,25,36" Style="{StaticResource BorderStyle}"/>
```

You can appreciate how easy is to set the style. Note that you are still defining the position using the `Margin` dependency property. If you want to have it predefined, you can move it and include it in your style. Now you can override the properties — this works as well and will change the background to red.

```
<Border Margin="32,91,25,36" Style="{StaticResource BorderStyle}"
Background="Red"/>
```

This is actually how the controls work internally. They have a predefined style that you can override, changing the properties: These are usually called *default styles*. Later on, you'll see how a combination of styles and skins makes the current controls look when you incorporate the control's visual states.

Now let's analyze a full example in which you can customize how your user control looks when customizing it with styles. For this you are going to use the login screen example. Your user control will change based on the condition, as shown in Figure 11-11. You will use a combination of XAML and managed code for this.

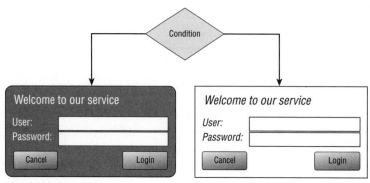

Figure 11-11

The following code implements this model. The first thing that you need is to define the styles; here you use two styles and store them in the user control resource dictionary.

```
<UserControl.Resources>

        <!-- Funky Style -->
        <Style TargetType="Border" x:Key="BorderFunkyStyle">
                <Setter Property="Background" Value="#FF1090B5"/>
                <Setter Property="CornerRadius" Value="20,20,20,20"/>
        </Style>

        <Style TargetType="TextBlock" x:Key="TitleFunkyStyle">
                <Setter Property="Foreground" Value="#FFFFFFFF"/>
        </Style>
```

```xml
        <!-- Classic Style -->
        <Style TargetType="Border" x:Key="BorderClassicStyle">
                <Setter Property="BorderBrush" Value="#FF050000"/>
                <Setter Property="CornerRadius" Value="0,0,0,0"/>
                <Setter Property="BorderThickness" Value="1,1,1,1"/>
        </Style>

        <Style TargetType="TextBlock" x:Key="TitleClassicStyle">
                <Setter Property="FontStyle" Value="Italic"/>
                <Setter Property="Foreground" Value="#FF86451B"/>
        </Style>

</UserControl.Resources>
```

> Note that the styles should always have an x:Key attribute because Silverlight does not support implicit styles using the target type as WPF does.

Because you don't know which style you are going to use at design time, you define them in the code behind. In this scenario, you add a random algorithm in order to present the different styles. For this you handle the user control loaded event. The code looks like this:

```csharp
private void UserControl_Loaded(object sender, RoutedEventArgs e)
{
        // Our powerfull algorithm :)
        long CurrentTick = DateTime.Now.Ticks;

        // Selects the correct style
        if ((CurrentTick & 1) == 1)
        {
                // Funky Style
                MainBorder.Style = (Style)Resources["BorderFunkyStyle"];

                // Fonts can not be specify by XAML styles
                lblWelcome.FontFamily = new FontFamily("Verdana");

                lblWelcome.Style = (Style)Resources["TitleFunkyStyle"];
                lblUser.Style = (Style)Resources["TitleFunkyStyle"];
                lblPassword.Style = (Style)Resources["TitleFunkyStyle"];
        }
        else
        {
                // Classic Style
                MainBorder.Style = (Style)Resources["BorderClassicStyle"];

                // Fonts can not be specify by XAML styles
                lblWelcome.FontFamily = new FontFamily("Courier New");

                lblWelcome.Style = (Style)Resources["TitleClassicStyle"];
                lblUser.Style = (Style)Resources["TitleClassicStyle"];
                lblPassword.Style = (Style)Resources["TitleClassicStyle"];
        }
```

```
                lblUser.FontFamily = lblWelcome.FontFamily;
                lblPassword.FontFamily = lblWelcome.FontFamily;
    }
```

As you can see, you can set the style at run time, changing the `Style` dependency property, but at this stage, you may have noticed that you are not adding the font family within the style. This is due to a technical limitation: the font family object cannot be parsed in XAML. The same thing happens, for example, with the `IsEnabled` dependency property because it is a `bool?` type that cannot be parsed either. The default template for the button uses this technique to assign the font. There is one exception to this rule; if you deliver the font with your package, you can make a reference as follows:

```
    <Setter Property="FontFamily" Value="/fonts/YouCustomFont.ttf "/>
```

Styles can really help you customize the look-and-feel predefining properties, but the Silverlight implementation has some limitations that you should be aware of if you are comparing the control styling of WPF:

❑   The first one is that your style cannot be based on another style; therefore, the `BasedOn` attribute is not supported in Silverlight.

❑   The second and most important one is that the style can be overridden only once. This means that once you have set your custom style (overriding the default once), you cannot set it again. If you try to do so, you will receive an exception.

You have seen in this section how you can customize the look and feel of the control just by controlling the properties, but in certain scenarios, you may want to customize completely how your control looks but still keep the same functionality. In the previous example, you kept the buttons style in the original style. The next section shows you how you can take the customization even further.

Customizing with Skins

Sometimes you want to customize your controls beyond changing properties or just applying different styles. For this reason, WPF and Silverlight allow you to do control skinning, sometimes called *templating*. This technique is also used in the default templates that you can find in your common controls.

In Silverlight 2, the skinning process is achieved using the `ControlTemplate` control, creating a completely new look and feel without changing the code behind. The template can also be stored as a resource or created dynamically using the code behind, as the `Control` object has the public dependency property called `Template`.

Figure 11-9 has shown you how you can transform the default button into a completely new layout; here's the code involved:

```
    <ControlTemplate x:Key="Customized" TargetType="Button" >
            <Grid x:Name="LayoutRoot">
                    <Ellipse Height="43.555" HorizontalAlignment="Left"
                            VerticalAlignment="Top" Width="99.556" Stroke="#FF22FFDC">
                            <Ellipse.Fill>
```

```
                              <LinearGradientBrush EndPoint="0.5,1"
                                                   StartPoint="0.5,0">
                               <GradientStop Color="#FFFFFFFF"/>
                               <GradientStop Color="#FF5ABBFF" Offset="1"/>
                              </LinearGradientBrush>
                         </Ellipse.Fill>
                    </Ellipse>
               </Grid>
          </ControlTemplate>
```

The control template object is very simple to create and manipulate. The important information is the target type, which has the same functionality as the style target type. With that information plus the key name for our resource dictionary, we are ready to use the template. The content of the template is the visual model that will represent the template; in this case, you are giving the button an elliptical look with a gradient background. Now it is time to consume the template:

```
<Button Template="{StaticResource Customized}"
        Foreground="Chocolate" Height="45"
        HorizontalAlignment="Right" Margin="0,30,25,0" VerticalAlignment="Top"
        Width="130" x:Name="cmdCustomizedButton"/>
```

The button now will divert the rendering to the content of the template. Remember that you can also assign the template via code behind as it shows the next code snipped. One very interesting feature is that you can change the template on the fly as many times as you want.

```
Private ControlTemplate previousControl;

if (previousControl == null)
{
        previousControl = cmdDefaultButton.Template;
        cmdDefaultButton.Template = (ControlTemplate)Resources["Customized"];
}
else
{
        cmdDefaultButton.Template = previousControl;
        previousControl = null;
}
```

Using skins to customize your control still allows you to set the properties of the control, but you will notice that they may not have the same desired effect. If, for example, you change the background color of the new button, you will notice that it does not change because the control does not know what to do with the value of that property, which may not fit the new template. But what if you still want that functionality? You can link it using `TemplateBinding`, which will allow you to copy the values from the source properties into your new template schema. You are going to change the original example using the template binding as it is shown in Figure 11-12.

Figure 11-12

To change the foreground color of the text on the button, we can still use the foreground color property that the designer is used to; it is considered best practice to allow this as it is the expected behavior. The code now looks like this:

```
<ControlTemplate x:Key="Customized" TargetType="Button">
        <Grid x:Name="LayoutRoot">
                <Ellipse Height="43.555" HorizontalAlignment="Left"
                        VerticalAlignment="Top" Width="99.556" Stroke="#FF22FFDC">
                        <Ellipse.Fill>
                                <LinearGradientBrush EndPoint="0.5,1"
                                                        StartPoint="0.5,0">
                                        <GradientStop Color="#FFFFFFFF"/>
                                        <GradientStop Color="#FF5ABBFF" Offset="1"/>
                                </LinearGradientBrush>
                        </Ellipse.Fill>
                </Ellipse>
                <TextBlock Text="Click Me!"
                        Foreground="{TemplateBinding Foreground}"
                        HorizontalAlignment="Left" Margin="15,10,0,0" Width="73"
                        FontSize="16" FontFamily="Comic Sans MS"
                        VerticalAlignment="Top" Height="18"/>
        </Grid>
</ControlTemplate>
```

Now, as you can see, you are hard-coding the text for the button; if you use `TemplateBinding` on the text, you must be sure that the content is supported — in other words, a string. You can change the example to use the template binding as follows:

```
<TextBlock Text="{TemplateBinding Content}"
        Foreground="{TemplateBinding Foreground}"
        HorizontalAlignment="Left" Margin="15,10,0,0" Width="73"
        FontSize="16" FontFamily="Comic Sans MS"
        VerticalAlignment="Top" Height="18"/>
```

But if you are looking for an extendable solution, you need to allow the designer to add any type of content. The content of the control can be another control or a hierarchy of multiple controls. This poses a problem when the text is expecting a string! If you want to add the content, you will need a `ContentPresenter` control.

The control presenter will do what it says on the label: It will allow you to render content within your template using the template binding command. Use the following code to incorporate this feature:

```
<ContentPresenter Content="{TemplateBinding Content}"
                HorizontalAlignment="Center" Margin="0,0,0,0"
                Width="73"                VerticalAlignment="Center" Height="25"/>
```

Note how you can extend the property binding to the font objects, which is not as limited as the styling. When you alter the source control with the following changes, you have a fully customized button control, as shown in Figure 11-13.

```
<Button Template="{StaticResource Customized}"
        Content="Login" FontSize="16"
```

```
Foreground="White" Height="45" HorizontalAlignment="Right"
Margin="0,30,25,0" VerticalAlignment="Top" Width="130"
x:Name="cmdCustomizedButton"/>
```

Figure 11-13

Putting Everything Together

Now that you understand how you can customize the look and feel of the control, you are going to use all these techniques to change the appearance of a control by mixing styling and skinning. Combining the techniques, you'll create a fully flexible control that can be reused in multiple applications without limiting the designers.

If you mix the style and the skin, you can have a control that applies a default style and template, allowing further changes if necessary. The following code defines the default behavior of the button and the default template:

```
<UserControl x:Class="Chapter11.Controls.StyleAndSkinDemo"
    xmlns="http://schemas.microsoft.com/winfx/2006/xaml/presentation"
    xmlns:x="http://schemas.microsoft.com/winfx/2006/xaml"
    FontFamily="Trebuchet MS" FontSize="11"
    Width="400" Height="300"
    xmlns:d="http://schemas.microsoft.com/expression/blend/2008"
    xmlns:mc="http://schemas.openxmlformats.org/markup-compatibility/2006"
    mc:Ignorable="d">

<UserControl.Resources>
    <Style x:Name="FunkyButton" TargetType="Button">
        <Setter Property="Content" Value="No name"/>
        <Setter Property="Background">
            <Setter.Value>
                <LinearGradientBrush EndPoint="0.5,1"
                                     StartPoint="0.5,0">
                    <GradientStop Color="#FFFFFFFF"/>
                    <GradientStop Color="#FF3094E8"
                                  Offset="0.513"/>
                    <GradientStop Color="#FFFFFFFF"
                                  Offset="0.987"/>
                </LinearGradientBrush>
            </Setter.Value>
        </Setter>
        <Setter Property="IsTabStop" Value="true"/>
        <Setter Property="Template">
            <Setter.Value>
                <ControlTemplate TargetType="Button">

<!--- Control Template -->
<Grid x:Name="LayoutRoot" Background="White">
    <Border Background="{TemplateBinding Background}"
```

```
                                HorizontalAlignment="Stretch"
                                VerticalAlignment="Stretch"
                                CornerRadius="10,10,10,10"
                                BorderThickness="2,2,1,1">
                            <Border.BorderBrush>
                                    <LinearGradientBrush EndPoint="0.5,1"
                                                         StartPoint="0.5,0">
                                    <GradientStop Color="#FFBECDE8"
                                                  Offset="0.004"/>
                                    <GradientStop Color="#FF1264F5" Offset="1"/>
                                    </LinearGradientBrush>
                            </Border.BorderBrush>
                            </Border>
                            <TextBlock HorizontalAlignment="Center"
                                    VerticalAlignment="Center"
                                    FontFamily="Lucida Sans Unicode"
                                    FontSize="{TemplateBinding FontSize}"
                                    Text="{TemplateBinding Content}"
                                    TextAlignment="Center"
                                    TextWrapping="Wrap"/>
                        </Grid>
                        </ControlTemplate>
                    </Setter.Value>
                    </Setter>
            </Style>
    </UserControl.Resources>

    <!--- Presentation -->
    <Grid>
            <StackPanel Orientation="Vertical" VerticalAlignment="Center">
                    <Button Width="200" Height="50"
                            Content="Silverlight Default Style" FontSize="14"/>
                    <Button Style="{StaticResource FunkyButton}" Width="200"
                            Height="50" FontSize="14"/>
                    <Button Style="{StaticResource FunkyButton}" Background="White"
                            Width="200" Height="50" Content="My customized version"
                            FontSize="14"/>
            </StackPanel>
    </Grid>
    </UserControl>
```

Adding a full example mixing both techniques shows you how to add values of type content; you can see how the default background is the definition of a brush. The user has changed the background brush upon the third instance of the button, but the second one, where the user has not changed it, is using the default gradient brush. When you run this example, you will get the results shown in Figure 11-14.

Figure 11-14

Visual States

So far you have seen how you can customize the visual aspects of a control, but after running the examples and playing with them, you may have noticed that the default styles includes different visual styles depending on the *state* of the button. Indeed, what if you want to trigger animations? For this reason, Silverlight includes the visual states that you can define for your controls.

Each of the target controls that you are using publishes a list of visual states that you can consume. This means that you can override how the control will look when there is a state transition without altering how this transition is calculated. For example, in the button example, you can see the visual states published:

```
[TemplateVisualStateAttribute(Name = "Unfocused", GroupName = "FocusStates")]
[TemplateVisualStateAttribute(Name = "MouseOver", GroupName = "CommonStates")]
[TemplateVisualStateAttribute(Name = "Pressed", GroupName = "CommonStates")]
[TemplateVisualStateAttribute(Name = "Focused", GroupName = "FocusStates")]
[TemplateVisualStateAttribute(Name = "Disabled", GroupName = "CommonStates")]
[TemplateVisualStateAttribute(Name = "Normal", GroupName = "CommonStates")]
public class Button : ButtonBase
```

It is important to note the attribute name and the group because they can be used to override the visual changes when you customize the control.

To understand how the visual states are managed, you first need to look into the `VisualStateManager`. This object will help you organize the visual states and transitions, adding the necessary storyboards that will occur during the state changes. The Visual State Manager is included in the `System.Windows` namespace; therefore, the first thing that you need to do is add the namespace to your control:

```
xmlns:vsm="clr-namespace:System.Windows;assembly=System.Windows"
```

With this namespace, you can start declaring the visual states in the control template. The first definition is the visual state groups container, `VisualStateManager.VisualStateGroups`, which will contain all the visual groups. If you review the list of states exposed in the button control, you will notice that there is a group name, which is the one defined by the individual group object called `VisualStateGroup`. The following example shows how you can add a color transition animation when the mouse hovers over the new customized button:

```
<VisualStateManager.VisualStateGroups>
        <VisualStateGroup x:Name="CommonStates">
                <VisualState x:Name="MouseOver">
                    <Storyboard>
                            <ColorAnimation Storyboard.TargetName="MainBorder"
                            Storyboard.TargetProperty =
                            "(Border.BorderBrush).(SolidColorBrush.Color)"
                            To="Black"/>
                    </Storyboard>
                </VisualState>
        </VisualStateGroup>
</VisualStateManager.VisualStateGroups>
```

In this case, when the target button triggers the state change to `MouseOver`, the animation will be triggered, changing the border color to black — again, without you having to change a single line in the code behind.

You can add a state transition storyboard if you want to trigger a visual change while the control is transitioning from one state to the other. The object responsible for grouping the transitions is `VisualState Group.Transitions`. Each transition is represented by a `VisualTransition` object that allows you to define the states to monitor and the duration of the intervention. The following code shows how you can add an extra color transition while the control is moving from the `MouseOver` state to the `Normal` state:

```
<VisualStateGroup.Transitions>
        <VisualTransition From="MouseOver" To="Normal"  GeneratedDuration="0:0:1.5">
            <Storyboard>
                    <ColorAnimation Storyboard.TargetName="MainBorder"
                    Storyboard.TargetProperty =
                    "(Border.BorderBrush).(SolidColorBrush.Color)" To="Red"/>
            </Storyboard>
        </VisualTransition>
</VisualStateGroup.Transitions>
```

Blend 2.5 also offers visual state management functionality to make it easier to design and visualize the changes using the user interface. Figure 11-15 shows how you can change the visual state.

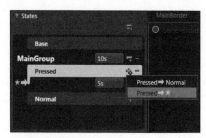

Figure 11-15

Blend lists the main states inherited from the base control and allows you to graphically add new visual state groups, visual states, and the transitions between them. This really helps you to reduce the amount of plumbing code that you need to write, as this generates all the XAML for you.

Now, you can alter the original example to add a visual state change when the user moves the mouse over your new customized button. The code shows you how you can integrate the visual states within your project:

```
<ControlTemplate TargetType="Button" >
        <Grid x:Name="LayoutRoot" Background="White">
        <VisualStateManager.VisualStateGroups>
            <VisualStateGroup x:Name="CommonStates">
                <VisualStateGroup.Transitions>
                    <VisualTransition From="MouseOver"
                            To="Normal"  GeneratedDuration="0:0:1.5">
                            <Storyboard>
                                    <ColorAnimation
                                    Storyboard.TargetName="MainBorder"
                                    Storyboard.TargetProperty =
                        "(Border.BorderBrush).(SolidColorBrush.Color)"
                                    To="Red"/>
```

```
                                      </Storyboard>
                                  </VisualTransition>
                          </VisualStateGroup.Transitions>

                          <VisualState x:Name="MouseOver">
                                  <Storyboard>
                                          <ColorAnimation
                                                  Storyboard.TargetName="MainBorder"
                                                  Storyboard.TargetProperty =
                                          "(Border.BorderBrush).(SolidColorBrush.Color)"
                                                  To="Black"/>
                                  </Storyboard>
                          </VisualState>
                          <VisualState x:Name="Normal">
                                  <Storyboard>
                                          <ColorAnimation
                                                  Storyboard.TargetName="MainBorder"
                                                  Storyboard.TargetProperty =
                                          "(Border.BorderBrush).(SolidColorBrush.Color)"
                                                  To="#FFBECDE8"/>
                                  </Storyboard>
                          </VisualState>
                  </VisualStateGroup>
          </VisualStateManager.VisualStateGroups>

          <Border x:Name="MainBorder" Background="{TemplateBinding Background}"
                  HorizontalAlignment="Stretch" VerticalAlignment="Stretch"
                  CornerRadius="10,10,10,10" BorderThickness="2,2,1,1">
                  <Border.BorderBrush>
                          <SolidColorBrush Color="#FFBECDE8"/>
                  </Border.BorderBrush>
          </Border>

          <TextBlock x:Name="MainContent"
                      HorizontalAlignment="Center"
                      VerticalAlignment="Center"
                      FontFamily="Lucida Sans Unicode"
                      FontSize="{TemplateBinding FontSize}"
                      Text="{TemplateBinding Content}"
                      TextAlignment="Center"
                      TextWrapping="Wrap"/>
          </Grid>
  </ControlTemplate>
```

Custom Controls

This custom controls section is the last part of the chapter, as it uses all the features that you've learned in this chapter. If you have been following the examples and the code, you may have noticed that in certain scenarios, the default behavior of a control is not good enough. At times, grouping them in user controls or changing how they look is not enough.

The Silverlight team adopted the WPF model of free customization completely open to developers. This means that there are no complex or undocumented models because the same techniques that the Silverlight team used to create the default toolbox can be used by developers and designers. You will discover how much easier it is to develop fully customized controls using Silverlight 2 than ASP.NET.

What Is a Custom Control?

Imagine that you are part of the Silverlight team and that your first task is to create the textbox control. You have learned all the previously discussed techniques around user controls and visual customization, but you may struggle to implement them without the basic controls. This is the place to start coding a full control from scratch; this means that you will be responsible for defining the functionality and how the control will look, always considering the extensibility model that WPF and Silverlight bring to the scene.

Now you need to code all the control logic based on the `Control` base class instead of the `UserControl` as presented so far in this chapter. Figure 11-16 is a visual representation of the control logic and presentation up to this point.

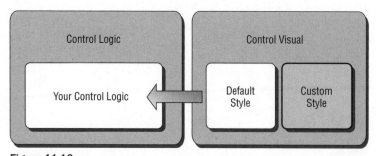

Figure 11-16

Figure 11-16 shows that now you own the control logic and the default style. When the designer implements your control, she should be able to override the visuals and still interact with the control logic and the state transitions. It seems like a lot of work, but trust us, you will see how the internal architecture allows you to customize it with minimal pain.

Because the custom control will not be included by default in the designer's toolbox, it is important to distribute the control and add it to the project. This leads you to the best practice of grouping all the custom controls in different assemblies so that you can reuse them in several projects. The assembly will be incorporated into the XAP Package and delivered to the final users with all the necessary resources.

> Note that since you are building a custom control, you can use other framework elements in your customization. For example, the `Calendar` control uses text blocks and buttons and is a fully customized control.

Scenarios

Deciding when to create a custom control is not easy; it will have a real impact on your project because you will need to dedicate effort to designing the control logic and appearance. At the same time, you need to think about what should be further customizable. The more options you offer, the more chances you create for something to go wrong.

One of the main scenarios in which we suggest using custom controls is when you really need functionality that requires custom logic that can be easily redeployed and used in other projects, for example, a thumbnail photo viewer. Such a control should not exist in the current toolbox, and there is a need for visual customization. With all these variables in place, the first scenario that can be addressed is when your business is selling custom controls. There are many companies that today are taking advantage of the lack of even basic controls in Silverlight and producing them in mass. You can see today that controls like combo boxes, visual sliders, and complex grids are not present by default, but they are already available for purchase. This leads us to another recommendation: If the control already exists, buy it. Trust us, controls are not very expensive, and a company has already gone through the pain of customizing it, testing it, and supporting it. This can really reduce the risk in your project.

Check to see if your requirement can be fulfilled with a simple user control. When evaluating a control, the rule of thumb is that if the control requires a lot of complexity and multiple controls, you will be better off using a user control. If the control is quite simple and has a simple and well-defined objective, you are probably in the custom control arena.

Your First Custom Control

In this section, you'll learn to develop a new custom control. We have identified that we need a value scroller that will present the content in a visually rich style.

For this project, we are going to start from the basics of creating a custom control, adding more functionality and complexity using the techniques you learned earlier in this chapter. (It would be a good idea to review them if you just jumped into this section.) Finally, we'll introduce new concepts around the interaction between the visuals and the control logic.

The custom control has been evaluated, and here are the requirements:

1. It will be presented as a simple control that can be reused in multiple projects and can be customized by the designers.

2. It will scroll content presenting one item at a time.

3. It will have two buttons to move the content forward and backward.

The completed custom control will look like Figure 11-17.

Figure 11-17

Now that you have all the details, you can start building the custom control. The first thing that you need to do is add a new item to your Silverlight project. If you want, you can create a separate assembly for it, as the steps are the same except that you need to add the reference and change the custom namespace on your control.

Use the following code to create a new class and rename it `ValueScroller`. It needs to inherit from `Control` to be recognized as a valid `UIElement`:

```
public class ValueScroller : Control
{
        public ValueScroller()
        {
                this.IsTabStop = true;
        }
}
```

`IsTabStop` specifies that you want your control to be included on the tab list. Now you switch to your user control that will present your custom control and add the namespace so it can be parsed:

```
<UserControl x:Class="Chapter11.Controls.CustomControlDemo"
    xmlns="http://schemas.microsoft.com/winfx/2006/xaml/presentation"
    xmlns:x="http://schemas.microsoft.com/winfx/2006/xaml"
    xmlns:custom="clr-namespace:Chapter11.Controls"
    FontFamily="Trebuchet MS" FontSize="11"
    Width="400" Height="300" Background="White">

  <Grid Width="400" Height="200" Background="White">
      <StackPanel Orientation="Vertical" VerticalAlignment="Center">
              <custom:ValueScroller Width="200" Height="25"/>
      </StackPanel>
    </Grid>
</UserControl>
```

As soon as the namespace is included, you can access it in your XAML designer. You may have noticed that some properties in the control are inherited from `Control`, for example, the width and the height. The project will compile without problems, but nothing will be rendered because you have just created the skeleton for the control logic.

Previously, you customized the visual parts of a control through styles and skins using control templates. In this control, you take the same approach. When you drag and drop a button, for example, the default template is applied; in our case, it is exactly the same as we will need in a default view. How do you define the default style? Let's explore the built-in style model.

Built-in Style

The default style is grouped in a file called *generic.xaml*; this is the same model that you may find in WPF. This file contains the default built-in style for your custom control. Note that this file may have more than one definition.

This file is just a resource dictionary with styles and templates that will be consumed by custom controls. Because the contents are resources, you should treat it as a resource file and should not compile it as a traditional XAML file.

Go back to the project, and create a new folder called *Themes*; then add a new XML file and rename it *generic.xaml*. Once the file is included, just go to the Properties section and change the build action to `Resource`. Also, remove the `Custom Tool` entry because you do not need it.

You need to define the dictionary in the same way you would in an application or user control dictionary. For this go to the generic.xaml file, and change the content as follows:

```
<ResourceDictionary
    xmlns="http://schemas.microsoft.com/winfx/2006/xaml/presentation"
    xmlns:x="http://schemas.microsoft.com/winfx/2006/xaml"
    xmlns:custom="clr-namespace:Chapter11.Controls">
</ResourceDictionary>
```

You are adding the custom namespace where your control is located because you will need it to define the target type in your styles and templates. Now you can start designing your control. Inside the resource dictionary, we are going to add a new style. The following code shows you how to do it:

```
<ResourceDictionary
    xmlns="http://schemas.microsoft.com/winfx/2006/xaml/presentation"
    xmlns:x="http://schemas.microsoft.com/winfx/2006/xaml"
    xmlns:custom="clr-namespace:Chapter11.Controls">

<!-- Built-in Style -->
<Style TargetType="custom:ValueScroller">
        <Setter Property="Template">
        <Setter.Value>
                <ControlTemplate TargetType="custom:ValueScroller">
                    <Grid x:Name="MainRoot" Background="White">
                        <Border x:Name="MainBorder"
                                HorizontalAlignment="Stretch"
                                VerticalAlignment="Stretch"
                                BorderBrush="#FF5E5E5E"
                                BorderThickness="1,1,1,1">
                        </Border>

                        <TextBlock  x:Name="MainText"
                                FontFamily="Verdana"
                                FontSize="14"
                                FontStyle="Normal"
                                TextWrapping="Wrap" Height="17"
                                HorizontalAlignment="Center"
                                VerticalAlignment="Center" />

                        <Button x:Name="RightButton"
                                HorizontalAlignment="Right"
                                VerticalAlignment="Stretch" Width="24"
                                BorderBrush="#FFC6BDBD">
                                <Grid>
                                        <Image Source="RightArrow.png"
                                                Width="16" Height="16"/>
                                </Grid>
                                </Button>
                        <Button x:Name="LeftButton"
```

```
                                        HorizontalAlignment="Left"
                                        VerticalAlignment="Stretch"
                                        Width="24" BorderBrush="#FFC6BDBD">
                        <Grid>
                            <Image Source="LeftArrow.png"
                                    Width="16" Height="16"/>
                        </Grid>
                    </Button>
                </Grid>
            </ControlTemplate>
        </Setter.Value>
        </Setter>
    </Style>
    </ResourceDictionary>
```

You should be familiar with this syntax by now. The important area to highlight is the `TargetType`, which is the new custom control. With the generic.xaml file added to your project, now you need to link your control to the style. For this go back to the code behind, and add the following in the constructor:

```
public ValueScroller()
{
        this.IsTabStop = true;
        this.DefaultStyleKey = typeof(ValueScroller);
}
```

When you run the project now, you can see that the control has a visual identity!

Custom Properties

To extend the default properties that you are publishing using the base class `Control`, you need to add new properties to your control. In this example, you add two types of properties. The first one will be a dependency property and the second one a standard property. The idea is to show you how you can interact with both types.

The dependency property is necessary if you want to allow any type of binding in your control including template binding for customizing the style. In this case, you have a demo text property that will be rendered when the control is first rendered. If you open the code behind, just add the following inside the control class:

```
public static DependencyProperty DemoTextProperty =
        DependencyProperty.Register("DemoText", typeof(string),
        typeof(ValueScroller), null);

/// <summary>
/// Demonstration text
/// </summary>
public string DemoText
{
        get { return (string)GetValue(DemoTextProperty); }
        set { SetValue(DemoTextProperty, value); }
}
```

We have just declared the dependency property and the traditional property accessor. Now you can use the property in your built-in template as well as in our control presentation. The example below shows you how you can change the generic.xaml file in order to use the property:

```
<!- - Generic.XAML -->

<Style TargetType="custom:ValueScroller">
        <Setter Property="DemoText" Value="Start Scrolling!"/>
        <Setter Property="Template">
            <Setter.Value>
                <ControlTemplate TargetType="custom:ValueScroller">
                    <!- - Other code removed -- >
                    <TextBlock  x:Name="MainText"
                            FontFamily="Verdana" FontSize="14"
                            FontStyle="Normal"
                            Text="{TemplateBinding DemoText}"
                            TextWrapping="Wrap" Height="17"
                            HorizontalAlignment="Center"
                            VerticalAlignment="Center" />
                </ControlTemplate>
            </Setter.Value>
        </Setter>
</Style>
```

When we consume the custom control on our user control container, we can also access the property that we have just added:

```
<!- - Control Implementation -->

<StackPanel Orientation="Vertical" VerticalAlignment="Center">
        <custom:ValueScroller x:Name="MyControl"
                            Width="200" Height="25"
                            DemoText="Current Item"/>
</StackPanel>
```

This does not stop you from using normal properties. In this example, you are going to add the source of the scrolling object using an array of strings. For this you can add the property and then handle the event using the code behind your implementation. The array declaration should be located on the new custom control code behind as it is shown in the following code:

```
private string[] source;
/// <summary>
/// Source
/// </summary>
public string[] Source
{
        get { return this.source; }
        set { this.source = value; }
}
```

We can now use the property of the code behind of the user control that is containing your custom control. In our example, we are going to fill the array with a default list; for this we need to handle the "Loaded" event as follows:

```
private void UserControl_Loaded(object sender, RoutedEventArgs e)
{
        MyControl.Source = new string[] { "Easy", "Medium", "Hard" };
}
```

Now you have a control that can expose a property and present the visual style. It's time to add the custom logic and the link between the visuals and the logic. For this you need to understand the parts model in Silverlight 2.

Parts Model

One thing that you may have noticed is that you don't have that seamless link between the XAML page and the code behind that you are used to in the user control environment. The XAML code is stored in generic.xaml, and you are linking it to the code behind using the `TargetType` at the moment.

But, how can you link the control logic when the user clicks on one of the scrolling buttons? The answer is located in the parts model.

The parts model is divided into two groups: The first one is the elements parts, where you define which elements your control needs to work. These elements should exist in the XAML template. Without them, the control may lose the functionality. (Note that we are saying *should* as a reminder that you can slightly change how the control works by using the visual styles and the templating model used earlier in the button example.)

The other group is the state parts. These parts define the control states that can be used with the Visual State Manager.

The parts model defines the contract between the control logic and the visuals, giving you a clear separation between the implementations. There is no other link between them. This is an excellent approach to dividing the effort of the developers and the designers.

Elements Parts

The elements parts allow you to define which object you are going to need to execute the logic of your control. This means that the visual template should incorporate them in order to get them at run time. Figure 11-18 shows the relationship when the control initializes.

When the control initializes, it will look for the parts by name in the current instance. This will give you access to the controls in order to handle the events or to perform alteration to the properties, for example, to change the content of the text block.

It is important to define the elements parts as attributes of your control; in this way, a designer or external tools can query the different elements that your control will need. The following code shows how you add the elements in the code behind the `ValueScroller` example:

```
[TemplatePart(Name = "MainBorder", Type = typeof(FrameworkElement))]
[TemplatePart(Name="MainRoot", Type=typeof(FrameworkElement))]
```

```
[TemplatePart(Name="LeftButton", Type=typeof(Button))]
[TemplatePart(Name = "RightButton", Type = typeof(Button))]
[TemplatePart(Name = "MainText", Type = typeof(TextBlock))]

[TemplatePart(Name = "LostFocusAnimation", Type = typeof(Storyboard))]
[TemplatePart(Name = "FocusAnimation", Type = typeof(Storyboard))]
public class ValueScroller : Control
```

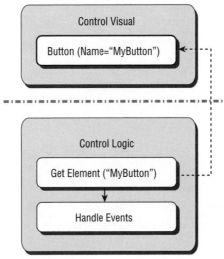

Figure 11-18

The template elements parts can be of the type that you need. Here you are looking for generic framework elements. (This is considered a best practice because you allow the designer to add any control he or she needs.) You are also looking for some specific types and a couple of storyboards to control the focus animation.

Because you already defined the templates as attributes, you need to add the necessary code to get the instance and to start adding the logic around them. For this you need to override the method OnApply Template that is exposed by your base class. This method will be executed once the default or custom template is applied on your control — perfect timing for your customization. The following code shows our ValueScroller code behind after overriding OnApplyTemplate:

```
private FrameworkElement mainBorder;
private Storyboard focusAnimation;
private Storyboard lostfocusAnimation;
private FrameworkElement mainRoot;
private Button leftButton;
private Button rightButton;
private TextBlock mainText;

public override void OnApplyTemplate()
{
        base.OnApplyTemplate();

        // Get the parts
```

```
        mainRoot = (FrameworkElement)GetTemplateChild("MainRoot");
        mainBorder = (FrameworkElement)GetTemplateChild("MainBorder");
        leftButton = (Button)GetTemplateChild("LeftButton");
        rightButton = (Button)GetTemplateChild("RightButton");
        mainText = (TextBlock)GetTemplateChild("MainText");

        // Get the resources
        if (mainRoot != null)
        {
                focusAnimation = (Storyboard)mainRoot.Resources["FocusAnimation"];
                lostfocusAnimation =
                        (Storyboard)mainRoot.Resources["LostFocusAnimation"];
        }

        InitInternalEvents();
}

private void InitInternalEvents()
{
        this.MouseEnter += new MouseEventHandler(ValueScroller_MouseEnter);
        this.MouseLeave += new MouseEventHandler(ValueScroller_MouseLeave);

        if (leftButton != null)
                leftButton.Click += new RoutedEventHandler(leftButton_Click);

        if (rightButton != null)
                rightButton.Click += new RoutedEventHandler(rightButton_Click);
}
```

The code shows how you can get the elements calling the GetTemplateChild function; remember that the names should match in order to receive the instance. Keep in mind that the designer may not implement all the elements; therefore, some of them may return null. For this reason, when you are querying resources like the storyboards, you need to check whether the element exists.

You can see how you can also access the element's resources using the object instances that you have just obtained. In this example, you are using two animations to change the background. Here is an example of one of them that will be accessed by key:

```
<Grid.Resources>
        <Storyboard x:Key="FocusAnimation">
                <ColorAnimationUsingKeyFrames BeginTime="00:00:00"
                Storyboard.TargetName="MainBorder"
                Storyboard.TargetProperty =
                "(Border.Background).(GradientBrush.GradientStops)[0].
                  (GradientStop.Color)">
                <SplineColorKeyFrame KeyTime="00:00:00" Value="#FFCECECE"/>
                <SplineColorKeyFrame KeyTime="00:00:01" Value="#FFFFFBFB"/>
                </ColorAnimationUsingKeyFrames>
        </Storyboard>
</Grid.Resources>
```

Finally, with the object instances in your hands, you can start adding the control logic. You can see how easy it is to link the visual styles with the control logic without coupling the two files. This is amazing architecture that really simplifies the efforts involved in developing a custom control.

```csharp
#region Event Handling
        void rightButton_Click(object sender, RoutedEventArgs e)
        {
                MoveNext();
        }

        void leftButton_Click(object sender, RoutedEventArgs e)
        {
                MovePrevious();
        }

        void ValueScroller_MouseLeave(object sender, MouseEventArgs e)
        {
                lostfocusAnimation.Begin();
        }

        void ValueScroller_MouseEnter(object sender, MouseEventArgs e)
        {
                focusAnimation.Begin();
        }
#endregion

#region Control Logic
        /// <summary>
        /// Next item
        /// </summary>
        private void MoveNext()
        {
                if (++currentIndex > Source.GetUpperBound(0))
                        currentIndex = 0;

                ShowContent(currentIndex);
        }
        /// <summary>
        /// Previous item
        /// </summary>
        private void MovePrevious()
        {
                if (--currentIndex < 0)
                        currentIndex = Source.GetUpperBound(0);

                ShowContent(currentIndex);
        }
        /// <summary>
        /// Shows the content
        /// </summary>
        /// <param name="index"></param>
```

```
            private void ShowContent(int index)
            {
                if (Source != null)
                {
                    if (index >= Source.GetLowerBound(0) &&
                        index <= Source.GetUpperBound(0))
                    {
                        mainText.Text = Source[index];
                    }
                    return;
                }
            }
        }
    #endregion
```

The code behind now is fully functional, and the default template can be overridden by a new template if necessary, because your logic will not break. Now, to provide consistent behavior to allow proper state overriding, you need to implement the necessary attributes and logic to interact with the Visual State Manager.

Visual State Parts

In this example, you have seen how you can obtain resources and trigger changes based on the control logic. But there is a more elegant way to perform these operations that will give the designer better control over how each state should look. Providing visual states allows the designer to override completely how the control looks in each state.

To define the different states, you need to add the visual state parts. These parts are defined using attributes; in this case, you are not using `TemplatePart`; instead, you use `TemplateVisualState`.

To apply the technique in this example, replace the elements parts that were defining the storyboards with the new visual state in the control code behind:

```
[TemplatePart(Name = "MainBorder", Type = typeof(FrameworkElement))]
[TemplatePart(Name="MainRoot", Type=typeof(FrameworkElement))]
[TemplatePart(Name="LeftButton", Type=typeof(Button))]
[TemplatePart(Name = "RightButton", Type = typeof(Button))]
[TemplatePart(Name = "MainText", Type = typeof(TextBlock))]

[TemplateVisualState(Name = "Normal", GroupName = "CommonStates")]
[TemplateVisualState(Name = "MouseOver", GroupName = "CommonStates")]
public class ValueScroller : Control
```

Now your control has two states: the normal state and the mouse over state. You can group the states using the group names. This is sometimes useful when you have multiple states and substates; defining a correct group hierarchy can help designers understand the logic behind them.

Change the generic.xaml file to transform those resources into two states using the Visual State Manager like this:

```
<vsm:VisualStateManager.VisualStateGroups>
        <vsm:VisualStateGroup x:Name="CommonStates">
            <vsm:VisualState x:Name="Normal">
```

```
                <Storyboard>
                    <ColorAnimationUsingKeyFrames BeginTime="00:00:00"
                    Storyboard.TargetName="MainBorder"
                    Storyboard.TargetProperty =
                    "(Border.Background).(GradientBrush.GradientStops)
                     [2].(GradientStop.Color)">

                        <SplineColorKeyFrame KeyTime="00:00:00"
                            Value="#FF00749F"/>
                        <SplineColorKeyFrame KeyTime="00:00:01"
                            Value="#FFFFFFFF"/>
                    </ColorAnimationUsingKeyFrames>
                </Storyboard>
            </vsm:VisualState>
            <vsm:VisualState x:Name="MouseOver">
                <Storyboard>
                    <!- - Removed for simplicity -- >
                </Storyboard>
            </vsm:VisualState>
        </vsm:VisualStateGroup>
</vsm:VisualStateManager.VisualStateGroups>
```

Note that we have removed some of the code for simplicity; you can find the full source code on the examples web site (wrox.com). But it is clear now how you are moving the storyboards from the resources to the Visual State Manager. Remember to add the Visual State Manager namespace in the generic.xaml. Otherwise, the vsm namespace will not be recognized!

```
xmlns:vsm="clr-namespace:System.Windows;assembly=System.Windows"
```

The last thing missing is how you change states within your control logic. You have access to the VisualStateManager object within your code; you can use it to transition from state to state. The first parameter is the control where the state is changing, the second is the name of the new visual state, and the third refers to the triggering transitions, which you can disallow if you need to do so. The code now looks like this:

```
void ValueScroller_MouseLeave(object sender, MouseEventArgs e)
{
        VisualStateManager.GoToState(this, "Normal", true);
}

void ValueScroller_MouseEnter(object sender, MouseEventArgs e)
{
        VisualStateManager.GoToState(this, "MouseOver", true);
}
```

As you can see, this code is much more elegant and allows the designer to trigger more than one storyboard if necessary instead of having the static ones derived from the elements parts.

With the knowledge and the tools to conquer the custom controls space, it is time for you to start experimenting for yourself and come up with awesome controls!

Summary

This chapter has been a journey. The idea was to discover what is possible with Silverlight 2 — learning individual features and trying to find the best implementation for each.

You have been exploring how the user controls work and in which scenarios they are useful. This is a concept that you may be quite familiar with because ASP.NET developers constantly use it. Grouping controls in parent controls is the most common customization that you may encounter. It is powerful and very simple with Silverlight 2.

Visual aspects in the rich internet application world are extremely important. For this reason, you looked at how you can customize controls using styles and skins. Sometimes the default look and feel is not good enough, but the control logic is spot on. This is a common technique that allows designers to easily change how their application looks. We have introduced the visual states and the tools of the trade that can help you to understand the internal logic of a control, customizing each state with one or more animations.

Finally, we put everything together in a discussion of custom controls. In this section, we described the special scenarios where this technique is useful and provided a simple example that applied each feature. The introduction of the generic.xaml is an important milestone in your learning as it is the heart of the built-in styles that you see in each control. Finally, you learned how to create custom states and how your control can trigger changes in it, allowing the designer to fully customize your newly created custom control.

Securing Your Silverlight Application

With the release of Silverlight has come a renewed excitement for picking up a technology and writing some rather rapid, visually pleasing applications. This attitude in picking up Silverlight and just going with it is reminiscent of a pre-Internet age when developers didn't have the constant pressures of having to weave security logic into their applications from the beginning. In the pre-Internet days, security was still of importance, but applications just didn't have the same levels of exposure as they do today. In today's world, there is much more of a defined line and differing expectations between the professional developer and the hobbyist.

Of course, being an ASP.NET developer, it is pretty typical for you to expect a high level of application exposure, and so you will constantly have security implications at the back of your mind. It's not a job that everybody enjoys doing, but it's a necessity.

Security comes in many guises and at many different levels. This chapter focuses on the different levels of security that you will want to be aware of during your Silverlight development. Some of these techniques you will be used to from your ASP.NET development, and where this is the case, you will see how you can extend the ASP.NET security model into your Silverlight client application.

This chapter begins by taking a look at application security as a whole and then starts looking at the core details of the security model introduced by Silverlight. Once this basis has been formed, the more subtle security features are discussed, along with how you can build on your security knowledge as an ASP.NET developer. There will be several concrete examples along the way to demonstrate the code blocks you can expect to use as a Silverlight developer.

You're under Attack!

To begin with, it is worth setting the scene to discuss what exactly is meant by "securing your Silverlight application." From whom do you need to secure it? What are the key areas of exploitation you need to guard against?

To take the example of a typical ASP.NET web application, you will know that you have to be aware of security at varying degrees of levels. This can be as low level as securing your resources with Access Control Lists (ACLs), securing the transport (e.g., SSL), securing who has access (authentication), and securing what authenticated users can access (authorization), among others. Although securing your applications across these different levels can be quite a daunting task, in larger organizations at least, you will tend to have people dedicated to such infrastructure-level security. As a developer, however, your responsibility is to take care of security concerns at the code level. This chapter is about how you should go about securing your Silverlight application at the code level. You will, of course, continue to use your existing ASP.NET security techniques, but will also need to extend these into your Silverlight code.

Before getting into the specific details of securing your code, it is worth taking a step back and first having a look at what it is you are guarding your application from.

Over the years, there have been many common attack areas exploited. These have included SQL injection, HTML injection, cross-domain scripting, cross-frame scripting, and distributed denial of service (DDOS) — to name but a few. You also have the possibility of people taking advantage of specific browser vulnerabilities. The responsibility of each of these attack points tends to fall naturally into some people's laps more easily than others. For example, it would be primarily the responsibility of the developer to ensure that SQL injection was not an option for an attacker, but it would be the primary responsibility of the browser vendor to ensure that their software was not vulnerable (or, realistically, that it gets patched sooner rather than later). When you start to look at cross-domain scripting, though, the lines are a little more blurred.

Does the responsibility fall to the developer, the browser vendor, or the user? Well, it would be a brave person to say it fell to the user, and an even braver person to tell users that the reason their data had been compromised was their fault! Fortunately, the baton of responsibility is (and should be) picked up by the other parties — namely, the browser vendor and, in the case of Silverlight, Microsoft. If you have already written a pretty simplistic Silverlight application, you maybe already know that there are compelling reasons for wanting the ability to communicate across domains. Chapter 9 has already explained how you can achieve this goal in Silverlight, but this will be mentioned again later in this chapter to complete the security story. Next comes the question of "who" the people are who might attack your applications. Well, this can depend on what your application does. For example, if you have a government site, perhaps your attackers would be people of differing political views. If your site was an online banking application, your attackers could be an organized criminal gang. Or perhaps your attackers are simply curious kids. The truth is that it doesn't really matter *who* compromises your application — if it is compromised, then the integrity of your company, and you as a developer, is at stake. In fact, it is pretty common for companies to keep such successful attacks under their hats if at all possible.

> These questions, and more, can be asked and answered in a more formal way by following an approach known as *threat modeling*. Threat modeling is usually introduced to the software development life cycle in order to reduce any weak areas of security within your application. It is outside the scope of this book to discuss this in detail, but if you are interested in finding out more about this, the following article is a good place to begin: http://msdn.microsoft.com/en-us/library/ms978516.aspx.

So with these exploits in mind, it is time to take a look at how you can barricade your application, while still letting in the good guys.

The Security Model

There are many levels of security to consider when building an application. This section focuses on the security model offered by the .NET Framework. In the desktop implementation of the .NET Framework, there are two models you might be familiar with: role-based security and code-access security.

Role-based security is provided in the desktop Framework to allow for a developer to specify the role in which the calling user must be a member in order to execute a particular piece of code (assembly, class, or method). In the Silverlight .NET Framework, role-based security is one of those features that has been removed. It is a feature that just does not make sense in an Internet-available, client-executed application.

To explain this further, the scenarios in which role-based security is used need to be addressed. Such security checks tend to be made either to restrict the information that is presented to a user or to prevent the user from performing an operation that they are not allowed to do.

For the former, the information restriction comes on the server side. The user is running under the security context of his or her browser, and the level of information supplied to him or her is determined on the server. If the application is available via the Web, then it is possible that your users are using anonymous authentication anyway. However, there are times when you do want the features provided by a role-based mechanism (perhaps your site uses Forms Authentication), in which case, this can be handled by the ASP.NET layer (or whichever server-side technology you may be using). This scenario is discussed further in the "Integrating with ASP.NET Security" section.

The other scenario for wanting role-based security is perhaps to determine certain operations a user can perform. First of all, these operations are those that can be performed on the user's own computer (e.g., reading/writing to a file). Security at this level is not required within a Silverlight application because it executes within a sandboxed environment (which is discussed in more detail in the next section). In other words, these security concerns are taken care of at another level. None of this, of course, means that you can't still implement this level of security on the server, where you are still working with the ASP.NET technology with which you are familiar.

So, with role-based security no longer involved, that just leaves code access security (CAS), right? Well, not exactly. If you have had the pleasure of configuring CAS in both the desktop and ASP.NET worlds, you will probably be pleased to hear there is a much simpler model in use for Silverlight. Despite the new model being a fresh implementation, you will notice some familiarity with some of the classes used in the desktop model. Before delving into the Silverlight security model, it is worth providing a brief overview of the traditional CAS model so that it becomes more apparent as to what is being left behind. This is by no means an in-depth look at the desktop model, but it should give you a quick refresher.

Code access security gives the developer (and a machine administrator) the ability to say what code can execute on a machine and what resources that code has access to at varying levels. This is largely unnecessary in the case of buying some software from a vendor that as an end-user you trust, but what about an application from a vendor you have never heard of that you download off the Internet? Take, for example, the scenario in which you are looking for an application to perform a particular task that would save you lots of time. You do a search in your favorite search engine, and you find an application that seems to do exactly what you want — great! So you go about executing this application in the hope that it will solve this particular problem, but how do you really know what that application will do? It could, for example, go ahead and overwrite a load of system files, modify some registry settings, or who knows what! Well, code access security can tackle this scenario by restricting the permissions of the application from a certain source (based on some "evidence"). Permissions can be grouped into permission sets and are associated with a "code group." *Evidence* is the information the CLR pulls from an assembly at load time. It can include information such as the URL where the assembly was found, the associated publisher, and so on — this information allows the run time to determine which "Code Group" the assembly is associated with. A Code Group has an associated set of permissions, which determine what exactly the assembly is allowed to do. As you can see, this can start to get a little complicated.

The CAS policies of the user's machine can be configured by either the MMC snap-in tool (`mscorcfg.cfg`) or the command-line tool (`caspol.exe`). For your ASP.NET applications, these settings are configurable via an AppDomain policy. The settings of these policies are found within the C:\Windows\Microsoft.NET\Framework\<Framework Version>\CONFIG folder in the web.config file. In this file, you will see some contents resembling the following:

```
<location allowOverride="true">
    <system.web>
        <securityPolicy>
            <trustLevel name="Full" policyFile="internal"/>
            <trustLevel name="High" policyFile="web_hightrust.config"/>
            <trustLevel name="Medium" policyFile="web_mediumtrust.config"/>
            <trustLevel name="Low" policyFile="web_lowtrust.config"/>
            <trustLevel name="Minimal" policyFile="web_minimaltrust.config"/>
        </securityPolicy>
        <trust level="Full" originUrl=""/>
    </system.web>
</location>
```

For each trust level you will find a further file that determines the permission sets associated with that trust level. One thing you may notice from this file is that, by default, your ASP.NET applications will be executing under Full Trust. This might go against the "secure by default" initiative (discussed in the next section), although you should bear in mind that this CAS level does not allow your application to do anything more than what is provided by the security context in which the host process is running. The thing to remember here is that although Silverlight has a new security model, ASP.NET will still be configured by the more traditional CAS security implementation.

The CAS functionality is hosted within the `System.Security` namespace, and this is where the Silverlight model can also be found.

As already mentioned, Silverlight security takes you away from this somewhat complex model. In Silverlight, each and every assembly, class, and method runs under one of the following security levels, which form the pillars of this model:

❑ **SecurityTransparent** — Code defined at this level can only call other SecurityTransparent code or code labeled SecuritySafeCritical. Code running at this level is deemed to perform operations that will not have an impact on the stability or security of the hosting operating system.

❑ **SecuritySafeCritical** — This level is a new edition to Silverlight and can be seen as the channel between SecurityTransparent (above) and SecurityCritical (below). As Transparent code is not allowed by the Security run time to call directly into Critical code, this level acts as the go-between. This layer has the ability to restrict access to only the crucial Critical APIs required by the Transparent code. In addition, it should perform any validation checks on what the Transparent code is passing in to ensure that there are no malicious or otherwise insecure calls being made. Only Microsoft-signed assemblies are able to use this security level.

❑ **SecurityCritical** — This level is reserved for any code that is performing any potentially dangerous calls. Such calls tend to be I/O operations or low-level direct calls into the operating system (in the case of Windows, Platform Invocation calls). SecurityTransparent code does not have the necessary level of access to call into code of this security level. Any attempts to do so will result in a `MethodAccessException`. Only Microsoft-signed assemblies are able to use this security level.

These various levels are, in fact, just attributes, which are added to the class definitions. These attributes are available in the desktop .NET Framework with the exception of SecuritySafeCritical. It is important to note that any code you write will, by default, be executed as being "Transparent." If you try to override this behavior and specify a level other than this, it will be ignored (resistance is futile!). This really means that there is no real reason for you to specify such an attribute on your code as it is effectively always going to be run as SecurityTransparent.

Although some of these attributes are available in the desktop CLR/CAS, they do form a subtly different piece of the puzzle. In CAS there was a concept of a stack-walk whereby the security run time performed a check on the calling code to ensure that code at a lower security level was not getting another API call to perform higher-privileged work. This concept has disappeared in Silverlight along with the rest of the CAS concepts.

With these points in mind, it is time for an example. The snippet of code below will illustrate how, as a user, you are unable to write directly to the disk using techniques you will be used to:

```
try
{
    using(FileStream fs = new FileStream("c:\\output.txt",
        FileMode.CreateNew))
    {
        using(StreamWriter sw = new StreamWriter(fs))
        {
            sw.WriteLine("Hello World!");
        }
    }
}
catch (Exception ex)
{
    DisplayError(ex);
}
```

This code demonstrates the best practice of including the "using" statement, which is used with classes that implement the Dispose pattern. This removes the burden of having to manually call Dispose on each object.

To get this code running on your machine, simply drop it into your `Page_Loaded` event handler in your code behind and add the `System.IO` namespace. You will also need to complete the `DisplayError` method in order to display some meaningful information out to the UI (which is omitted here for readability).

Upon executing this pretty simple-looking code, you will find that an exception is raised at the point of trying to create the file on the following line:

```
FileStream fs = new FileStream("c:\\output.txt",
                    FileMode.CreateNew
```

The exception raised is the aforementioned `MethodAccessException`, and if you output the exception message, you will see that it is raised upon the `FileStream` constructor. This is evidence that the `FileStream` class implemented by Microsoft does, in fact, have a `SecurityCritical` attribute applied to it.

You can go one step further here to prove this by opening up the .NET `Reflector` tool, browsing to the Silverlight directory (C:\Program Files\Microsoft Silverlight\<version>), and opening up the Silverlight .NET Base Class Library, which is contained within mscorlib.dll. By expanding the CommonLanguage RuntimeLibrary, followed by `System.IO` and then the `FileStream` class, if you view the Disassembly pane (Tools ⇨ Disassemble), you will see that the static constructors are all marked with this attribute, as shown in Figure 12-1.

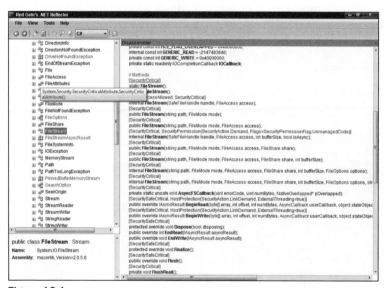

Figure 12-1

Working in a Sandbox

During the 1990s, Microsoft began to suffer from a lot of bad publicity about security vulnerability in its software. There was a feeling that the company had not practiced what it preached and had strayed down the route of bolting on security features. Of course, things are not always so black and white, and sure, security would have been considered from the design phase of applications, but it was the Microsoft Trustworthy Computing initiative that was required to bring back the emphasis on security into its applications. In fact, development of several flagship applications was halted while a full security assessment took place. The three tenets of this initiative were to be secure by design, secure by default, and secure by deployment. A brief description of each of these is given below:

❑ **Secure by Design** — This is pretty self-explanatory. It involves security being considered as a first-class citizen during the design phase of the application. Security should be at every level of the application design, from the high-level architecture right down to the API calls used.

❑ **Secure by Default** — Traditionally, applications would ship with every single feature enabled. This resulted in a larger surface area for attacks. This particular tenet dictates that only the core features of the application should be enabled by default. A great example of this is Internet Information Services (IIS) 7.0. IIS 7.0 has a very modular design, which allows you to easily configure the features you want to enable at a very granular level, many of which are turned off by default. You also get some welcome side effects from using such an architecture in that the memory footprint is reduced.

❑ **Secure by Deployment** — This is much more on guidance in deploying the application. This can include how to securely configure the application, which may mean providing tools and documentation to aid in that process.

With these points in mind, what is a sandbox, and under which of these points does it fall?

You now know that you cannot directly write to the filesystem because the APIs that allow you to do this are marked with the `SecurityCritical` attribute, yet your code is only given the level of Security Transparent. What you ideally need is an API that you can call with the `SecuritySafeCritical` attribute that could then perform adequate checks on the parameters you are passing in or restrict you to a safe level of functionality. This API is found within the `System.IO.IsolatedStorage` namespace.

In the example given in the last section, the call failed once you tried to create a file via the `FileStream` class. This file was located at c:\output.txt. The `IsolatedStorage` namespace will not let you write to the root of your hard disk, but it will allow you to create and write to this file at some other location. That location is provided as part of the Silverlight sandbox, whose location will be discussed in a little while. To start to prove that this is possible, take a look at the following snippet of code. Its functionality is the same as the previous example, except it uses `IsolatedStorage` and succeeds.

If you are compiling this code yourself, remember to include the `System.IO.IsolatedStorage` namespace. You will also need to complete the `DisplayOutput` method, which simply displays the string read out of the file to the screen.

```
using (IsolatedStorageFile isf =
IsolatedStorageFile.GetUserStoreForApplication())
    {
        using (IsolatedStorageFileStream ifs = new
IsolatedStorageFileStream("output.txt", FileMode.Create, isf))
        {
            using (StreamWriter sw = new StreamWriter(ifs))
            {
                sw.WriteLine("Hello World!");
            }
        }

        using (IsolatedStorageFileStream ifs = new
IsolatedStorageFileStream("output.txt", FileMode.Open, isf))
```

```
                    {
                        using (StreamReader sr = new StreamReader(ifs))
                        {
                            string firstLine = sr.ReadLine();
                            DisplayOutput(firstLine);
                        }
                    }
                }
```

There are some notable, yet simple, additions to this code that have been added in order to make use of Isolated Storage. Once you have added the System.IO.IsolatedStorage namespace reference, the first difference over the original code sample is the following piece of code:

```
IsolatedStorageFile isf = IsolatedStorageFile.GetUserStoreForApplication()
```

This line of code is requesting a storage location for the file that you are about to create. By default, any Silverlight application will have a maximum quota of 1 MB in which to save files, and access to this area is provided by the IsolatedStorageFileStream class. In fact, if you set a breakpoint on this line of code in the debugger, you will notice that the instance variable (in this case, ifs), has a property named *m_FullPath*, which shows the exact location of the file on your local filesystem. You won't need to worry about this for the most part, although it can be useful when you need to get your hands dirty with some debugging.

If you try to exceed the 1-MB storage quota from within your application, then a System.IO.Isolated Storage.IsolatedStorageException will be raised, indicating that you have tried to exceed this quota. There is a way around this, and that is to call the IsolatedStorageFile.IncreaseQuotaTo() method. This method accepts a *long* value and allows you to specify a new quota in bytes; however, there is a caveat to be aware of here. You cannot just call this from anywhere within your code — it must be called within an event handler that gets raised as a result of user input. This is because to raise the quota, you need the user's permission. If you make this call within, say, a button event handler, the user will be presented with a dialog telling him or her that your application has requested more space, and will they allow you to have this extra space (see Figure 12-2)?

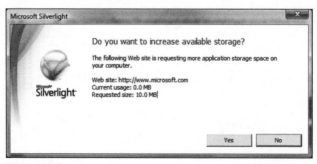

Figure 12-2

As a result, IncreaseQuotaTo returns a Boolean to signify whether they have given you these privileges or not, so your code logic should take this response into account.

Besides the dialog prompting the user to increase the quota for your application, there are other areas where the user can configure the quota. For example, if users begin to run low on disk space, they can either delete all the storage associated with your site, or they can disable Isolated Storage altogether. This is achieved in the configuration options for the Silverlight plug-in and can be seen in Figure 12-3.

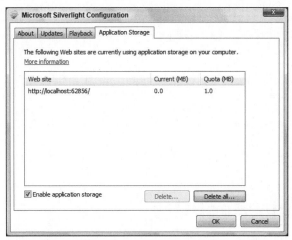

Figure 12-3

The next line of the security-friendly code starts to look a little more familiar (and the using statement continues to be omitted for clarity):

```
IsolatedStorageFileStream ifs = new IsolatedStorageFileStream("output.txt",
    FileMode.CreateNew, isf)
```

This code looks pretty similar to the FileStream line used in the previous example, except of course that the SafeCritical `IsolatedStorageFileStream` class is being used instead. This class has several over-loaded constructors, but in the simple case above, there is just one extra parameter when compared to the FileStream example, and this is simply the passing of the `IsolatedStorageFile` object so that the Stream knows where to read or write to.

Following this code, the sample is pretty much identical to the FileStream example. The addition in this sample is the code to read back out the value, which is there simply to prove that some data has been written.

This example has given a bare-bones look at the Isolated File Storage API, although you should be aware that there is more to the classes it exposes than is shown. For example, there will be scenarios in which you need to provide a richer file structure than the flat structure outlined above. You can achieve this by creating directories (via the `IsolatedStorageFile` class). When creating and reading folders and files, you should note that as you are working in a sandbox, you will only ever specify relative path names. This is why there was no sign of c:\output.txt in the above example, but rather, output.txt.

One interesting area to discuss regarding IsolatedStorage is the details surrounding the subfolders under c:\users\<username> \AppData\Local\IsolatedStorage. This becomes more important when you are relying on multiple browsers on the client machine to pick up the files from the same location. It is true that such scenarios may be quite rare, but it is good to know that this is taken care of for you. In such instances, a Silverlight application running under User A will always store its data in the same place. This example is using the Windows filesystem structure as an example, but continuing in this vein, your data would be safe from other users on the same machine as NTFS permissions would restrict you from looking into another user's folder under c:\users (unless, of course, you were the machine administrator).

Although you are restricted regarding where you can save files to and open files from, you are able to stretch a little further and put your trust in the users by providing them with a File Dialog for choosing files on their local drive. This ability is provided by the OpenFileDialog class and allows you to select a file just as you can in any other file-based operation outside of Silverlight. You may want to influence the user in some way here and point them in the right direction. You can do this by providing a filter on the types that the dialog will display by default. You can also allow the user to select one or multiple files, and you can then, of course, hold the files they selected in a collection for further processing.

One thing to note is that you do not have an equivalent SaveFileDialog class for saving files.

Cross-Domain Security

You are probably not going to be bitten by cross-domain security restrictions immediately as you will be confined to a development environment where your services and client code all reside on the one machine. The problems will start to arise when you try to consume services out on the Net, or elsewhere within your organization.

Chapter 9 showed the security mechanism in place to prevent the Silverlight run time from making any cross-domain network calls at both the HTTP and Socket levels. It also showed the approach you need to take on the server for each in order to make such calls possible. One of the important points to remember when you are starting to develop a cross-network Silverlight application is just how these restrictions manifest themselves without the appropriate policy files and policy server in place. For the purpose of the examples that are discussed later, you should remember that a Web Service client will receive a CommunicationException if it is unable to locate a cross-domain policy file. Fortunately in this situation, the error message should point you in the right direction if this is the case.

Integrating with ASP.NET Security

Some of the concepts covered up until now may have been familiar to you even if you hadn't dealt with them within the context of Silverlight. For example, you may have hit the cross-domain issue in the past when using the ASP.NET AJAX extensions or maybe even as part of some Flash development. If you hadn't covered these issues before, you should now have a good understanding of them. This section concentrates on an area of security you will almost certainly be familiar with if you are an ASP.NET developer, and that is ASP.NET's Provider model and, in particular, its out-of-the-box security providers. Before entering this discussion, a brief overview will be given of this model in case you are not so familiar with this area.

Putting security aside for a moment, ASP.NET introduces the developer to the provider pattern. This is a well-known pattern used throughout ASP.NET (and beyond) whereby the developer can code against a common API for a particular task or feature but is abstracted away from the concrete implementation, usually via some kind of Data Abstraction Layer. This allows for an extremely flexible and pluggable architecture so that if a store or end resource were to be changed, all that is involved is a configuration change, allowing the API to remain the same.

To bring security into this model, you can take, for example, the role provider. The *role provider*, as the name implies, is a feature to allow users to be placed in roles defined by the application designer in order to restrict access to certain parts of the system. Why does this need to use the provider model? Well, because it is useful to have the flexibility to store this information in differing locations depending on your environment. These locations could include a database, Active Directory, or elsewhere. The developer doesn't really need to worry about this. They can just write some code as demonstrated below that follows the contract of the API, and everything else happens behind the scenes:

```
Roles.AddUserToRole("cbarker00", "Administrators");
```

Before you start to use roles, you will need to authenticate the users accessing your application — that is to say, "Who is this person?" This is tackled by another provider: the membership provider. Again, this may seem familiar to you from its use in the ASP.NET world, but you will now be presented with the challenge of extending this into your Silverlight application.

An example will now be given as to how you secure your ASP.NET applications in this way. The Calculator example can be used as the sample application and can be found with the code that accompanies this chapter. Once the service has been tweaked to allow for this functionality, a look will be taken at the consuming Silverlight client and how it can be configured to interact with the newly secured service.

Introducing the membership provider into your Calculator Web Service is made trivial by the Visual Studio .NET IDE. If you are working along with this example, all you need to do is open up your Calculator project along with your Silverlight client.

There are several ways in which you could carry out the following steps, including using command-line tools and manually modifying the web.config file. However, this example will use a simple UI approach which will allow you to get up and running more quickly.

First of all, you want to enable the membership and role providers, and for this example, you will use Forms authentication. Right-click on your Calculator project, and select the "Set as Startup Project" option. Next, click on the "Project" toolbar option, and select "ASP.NET Configuration." Once the Web Site Administration Tool has opened up, select the "Security" option, as illustrated in Figure 12-4.

Upon selecting the "Security" option, you will need to set the "authentication type" in the "Users" box to "From the Internet." This indicates to ASP.NET that you would like to use Forms Authentication rather than Windows Authentication, and the tool inserts the following line into your web.config file:

```
<authentication mode="Forms" />
```

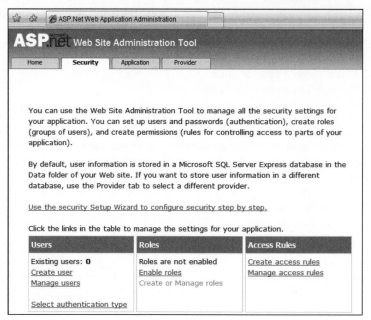

Figure 12-4

Following this, you will create a user that has access to the application, so click "Create user." On the next page, enter some user credentials that you will use to log in to the application. Now select "Enable roles" and add a role called **Administrators**. You should now add the user you created to the Administrators role either by selecting "Manage roles" or "Manage users." Because you will be using the provider defaults, all the information relating to users and roles will be stored within a SQL Server Express database. You can first of all see that the store is indicated in the provider name by clicking on the Provider tab and clicking the "Select a different provider for each feature (advanced)" option. The membership provider you are using is the AspNetSqlMembershipProvider, and the role provider is the AspNetSqlRoleProvider. The membership provider is what takes care of authenticating to your application, and the role provider helps you to take care of authorizing certain roles within your application. The default store for Forms authentication is SQL Server, which is why AspNetSqlMembershipProvider is being used. SQL Server is also used for storing the role information, which is why AspNetSqlRoleProvider is used. To examine this further, you will find that upon accessing and configuring this information within the tool, a database will have appeared under your AppData directory in Visual Studio. If you can't see this, then select the "Show All Files" option in the Solutions Explorer, and expand AppData. This can be seen in Figure 12-5.

You've created your user and you've created your role. So what else is there left to do? You need to restrict unauthorized access to your site, and you must provide the users a means of authenticating themselves to the application. You want to first enable members of your "Administrators" role access to your entire application, so click on the "Create access rules" option, select "Rule applies to: Administrators," and give this a permission of **Allow**. You can then click on OK. Next, you want to deny people who are not authenticated (and therefore not in this role). To do this, select "Create access rules," select "Anonymous users," and give a permission of "Deny." You may now click "Done" and close the Web Site Administrative Tool. Now take a look at what configurations have been added to your web.config file in your Calculator project:

```
<authorization>
    <allow roles="Administrators" />
```

```
    <deny users="?" />
</authorization>
<roleManager enabled="true" />
<authentication mode="Forms" />
```

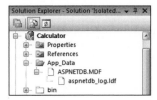

Figure 12-5

You can see that the "Administrators" role is allowed access to the entire application, and that "?" is denied access to the application. The "?" simply means "not authenticated" or "guest." You can also see that the `roleManager` property is enabled. This is enabled as a result of the step you took via the UI to enable roles.

The last step needed to enable this basic level of security in your application is to give the user the ability to authenticate. In order to authenticate, ASP.NET's Forms Authentication mechanism by default will look for a page called *Login.aspx*. This is configurable, but for the purposes here, this name is fine. You need to add this page by right-clicking on your project and selecting "Add new item." Next, select "Web Form," and give it a name of **Login.aspx**. Now simply drag a "Login" control into your new page, and you are good to go.

To test that this all works, try to access your Web Service directly (Calculator.svc). You should be redirected to your login page. Once you enter the credentials for your user, you will be authenticated. As you are a member of the Administrators role and can access the site, you will get redirected to the page you originally requested, which is your Calculator.svc Web Service.

Now on to the fun part — getting your Silverlight client to talk to your newly secured Web Service.

To start with the simplest scenario, you are going to have two files that may look something like this:

❑   **Calculator.svc** — The Web Service your client will call.

❑   **AuthenticationTestPage.aspx** — The client page hosting the Silverlight control.

Your managed code is going to be called as a result of the control within AuthenticationTestPage.aspx. This control is going to call your Calculator Web Service via the web proxy. If your AuthenticationTest Page.aspx page is sitting in the same web application as the Web Service, there is not going to be a problem because the user will not be authenticated when hitting AuthenticationTestPage.aspx and so will get re-directed to the login page in order to authenticate themselves. Once the user has logged in, the call to invoke the Web Service is going to succeed because it will be running in the context of an authenticated user. Just to be clear, the following code is going to succeed:

```
CalculatorClient calc = new CalculatorClient();

calc.AddCompleted +=
new EventHandler<AddCompletedEventArgs>(calc_AddCompleted);

calc.AddAsync(1, 2);
```

However, having the client page in the same web application as the Web Service is not a very realistic real-world scenario. The chances are that you are going to have your client application sit somewhere remotely, and once you have overcome the cross-domain issue, you are going to hit a new problem. The problem is going to be that your remote client application has no security credentials set up on it. This would result in the application getting re-directed because it is the assembly in which the client code is housed that makes the call to the Web Service. Running the code in this manner is going to result in a `CommunicationException`, with essentially the same message you would see as if there were no cross-domain policy file configured. This is because the run time will request the policy file, but as it gets re-directed to the login page, it is not able to find it and the request fails.

It is because of such error messages that being aware of this particular scenario is essential. You know in this very simple case why this is happening, but if you consider a more complex application with nested calls, this would be a tricky situation to debug. This chapter isn't about debugging (which is covered in Chapter 15). The discussion here is about how you go about authenticating your Silverlight client against the secured ASP.NET Web Service.

This may seem familiar territory if you have ever tried to tackle this problem from an ASP.NET AJAX client. As both technologies are based on the client, the challenges are logically the same in terms of having the requirement of telling the server who you are. The following sections will take you through the implementation steps you will need to take in order to expose your ASP.NET application in the appropriate way and how to instruct Silverlight to fulfill its obligations.

The first thing you need to do is to expose the appropriate ASP.NET application services to the client.

> *As covered elsewhere in the book, Application Services are the Web Services that can be enabled in ASP.NET applications to expose the authentication, role, and profile features of ASP.NET outside the server environment. These Web Services can be configured to communicate using both the JSON and SOAP formats, which allows for a wider client audience.*

To keep the theory relatively straightforward, this walk-through is going to focus solely on getting the membership provider exposed to the client, rather than the role provider. Also, to avoid any confusion, the membership provider is exposed via the authentication service.

> **Some of these steps have been covered in more depth in Chapter 5 when exposing the Profile application service. The principles are the same, and this section will use the same concepts in order to expose and consume the Authentication application service.**

As you have seen previously, the ASP.NET application services are built on WCF, and so the first steps you will need to take are to expose the authentication service as a WCF endpoint by first off creating a dummy AuthenticationService.svc service, which contains the following line of code:

```
<%@ ServiceHost Language="C#" Service="System.Web.ApplicationServices.
AuthenticationService" %>
```

This line is pointing your service to the implementation that comes out-of-the-box with ASP.NET. You then need to configure this WCF service, bindings, and behavior by adding the following elements in the appropriate places:

```
<service name="System.Web.ApplicationServices.AuthenticationService"
         behaviorConfiguration="AuthenticationServiceTypeBehaviors">
  <endpoint contract="System.Web.ApplicationServices.AuthenticationService"
            binding="basicHttpBinding" bindingConfiguration="userHttp"
            bindingNamespace="http://asp.net/ApplicationServices/v200"/>
</service>

<bindings>
  <basicHttpBinding>
    <binding name="userHttp">
      <security mode="None"/>
    </binding>
  </basicHttpBinding>
</bindings>

<behavior name="AuthenticationServiceTypeBehaviors">
  <serviceMetadata httpGetEnabled="true"/>
</behavior>
```

> You should already have an existing service and behavior configured in your application for the Calculator service as this would have been produced for you by Visual Studio. You can use the configuration settings created for this service as a basis for adding the authentication service details as shown above.

You next need to enable the authentication service for script (and Silverlight) based clients. To do this, you need to add the following configuration section to your web.config file:

```
<system.web.extensions>
  <scripting>
    <webServices>
      <authenticationService enabled="true" />
    </webServices>
  </scripting>
</system.web.extensions>
```

For this to work, you need to make sure that you have the appropriate configuration sections defined within your web.config. The xml that defines these configuration sections can be seen below:

```
<configSections>

  <sectionGroup name="system.web.extensions"
type="System.Web.Configuration.SystemWebExtensionsSectionGroup,
System.Web.Extensions,
Version=3.5.0.0, Culture=neutral,
PublicKeyToken=31BF3856AD364E35">
```

```
        <sectionGroup name="scripting"
type="System.Web.Configuration.ScriptingSectionGroup,
System.Web.Extensions,
Version=3.5.0.0,
Culture=neutral,
PublicKeyToken=31BF3856AD364E35">

            <sectionGroup name="webServices"
type="System.Web.Configuration.ScriptingWebServicesSectionGroup,
System.Web.Extensions,
Version=3.5.0.0,
Culture=neutral,
PublicKeyToken=31BF3856AD364E35">

            <section name="authenticationService"
type="System.Web.Configuration.ScriptingAuthenticationServiceSection, System.Web.
Extensions,
Version=3.5.0.0,
Culture=neutral,
PublicKeyToken=31BF3856AD364E35" requirePermission="false"
allowDefinition="MachineToApplication"/>

        </sectionGroup>
      </sectionGroup>
    </sectionGroup>
  </configSections>
```

You now need to glue all of this together. The steps above should have exposed the authentication service to your Silverlight client in much the same way as the Calculator service has been. So, the next steps are to simply add a new Service Reference to the AuthenticationService.svc service that you have created.

> **One interesting problem here is that you may not be able to add the Service Reference if the page sits in the site that requires authentication. In this instance, you can allow anybody to access the AuthenticationService.svc endpoint by entering the following configuration into your web.config:**
>
> ```
> <location path="AuthenticationService.svc">
>   <system.web>
>     <authorization>
>       <allow users ="*" />
>     </authorization>
>   </system.web>
> </location>
> ```
>
> **If you are making the request cross-domain, you will also need to make a similar exception for your policy file.**

The scene is now set for you to pass in your authentication details. You could obviously hard-code this, or provide some user input via XAML as demonstrated below:

```
<Grid x:Name="LayoutRoot" Background="White">
```

```xml
<Grid.RowDefinitions>
    <RowDefinition Height="20" />
    <RowDefinition Height="20" />
    <RowDefinition Height="20" />
    <RowDefinition Height="20" />
    <RowDefinition Height="20" />
    <RowDefinition Height="20" />
    <RowDefinition Height="20" />
    <RowDefinition Height="20" />
</Grid.RowDefinitions>

<Grid.ColumnDefinitions>
    <ColumnDefinition />
    <ColumnDefinition />
</Grid.ColumnDefinitions>

<TextBlock Text="Username" Grid.Row="0" Grid.Column="0" />
<TextBox x:Name="txtUsername" Grid.Row="0" Grid.Column="1" />

<TextBlock Text="Password" Grid.Row="1" Grid.Column="0" />
<TextBox x:Name="txtPassword" Grid.Row="1" Grid.Column="1" />

<Button x:Name="btnLogin" Content="Login" Grid.Row="2" Grid.Column="1"
Click="btnLogin_Click" />

<TextBlock x:Name="LoginSuccess" Grid.Row="3" Grid.Column="1" />

<TextBlock Text="Number1:" Grid.Row="4" Grid.Column="0" />
<TextBox x:Name="txtNum1" Grid.Row="4" Grid.Column="1" />

<TextBlock Text="Number2:" Grid.Row="5" Grid.Column="0" />
<TextBox x:Name="txtNum2" Grid.Row="5" Grid.Column="1" />

<Button x:Name="btnAdd" Content="Add" Grid.Row="6" Grid.Column="1"
Click="btnAdd_Click" />

<TextBlock Text="Result:" Grid.Row="7" Grid.Column="0" />

<TextBlock x:Name="txtResult" Grid.Row="7" Grid.Column="1" />

</Grid>
```

You will need to add the appropriate event-handler hookups here, which you can see from the code samples associated with the chapter, but the key piece of code that provides the call to the authentication service can be seen below:

```
svc = new AuthenticationServiceClient();
svc.LoginCompleted +=
new EventHandler<LoginCompletedEventArgs>(svc_LoginCompleted);
svc.LoginAsync(txtUsername.Text, txtPassword.Text, "", false);
```

The svc_LoginCompleted event handler will allow you to see if the login has succeeded. You can figure this out by testing the LoginCompletedEventArgs.Result property for a Boolean value.

You will notice that there are four parameters passed in to the `LoginAsync` method above. These follow a signature of `LoginAsync(username, password, customCredential, isPersistent)`. The first two parameters are self-explanatory, but the third (`customCredential`) is there to allow you to pass in some further custom parameters to an authentication service that has been configured to accept more than just a username and password. The fourth parameter, `isPersistent`, is stating whether or not a cookie should be created to persist the user's authenticated state.

You now have all of the components required for authenticating a user from a Silverlight client. In the accompanying sample, you will find that calls to the Calculator service will fail with the now familiar CommunicatioException until the user has authenticated himself via the provided form.

In order to use the samples successfully, you should refresh the Service References to ensure that they are pointing to the correct location, and you should add a set of user credentials to the application using the ASP.NET Configuration Tool as directed previously. A pre-requisite to running these samples is that you have SQL Server 2005 Express Edition installed as this is required for the authentication repository.

Obfuscation

In the ASP.NET world, the majority of your intellectual property (IP) is kept on the server in the form of assemblies. All the client sees is the HTML that is rendered in his or her browser. In traditional WinForm applications, developers are sometimes a little more cagey. In other words, when they ship their application, their assemblies are being deployed to a client machine. The conceived problem with this is that the Microsoft Intermediate Language (MSIL) contained within the assemblies makes it almost trivial to reverse-engineer the application to discover its code and logic. A developer's code and its associated intellectual property have always seemed to be at odds with each other. Should it be the code that is protected, or should it be the actual idea? Well, that is a debate for another day. This section describes one of the techniques developers take to try to protect their .NET assemblies from prying eyes: *obfuscation*. Your Silverlight assemblies are going to find their way to the end-users' machines in order to execute. Therefore, you should consider your obfuscation options to protect your intellectual property.

There are many obfuscation tools on the market at the moment, each using a varying degree of methods to hide your code from decompilers. However, your code obviously needs to compile and execute, so in the .NET world, the obfuscated code must still be valid MSIL, assuming that you are not using `ngen.exe` to generate a native image of your assembly. With your obfuscated code still being in MSIL, it can be read by decompilation tools such as Red Gate's Reflector, but it should be much less intuitive as to what the code actually does. There are various techniques used to hide what your code does, including simple type, method and field renaming, string encryption, and the more complex control flow coding. The latter is a way of allowing your code to perform logically in the same manner, but the physical code to achieve this is obscured so that your actual code logic is not so directly exposed. Of course, despite all of these levels of obfuscation, all you are really doing is making your assemblies more difficult to decrypt. If a hacker, competitor, or anyone else were determined enough and had a large amount of time on their hands, they could work out the various algorithms you have used to hide this code. *Obfuscation* is essentially "security by obscurity." If you have areas of your application that you really would not be happy about being decompiled and understood, you should consider hosting that logic on the server to reduce the likelihood further of this falling into the wrong hands. This could be code that is exposed via a Web Service or sockets, or it could be dynamically generated XAML.

If you have used obfuscation tools in the past, you probably know that there is a "Community Edition" of the Dotfuscator tool included with Visual Studio. Unfortunately, in the Visual Studio .NET 2008 RTM release, this version does not offer support for Silverlight assemblies. The first version of Dotfuscator that allows this is v4.1.

Cryptography

When it comes to working with the cryptography classes, you will again find that you are working with a subset in Silverlight. They are still located in the familiar namespace of `System.Security.Cryptography`, and `System.Security.Cryptography.X509Certificates`, however. The latter namespace allows you to import, export, and read in a certificate from a file, which you can then use to extract information from it.

The former namespace provides a number of functions such as being able to generate a random number, to generate hashes off data (using the `SHA1Managed` and `SHA256Managed` classes), and to encrypt data (using the `AesManaged` class).

The `AesManaged` class is the only symmetric encryption class you are provided with in Silverlight. A symmetric encryption algorithm is one whereby the key used to *encrypt* the data is the same as that which is used to *decrypt* the data. This can work well when being used between your server and Silverlight client application, as it allows for you to store any encrypted data in the isolated storage area of the client if required. The important point to realize here, however, is the safety of the public key. In other words, you should keep this separate from the encrypted data. One suggestion here is that you use some input that the user knows about, such as a passkey, such that the user can unlock the data that belongs to them as and when required.

Although this is a drastically cut-down library over the fully fledged version in the desktop .NET framework, it does provide you with some fundamental building blocks to ensure that your data is not tampered with as it is sent over the wire between the server and the client.

Summary

This chapter has taken the security surrounding a Silverlight application and sliced it up into some fairly chunky topics. These topics by and large are probably not new to you, but the way in which you tackle them might be. What you have seen discussed is the attacks likely to be made against your application, and how there are certain measures tackled within the Silverlight framework. Once you move past this foundational level of security, you are into the custom aspect of securing your application from an authentication and authorization point of view. Once these security blocks are in place, you need to secure the data that is passed to the client — perhaps a subtly different way of thinking in the world of Rich Internet Applications.

Although you have been guided through all the major pillars of security in a Silverlight application, the most important rule of all is to code securely from day one and not as an afterthought.

13

Audio and Video

Perhaps one of the most compelling features of Silverlight is its ability to allow you to easily embed high-fidelity audio and video within your ASP.NET application. With the prevalence of broadband Internet access, most users have come to expect rich content such as this, with audio and video used for advertising, previewing, entertaining, and even training end-users.

This chapter will show you how to work with audio and video by dissecting the `MediaElement` object and explaining how to explicitly control playback of your chosen media. Details of all the supported formats will be given in conjunction with a brief tutorial on the use of Microsoft Expression Encoder. As well as using the `MediaElement` control from directly within your Silverlight application, the ASP.NET Media Server Control will also be demonstrated, negating the need for you to write a Silverlight application if you simply want to embed media in your ASP.NET web site.

On a more advanced note, providing synchronization points within your media will be shown before taking a look at streaming content in Silverlight and how you can leverage the Microsoft Silverlight Streaming service to easily deliver and scale media within your ASP.NET application.

First Steps

The next few sections will show you how to embed audio and video in your ASP.NET applications using the Silverlight `MediaElement` control. The supported formats are listed, and the properties required for loading and playing your chosen media are shown and discussed. Following this, the methods and properties used to take finer control of your media are walked through.

Embedding Audio and Video in Your ASP.NET Application

The delivery of different types of media within your ASP.NET application is provisioned through the `MediaElement` object. In the simplest terms, this object provides you with the ability to specify a media file via a URI and either display it in a rectangular region within the Silverlight UI (in the case of video) or simply play and control the playback without a visual representation (in the case of audio). As well as using the `MediaElement` object within Silverlight, later in the chapter, you will see the use of the Media Server Control provided within the ASP.NET 3.5 Futures download.

Supported Formats

Before diving into the `MediaElement` object and its usage, a quick note regarding the supported media formats. A variety of audio and video formats are catered to, as listed below:

❑ Audio formats

   ❑ **WMA 7** — Windows Media Audio 7

   ❑ **WMA 8** — Windows Media Audio 8

   ❑ **WMA 9** — Windows Media Audio 9

   ❑ **WMA 10** — Windows Media Audio 10

   ❑ **MP3** — MPEG-1 Audio Layer 3

❑ Video formats

   ❑ **WMV1** — Windows Media Video 7

   ❑ **WMV2** — Windows Media Video 8

   ❑ **WMV3** — Windows Media Video 9

   ❑ **WMVA** — Windows Media Video Advanced Profile, Non-VC-1

   ❑ **WMVC1** — Windows Media Video Advanced Profile, VC-1

As well as the above selection, `MediaElement` also supports Windows Media Metafiles (Advanced Stream Redirector files, ASX). An ASX file is nothing more than an XML file that contains a list of Windows Media files to play. It's a playlist if you like.

Silverlight doesn't support certain ASX features, though. For the full list, please consult the MSDN documentation.

MediaElement

`MediaElement` derives from `FrameworkElement`, which, in turn, derives from `UIElement`. These two classes provide derived controls with their layout abilities, including input (keyboard, mouse, and stylus) and focusing characteristics as well as sizing information via `Width` and `Height` properties.

Of course, as well as the standard input, visual and layout abilities, `MediaElement` adds a host of properties, methods, and events that are used to select and control media within your application, the starting point of which is `Source`.

Source

By default, the Source property is set to null but expects an argument of type String, which should be set to a valid URI.

> The Source property expects a string to be in the URI (Uniform Resource Identifier) format. This means that it must use characters within the US-ASCII set. Internationalized Resource Identifiers (IRIs), on the other hand, were introduced to allow developers and users to specify resource locations in their own languages using the Universal Character Set (Unicode). Even though IRI strings are functionally supported, they are not part of the US-ASCII set. The upshot of this is that if you want to use characters in your URI that are not within US-ASCII, you will need to encode them explicitly.

So, to select and play media, you need first to instantiate a MediaElement object and then set its Source property to a URI defining the location of your media file. The following XAML shows how to do this:

```
<UserControl x:Class="Chapter13.Page"
    xmlns="http://schemas.microsoft.com/winfx/2006/xaml/presentation"
    xmlns:x="http://schemas.microsoft.com/winfx/2006/xaml"
    Width="400" Height="300">

    <Canvas x:Name="LayoutRoot" >
        <MediaElement x:Name="MyMedia"
                      Canvas.Left="100"
                      Canvas.Top="100"
                      Source="/Assets/Butterfly.wmv">

        </MediaElement>
    </Canvas>

</UserControl>
```

As you can see, the MediaElement object is instantiated and an x:Name provided in case you want to access it from code. It's positioned 100 pixels from the top and 100 pixels from the left of the Canvas, and the Source is set to locate Butterfly.wmv in the Assets folder within the ClientBin directory. As shown above, relative URIs can be used within the Source property, in which case, the starting location will be relative to the .xap file currently loaded.

> As well as relative URIs, you can also access media cross-domain by using the http: moniker, content from Microsoft Media Server using the mms: moniker and content over Real Time Streaming Protocol using the rtsp: and rtspt: monikers.

If you compile and run this code, you should see the video automatically begin to play in your browser window as in Figure 13-1.

Figure 13-1

AutoPlay

By default, the media specified in the `Source` property will automatically begin to play. This is because the Boolean `AutoPlay` property of `MediaElement` defaults to `True`. Simply set this to `False` if you would like to control directly when the media should begin to play back, as shown in the Controlling Playback section further on in this chapter.

```
<MediaElement x:Name="MyMedia"
              Canvas.Left="100"
              Canvas.Top="100"
              Source="/Assets/Butterfly.wmv"
              AutoPlay="False">

</MediaElement>
```

Position

Whenever you set the `Source` property, `MediaElement` re-sets its `Position` property to `00:00:00`. This property expects a `TimeSpan` value that denotes the amount of time from the very start of the media referenced by `Source` to begin playback from. Be aware, however, that if the media you are referencing does not support seeking — for instance, if it is streaming — setting this property will have no effect at all.

You can check to see if the media you are playing supports seeking by checking the Boolean property `CanSeek`. This will return `True` if the media supports seeking and `False` if not. Until the media has actually been loaded, however, it's impossible to tell what the value of `CanSeek` will be, and so you should listen for the `MediaOpened` event and then check the value there.

This implies that setting the `Position` property in XAML isn't really the right thing to do, as you have no way of knowing at this point whether setting this value will have any effect. Instead, the `Position` property should be used from the code behind once the media has been opened and tested for seeking ability.

The following XAML and code show the handling of the `MediaOpened` event and determining if the media supports seeking. If it does, the media's position is set to 5 seconds from the start. The media is then instructed to play either way.

```xml
<UserControl x:Class="Chapter13.Page"
    xmlns="http://schemas.microsoft.com/winfx/2006/xaml/presentation"
    xmlns:x="http://schemas.microsoft.com/winfx/2006/xaml"
    Width="400" Height="300">

    <Canvas x:Name="LayoutRoot" >

        <MediaElement x:Name="MyMedia"
                    Canvas.Left="100"
                    Canvas.Top="100"
                    Source="/Assets/Butterfly.wmv"
                    MediaOpened="MyMedia_MediaOpened"
                    AutoPlay="False">

        </MediaElement>

    </Canvas>

</UserControl>
```

Note the wiring up of the `MediaOpened` event in the above XAML. The code below shows the `CanSeek` property being tested in the `MediaOpened` event, where the value it returns can be relied on. If it is seekable, a `TimeSpan` value is assigned to the `Position` property to set the media to be 5 seconds. The media is then played.

```csharp
using System;
using System.Collections.Generic;
using System.Linq;
using System.Net;
using System.Windows;
using System.Windows.Controls;
using System.Windows.Documents;
using System.Windows.Input;
using System.Windows.Media;
using System.Windows.Media.Animation;
using System.Windows.Shapes;

namespace Chapter13
{
    public partial class Page : UserControl
    {
        public Page()
        {
```

```
                InitializeComponent();
        }

        private void MyMedia_MediaOpened(object sender, RoutedEventArgs e)
        {
            //If seekable, set position
            if (MyMedia.CanSeek)
            {
                MyMedia.Position = new TimeSpan(0, 0, 5);
            }
            //Either way, instruct the media to being playing
            MyMedia.Play();
        }
    }
}
```

NaturalDuration

But what if you don't know how long the media in question is? MediaElement takes care of this requirement by providing the NaturalDuration property. This property returns a type of Duration, the contents of which can be TimeSpan, Automatic, or Forever.

Prior to the MediaOpened event firing, the NaturalDuration property will be set to its default value of Automatic. This value will remain Automatic if the media opened is live streaming or has no known duration. In this case, the media will simply continue to play until it is finished.

The following code shows how this can be used to write the duration of the media to a TextBlock:

```
private void MyMedia_MediaOpened(object sender, RoutedEventArgs e)
{
    //If seekable, set position
    if (MyMedia.CanSeek)
    {
        MyMedia.Position = new TimeSpan(0, 0, 5);
    }

    Duration duration = MyMedia.NaturalDuration;
    //If the duration can be ascertained
    if (duration != Duration.Automatic)
    {
        TimeSpan ts = duration.TimeSpan;
        MediaInfo.Text = ts.ToString();
    }
    else
    {
        MediaInfo.Text = "Cannot ascertain duration";
    }

    //Either way, instruct the media to being playing
    MyMedia.Play();
}
```

Height and Width

Although it is possible to set the inherited `Height` and `Width` properties on the `MediaElement` object, you should refrain from doing so for performance reasons. The fastest way to display media is to have it displayed at its natural size, which is the size it was originally encoded to display at. If this size is not desirable, you should consider re-encoding the media to the size required, using a tool such as the Expression Media Encoder.

Once the `MediaOpened` event has fired, you can access the values held within the `NaturalVideoHeight` and `NaturalVideoWidth` properties, which each contains a `double` value specifying the video's natural render resolution, as shown in the following example:

```
private void MyMedia_MediaOpened(object sender, RoutedEventArgs e)
{
    double naturalHeight = MyMedia.NaturalVideoHeight;
    double naturalWidth = MyMedia.NaturalVideoWidth;

    MediaInfo.Text = String.Format("Height: {0}, Width: {1}",
        naturalHeight,
        naturalWidth);

    MyMedia.Play();
}
```

If you run this code, you will see Figure 13-2.

Figure 13-2

Volume

In order to control the volume at which the media plays, you can set the Volume property of the Media Element object. This property expects a value of type double and can be set to a value between 0 and 1, where 0 is quietest and 1 is loudest. The default value for this property is 0.5.

Keep in mind, however, that a value of 0.5 might not equate to the same true volume across different media files. This is because each media file is recorded with its own baseline volume setting. It's important to test your application and set the desired volume appropriately for each media file, or make sure that you encode all of your media files with the same baseline volume.

You can also opt to switch the volume on or off completely by setting the IsMuted property to False or True, respectively.

Finally, you can use the Balance property of the MediaElement object to alter the volume between the left and right speakers. This property requires a value of type double between –1 and 1, where –1 is full volume on the left speaker and 1 is full volume on the right speaker. The default value is 0 which means that the volume will be the same from each speaker.

The following example shows the usage of these properties in a basic example that uses Slider objects to control the overall volume and the balance between the speakers:

```
<UserControl x:Class="Chapter13.VolumeControlExample"
    xmlns="http://schemas.microsoft.com/winfx/2006/xaml/presentation"
    xmlns:x="http://schemas.microsoft.com/winfx/2006/xaml"
    Width="400" Height="300">

    <Grid x:Name="LayoutRoot" Background="White">

        <Grid.ColumnDefinitions>
            <ColumnDefinition Width="*" />
            <ColumnDefinition Width="5*"/>
        </Grid.ColumnDefinitions>

        <Grid.RowDefinitions>
            <RowDefinition Height="*" />
            <RowDefinition Height="*" />
            <RowDefinition Height="8*"/>
        </Grid.RowDefinitions>

        <TextBlock Text="Volume"
                Grid.Row="0"
                Grid.Column="0" />

        <Slider x:Name="VolumeSlider"
                Grid.Row="0"
                Grid.Column="1"
                Orientation="Horizontal"
                Minimum="0"
```

```
                        Maximum="1"
                        Width="200"
                        SmallChange="0.1"
                        LargeChange="0.2"
                        ValueChanged="VolumeSlider_ValueChanged"/>

            <TextBlock Text="Balance"
                        Grid.Row="1"
                        Grid.Column="0" />

            <Slider x:Name="BalanceSlider"
                        Grid.Row="1"
                        Grid.Column="1"
                        Orientation="Horizontal"
                        Minimum="-1"
                        Maximum="1"
                        Width="200"
                        SmallChange="0.1"
                        LargeChange="0.2"
                        ValueChanged="BalanceSlider_ValueChanged"
                        Value="0"/>

            <MediaElement x:Name="MyMedia"
                        Canvas.Left="100"
                        Canvas.Top="100"
                        Source="/Assets/Butterfly.wmv"
                        AutoPlay="True"
                        Grid.Row="2"
                        IsMuted="False"
                        Volume="0"
                        Grid.ColumnSpan="2"
                        Balance="0"/>
        </Grid>

</UserControl>
```

The code behind is now listed. The two handlers for each Slider control take care of altering the values of the Volume and Balance properties using the NewValue provided by each slider.

```
using System;
using System.Collections.Generic;
using System.Linq;
using System.Net;
using System.Windows;
using System.Windows.Controls;
using System.Windows.Documents;
using System.Windows.Input;
using System.Windows.Media;
using System.Windows.Media.Animation;
using System.Windows.Shapes;
```

```
namespace Chapter13
{
    public partial class VolumeControlExample : UserControl
    {
        public VolumeControlExample()
        {
            InitializeComponent();
        }

        private void VolumeSlider_ValueChanged(object sender,
                                    RoutedPropertyChangedEventArgs<double> e)
        {
            MyMedia.Volume = e.NewValue;
        }

        private void BalanceSlider_ValueChanged(object sender,
                                    RoutedPropertyChangedEventArgs<double> e)
        {
            MyMedia.Balance = e.NewValue;
        }
    }
}
```

Figure 13-3 shows the UI including the two new Slider controls. Try changing the values of both to hear the effect.

Figure 13-3

Finer Control

It's unlikely that having your media files simply burst into life at the very beginning and play through to the end is going to be desirable in all scenarios. `MediaElement` provides you with fine-grained control over the playback of your media files via a selection of properties and events.

Controlling Playback

As you'd expect, playback of your media can be controlled using the universal `Play`, `Pause`, and `Stop` commands.

Play

The `Play` command will cause the media specified in `Source` to start playing if it hasn't done so already, or to resume playing if the media is in a paused state. If the media is playing when this command is called, no action will occur.

This method is void and accepts no arguments:

```
MyMedia.Play();
```

Pause

Nothing too taxing here. As you'd guess from the name, issuing the `Pause` command causes the media that is currently playing to enter a paused state, from which `Play` can be used to then continue. `MediaElement` also provides the `CanPause` property, which will return `False` for live streaming media. If you issue the `Pause` command on media that has a `CanPause` property of `False`, the command will effectively be ignored.

`Pause` is void and accepts no arguments, and `CanPause` accepts no arguments and returns a Boolean value:

```
MyMedia.Pause();
bool CanPause();
```

Stop

The `Stop` command causes the media that is currently playing to stop. If the media is in a paused or playing state when the `Stop` command is issued, the `Position` is set back to the beginning. Issuing the `Stop` command on media that is already stopped is simply ignored and will have no effect.

This method is void and accepts no arguments:

```
MyMedia.Stop();
```

Putting It All Together

You'll now step through a basic example that demonstrates the usage of these playback commands. This example will use a few custom shapes to denote the Play, Pause, and Stop functionality.

The following XAML shows how you could lay out this functionality in Silverlight and is available in the Chapter 13 source code within the ControlPlayback.xaml file.

```
<UserControl x:Class="Chapter13.ControlPlayback"
    xmlns="http://schemas.microsoft.com/winfx/2006/xaml/presentation"
    xmlns:x="http://schemas.microsoft.com/winfx/2006/xaml"
    Width="640" Height="480">

    <Canvas x:Name="LayoutRoot">

        <!-- Media Navigation Commands -->
        <!-- STOP -->
        <Canvas MouseLeftButtonDown="NavButtonPressed"
                MouseLeftButtonUp="StopPlayback"
                Canvas.Left="10"
                Canvas.Top="10">

            <Rectangle Stroke="Black"
                       StrokeThickness="3"
                       Height="30"
                       Width="30"
                       Fill="Red" />

        </Canvas>

        <!-- PAUSE -->
        <Canvas MouseLeftButtonDown="NavButtonPressed"
                MouseLeftButtonUp="PausePlayback"
                Canvas.Left="100"
                Canvas.Top="10">

            <Rectangle Stroke="Black"
                       StrokeThickness="3"
                       Height="30"
                       Width="10"
                       Fill="Orange"
                       Canvas.Left="0" />

            <Rectangle Stroke="Black"
                       StrokeThickness="3"
                       Height="30"
                       Width="10"
                       Fill="Orange"
                       Canvas.Left="10" />

        </Canvas>
```

```xml
            <!-- PLAY -->
            <Canvas MouseLeftButtonDown="NavButtonPressed"
                    MouseLeftButtonUp="PlayPlayback"
                    Canvas.Left="190"
                    Canvas.Top="10">

                <Polygon Points="0 0, 30 15, 0 30"
                         Fill="Green"
                         Stroke="Black"
                         StrokeThickness="3" />

            </Canvas>

            <TextBlock TextAlignment="Right"
                       Canvas.Left="240"
                       Canvas.Top="10"
                       x:Name="MediaDuration">
            </TextBlock>

            <!-- Our Media Object -->
            <MediaElement x:Name="MyMedia"
                          Source="/Assets/Butterfly.wmv"
                          AutoPlay="False"
                          MediaOpened="MyMedia_MediaOpened"
                          Canvas.Left="10"
                          Canvas.Top="100">

            </MediaElement>

        </Canvas>

    </UserControl>
```

The main layout control in use is the `Canvas`, and as such, the constituent parts of the basic media player are absolutely positioned on it. The media navigation icons appear first. We've chosen to wrap each of these in their own `Canvas` and then simply draw them within this child `Canvas` using a `Rectangle` object for the stop icon, two `Rectangle` objects to represent the pause icon, and a `Polygon` to draw the play button.

The `MouseLeftButtonDown` and `MouseLeftButtonUp` events are handled at the child `Canvas` level and take care of calling the generic `NavButtonPressed` method and the command-specific `[command]Playback` methods, respectively, an explanation of which appears following the source code listing below.

```csharp
using System;
using System.Collections.Generic;
using System.Linq;
using System.Net;
using System.Windows;
using System.Windows.Controls;
using System.Windows.Documents;
using System.Windows.Input;
```

```csharp
using System.Windows.Media;
using System.Windows.Media.Animation;
using System.Windows.Shapes;

namespace Chapter13
{
    public partial class ControlPlayback : UserControl
    {
        public ControlPlayback()
        {
            try
            {
                // Required to initialize variables
                InitializeComponent();
            }
            catch (Exception ex)
            {
                string errorMessage = ex.Message;
                //appropriate error handling in here : )
            }
        }

        //Media is loaded and information (if any) should now be available
        private void MyMedia_MediaOpened(object sender, RoutedEventArgs e)
        {
            TimeSpan ts = MyMedia.NaturalDuration.TimeSpan;

            MediaDuration.Text = String.Format("{0} - {1}:{2}:{3}",
                    "Media Duration",
                    ts.Hours.ToString().PadLeft(2, '0'),
                    ts.Minutes.ToString().PadLeft(2, '0'),
                    ts.Seconds.ToString().PadLeft(2, '0')
                );

            ts = MyMedia.Position;
        }

        private void StopPlayback(object sender, MouseButtonEventArgs e)
        {
            MyMedia.Stop();
            this.NavButtonReleased(sender, e);
        }

        private void PausePlayback(object sender, MouseButtonEventArgs e)
        {
            MyMedia.Pause();
            this.NavButtonReleased(sender, e);
        }

        private void PlayPlayback(object sender, MouseButtonEventArgs e)
```

```
        {
            MyMedia.Play();
            this.NavButtonReleased(sender, e);
        }

        private void NavButtonPressed(object sender, MouseButtonEventArgs e)
        {
            foreach (UIElement element in ((Canvas)sender).Children)
            {
                Shape shape = element as Shape;
                if (shape != null)
                {
                    shape.Stroke = new SolidColorBrush(Colors.Gray);
                }
            }
        }

        private void NavButtonReleased(object sender, MouseButtonEventArgs e)
        {
            foreach (UIElement element in ((Canvas)sender).Children)
            {
                Shape shape = element as Shape;
                if (shape != null)
                {
                    shape.Stroke = new SolidColorBrush(Colors.Black);
                }
            }
        }

    }
}
```

The first method of note is MyMedia_MediaOpened, which will occur when the media has been loaded. At this point, certain information about the media in question should be available. For this example, you'll note that the NaturalDuration is queried and formatted for display.

There are then three event handlers that are fired directly from the navigation icons in the display: StopPlayback, PausePlayback, and PlayPlayback. Each of these handlers begins by calling the relevant command against MediaElement, Stop(), Pause(), and Play(), respectively. They then call the generic NavButtonReleased method, passing the event parameters through.

Basically, to make the icons look like they've been clicked, the code in NavButtonPressed (fired from MouseLeftButtonDown) alters their Stroke property to Colors.Gray. When the button is released, both the media command and the NavButtonReleased generic method are called. This method simply sets the Stroke back to the original color of Colors.Black. This provides a very rudimentary highlighting mechanism for the custom icons.

Figure 13-4 shows this most basic of media players in action.

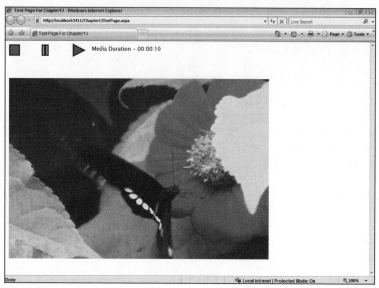

Figure 13-4

Stretch

MediaElement also provides a Stretch property, the value of which dictates how and if the video being loaded will be stretched to fit the MediaElement object itself. This property is of type System.Windows .Media.Stretch and is an enumerated type that holds the following values:

- ❑ None — The video will not be stretched to fill the MediaElement.

- ❑ Uniform — The video will be stretched uniformly until one side reaches the MediaElement border. The video will stay in proportion.

- ❑ UniformToFill — The video will be stretched uniformly to fill the MediaElement completely, and as such, some clipping may occur.

- ❑ Fill — The video will be stretched potentially non-uniformly until the MediaElement is filled. The video may appear out of proportion.

The Chapter 13 source code contains a XAML file called *StretchExample*. This is intended to show the effect that each of these settings has by simultaneously displaying the video in four separate MediaElement objects. The MediaElement has been set to a different width and height ratio than the video itself to better demonstrate this.

The XAML below demonstrates the layout for this page:

```
<UserControl x:Class="Chapter13.StretchExample"
    xmlns="http://schemas.microsoft.com/winfx/2006/xaml/presentation"
    xmlns:x="http://schemas.microsoft.com/winfx/2006/xaml"
```

```
                Width="400" Height="300">

        <Canvas x:Name="LayoutRoot"
                Background="Gray">

            <!-- Stretch.None -->
            <MediaElement x:Name="MediaStretchNone"
                          Canvas.Left="0"
                          Canvas.Top="10"
                          Width="300"
                          Height="150"
                          Source="/Assets/Butterfly.wmv"
                          Stretch="None" />
            <!-- End Stretch.None -->

            <!-- Stretch.Uniform -->
            <MediaElement x:Name="MediaStretchUniform"
                          Canvas.Left="350"
                          Canvas.Top="10"
                          Width="300"
                          Height="150"
                          Source="/Assets/Butterfly.wmv"
                          Stretch="Uniform" />
            <!-- End Stretch.Uniform -->

            <!-- Stretch.UniformToFill -->
            <MediaElement x:Name="MediaStretchUniformToFill"
                          Canvas.Left="0"
                          Canvas.Top="200"
                          Width="300"
                          Height="150"
                          Source="/Assets/Butterfly.wmv"
                          Stretch="UniformToFill" />
            <!-- End Stretch.UniformToFill -->

            <!-- Stretch.Fill -->
            <MediaElement x:Name="MediaStretchFill"
                          Canvas.Left="350"
                          Canvas.Top="200"
                          Width="300"
                          Height="150"
                          Source="/Assets/Butterfly.wmv"
                          Stretch="Fill" />
            <!-- End Stretch.Fill -->

        </Canvas>

    </UserControl>
```

This results in the display shown in Figure 13-5.

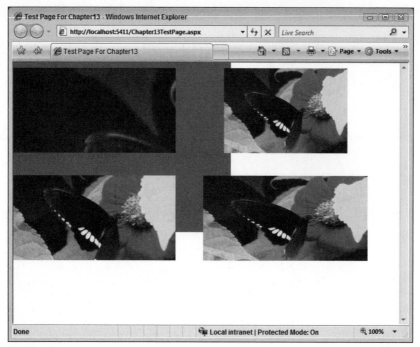

Figure 13-5

Inherited Properties

It's worth keeping in mind also that as mentioned earlier in this chapter, MediaElement itself derives from UIElement, and as such has all of the properties you would expect of such a child object. For example, you're free to apply settings to alter the Opacity of your MediaElement.

```
<UserControl x:Class="Chapter13.AlterProperties"
    xmlns="http://schemas.microsoft.com/winfx/2006/xaml/presentation"
    xmlns:x="http://schemas.microsoft.com/winfx/2006/xaml"
    Width="400" Height="300">

    <Canvas x:Name="LayoutRoot" >

        <MediaElement x:Name="MyMedia"
                    Canvas.Left="10"
                    Canvas.Top="10"
                    Source="/Assets/Butterfly.wmv"
                    Opacity="0.3" />

    </Canvas>

</UserControl>
```

The Opacity property accepts a value of type double between 0.0 and 1.0, where 0 is fully transparent and 1 is fully opaque.

Figure 13-6 shows how a value of 0.3 affects the video display.

Figure 13-6

And you don't have to settle for a rectangular display for your video. Using the `Clip` property provided by `UIElement`, you can define a region outside of which the content will be clipped. Consider the following example:

```xml
<UserControl x:Class="Chapter13.ButterflyClip"
    xmlns="http://schemas.microsoft.com/winfx/2006/xaml/presentation"
    xmlns:x="http://schemas.microsoft.com/winfx/2006/xaml">

    <Grid x:Name="LayoutRoot" Background="White">

        <MediaElement x:Name="MediaClipButterfly"
                    Canvas.Left="10"
                    Canvas.Top="10"
                    Source="/Assets/Butterfly.wmv">

            <MediaElement.Clip>
                <EllipseGeometry Center="200,200" RadiusX="200" RadiusY="200" />
            </MediaElement.Clip>
        </MediaElement>
```

```
        </Grid>

    </UserControl>
```

In XAML, the `MediaElement.Clip` property is set to an `EllipseGeometry` object that defines an `Elipse` whose center is at 200, 200 and whose radius in both directions is 200 — therefore a circle.

Figure 13-7 shows the resulting output.

Figure 13-7

Controlling Playback from ASP.NET

If you wanted to control the `MediaElement` object from the containing page, you could, of course, use the ability discussed in Chapter 4, whereby a client script can access correctly decorated types and members within your Silverlight application. This will work fine.

However, embedding media into your ASP.NET page is a common requirement, especially with the prevalence of broadband Internet access. Because of this, there is an ASP.NET server control that takes care of utilizing the Silverlight `MediaElement` for you and embedding the plug-in. This is the ASP.NET Media Control, and all you need to do is add this control to your ASP.NET page.

This control is shipped as part of the ASP.NET Futures download, freely downloadable from the Microsoft site.

ASP.NET Media Server Control

The beauty of this control is that it allows you to embed your audio and video files directly into your web page without requiring any knowledge whatsoever of either client-side JavaScript or, indeed, XAML/Silverlight. The control then takes care of generating all of the Silverlight markup and code behind required to get your media running.

The control also supports skinning as well as allowing the inclusion of Chapters, Markers, and Captions.

Once you have installed the ASP.NET Futures toolkit, opt to create a new project, and in the web project templates, you should see the ASP.NET AJAX Futures Web Application available for selection, as shown in Figure 13-8.

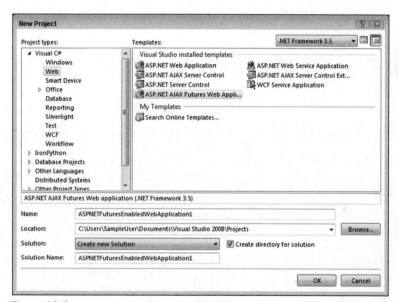

Figure 13-8

Once you have created this project, you're free to use the ASP.NET Media Control within your page, as shown in the following HTML:

```
<%@ Page Language="C#" AutoEventWireup="true"
        CodeBehind="Default.aspx.cs"
        Inherits="TestMediaControl._Default" %>

<!DOCTYPE html PUBLIC "-//W3C//DTD XHTML 1.0 Transitional//EN"
"http://www.w3.org/TR/xhtml1/DTD/xhtml11-transitional.dtd">

<html xmlns="http://www.w3.org/1999/xhtml" >
<head runat="server">
```

```
    <title>Untitled Page</title>
</head>
<body>
    <form id="form1" runat="server">
        <asp:ScriptManager ID="ScriptManager1" runat="server" />
    <div>
        <asp:Media ID="MyMedia"
                    MediaUrl="~/Bear.wmv"
                    runat="server"
                    Width="100%"
                    Height="100%" />
    </div>
    </form>
</body>
</html>
```

Notice how no Silverlight project is needed and you haven't needed to touch XAML at all. This is all taken care of by the Media Control. Figure 13-9 shows the media player in action — it looks a little better than the one you created earlier, you'll agree!

Figure 13-9

Timeline Markers

Timeline markers allow you to associate multiple specific points in a media file with any 'useful' information. They are typically used as a form of synchronization mechanism, for instance, to enable seeking through the media to a specific point, or even to allow you to synchronize the media with other items at set times (advertising being a good example — a car chase in a movie could signal via a timeline marker that it's time to show the BMW advert on the right-hand side).

You could also use timeline markers to allow you to show the right portion of a transcript below a training movie or such.

You get the idea.

Timeline markers are created and stored in the media itself. Microsoft provides both the Windows Media File Editor (which comes with Windows Media Encoder 9 installation) and Microsoft Expression Encoder. Before looking at the consumption of these markers within your Silverlight application, you'll first see both the Windows Media File Editor and Expression Encoder used to add timeline markers to a media file.

Windows Media File Editor

This handy tool comes with the Windows Media Encoder 9 installation package and allows you to open and edit media files that end with the .wmv, .wma, and .asf file extensions. When you run the application, you will be presented with the screen shown in Figure 13-10.

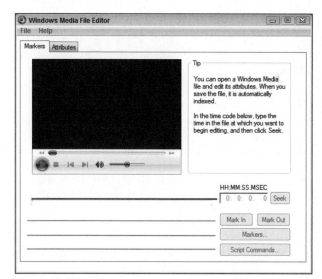

Figure 13-10

The file you're going to see opened and edited in this example is, like the Butterfly.wmv that you've seen thus far, installed along with Windows Vista and is called *Bear.wmv*. Once the file is opened in

Windows Media File Editor, the Markers button becomes enabled. Clicking this button opens the Markers dialog, which allows you to create arbitrary markers at set points in the media file. Figure 13-11 shows this process.

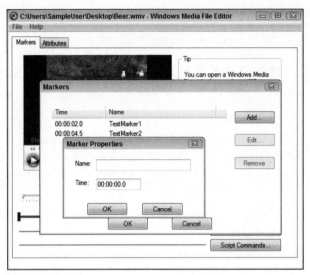

Figure 13-11

As you can see, as well as listing the created markers with their string data and time, the timeline alongside the Markers button also shows the points where your created markers are positioned. The edited version of this file was saved as *BearWithMarkers.wmv* and placed into the Assets directory in the Chapter 13 source code.

Expression Encoder

Expression Encoder gives you the ability to easily get your video project Web-enabled and is especially suited for taking full advantage of the rich graphic and interactive capability within Silverlight playback scenarios. You can even generate content that is suitable for playback on a Zune.

As well as creating media files, you can also create live multimedia sessions that can be streamed from a workstation, or from a Windows Media Server. This example will simply add markers to a media file and encode it.

Expression Encoder uses jobs to allow you to create your work. You create a new job, which is effectively a session, import your videos, make changes and add markers, encode and output.

Figure 13-12 shows the UI after Bear.wmv is imported into a new job.

As you can see from the rich UI, there are a host of features available. However, since this book is not intended to be a tutorial for Expression Encoder, we won't go over them here.

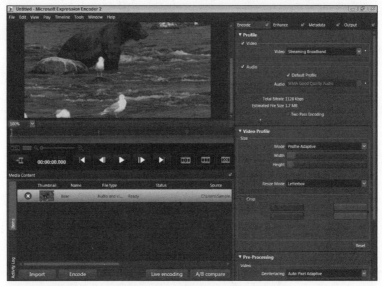

Figure 13-12

In order to work with markers, you can either select Timeline — Add Marker from the menu bar or select the Metadata tab in the top right and use the Marker panel beneath. Figure 13-13 shows the UI after importing another video and adding two markers to Bear.wmv.

Figure 13-13

Once you have added your markers (and presumably made any other changes required), you can choose to encode the new media. Figure 13-14 shows the encoding panel during this operation.

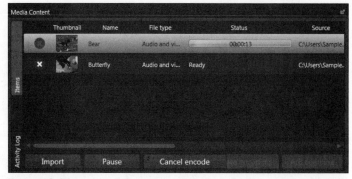

Figure 13-14

The newly encoded files will be output according to the output panel options, shown in Figure 13-15.

Figure 13-15

Timeline Markers via Code

The code to demonstrate the use of timeline markers in your Silverlight application is listed here, but feel free to download and peruse it at your leisure. The file in question is TimelineMarkers.xaml in the Chapter 13 source code.

```
<UserControl x:Class="Chapter13.TimelineMarkers"
    xmlns="http://schemas.microsoft.com/winfx/2006/xaml/presentation"
    xmlns:x="http://schemas.microsoft.com/winfx/2006/xaml"
    Width="400" Height="300">

    <Canvas x:Name="LayoutRoot" >
```

```
              <MediaElement x:Name="MyMedia"
                            Canvas.Left="10"
                            Canvas.Top="70"
                            Source="/Assets/BearWithMarkers.wmv"
                            MarkerReached="MyMedia_MarkerReached">

        </MediaElement>

        <TextBlock x:Name="StatusText"
                   Canvas.Left="0"
                   Canvas.Top="0"
                   FontSize="10"/>
    </Canvas>

</UserControl>
```

The code above adds two controls to the root Canvas object, a MediaElement and a Textblock control. The MediaElement declaration includes the MarkerReached event being wired up to a handler called MyMedia_MarkerReached. This event will fire whenever a marker is encountered in the media file during playback.

The TextBlock is included so you can see the information returned by each marker. The following code shows how the MarkerReached event is handled to output marker information to the screen:

```
using System;
using System.Collections.Generic;
using System.Linq;
using System.Net;
using System.Windows;
using System.Windows.Controls;
using System.Windows.Documents;
using System.Windows.Input;
using System.Windows.Media;
using System.Windows.Media.Animation;
using System.Windows.Shapes;

namespace Chapter13
{
    public partial class TimelineMarkers : UserControl
    {
        public TimelineMarkers()
        {
            InitializeComponent();
        }

        private void MyMedia_MarkerReached(object sender,
                                           TimelineMarkerRoutedEventArgs e)
        {
            StatusText.Text += String.Format(
                " Time: {0}, Type: {1}, Text: {2}\n",
                e.Marker.Time.Seconds.ToString(),
                e.Marker.Type,
                e.Marker.Text);
        }
    }
}
```

The `MyMedia_MarkerReached` handler accepts two parameters, the usual sender object and a `Timeline MarkerEventArgs` parameter. This object contains a `Marker` object, which exposes the `Time`, `Type`, and `Text` properties for you to ascertain.

The code above simply extracts the appropriate values and lists them in the `TextBlock` as the media is played.

Figure 13-16 shows the result.

Figure 13-16

You also have direct programmatic access to the `Marker` property within `MediaElement`, which contains a collection of `TimelineMarker` objects. This collection contains all the markers that have been embedded within the media file, but it also allows you to dynamically add markers to the media file. The markers that you add in this way are transient only and will be removed whenever a different media file is loaded into the `MediaElement` object.

DynamicMarkers.xaml shows this technique. The XAML itself defines a `MediaElement` object and a `TextBlock` to output information to:

```
<UserControl x:Class="Chapter13.DynamicMarkers"
    xmlns="http://schemas.microsoft.com/winfx/2006/xaml/presentation"
    xmlns:x="http://schemas.microsoft.com/winfx/2006/xaml"
    Width="400" Height="300">

    <Canvas x:Name="LayoutRoot" >

        <MediaElement x:Name="MyMedia"
                    Canvas.Left="10"
                    Canvas.Top="70"
                    Source="/Assets/Bear.wmv"
```

```
                            MarkerReached="MyMedia_MarkerReached"
                            MediaOpened="MyMedia_MediaOpened">

        </MediaElement>

        <TextBlock x:Name="StatusText"
                   Canvas.Left="0"
                   Canvas.Top="0"
                   FontSize="10"/>
    </Canvas>

</UserControl>
```

The media file /Assets/Bear.wmv is clear of markers at this point. In the code behind, the MediaLoaded event is handled. The Markers collection of MediaElement is only considered valid once the MediaLoaded event has fired, and so the code to dynamically add new TimelineMarker objects to this collection is located within here.

```
using System;
using System.Collections.Generic;
using System.Linq;
using System.Net;
using System.Windows;
using System.Windows.Controls;
using System.Windows.Documents;
using System.Windows.Input;
using System.Windows.Media;
using System.Windows.Media.Animation;
using System.Windows.Shapes;

namespace Chapter13
{
    public partial class DynamicMarkers : UserControl
    {
        public DynamicMarkers()
        {
            InitializeComponent();
        }

        private void MyMedia_MarkerReached(object sender,
                                                TimelineMarkerRoutedEventArgs e)
        {
            StatusText.Text += String.Format(
                " Time: {0}, Type: {1}, Text: {2}\n",
                e.Marker.Time.Seconds.ToString(),
                e.Marker.Type,
                e.Marker.Text);
        }

        private void MyMedia_MediaOpened(object sender, RoutedEventArgs e)
        {
            TimelineMarker marker = new TimelineMarker();
            marker.Type = "Added Via Code";
            marker.Time = new TimeSpan(0, 0, 6);
```

```
                  marker.Text = "Hello, World!";

                  MyMedia.Markers.Add(marker);

                  TimelineMarker marker2 = new TimelineMarker();
                  marker2.Type = "Annotation";
                  marker2.Time = new TimeSpan(0, 0, 2);
                  marker2.Text = "Test annotation";

                  MyMedia.Markers.Add(marker2);
            }
        }
    }
```

Adding dynamic markers is as easy as instantiating a new `TimelineMarker` object and setting its `Type`, `Time`, and `Text` properties to values of your choice, before adding it to the `Markers` collection.

Figure 13-17 shows the result.

Figure 13-17

Timeline markers can also be used to allow the user or developer to immediately position the media file at a specific point, for example, skipping to Step 2 of a tutorial. The code to do this is as simple as setting the `MediaElement.Position` property to the `TimeSpan` value held in the appropriate `TimelineMarker` object:

```
MyMedia.Position = MyMedia.Markers[1].Time;
```

By iterating over the available markers and displaying them in a content list, users can move easily between the different points in a media file or even dynamically add their own markers at points of interest as they watch or listen.

MediaElement *Events*

MediaElement exposes several useful events for you to handle. You've already seen the MediaOpened and MarkerReached events many times in the examples thus far. Other events that you should be aware of are now discussed, followed by some sample code showing them in action.

CurrentStateChanged

This event fires whenever the CurrentState property of the MediaElement object changes. This property is of type MediaElementState, which is an enumerated type. Common states are listed below:

- ❑ MediaElementState.Buffering — Media is currently being loaded. If media was playing when this state is entered, the last frame is displayed.

- ❑ MediaElementState.Closed — The MediaElement does not have any media loaded and will simply display a transparent frame.

- ❑ MediaElementState.Opening — Media specified in the Source URI is being loaded. Any Play, Pause, and Stop commands are queued up and executed upon successful opening.

- ❑ MediaElementState.Paused — The Position property of MediaElement will not advance. If the media was playing, the last frame will continue to be displayed.

- ❑ MediaElementState.Playing — The Position property increases and the media is played.

- ❑ MediaElementState.Stopped — If the media is of type video, the first frame is displayed. The Position property is set to 0 and does not increase.

  This signature for this event is:

  ```
  void CurrentStateChanged(object sender, RoutedEventArgs e);
  ```

MediaEnded

This event is raised when the media that is currently playing ends.

```
void MediaEnded(object sender, RoutedEventArgs e);
```

MediaFailed

This event is raised when there is an error with the MediaElement Source. The signature includes a parameter of type ErrorEventArgs that allows you to ascertain the Type, Code, and Message relating to the error:

```
void MediaFailed(object sender, ErrorEventArgs e);
```

BufferingProgressChanged

This event will be fired more than once during a download, as a set amount of the media file has been buffered (value increase by 0.05 or more since the event was last raised):

```
void MyMedia_BufferingProgressChanged(object sender, RoutedEventArgs e)
```

DownloadProgressChanged

Like `BufferingProgressChanged`, this event is more than likely to occur repeatedly during a progressive download and will fire whenever the total downloaded content increases by 0.05 or more.

```
void MyMedia_DownloadProgressChanged(object sender, RoutedEventArgs e)
```

Simply wire these events up in your XAML markup (or in code if you really want to), and you're ready to roll.

```
<!-- Our Media Object -->
<MediaElement x:Name="MyMedia"
              Source="/Assets/Butterfly.wmv"
              AutoPlay="False"
              MediaOpened="MyMedia_MediaOpened"
              Canvas.Left="10"
              Canvas.Top="100"
              CurrentStateChanged="MyMedia_CurrentStateChanged"
              MediaEnded="MyMedia_MediaEnded"
              MediaFailed="MyMedia_MediaFailed">

</MediaElement>
```

The handlers below do nothing more than output information to a `TextBlock` when each of these errors occurs:

```
//Listen for the media current state changing and output state to textblock
private void MyMedia_CurrentStateChanged(object sender, RoutedEventArgs e)
{
    MediaElementState state = MyMedia.CurrentState;
    MediaState.Text = state.ToString();
}

private void MyMedia_MediaEnded(object sender, RoutedEventArgs e)
{
    MediaState.Text = "Media Ended";
}

private void MyMedia_MediaFailed(object sender, ErrorEventArgs e)
{
    MediaState.Text = String.Format("Error Code: {0}, Error Message: {1}, Error
      Type: {2}",
    e.ErrorCode.ToString(),
    e.ErrorMessage,
    e.ErrorType.ToString());
}
```

SetSource

So far you've always set the media file referenced by the `MediaElement` object via the `Source` property. The problem with this technique, though, comes if the media file is large in size (and face it, media files often are). When a Silverlight application loads, no XAML at all is displayed to the user until all the

XAML and associated assets have been downloaded. This means that the user can be waiting a long time with nothing showing should the XAML and assets be large in size, which does not make for a good user experience.

To overcome this issue, you can write your Silverlight application so that it doesn't link directly to the media file in question, but instead downloads the media asynchronously. The SetSource method of the MediaElement class accepts a Stream object, which you can provide by using the WebClient object to download the media file asynchronously. You might remember this code from Chapter 4, where it was used to download .xap files on demand. The following code shows how you can use the SetSource method and the WebClient class to download your media files without stalling the UI:

```csharp
using System;
using System.Collections.Generic;
using System.Linq;
using System.Net;
using System.Windows;
using System.Windows.Controls;
using System.Windows.Documents;
using System.Windows.Input;
using System.Windows.Media;
using System.Windows.Media.Animation;
using System.Windows.Shapes;

namespace Chapter13
{
    public partial class SetSourceExample : UserControl
    {
        public SetSourceExample()
        {
            InitializeComponent();
        }

        private void UserControl_Loaded(object sender,
            RoutedEventArgs e)
        {
            WebClient webClient = new WebClient();

            webClient.OpenReadCompleted +=
                new OpenReadCompletedEventHandler(webClient_OpenReadCompleted);

            webClient.OpenReadAsync(
                new Uri("Assets/Bear.wmv", UriKind.Relative)
                );
        }

        void webClient_OpenReadCompleted(object sender,
            OpenReadCompletedEventArgs e)
        {
            MyMedia.SetSource(e.Result);
            MyMedia.Play();
        }
    }
}
```

Streaming

The MediaElement control supports streaming of media files from a Windows Media Server. Streaming will be attempted first if the scheme in the URI is specified as mms (Microsoft Media Services). If the file cannot be streamed, then MediaElement will fall back to progressively downloading the media file. Conversely, if http or https is specified as the scheme, a progressive download is attempted first, followed by streaming.

Perhaps the easiest way of streaming media in your Silverlight application is to take advantage of the free companion service to Silverlight: Microsoft Silverlight Streaming by Windows Live.

The streaming service provides you with a platform to host and stream your media, and it can be accessed from either the administration web site or via a REST API. Unlimited streaming is available for free with advertising, or without advertising when coupled with a fee payment. Check out the site http://dev.live.com/silverlight/ for the latest pricing information and technical documentation explaining how the service can be utilized.

Summary

Thus concludes the audio and video chapter. At the start of this chapter, you learned about the key object in the Silverlight programming model that enables the display of high-quality media: the MediaElement object. You discovered how to control the different settings for both audio and video and the different formats that are supported within Silverlight.

As media files are likely to be large, by default referencing them via the Source property can cause a performance problem at the client, as the full XAML and media asset has to be brought down before anything can be displayed. You learned how to mitigate this by taking advantage of the SetSource property and improving the client user experience.

A common requirement within a media-enabled ASP.NET application is to be able to synchronize your chosen media with other UI events and objects — for instance, the timely display of advertising features while a movie is playing — or to synchronize a transcript with a training video. You saw how this can be accomplished by first creating timeline markers within your media, using both Microsoft Expression Encoder and the Windows Media File Editor. These markers, which effectively act as synchronization points, can then be easily consumed within your Silverlight application, and the appropriate action can be taken.

As the embedding of media within an ASP.NET application is a common scenario, you saw how the ASP.NET Media server control allows you to do just this, without writing a single line of either XAML or JavaScript.

You also saw how media can be streamed via mms as well as progressively downloaded, and you took a brief look at streaming by Windows Live, the companion service provided by Microsoft to enable you to deliver and host media-enabled Silverlight applications.

The next chapter, "Graphics and Animation," will show you how to create and use custom graphics to spice up your UI, as well as bring them to life by using animation.

14

Graphics and Animation

In Chapter 3, "XAML Condensed," you took your first look at drawing in Silverlight, albeit a basic one that covered the `Ellipse`, `Rectangle`, and `Line` objects. This chapter will begin by expanding on that material, taking you through the `Shape` base class and then going over the `Path`, `Polyline`, and `Polygon` objects used for drawing more complex shapes to screen.

As well as `Shape`-derived objects that are able to participate in layout and render themselves to screen, there are also `Geometry`-derived objects, able to describe various shapes but unable on their own to render and participate in layout. You'll look at their uses here.

Next up is an examination of `Brush` objects and how they're used to paint regions of the display, including how to use both images and even videos as a brush.

You'll then have a look at image handling in Silverlight, including the supported image types and how images can be asynchronously as well as synchronously downloaded. Advanced panning and zooming of images using `DeepZoom` is also covered here.

Finally, you'll move on to Silverlight's ability to animate your user interface and learn about the two main types of animation, "From/To/By" and "key frame." You'll look at the different properties that each of these animation types allows you to animate and the timing options available for each. You'll also see how you can create a per-frame callback mechanism in your animations, useful for games programming.

Breathing Life into ASP.NET

This first section is intended to help you position Silverlight and its capabilities against current technologies, as well as discuss some of the benefits that Silverlight can bring to your ASP.NET estate.

Before Silverlight

It would be naive to think that the Web was a boring, static place before Silverlight came along, because that's simply not the case. Prior to Silverlight, a variety of technologies could be used to provide high-impact graphics, animation, and rich content, most notably Flash and Java Applets.

Flash opened programming rich Web UIs up to the masses with its easier-than-most programming model and heavy focus on graphics and animation. Java Applets could provide the same thing, and then some. However, the learning curve for jumping straight into Java was seen by a lot of people as too much of a hurdle.

As well as these two technologies, graphics, media, and animation support on the Web could be provided by a little-used language called XHTML + SMIL.

SMIL (Synchronized Multimedia Integration Language) is an XML-based language that can be used to provide timing and animation as well as the embedding of multimedia content. XHTML + SMIL is the current W3C specification for including SMIL within HTML pages. Originally, Microsoft, Macromedia, and Compaq/DEC submitted a proposal to the W3C on integrating SMIL with HTML, which at that time was termed *HTML + TIME*. XHTML + SMIL built on this and added other features, and hence, XHTML + SMIL became the current standard for doing so.

For a detailed look at this technology, check out the W3C note at `www.w3.org/TR/XHTMLplusSMIL/`.

Silverlight-Enabled Graphics and Animation

Silverlight solves the problem of rich functionality coming at the price of a steep learning curve. As has already been mentioned, the separation of UI layout and procedural code via XAML and .NET code behind means that designers can quickly pick up the technology, either by hand or using the Expression suite of development tools. .NET developers (who are too numerous to count) can then be left with the task of writing any plumbing code that is required.

Silverlight can enable you to create "break the mold" UIs. Each one can be completely customized rather than relying on built-in controls/shapes to churn out another run-of-the-mill site or add-in. The complex two-dimensional (2D) graphics support that you're about to delve into allows you to easily render any shape possible to screen, without writing a single line of procedural code. And the full-featured animation API will then allow you to bring your content to life, easily moving multiple controls around the screen at precise time intervals while smoothly changing colors, for example.

In short, Silverlight will help you to easily breathe life into your existing ASP.NET sites by giving you integrated design time support, rich graphics and animation APIs, and ease of use by your designers.

Graphics in Silverlight

There comes a time in UI development when relying on the standard built-in controls simply won't suffice. Perhaps your design team would prefer input control to look like their corporate logo — you know the one, with the rounded edges and stuff. Or perhaps your image/video would look better if it fit inside this specially shaped container, rather than a plain old rectangle.

Whatever the reason, your needs are catered to in Silverlight, as the following sections will explain.

The Shape Class

The System.Windows.Shapes.Shape class acts as the base class for all six of the fundamental shape types in Silverlight — Ellipse, Rectangle, Line (discussed in Chapter 3), Polyline, Polygon, and Path. Shape inherits from FrameworkElement and therefore UIElement, and as such comes with the ability to receive input and focus and participate in layout — in short, it can render to screen.

Shape adds to the base class mix various properties, including the ability to be painted within, provided via its Fill property; the ability to be stretched in certain ways to fill its containing space, provided via the Stretch property; and the ability to specify how the shape's outline is rendered, provided via the Stroke and StrokeThickness properties. You'll see each of these in action as you learn about more of the derived shapes below and later in the section on painting with Brush objects.

Shape is an abstract class, which means that it cannot be instantiated in its own right. It has to be derived from in order to be used.

Polygon *Objects*

The Polygon class enables you to draw an enclosed shape comprised of multiple lines. You use the Points property to specify a series of Point objects that each defines the corner or connecting points of your Polygon shape to draw. Consider a simple example, that of drawing a triangle. To draw a triangle, three points need to be specified. The following XAML shows how to draw a triangle whose three points are specified as {50, 50}, {400, 200}, and {25, 200}. The triangle is red.

```
<UserControl x:Class="Chapter14.PolygonExample"
    xmlns="http://schemas.microsoft.com/winfx/2006/xaml/presentation"
    xmlns:x="http://schemas.microsoft.com/winfx/2006/xaml"
    Width="400" Height="300">

    <Grid x:Name="LayoutRoot" Background="White">

        <Polygon Points="50,50 400,200 25,200"
                Fill="Red" />

    </Grid>

</UserControl>
```

Note that the Points property allows for the convenient short-hand syntax shown above when written in XAML, that is, a comma between the X and Y values and then a space between the points themselves. This could have been specified more verbosely, of course.

And the same polygon can be described programmatically using code, although you'll agree that this is the more clunky option:

```
private void UserControl_Loaded(object sender, RoutedEventArgs e)
{
    Polygon polygon = new Polygon();
    polygon.Points.Add(new Point(50, 50));
```

```
polygon.Points.Add(new Point(400, 200));
polygon.Points.Add(new Point(25, 200));
polygon.Fill = new SolidColorBrush(Colors.Red);

LayoutRoot.Children.Add(polygon);
}
```

Both of these methods will result in the triangle shown in Figure 14-1 being drawn.

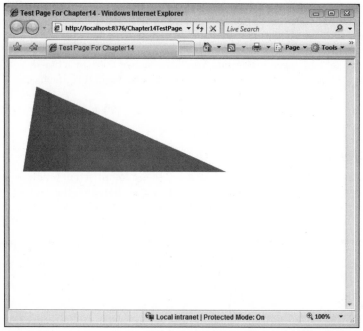

Figure 14-1

As odd as it may seem, `Polygon` actually allows you to specify only two points in the `Points` property:

```
<!-- Triangle -->
<Polygon Points="50,50 400,200 25, 200"
        Fill="Red" />

<!-- Only two points, so essentially a Line -->
<Polygon Points="25,300 400,300"
        StrokeThickness="5"
        Stroke="Blue" />
```

If you do this, however, be aware that you're essentially describing a line, and the `Line` object exists for this purpose. The line that you draw in this manner will only be rendered if a non-zero value is specified for the `StrokeThickness` property. The output will now be that shown in Figure 14-2.

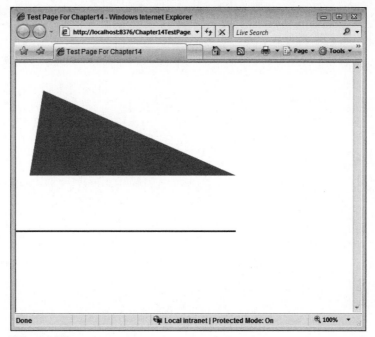

Figure 14-2

You can, if you choose, create a polygon with only one point specified. Be aware, however, that this polygon will not render. If, in fact, you want to render a small point on screen, you can use an `Ellipse` and size it appropriately.

Polyline *Objects*

Like the `Polygon` class, `Polyline` allows you to specify a series of points that will render as a series of connected lines. The key difference then between `Polygon` and `Polyline` is that in the case of `Polyline`, the lines do not ultimately have to join to form a closed shape.

Figure 14-3 shows the output of the following XAML:

```
<UserControl x:Class="Chapter14.PolylineExample"
    xmlns="http://schemas.microsoft.com/winfx/2006/xaml/presentation"
    xmlns:x="http://schemas.microsoft.com/winfx/2006/xaml"
    Width="400" Height="300">

    <Grid x:Name="LayoutRoot" Background="White">

        <Polyline Points="80,20 20,150 100,300"
                Stroke="Red" StrokeThickness="5" />

    </Grid>

</UserControl>
```

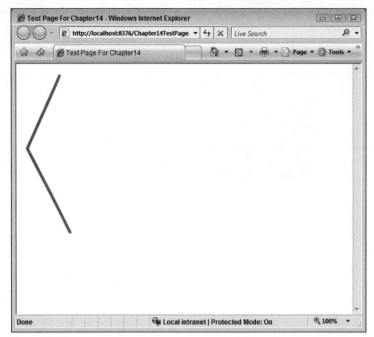

Figure 14-3

This `Polyline` has three `Point` objects specified. As you can see from Figure 14-3, the last and first points are not automatically joined to form a closed shape. Instead, it's left open. How does this affect the `Fill` property then? Can a closed shape only act on this value? Consider the following XAML:

```
<UserControl x:Class="Chapter14.PolylineExample"
    xmlns="http://schemas.microsoft.com/winfx/2006/xaml/presentation"
    xmlns:x="http://schemas.microsoft.com/winfx/2006/xaml"
    Width="400" Height="300">

    <Canvas x:Name="LayoutRoot"
            Background="White">

        <Polyline Points="80,20 20,150 100,300"
                Stroke="Red" StrokeThickness="5"
                Fill="Blue"
                Canvas.Left="0"
                Canvas.Top="0" />

        <Polyline Points="110,200 200,200 250,170 110,200"
                Stroke="Red" StrokeThickness="5"
                Fill="Blue"
                Canvas.Left="0"
                Canvas.Top="0" />

    </Canvas>

</UserControl>
```

Two shapes are specified, one that will form a closed shape as the first and last points match, and one that will not. Both have their `Fill` property set to the color blue. Figure 14-4 shows how Silverlight deals with this.

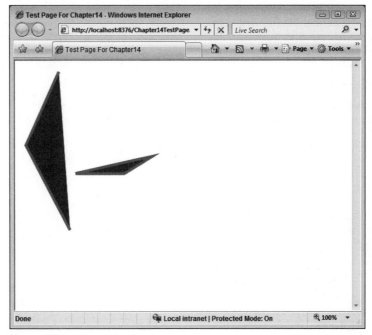

Figure 14-4

As you can see, both shapes honor the `Fill` property. In the case of the shape that doesn't close, an imaginary line is drawn between the last and first points where the `Fill` property should run up to.

As with the `Polygon`, you can create and specify a `Polyline` with only one point. However, this `Polyline` will not render.

Path *and* `Geometry` *Objects*

The `Path` class gives you the freedom to draw the most complex shapes of all, comprising not only a series of connected lines, but also curves, rendering either closed or open shapes.

In order to draw a shape using the `Path` object, a `Geometry` object is used to define the shape and is passed to the `Path` object's `Data` property. Much like `Shape` objects, `System.Windows.Media.Geometry` objects are used to describe two-dimensional (2D) shapes. The key difference between `Geometry` objects and `Shape` objects, however, is that `Shape` objects can render themselves to screen as they derive from `UIElement`, whereas `Geometry` objects cannot unless paired with a Path object. `Geometry` objects can only be used to describe a shape on their own. However, when coupled with a `Path` object, a `Geometry` object can be rendered to screen. `Geometry` objects are more lightweight than their fully fledged `Shape` counterparts and should be used whenever a `Shape` is needed but will potentially not be rendered. You will commonly see `Geometry` objects used to describe clip regions, for example. So, if you need programmatic access to shapes but don't need to display them, take advantage of the `Geometry` objects instead.

There are three types of basic `Geometry` object: RectangleGeometry, EllipseGeometry, and LineGeometry. For more complex shapes that are comprised of lines, curves, and arcs, `PathGeometry` is used. As well as this, the `GeometryGroup` object is provided, which allows you to compose a shape from multiple different geometries.

The following few sections take you very briefly through these objects to get you familiar with them and how they can be rendered. Importantly, though, `Geometry` objects can also be used for clipping items such as images, and thus are more versatile than `Shape` objects.

RectangleGeometry

As the name suggests, the `RectangleGeometry` object is used to describe a 2D rectangle. The following example shows how this object can be passed to `Path.Data` in order to render it to screen:

```xml
<UserControl x:Class="Chapter14.PathExample"
    xmlns="http://schemas.microsoft.com/winfx/2006/xaml/presentation"
    xmlns:x="http://schemas.microsoft.com/winfx/2006/xaml"
    Width="400" Height="300">

    <Grid x:Name="LayoutRoot" Background="White">

        <Path Fill="Blue">
            <Path.Data>
                <!-- Position is 100,50 height and width are both 200 -->
                <RectangleGeometry Rect="100, 50, 200, 200" />
            </Path.Data>
        </Path>

    </Grid>

</UserControl>
```

EllipseGeometry

The `EllipseGeometry` object is used to describe a 2D ellipse by assigning its center point and both the *X* and *Y* radii:

```xml
<UserControl x:Class="Chapter14.PathExample"
    xmlns="http://schemas.microsoft.com/winfx/2006/xaml/presentation"
    xmlns:x="http://schemas.microsoft.com/winfx/2006/xaml"
    Width="400" Height="300">

    <Grid x:Name="LayoutRoot" Background="White">

        <Path Fill="Blue">
            <Path.Data>
                <EllipseGeometry Center="100,100"
                                 RadiusX="40"
                                 RadiusY="80" />
            </Path.Data>
        </Path>

    </Grid>

</UserControl>
```

LineGeometry

The LineGeometry object is the simplest of the Geometry objects and describes a line:

```xml
<UserControl x:Class="Chapter14.PathExample"
    xmlns="http://schemas.microsoft.com/winfx/2006/xaml/presentation"
    xmlns:x="http://schemas.microsoft.com/winfx/2006/xaml"
    Width="400" Height="300">

    <Grid x:Name="LayoutRoot" Background="White">

        <Path Stroke="Blue"
            StrokeThickness="5">
            <Path.Data>
                <LineGeometry StartPoint="10,10"
                              EndPoint="200,200" />
            </Path.Data>
        </Path>

    </Grid>

</UserControl>
```

GeometryGroup

The GeometryGroup object is used to compose a shape from multiple different geometry objects:

```xml
<UserControl x:Class="Chapter14.PathExample"
    xmlns="http://schemas.microsoft.com/winfx/2006/xaml/presentation"
    xmlns:x="http://schemas.microsoft.com/winfx/2006/xaml"
    Width="400" Height="300">

    <Grid x:Name="LayoutRoot" Background="White">

        <Path Fill="Blue" Stroke="Yellow" StrokeThickness="2">
            <Path.Data>
                <GeometryGroup FillRule="EvenOdd">
                    <RectangleGeometry Rect="30, 30, 100, 50" />
                    <RectangleGeometry Rect="20, 20, 30, 80" />
                    <EllipseGeometry Center="60, 60"
                                     RadiusX="100"
                                     RadiusY="50" />
                    <LineGeometry StartPoint="0,0"
                                  EndPoint="100, 20" />
                </GeometryGroup>
            </Path.Data>
        </Path>

    </Grid>

</UserControl>
```

Figure 14-5 shows the output of this markup when the `FillRule` property of `GeometryGroup` is set to `EvenOdd`. Figure 14-6 shows the output when this property is set to `NonZero`.

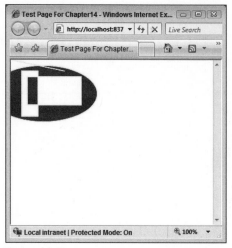

Figure 14-5

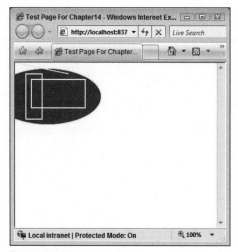

Figure 14-6

PathGeometry

`PathGeometry` allows you to use lines, arcs, and curves to describe a 2D shape and as such is used for creating the most complex shapes (open or closed). In order to create a `PathGeometry` object, you need to create a collection of `PathFigure` objects that `PathGeometry` will use. Each of these `PathFigure` objects is responsible for drawing a portion of the overall shape.

A `PathFigure` object, in turn, is made up of several `PathSegment` objects, which can be an `ArcSegment`, `BezierSegment`, `LineSegment`, `PolyBezierSegment`, `PolyLineSegment`, `PolyQuadraticBezier Segment`, or a `QuadraticBezierSegment`. Each of these is used for drawing different lines, arcs, and curves.

When drawing a shape using `PathGeometry`, the `PathSegment` objects within each `PathFigure` are connected to each other in sequence nose to tail.. The following code shows a `PathGeometry` comprised of two `PathFigure` objects. The first contains a simple `LineSegment` only; the second contains both an `ArcSegment` and a `BezierSegment`. Notice how the `BezierSegment` starts at the endpoint of the `ArcSegment` in Figure 14-7.

```xml
<UserControl x:Class="Chapter14.PathGeometryExample"
    xmlns="http://schemas.microsoft.com/winfx/2006/xaml/presentation"
    xmlns:x="http://schemas.microsoft.com/winfx/2006/xaml"
    Width="400" Height="300">

    <Grid x:Name="LayoutRoot" Background="White">

        <Path Stroke="Black" StrokeThickness="3">
            <Path.Data>
                <PathGeometry>
                    <PathGeometry.Figures>
                        <PathFigure StartPoint="0, 0">
                            <PathFigure.Segments>
                                <LineSegment Point="30, 100" />
                            </PathFigure.Segments>
                        </PathFigure>

                        <PathFigure StartPoint="30, 100">
                            <PathFigure.Segments>
                                <ArcSegment IsLargeArc="False"
                                            Size="175, 135"
                                            RotationAngle="45"
                                            SweepDirection="Counterclockwise"
                                            Point="200, 50"/>

                                <BezierSegment Point1="300, 50"
                                               Point2="250, 80"
                                               Point3="300, 60" />

                            </PathFigure.Segments>
                        </PathFigure>
                    </PathGeometry.Figures>
                </PathGeometry>
            </Path.Data>
        </Path>

    </Grid>

</UserControl>
```

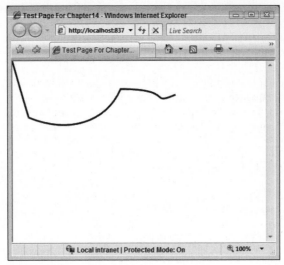

Figure 14-7

Painting with *Brush Objects*

If you're doing any custom drawing in Silverlight, you're more than likely going to need to "fill" your custom shapes with some kind of content, be it a simple solid color or perhaps something more advanced like a gradual color gradient. To enable this, Silverlight provides various Brush objects. All brushes in Silverlight inherit from the abstract Brush class, which is used to define an object that can paint regions of the screen. Silverlight ships with five main types of derived Brush implementation.

SolidColorBrush

The SolidColorBrush object can be thought of as the most basic of the Brush objects as it allows you to simply paint a region of the screen with a specific solid color. There is a plethora of ways to specify a solid color, both declaratively in XAML and in code. The following XAML shows the different techniques that can be used for specifying a solid color via the Fill property of a series of Rectangle objects. As you can probably guess, because there are many ways of providing this information to the single Fill property, TypeConverters are playing a key role in converting the values passed into Brush objects.

```xaml
<UserControl x:Class="Chapter14.PaintingWithBrushes"
    xmlns="http://schemas.microsoft.com/winfx/2006/xaml/presentation"
    xmlns:x="http://schemas.microsoft.com/winfx/2006/xaml"
    Width="400" Height="300">

    <Grid x:Name="LayoutRoot" Background="White">

        <StackPanel>

            <!-- Specify using set Brush Color -->
            <Rectangle Width="200"
```

```
                                    Height="40"
                                    Fill="DarkGreen" />

                    <!-- Specify using Red, Green and Blue hex values -->
                    <Rectangle Width="200"
                               Height="40"
                               Fill="#F0F" />

                    <!-- Specify using Alpha, Red Green and Blue hex values -->
                    <Rectangle Width="200"
                               Height="40"
                               Fill="#5F0F" />

                    <!-- Specify using Red, Green and Blue hex values
                         (2 digits per value)-->
                    <Rectangle Width="200"
                               Height="40"
                               Fill="#FF0712" />

                    <!-- Specify using Alpha, Red, Green and Blue
                         hex values (2 digits per value) -->
                    <Rectangle Width="200"
                               Height="40"
                               Fill="#FF00FF00" />

                    <!-- Specify Red, Green and Blue using scRGB format -->
                    <Rectangle Width="200"
                               Height="40"
                               Fill="sc#0.3, 0.8, 0.2" />

                    <!-- Specify Alpha,  Red, Green and Blue using scARGB format -->
                    <Rectangle Width="200"
                               Height="40"
                               Fill="sc#1.0, 0.3, 0.8, 0.2" />

        </StackPanel>

    </Grid>

</UserControl>
```

As you can see, at a high level, there are three common techniques for specifying color. First off, you can use the string name of one of the predefined colors, such as Red, Green, or DarkGreen as in the example. Next up you can specify the color using RGB hex values, with either one or two digits used for each red, green, or blue color component. You can also add an Alpha component to the front of your RGB values, which dictates the level of transparency in the color, with 0 being fully transparent. Finally, you can use scRGB syntax to specify a color, where each component is specified with a value between 0 and 1.

Take a look now at how a SolidColorBrush can be created in code. The following example uses SolidColorBrush to set both the Fill and Stroke property of a Rectangle object. For the Fill property, a color is specified using the Color.FromArgb static method, which allows you to provide the A, R, G, and B color components as byte parameters. The Stroke property, however, is set using one of the static `Colors.[ColorName]` properties. Both of these techniques return a `Color` object, which, in turn, is used by the `SolidColorBrush` when rendering to screen:

```
private void UserControl_Loaded(object sender, RoutedEventArgs e)
{
    Rectangle rectangle = new Rectangle();
    rectangle.Height = 40;
    rectangle.Width = 200;
    rectangle.StrokeThickness = 3;
    rectangle.Stroke = new SolidColorBrush(Colors.Black);
    rectangle.Fill = new SolidColorBrush(
        Color.FromArgb(0, 120, 120, 255));

    RectContainer.Children.Add(rectangle);
}
```

LinearGradientBrush

As well as the provision of painting with a single, solid color, you also have the option of painting an area with (*n*) different colors, each of which blends into the next as gradually or as suddenly as you dictate. `LinearGradientBrush` allows you to specify how multiple colors are blended into one another along a single straight axis, which runs from the top-left corner of the area being painted to the bottom-right corner of the area being painted by default. The different colors and their position along the gradient are specified using `GradientStop` objects. The following example shows how a `LinearGradientBrush` is used to paint a `Rectangle` object with a color blended smoothly from yellow to red along the default diagonal linear gradient axis:

```
<UserControl x:Class="Chapter14.LinearGradientBrushExample"
    xmlns="http://schemas.microsoft.com/winfx/2006/xaml/presentation"
    xmlns:x="http://schemas.microsoft.com/winfx/2006/xaml"
    Width="400" Height="300">

    <Grid x:Name="LayoutRoot" Background="White">

        <Rectangle Width="200" Height="200">
            <Rectangle.Fill>
                <LinearGradientBrush>
                    <GradientStopCollection>
                        <GradientStop Color="Yellow"
                                      Offset="0.5" />
                        <GradientStop Color="Red"
                                      Offset="1.0" />
                    </GradientStopCollection>
                </LinearGradientBrush>
            </Rectangle.Fill>
        </Rectangle>

    </Grid>

</UserControl>
```

Figure 14-8 shows the output of this XAML.

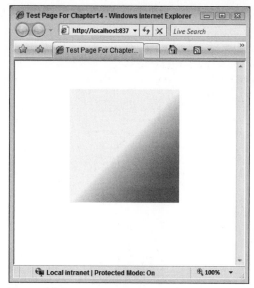

Figure 14-8

Notice how the colors are blended along the default axis. To reiterate, by default, this axis runs from the top-left of the area being painted — deemed point (0, 0) — to the bottom-right of the area being painted — deemed (1, 1) — see Figure 14-9.

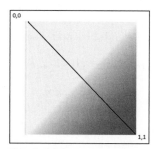

Figure 14-9

If you'd like to change the default axis, you can simply alter the StartPoint and EndPoint properties of the LinearGradientBrush in question. The following XAML shows how this axis has been altered to start at the top-right (1, 0) and run to the bottom-left (0, 1):

```
<Grid x:Name="LayoutRoot" Background="White">
    <Rectangle Width="200" Height="200">
        <Rectangle.Fill>
            <LinearGradientBrush StartPoint="1,0" EndPoint="0,1">
                <GradientStopCollection>
                    <GradientStop Color="Yellow"
```

```
                                        Offset="0.5" />
                        <GradientStop Color="Red"
                                        Offset="1.0" />
                    </GradientStopCollection>
                </LinearGradientBrush>
            </Rectangle.Fill>
        </Rectangle>
    </Grid>
```

Figure 14-10 shows the output and new axis.

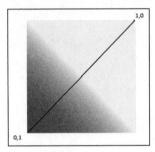

Figure 14-10

RadialGradientBrush

RadialGradientBrush allows you to specify how multiple colors are blended together using an ellipse as the axis, therefore specifying Offset 1.0 in a child GradientStop referring to the entire circumference of the axis. The default center (GradientOrigin) is set to (0.5, 0.5). The following example leaves the GradientOrigin unchanged and blends blue and green together:

```
<UserControl x:Class="Chapter14.RadialGradientBrushExample"
    xmlns="http://schemas.microsoft.com/winfx/2006/xaml/presentation"
    xmlns:x="http://schemas.microsoft.com/winfx/2006/xaml"
    Width="400" Height="300">

    <Grid x:Name="LayoutRoot" Background="White">

        <Rectangle Height="300"
                Width="300">

            <Rectangle.Fill>
                <RadialGradientBrush>
                    <GradientStopCollection>
                        <GradientStop Color="Blue" Offset="0.5" />
                        <GradientStop Color="Green" Offset="1.0" />
                    </GradientStopCollection>
                </RadialGradientBrush>
            </Rectangle.Fill>

        </Rectangle>
```

```
        </Grid>

    </UserControl>
```

Figure 14-11 shows the output.

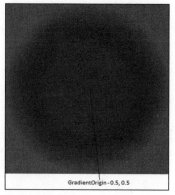

GradientOrigin - 0.5, 0.5

Figure 14-11

If you change the `GradientOrigin` to be (0.0, 0.0), you can see how the output changes to reflect this in Figure 14-12.

Figure 14-12

It can be useful to think of the `GradientOrigin` as representing the origin of a light source, as the colors will be spread out from this point along the ellipse specified.

ImageBrush

So you've seen how you can paint an area of the screen with either a solid single color or a color comprised of multiple colors that have been blended together along a specified axis. You can also use the `ImageBrush` class to enable you to paint an area with a specified image. This is a useful technique for painting a textured surface, perhaps the bricks in a wall, for example.

The following example shows how an image can be used to paint inside a rectangle. By default, the image will not be tiled and will be stretched to fill the entire area, although these can be changed by altering the `Stretch` and `TileMode` properties.

```xml
<UserControl x:Class="Chapter14.ImageBrushExample"
    xmlns="http://schemas.microsoft.com/winfx/2006/xaml/presentation"
    xmlns:x="http://schemas.microsoft.com/winfx/2006/xaml"
    Width="400" Height="300">

    <Grid x:Name="LayoutRoot" Background="White">

        <Rectangle Width="400"
                   Height="300"
                   Stroke="Yellow"
                   StrokeThickness="2">
            <Rectangle.Fill>
                <ImageBrush ImageSource="bricks.jpg" />
            </Rectangle.Fill>
        </Rectangle>

    </Grid>

</UserControl>
```

Figure 14-13 shows the output. Note that the image has been stretched to fill the rectangle border colored yellow in the image (when viewed on your screen).

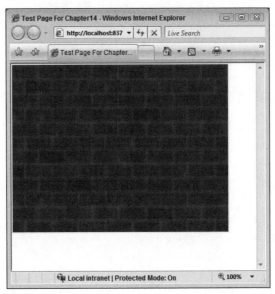

Figure 14-13

By altering the `Stretch` property to be `None`, the image will be painted once inside the rectangle at its native size, as shown in Figure 14-14.

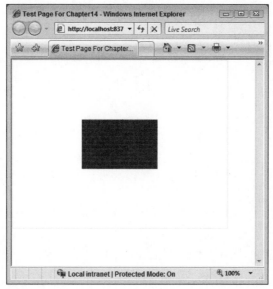

Figure 14-14

VideoBrush

You also have the option to paint a specified region of the screen with the contents of a video via the `VideoBrush` object. There are a couple of points you need to take into account when using this object. First and foremost, the `VideoBrush` works hand-in-hand with a `MediaElement` object. It's the `Media Element` object that takes care of loading and controlling the video that the `VideoBrush` will use to paint the specified area. You'll look at `MediaElement` in more detail in the next chapter. Secondly, unless you take action, both the `MediaElement` and the area being painted will simultaneously display the selected video. You'll see how to hide the `MediaElement` object in the example that follows:

```
<UserControl x:Class="Chapter14.VideoBrushExample"
    xmlns="http://schemas.microsoft.com/winfx/2006/xaml/presentation"
    xmlns:x="http://schemas.microsoft.com/winfx/2006/xaml"
    Width="400" Height="300">

    <Grid x:Name="LayoutRoot" Background="White">

        <!-- The MediaElement object to control t-->
        <MediaElement x:Name="BearVideo"
                    Source="Bear.wmv"
                    Opacity="0.0"
                    IsMuted="False" />
```

```xml
<StackPanel>
    <Path>
        <Path.Fill>
            <VideoBrush SourceName="BearVideo" Stretch="UniformToFill" />
        </Path.Fill>
        <Path.Data>
            <EllipseGeometry Center="100,100"
                             RadiusX="50"
                             RadiusY="50" />
        </Path.Data>
    </Path>

    <TextBlock Text="Silverlight Rocks"
               FontSize="30">
        <TextBlock.Foreground>
            <VideoBrush SourceName="BearVideo" Stretch="UniformToFill" />
        </TextBlock.Foreground>
    </TextBlock>
</StackPanel>

    </Grid>

</UserControl>
```

This XAML uses a `VideoBrush` in two different places — to paint the area described by an `Ellipse Geometry` and to paint the `Foreground` of a string of text. Remember that both are controlled ultimately by the `MediaElement` that they both use.

In order to prevent both the `MediaElement` from being displayed as well as the areas painted by the `VideoBrush` objects, its `Opacity` property is set to 0.0 to make it fully transparent. Figure 14-15 shows the application running with the `MediaElement.Opacity` changed to 0.5.

Figure 14-15

Transforms

Applying a Transform to an element allows you to alter its position and/or size within the coordinates defined by the UI. For example, you could rotate an object such as a Rectangle 90 degrees, scale up an element to twice its size, or simply move some text to the right.

Under the covers, transformations work by utilizing matrices to describe an object's position in 2D coordinates. By altering the individual values of an object's matrix, its position and size can be adjusted. Silverlight allows you to edit an object's transformation matrix manually using the MatrixTransform class. However, there are Transform-derived implementations that cover the most common scenarios, and you'll look at them in this section.

RotateTransform

Use the RotateTransform class to rotate an element by an angle you specify. The actual rotation point of the object defaults to the origin of its container (0, 0). If you want your object to rotate in place about its center or to rotate about an arbitrary point of your choosing, you can specify the CenterX and CenterY properties of RotateTransform to provide the new rotation point:

```xml
<UserControl x:Class="Chapter14.TransformsExample"
    xmlns="http://schemas.microsoft.com/winfx/2006/xaml/presentation"
    xmlns:x="http://schemas.microsoft.com/winfx/2006/xaml"
    Width="400" Height="300">

    <Grid x:Name="LayoutRoot" Background="White">

        <TextBlock Text="Silverlight Rocks">
            <TextBlock.RenderTransform>
                <RotateTransform Angle="45" />
            </TextBlock.RenderTransform>
        </TextBlock>

    </Grid>

</UserControl>
```

Notice in this XAML how the RotateTransform object is applied to the RenderTransform property of the TextBlock. If you were to apply this same transformation to a Geometry-based object, you would need to set it against the Transform property of the object, as Geometry-based objects do not support the RenderTransform property. Figure 14-16 shows the before-and-after state of the TextBlock being transformed.

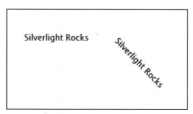

Figure 14-16

The following XAML shows a similar transformation being applied to a `RectangleGeometry` object that is being rendered via a `Path` object. Notice how the transformation is applied to the `Transform` property, rather than the `RenderTransform` property, which exists only on objects that inherit from `UIElement`.

```
<Path Grid.Row="1" Fill="Blue">
    <Path.Data>
        <RectangleGeometry Rect="0,0,100,30">
            <RectangleGeometry.Transform>
                <RotateTransform Angle="90" />
            </RectangleGeometry.Transform>
        </RectangleGeometry>
    </Path.Data>
</Path>
```

SkewTransform

`SkewTransform` allows you to stretch an object by a number of degrees around the specified axis. For example, you could stretch a `Rectangle` 45 degrees along the X-axis. The following XAML shows how a rectangle can be skewed about its X-axis and Y-axis negatively and positively:

```
<UserControl x:Class="Chapter14.TransformsExample"
    xmlns="http://schemas.microsoft.com/winfx/2006/xaml/presentation"
    xmlns:x="http://schemas.microsoft.com/winfx/2006/xaml"
    Width="400" Height="300">

    <Grid x:Name="LayoutRoot" Background="White">

        <Canvas Background="White" >

            <Rectangle Fill="Black"
                    Width="200"
                    Height="30"
                    Canvas.Top="50"
                    Canvas.Left="50">
            </Rectangle>

            <Rectangle Fill="Black"
                    Width="200"
                    Height="30"
                    Canvas.Top="150"
                    Canvas.Left="50">
                <Rectangle.RenderTransform>
                    <SkewTransform AngleX="25" />
                </Rectangle.RenderTransform>
            </Rectangle>

            <Rectangle Fill="Black"
                    Width="200"
                    Height="30"
                    Canvas.Top="250"
                    Canvas.Left="50">
                <Rectangle.RenderTransform>
                    <SkewTransform AngleY="25" />
                </Rectangle.RenderTransform>
```

```
            </Rectangle>

            <Rectangle Fill="Black"
                    Width="200"
                    Height="30"
                    Canvas.Top="350"
                    Canvas.Left="50">
                <Rectangle.RenderTransform>
                    <SkewTransform AngleY="-25" />
                </Rectangle.RenderTransform>
            </Rectangle>
        </Canvas>

    </Grid>

</UserControl>
```

Figure 14-17 illustrates the result.

Figure 14-17

ScaleTransform

Using the `ScaleTransform` object, you can scale an object up or down along both its X-axis and Y-axis. This implies that you can use this object not only to scale an object evenly up or down, but also to stretch it along its axis also, as the following XAML demonstrates:

```
<UserControl x:Class="Chapter14.ScaleTransformExample"
    xmlns="http://schemas.microsoft.com/winfx/2006/xaml/presentation"
    xmlns:x="http://schemas.microsoft.com/winfx/2006/xaml"
    Width="400" Height="300">

    <Canvas x:Name="LayoutRoot" Background="White">

        <TextBlock Text="Scale Me!"
                FontSize="25"
                Canvas.Left="50"
                Canvas.Top="50"/>
```

```xml
        <TextBlock Text="Scale Me!"
                FontSize="25"
                Canvas.Left="50"
                Canvas.Top="100">
            <TextBlock.RenderTransform>
                <ScaleTransform ScaleX="2" />
            </TextBlock.RenderTransform>
        </TextBlock>

        <TextBlock Text="Scale Me!"
                FontSize="25"
                Canvas.Left="50"
                Canvas.Top="150">
            <TextBlock.RenderTransform>
                <ScaleTransform ScaleY="2" />
            </TextBlock.RenderTransform>
        </TextBlock>

            <TextBlock Text="Scale Me!"
                FontSize="25"
                Canvas.Left="50"
                Canvas.Top="200">
            <TextBlock.RenderTransform>
                <ScaleTransform ScaleY="2" ScaleX="2" />
            </TextBlock.RenderTransform>
        </TextBlock>

    </Canvas>

</UserControl>
```

Figure 14-18 shows the output of the various transformations.

Figure 14-18

TranslateTransform

Using the `TranslateTransform` object, you can specify how far to move the element in question along both its *X*-axis and *Y*-axis:

```xml
<UserControl x:Class="Chapter14.TranslateTransformExample"
    xmlns="http://schemas.microsoft.com/winfx/2006/xaml/presentation"
    xmlns:x="http://schemas.microsoft.com/winfx/2006/xaml"
    Width="400" Height="300">

    <Canvas x:Name="LayoutRoot" Background="White">
        <Rectangle Width="100"
                Height="30"
                Canvas.Top="50"
                Canvas.Left="50"
                Fill="Black">

        </Rectangle>

        <Rectangle Width="100"
                Height="30"
                Canvas.Top="50"
                Canvas.Left="50"
                Fill="Black">
            <Rectangle.RenderTransform>
                <TranslateTransform X="150" Y="0" />
            </Rectangle.RenderTransform>
        </Rectangle>

        <Rectangle Width="100"
                Height="30"
                Canvas.Top="50"
                Canvas.Left="50"
                Fill="Black">
            <Rectangle.RenderTransform>
                <TranslateTransform X="150" Y="50" />
            </Rectangle.RenderTransform>
        </Rectangle>

    </Canvas>

</UserControl>
```

This XAML defines three `Rectangle` objects, each of which begins in the same place. The second and third, however, have a `TranslateTransform` applied, with the second moving along the *X*-axis by 150 pixels and the third moving along the *X*-axis by 150 pixels and the *Y*-axis by 50 pixels. Figure 14-19 illustrates the result.

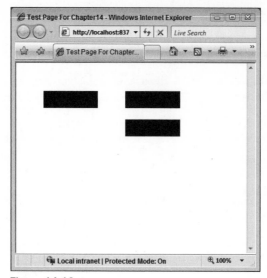

Figure 14-19

Image Handling

In order to display a standard image on screen in Silverlight, you have two main choices, one of which you have already seen in this chapter. You can elect to "paint" an area of the screen with an ImageBrush, or you can use the System.Windows.Control.Image class to specify and display your image. Generally speaking, if you just need to load and display an image in your UI, the Image class will do the job. If you want to use an image to paint within an existing element, to set the Background of your page, for example, then you will need to use the ImageBrush object, which can be used wherever an instance of a Brush is required.

There is a third option for image display within Silverlight also, a rather specialized option that allows you to load a high-resolution image and zoom and pan around it at will. This option involves a few steps to both create the files necessary and to program the panning and zooming, which you can look at in the MultiScaleImage and DeepZoom section further down.

Image *and* BitmapImage

Both Image and ImageBrush use an object of type ImageSource to specify which image to load, Image via its Source property and ImageBrush via its ImageSource property. When set in XAML, this can be passed in as a URI that is converted using a TypeConverter to an ImageSource object. In actual fact, ImageSource is an abstract class, and the type that is ultimately used is BitmapImage.

At present, `BitmapImage` only supports JPEG and PNG file formats.

```
<Grid x:Name="LayoutRoot" Background="White">
    <Image Source="bricks.jpg" />
</Grid>
```

The simplest way to load and display an image in your UI is to just drop the `Image` element on and specify the URI in the `Source` property. Under the covers, an instance of `BitmapSource` is used to attempt to load the image. If the image cannot be loaded, the `ImageFailed` event will be raised. If the `Height` and `Width` properties of the image are not specified, the image will be loaded at its native size.

As well as synchronously loading an image by setting the `Source` property directly, you can asynchronously download the image as a stream and then apply this to a `BitmapImage` object by using its `SetSource` method. If you have a large image that may take a little while to download, this technique will allow the UI to draw and remain responsive while the image file is loading.

The technique for loading the image resource on demand is the same as both loading an assembly on demand and loading media content on demand. First off, you use a `WebClient` object to locate and download the resource in question. The `OpenReadCompleted` and `DownloadProgressChanged` handlers can then be used to allow you to obtain the fully downloaded stream and to track the progress of the download, respectively. The following code demonstrates this technique:

```
using System;
using System.Collections.Generic;
using System.Linq;
using System.Net;
using System.Windows;
using System.Windows.Controls;
using System.Windows.Documents;
using System.Windows.Input;
using System.Windows.Media;
using System.Windows.Media.Animation;
using System.Windows.Shapes;
using System.Windows.Media.Imaging;

namespace Chapter14
{
    public partial class ImageExample : UserControl
    {
        public ImageExample()
        {
            InitializeComponent();
        }

        private void LoadAndDisplayImage()
        {
            System.Net.WebClient client = new System.Net.WebClient();
```

```
                    client.DownloadProgressChanged +=
                        new System.Net.DownloadProgressChangedEventHandler(
                            client_DownloadProgressChanged);

                    client.OpenReadCompleted +=
                        new System.Net.OpenReadCompletedEventHandler(
                            client_OpenReadCompleted);

                    client.OpenReadAsync(new Uri("bricks.jpg", UriKind.Relative));
                }

                void client_OpenReadCompleted(object sender,
                    System.Net.OpenReadCompletedEventArgs e)
                {
                    BitmapImage bmpImage = new BitmapImage();
                    bmpImage.SetSource(e.Result);

                    MyImage.Source = bmpImage;
                }

                void client_DownloadProgressChanged(object sender,
                    System.Net.DownloadProgressChangedEventArgs e)
                {
                    PercentageComplete.Text = e.ProgressPercentage.ToString();
                }

                private void UserControl_Loaded(object sender, RoutedEventArgs e)
                {
                    this.LoadAndDisplayImage();
                }
            }
        }
```

Notice how in the OpenReadCompleted handler a BitmapImage is instantiated and its SetSource method is called, passing in the Stream that is provided by the OpenReadCompletedEventArgs.Result property. The DownloadProgressChangedHandler shows how you can access the DownloadProgressChanged EventArgs.ProgressPercentage to track the progress of the download, perhaps to update a progress bar or similar if the download is sufficiently large to take some time.

Advanced Panning and Zooming with Deep Zoom

The basic premise behind Deep Zoom is this: Imagine that you have a large image file that you want to display in your Silverlight application, perhaps a map or a detailed graphic. Rather than sending the image to the browser in one operation, Deep Zoom allows you to send only the specific portion of the image that the user has elected to view or that would be visible on screen, saving time and bandwidth and improving performance. As well as this, Deep Zoom allows users to pan and zoom smoothly around the large image file in question. Is that cool or what?

To provide these abilities, Deep Zoom relies on the image file in question being split into several smaller tiles in a specific format and folder structure. It is these tiles that are sent to the user as they are needed, rather than the full image in question.

In order to help you create the correct tiles and file structure, the Expression team came up with the Deep Zoom Composer. To give you an overview of this tool and using Deep Zoom in Silverlight, an example is required.

To start with, you're going to need a test image and to have the Deep Zoom Composer installed. I've included a test image in the Chapter 14 source code called *aircraft.jpg*, but you're free to use one of your own. To install Deep Zoom Composer, simply download it for free from the Microsoft site.

Once installed, fire it up, and you will be presented with the opening screen shown in Figure 14-20.

Figure 14-20

Select "New Project," and enter an appropriate project name, as shown in Figure 14-21.

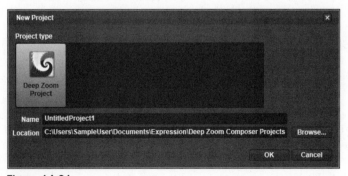

Figure 14-21

When working with the Deep Zoom Composer, there are three distinct steps that need to be followed to create the desired output — Import, Compose, and Export.

The Import tab will be selected by default at this stage, and there will be one option available, "Add Image." Select this option, and use the standard open file dialog to browse to an image of your choice. Figure 14-22 shows the Deep Zoom Composer with a single image imported and ready for use.

Figure 14-22

Now, if you have multiple different images to compose into a single Deep Zoom image, you would do this in the Compose tab. In this example, you're just going to use a single image, and so you can ignore this tab for now. Figure 14-23 shows the Compose workspace for your reference.

Finally, you have the Export tab and workspace, which allow you to specify various options for the export of the Deep Zoom image tiles, supporting directory structure and files. Figure 14-24 shows this workspace with the Name property set to AircraftExport and the option selected to have the composer create both the Deep Zoom files and a Silverlight project to view it in, using the `MultiScaleImage` control.

Once you have entered the relevant property values, simply click on the Export button, and Deep Zoom Compose will take care of the rest. The Chapter 14 source code contains a project called *aircraftexport*. Open this project, build and run it, and you will be presented with the image in question in all its glory. Try zooming in by clicking on the left mouse button, or zooming out by holding Shift while you click on the left mouse button. You can also use the mouse to drag and effectively pan around the image. Figure 14-25 shows the image zoomed in with a couple of clicks.

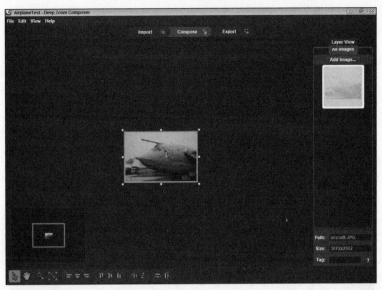

Figure 14-23

Figure 14-24

Figure 14-25

The following XAML shows the markup required to use a Deep Zoom Composer output. Note the `MultiScaleImage` control element.

```xml
<UserControl x:Class="DeepZoomProject.Page"
    xmlns="http://schemas.microsoft.com/winfx/2006/xaml/presentation"
    xmlns:x="http://schemas.microsoft.com/winfx/2006/xaml"
    Width="800" Height="600">
    <Grid x:Name="LayoutRoot" Background="White">
        <Border BorderBrush="#FF727272" BorderThickness="1,1,1,1">
                <MultiScaleImage Height="600" x:Name="msi" Width="800"/>
        </Border>
    </Grid>
</UserControl>
```

The code behind takes care of setting the actual image source (shown below) and also providing the sample code for zooming and panning around the image. If you're interested, take a look in the source file, copy and paste it, and use it in your own projects if required.

```
this.msi.Source = new DeepZoomImageTileSource(
new Uri("GeneratedImages/dzc_output.xml", UriKind.Relative));
```

Animating Your User Interface

Silverlight provides two main types of animation for you to utilize, "From/To/By" and the "key frame," both of which you'll look at in detail in the sections that follow. First off, though, it's worth pointing out that *all* animations in Silverlight, whether they are of type "From/To/By" or "key frame," ultimately derive from the `System.Windows.Media.Animation.Timeline` class.

Timeline

The `Timeline` class, as its name suggests, is used to represent a portion of time. The various properties provided by this class include the ability to specify the length of time the `Timeline` represents (`Duration`), the rate at which time should progress (`SpeedRatio`), whether the `Timeline` should repeat (`RepeatBehavior`), and what should happen when the animation ends (`FillBehavior`), among other things. `Timeline` also provides the `Completed` event, which will fire when the animation has completed.

`Timeline` is an abstract class and thus cannot be instantiated, so it is used solely to help build the animation classes provided within Silverlight.

From/To/By Animations

The first main category of animation is known as a *From/To/By* animation, and is named thus because you can use it to alter an object's property from one value to another over a period of time, such as an image's `Opacity`, for example. There are several different combinations of the `From`, `To`, and `By` properties that can be set to decide how the property value being animated changes, as shown in Table 14-1.

Table 14-1

Property Combination Set	Animation Behavior
`From` property only	The property being animated will move from the `From` value specified to whatever the default value of that property is. For instance, if you set the `From` property for the `Opacity` property to 0.0 and do not specify either `To` or `By` values, it will move from 0.0 to the default value, which is 1.0.
Both `From` and `To` properties set	The property value being animated will start at the `From` value and move to the `To` value over the `Duration` specified.
Both `From` and `By` properties set	The property value being animated will start at the `From` value and move to the sum of the `From` and `By` values over the set `Duration`. For example, if you set the `From` value to 0.1 and the `By` value to 0.2, the property value being animated will move from 0.1 to 0.3, the sum of these two values.
`To` property only	The property value being animated will move from its default value to the value specified in the `To` property.
`By` property only	The property value being animated will move from its default value to the sum of the default value and the `By` property.

Within this category of animation, the only properties that can be "animated" are those that are of the Color, Double, or Point type, and these are represented by the ColorAnimation, DoubleAnimation, and PointAnimation classes, respectively.

An example of this type of animation would be fading an image in or out of view by gradually changing its Opacity property from completely transparent to fully opaque over a set period of time.

StoryBoard

In order for an animation to be used, it needs to be contained within a StoryBoard object. This object provides two key areas of functionality to an animation — the ability to actually specify which object properties should be animated and the ability to control the animation's playback via Begin, Stop, Pause, and Resume methods. Two attached properties are provided by this class to control object/property targeting for From/To/By animations, TargetName and TargetProperty. A StoryBoard object cannot exist as content within a container control such as a Grid and instead has to be placed within the Resources section of the containing control ready for use.

DoubleAnimation

The following example shows how to use a DoubleAnimation and containing StoryBoard to gradually fade an Image control within a Silverlight page. A DoubleAnimation can be used to animate any property value that is of type Double.

```xml
<UserControl x:Class="Chapter14.AnimationExamples"
    xmlns="http://schemas.microsoft.com/winfx/2006/xaml/presentation"
    xmlns:x="http://schemas.microsoft.com/winfx/2006/xaml"
    Width="400" Height="300">

    <Grid x:Name="LayoutRoot" Background="White">

        <Grid.RowDefinitions>
            <RowDefinition />
            <RowDefinition />
        </Grid.RowDefinitions>

        <Grid.Resources>
            <Storyboard x:Name="FadeImageStoryboard">
                <DoubleAnimation From="1.0"
                                 To="0.0"
                                 Duration="0:0:5"
                                 RepeatBehavior="Forever"
                                 AutoReverse="True"
                                 Storyboard.TargetName="MyImage"
                                 Storyboard.TargetProperty="Opacity" />
            </Storyboard>
        </Grid.Resources>

        <Image x:Name="MyImage"
               Source="Desert Landscape.jpg"
               Grid.Row="0"/>
```

```
          <Button x:Name="StartAnimation"
                  Content="Start Animation"
                  Click="StartAnimation_Click"
                  Grid.Row="1"
                  Width="100"
                  Height="20" />

    </Grid>

</UserControl>
```

The first noteworthy item is the StoryBoard and DoubleAnimation defined within the Grid.Resources section of the page. The StoryBoard comprises a single DoubleAnimation (but it could contain many animations) that specifies an animation time of 5 seconds repeating indefinitely, altering the value of the MyImage.Opacity property from 1.0 to 0.0 each 5-second iteration. (MyImage is defined further down the XAML.) This will effectively fade the image out and then back into view indefinitely, courtesy of the AutoReverse property being set to True and the RepeatBehavior set to Forever.

Next, you can see the image object definition that is the target of the animation, followed by a Button object, which you use to kick-start the animation in its Click event handler:

```
private void StartAnimation_Click(object sender, RoutedEventArgs e)
{
    FadeImageStoryboard.Begin();
}
```

The net result of this is that when the button on the page is clicked, the image will fade in and out indefinitely, as illustrated by Figure 14-26.

Figure 14-26

PointAnimation

The PointAnimation class of animation allows you to animate any property that is of type Point, and it works in exactly the same way as DoubleAnimation. The following example uses this type of animation to alter the StartPoint of a LineGeometry object:

```xml
<UserControl x:Class="Chapter14.PointFromByToAnimation"
    xmlns="http://schemas.microsoft.com/winfx/2006/xaml/presentation"
    xmlns:x="http://schemas.microsoft.com/winfx/2006/xaml"
    Width="400" Height="300">

    <Canvas x:Name="LayoutRoot" Background="White">

        <Canvas.Resources>
            <Storyboard x:Name="PointAnimationExample">
                <PointAnimation From="50, 50"
                                To="300, 300"
                                Duration="00:00:05"
                                Storyboard.TargetName="TheLine"
                                Storyboard.TargetProperty="StartPoint" />
            </Storyboard>
        </Canvas.Resources>

        <Path Stroke="Black"
              StrokeThickness="3"
              Loaded="Path_Loaded">
            <Path.Data>
                <LineGeometry x:Name="TheLine"
                              StartPoint="50, 50"
                              EndPoint="50, 300" />
            </Path.Data>
        </Path>

    </Canvas>

</UserControl>
```

In this example, the animation is kicked off from the Loaded event of the LineGeometry object, rather than having the user click a button or other UI element.

ColorAnimation

The last of the built-in From/To/By animation types, ColorAnimation allows you to animate the Color property of an object. Again, this animation works in the same way as the previous two From/To/By animation types. The following example demonstrates the usage of a special syntax for targeting properties that haven't been explicitly named in XAML:

```xml
<UserControl x:Class="Chapter14.ColorFromToByAnimationExample"
    xmlns="http://schemas.microsoft.com/winfx/2006/xaml/presentation"
    xmlns:x="http://schemas.microsoft.com/winfx/2006/xaml"
    Width="400" Height="300">

    <Grid x:Name="LayoutRoot" Background="White">
```

```
        <Grid.Resources>
            <Storyboard x:Name="ColorAnimationStoryboard">
                <ColorAnimation From="Yellow"
                                To="Red"
                                Duration="00:00:05"
                                AutoReverse="True"
                                RepeatBehavior="Forever"
                                Storyboard.TargetName="MyRectangle"
    Storyboard.TargetProperty="(Rectangle.Fill).(SolidColorBrush.Color)" />
            </Storyboard>
        </Grid.Resources>
        <Rectangle x:Name="MyRectangle"
                   Width="300"
                   Height="200"
                   Fill="Yellow"
                   Loaded="MyRectangle_Loaded" />

    </Grid>

</UserControl>
```

The key point to look at is the value passed into the `Storyboard.TargetProperty` property. Notice how the syntax allows you to specify the `(object.property)` to animate followed by the `(type_to_use.property)`. In the above example, these are `(Rectangle.Fill)` and `(SolidColorBrush.Color)`, respectively. This is required in this instance because the `Fill` property has been set inline. If the `Fill` property had been set more verbosely, with a named `SolidColorBrush` specified, the standard syntax of setting the named object would have sufficed.

Multiple From/To/By Animations

It's perfectly acceptable for a Storyboard to contain multiple animation objects, each of which can run in parallel. The following example shows how multiple different animations have been applied to two separate `Ellipse` objects. The second `Ellipse` contains both a `TranslateTransform` and a `RotateTransform`, which have been animated also.

```
<UserControl x:Class="Chapter14.MultipleFromToByAnimationExample"
    xmlns="http://schemas.microsoft.com/winfx/2006/xaml/presentation"
    xmlns:x="http://schemas.microsoft.com/winfx/2006/xaml"
    Width="400" Height="300">

<Canvas x:Name="LayoutRoot"
        Background="White"
        Loaded="LayoutRoot_Loaded">

    <Canvas.Resources>
        <Storyboard x:Name="AnimationController">
            <PointAnimation From="100, 100"
                            To="100, 450"
                            Duration="00:00:02"
                            AutoReverse="True"
                            RepeatBehavior="Forever"
                            Storyboard.TargetName="Ball1"
                            Storyboard.TargetProperty="Center" />
```

```xml
            <ColorAnimation From="Red"
                            To="Yellow"
                            Duration="00:00:05"
                            AutoReverse="True"
                            RepeatBehavior="Forever"
                            Storyboard.TargetName="MyPath"

Storyboard.TargetProperty="(Path.Fill).(SolidColorBrush.Color)" />


            <DoubleAnimation From="0"
                             To="360"
                             Duration="00:00:03"
                             RepeatBehavior="Forever"
                             AutoReverse="True"
                             Storyboard.TargetName="Ball2Rotate"
                             Storyboard.TargetProperty="Angle" />

            <DoubleAnimation From="100"
                             To="300"
                             Duration="00:00:05"
                             AutoReverse="True"
                             RepeatBehavior="Forever"
                             Storyboard.TargetName="Ball2Translate"
                             Storyboard.TargetProperty="X" />

            <DoubleAnimation From="120"
                             To="200"
                             Duration="00:00:05"
                             AutoReverse="True"
                             RepeatBehavior="Forever"
                             Storyboard.TargetName="Ball2Translate"
                             Storyboard.TargetProperty="Y" />
        </Storyboard>
    </Canvas.Resources>

    <Path x:Name="MyPath"
          Fill="Red">
        <Path.Data>
            <GeometryGroup>
                <EllipseGeometry x:Name="Ball1"
                                 Center="100, 100"
                                 RadiusX="50"
                                 RadiusY="50" />
            </GeometryGroup>
        </Path.Data>
    </Path>

    <Ellipse x:Name="Ball2"
             Width="100"
             Height="30"
             Canvas.Top="120"
             Canvas.Left="100"
             Fill="Blue">
        <Ellipse.RenderTransform>
```

```
                    <TransformGroup>
                        <RotateTransform x:Name="Ball2Rotate" />
                        <TranslateTransform x:Name="Ball2Translate" />
                    </TransformGroup>
                </Ellipse.RenderTransform>
            </Ellipse>
        </Canvas>

    </UserControl>
```

The code begins by creating a `Storyboard` object within the `Canvas.Resources` section. Within this `Storyboard`, one color and three double animation types are specified, each of which acts on elements within the UI itself. These UI elements are then defined within the `Canvas`, and the whole thing is kicked off from the `LayoutRoot_Loaded` method in the code behind, as wired up from within the main `Canvas` element's Loaded event.

Key Frame Animations

Now that you're comfortable with From/To/By animations, it's time to turn your attention to the more advanced animation type: key frame animations. The big drawback with From/To/By type animations is that they only allow you to specify two values for your chosen property to move between. Key frame animations, however, allow you to specify (n) values that are stepped through in order to create the animation. This functionality allows you to create much more complex animations, as not only can you specify more steps for your property to transition between, but you can also control how each step is actually transitioned, whether it's smooth, abrupt, or a mixture of the two.

Key Frame Animation Types

There are four types of key frame animation that you can use in Silverlight.

❑   `ColorAnimationUsingKeyFrames` — Allows you to animate a specific `Color` property via a series of `KeyFrame` steps over a specified duration.

❑   `DoubleAnimationUsingKeyFrames` — Allows you to animate a specific `Double` property via a series of `KeyFrame` steps over a specified duration.

❑   `PointAnimationUsingKeyFrames` — Allows you to animate a specified `Point` property via a series of `KeyFrame` steps over a specified duration.

❑   `ObjectAnimationUsingKeyFrames` — Allows you to animate a property by changing the object that is applied to it via a series of `KeyFrame` steps, for example, swapping a `SolidColorBrush` for a `RadialGradientBrush`.

The `KeyFrames` Collection

Each `KeyFrame` animation contains a collection of objects that derive from either the `DoubleKeyFrame`, `PointKeyFrame`, `ColorKeyFrame`, or `ObjectKeyFrame` abstract classes. Which one they derive from depends, of course, on the type of `KeyFrame` animation they are going to exist within — `DoubleKeyFrame` within a `DoubleAnimationUsingKeyFrames` animation, for example.

To recap, a `KeyFrame` animation contains a collection of (n) `KeyFrame` objects, each of which derives from an abstract base class specific to the `KeyFrame` in use. Now, you also need to know that each of these `KeyFrame` objects (apart from `ObjectKeyFrame` — more on this shortly) can be one of three main subtypes — `Linear`, `Discrete`, or `Spline`. Which one you choose depends on how you want the `KeyFrame` objects to transition to one another. The nine different permutations for `Double`, `Point`, and `Color` `KeyFrame` types are shown below:

- ❑   `Linear[Double | Color | Point]KeyFrame`
- ❑   `Discrete[Double | Color | Point]KeyFrame`
- ❑   `Spline[Double | Color | Point]KeyFrame`

So which of the three key frame types would you use for each step of your animation? The difference between them is how the value they specify is transitioned to. For `Linear`, the value is transitioned to smoothly, in the same way as standard From/To/By animation transitions values. For `Discrete`, the transition is abrupt, moving from one value to the next instantly. For `Spline`, you get to specify how the transition occurs, incorporating acceleration, for example.

Therefore, if you want to smoothly transition the color of an object between yellow and blue, you use a `LinearColorKeyFrame`. If you then want to abruptly change the color to red, you add a `DiscreteColor KeyFrame`. Finally, if you want to start slowly changing the color to orange but then speed up toward the end of the transition, you achieve this by adding a `SplineColorKeyFrame`.

For `ObjectAnimationUsingKeyFrame` animations, only `DiscreteObjectKeyFrame` objects exist. It is too complex to implement either `Linear` or `Spline` interpolation on arbitrary objects.

Each key frame usually holds two values, `Value` and `KeyTime`. `KeyTime` is the time at which the transition should be complete, and `Value` is the new value to transition to. The `Spline`-based key frames have a third value, however: `KeySpline`. In order to understand this value's usage, you need to understand how cubic Bézier curves work. A full explanation is outside the scope of this book, but imagine drawing a line and then specifying two control points along that line that dictate how the line will be "pulled" into a curve. This is the essence of creating a Bézier curve. With the `KeySpline` property, you get to set two control points along a line that represents the time between the start and the end of the transition. In this way, you can affect the speed of the transition, as the rate of change against time alters in line with your "curve," providing more real-world acceleration or deceleration than a constant change.

More information on Bézier curves can be found at `http://en.wikipedia.org/wiki/B%C3%A9zier_curve`.

Color Animation Using Key Frame Example

The following XAML uses `Discrete`, `Linear`, and `Spline` interpolation to animate the color property of an `Ellipse`, moving gradually from yellow to blue, then abruptly from blue to red, before gradually moving back toward yellow, speeding up as it does so using a `Spline` key frame:

```
<UserControl x:Class="Chapter14.ColorKeyFrameAnimationExample"
    xmlns="http://schemas.microsoft.com/winfx/2006/xaml/presentation"
    xmlns:x="http://schemas.microsoft.com/winfx/2006/xaml"
    Width="400" Height="300">

    <Canvas x:Name="LayoutRoot"
            Background="White"
            Loaded="LayoutRoot_Loaded">
```

```
        <Canvas.Resources>
            <Storyboard x:Name="AnimationController">
                <ColorAnimationUsingKeyFrames BeginTime="00:00:00"
                                        Storyboard.TargetName="Ball"
    Storyboard.TargetProperty="(Shape.Fill).(SolidColorBrush.Color)">

                    <LinearColorKeyFrame Value="Blue"
                                    KeyTime="00:00:05" />

                    <DiscreteColorKeyFrame Value="Red"
                                    KeyTime="00:00:10" />

                    <SplineColorKeyFrame Value="Yellow"
                                    KeySpline="0.1,0.0   0.8,0.0"
                                    KeyTime="00:00:13" />

                </ColorAnimationUsingKeyFrames>

            </Storyboard>
        </Canvas.Resources>

        <Ellipse x:Name="Ball"
                Width="100"
                Height="100"
                Canvas.Left="200"
                Canvas.Top="200"
                Fill="Yellow"/>
    </Canvas>

</UserControl>
```

Per-Frame Animation Call Back

If you're using Silverlight to help you write online games or perform custom intensive animations, then it's likely that you're going to need to create a rendering or game loop. In Silverlight, the creation of a game loop is a relatively easy task, with the help of the CompositionTarget class.

CompositionTarget itself is used to represent the display surface on which your user interface is being rendered. It has one very useful event that you can hook up to, Rendering. This event fires whenever the user interface is rendering the items in the visual tree and thus can act as a good way of allowing you to perform actions on a per-frame or per-set time limit basis.

Simply wire up the CompositionTarget.Rendering event to an appropriate handler, and then extract the RenderingTime from the event arguments, as shown in the following code sample. In every frame, the code simply writes the current rendering time to a TextBlock.

```
using System;
using System.Collections.Generic;
using System.Linq;
using System.Net;
using System.Windows;
using System.Windows.Controls;
using System.Windows.Documents;
```

```
using System.Windows.Input;
using System.Windows.Media;
using System.Windows.Media.Animation;
using System.Windows.Shapes;

namespace Chapter14
{
    public partial class PerFrameCallback : UserControl
    {
        public PerFrameCallback()
        {
            InitializeComponent();
            CompositionTarget.Rendering +=
                        new EventHandler(CompositionTarget_Rendering);
        }

        void CompositionTarget_Rendering(object sender, EventArgs e)
        {
            TimeSpan renderingTime = ((RenderingEventArgs)e).RenderingTime;
            tbDisplay.Text = renderingTime.ToString();
        }
    }
}
```

Summary

And thus concludes the "Graphics and Animation" chapter.

In this chapter, you walked through the Graphics API provided by Silverlight, starting off by looking at the remaining Shape-derived objects not shown in Chapter 3 — Polygon, Polyline, and Path. You saw how a Path object requires a Geometry object in order to render itself to screen, and that Silverlight provides various Geometry-derived objects out-of-the-box, such as RectangleGeometry, EllipseGeometry, LineGeometry, and PathGeometry. These objects can also be grouped together in a GeometryGroup object to create more complex shapes.

You also learned that if your application needs to work with shapes but *not* necessarily to render them to screen, using the Geometry objects is a more lightweight approach for doing so.

Next up was a look at Brush objects and the different types that enabled you to paint either with a solid single color (SolidColorBrush) or transition through various colors, either along a line (Linear GradientBrush) or spreading out from a central point (RadialGradientBrush). You also saw how you could paint with both images and video, using the ImageBrush and VideoBrush objects, respectively.

Finally in this section, the advanced panning and zooming capabilities of DeepZoom were explained, including the utilization of the DeepZoom Composer to prepare your image content for use with this technology.

You then began an examination of the animation API, kicking off with a brief look at the `Timeline` and `Storyboard` objects before moving on to the simpler of the two types of animation — From/To/By. You saw how this animation type allows you to animate values of type `Double`, `Point`, and `Color` and also how animations can be controlled via their containing `Storyboard` object.

You then looked at key frame animation types, which allow you to create much more complex animations that move through (*n*) different steps via `Linear-`, `Discrete-`, or `Spline`-based transitions. You saw how, in addition to animating `Double`, `Point`, and `Color` types, key frame animations allow you to animate `Object` types, but only with `Discrete` transition types because of the inherent complexity of providing any other transition on an arbitrary type.

Finally, you saw how you can programmatically hook up to the rendering of each frame of your user interface by handling the `CompositionTarget.Rendering` event, which is useful for the creation of a game loop or other customer intensive drawing routines.

The next chapter, "Troubleshooting," will instruct you on how to find and fix the bugs that find their way into your application. Enjoy!

15

Troubleshooting

Whether you are learning a new technology or writing an application based on a technology you have been using for years, there comes the time when things just aren't working and you need to take a step back and do some troubleshooting. Things are no different with Silverlight, and because it is fundamentally a .NET technology, you are going to be able to get by in many cases using the skills you have today. If you are coming from an ASP.NET background, you may be in an even better position than the average .NET developer, as you have the same concept of data being transferred over the wire and you may in the past have had to take a look at this data.

This chapter covers a variety of tools that you will want to add to your toolbox. Of course, the first tool to be discussed will be Visual Studio, and the support it brings for debugging a Silverlight application. Aside from Visual Studio, though, there are lots of free tools for helping you dissect your application further and allowing you to see what your application is doing from a different perspective.

The multi-platform, multi-browser nature of Silverlight is great for the end-user, but it can introduce complications from a development and troubleshooting point of view — not least that you will need to test your application in a varying degree of environments. The good news is that from day one, there has been debugging support built into Silverlight for the multiple platforms it supports.

So, without further ado, it's time to look at these points in more detail and find out how you can get that broken application up and running again in as little time as possible.

This chapter is broken up into four main sections, each looking to answer four key questions:

❑ How do you know when there is a problem with your application?

❑ What classifications of problem are you likely to see?

❑ What tools are available to help you?

❑ What can you do to reduce potential problems?

The first two questions are really all about setting the scene, before the subsequent sections put some meat on the bones and show you how to tackle the types of issues raised.

Is There a Problem?

This question sounds as though it would have a pretty obvious answer, but there are several different types of problems that your application could face, and depending on what those problems are, they are not always apparent.

The most obvious type of problem is when an error manifests itself to the end-user via a Silverlight error dialog. These error messages are not always very obvious, but at least you know there is a problem to solve.

A much less apparent problem is when an exception occurs within your code, but it is getting swallowed up either by your own code or by the Silverlight run time. These problems can manifest themselves in various ways — perhaps the user is clicking a button and it's not doing anything, or the application is rendered incorrectly. A more concerning problem could be if the user understands an action to have been performed (say, calling out to a Web Service, or something considered critical like starting off a financial transaction), and it fails silently. This type of error leads you to think about two mitigating actions: (1) Ensure that your code has appropriate Error/Exception Handling, and (2) consider instrumenting your code to provide useful diagnostic information.

Another type of problem is if the end-user is complaining about the application not functioning in the expected way. If you read that sentence again, care has been deliberately taken to distinguish between a *problem* and an *error*. A problem for users could be that they are not using the application in the intended way (in which case, you might want to reconsider your UI design). However, perhaps they have tried to perform a certain action, and the application is genuinely doing something it shouldn't be. Well, first of all, if such problems are occurring after the application has been released and is in use by end-users, the application could prove quite timely and expensive to fix. One of the first questions you will be asking yourself and your user is the specific actions they carried out, so that you can reproduce the problem back at base. You have tested your application before release, so everything must work, right? Well, it is the dynamic nature of an application to have many code paths, which makes it virtually impossible to test all scenarios. One action that you can take to help mitigate against this type of problem is to introduce formal unit testing into your application. This will be discussed in the last section.

With your applications having this dynamism, it is not going to be possible to predict every sign of a problem, although the list above gives you some of the more common forms. It is also useful to consider some of the more common "types" of problems that you may encounter. These are discussed next.

Common Types of Problems

What has just been discussed is how different problems manifest themselves. What comes next is a discussion of the possible causes of these problems. For the most part, the problems you will encounter will be divided into the following categories:

- ❑ Design-time issues
- ❑ Compile-time issues
- ❑ Runtime issues

The first two types of problem are something a developer experiences on a fairly regular basis. These types of issues are going to be less expensive to fix, and you should have the intelligence of the Designer (such as Microsoft Expression Blend) or the Compiler (via Visual Studio) to give you some vital clues as to why the tools are failing to deal with your code and markup in some way.

The last type of issue is the wilder beast. If you are lucky, you will experience a problem within the first few clicks of your application, but more often the reproduction scenarios will be much more complex. In other words, certain actions have to be performed in a certain order, and the application has to be in a certain state for it to fail. What further complicates runtime issues is that they can be either:

- ❏ **Transient** — The problems can be short-lived. Maybe they don't happen all of the time. It could even be a one-off.

- ❏ **Nontransient** — This type of issue is repeatable. If you perform the exact same actions every time, you can be sure to hit the same problem.

Transient issues are by far the most difficult to troubleshoot. It may be that for one reason or another the application fails in a certain way just once. What is worse is if it fails more often, but not every time. This kind of issue is similar to nontransient issues that occur much less frequently in that both are difficult to debug.

Design-time and compile-time problems will not be examined more closely here as you should, hopefully, have adequate support provided by the environment on where to look next to troubleshoot. For runtime bugs, errors, and the like, you should consider the following possible sources of error:

- ❏ Your code
- ❏ The network
- ❏ The environment

Problems arising from code defects are pretty much always going to fall into the "nontransient" category. Difficulties will arise however when they don't occur frequently. To debug coding problems, you are going to need to use a range of tools and techniques, which are discussed throughout the rest of the chapter. These include using your debugger (e.g., Visual Studio), writing some diagnostic information out, writing unit tests to catch the problems early, and other techniques.

It may be that you are using some third-party code that you suspect is causing the problems. If this is the case, your first port of call should be with that vendor, but this is not always possible. In some cases, you may need to take a look into the third-party assemblies using tools such as Reflector (and hope that the assemblies have not been obfuscated to make your job more difficult). If the code isn't yours, it's going to be pretty difficult to fix, but understanding what it is doing can at least give you some clues as to how you might use it differently to get the desired results.

In today's modern Internet, there is a much greater sense of community, and so perhaps you are using some Open Source code, in which case, you can feed any bugs or problems back into the community and query the forums for further information.

So you have ruled out any coding defects, but you are still encountering strange behavior with your application. A source of problems that falls very neatly into the "transient" category is that of the network. Because your Silverlight application is executed on the client, it is going to be a lot less "chatty" than your traditional ASP.NET web applications, which need to query the server for each new page. There are going to be times, though, when your Silverlight application needs to phone home and make a request back to the server or maybe even make a Web Service call to another service out there on the Internet. Depending on what kind of developer you are and the type of application you are writing when coding an Internet application, there is a certain degree of trust you are putting into other service providers. If you are writing a Silverlight application within the Enterprise, you (your business) will pretty much have full control over the servers that your application talks to. You may even be talking to another business, but in such cases, you are likely to have some kind of Service Level Agreement (SLA) with that company. If your application starts failing because their server is down, you would expect a notification that they have the problem and be given an estimate as to when the server will be back up and running again.

For a consumer-type application out there on the Web that talks to many different services (think along the lines of a mash-up), for the most part, you are not going to have available such SLAs. Therefore, any problems you encounter can be largely up to you to identify. The trouble with this is that you won't necessarily know if the problem is on the server side, on your client, or anywhere in between such as with your Internet Service Provider. Diagnosing a rarely occurring network problem can be one of the more difficult issues to troubleshoot. Instrumenting your code can help (around network calls), and if you are lucky enough to reproduce the problem, you can use some of the HTTP Tracer tools discussed later to help further.

The third main type of problem source is the environment. The environment typically is going to be the client, as you are using Silverlight, but this does not rule out the server environment, because, of course, your Silverlight resources have to be hosted off somewhere in order to be pulled down to the client for execution. Silverlight is pretty much aimed at being client-agnostic (within reason), and therefore if you hit a problem in Internet Explorer, you would expect to hit it in Firefox. If you hit a problem on the PC, you would expect to hit on the Mac. If you don't get this kind of consistency across platform and browser and you are running within a Silverlight-supported client environment, you should raise this matter with Microsoft. If you can consistently reproduce the problem, you should look to use some of the same techniques as for the other problem types. These other techniques are largely browser-agnostic (excluding the Web Development Helper tool and Firebug), and you can even use Visual Studio remotely to debug Silverlight applications on the Mac.

At this point, it's time to start backing up the theory with some real tools and techniques that you will want to use to get your application up and running again.

Your Toolkit

Every developer needs a good chest of tools to help him or her troubleshoot problems with their applications. Besides having the correct tools, though, the real skill comes in knowing when to use which tool. This section looks at the options you have available and describes the circumstances when you will need to think about using a particular type of debugger. First and foremost comes Visual Studio. You should be familiar with the IDE from a coding and development perspective, but maybe not so much from a Silverlight debugging point of view.

Visual Studio

This section takes you through setting up Visual Studio to be ready to act as a debugger for your Silverlight applications. By this stage, you have probably created several Silverlight projects, and if you have, you have almost certainly done this via the templates supplied as part of the Silverlight Tools for Visual Studio. What this means is that you have immediately been presented with a choice of debugging and testing options for your project. To begin examining these options, see Figure 15-1.

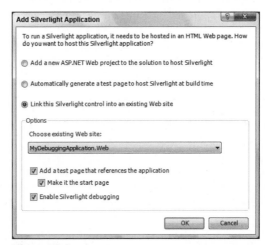

Figure 15-1

The option names give an indication as to what they each do, but a more detailed description is required to understand each of these fully and their implications.

"Add a New ASP.NET Web Project to the Solution to Host Silverlight"

This option is similar in some ways to the third option, "Link this Silverlight control into an existing Web site," albeit with fewer associated options. The third section will be described shortly, but the first option should be chosen if you are starting a project from scratch, where you have the requirement to host your Silverlight plug-in within a web page, but do not have an existing site to point it at.

You are first of all presented with the "Type" of project you would like to create. These options will again be familiar to an ASP.NET developer, but just to recap, you have two basic ways in which to host your site: (1) as a web site or (2) as a web application project. The first option provides a quick and easy way to pick up and deploy a web site using XCOPY deployment; that is, it's very much an isolated and self-contained site that uses a special file structure in order to be able to build on-the-fly. An example of this is the ability to use an "App_Code" folder. In this folder, you can play ASP.NET source files such as MyLibrary.cs, and these will get built into temporary assemblies at run time. The key difference between this option and the web application project is that there is no associated project file.

The Project file of the second option is often seen as a large benefit, especially when you are working on larger-scale projects and you somehow need to incorporate your web site into an automated build and deployment process. You can simply point your build environment at the project file, and the project file knows all the assets associated with the web application; it can go ahead and build everything it needs to with relative ease.

Once you have made your decision here, the Wizard will create all the assets required to host your plug-in within a test web page. This is described in more detail in the "Link This Silverlight Control into an Existing Web Site" section.

"Automatically Generate a Test Page to Host Silverlight at Build Time"

If you have or are creating a project using this option, you will notice that a single project is created that contains two standard XAML files, their respective code-behind files, an AppManifest.xml file, an AssemblyInfo file, and the appropriate assembly references. This is fine for developing your application, but the Silverlight control needs to have a host in order for it to be displayed. This is achieved by dynamically generating the test page at build time.

If you take a look at the properties for your project and select the Debug tab, you will notice that the Wizard has set a Start Action for your project of "Dynamically generate a test page." This raises the question of how it is actually creating this test page. To find the answer to this, you can do some delving into the Visual Studio project file. All projects in Visual Studio declare their settings in XML, which follows a schema that is recognized by MSBuild — Microsoft's software build technology.

So, if you use Windows Explorer to locate your build project file (which will have an extension of `.csproj` for a C# project and .vbproj for a VB.NET project) and then open this up in Notepad, you will notice a file containing the various settings and configuration information for your project, all stored as XML. When you click on the Build option in Visual Studio, this is the file that is being read by MSBuild. But why do you need to know this? Well, here you will see a property that looks as follows:

```
<CreateTestPage>true</CreateTestPage>
```

Visual Studio doesn't know to read this property without the assistance of the Visual Studio Tools for Silverlight. If you look further down the file, you will see a reference to a Silverlight build helper file:

```
<Import Project="$(MSBuildExtensionsPath)\Microsoft\Silverlight\v2.0\
Microsoft.Silverlight.Csharp.targets" />
```

It is beyond the scope of this discussion to go into MSBuild in any depth, but the above line contains a property called *MSBuildExtensionsPath*, which by default will be something like *C:\Program Files\MSBuild*. If you open the subsequent *Microsoft.Silverlight.Csharp.targets* file, you will see that this imports `Microsoft.Silverlight.Common.targets`, which, in turn, imports a task from a managed assembly:

```
<UsingTask
TaskName="Microsoft.Silverlight.Build.Tasks.CreateHtmlTestPage"
AssemblyFile="Microsoft.Silverlight.Build.Tasks.dll" />
```

It is the task that sits inside this assembly that will be called when the `CreateTestPage` property is evaluated as being equal to `true`. As a result, you will be provided with a dynamic web page to host your application. If you build and execute your project and take a look in the ClientBin folder, you will see the files that this task has generated for you — namely, a TestPage.html, which will be the host for your application. This HTML page will contain some markup that looks similar to the following:

```
<object data="data:application/x-silverlight," type="application/
x-silverlight-2"    width="100%" height="100%">
    <param name="source" value="MySilverlightApplication.xap"/>
    <param name="onerror" value="onSilverlightError" />
    <param name="background" value="white" />
</object>
```

The object tag should look familiar to you if you have used ActiveX plug-ins as part of your web pages in the past. The "type" parameter is indicating to the browser which control should be fired up at run time (in this case, Silverlight). It is then passing in the relevant parameters to the control, such as the package name (*MySilverlightApplication.xap* in this case).

The advantage of the "Automatically generate a test page to host Silverlight at build time" option is that you have a simple test harness in which to test your application. If, however, you would like to see how your Silverlight control is rendering within the context of an existing web application, you need to select the first or last option in the initial Silverlight template or change your "Start Action" setting within the properties of your project.

"Link This Silverlight Control into an Existing Web Site"

In the real world, you may have more than your Silverlight application sitting on a plain web page. Perhaps you have a web application that uses Web Parts, and each of those Web Parts has its own Silverlight control. The previous option would not have given you the ability to test this.

If you do have an existing web application or web site, you might want to enhance this application using Silverlight and build on the integration into the host web application. If this is the case, you should select the second option in the Silverlight Application Wizard. Selecting this option will enable you to select several additional checkboxes, which are described below:

❑   **Choose Existing Web Site** — This option is pretty self-explanatory and allows you to select the existing web site that you want to host your Silverlight application within.

❑   **Add a Test Page That References the Control** — This option specifies whether you would like a test page to be inserted into the existing web site. If you uncheck this option and the options below it, you will find that your Silverlight project is added to the existing web site solution. Once you build your solution, the Silverlight package will be placed in a ClientBin subfolder under the web site. If you change your mind after you have gone through the Wizard, you have the ability to change your options by right-clicking on the web site project and selecting "Properties." You will then see down the left-hand pane a tab called *Silverlight Applications*. If you select this tab and then click on the "Add" button, you will see the dialog presented that you see in Figure 15-2.

If you check the "Add a test page that references the control" option, the package that results from building your Silverlight project is automatically copied to the "Destination Folder," which by default is "ClientBin." In addition to this, a hosting test page is created. This test page is an ASP.NET page, which contains an asp:Silverlight control, which references your built .xap Silverlight package sitting in the Destination folder.

Figure 15-2

❑ **Make It the Start Page** — This option simply makes the test page that is generated by the previous checkbox the start-up page within your web site. This can be adjusted in the usual way via the web site project properties.

❑ **Enable Silverlight Debugging** — This option tells Visual Studio that you would like to enable Silverlight debugging in your web site project. If you wish to enable/disable this option at a later time, you can find it in your web site project properties, on the "Web" tab, and under Debuggers, there is a checkbox called *Silverlight*.

So what does this actually do? Well, quite simply, having this checkbox ticked allows you to set breakpoints within your Silverlight code-behind files, and the debugger will break into these when they are hit. In other words, you can debug your application seamlessly as you would do a more traditional application.

What this is doing behind the scenes is twofold:

❑ dbgshim.dll and mscordbi.dll are loaded to aid Visual Studio in debugging your application. These DLLs can be located in various places, but you should be able to find them under the Silverlight installation folder at C:\Program Files\Microsoft Silverlight\<version number> (by default).

❑ It also enables script debugging in your browser, which allows for debugging your script-based JavaScript pages. The added benefit of using Visual Studio .NET 2008 here is that you get some really cool support for setting breakpoints in your script.

Debugging Your Application

Now that you have gotten your application into a state where you are ready to debug, the next steps can be discussed. There are some further options for you to consider before you start your debugging.

When you come to deploy your application, you should set the build type to "Release" within the IDE. This tells the compiler to build your Silverlight assemblies in Release mode. What setting the Release mode actually does depends on the respective compiler. For example, the C# compiler might perform different compilation actions from the VB.NET compiler. By setting this option, you are setting a flag of intent: You are telling the compiler what type of build you want to produce. If the compiler sees that you have set the type to Release, it knows that it is free to optimize the MSIL (Microsoft Intermediate Language) code that it produces, and it doesn't need to worry about keeping the code in a more readable form for a human. What it actually does during this optimization process doesn't really need a discussion here, although you will often notice that the size of the Release assembly is smaller than the size of the Debug assembly (although optimizations are not just about assembly size).

Another difference between these build types is the symbol file that is produced. A symbol file is the file with the extension of .pdb (Program Database), and you should have a matching .pdb file for each assembly that you have built. A symbol file can be passed to the debugger when you come to troubleshoot an application, and it provides the glue between the built assembly and your source code. Even from a Release build, a symbol file will be produced, although it will have less information in it relating to the source code. Examples of the information that is omitted include things like source-code line numbers, paths, and so on. Symbol files are very useful when it comes to debugging, although they have lost their value somewhat in the managed world because you can now use reflection to find certain pieces of information that were traditionally not accessible in an unmanaged application.

> In .NET the metadata describing the classes, methods, and types (etc.) are held within the assembly that they describe. Because the metadata sits beside the actual structures it describes, you can be confident that the two are synchronized. The .NET framework exposes methods for querying this information at run time, and this is the process known as *.NET reflection.*
>
> This powerful feature allows you to retrieve information that traditionally (in the unmanaged world) was only possible at run time (or thereafter) via the use of symbol files. Symbols still maintain some value in the managed world by retrieving information the metadata does not store, such as code line numbers and paths, as already described.

There are certain rules that you should follow when using symbol files:

❑ Always produce symbol files as part of your build to allow for debugging at a later stage against a specific build.

❑ If your code doesn't change and you rebuild, you should still generate a new symbol as compiler optimizations can result in the symbols becoming out of sync with the code.

❑ Do not distribute your debug symbols to third parties — only your release symbols. This is for security reasons because it can expose information you would not necessarily want the public to know.

One of the most useful applications of symbol files is if you have a remote user accessing your application and finding that it fails in some way. It can sometimes be useful to have the remote user take a snapshot of the application memory at the point of failure and have him or her send you this snapshot. This snapshot is referred to as a *memory dump,* and the symbol file allows you to take a look at your application in great depth at the point of failure.

> As Silverlight is going to be hosted in a browser, you would also need symbols for the browser. Microsoft makes its "Release" symbols available on a public server, should you need to go down this route.

As you are developing your application, you are going to have all of the relevant debug environment on hand in the form of Visual Studio.

It may be the case that you are writing some client script within your web application to either act separately or complement your Silverlight application. With the HTML "bridge" in Silverlight, your managed code can communicate with the browser's HTML document object model and any JavaScript content. This means that you may also sometimes need to do some script debugging as part of your troubleshooting process. The Visual Studio environment is a great tool to help you here, but there are some things to watch out for. First and foremost, you cannot debug your managed code *and* your script within the same debug process. This means that if you are setting a break point on your XAML code-behind and you have Silverlight debugging enabled, the breakpoint will be hit appropriately. However, if you have also set break points within your script, these will not be hit while "Silverlight" debugging is enabled. To use Internet Explorer as an example, you should follow the steps below to ensure that you can hit the break points within your client-side script:

1. In your web application, which hosts the Silverlight control, go to the Project Properties and browse to the Web tab. Under the Debuggers section, ensure that the Silverlight box is cleared, as shown in Figure 15-3.

Figure 15-3

2. The next step is to ensure that the browser is configured to allow for script debugging. In the case of Internet Explorer, fire up the browser and go to the Tools tab, followed by "Internet Options." On the Advanced tab, ensure that the "Disable script debugging (Internet Explorer)" and "Disable script debugging (Other)" checkboxes are clear. This is illustrated in Figure 15-4.

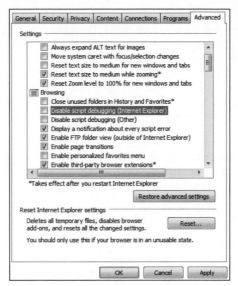

Figure 15-4

3. The last step is to simply set a break point on your script as you would do for any other code and then execute your application. This gives you all the benefits of a rich debug environment such as being able to view the call stack and take a look at the values of local variables. Figure 15-5 shows what this might look like for a simple function.

Figure 15-5

An environmental issue you need to be aware of is the hosting web server of your application. By default, Visual Studio is going to execute your Silverlight application in the Cassini Web server. There will come a time when you move your application throughout the deployment process and into a UAT or Staging environment. In these environments, you are going to be using a larger-scale Web Server (IIS, Apache, etc.). You should ensure that your web server has the correct MIME types configured for serving up a Silverlight application. In short, you are going to need to add a MIME type mapping as follows to your web server: File Extension: `.xap`, MIME Type: `application/x-silverlight-app`.

> *Cassini* is the name of the local web server that hosts web projects in Visual Studio to save you configuring your application at development time in a more complex server environment like IIS or Apache. A sure sign that you are using Cassini is by the appearance of the small icon in the system tray, labeled "ASP.NET Development Server."

You are not always going to hit issues in the debug environment, and sometimes you may be lucky enough to be able to readily reproduce the problem, but rather than executing your application by hitting [F5], it may be more convenient to attach to an existing browser process.

To attach Visual Studio as a debugger to another process, you need to select the Debug tool option, followed by "Attach to Process." This will present you with a list of processes running on the system. It is likely that you will be executing the browser in the context of your own user account, but if you are not, be sure to check the "Show processes from all users" and "Show processes from all sessions" options so that you can find the process that you need to debug.

This section has discussed some of the steps you will need to go through to get started debugging your application. This should be a familiar position if you have debugged other types of applications within Visual Studio. The next few tools that are discussed are ones that you might not be as familiar with. These are not Microsoft Products, but are essential tools for development, particularly web development.

HTTP Tracers

Sometimes your application may fail, and you will be unsure at which point in the life cycle of a particular method call it failed. For example, you may click a button in your application that will process some page logic and then, based on this logic, make a call to a particular Web Service in order to retrieve some further information. If you click that button and get either a handled or unhandled exception, you may already be on the trail of the problem. However, perhaps there is no exception raised, there is a silent failure, or you do not see the expected behavior — what do you do? In this situation, you can trace through your code, but you may want to then check whether the request is actually leaving the client, and if so, what is getting sent and received. There are plenty of tools available to help you do this. For example, you could use a tool such as Ethereal (www.ethereal.com) or Microsoft's Network Monitor tool, but for a Silverlight application, these are going to probably be a little too verbose in that they will report communication information too low down the network stack.

What you ideally want is a similar tool, but one that targets the HTTP protocol specifically. There are several options here, but my favorite tools are Fiddler (www.fiddler2.com) and Nikhil Kothari's Web Development Helper tool (www.nikhilk.net/Project.WebDevHelper.aspx).

Another very useful tool to add to your arsenal, if you are using the FireFox browser is `Firebug()`. Firebug is more than just an HTTP tracer as it allows you to debug the browser object model in real time, and also code JavaScript against it. It will also be discussed in this section because it does provide a useful network tracing feature.

A description of each of these tools follows, although for more in-depth information, you should see the respective web sites.

The Calculator Web Service sample has been referred to already in earlier chapters, and this sample will now be used as a basis to show how you can extract some useful information from your application using the various tools described below.

Web Development Helper

The Web Development Helper tool is a great tracing tool that integrates well into Internet Explorer. This allows you to take a look at the requests and responses from a page, and it really does have all the basic functionality you need to help troubleshoot problems that relate to the network communication between your client application and the server.

To show how this tool can be used to diagnose a problem, the authentication sample from Chapter 12 will be used. Just as a recap, this sample had a Calculator Web Service being hosted on a separate domain, and also required you to authenticate yourself within your Silverlight client before being able to make a successful call.

The problem that is going to be simulated here is where the clientaccesspolicy.xml file has not been explicitly enabled to be accessed from all users. In other words, the following lines have not been added to the web.config file:

```
<location path="clientaccesspolicy.xml">
  <system.web>
    <authorization>
      <allow users="*"  />
    </authorization>
  </system.web>
</location>
```

So, if you fire up the application in Internet Explorer and enable the tool by going to "Tools" and then selecting "Web Development Helper," you should see the tool load up in a separate pane at the bottom of the page. You then need to tell it to start tracing so that it tracks the traffic between your client and the Web Service on the server. If you enter some valid credentials and then select "Login," you would ordinarily expect that you are authenticated, and thus be able to perform the Add operation by entering in two numbers, and clicking on the "Add" button. However, you will see that by clicking on the "Login" button, a CommunicationException shows that not all is well. If you continue on through that exception, you will see this is further backed up by the Web Development Helper.

You can see what the application and tool output should look like in Figure 15-6.

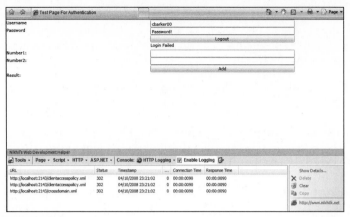

Figure 15-6

The tool is showing that a request is being made to `http://localhost:<port>/clientaccess policy.xml` and that the HTTP response to this request has a status code of 302. First of all, you know that your application has not explicitly requested this resource, and that it is the Silverlight run time doing a check for the presence of the clientaccesspolicy.xml file as part of its security remit. What is less clear is why a status code of 302 is being returned. (OK, you have an idea of why this is because of the steps taken in the web.config, but just go with this for now.)

The HTTP Status Code 302 actually translates to a resource being found, but not at the requested location. In other words, there has been a re-direction. If you double-click on the HTTP request item in the tool, a dialog will pop up with some more information. This is shown in Figure 15-7.

As you can see, the dialog is divided into two panes. The upper pane shows the Request to the server, and the lower pane shows the Response from the server. The key value that you see in the upper pane is the resource being requested — "`GET /clientaccesspolicy.xml HTTP /1.1`." This line shows that the HTTP verb being used is the `GET` verb (i.e., we are requesting a resource), the resource we are requesting is located at /clientaccesspolicy.xml, and we are communicating over HTTP version 1.1.

The web server is responding to this request with a value of "`HTTP /1.1 302 Found`" to indicate the protocol being used and the status code it is returning. The most interesting piece of information here is the "Location" value of "/login.aspx?ReturnUtl=%2fclientaccesspolicy.xml," which is showing you the address to which you have been re-directed. The Silverlight run time is effectively getting returned a login page instead of a policy file, and as a result, it fails over looking for the policy file in a different location. The run time actually searches its series of paths, but always gets referred back to the login page, and thus the user will never successfully be authenticated. In this particular instance, the status code would lead you to investigate where you were getting re-directed to, by which point you would have a good understanding of why the behavior was occurring. You could use these techniques to troubleshoot a whole range of problems.

If you re-add the original lines of the web.config to provide an exception rule to the policy file, you will find that the trace successfully shows a call to your authentication service.

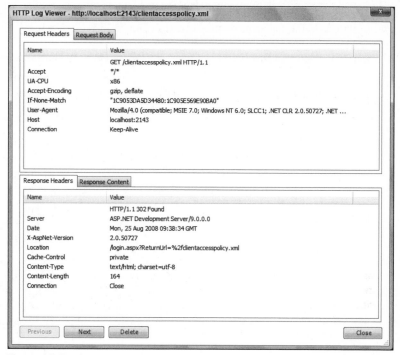

Figure 15-7

Fiddler

Fiddler is another web tracing tool, but it could perhaps be considered richer than the previously mentioned Web Development Helper. The previous tool will be sufficient for the most part, although Fiddler provides additional features such as being able to build up requests and post these to sites to see what they return with — a nice feature, but not something that is always going to be required.

Fiddler isn't simply a web tracing tool but, rather, a proxy tool. In other words, it sits in between your application and the target web site, Web Service, and so on.

You may already be familiar with this tool if you have done any AJAX (Asynchronous JavaScript and XML) programming in the past. Although there are tools that allow you to simply trace HTTP Request/Response messages, Fiddler can also trace AJAX requests (which are typically sent via the XMLHTTPRequest object). Again, this is because it is acting as a proxy.

Unlike Web Development Helper, Fiddler sits beside your browser in a separate process, allowing you to use it in conjunction with a large number of browsers and other HTTP requesting client applications.

To get an initial feel for Fiddler, you can start it up alongside the sample application used in the previous section when demonstrating the Web Development Helper. Simply load up the application, and from the Tools menu, select "Fiddler2," which will then fire up Fiddler in a separate process. If you type in a set of valid credentials into the Silverlight client, and click "Login" (assuming that you still have the policy file available to everyone), you should see a successful call being placed, and in Fiddler, you will see two new requests being made, as demonstrated in Figure 15-8.

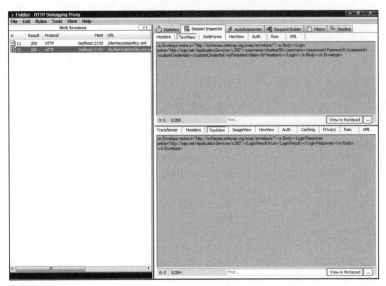

Figure 15-8

To break this screen down a little, you can see the HTTP requests being made in the left-hand pane, and the right-hand pane is being broken into Request (top pane) and Response (lower pane). On the left-hand side, you can see the successful OK status code of 200 for the request to the policy file, and to the Authentication Web Service. In the right-hand panes, you can see the actual SOAP messages that are being sent to and from the server. If you look closely, you can see the credentials being sent over the wire in the request, and a successful "LoginResult" in the response, which is set to "true." This also highlights why you may consider transporting your messages over a secure connection like SSL for sensitive information. This would result in an encrypted channel such that the information is not sent in clear text as it is here.

> You will notice that in this particular example, the HTTP requests are being made against "testhost" rather than "localhost." This is because Fiddler will not trace any calls made on the local machine. A way around this is to fool it into thinking that you are making a request to another machine. On Windows you can do this by opening up the C:\Windows\System32\drivers\etc\hosts file and adding in the following line:
>
> ```
> 127.0.0.1               testhost
> ```
>
> This resolves any calls to "testhost" that are made on your machine to the loopback IP address of 127.0.0.1, which effectively is the same as a request to "localhost."

Firebug

In keeping with the previous two examples, a demonstration will now be shown with the Firebug debugger. As mentioned, this tool provides a range of different features, which you should take the time to explore if Firefox is your browser of choice. The sample below, however, will take a look at the output gained from the networking component.

If you browse to the sample application that you have been using, you can then open up Firebug inside of Firefox by going to Tools, selecting Firebug, and then "Open Firebug." This will then open up in the lower pane, similarly to the Web Development Helper. To get to the networking functionality, simply select "Net," and then log into the sample application using some valid credentials. This should present you with a screen similar to Figure 15-9.

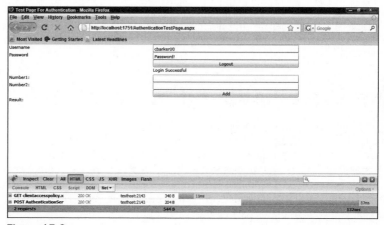

Figure 15-9

This screen is a little easier to read than the previous tools, and it gives a nice graphic indicating the time taken to load each request (see the bar to the right of each resource requested). You can also expand each request to retrieve further details relating to the headers and response message.

Using a technology such as Silverlight, you could potentially be communicating across the network quite a lot, and these tools are going to provide you with a great head start when troubleshooting any problems that may arise.

Red Gate's Reflector

Red Gate's Reflector tool has been used in examples throughout the book already, but its usefulness really does need highlighting. If you have been doing .NET development (not just web) for a while, you most likely have used Reflector at one time or another. On this author's machine, it sits beside the short-cuts to Outlook and Media Player on the Task Bar, and rightly so!

So, what does it do? Well, using .NET Reflection, it extracts all the pertinent information from an assembly and puts it into a friendly, human-readable format on the screen. The UI is not so dissimilar to the Visual Studio Class View, but its real benefits come from extracting the assembly's MSIL and translating this into your .NET language of choice (such as C#).

By providing such a translation, you can better understand code that you have not written and realize how you should be interacting with it. This, of course, is no replacement for documentation and should only be used as a last resort. Documentation often stops short of the inner workings of a piece of code and usually just describes the public interfaces, which gives you a black box perspective of the code you are working with. This is suitable for most purposes, but there are times when you need to know what is going on behind the scenes or are just plain curious!

Yes, vendors can obfuscate the code, and yes, the translated C# is not always entirely representative of the original code (owing to compiler optimization, etc.), but the latter point should not prove to be a block in understanding what an assembly actually does.

When Microsoft announced .NET and the idea of reflection came to light, there was quite a fuss made of people losing their Intellectual Property (IP) to competitors. The main argument against this perspective is that unless you are writing some ground-breaking algorithm, the code should really just be an implementation of a great idea. Of course, the majority of Microsoft's managed assemblies are not obfuscated in any way, which helps reiterate the point.

Reducing the Likelihood of Problems

It is always good to be able to troubleshoot a problem when it inevitably occurs. It is even better to reduce the likelihood of them occurring in the first place. There are various coding methodologies and techniques in use today that have testing at their heart, none more so than Test Driven Development (TDD). Test Driven Development works on the basis of writing a test case before you have written a piece of code to satisfy that test case. This section concentrates more on the types of test you might write to ensure increased confidence in the integrity of your code, leaving you free to decide for yourself the type of technique you wish to use as part of your development process.

Unit Testing

Unit Testing is something that middle-tier or component developers are more familiar with writing, whereas a typical ASP.NET developer may be more familiar writing UI tests of some form. However, if you have developed multiple layers in your applications before, you may have already had Unit Testing exposure.

To begin with, what is a Unit Test? Well, it's pretty much one of the lowest levels of testing you will write, and a Unit Test's sole purpose is to ensure that your code is performing a very particular piece of functionality, often at the method or class level.

Unit Testing should be a key part of your development process and can help you to identify issues before they become expensive to fix. Figure 15-10 illustrates some relative costs for fixing bugs through each stage of the development process.

In the Developer and Test Editions of Visual Studio, you are given a lot of support in the way of getting your Unit Tests up and running. It is beyond our scope here to discuss these great features, so it is suggested that you read up on these at `http://msdn2.microsoft.com/en-us/library/ms379625(VS.80).aspx`. Before you get stuck in that article, though, read on.

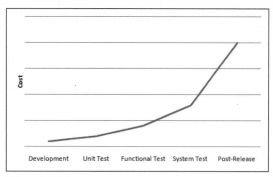

Figure 15-10

If you try this Unit Test framework against your Silverlight source code, you will find that the usual Generate Unit Tests dialog box appears but is empty. The reason this does not work is because your test project is using the Desktop CLR, but the project you are referencing is using Silverlight's CoreCLR, and the two are not binary-compatible. At this point, you are probably thinking this is going to be quite a short section. Cue `Microsoft.Silverlight.Testing`.

In a non-Silverlight application, there are various testing assemblies (such as Microsoft.VisualStudio. QualityTools.UnitTestFramework.dll) used to provide Unit Testing support and IDE integration. These assemblies have all been built against the Desktop CLR, so when you try to use them against a Silverlight application, which, of course, uses the CoreCLR, you are going to hit some problems.

The Silverlight product team had to test their controls as they underwent development, and so they developed their own test framework to help support this. The entry point into this framework is the aforementioned `Microsoft.Silverlight.Testing` assembly.

> **You will not find the Silverlight Unit Testing assemblies as part of the SDK, where you might expect them. The framework was developed alongside of Silverlight and can be found as part of the Silverlight Toolkit as a separate, free download at** `www.codeplex.com/Silverlight/`.

For the most part, the test framework uses the standard test attributes that you have used against the Desktop CLR, although as always, this is a smaller subset. The Silverlight test framework has been built against the CoreCLR, and therefore will support your testing needs. One downside to the Silverlight framework, however, is the lack of integration into the Visual Studio IDE. This means that you will have to create your test projects yourself and then apply the relevant set of attributes on your classes and methods. This section will help to get you on your feet and put you into a position where you are ready to start writing some Unit Tests against your code.

> **To help author your Unit Tests within the IDE, you can look to use the** `TestDriven.NET` **add-in for Visual Studio found at** `www.testdriven.net/`. **The** `TestDriven.NET` **tool will not be used here, but you should be aware of its existence and the potential for it to make your life a little easier.**

To get up and running, you are going to need three things:

❑ The Silverlight test framework assemblies downloaded as part of the Silverlight Toolkit

❑ A Silverlight project to test

❑ A Silverlight project that will host your tests

When you have created a project to host your tests, you'll have to add in the relevant assemblies, and so, to be clear, here are the two files that you are interested in:

❑ **Microsoft.Silverlight.Testing.dll** — This assembly houses the Silverlight Test Engine and Test Harness and is therefore more focused around the execution of the tests and generating their results.

❑ **Microsoft.VisualStudio.QualityTools.UnitTesting.Silverlight.dll** — This assembly, among other things, holds the various Assert methods and attributes that you can set on your tests, and is basically scoped around the syntax available to you within Visual Studio.

The next thing you need to do is either open up an existing Silverlight solution or just quickly create a dummy one that, say, has two textboxes and a button to allow you to add two numbers together. (This will really make you feel the power of Silverlight!)

When you come to create the Silverlight project to host your tests, there is a cheat. Ordinarily, you would have to tweak the project that gets created by the Silverlight template, although Jeff Wilcox (who produced the testing framework) has made available some templates that you can use to get you set up. You can download the latest templates from his blog at www.jeff.wilcox.name/. Besides this, though, his blog is a great place to look for further information around the testing framework.

> A common convention when creating your test project is to name it the same as the project you are targeting, but append .Test to the end. For example, if your target project is called *Calculator*, your test project would be called Calculator.Test.

Before you start writing any tests, you need to understand some of the glue between Silverlight and the test framework. An initial description is given based on the code that the test template generates for you.

The first thing you will notice is that the created Silverlight project has, in addition to the usual assemblies, references to the two Silverlight test framework assemblies. You will also see that there is a Test.cs file generated that looks something like the following:

```
using System;
using System.Collections.Generic;
using Microsoft.VisualStudio.TestTools.UnitTesting;

namespace Calculator.Test
{
    [TestClass]
    public class Test
    {
        [TestMethod]
        public void TestMethod()
```

```
        {
            Assert.Inconclusive();
        }
    }
}
```

This is a very simplistic file, but it introduces you to some of the Unit Testing conventions if you are not already familiar with them. You can see a reference to the UnitTesting namespace in this code. This namespace reflects what you would usually use in a non-Silverlight project, but it is, of course, using the Silverlight implementation of the assembly.

The name of the class will typically be the name of the class you are testing with the "Test" extension. So, if you are testing a Calculator class, your test class will be Calculator.Test. When it comes to the method names, a similar convention applies, although it may be that for a specific target method, you have multiple test methods. As an example, imagine that you have the following method within your Calculator class:

```
public double Divide(double i, double j)
{
    if ((i / j) == double.PositiveInfinity)
    {
        throw new System.DivideByZeroException();
    }
    else
        return i / j;
}
```

Although this is a very simplistic example, it may be that you have the following tests for this method:

```
[TestMethod]
[ExpectedException(typeof(System.DivideByZeroException))]
public void DivideCheckForDivideByZero()
{
    double Actual = 0;

    Page calc = new Page();

    Actual = calc.Divide(5, 0);

}

[TestMethod]
public void DivideCheck()
{

    double Actual = 0;
    double Expected = 2;

    Page calc = new Page();

    Actual = calc.Divide(6, 3);

    Assert.AreEqual(Actual, Expected);
}
```

The first test is checking that a number is not being returned when trying to divide 5 by 0. The second test is checking that the `Divide` method correctly returns 2 when trying to divide 6 by 3. In the fully fledged "non-Silverlight" test environment, you would probably just have the one test here, and bind it to a data source that passes in a sequence of values to the method. Unfortunately, the Silverlight version of the test framework does not allow for binding to a data source.

There are some attributes that were specified on the previous classes and methods, which should be explained briefly. The attribute of the class (`TestClass`) is simply telling the test framework that this assembly contains some tests. The attribute of the methods (`TestMethod`) is similarly telling the framework that these methods should be executed as part of the tests.

In the first "Divide" test, there is an additional attribute called `ExpectedException`. As its name implies, this attribute is telling the test framework to expect an exception (in this case, `System.DivideByZero Exception`), and if the test framework does encounter this exception, it should not fail. In fact it goes further than this, and if it does not encounter the exception, it will fail. Unfortunately you will find that when running this code, Visual Studio by default will break into the debugger at the point where the exception is thrown, which is no good for automated testing. To prevent this, you can tell Visual Studio not to break on Managed Exceptions by going into the Debug ⇨ Exceptions menu, and de-selecting the Common Language Runtime Exceptions checkbox for 'User-unhandled.'

A more common test approach is to make an "assertion" on the method results by using the `Assert` class. You can see an example of the `Assert` class in the second Divide test method. This class is asserting a specific result. If that criterion is not fulfilled, the test will fail.

So, that is a guide on how you might configure a test class, but you need a harness in which to run the tests. As already mentioned, there is no tight integration into the IDE for Silverlight, but the framework does provide its own harness for executing the tests. To see the linking piece between the harness and the tests, you can turn your attention to the App.xaml code-behind file (App.xaml.cs for C#), which was generated by the template.

Besides the test framework references in the code-behind file, the interesting section of code looks as follows:

```
private void Application_Startup(object sender, StartupEventArgs e)
{
        this.RootVisual = UnitTestSystem.CreateTestPage(); }
```

You don't need to understand the inner workings of this static method, except you should know that it is responsible for setting up the test page, executing your tests, and reporting on the results. You can see what this test page looks like in Figure 15-11.

Figure 15-11

You may think that the previous figure shows a lot of white space, but this is the area in which any Silverlight UI would be displayed during the test. This is something explored in the following section on user interface testing.

The two tests executed in this particular run both succeeded, but if they failed, you would see these flagged in red, and you would be provided with some details as to the cause of the failure to help you troubleshoot further.

> **One of the features of Visual Studio that isn't currently hooked into the Silverlight test framework is the ability to apply Code Coverage to your code.**

These samples have been targeting logic within your Silverlight application, but it may be that you farm out your logic to the server, or even that you keep the logic locally, but also have a requirement to test the user interface of your Silverlight application. This is discussed in the following section.

UI Testing

Coming from the Web Developer world, you may be used to using tools such as Mercury LoadRunner, Microsoft Application Center Test (ACT), or Visual Studio Test Edition (Web Testing). All of these tools provide you with the ability to browse to a web site, select a few options, and record those actions in a macro-like manner. Depending on the tool, you can then tinker with the recorded macro in code and perform a number of advanced replay steps to replay hits against the site. These kind of tools are really beneficial for stress testing (imagine replaying tens, hundreds, or even thousands of these actions against a site), but they can also be useful in regression testing.

These tools work by replaying HttpRequests against the server, and with your Silverlight application being client-based, you have to turn to other techniques. While the last section will prove useful for testing any business logic, you are more likely to be in the Silverlight game for the user interface richness it can provide your applications with. This section builds on the framework introduced in the previous section and shows you how you can use this framework to test your UI.

As always, it's best to work through an example to get these ideas across, so that is what will be done here. The example will be to test that a button performs correctly once it is pressed. The actions this button will perform when it is pressed are:

1. It will animate itself by getting smaller.
2. It will then animate itself back to its original size.
3. It will then set the value of a TextBlock to "Completed" to signal that the button's processing has completed.

This may sound a little contrived, but it is really a very simple form of the same process used in more complex operations. To illustrate what this looks like when executed, follow the sequence of diagrams through in Figure 15-12.

Once this application has been set up, you can create a test class much in the same way as you did for a logic-based Unit Test. An illustration of the project structure can be seen in Figure 15-13.

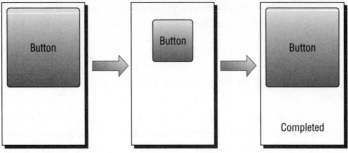

Figure 15-12

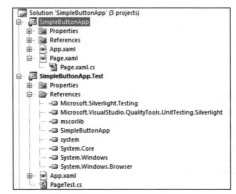

Figure 15-13

The next thing to do is write your Unit Test class. The template that was described previously still leaves a small amount of work here. For example, you will need to derive your Test Class from `SilverlightTest` (found in the `Microsoft.Silverlight.Testing` namespace) in order to get easy access to the Test Surface and some other features that you will need for any UI testing. You are also going to need to include the relevant namespaces for the controls you are using during your test. Before looking at the testing code further, the snippet below shows what the actual code behind of the application page might look like:

```
public bool buttonCompleted; //TODO: Make private

//TODO: Make private
public void myButton_Click(object sender, RoutedEventArgs e)
{
    buttonCompleted = false;
    buttonDownSB.Begin();
    buttonDownSB.Completed += new EventHandler(buttonDownSB_Completed);
}

void buttonDownSB_Completed(object sender, EventArgs e)
{
    buttonDownReverseSB.Begin();
    buttonDownReverseSB.Completed += new
```

```
        EventHandler(buttonDownReverseSB_Completed);
    }

    void buttonDownReverseSB_Completed(object sender, EventArgs e)
    {
        myTextBlock.Text = "Completed";
        buttonCompleted = true;
    }
```

This code snippet raises a few points for discussion, which are highlighted by the two TODO comments. Notably, the member variable and event handlers shown would typically be encapsulated within the class so that they would be both given a private access modifier. However, by declaring them as private, you take away the ability of the test framework to access them directly. In the full desktop version of the test framework, there is a notion of private accessors that get generated to allow for such access, but the Silverlight security model does not allow for this here. The best practice to enable your test to access the private code would be to use the InternalsVisibleTo attribute found in the System.Runtime.CompilerServices namespace. This attribute can be set on your assembly and allows you to specify a remote assembly that you want to give access to. For the sake of simplicity and to avoid these steps, the snippets above just use public modifiers.

As you can see from the code above, there is a simple chain of events that occur. The user clicks a button, and this starts the storyboard animation of the button getting smaller. Once this storyboard has completed, a second begins that restores the button to its original size. Once this completes, the textblock is updated to reflect the completion of the animation. There is also a Boolean flag that is set to indicate completion. While this is useful to have within your code anyway, you will need some kind of completion marker in your real-world code. The code below shows how the code looks with the Boolean flag (buttonCompleted):

```
using System;
using System.Collections.Generic;
using System.Windows;
using System.Windows.Controls;
using Microsoft.VisualStudio.TestTools.UnitTesting;
using Microsoft.Silverlight.Testing;
using SimpleButtonApp;

namespace SimpleButtonApp.Test
{
    [TestClass]
    public class PageTest : SilverlightTest
    {
        [TestMethod]
        [Asynchronous]
        public void myButtonTest()
        {
            Page page = new Page();

            Silverlight.TestSurface.Children.Add(page);

            string ExpectedStart = "";
            string ActualStart;
            string ExpectedEnd = "Completed";
```

```
TextBlock myTextBlock = page.FindName("myTextBlock") as TextBlock;

ActualStart = myTextBlock.Text;

Assert.AreEqual(ActualStart, ExpectedStart);

page.myButton_Click(this, null);

EnqueueConditional(() => page.buttonCompleted);

EnqueueCallback(() => Assert.AreEqual((page.FindName("myTextBlock") as
    TextBlock).Text, ExpectedEnd));

EnqueueTestComplete();
        }
    }
}
```

Approaching this test code for the first time can raise many questions. You should now be familiar with a number of the attributes, references, and target class instantiations, as these are concepts introduced in the previous section. However, for the user interface testing, there are some more complex techniques to learn. To help understand this code, a diagram is shown in Figure 15-14.

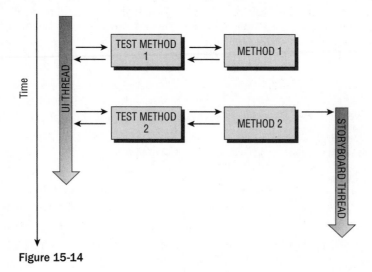

Figure 15-14

Test Method 1 represents a standard, synchronous Unit Test. That is, the Silverlight Test Harness is running off the UI Thread, and it executes Test Method 1, which, in turn, executes Method 1. Method 1 returns a value, Test Method 1 makes an assertion on this value, and the Test Harness can display the result in the UI.

Complications arise in UI Testing where you might have an event firing as part of your target method or maybe some other kind of asynchronous action like waiting for a storyboard to complete. This is what is represented by Method 2 in Figure 15-14, and it is this scenario that is introduced by the code in Figures 15-12 and 15-13. As you can see from the diagram, the Storyboard thread may still be executing when the Test UI thread completes. Upon completion of a test method, the Test Harness will ordinarily tear down the test surface, which will effectively pull the rug out from under the ongoing storyboard. This will prevent you from being able to perform an accurate assert on any values that are set as part of, or at the end of, the storyboard's execution — in the case of the previous example, an assertion on the value of the TextBlock will not be accurate because the UI Thread will have moved on to the next test method before the value could have been set.

In order to resolve this issue, the test framework has the ability to deal with methods whose actions are asynchronous in nature. To test such a method, you need to set the `Asynchronous` attribute on your test method to signify your intent to the test engine. By setting this attribute, you have access to the `Enqueue*` methods that you see throughout the code in the previous code snippet. An explanation will now be given as to what these lines of code are actually doing.

The first thing you need to do is make your method call. This is pretty simple stuff and is being done in the following line by making the direct call to the event handler:

```
page.myButton_Click(this, null);
```

This is going to start off the sequence of storyboard executions. At this point, you want to tell the test engine that you haven't finished yet and that it shouldn't move on to the next test. You can signify that the test engine must wait for the Storyboard/Button-Click completion by making the following call to `EnqueueConditional`:

```
EnqueueConditional(() => page.buttonCompleted);
```

This is using the `buttonCompleted` flag that is defined within the target application. Once this is set to `true`, the test engine knows that it is safe to continue through the test method.

> You may not be familiar with the syntax shown in the previous method call as it uses the notation `() => page.buttonCompleted`. This is called a lambda expression, a feature introduced in C# 3.0. In short, a lambda expression in this instance is shorthand for declaring an anonymous delegate, and it therefore saves several lines of code. A lambda expression follows the syntax shown below:
>
> ```
> Params => Expression
> ```
>
> This reads as, "I would like to pass these Params to this Expression." In the above case, you are indicating that no parameters should be passed to the expression by using the empty parentheses. For an introduction to lambda expressions, see the MSDN article, "Lambda Expressions" (http://msdn2.microsoft.com/en-us/library/bb397687.aspx).

Once the storyboard has completed, you are free to perform your assert. In keeping with the asynchronous testing model, you need to pass the operation (in this case an Assert) as part of a delegate to the test engine. By doing this, the test engine can add that operation as a piece of work to its queue, which will then be executed by the dispatcher on the UI thread at the appropriate time. This action is performed in the following code:

```
EnqueueCallback(() => Assert.AreEqual((page.FindName("myTextBlock") as
    TextBlock).Text, ExpectedEnd));
```

This is not dissimilar to how you would do this in a synchronous test, except you are now plugging the assertion into the test engine as part of a delegate.

Once you have performed your assertion, you need to notify the engine that your test is complete, and it can then clean up the test surface appropriately (although, as a best practice, you should also consider doing this cleaning up yourself, too). The completion code is a simple call to `EnqueueTestComplete`.

> It is important to note that the target code should not have any dependencies on the test code; nor should it contain any code that is specific to a test. In other words, it should remain isolated from the test environment and merely be a potential target of a test. The aforementioned `InternalsVisibleTo` attribute could be seen as being an exception to this rule because you are given little choice in testing against a Silverlight assembly. This attribute also allows you to give a specific assembly name, which would be your test assembly.

Accessibility

There is actually another option for testing your UI over and above what has just been discussed.

It is important to make your application accessible to the widest audience possible, and you should be sensitive to the needs of your audience. One such audience that you should cater to is users with disabilities. If, for example, you have blind users navigating your site, they may have a text reader to help them read what is on a page. A text reader can make sense of a standard HTML page fairly simply since it can read the appropriate text and translate this to human voice. The problem arises with embedded plug-ins like Silverlight — that text-reading piece of software has no knowledge of what is inside the plug-in and what it should be reading out. There are many more reasons for providing accessibility to this information, but it is useful to know that Silverlight provides you with the ability to expose information about your controls to external applications via the `System.Windows.Automation.*` namespaces.

The example shown in the previous section enabled you to raise the button click events manually, but you did have to jump through some hoops to achieve this.

What would be preferable is to have a more formal interface into the controls and their behavior. Fortunately, the Silverlight controls expose their properties via specific "Automation Peer" classes, which do exactly this. Furthermore, if you are writing your own control, you can implement your own Automation Peer and expose your controls functionality by overriding the `UIElement.OnCreate AutomationPeer` method.

You can find a list of the Silverlight controls that implement their own Automation Peers in the `System .Windows.Automation.Peers` namespace. Although not targeted for testing specifically, automation certainly does have a small overlap with the Unit Testing framework, and so it is possible to envisage that in future versions, these two features may become better acquainted.

Exception Handling

When you start writing Silverlight applications and are becoming familiar with its Application Model, you may notice that you receive a lot of silent failures. As in any managed application, exceptions will bubble up the stack until they reach an exception handler. You will notice that the Silverlight run time occasionally swallows up exceptions from user code, so it is important to ensure that you handle exceptions properly. (In fact, this should always be the case anyway.) The first thing you should do is wrap up any potential problem calls within an appropriate `try/catch` block; this way you get to handle any problems the way you want. Maybe this involves notifying the user via a pop-up in some way, or maybe it could involve sending an error notification to the server (if the error wasn't network-based, of course!).

It's not always practical to wrap up all of your code individually, so Silverlight offers an "unhandled exception handler" to be defined at the application level. This is somewhat similar to your global exception handlers in an ASP.NET application. If you look at the code behind your App.Xaml, you will see something that looks like the following:

```
this.UnhandledException += this.Application_UnhandledException;
```

You can then perform the appropriate actions for the more generic failures in your application.

Instrumentation

Another useful troubleshooting technique is to instrument your code. The way you might do this in a Silverlight application is to use the familiar `System.Diagnostic` namespace. For example, if you feel it is not appropriate to notify the users of a particular failure, you could use the `Debug` class to pass some output to any debug listeners that are attached.

So, your code might look something like the following:

```
private void Application_UnhandledException(object sender,
    ApplicationUnhandledExceptionEventArgs e)
{

    Debug.WriteLine(e.ExceptionObject.Message);

}
```

This would output the message generated by the exception to anything that listens to the underlying output. If you had Visual Studio attached to the process, this message would be visible in the Output window, although there are several applications that can also listen to such silent error messages.

Summary

This chapter has intentionally steered away from any real-world problem discussions and instead focused on the techniques and tools that you should be thinking about should you come across any bugs or other problems. This should have equipped you well so that you can develop your code in such a way as to reduce problems in the first place. Should your application fail in any way, you will, hopefully, now catch this early, but either way, you will have a better idea what tool to use in which circumstance.

The software industry is one of the fastest-paced industries around, and even more so in today's connected world. There will be continual development efforts by community members to produce tools to help you fix and diagnose problems, so be sure to keep your eyes on the forums for the latest killer diagnostic tools.

16

Performance

When it comes to considering the performance of a Silverlight application, the mindset is much more similar to that on the performance of a desktop application, rather than the ASP.NET Web Application performance-tuning that you may be used to. The obvious reason for this is that the majority of the processing will be done on the client machine and not centralized on a server farm somewhere. The performance of an application should not be a development afterthought; that is, as a developer, it should be something you are conscious of before you even write your first line of code — at the design stage. With that said, there are still several steps you can take to tune an application once development is complete. This chapter aims to tackle performance tuning from both angles: decisions you should be conscious of while writing your application and steps you can take in retrospect.

The strange thing about performance is that every developer and project manager wants their application to be performative, but if you dig a little deeper and ask for some metrics on the performance they are aiming for, you can sometimes be faced with silence, or at best, vague replies. It is important to get a clear understanding of the performance you are hoping to achieve from the outset. In a centralized ASP.NET application, this may have been metrics such as the number of concurrent users your application can service, page response times, and so on. In a Silverlight application, you may choose to gauge your performance on the number of frames per second an animation should serve to the end-user. As the processing is largely done on the client in Silverlight, you should also keep in mind client hardware specifications, which could be nontrivial in the web environment. The key step to take here is to identify your target audience. Once you have done this, you should aim your hardware specification toward the software the critical mass of your audience is running. This is not all that dissimilar to sites in the past stating that they are "best viewed with a resolution of 1024 × 768."

This chapter is structured such that the common bottlenecks of a Silverlight application are initially outlined. Subsequent sections then discuss how you can retrieve further information on the performance your application is hitting via instrumentation. Finally, the latter part of this chapter discusses what it is you can actually do to increase the performance of your application. Again, *performance*, at this stage, will no longer be a generic term, but a more concrete performance benchmark that you have decided your application needs to meet.

Performance Bottlenecks

As discussed throughout previous chapters, there are many benefits brought to you by Silverlight — the more groundbreaking of these benefits being the reach of the applications across multiple platforms and browsers. It would be nice to live in a world of all pro's and no con's, but the downside to the reach of Silverlight is that there has to be a compatibility layer between your application and the target platform. This layer means that you cannot target specific hardware and cannot make use of specific software; what you are writing has to be generic to a certain extent to prevent it from working in one environment and breaking in another. Fortunately, this abstraction layer from the platform is taken care of for you by the Silverlight run time, and, in fact, one of the goals of the product teams developing Silverlight was to keep performance between platforms as close as possible. This, however, is not an excuse to avoid testing your application across those platforms, as differences will invariably exist.

One example of this is that the different browsers and platforms have different underlying graphics technologies, and the interoperability between Silverlight and these lower layers can be somewhat different depending on the actions you are performing. This means that when designing an application, you must test that your animations, videos, and the like perform as well on a machine running on a Mac and Firefox as they do running on Windows and Internet Explorer. Another thing to be aware of is that Silverlight does not currently support any graphics hardware acceleration.

You may not always hit the performance levels that you are after, but so long as you have a lower bar that you are not willing to drop below, then you have your target metric, ready for tuning and coding toward.

Developers versus Designers

The title of this section is playing playing Devil's advocate a little. That is because it gives the impression of a face-off between the development teams and the designers, but, of course, this shouldn't be the case. Silverlight has been designed from the bottom up to separate concerns; you let your designers put together your XAML, and you let your developers write the coding logic in the code-behinds. This level of separation is good because it lets the people with the best skills focus on what they are good at, and they don't have to trawl through code or markup that they either don't understand or don't necessarily care about. These are, however, the reasons for the separation, and the two teams should still work very closely together.

Your designers will put together some great-looking applications that may have many MediaElements, animations, and maybe even custom controls, but it will probably come down to you as the developer to evaluate performance impacts that these designs may have on the application. On first appearance, it is a balancing act of Visual prowess versus application performance, but this is not always the case. For example, even though your designer has put together a video on your application background, there are still a number of steps you can take to maintain this visual impact, while reducing the performance impact. This particular problem and others will be identified as you progress through the chapter. Before moving on to instrumentation and improving performance, it is first worth taking a look at the areas in which a performance issue may start to manifest itself.

The main symptoms you can expect of an application that performs poorly include the following:

❏ High processor usage

❏ Lack of smooth animation and media playback

❏ Unresponsive user interface

Depending on the specific scenario, the causes of these symptoms can vary greatly. A brief discussion of each of these symptoms is given here:

High Processor Usage

Without graphics acceleration, the key hardware indicator of a poorly performing application is the processor usage. The causes of this are endless, but by measuring this rate throughout the lifetime of your application, you can start to see where it is struggling with the amount of processing there is to be done. Instrumenting your application may point you to the sources of the problems, but there will likely be various solutions, or choices to be made. Some causes can be put down to poor usage of elements within a page, but other causes may be due to more genuine blocks of heavy code. In the latter case, you should look to break the code out into smaller tasks.

The Silverlight run time itself has a good performance history, and so for the most part you are going to be able to get over any hurdles yourself by following through the steps in this chapter.

Low Frame Rate

Generally, any performance hits you see are going to be the result of the aforementioned high processor usage. This is not true in every single case, however, because the problem maybe I/O bound rather than processor bound — in other words, rather than the processor being the bottleneck, it could be that you are taking a hit in the UI because you are waiting for some data to be pulled down. With some tweaks, this is pretty simple to avoid given the communications model you are driven to use by Silverlight, and this is something that is discussed in detail in the section on improving performance.

If you are an end-user, you are probably not going to notice the processor usage as a first indicator of the poor performance; you are going to start seeing either a poor frame rate or poor responsiveness of the user interface.

When the processor starts experiencing a high volume of work, the Silverlight renderer will begin to drop frames. This is something you should catch during your testing, or earlier proof-of-concept work, and should therefore, hopefully, not be something your users will see.

Unresponsive UI

An unresponsive user interface (UI) has two primary causes (with a possible third). The first is high processor utilization, and the second is that the main user interface thread is blocking on the network (which should occur in a minimal number of cases because of the communications model Silverlight uses). A third possibility is that bugs in the code may block the UI indefinitely, and therefore control over the UI would never return. The latter should certainly be something that is picked up during testing, and maybe something that would be detected by the testing techniques discussed in Chapter 15.

Instrumentation

Instrumentation is basically the steps you can take to gain some kind of feedback from your application, usually through the development progress. You can instrument your code to gather debug information or, in this case, performance-related statistics. Such instrumentation can be divided into configuration settings provided with Silverlight, or those that you instruct your application to emit at run time (maybe only under a debug build).

Monitoring the Frame Rate

The Silverlight plug-in provides a few different settings on the frame rate of your application, which can be essential for tuning your application. The various settings pertaining to this are discussed below.

EnableFrameRateCounter *and* MaxFrameRate

One of the first settings that you should enable during the development process is the `EnableFrame RateCounter` setting, which you set on the Silverlight plug-in. If you were using the ASP.NET Silverlight control, this would look something like:

```
<asp:Silverlight ID="Xaml1" runat="server" Source="~/ClientBin/TextAnimation.xap"
        Version="2.0" Width="100%" Height="100%" EnableFrameRateCounter="true" />
```

If you are creating the object directly, specify an object parameter, like this:

```
<object data="data:application/x-silverlight," type="application/x-silverlight-2"
        width="100%" height="100%">
...
<param name="enableframeratecounter" value="true" />
...
```

This gives you a handy frame rate indicator in the status bar of your browser.

> **Please note that this status bar indicator will only work in Internet Explorer–based browsers.**

An example of the format of this indicator is shown in Figure 16-1.

The numbers are following the notation *fps:currentframerate/maximumframerate*. This presents an obvious question: how can the current frame rate be higher than the maximum? Well, the actual meaning of the first number is that this is the frame rate the application would be operating at given the chance. This is being restricted by the default value of 60 fps (frames per second) in this example. So, the way to interpret this in your application is that the lower value of the two is the actual rate at which your application is operating. This begs the question of how to override the default maximum frame rate. Well, this is just another simple parameter called `MaxFrameRate`. You can test the effects of this by setting the `MaxFrameRate` to a value of just 1 and then by execute the sample application called BouncingBall. The BouncingBall sample is a simple application, which does exactly as you would imagine; it is a ball that bounces around inside a `Canvas` control. This is not done via a traditional animation as its trajectory is dynamic and therefore uses a per-frame callback event handler.

As with any more traditional animation, however, it *does* depend on a suitable frame rate to execute in a smooth manner. When you execute it at varying maximum rates, the suitability of the frame rate should become apparent.

Figure 16-1

> An important point to be aware of here is that, where possible, you should use a standard Silverlight animation rather than writing your own animation code. In scenarios in which a traditional animation can be used, there will be performance gains.

Where these counters come in useful is in testing the performance of your application on different machines and different browsers (in the case of MaxFrameRate). For example, you may know that on a certain configuration of browser and Operating System, you can get a throughput of 50 fps. It is quite possible that you have a top-end machine that could deal with this with no problem, but during development, you could set the MaxFrameRate value to something much lower, such as 15, in order to make sure your application user experience at this level is suitable. This gives you peace of mind that when lower-end machines run your application, they are going to be able to use the application as intended.

EnableRedrawRegions

Another interesting setting that you can set up on the Silverlight plug-in is the EnableRedrawRegions setting. This is turned off by default, but by enabling it (setting it equal to true), you will get a visual indicator of the regions being re-drawn through each frame change of your application. By enabling this setting in conjunction with a MaxFrameRate setting of 1, you can see that the ball region is being re-drawn per frame. This is illustrated in Figure 16-2.

Figure 16-2

As you can see from this illustration, the areas that are redrawn are being shaded. It is good to know, though, that Silverlight is not re-drawing the entire screen per frame and is therefore not using up valuable CPU clock cycles.

Manual Timing

The previous approach is the recommended way to test the frame rate of your application, but you can complement this information if you need to time a particular task within your application, or if you need some comparable numbers between Internet Explorer and Firefox (which, as already mentioned, does not support the EnableFramerateCounter parameter). In order to time a particular task, you can write some simple timing code; this is not something specific to Silverlight because you can use the DateTime.Now.Ticks method, which you may be familiar with from previous .NET Framework development work. The TimerAndText sample code included demonstrates how you might achieve this timing for a storyboard.

In the sample code, you will see four simple animations sitting within a storyboard. Each animation spins and enlarges a TextBlock on top of MediaElement — nothing too complicated for the processor to deal with, but it gives it something to think about. The last animation finishes after 1.6 seconds, but because the code set AutoReverse equal to true, you can expect the total time for the Storyboard to complete to be 3.2 seconds. The storyboard code wraps some simple timing code as previously described, which can be seen in the following snippet:

```
void Page_Loaded(object sender, RoutedEventArgs e)
{

    ...
    storyBoard1.Completed += new EventHandler(storyBoard1_Completed);
    storyBoard1.AutoReverse = true;
    storyBoard1.Begin();

}
```

```
void storyBoard1_Completed(object sender, EventArgs e)
{

ticks = DateTime.Now.Ticks - ticks;
timer.Text = ticks.ToString();
ticks = DateTime.Now.Ticks;
storyBoard1.Begin();

}
```

So, all the code does is start a timer off, and once the storyboard has completed, it displays a differential between the number of ticks at the time of starting the storyboard being started, and at its end, and then puts that value in a `TextBlock`. The storyboard is then kicked off again. Keeping in mind that the units of `DateTime.Now.Ticks` are nanoseconds, some simple math tells you that `timer.Text` should be equal to $3.2 \times 10,000,000 = 32,000,000$. For the most part, this will be true, although when running the sample, you will find that this is not always the case. For example, on a rather mid-market laptop, we found the time to vary by anything up to 50,000 ns (nanoseconds), or 0.005 seconds, which is pretty reasonable, and unlikely to be anything the end-user would notice. But, of course, this is a relatively lightweight application despite some attempts to make it otherwise. Where things get interesting is if you open up multiple browser windows to start really stressing the application on the client. Without any graphical hardware acceleration, you will find that the CPU really starts to suffer. Figure 16-3 shows a screenshot of multiple browser windows being open, hitting this test sample at the same time.

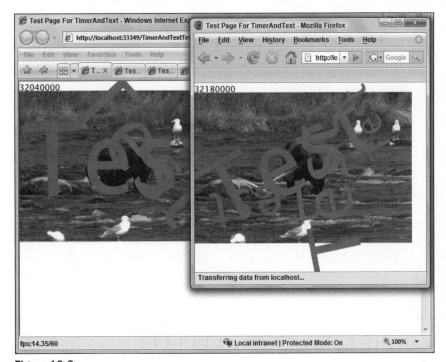

Figure 16-3

In this particular example, you can see that the Firefox metric shows a value of 32,180,000, which is a value of 0.018 second over the preferred amount of time. Although this is not a massive difference and this example is slightly contrived, it is not difficult to imagine a user having a slower machine with maybe just a couple of windows open to a few other sites. This is really just referring back to the point on testing on a wide range of realistic hardware and platforms in order to get a good feel for how your application performs across the board. The 0.018 seconds may not have seemed a big figure, but in the same illustration you can see just how poor the current frame rate is — a meager 14.35 fps. The user is likely to notice such a low frame rate, but the main reason for this will be because of the lack of a *consistent* frame rate. In other words, if the frame rate was consistently at 14 fps, the user may realize it, but it may not greatly impact the experience. If the frame rate is switching aggressively between 14 fps and 60 fps, then the performance hit is going to be highlighted much more.

You could easily have reproduced the end result of a low frame rate using the aforementioned techniques, but until you actually put stress on your application, it's difficult to see just how far it can be pushed.

Another interesting metric during this test, which you could take a look at, is the Process Utilization. You can simply use Windows Task Manager to do this, but you get a far more accurate figure by setting up some Performance Monitor counters. Figure 16-4 shows the respective performance data for the previous stress test.

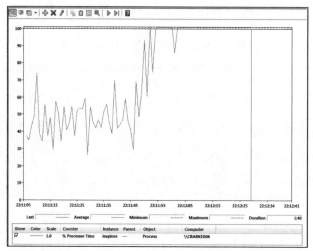

Figure 16-4

It shouldn't take a data analyst to figure out at which point the other instances of the application were fired up. Also note that the load is spread over all cores/CPUs.

Improving Performance

This section takes you through various ways you can increase the performance of your application during and after your application development. It is also a useful section to read before any serious development commences because it will provide you with a catalog of areas to be wary of during your design. The general guidance here is that if you are unsure of the effects of a particular feature in your application, then it may be a good idea to write a small proof of concept application in advance of your main design to prove its ability to function as you expect. There is always the all-important point of testing this cross-browser, and cross-platform too, which cannot be reiterated enough.

In many of the points that follow, you may find yourself in the position of having to make trade-offs, but this isn't always the case. As an example, when designing your media, you should always try to lower the quality of it in terms of an encoding point of view to see just how much you can get away with. Lowering quality isn't usually a term associated with good application design, but the key thing to remember here is that the user experience could be greatly improved with relatively few, if any, visible differences. Again, consider the point about frame rate consistency over having a high frame rate for short bursts.

So, now it's time to break the application up into some common features and pitfalls, which will allow you to begin on your path to creating a responsive and visually appealing application.

Animation

One of the richer features of a Silverlight application is animation; it brings the interface to life for a user and can make the interaction with your application much more intuitive. The baggage that comes with this is the possible performance impact of having a large number of animations occurring at the same time, and when animating certain types of elements (such as text, which is described shortly). This section explains some of the traps to watch out for, most of which are good to know about before you start development, as they can be quite costly to fix further down the line.

Text

In the TimerAndText sample that you have already looked at, there are four text animations occurring as part of the storyboard. These were used intentionally as a stress scenario while the timing data was collated because animating text can actually have a performance impact. When text is rendered within Silverlight, it undergoes a process known as *hinting*. *Hinting* is the way font developers associate information with the font so that for a certain font size, each glyph has a number of primary pixels associated with it to use to render a rasterized display. To clarify the meaning of this sentence, a definition of some of those terms is required.

First of all, a *glyph* is a representation of a character (as you may know if you have used the Glyphs element within Silverlight). To put this into context, the character *A* can be used as an example. In the simple case, *A* could have two associated glyphs — one for its uppercase representation and one for its lowercase representation. Now, if you think about a PC display, you know that it is built up of a matrix of elements called *pixels* — this is essentially a *rasterized* display. When a graphics driver comes to render content onto this display (in this case, a glyph), it must take the graphical information, which may not conform strictly to the target matrix of pixels, and it must use an algorithm in which to lay those glyphs onto the matrix to reflect the source as accurately as possible. This interpolation process can be seen in Figure 16-5.

In Figure 16-5, each square represents a pixel. In this particular example, the rendered character **A** on the right has become distorted from its source (on the far left) as it has been transformed. Obviously, the greater the number of squares in the matrix (i.e., the higher the resolution), the less apparent the distortion is to the user. When developing a font, the designer has the ability to associate a number of "hints" with a glyph such that for a certain size, it can say exactly which of those pixels should be rendered.

Taking Figure 16-5 as an example again, the distorted glyph on the right could be tidied up by rendering some of the pixels slightly differently.

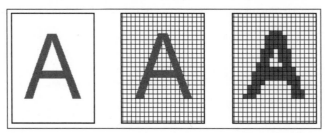

Figure 16-5

> **Various techniques can be used to improve the appearance of the glyphs, such as anti-aliasing, which provides a smooth edge to the rendered glyphs.**

So, now that these terms have been explained, it's time to revisit why this is important. The fact is that in animating text within Silverlight, the rendering engine performs hinting for each frame. This can get expensive in terms of the amount of processing that has to be done. While you may not notice the impact of this for a smaller animation, you should bear this hit in mind. The symptoms of this behavior will be high CPU usage, and frames will be dropped. This is the behavior that you will have seen by stressing the TimerAndText sample previously.

One solution to this is to use `Path` element instead of font-based text elements such as the `TextBlock`. This obviously has an associated development overhead, and so it may require some proof-of-concept work in advance of your main application design if you are considering using these features.

Game Loops

The requirements of your application could be very different depending on whether your application is going to be a line-of-business application or something like an interactive game. Most games that require any interactive movement directed by the player require something called a *game loop*. You have seen an example of this in the Instrumentation section, but this is worth revisiting here in order to understand the options you have available.

A game loop allows you to perform your game logic at a regular frequency, and as the game will run over a period of time; these checks are usually contained within some kind of looping code. In the example of the BouncingBall, no user input was expected, but it still needed to use a game loop because its movement is highly dynamic, and each run is different. It would have been possible to have used an animation to do this, although it would have required quite a bit more work, and the overall feeling as a developer doing this would be that you were working against the grain somewhat.

There are a few different options to you when developing a game loop, the more common of which are mentioned below:

❑ Create a storyboard of "0" duration, and use the storyboard's completed event as your game loop pulse. This works quite well, but as the application starts to get stressed, your game loop performance will start to degrade quite badly.

❑ Create a new thread, and within that thread make a looping call to check for a user's input, and move the objects on the screen accordingly. Because your work will be done on a separate thread and you need to manipulate UI elements, you have to marshal your calls to the UI thread using `Dispatcher.BeginInvoke()`. This allows you to place a delegated function into the UI's message queue ready for execution. This approach usually means introducing a `Thread.Sleep()` in the spawned thread to avoid it overflowing the UI thread with messages, in which case, your application may appear to freeze up, and nothing gets updated.

❑ Create a `DispatcherTimer` instance, and fire a call to your logic after a set number of milliseconds. Setting the `Interval` property and then hooking into the `OnTick` event can do this. `DispatcherTimer` is a high-resolution timer and can therefore give you a high number of opportunities per second in which to influence the game's activities. Quite obviously, the more logic you place in your event handler and the lower the timer interval, the more strain you are going to be placing on your application.

❑ Create a per-frame callback using `CompositionTarget.Rendering`. Within the callback function, gather the input from the user/player, and then move the objects on the screen as required.

There are other approaches you can take to generate these game loops, but they tend to become quite contrived. The preferred approach to take is the last option on this list, which is to perform your logic in the per-frame callback. This approach is highly flexible and inherently prevents you from calling your game logic more often than needed — in other words, taking the example of the Bouncing Ball, why would you need to update its position more frequently than the frames change to render the movement? The answer is that you wouldn't need to do this, as it would be a waste of cycles. If there is a certain piece of game logic that does need to be performed at a higher frequency, then you can still use `DispatcherTimer` in parallel if required.

The Bouncing Ball sample demonstrates the use of the per-frame callback technique, but in its most basic form, it is implemented simply as follows:

```
void Page_Loaded(object sender, RoutedEventArgs e)
{
    CompositionTarget.Rendering += new
        EventHandler(CompositionTarget_Rendering);
}

void CompositionTarget_Rendering(object sender, EventArgs e)
{
// TODO:  Implement per-frame callback rendering code.
}
```

In the case of the Bouncing Ball, the code to position the ball is done within the `CompositionTarget_` `Rendering` event handler.

If you take a look inside the Bouncing Ball sample, you will see how the game loop can be implemented as a zero-duration storyboard (within the commented-out code). This is not the recommended approach, but to give you the idea, the main skeleton of this code looks like the following:

```
void Page_Loaded(object sender, RoutedEventArgs e)
{

    storyBoard1.Completed += new EventHandler(storyBoard1_Completed);
    storyBoard1.Begin();


}

void storyBoard1_Completed(object sender, EventArgs e)
{

    // TODO:  Implement rendering and positioning code.

    storyBoard1.Begin();
}
```

storyBoard1 is simply defined in XAML as follows:

```
<UserControl.Resources>
        <Storyboard x:Name="storyBoard1" BeginTime="0:00:00" Duration="0:00:00" />
</UserControl.Resources>
```

As already discussed, however, the best practice here is to use the CompositionTarget approach, so the other techniques will not be discussed in detail.

Windowless

If you take another look at the Bouncing Ball example, you will notice that one of the parameters passed to the Silverlight plug-in on the test page is `Windowless="true"`. This setting tells the Silverlight plug-in to execute as a Windowless control within the browser. What this means is that in the underlying Win32 API, no Windows handle is associated with the plug-in. This reason alone is not enough to want to set this option to `true`; where it becomes really useful is in its ability to allow integration with the HTML elements of your web page. Essentially, by setting `Windowless="true"`, you gain the ability to set a Z-index on the hosting plug-in such that it appears either behind or in front of existing HTML content. This becomes useful when you want to, say, have an HTML dropdown list box sitting on top of your Silverlight control. You can, of course, link the two pieces seamlessly together using the HTML "bridge," and so for the user, the appearance of the HTML and the Silverlight content is in unison. The same is going to apply with any of the ASP.NET controls that you want to use in conjunction with your Silverlight application.

The downside to setting this value is the performance impact caused by the rendering engine. With that said, you are left with no choice when running your application on a Mac; even if you explicitly set the value to `false` (which is the default value, anyway), it will still have the behavior of a Windowless plug-in running inside a browser on the Mac. The reason for this is that a Windowless plug-in isn't directly tied to Silverlight but, rather, ActiveX and the underlying Windows platform. On the Mac, the plug-in has no notion of being "Windowed."

It is worth pointing out here, that despite your not having the ability to disable this on the Mac, it does not mean that the performance will be any worse when run on the Mac when compared to a PC or otherwise, as it is really about how the underlying Operating System APIs deal with the rendering. The rule of thumb here, though, is to set this value to `false` unless you have requirements within your application to have the ability to overlay Silverlight on top of HTML content, or vice versa.

> **The main example used here outlined that the reason for enabling this setting is to allow an HTML/Silverlight interaction. The setting actually allows for even more flexibility than that, and you could use it to overlay Silverlight and Flash plug-ins over each other.**

The Windowless setting is often used in conjunction with another performance-impacting offender: Transparent Backgrounds.

Transparent Backgrounds

The previous section detailed some scenarios whereby you might want to overlay some Silverlight content over your HTML content. Well, to improve on the visual integration between the two worlds, you may also choose to set the `PluginBackground` color to Transparent on your Silverlight plug-in. This is really only worth setting on the plug-in if you are overlaying some content, and hence the tight relationship with the Windowless parameter. You can achieve some pretty nice effects by having a transparency in the plug-in background — even something simple like a menu, as demonstrated in Figure 16-6, can soften the impact of a page.

Figure 16-6

Something as static as a menu probably isn't going to hit your application too hard, but certainly animations are a different story. To fully understand why you get the performance hit with transparencies, it is worth explaining fundamentally what they are. So, on your Silverlight control, you may have the parameter specified as follows:

```
<asp:Silverlight ID="Xaml1" runat="server" Source="~/ClientBin/Transparency
.xap"
        Version="2.0" Windowless="true" PluginBackground="Transparent"
        EnableFrameRateCounter="true"/>
```

If you are using the <object> tag notation here, the equivalent parameter name is *background*. As with any other named colors, *Transparent* is just an alias for an underlying value. Where you may be used to specifying RGB (red, green, blue) values in the ASP.NET world, you may not be used to the extra component that is being wrapped up here, and this is the *A* in *ARGB*, which is an Alpha value. Each color and the Alpha holds an associated 8-bit value, which is addressed by a base-16 value ranging from 00 through to FF. So when you use the Transparent alias, this actually translates to 00FFFFFF, where the first two *F* characters are representing the Alpha value as shown here:

```
<asp:Silverlight ID="Xaml1" runat="server" Source="~/ClientBin/Transparency.xap"
        Version="2.0" Windowless="true" PluginBackground="#00FFFFFF"
        EnableFrameRateCounter="true"/>
```

In fact, when the first two characters of the *ARGB* are set to 0×0, it doesn't matter what the rest of the values are set to as they will not be visible. If you increase the Alpha value to 0×80, which equates to a decimal value of 128 (of the 256 possible values), then the remaining values start to come into play. By keeping the rest of the values set to $0 \times FF$, you will notice a translucent white color as *#FFFFFF* evaluates to White. You can see from the Transparency sample solution a couple of different translucent colors provided by the Alpha value.

So, the performance hit with transparencies comes when the renderer must make a special effort to "blend" the image of the foreground and the image of the background together to provide the transparency effect. With an animation, each frame must be reblended, and so this can build up into quite an impact. As always, the key thing to remember here is to test across platforms and browsers, as some combinations may be hit harder than others.

> **Although any transparency is going to result in an increase in processing, the biggest hit comes from plug-in transparency rather than that of transparency within the plug-in itself.**

Alpha values are not purely associated with the Transparent alias in Silverlight, as they can also be set by other means such as setting an Opacity value.

Opacity and Visibility

The Tranparent color alias tends to be set on properties such as Background, Foreground, and as you have just seen, PluginBackground. These properties all allow you to set the colors and the Alpha value all under one property.

> Although the color names can be thought of as *aliases*, these do not always have to be colors. What is actually happening behind the scenes is that these string representations are undergoing a type conversion from the string representation into a `SolidColorBrush`.

Another property that allows you to set the Alpha property individually is the `Opacity` property. This property is available to all `UIElements`, and you won't find it on the Silverlight plug-in itself. Whereas `Opacity` is available on all `UIElements`, properties such as `Background` aren't. For example, you can set both the `Opacity` and the `Background` on a grid layout, but you can only set the `Opacity` on a `TextBlock`. The `Opacity` is set on a scale of 0 to 1.0, with 1.0 being fully opaque, and 0 being fully transparent. So, what is the difference between setting the `Background` property on a grid to `Transparent`, and setting its `Opacity` property to 0? Well, the latter is going to alter the visibility of both the background and foreground of the grid (or target `UIElement`), whereas the former will only make the background transparent.

> For finer control over exactly which part of the element you make translucent, you can set the `OpacityMask` property and use a brush to instruct the area you wish to affect.

In the last section, it was highlighted that although reducing the Alpha value within the Silverlight control will result in an increase in processing, it is not going to have a hit on the scale like reducing the Alpha value on the Silverlight Plug-in, so why mention `Opacity` in this section? Well, it is a useful property to have from an aesthetics perspective, but you, again, must use it wisely. A poor use of `Opacity` would be to use it to hide elements in your display. The reason that this is such a bad practice is because the renderer is still essentially performing some rendering around this element despite its lack of visibility to the user. So, if you are intending to hide elements, you should, in fact, set their `Visibility` property to a value of `System.Windows.Visibility.Collapsed`.

Full-Screen Mode

The ordinary end-user isn't going to care too much about the technology sitting behind his or her web experience, but they are going to be impressed with the improved web experience that it can bring. To achieve this experience, you will no doubt design lots of fancy animations, template the existing controls, and probably start to write your own controls. Using the techniques discussed already in this chapter and throughout the book, you are also going to want to blend your application seamlessly into today's Web. You have seen how some of these techniques can affect your application's performance and are now aware of what you can do to counter these performance bear traps. Another approach you may take to integrate your application into the end-user's web experience is to give your application the ability to switch into Full-Screen mode. This is nothing new to Silverlight, and, in fact, if you hit [F11] on Windows in any of the big browsers, you will see that you get a Full-Screen view of the browser, where most, if not all of the browser toolbars disappear. Traditional uses of a Full-Screen mode have been found in a whole range of applications, such as Internet Café browsing, through to machines dedicated to running a single web application; it gives sole focus to a particular application. It may not necessarily be the case that you want to force users to go Full Screen but, rather, provide them with the option to do so should they choose.

It is all well and good being able to hit a shortcut key in your browser to go Full Screen, but you can bring this ability into your application using Silverlight. The slightly hidden property within the Silverlight object model allows you to instruct your browser to go Full Screen:

```
App.Current.Host.Content.IsFullScreen = true;
```

You will probably execute this code as the result of some kind of input event; for example, if the user hits a particular key, or if they click a certain button. You should, of course, provide them with a way of returning from Full-Screen mode (by setting the property to `false`), but as a fallback, the Silverlight run time at least allows you to hit [Esc] to return from this.

> **You cannot execute this line of code during any of the start-up events. This has been prevented as a security measure in order to prevent extreme attacks such as a malicious site replicating your desktop and accepting input under false pretences.**

When you go Full Screen, there are several common steps that you will likely undertake. You will first of all probably want to rescale any controls, shapes, and the like in order to take advantage of the extra screen real estate. You can do this by hooking up your code to the `FullScreenChanged` event like so:

```
public Page()
{
    InitializeComponent();
    this.Loaded += new RoutedEventHandler(Page_Loaded);
    App.Current.Host.Content.FullScreenChanged+=new
        EventHandler(Content_FullScreenChanged);
}

private void btn1_Click(object sender, RoutedEventArgs e)
{
    if (App.Current.Host.Content.IsFullScreen == false)
    {
        App.Current.Host.Content.IsFullScreen = true;
    }
    else
    {
        App.Current.Host.Content.IsFullScreen = false;
    }
}

void Content_FullScreenChanged(object sender, EventArgs e)
{
    if (App.Current.Host.Content.IsFullScreen == true)
    {
        //TODO: Write scale-up code
        //TODO: Hide unwanted elements
    }
    else
    {
        //TODO: Write scale-down code
        //TODO: Bring back previously hidden elements
    }
}
```

As discussed, you can use a keyboard shortcut in most browsers to switch to Full-Screen mode. One thing to be aware of is that these will bypass the Silverlight run time if executed directly, and so your Silverlight event handlers will not be run as a result. Therefore you should look to drive screen switching through your application rather than through the browser directly.

Another one of the actions you are likely to take is to hide some of the elements on the display. An example of why you might do this is if you had a number of toolbars for your application that didn't lend themselves well to Full Screen, or just plain well don't make sense. You can see from the //TODO comments exactly where you might hide/unhide those elements, but a couple of options are available to you. From the previous section on "Opacity and Visibility," you know what you shouldn't do from a performance perspective, but there is another option open to you besides setting the Visibility to Collapsed on the elements you wish to hide: that is to remove the elements from the Visual Tree. You can do this quite simply by executing some code like this:

```
LayoutRoot.Children.Remove(textBlock);
```

There are pros and cons in taking this option over setting the Visibility property, depending on the usage of your application. For example, if you are in a situation whereby there are many elements that you wish to hide during a Full Screen and you know that it is likely your application is going to be used in a Full-Screen state for a large proportion of the time, then it could be beneficial to remove the elements from the tree. This will reduce the burden on the run time as there will not be so many elements to enumerate within the tree, and this will, of course, also reduce memory consumption. However, this is really only going to be worth doing if you *do* meet this strict criterion; that is, you will be in Full Screen for a long period of time, and you have a large number of elements that you wish to hide. This is because presumably when you return from Full Screen you are going to want these elements to reappear. If these elements have previously only been given a Visibility value of Collapsed, then they are already in the Visual Tree, and it is just a case of switching this property back to Visible. However, if you have removed them from the tree and they have subsequently gone out of scope and been garbage-collected, then you are going to have to go through the costly process of reconstructing the objects and placing them at the correct point within the tree; this could burn a number of cycles, particularly when you are looking at a large number of elements.

So again, there is no silver bullet here, but these are considerations you need to bear in mind, and armed with this knowledge, you should be able to make the right decisions at design time.

Height and Width

A fairly common mistake often experienced by novice web developers, even in the pre-ASP.NET days, was to take a relatively large image file and use it on a web page. It didn't need to be so large, and, in fact, the developer may have rescaled this using HTML or setting the style on the image. What the end-user got in this case was an extremely slow-loading page, and at the end of it, a tiny image hidden away in the corner somewhere. This is, of course, something that should still be avoided today, but there is the extra trap to avoid, which is not setting the height and width of media elements. It doesn't matter if you are setting a large piece of media smaller, or a small piece of media larger — either way you are walking into a performance problem. It may not be a notable performance problem, but as with all of these potential issues, they can snowball if the behavior is exhibited hundreds or even thousands of times within an application.

The reason for the hit is that when the Silverlight renderer comes to display the element, whether it be an image or a video, it has to perform an extra step in its pipeline. That is, it decodes the element and then has to resize it to the specified boundaries, before it is able to render it. The ultimate taboo here would be to animate the height and width of the media element as you would take this hit for every frame, with the possibility of also undergoing the hit of blending the media per animation frame.

When facing this issue, your friend is a tool such as Expression Encoder. This allows you to encode your media at the new size at design time, and therefore removes the hit at run time; of course, this is not going to help you should you wish to animate the media size as well, but this will be, hopefully, a niche requirement.

XAML versus Images

In the design phase of your application, you may have either in-house or third-party designers putting together prototypes of what your application should look like from a graphical perspective. These designs may be presented to the project leader, who then coordinates the development effort in bringing these images to life. It may be, however, that your designers are "mocking up" some screens using Microsoft Expression Blend or Microsoft Expression Design, and therefore your project leader gets handed a set of XAML files. This leads to an important design decision about which parts of your application should render graphics from the XAML and which parts should use plain old images. The choice you make will have a direct bearing on the performance of your application, and as always, there's not a "one size fits all" approach.

The XAMLvsImage sample in the Performance solution is used to show some of the size differences between an image represented as XAML, and one represented as a JPEG. The project isn't intended for execution but, rather, to prove the design-time concepts. What you can see in the project are two XAML files, one named *simple.xaml* and one named *complex.xaml*. These have respective representations as JPEG images in the Images folder named *image_simple.jpg* and *image_complex.jpg*. All files were produced using Expression Design, and their file sizes are shown in the following table:

Filename	Simple (bytes)	Complex (bytes)
XAML	799	357,193
JPEG	7431	14,305

This example shows just how extreme the sizes can be, depending on the format. In the simple graphic, the XAML is smaller, but in the more complex graphic, the XAML is many times bigger. The reason for this is twofold: The JPEG format by its nature undergoes a level of compression, but also the XAML representation is using a Path element to get the complex outline of the text, and this involves a lot of associated data, which is, of course, stored as a text string. The performance story here is pretty obvious from the fact that if you had to pull the complex XAML graphic over the network, it would have a much greater impact than that of the JPEG (although if the XAML were contained in a XAP file, it would also undergo a level of compression). From the simple graphic example, though, you can see that there is not always a rule of thumb to follow with regard to the size of the asset.

The performance decision you have to make is not always going to be about the size of the asset, though. If, for example, you wish to resize the graphic, the XAML vector graphic is going to fare better than the JPEG raster image. On the flip side, if you simply need a representation of your company's logo, it is unlikely that it is going to need to be resized, and will quite likely be a smaller resource for downloading.

> Much the same as there is a performance hit in setting the `Height` and `Width` of a `MediaElement`, there is also an impact in setting the `Height` and `Width` of a `Path` element. If you need to resize a `Path` element, then you should do this via the coordinates of the `Data` attribute.

If you do choose to use an image such as a JPEG, you could increase performance further by downloading it via the `WebClient` class so that you do not hold up the UI thread while it is being downloaded.

Threading

You saw the various threading options available to you in Chapter 4. You should keep these concepts in mind when considering the performance of your application. As always, there is a balancing act when it comes to the performance of your application and threading. For example, if you are performing a lot of complex logic on the main UI thread, it is going to result in the user interface becoming unresponsive and frustrating for the end-user. The solution here is to use one of the approaches discussed in Chapter 4 to separate the complex logic and hand it off to another thread. Creating threads, however, is an expensive operation in itself, so they should be used sparingly and with consideration. The general rule of thumb is that if you have a long-running, blocking operation within your custom logic, you should consider using a separate thread. The Silverlight framework helps enforce some of these practices by use of the Async Pattern, which is visited later in this chapter.

JavaScript versus Managed Code

Coming from an ASP.NET background, you have probably been exposed to JavaScript fairly frequently when you have needed to save round-trips to the server, and needed to do some calculations on the client. Now that Silverlight 2 brings a managed environment to the client, you can for the most part start to concentrate all your development effort in your .NET language of choice. There will, however, be the odd time when you need to develop some code in JavaScript. There are a few reasons for you having to do this, including a couple outlined here:

❑ You want to perform some logic/operations before your Silverlight application has loaded. Maybe this is on some custom plug-in start-up code, or maybe it is trying to do something a little more complex with a splash screen (which in its nature comes before your application and the managed run time are loaded).

❑ You may have some existing investment in some HTML controls that require JavaScript, and part of your migration strategy means that you cannot port these to Silverlight immediately.

Whatever the reason, it's worth knowing just how the performance of the compiled, managed code performs against the interpreted script. As part of the sample code at `wrox.com`, you will find a Silverlight project named *JSvsCS*, which represents a JavaScript/C# comparison project. The project presents you with a page and allows you to click a button to calculate the first 28 numbers of the Fibonacci sequence in either JavaScript or C#.

> To keep the test fair, the timing code was wrapped as tightly as possible around the Fibonacci algorithm code; in other words, the timings do not take into consideration enumerating the Visual Tree in order to display the results.

After the calculation has been performed, the results are shown, along with the time it took to calculate the results.

> You may be asking yourself why it is the first 28 numbers that are being calculated since this is not a very round number. The reason for this is that during testing, Internet Explorer detected that the time taken to calculate 29 numbers was too long, and a prompt would continue to appear asking whether the long-running script should be terminated. This was within the JavaScript code only, but to keep the tests fair, both sets of code perform the calculations based on the first 28 numbers of the sequence.

The code implementation of the JavaScript algorithm can be seen here:

```
// JavaScript Implementation of Fibonacci Sequence

function main(j)
{
    var strFib;
    var dateStart = new Date();
    var startTime = dateStart.getTime();

    for(i=0; i<j; i++)
    {
        strFib = strFib + fib(i) + ", ";
    }

    var dateEnd = new Date();
    var endTime = dateEnd.getTime();

    var plugin = document.getElementById("Xaml1");

    var JSFib = plugin.Content.FindName("txtJSFib");
    var JSTimer = plugin.Content.FindName("txtJSTimer");

    JSFib.Text = strFib;
    JSTimer.Text = endTime - startTime + " ms";
}

function fib(n)
{
    if(n < 2)
    {
        return n;
    }
    else
    {
        return fib(n-1) + fib(n-2);
    }
}
```

The C# implementation of the same algorithm can be seen here:

```csharp
// C# Implementation of Fibonacci Sequence

private void btnCSGo_Click(object sender, RoutedEventArgs e)
{
    StringBuilder sb = new StringBuilder();
    DateTime startTime = DateTime.Now;

    for (int i = 0; i < FIB_RUNS; i++)
    {
        sb.Append(fib(i));
        sb.Append(", ");
    }

    DateTime endTime = DateTime.Now;

    txtCSFib.Text = sb.ToString();
    txtCSTimer.Text =
        endTime.Subtract(startTime).Milliseconds.ToString() + " ms";
}

private long fib(long n)
{
    if (n < 2)
    {
        return n;
    }
    else
    {
        return fib(n - 1) + fib(n - 2);
    }
}
```

> The code implementation could be written more efficiently for the C# implementation, but the coding constructs have been kept as similar as possible to those of the JavaScript to provide a more obvious comparison, and a potentially fairer test.

You can see from both snippets that the actual fib function/method is practically identical. The calling functions then make a looping call to this method a variable number of times (which, as already explained, turns out to be 28). Immediately on either side of the loop code is the assignment of the current time to a variable, where a differential is taken upon completion and output to the Silverlight Application Window. The JavaScript code is being called from the Silverlight Browser bridge with the following simple line of code:

```
HtmlPage.Window.Invoke("main", FIB_RUNS);
```

This line of code pretty much ties up the link between the buttons of the form, and the JavaScript implementation getting called and iterated the same number of times as the C# implementation (i.e., it is directed by the FIB_RUNS constant).

So, now that the implementation details have been discussed, how exactly do the two compare when it comes to performance? Well, Figure 16-7 shows the results, which also gives you an idea of how the test harness looks.

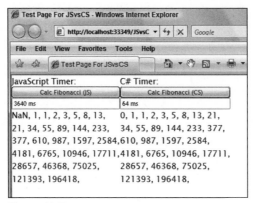

Figure 16-7

So, the JavaScript implementation takes 3,640 ms (milliseconds) to complete, whereas the C# code producing the same output, executing the same algorithm, takes a mere 64 ms. Well, actually, that is not strictly true. The first time the C# test was run, it took around 150 ms, with all subsequent runs taking about 64 ms; this is perfectly reasonable given that the code must be Just-In-Time compiled, and possibly cached along the way. Despite this, even the initial run is many times quicker than its JavaScript counterpart.

> **These timings are ballpark figures after running the tests several times. These timings will vary depending on the hardware specification of the machine they were run on, but you should be able to get the tests running on your own machine in no time at all.**

The really interesting discovery comes when you start to run the same test across different browsers. The test figures just quoted were those against Internet Explorer 7. The following table shows the same test being run on Windows Vista in Firefox and in Safari.

Browser	JavaScript (ms)	C# – Second Run (ms)
Internet Explorer 7	3,640	64
Firefox 3.0.1	301	64
Safari 3.1.2	705	66

> **Running Silverlight 2 within Safari 3.1.2 on Windows is not a supported configuration, but is used here for a deeper comparison.**

Although these tests can't be considered scientific with regard to the algorithm logic, which isn't entirely fair, and with the hardware and software configured on the machine, two key points become quite apparent:

❑   The Internet Explorer implementation is about five times slower than Safari, and a massive 12 times slower than Firefox.

❑   As you probably anticipated, the C# implementation is comparable across browsers. In fact, the results are so close that there is no clear winner.

So what conclusions can be drawn from this? Well, again, it's that old point, stressing the importance of testing your application across multiple browsers. It also reiterates that you should strive to use managed code, certainly for your logic, wherever possible because it is many times quicker than JavaScript and is a lot more consistent when you go cross-platform.

To save you getting the calculator out, the managed code was more than 50 times faster than the JavaScript in Internet Explorer in this case.

Hopefully, this news won't have come as a massive shock to you, but if you do enjoy writing in JavaScript, you have the option of porting your code to managed JavaScript, which sits on top of the Dynamic Language Runtime.

Element Reuse

Where possible, your designers should be looking to keep the complexity of the XAML to a minimum. This does not mean that you have to cut back on the features, but there are often ways to achieve the same visual effects with much cleaner-looking XAML. One way you have already seen in order to keep your XAML cleaner, and enabling reuse is through the use of Styles and Templates, which removes the need to define the look and feel of each control individually.

If you are looking to develop your own controls, then you can reduce the complexity of the XAML further by minimizing the use of the constituent elements that make up your control. Take, for example, a control that displays a star rating system, where the end-users hover over a series of five stars, lighting each of them up in a gold color as they go.

It seems obvious in this simple example, but as a designer, you would not be looking to design the same star element five times within your control — you would most likely define a control that was a star, such that it could be reused five times by a parent control. Also, you may look to achieve some kinds of effects on each one of those stars to give it the appearance of depth. Whereas you could do this by overlaying several shapes over it, it would be more easily achieved by using a simple gradient. You also have the inherent ability to add richness to the controls further by using the Visual State Manager. In short, there are often many ways to skin a cat, and so when defining your XAML, careful consideration should be given to the options available. Your designers may often be using tools to create their XAML, but this does not mean that they should shy away from what is being created behind the scenes. The tools are likely to only have a limited intelligence in their generation, and so there should be a phase in your development when the XAML is reviewed to see if it can be made more efficient in terms of reusability and maintainability.

Layouts

As you have already seen, Silverlight presents you with three layout panel options — a `Canvas`, a `StackPanel`, and a `Grid`. The most flexible of all these panels is the `Canvas`, as it lets you place child elements pretty much anywhere you like by specifying the `Canvas.Top` and `Canvas.Left` properties. From an application design perspective, you are discouraged from using the `Canvas` where possible because for the most part, a panel would address your needs more specifically. For example, imagine that you are designing some kind of form entry for a line of business application. The form may contain a set of labels for your customer's name and address, and these will be accompanied by a `TextBox` used for the input of this information. Although it's true that you could present this information inside a `Canvas`, it does not make sense from a design perspective, and it would involve more work for you as the developer to calculate things like row and column calculations. In Chapter 5, you also saw the associated calculation process that was made by a layout panel in order to render the child elements; this is the two-step layout process of measuring and arranging the children. In other words, the first pass is the layout asking the children how much room they want within the panel, and the second pass is the result of the panel actually calculating how much room they can have, and rendering them accordingly. With the `Canvas` being so flexible, it doesn't really do all that much work at the Arrange stage; it somewhat spoils its children by giving them what they want. This differs from the other layouts, such as the `Grid`, which has to do calculations to figure out which row and column an element should sit in, and it must ensure the elements do not fall outside those confines. As you can imagine, the extra calculations made by the stricter layouts actually mean they do not perform as well as the `Canvas`. Despite this, the key point to realize is that you could use the `Canvas` to get more performance, but then you are likely going to have to perform such Measure and Arrange steps in many cases yourself (using the form scenario as an example), and so you are going to lose most, if not all, of the performance gains anyway. The key thing to take away here is that you should always use the most appropriate panel for the task, and this often means avoiding the use of the `Canvas` layout.

The `Grid` and the `StackPanel` undergo several calculations in order to coordinate their children, so the positive performance impacts you can make are to consider how you might reduce the number of times the Measure and Arrange process occurs. In order to make an informed decision, you need to know what triggers the layout calculations in the first place, and these are:

- ❑ Adding or removing a child element to a layout

- ❑ Changing the values of certain element properties such as `Width` and `Height`

- ❑ Calling `UIElement.InvalidateMeasure`. This results in an implicit call to the following method.

- ❑ Calling `UIElement.InvalidateArrange`. This triggers an asynchronous update of the layout, if an `UpdateLayout` call does not follow.

- ❑ Calling `UIElement.UpdateLayout`. This differs from the above calls in that it triggers a synchronous update of the layout on the `UIElement`. It does this by checking for invalid Measure and Arrange values on the element, which can be set as being "dirty" by the two preceding method calls.

The layout process is always going to have to be performed after you add your element to the panel, so there is not a great deal you can do about this besides minimizing the amount of times you add and remove elements from the panel, which will depend on the design of your application. It may be the case, however, that you can avoid unnecessary resizing of your child elements. If your panel has hundreds of child elements and you are resizing one of these, you could be putting quite a large burden on the layout process.

If you wish to force a recalculation of the layout for a child element, then you can call UIElement .InvalidateMeasure, UIElement.InvalidateMeasure, or UIElement.UpdateLayout. These could be quite legitimate, but you should be aware of what this is actually doing behind the scenes. In general, these would only be called as part of advanced layout management within your code. For the most part, such calls will be taken care of for you by the run time.

Working with Data

The flexibility of the Silverlight run time gives scope for a great range of different types of applications. For example, it may be that you are developing a consumer application for the Web, or it may be that you are writing an Enterprise application for a bank. Traditionally, these two very different types of applications have had very different visual appearances; for example, a consumer web application such as YouTube.com has a compelling, visual user interface to support its focus on media. An Enterprise banking application has a much more conservative user interface, and quite typically is Forms-based. In the latter case, controls are an important aspect to support the everyday business requirements of working with data. No doubt moving forward with Silverlight, you will start to see some tasteful uses of graphics and animations in these applications, but only if they are adding business value to the application.

Although these different types of applications may take different approaches, there will no doubt be a crossover in functionality, and one thing to be careful of in both these instances — but probably more so in the Enterprise case — when it comes to manipulating data within your application. Perhaps your client's requirements are to store a large amount of customer relationship data, and you need your call center clerks to access this data. To add such functionality requires careful consideration when you are designing your application. Although it can be a good thing to reduce the number of calls to the server for data, it can also be a bad thing to store large amounts of data in the client browser's memory. In the code samples on wrox.com, you will see a sample project named *WorkingWithData*, which shows you some of the ill effects of having a large amount of data on the client. The sample is simulating the data, but the end results are the same. The sample uses the DataGrid control that comes with the Silverlight SDK, which you should now be familiar with as a result of reading the chapter on displaying data in your UI. The following snippet highlights the key lines of the code sample and is followed by an explanation of what it is doing, and breaks down the anticipated behavior of this:

```
public partial class Page : UserControl
{

    string[] firstNames = { "Chris", "Dave", "Matt" … };
    string[] lastNames = { "Barker", "Smith", "Doe" … };
    string[] cities = { "Derby", "Nottingham", "Manchester" … };
    const int GRID_ELEMENTS = 1000000;

    public Page()
    {
        InitializeComponent();

        this.Loaded += new RoutedEventHandler(Page_Loaded);
    }

    void Page_Loaded(object sender, RoutedEventArgs e)
```

```
        {

            // call to loop the media
            media1.MediaEnded += new RoutedEventHandler(media1_MediaEnded);

            XElement root = new XElement("Root");

            Random r = new Random(DateTime.Now.Millisecond);
            for (int i = 0; i < GRID_ELEMENTS; i++)
            {
                root.Add(new XElement("Customer",
                    new XElement("Firstname", firstNames[r.Next(firstNames.Length)]),
                    new XElement("Lastname", lastNames[r.Next(lastNames.Length)]),
                    new XElement("DOB.", r.Next(31).ToString()
                            + "/" + r.Next(12).ToString()
                            + "/" + r.Next(1900, 2008).ToString()),
                    new XElement("OfficeLocation", cities[r.Next(cities.Length)])
                    ));
            }

            var query = from customer in root.Descendants("Customer")
                select new Customer { Firstname = customer.Element("Firstname").Value,
                                Lastname = customer.Element("Lastname").Value,
                                DOB = customer.Element("DOB.").Value,
                                Office = customer.Element("OfficeLocation").Value };
            dataGrid1.ItemsSource = query;
        }

    }

    public class Customer
    {
        public string Firstname{ get; set; }
        public string Lastname { get; set; }
        public string DOB { get; set; }
        public string Office { get; set; }
    }
```

So, first up is a high-level explanation of what the code actually does. It displays a data grid, which is displaying some dummy customer data; there is a column for first name, last name, date of birth, and the customer's central office location. The data itself is randomly generated, with the names and office location being randomly taken from an array of possible values. On the subject of being random, there is a video of a bear to the right of the data grid. The video is there as a litmus test to show how performance might be affected by having a lot of data loaded into memory at once.

The first few lines in the previous code declare the arrays of strings, which house the first names, last names, and UK cities/towns in which the customer is based. The GRID_ELEMENTS constant is there to allow you to easily tweak the number of randomly generated elements that will appear in the data grid; the higher this number, the more you can expect the application to struggle. The data is initially built up into an XML tree using LINQ to XML, where the data looks something like this:

```
<Root>
    <Customer>
```

```
        <Firstname>Chris</Firstname>
        <Lastname>Barker</Lastname>
        <DOB.>18/8/1980</DOB.>
        <OfficeLocation>Derby</OfficeLocation>
    </Customer>
</Root>
```

A query expression is then used to project the data into the "Customer" entity. This query is then executed by the data grid by setting its value to the `ItemsSource` property. The grid itself performs well with a reasonably large number of elements. If you increase the number of elements, your application takes longer to start up, but once it is loaded, the media will play smoothly. The application starts to be put under load once you start scrolling through the data grid.

> **We ran this application with 1 million data grid elements on an Intel Dual Core 2.16 GHz processor, which had 2 GB of RAM. It was around this number of elements that the application really started to struggle when we scrolled through the grid.**

When you have stressed the application by increasing the number, and then scrolling, you will see that two of the initial bottlenecks are hit — that is, the processor usage shoots up, and frames are dropped. The latter behavior is apparent from the media element skipping quite dramatically, and by the frame rate counter in the status bar of Internet Explorer becoming very low. Another impact on the system when working with this data is the amount of memory being consumed by the browser process. If you take a look at the memory footprint of your process when you have 1 million elements, you should see consumption of approximately 250 MB.

This is a bare-bones example of a performance hit when using data, but some further considerations you should make when working with a lot of data are:

❑ Test your application with a realistic amount of data. There is no point in concluding that your application performs well if you test it with 10,000 rows of data on a high-end developer machine, if out in the wild it's going to be processing 1 million rows on a low-end consumer machine.

❑ Test the application in the context of the rest of your application. This example had nothing more than a data grid and a video in order to get across the core idea. In the real world, you may have many controls, animations, and so on on the screen, and so it could be unrealistic to expect the number of data rows used here. If you have applied any complex themes or templates to the data grid, consider that these could have a dramatic impact on performance.

A third point, and an area of consideration for improving performance when working with this amount of data, concerns how much you actually need on the client at any one time. Having so much data in a data grid is not particularly intuitive from a UI perspective. Users have to scroll through the data in order to find one particular record. For this reason, it might make sense to separate the data into multiple data grids. You could offer a filter on the data that allows you to categorize the rows into office locations, or even surnames beginning with a certain letter.

In a call center scenario, it may be that if a caller rings in, you are able to take the hit of going to the server for the data just for that one user. In an Enterprise scenario, this should be relatively quick, and would reduce greatly the amount of data being held on the client at any one time. Another option might be to cache the data locally. So, you could take the initial hit of pulling down the data when the application starts (or at least a large subset of the data), and you could then persist this data to Isolated Storage. You should still avoid loading all of this at once into the data grid, but the advantage here is that when you need the data, you don't have to go to the network and can just find the data you need locally on disk; this is going to be much less costly, particularly in a Web-based scenario.

Some further points to note on this test are that the DataGrid has some inherent performance optimizations in order to deal with large volumes of data. The key optimization the DataGrid uses is that of UI Virtualization. *UI Virtualization* is the term given whereby only the viewable data is processed by the control. For example, if you had 1,000 rows in your DataGrid, it is unlikely that owing to screen constraints you would be able to view all of these at once, and could perhaps only see a subset of 20. The virtualization technique means that the control is only going to process 20 rows, rather than the total 1,000, which vastly improves the performance of the application. Of course, when moving up to numbers of 1 million as demonstrated previously, the application needs to calculate and process the new viewable area at a potentially quick rate if you are scrolling several viewable areas at once, in which case, you are still going to see problems. In fact, if you had used a control such as the ListBox to view the data, you would have likely noticed worse performance because it does not use UI Virtualization.

> There are a number of control vendors out to market at the moment. One vendor, www.devexpress.com, offers you another free DataGrid control, which you may want to investigate further in terms of its features and comparable performance. You can register and download this from www.devexpress.com/Products/NET/Controls/Silverlight/Grid/.

Reduce Chatty Applications

The previous section discussed briefly how one way to reduce holding a large number of elements in memory is to query the server for the data when required. This can be a performance-saver but is not always the silver bullet to solve a problem. First of all, pretty much the most costly operation you will perform in a web application is going over the Web. In other words, any communications over the wire are going to be many times more expensive than simply picking your data directly from memory. The other point to note is that it isn't just data that is being referred; it could be any resource that your application relies on such as images, videos, and so on. Although it is good to reduce the number of round-trips your application makes to the server (and make it less "chatty"), you have to be careful not to hit the other extreme of pulling everything down at once; it's a balancing act. The main variables you need to consider juggling are as follows:

- ❏ How often is the data going to be required?
- ❏ How often might the data on the server be changed by other clients, and do you need to know about it?
- ❏ Do you really need all the data at once, or can you consider a subset?
- ❏ Can the data be persisted to disk locally, or stored efficiently in memory?

Up until now, it has been assumed that a chatty application is closely tied to large amounts of data, but this is not always the case. It may be that the data you need is very small yet changes frequently. The problem with data that changes frequently on the server is that you often need to know when it has changed so you won't be working with old data. One solution to this problem is to have your application poll the server periodically to check if the data has changed; if it has, it can notify the client. If you have a lot of clients running the same application on the network, this can start to become a burden on the network, and the real downside is that it could be a case of having 90 percent of poll requests determining that nothing has changed. Another option is to just cut your losses and have a rule whereby either the last client to modify the data wins, or even the first client to modify the data wins — either way, you remove the need for polling. This approach can have repercussions and certainly doesn't fulfill every business case, but you shouldn't assume by default that you need to know the second that any data has changed. Chapter 9 also introduced you to another option that you may not have been so familiar with as an ASP.NET developer, and that is having the server notify you of changes via sockets. This won't be revisited again here, but for completeness, consider it as an option for reducing chatty applications in certain scenarios.

Runtime Performance

It may seem as though a lot of the performance tuning is being placed on you as the developer, and therefore this section is here to outline some of the optimizations the Product Team has made in order to build a framework, which when treated right will give you the required performance for your application. It is useful to be aware of these optimizations, because by being aware of the underlying plumbing, you can make more informed decisions when it comes to building on top of it.

You are already aware of many of the design decisions that have been made with Silverlight to improve performance — that is, the cut-down version of the .NET Framework, which includes a reduction in the Base Class Library and the subset of XAML from Windows Presentation Foundation (WPF), in order to maintain the small, and appealing, plug-in size. This trend of optimizations continued throughout the development of Silverlight, and so it would not be realistic to cover all of these here. This section outlines some of the less well-known, but farther-reaching optimizations that Silverlight provides for you.

Multicore

One of the nice features of Silverlight is that it will make use of multiple processor cores on the machine in which it is executing. This is an important consideration when you are planning the hardware that your target audience will be running.

Async Pattern

If you have had the chance to write any code that communicates with the server, whether it be a Web Service call, using `WebClient`, or `HttpWebRequest`, then you will notice there is a shift in models from the traditional synchronous design to an asynchronous pattern. So in your traditional ASP.NET development, if you were calling an Add Web Method on your CalcService Web Service, your client code would look something like this:

```
private void btn1_Click(object sender, RoutedEventArgs e)
{
    CalculatorSoapClient svc = new CalculatorSoapClient();
    txtResult.Text = svc.Add(2,2).ToString();
}
```

Under the Silverlight model, you must now write more lines of code, which would look something like this:

```
private void btn1_Click(object sender, RoutedEventArgs e)
{
    CalculatorSoapClient svc = new CalculatorSoapClient(binding, addr);
    svc.AddCompleted += new EventHandler<AddCompletedEventArgs>(svc_AddCompleted);
    svc.AddAsync(2, 2);
}

void svc_AddCompleted(object sender, AddCompletedEventArgs e)
{
    txtResult.Text = e.Result.ToString();
}
```

You actually had the option of using this asynchronous pattern for more traditional web development, but it was relatively rare to find applications coded in this way. Besides the extra level of simplicity in calling a web method (or otherwise) synchronously, it actually didn't make so much sense to do this asynchronously in the average ASP.NET web application. The reason for this is that if you needed some information returned from the server, an entire page post-back would be required anyway. It was only during the move to AJAX that you started to have the ability to break out of the synchronous model, and that had its own way of doing things — via the XmlHttpRequest object. With the richness that Silverlight brings, you would not expect the whole page to refresh each time a server request was made, nor would you expect the user interface to freeze during such a request, and this is why it drives you down the route of solely using the asynchronous model, despite adding a few extra lines of code.

This decision really takes away the possibility of the developer blocking the UI thread during a long-running operation, and it helps to overcome one of the bottlenecks discussed at the beginning of the chapter. Under the covers, this pattern is actually firing up a new thread to make the request, but as this is such a common operation, you do not need to be exposed to the underlying complexities of the extra request thread.

XAML Parser

The XAML Parser at the core of the Silverlight run time has to provide good performance — after all, the XAML is pretty much the lifeblood of your application — certainly for the designers. There are times when you will need to manipulate the visual tree via your code-behind, which is perfectly valid. There is one thing to bear in mind when you load XAML via code and manipulate the visual tree, and that is you are writing in managed code, which means that behind the scenes you are going through an interop layer, which is relatively expensive in terms of performance. By declaring your UI in XAML directly, the XAML Parser reads the XAML and constructs the visual tree, the advantage being that the XAML Parser is written in native code and therefore does not have the added expensive of going through the interop layer. Of course, not everything is achievable directly in XAML, and there are times when you will have to take a hit, but it is a runtime behavior to be aware of if you are to avoid manipulating the visual tree via code unnecessarily.

Comparisons

There are a number of RIA frameworks available on the Web today, most notably Flash. Out of the available frameworks, it is interesting to compare the performance between each of these. There are a few sites on the Web that claim to offer a near close benchmark of an identical application running on each of the frameworks. It is important to be wary of such benchmarks, as one framework may be more performant in one area than another, and the code samples are not necessarily using the most optimal features of each language. But either way, to complete the performance picture, it is interesting to review these resources, and a couple of these are listed below:

❑ www.bubblemark.com/ — This site has an application not so dissimilar from the BouncingBalls sample you have in the code. It has the ability to increase and reduce the number of balls, and it tracks the frame rate in each of the underlying technologies.

❑ www.craftymind.com/guimark/ — GUIMark is another rendering test, but this has a lot of focus on displaying text and provides a focus to another area of the rendering engine performance for each of the tested technologies.

Summary

It is not possible to cover every single performance hit in every single application, but after reading this chapter, you should be aware of the most common pitfalls and know what your options are for avoiding them.

The aim of the chapter was to first outline the problems you can expect from a poorly performing application and then take you through the methods for diagnosing the cause of slow performance. Finally, there was an extensive set of Silverlight features visited, ranging from animations through to network communication. Best practices for performance exist in most of the features discussed, although as you will have found, these are not always in black and white. For the most part, there are trade-offs to make, although these trade-offs can be minimized once you have settled on the performance bar you are working toward in your application. This is not possible until you have identified the mainstream hardware of your users, and thus it is difficult to gauge the effectiveness of these steps until you have outlined the hardware, and finally, tested the impact of your application before and after making changes on the range of platforms and browsers for which you intend to have users enter your application.

Index

NUMBERS

3D tools, 56

A

absolute positioning, CSS, 131
Access Control Lists (ACLs), ASP.NET security, 462
Accessibility Checker, Expression Web, 122
ACLs (Access Control Lists), ASP.NET security, 462
ACT (Application Center Test), 581
ActiveX, 16
ad hoc queries, for data retrieval, 408
Add Service Reference, 398
Add Service References tool, Visual Studio 2008, 308–309
ADO.NET
  Data Services, 387, 399–401
  Entity Data Model, 400
  overview of, 16
  Silverlight not supporting, 409
Advanced Stream Redirector (ASX), 482
agcore.dll, 23
AJAX (Asynchronous JavaScript and XML)
  asynchronous web development, 618
  Control Toolkit, 206
  cross-domain calls, 289
  Fiddler and, 573
  modal screens, 274
  Silverlight integration with, 249–250
AJAX-style updates, 5
animation. see also graphics
  applying to UI elements with Expression Blend, 126
  color animation using key frame example, 554–555
  ColorAnimation, 550–551
  DoubleAnimation, 548–549
  Expression Blend and, 56
  From/To/By approach, 547–548
  key frame approach, 553
  KeyFrames collection, 553–554
  multiple From/To/By animations, 551–553
  performance and, 597
  per-frame animation call back, 555–556
  PointAnimation, 550
  StoryBoad object and, 548

  summary, 556
  Timeline and, 547
  types of, 547
Animation Workspace, Expression Blend
  applying animations to UI elements, 126
  overview of, 59
Application Center Test (ACT), 581
Application class, System.Windows namespace, 66–69
application level, setting styles at, 223–224
Application object, 223–224
application services, ASP.NET integration with Silverlight, 25
applications
  life cycle, 27–29
  localization, 161–164
  per instance customization, 436
  programming. see programming Silverlight applications
  reducing chatty applications, 616–617
AppManifest.xaml, 65–66
App.xaml page, 223–224
architectural awareness, in ASP.NET, 7
architecture, Silverlight, 9–29
  application life cycle, 27–29
  client platform, 11–12
  client/server model, 9–10
  data classes and, 22
  data-binding, 367–368
  DLR (Dynamic Language Runtime) and, 22–23
  illustration of, 12
  installed files, 23–24
  .NET Framework elements, 16–17
  .NET Framework features included/excluded in, 17–18
  networking and, 21–22
  overview of, 9
  platforms, 10–11
  presentation core, 13–16
  server platform, 11
  summary, 29
  updates, 28–29
  WPF (Windows Presentation Foundation) and, 18–21
artwork, Expression Design for, 129
ASCX files, 424

ASMX file, 301
ASMX services. *see* **ASP.NET Web Services**
`asp:Media`, **ASP.NET server controls for Silverlight, 27**
ASP.NET
  AJAX Control Toolkit, 206
  AJAX support for, 249
  application services, 25
  caching, 401
  composite controls, 25
  data framework, 362
  dynamically generating XAML and, 26
  Expression Web for accessing ASP.NET controls, 122
  `GET` and `POST` methods, 278
  graphics for adding life to, 515–516
  integration with. *see* integration with ASP.NET
  layout options, 130–131
  Media Server control, 500–502
  modal screens, 274
  .NET Framework and, 16
  playback control, 500–501
  Profile Provider, 235–239
  server controls for Silverlight, 27
  Silverlight communicating with, 26
  themes, 214
  traditional data handling, 407–408
  user controls, 424–426
  validation control, 417
ASP.NET Futures, 501
ASP.NET Web Services, 21
  ASMX file, 301
  calling with Silverlight, 308–310
  overview of, 301
  `WebMethods`, 302–303
`asp.Silverlight`, **ASP.NET server controls for Silverlight, 27**
`<asp:Silverlight>` **control, 69–70**
assemblies
  deploying user controls and, 427
  obfuscation techniques and, 478
Asset Library button, 126–127
Astoria, 387, 399–401
ASX (Advanced Stream Redirector), 482
Asynchronous JavaScript and XML. *see* **AJAX (Asynchronous JavaScript and XML)**
asynchronous pattern, for web development, 617–618
asynchrony, threading and, 95
ATOM (Atom Syndication Format), 333–335
  how it works, 334–335
  syndication feed classes, 335–337
Atom Syndication Format. *see* **ATOM (Atom Syndication Format)**
attached properties, XAML, 40–41
attacks/attackers, 462
attributes, application instantiation and, 70–71

audio formats, 201, 482
audio/video
  ASP.NET Media Server control, 500–502
  `AutoPlay` property, 484
  embedding in ASP.NET applications, 482
  Expression Encoder and, 504–506
  formats, 201, 482
  `Height` and `Width` properties, 487
  inherited properties, 498–500
  `MediaElement` control, 482
  `MediaElement` events, 511–512
  `NaturalDuration` property, 486
  overview of, 481
  playback controlled from ASP.NET, 500–501
  playback controls, 491–495
  `Position` property, 484–486
  `SetSource` method, 512–513
  `Source` property, 483–484
  streaming, 514
  `Stretch` property, 496–498
  summary, 514
  timeline markers, 503
  timeline markers via code, 506–510
  `Volume` property, 488–490
  Windows Media File editor, 503–504
authentication
  ASP.NET, 462, 474–478
  membership provider, 471–472
authorization, ASP.NET, 462
`AutoCompleteBox` **control, 206–207**
`AutoCompleteExtender` **control, ASP.NET, 206**
`AutoGenerateColumns`, **405**
`AutoPlay` **property,** `MediaElement`, **484**

B

`Background` **property, drawing in XAML, 42**
backgrounds, transparent, 601–602
`BackgroundWorker` **class, threading model, 95–100**
BAML, 13
Base Class Library (BCL), .NET Framework, 16, 617
base classess, Silverlight Object Model, 84–85
BCL (Base Class Library), .NET Framework, 16
Beginning JavaScript (McPeak and Wilton), 83
binding component, data-binding architecture, 368
`BitmapImage`, **540–542**
bitmaps. *see* **raster graphics**
Blend. *see* **Expression Blend**
`Border` **type, 438**
bottlenecks, performance, 590–591
bridging, code-behind binding and, 375
browsers
  interacting with browser from Silverlight, 105–110
  interacting with Silverlight from browser, 110–114

mouse handling properties and, 256

Brush class
ImageBrush, 531–533
LinearGradientBrush, 528–530
overview of, 526
RadialGradientBrush, 530–531
SolidColorBrush, 526–528
VideoBrush, 533–534

brushes, drawing in XAML, 44

bubbling routing strategy
routed events and, 92–94
Silverlight support for, 245

BufferingProgressChanged event, MediaElement, 511

built-in styles, custom controls, 451–452

Button control
adding Click event to, 170
Silverlight user input controls, 176–177
states, 227
System.Windows.Controls, 21

Button event handler
code-behine file and, 86–87
toggling between Embedded mode and Full-screen mode, 155–156

buttons
adding to Expression Blend design surface, 128
visual styles connected to button state, 445–447

C

caching, 401
calculator class, 111
Calendar control
customizing, 448
as Silverlight user input control, 183–185
System.Windows.Controls, 186

calls, Web Service
ASP.NET Web Service proxy, 308–310
creating WCF proxy, 305
making asynchronous calls with WCF proxy, 305–308

Canvas control, 136–143
adding/positioning elements in, 136–138
hosting page settings effectively overriding Canvas properties, 143
InkPresenter deriving from, 259–260
layout options in Silverlight, 132
layout performance issues, 612
nesting Canvas within Canvas, 138–139
overlapping elements within, 140–142
positioning elements with X and Y coordinates, 136

CaptureMouse( ) method, 254
CAS (code access security), 463–464
Cascading Style Sheets (CSS)
Expression Web support for, 122
layout options in ASP.NET, 130–131

case-sensitivity, XAML, 36
central location, styles at, 218–219
Chart control, 210–212
chatty applications, 616–617
CheckBox control, 178–179
child objects
adding/positioning on Canvas, 139
control trees for managing, 171
XAML (eXtensible Application Markup Language), 269

class definitions, security levels and, 465–466
classes, Silverlight data, 22
Click event, adding to Button control, 170
ClickMode properties, RepeatButton control, 181
client access policy, for socket server, 343–347
client platform, Silverlight architecture, 11–12
clientaccesspolicy.xml, 291
clients
access policy to socket server, 343–347
sockets on, 340–343

client/server architecture, 9–10
CLR (Common Language Runtime)
ASP.NET Web Services and, 301
calling Web Services and, 304
converting XML schema to, 320
data-binding performance considerations, 386–387
element of .NET Framework, 17
mapping data to CLR objects, 288
OOP (object oriented programming), 384

code
code level security, 462
event handling programmatically, 171–172
instrumentation of, 587
timeline markers created via, 506–510

code access security (CAS), 463–464
code behind
accessing Content data, 389
auto-generated method, 75–76
binding, 373–375
Button event handler and, 86–87
event handlers, 245
fade screen effect, 274
interacting with traditional properties, 246
XAML and, 46–49
x:class attribute for referencing, 72

code generators, 57
ColorAnimationUsingKeyFrames, 553–555
colors
ColorAnimation, 550–551
gray scale colors, 199
inline styles, 217
key frame example, 554–555
linear gradients, 528–530
options for specifying brush color, 527–528
radial gradients, 530–531

columns
   DataGrid control and, 192
   Grid control and, 144
   properties, 145–146
   sizing Row and Column elements, 146–149
COM components, 16
ComboBox control, 195–196
Common Language Runtime. see CLR (Common Language Runtime)
communication
   ASP.NET integration with Silverlight, 26
   with server. see server communication
   Silverlight features, 5
compile-time problems, 560–562
complex bindings, 378–381
composite controls, ASP.NET integration with Silverlight, 25
conditional statements, JavaScript, 79–80
consuming remote data, 396–399
container controls, 269
content files, local resources, 388
ContentControl, System.Windows.Controls, 20–21
ContentPresenter control, 442–443
contracts, WCF service
   data contract, 293–294
   service contract, 294–295
   WCF duplex service, 347–348
Control class
   as base class, 448
   customizing. see custom controls
   System.Windows.Controls, 20
control trees, for managing parent/child controls, 171
controls, Silverlight, 167–212
   <asp:Silverlight> control, 69
   AutoCompleteBox control, 206–207
   Button control, 176–177
   Calendar control, 183–185
   Chart control, 210–212
   CheckBox control, 178–179
   ComboBox control, 195–196
   DataGrid control, 191–193
   DatePicker control, 186–187
   defining in XAML, 169–170
   event handling declaratively, 170–171
   event handling programmatically, 171–172
   HyperlinkButton control, 177–178
   Image control, 199–200
   items controls, 188–189
   layout. see layout controls
   ListBox control, 189–191
   media controls, 198
   MediaElement control, 200–202
   MultiScaleImage control, 203–204
   overview of, 167–168

   PasswordBox control, 176
   Popup control, 196–198
   ProgressBar control, 202–203
   RadioButton control, 179–180
   RepeatButton control, 180–182
   rich control library in Silverlight, 5
   ScrollViewer control, 193–195
   Slider control, 182–183
   summary, 212
   TextBlock control, 173–174
   TextBox control, 174–176
   toolkit controls, 205–206
   ToolTip control, 187–188
   TreeView control, 208–210
   Type Library and, 16
   user input controls, 172–173
   Windowless, 600–601
   WrapPanel control, 207–208
   x:Name property, 74
ControlTemplate class
   creating new ControlTemplate, 225–226
   customzing with skins, 440–443
   overview of, 224
conversions, 382–384
coreclr.dll, 23
cross-domain calls, 289–290
   Flash cross-domain policy files, 290
   overview of, 289–290
   self-hosted WCF service and, 299–301
   Silverlight cross-domain policy files, 291–292
cross-domain security, 470
crossdomain.xml, 290
cross-platform support, 4
cryptography, 479
CSS (Cascading Style Sheets)
   Expression Web support for, 122
   layout options in ASP.NET, 130–131
culture parameter, in conversions, 383
CurrentStateChanged event, MediaElement, 511
custom controls, 423–460. see also user controls
   building, 450
   built-in style, 451–452
   composite controls compared with custom server control, 25
   custom properties, 452–454
   overview of, 423, 447–448
   parts model, 454
   requirements for, 449
   scenarios for use of, 447–448
   summary, 460
   visual states parts, 458–459
customizing current controls
   example mixing styling and skinning, 443–444
   overview of, 435

scanarios, 436–437
skins for, 440–443
styles for, 437–440
visual customization, 435–436
visual styles connected to button state, 445–447

D

data
accessible by Silverlight, 286
data-processing options, 288–289
performance issues when working with, 613–616
data classes, Silverlight, 22
data containers, creating custom, 362
data contract, WCF service, 293–294
data controls
data templates, 402–403
`DataGrid` control, 403–407
namespaces, 364
overview of, 401
`System.Windows.Controls`, 403
data entity classes, 294
data flow
conversions and, 382
in data binding example, 371
`OneWay, TwoWay,` and `One Time`, 369
overview of, 368
`PropertyPath and`, 370
data framework
ASP.NET, 362
creating custom data containers, 362
namespaces, 363–364
overview of, 361–362
data manipulation
binding from XML, 415
dynamic XAML with LINQ, 414–415
LINQ, 408–412
LINQ to XML, 412–414
overview of, 407
traditional handling, 407–408
data repositories
local data. see local data
overview of, 387–388
remote data. see remote data
Data Services, ADO.NET, 387, 399–401
data sources, binding item controls to, 189
data storage/retrieval
ADO.NET Data Services, 399–401
caching, 401
consuming remote data, 396–399
data repositories, 387–388
interacting with hosting computer, 394–396
isolated storage, 392–394

local data, 388
local resources, 388–391
overview of, 387
remote data, 396
site-of-origin resources, 396
data templates, 402–403
data-binding
architecture, 367–368
binding from XML, 415
code-behind binding, 373–375
complex bindings, 378–381
conversions and, 382–384
data flow and, 368–370
`DataContext` property, 375, 378
dependency properties and, 384–386
graphical view of, 366
`ListBox` control, 189–190
mixing binding techniques, 378
overview of, 365–367
performance and, 386–387
in practice, 370–372
validation, 419–420
XAML binding, 375–377
`DataContext`
data-binding example, 381
defining with XAML code, 378
inheritance and, 375
DataContractJsonSerializer class, 328, 330–332
DataGrid control, 403–407
adding extra information fields, 406–407
adding namespace for, 403
automatic column generation, 404–406
configuring data binding for, 403–404
data control namespaces, 364
overview of, 403
performance optimization and, 616
Silverlight items controls, 191–193
DataGridCheckBoxColumn, 404
DataGridTextBoxColumn, 404
DataSet control, ASP.NET, 301, 408
DataTemplate, 402–403
DatePicker control, 186–187
dates
`Calendar` control, 185
`DatePicker` control, 186
DateTime.Now.Ticks method, 594–595
dbgshim.dll, 23
Debug class, 587
debuggers. see also troubleshooting
debugging applications, 566–570
tools for working with XAML, 57
Visual Studio 2008 as, 563–566

declarative programming
event handling, 170–171
Silverlight applications and, 244
XAML and, 32
Deep Zoom Composer tool, 203–204, 544
DeepZoom, image handling, 542–546
default styles, 438
Delay values, RepeatButton control, 181
dependency properties
AutoGenerateColumns, 405
binding, 386
custom controls and, 452–454
data-binding performance considerations, 386
declaring, 384–385
interacting with, 247
overview of, 384
Setter object for setting, 437
user controls and, 432–433
Dependency Property Identifier, 385
DependencyObject class
Silverlight Object Model, 84, 384
System.Windows, 19
deploying Silverlight applications, 64–66
deploying user controls, 427
Design Workspace, in Expression Blend, 59
designers, vs. developers, 590
design-time problems, 560–562
developers
vs. designers, 590
XAML basics and, 31–32
development, ASP.NET for, 7
DHTML (Dynamic HTML), 3
Digg, 287, 310
digital media, Expression Media for managing, 129–130
Digital Rights Management. see DRM (Digital Rights Management)
Dispatcher object
interacting with properties, 246
System.Windows.Threading, 100–102
DispatcherTimer, 102–105, 599
display modes
Embedded display mode, 154
Full-screen display mode, 154–161
overview of, 154
DIV tags
CSS and, 130–131
sizing instructions and, 134–135
dll assembly, Microsoft.Windows.Controls, 205
DLLs, creating custom data containers, 365
DLR (Dynamic Language Runtime)
overview of, 22–23
Silverlight features, 5
validation using dynamic languages, 418–419
DnsEndPoint, 340–341

document object model. see DOM (document object model)
Document property, HtmlPage class, 106
DOM (document object model)
browser interaction and, 105–110
event handling, 80
integration with Silverlight, 15–16
JavaScript and, 77
manipulating with JavaScript, 80–83
domains
cross-domain communication, 289–290
cross-domain security, 470
Flash cross-domain policy files, 290
Silverlight cross-domain policy files, 291–292
supported by Silverlight, 286
dots per inch (DPI)
high-resolution monitors and, 256
resolution-independent rendering and, 132
DoubleAnimation, 548–549
DoubleAnimationUsingKeyFrames, 553
DownloadProgressChanged event, MediaElement, 512
downloads
DownloadProgressChanged event, 512
ProgressBar control, 202–203
DPI (dots per inch)
high-resolution monitors and, 256
resolution-independent rendering and, 132
drag-and-drop, user interaction via, 263–266
drawing basics, XAML
Ellipse object, 41–43
Line object, 45–46
overview of, 41
Rectangle object, 43–45
DrawingAttributes property, stroke options, 262
DRM (Digital Rights Management)
overview of, 14–15
PlayReady technology, 15
Silverlight features, 5
DropDownList control, ASP.NET, 195
duration, media, 486
Dynamic HTML (DHTML), 3
Dynamic Language Runtime. see DLR (Dynamic Language Runtime)
dynamic languages. see also DLR (Dynamic Language Runtime)
overview of, 22
validation, 418–419
dynamically loading XAML, 49–50, 87–89

E

e parameter, 245
ECMAScript, 77
effects, enhancing user navigation, 273–275

elements
adding/positioning on `Canvas`, 136–138
CSS methods for positioning, 131
`Margin` property, 151–152
overlapping on `Canvas`, 140–142
positioning with X and Y coordinates, 136
reusing, 611
sizing `Row` and `Column` elements, 146–149
stacking (`StackPanel`), 150–151
elements parts, parts model, 454–458
`Ellipse`
drawing with XAML, 41–43
`Shape` class and, 517
`EllipseGeometry, 522`
Embedded mode
display options, 154
toggling between Full-screen display mode, 155–157
embedding audio/video, in ASP.NET applications, 482
`EnableFrameRateCounter, 592–594`
`EnableRedrawRegions, 593–594`
encapsulation, user controls and, 428
encryption algorithms, 479
Enterprise Web Services, 21
Entity Data Model, ADO.NET, 400
environments, ASP.NET for, 7
eraser mode, Ink feature, 262–263
errors, 560. *see also* **troubleshooting**
Ethereal tool, 570
event handlers
declarative, 170–171
JavaScript, 80
media playback, 495
programmatic, 171–172
routed events, 93–94
user controls and, 434
user interaction, 244–245
for wiring up events, 90–92
events
keyboard events, 257
`MediaElement`, 511–512
mouse events, 251–252
routed events, 92–94
types of interaction events, 244
`UIElements` events, 244
wiring up, 90–92
exception handling, 586–587
exploitations, security, 461–462
Expression Blend, 123–129
add Text Block to design surface, 126
adding button to design surface, 128
adding controls, 126
adding rectangle to design surface, 124
adding/changing properties, 124–125
applying animations, 126

creating user controls, 424, 430
design environment and, 8
drawing objects with vector graphics, 129
interoperability with Visual Studio, 56, 59
Properties pane, 127–128
starting new project, 123
tools for working with XAML, 56–57
visual state management, 446–447
Expression Design, 129
Expression Encoder
converting audio/video formats, 201
overview of, 130
sizing at design time, 606
timeline markers, 504–506
Expression Media
Expression Encoder and, 130
overview of, 129–130
Expression Studio, 130
Expression Suite
compared with Visual Studio, 121–122
Expression Blend, 123–129
Expression Design, 129
Expression Encoder, 130
Expression Media, 129–130
Expression Studio, 130
Expression Web, 122
Expression Web, 122
eXtensible Application Markup Language. *see* **XAML**
(eXtensible Application Markup Language)
Extensible Markup Language. *see* **XML (Extensible**
Markup Language)
Extensible Stylesheet Language Transformation (XSLT)
LINQ and, 364
real-time standarads validation in Expression Web, 122
extensions
LINQ, 364
markup, 38–40

F

fade screen effect, 274
Fiddler, 573–574
Fielding, Roy, 287
`Fill` **property, drawing in XAML, 42**
Firebug, 575
fixed positioning, CSS, 131
Flash
animation and, 516
cross-domain policy files, 290
rich content and, 4
Flickr
REST and, 287, 310
retrieving XML data, 324–325
serializing/deserializing data, 321–324

FocusVisualElement, 226
fonts
   applying inline styles to, 216–217
   TextBox control, 175
formats, audio/video, 201, 482
form-based validation, 418
Forms authentication, 471–472
frame rates
   low, 591
   monitoring, 592–594
FrameworkElement class
   MediaElement deriving from, 482
   Shape class inheriting from, 517
   Silverlight Object Model, 84
   Style property, 219
   System.Windows, 20
free-hand drawing, 258
From/To/By animation
   ColorAnimation, 550–551
   DoubleAnimation, 548–549
   multiple From/To/By animations, 551–553
   overview of, 547–548
   PointAnimation, 550
   StoryBoad, 548
Full-screen display mode, 154–161
   how to activate, 154
   performance and, 603–605
   scaling contents to take advantage of, 159–161
   toggling between Embedded mode and, 155–157
   viewing current screen dimensions, 157–158
function keyword, 78
functions, JavaScript, 78

G

game loops, 598–600
generic.xaml
   built-in style, 450–451
   templating and, 227–232
Geometry objects
   EllipseGeometry, 522
   GeometryGroup, 523–524
   LineGeometry, 523
   overview of, 521–522
   Path class and, 521
   PathGeometry, 524–526
   RectangleGeometry, 522
   System.Windows.Media., 521
GeometryGroup, 523–524
getElementById method, 81
getElementByTagName method, 81
GetPosition method, 253–254
GetScreen method, 279

glyphs, 597–598
graphics. see also animation
   brushes, 526
   DeepZoom, 542–546
   EllipseGeometry, 522
   enlivening ASP.NET, 515–516
   Expression Design for advanced, 129
   Geometry objects, 521–522
   GeometryGroup, 523–524
   Image and BitmapImage, 540–542
   image handling, 540
   ImageBrush, 531–533
   LinearGradientBrush, 528–530
   LineGeometry, 523
   overview of, 515
   Path class, 521
   PathGeometry, 524–526
   Polygon class, 517–519
   Polyline class, 519–521
   RadialGradientBrush, 530–531
   RectangleGeometry, 522
   RotateTransform, 535–536
   ScaleTransform, 537–538
   Shape class, 517
   SkewTransform, 536–537
   SolidColorBrush, 526–528
   summary, 556
   transforms, 535
   TranslateTransform, 539–540
   VideoBrush, 533–534
gray scale colors, 199
Grid layout object, 143–149
   defining columns and rows, 144
   layout options in Silverlight, 132
   layout performance issues, 612
   placing TextBlock objects, 145
   setting row and column properties, 145–146
   sizing Row and Column elements, 146–149
   TABLE HTML element compared with, 143
grids
   DataGrid control (Silverlight), 191–193
   GridView control (ASP.NET), 191–192
GridView control, ASP.NET, 191–192

H

Handled parameter, 245
handwriting, Ink feature, 258
Height property
   drawing in XAML, 41
   MediaElement control, 487
   performance and, 605–606
hinting, 597

hosting computer

hosting page settings overriding Canvas
    properties, 143

local data and, 394–396

UI (user interface) and, 134–136

HTML (HyperText Markup Language)

ASP.NET layouts derived from, 130

challenge of creating rich user interface, 3

Silverlight providing HTML/Managed Code bridge, 5

standards, 10–11

types of data Silverlight can access and process, 286

HTML tables, layout options in ASP.NET, 131

HtmlPage class

Document property, 106

RegisterScriptableObject command, 111–112

System.Windows.Browser namespace, 255, 281

HTTP

polling duplex calls, 286

retrieving images from HTTP locations, 199

WCF polling duplex service, 347–348

HTTP tracers, 570–571

Fiddler, 573–574

Firebug, 575

overview of, 570–571

Web Development Helper, 571–573

HttpWebRequest class, 313–314

HttpWebResponse class, 313–314

HyperlinkButton control, 177–178

I

IDE (Integrated Development Environment), 7–8

IIS (Internet Information Services), 299

Image control

image handling, 540–542

loaded and failed events, 200

overview of, 199

Stretch property, 199–200

image formats, vs. XAML, 606–607

image handling, 540

DeepZoom, 542–546

Image and BitmapImage, 540–542

Image_ImageFailed, 200

ImageBrush object, 531–533, 540–542

ImageSource property, Image control, 540–542

ImplicitStyleManager, 239–241

inheritance

audio/video properties, 498–500

DataContext property and, 375

initialization, of .NET objects, 33

InitializeComponent code, 72–73

Ink feature, 258–263

eraser mode, 262–263

InkPresenter, 259–261

overview of, 258–259

stroke options, 261–262

InkPresenter, 259–261

inline styles

applying, 214–218

defined, 213

limitations of, 218

inline technique, for input validation, 416

input component, of presentation core, 15

input controls

Button control, 176–177

Calendar control, 183–185

CheckBox control, 178–179

DatePicker control, 186–187

HyperlinkButton control, 177–178

list of, 172–173

PasswordBox control, 176

RadioButton control, 179–180

RepeatButton control, 180–182

Silverlight control categories, 168

Slider control, 182–183

TextBlock control, 173–174

TextBox control, 174–176

ToolTip control, 187–188

input devices

drag-and-drop, 263–266

Ink feature, 258–263

keyboard, 257–258

mouse, 250–256

overview of, 250

stylus and touch screens, 256

input validation, 416–418

installed files, Silverlight, 23–24

instantiation

.NET objects, 33

Silverlight applications, 69–71

instrumentation, performance, 591–592

manual timing, 594–596

monitoring frame rate, 592–594

overview of, 591

instrumentation of code, 587

Integrated Development Environment (IDE), 7–8

integration with AJAX, 249–250

integration with ASP.NET, 470–478

application services, 25

authentication, 471, 474–478

communication, 26

composite controls, 25

dynamic generation of XAML from server, 26

membership provider, 471–472

multiple plug-in navigation, 280–282

overview of, 24, 235

integration with ASP.NET *(continued)*
   Profile Provider, 235–239
   Provider model for security, 470–471
   role provider, 471
   role-based security, 472–474
   server controls, 27
integration with DOM, 15–16
intellectual property (IP), 478
IntelliSense
   automating event handler with, 170
   tools for working with XAML, 57
interaction context, Silverlight, 243–244
Internet Information Services (IIS), 299
InteropServices.*, System.Runtime, 18
Interval values, RepeatButton control, 181
IP (intellectual property), 478
IScreen interface, 271
Isolated File Storage API, 469
isolated storage
   local data, 392–394
   security and, 467–469
items controls
   ComboBox control, 195–196
   data templates and, 402
   DataGrid control, 191–193
   list of, 188–189
   ListBox control, 189–191
   Popup control, 196–198
   ScrollViewer control, 193–195
   Silverlight control categories, 168

J

Java Applets, 516
JavaScript
   adding to a page, 77
   conditional statements, 79–80
   DOM (document object model), 77
   DOM manipulation, 80–83
   event handling, 80
   functions, 78
   vs. managed code, 607–611
   overview of, 76–77
   scripts for interacting with properties, 247–248
   Silverlight extensions, 5
   Silverlight integration with AJAX library, 249–250
   validation using dynamic languages, 418
   variables, 78
JavaScript Object Notation (JSON), 249–250
JPEG format, 199, 606
JScript, 77
JSON (JavaScript Object Notation), 249–250
   DataContractJsonSerializer class, 330–332
   overview of, 328–330
   REST and, 310
   serializing/deserializing data, 289
   types of data Silverlight can access and process, 286

K

key frame animation
   color animation using key frame example, 554–555
   KeyFrames collection, 553–554
   overview of, 553
   per-frame animation call back, 555–556
keyboard, 257–258
KeyDown, 257
KeyEventArgs, 257
KeyFrames collection, 553–554
KeyUp, 257

L

Label controls, ASP.NET and Windows Forms, 173
language-integrated query. see LINQ (language-integrated query)
languages, localization and, 162
layout
   ASP.NET options, 130–131
   performance and, 612–613
   process in Silverlight, 133–134
   Silverlight options, 131–132
layout controls
   Canvas control, 136–143
   Grid layout object, 143–149
   Margin property, 151–152
   overview of, 136
   Silverlight control categories, 168
   StackPanel, 150–151
   TabControl, 152–154
lazy load, 64
libraries
   BCL (Base Class Library), 16
   rich control library in Silverlight, 5
   SCL (Silverlight Class Library), 8
   Silverlight integration with AJAX library, 249–250
Line object
   drawing with XAML, 45–46
   Shape class and, 517
LinearGradientBrush, 528–530
LineGeometry, 523
LINQ (language-integrated query), 408–412
   data query mechanism in .NET Framework 3.5, 22
   data-processing options, 288
   dynamic XAML with LINQ, 414–415
   example manipulating data collection with, 410–412

namespaces, 364
new in .NET 3.5, 325
overview of, 408
Silverlight implementation, 409
Silverlight support for, 5
LINQ to objects, 409
LINQ to SQL, 294, 328
LINQ to XML, 412–414
example querying XML data, 412–414
overview of, 412
processing XML data, 325–328
serializing/deserializing data, 288–289
Silverlight support for, 409
list boxes. *see* **ListBox control**
ListBox control
data control namespaces, 364
data templates, 403
data-binding example, 380–381
scrolling capacity of, 194
Silverlight items controls, 189–191
Loaded event, Image control, 200
LoadRunner, Mercury, 581
local data
interacting with hosting computer, 394–396
isolated storage, 392–394
local resources, 388–391
overview of, 388
local resources, 388–391
localizable resources, 389
localization, of Silverlight applications, 161–164
look and feel. *see* **styles**
lookless controls, 224

M

Macromedia Flash, 4
managed code
accessing Content data, 389
adding event handler with, 245
code-behind binding, 373–375
interacting with properties, 246
JavaScript vs., 607–611
manual timing, performance instrumentation, 594–596
Margin property, 151–152
markup extensions, XAML, 38–40
markup views, Expression Blend, 56
mash-up applications, 289
MaxFrameRate, 592–593
measure and arrange algorithm, 133
media
Expression Media for managing media assets, 129–130
media component of presentation core, 13–14
unified media format, 6

media controls
Image control, 199–200
MediaElement control, 200–202
MultiScaleImage control, 203–204
overview of, 198
ProgressBar control, 202–203
Silverlight control categories, 168
System.Windows, 521
Media Server control, ASP.NET, 500–502
MediaElement control
AutoPlay property, 484
developers vs. designers, 590
events, 511–512
Height and Width properties, 487
NaturalDuration property, 486
overview of, 481–482
playback controls, 491–495
Position property, 484–486
SetSource method, 512–513
Silverlight media controls, 200–202
Source property, 483–484
Stream object, 513
streaming services supported, 514
Stretch property, 496–498
VideoBrush and, 533–534
Volume property, 488–490
MediaEnded event, 511
MediaFailed event, 511
membership provider, ASP.NET, 471–472
memory dump, 567
Mercury LoadRunner, 581
Microsoft Application Center Test, 581
Microsoft Deep Zoom Composer tool, 203–204, 544
Microsoft Expression Blend. *see* **Expression Blend**
Microsoft Intermediate Language (MSIL), 478
Microsoft Media Services (mms), 514
Microsoft Silverlight Streaming by Windows Live, 514
Microsoft Trustworthy Computing initiative, 466–467
Microsoft.VisualBasic.dll, 23
Microsoft.Windows.Controls
dll assembly, 205
themes, 239–241
mms (Microsoft Media Services), 514
mobile support, Silverlight features, 5
modal screens, 275–276
mode component, data-binding architecture, 368
Model View Controller (MVC), 365
Model View Presenter (MVP), 365
ModifiersKeys, 258
monitoring frame rate, 592–594
mouse, 250–256
browser and platform compatibility and, 256
capturing, 254, 260–261

mouse *(continued)*
events, 251–252
getting relative positions, 253–254
mouse wheel, 254–256
overview of, 250
triggering storyboards, 252–253
MouseButtonEventArgs, 251
MouseEnter
drag-and-drop and, 266
mouse events, 251–252
MouseEventArgs, 251
MouseLeave
drag-and-drop and, 266
mouse events, 251–252
MouseLeftButtonDown, 251–252
MouseLeftButtonUp
HitTest, 266
mouse events, 251
MouseMove
capturing mouse, 254
overview of, 251
MouseOver, visual states and, 445–446
MP3 format
audio/video formats, 482
MediaElement control, 200
Silverlight support for, 6
mscordaccore.dll, 23
mscordbi.dll, 23
mscorlib.dll, 23
mscorrc.debug.dll, 23
mscorrc.dll, 23
MSIL (Microsoft Intermediate Language), 478
multicore processors, 617
multiple From/To/By animations, 551–553
multiple plug-in navigation
integration with ASP.NET, 280–282
overview of, 280
services for, 282–283
MultiScaleImage control, 203–204
MVC (Model View Controller), 365
MVP (Model View Presenter), 365

N

namespaces
overview of, 363
XAML, 33–34
xmlns command for adding, 375
naming conventions, for user controls, 430
NaturalDuration property, MediaElement control, 486
navigation
ASP.NET environment and, 266–267
multiple plug-in navigation, 280

overview of, 266
single plug-in navigation. *see* single plug-in navigation
nesting, Canvas within Canvas, 138–139
.NET assemblies. *see* assemblies
.NET Framework
ASP.NET Web Services and, 301
code access security, 463–464
data classes, 22
DLR (Dynamic Language Runtime) and, 22–23
elements, 16–17
LINQ support added to, 408
networking, 21–22
role-based security, 463
Silverlight based on subset of, 5
what is included/excluded in Silverlight, 17–18
WPF (Windows Presentation Foundation) and, 18–21
XAML for instantiation and initialization of .NET objects, 33
.NET reflection, 378, 567, 575–576
.NET Reflector Tool, 19
Network Monitor utility, Microsoft, 570
network sockets. *see* sockets
networking, 21–22
ASP.NET. *see* ASP.NET Web Services
built-in features, 285–286
cross-domain calls, 289
WCF service. *see* WCF service
ngen.exe, 478
nodes, JavaScript, 80–81
npctrl.dll, 23

O

obfuscation techniques, 478–479
object models
DOM. *see* DOM (document object model)
Silverlight. *see* Silverlight Object Model
object oriented programming (OOP), 384
OBJECT tags
application instantiation and, 70–71
sizing instructions and, 135–136
object tree, Silverlight Object Model, 85–87
ObjectAnimationUsingKeyFrames, 553
objects
dragging, 264–265
overview of, 36
property syntax, 61
XAML, 36–37
OleView, 16
on-demand XAP loading, 114
OneTime data flow, 369
OneWay data flow, 369
OOP (object oriented programming), 384

Opacity property, 498, 602–603
Open File dialog box, 394
overlapping elements, within Canvas control, 140–142
overriding set styles, 222–223

P

packaging Silverlight applications, 64–66
page
  adding JavaScript to, 77
  basic Silverlight page, 72–76
  setting styles at page level, 219–222
Page.xaml file, 72–76
Panel control, 136
parameter, 383
parent elements
  adding/positioning on Canvas, 139
  control trees for managing, 171
parser, XAML, 618–619
parsing data, 288
parts model
  elements parts, 454–458
  overview of, 454
  visual states parts, 458–459
PasswordBox control, 176
Path class, 521
path component, data-binding architecture, 368
PathGeometry, 524–526
Pause command, MediaElement playback, 202, 491, 495
.pdb (Program Database) files, 567–568
performance, 589–619
  animation and, 597
  bottlenecks, 590–591
  chatty applications, 616–617
  data-binding and, 386–387
  data-related applications and, 613–616
  element reuse, 611
  full screen mode, 603–605
  game loops and, 598–600
  height and width and, 605–606
  improving, 596–597
  instrumentation, 591–592
  JavaScript vs. managed code, 607–611
  layouts and, 612–613
  manual timing, 594–596
  monitoring frame rate, 592–594
  opacity and visibility and, 602–603
  overuse of assemblies and, 427
  overview of, 589
  resources for, 619
  runtime, 617–618
  summary, 619
  text animation and, 597–598

threading and, 607
transparent backgrounds, 601–602
Windowless controls and, 600–601
XAML vs. images, 606–607
per-frame animation call back, 555–556
pixels
  device-independent, 132
  raster graphics and, 597–598
platforms
  client platform, 11–12
  mouse handling properties and, 256
  overview of, 10–11
  server platform, 11
Play command, MediaElement playback, 202, 491, 495
playback control
  ASP.NET, 500–501
  MediaElement, 491–495
PlayReady technology, DRM (Digital Rights Management), 15
plug-ins
  attributes, 70–71
  displaying Silverlight plug-in, 134–136
  multiple plug-in navigation. see multiple plug-in navigation
  single plug-in navigation. see single plug-in navigation
  Windowless controls and, 600–601
PNG format, 199
PointAnimation, 550
PointAnimationUsingKeyFrames, 553
policies
  client access policy for socket server, 343–347
  cross-domain policy files, 290–292
Polygon class, 517–519
Polyline class, 519–521
Popup control, 196–198
Position property, MediaElement control, 484–486
positioning methods, 263–266
POX (Plain Old XML), 310
predefined styles, 218–219
presentation core
  DOM integration component, 15–16
  DRM (Digital Rights Management) component, 14–15
  input component, 15
  media component, 13–14
  overview of, 13
  UI Core, 13
  XAML parser, 13
previews, 245
Primitives.ButtonBase, System.Windows.Controls, 21
problems. see also troubleshooting
  vs. errors, 560
  types of, 560–562

processors
  multicore, 617
  performance issues, 591
Profile Provider, ASP.NET, 235–239
programming languages
  event handling, 171–172
  XAML (eXtensible Application Markup Language) as, 32
programming Silverlight applications
  `BackgroundWorker`, 95–100
  basic Silverlight page, 72–76
  components of Silverlight applications, 63–64
  `DispatcherTimer`, 102–105
  dynamically loading XAML, 87–89
  events, 90–92
  instantiating applications, 69–71
  interacting with browser from Silverlight, 105–110
  interacting with Silverlight from browser, 110–114
  JavaScript and. see JavaScript
  object model base classess, 84–85
  on-demand XAP loading, 114
  overview of, 63
  packaging Silverlight applications, 64–66
  routed events, 92–94
  summary, 116–117
  `System.Net.WebClient`, 114–115
  `System.Windows.Application` class, 66–69
  `System.Windows.Threading`, 100–102
  threading model, 95
  walking object tree, 85–87
`ProgressBar` control, 202–203
projects, creating, 64
properties
  adding/changing in Expression Blend, 124–125
  attached properties, 40–41
  custom controls, 452–454
  managed code for interacting with, 245–246
  scripts for interacting with, 247–248
  stroke options, 261–262
  syntax, 37
  XAML, 36–37
Properties pane, Expression Blend, 127–128
`PropertyPath` , 370
Provider model, ASP.NET
  membership provider, 471–472
  overview of, 470–471
  role provider, 471
  role-based security and, 472–474
proxies, Web Services
  ASP.NET Web Service, 308–310
  creating WCF proxy, 305
  making asynchronous calls with WCF proxy, 305–308

Q

queries, for data retrieval, 408

R

`RadialGradientBrush` control, 530–531
`RadioButton` control, 179–180
raster graphics
  overview of, 132–133
  pixels and, 597–598
reach, Web, 4
Really Simple Syndication (RSS)
  how it works, 333–334
  syndication feed classes, 335–337
receiver class, WCF duplex service, 352–357
`Rectangle` object
  adding to Expression Blend design surface, 124
  adding/positioning elements on `Canvas`, 136–138
  drawing with XAML, 43–45
  overlapping elements on `Canvas`, 142
  `Shape` class and, 517
`RectangleGeometry` object, 522
Red Gate's Reflector tool, 575–576
references
  adding service and web references, 279
  Web Reference support, 57
Reflector tool, Red Gate, 575–576
RegisterScriptableObject command, `HtmlPage` class, 111–112
relative positioning, CSS, 131
remote data
  ADO.NET data services, 399–401
  consuming, 396–399
  overview of, 396
  site-of-origin resources, 396
Remoting, `System.Runtime`, 18
rendering, resolution-independent, 132
`RepeatButton` control, 180–182
Representational State Transfer. see REST (Representational State Transfer)
resolution, 132
resources
  local resources, 388–391
  site-of-origin resources, 396
  `StaticResources` command, 376–377
REST (Representational State Transfer), 310–314
  ADO.NET Data Services and, 399, 400
  development of, 287
  `HttpWebRequest` and `HttpWebResponse` classes, 313–314
  options for calls between Silverlight applications and data repository, 286

Silverlight support for, 22
transforming DataContracts into XML, 399
Web Services and, 310
`WebClient class`, 311–313
reusability
of elements, 611
of user controls, 428
RIAs (Rich Internet Applications)
comparing performance of, 619
Silverlight support for, 4
transforming web application into, 24
rich clients, Web reach compared with, 4
**Rich Internet Applications. *see* RIAs (Rich Internet
Applications)**
Roeder, Lutz, 19
role provider, ASP.NET, 471–472
role-based security
ASP.NET, 472–474
code access security compared with, 463
root elements, of controls, 226
`RotateTransform`, **535–536**
routed events
bubbling routing strategy, 92–94
example of, 171
user interaction and, 245
rows
defining in `Grid`, 144
properties, 145–146
sizing `Row` and `Column` elements, 146–149
RSS (Really Simple Syndication)
how it works, 333–334
syndication feed classes, 335–337
runtime performance, 617–619
runtime problems, 560–561

S

SaaS (Software as a Service), 6
sandbox environment
security and, 467–470
Silverlight running in, 244
`ScaleTransform`, **537–538**
scaling contents, display modes and, 159–161
scenarios
custom controls, 447–448
customizing current controls, 436–437
user controls, 428
SCL (Silverlight Class Library), 8
screen dimensions, 157–158. *see also* display modes
screens on demand, from serve, 276–280
`<script>` **tags, 77**
scripting languages, 77. *see also* JavaScript
scripts, for interacting with properties, 247–248

`ScrollViewer` **control, 193–195**
**Secure by Default, Microsoft Trustworthy Computing
initiative, 467**
**Secure by Deployment, Microsoft Trustworthy
Computing initiative, 467**
**Secure by Design, Microsoft Trustworthy Computing
initiative, 467**
security
class definitions and, 465–466
code access security, 463–464
cross-domain, 470
cryptography, 479
exploitations, 461–462
integration with ASP.NET, 470–478
levels in Silverlight, 464–465
Microsoft Trustworthy Computing initiative, 466–467
obfuscation techniques and tools, 478–479
overview of, 461–479
role-based security, 463
sandbox environment and, 467–470
summary, 479
what you continue to use ASP.NET for, 6–7
SecurityCritical level, Silverlight security levels, 465
**SecuritySafeCritical level, Silverlight security levels,
464–465**
**SecurityTransparent level, Silverlight security levels,
464**
`sender` **parameter, 245**
serializing/deserializing data
ASP.NET Web Services and, 301
`DataContractJsonSerializer` class, 328–329
serialization namespaces, 364
Silverlight options for, 288–289
`System.Runtime`, 24
`XmlSerializer` class, 318–325
server communication, 285–359
ASP.NET. *see* ASP.NET Web Services
client access policy socket server, 343–347
cross-domain support, 289–290
data-processing options, 288–289
domains and URLs supported, 286
Flash cross-domain policy files, 290
JSON data, 328–332
LINQ to XML, 325–328
making RESTful calls, 310–314
options for, 286–288
overview of, 285
RSS and ATOM syndication feeds, 333–335
services for, 292
Silverlight cross-domain policy files, 291–292
sockets for communicating over TCP, 337–338
sockets in a Silverlight client, 340–343
sockets on a server, 338–340

server communication *(continued)*
summary, 343–347
syndication feed classes, 335–337
syndication feeds, 332
WCF duplex service for Silverlight. *see* WCF duplex service for Silverlight
WCF service. *see* WCF service
what types of data are accessible by Silverlight, 286
XML data, 314
`XmlReader` class, 314–318
`XmlSerializer` class, 318–325
server controls, ASP.NET integration with Silverlight, 27
server platform, Silverlight architecture, 11
servers, sockets on, 338–340
server-side pages, referencing, 50–55
service contract, WCF service, 294–295
service factory, WCF duplex service, 350–352
Service Level Agreements (SLAs), 562
services, for multiple plug-in navigation, 282–283
`SetSource` method, 512–513
`Setter` object, 219, 437
`Setter` proprety, `Style` object, 219
shapes
`Ellipse` object, 41–43
`Geometry` objects compared with, 521
`Line` object, 45–46
overview of, 517
overview of `Shape` class, 41
`Polygon` class, 517–519
`Polyline` class, 519–521
`Rectangle` object, 43–45
`Shape` class, as base class, 41
`System.Windows.Shapes`, 517
Silverlight, introduction to
challenge of creating rich user interface, 3–4
development environment, 7–8
high-level features, 4–5
impact on existing ASP.NET applications, 5
overview of, 3
rich client vs. Web reach, 4
summary, 8
what you continue to use ASP.NET for, 6–7
Silverlight Class Library (SCL), 8
Silverlight Object Model
base classess, 84–85
dynamically loading XAML, 87–89
overview of, 84
walking object tree, 85–87
Silverlight resources, 389
Silverlight Tools for Visual Studio 2008
'Add a New ASP.NET Web Project to the Solution to Host Silverlight', 563–564
'Automatically Generate a Test Page to Host Silverlight at Build Time', 564–565

debugging applications with, 566–570
'Link This Silverlight Control into an Existing Web Site', 565–566
overview of, 7
`Silverlight.Configuration.exe`, 23
`Silverlight.ConfigurationUI.dll`, 23
single plug-in navigation
effects for enhancing user navigation, 273–275
overview of, 267–268
screens on demand from server, 276–280
simulation of modal screens, 275–276
transitioning user controls, 268–273
site-of-origin
cross-domain calls and, 289
resources, 396
`SkewTransform`, 536–537
skins. *see also* templating
of controls, 213
customizing current controls, 440–443
example mixing styling and skinning, 443–444
lookless controls, 24
SLAs (Service Level Agreements), 562
`Slider` control
for media volume and balance, 489–490
Silverlight user input controls, 182–183
`slr.dll.managed_manifest`, 24
SMIL (Synchronized Multimedia Integration Language), 516
SOAP (Simple Object Access Protocol)
ASP.NET Web Service proxy and, 309
ASP.NET Web Services and, 301
calling Web Services and, 304
data-processing options, 288
REST and, 310
types of data Silverlight can access and process, 286
SOAP messages, 21
sockets
client access policy for, 343–347
for communicating over TCP, 337–338
on a server, 338–340
in a Silverlight client, 340–343
Software as a Service (SaaS), 6
`SolidColorBrush`, 526–528
`sos.dll`, 23
source component, data-binding architecture, 368
`Source` property, `MediaElement` control, 483–484
SSL, 462
`StackPanel` control
layout options in Silverlight, 132
layout performance issues, 612
orientation setting for `ListBox` control, 191
overview of, 150–151
`ScrollViewer` control and, 193

standards
Expression Web validation, 122
HTML, 10–11
states
`MediaElement` events, 511
visual styles connected to button state, 445–447
static positioning, CSS, 131
`StaticResources` **command, 376–377**
`Stop` **command,** `MediaElement` **playback, 202, 491, 495**
storage. see data storage/retrieval
`StoryBoad` **object, 548**
storyboards
animation contained in `StoryBoard` object, 548
creating new, 59
triggering, 252–253
`Stream` **object,** `MediaElement`**, 513**
streaming media
services, 514
Silverlight features, 5
`Stretch` **property**
`Image` control, 199–200
`MediaElement` control, 496–498
strings, converting string values into object types, 37
strokes
creating new stroke objects, 261
drawing in XAML, 42
modifying properties of, 261–262
`Style` **object**
customizing with, 437
overriding set styles, 222–223
predefined styles, 218–219
`Setter` property, 219
setting styles at page level, 219–222
`Style` **property,** `FrameworkElement` **class, 219**
Style Sheets, 213
styles, 212–224
applying inline styles, 214–218
built-in styles, 451–452
customizing current controls, 437–440
default styles, 438
`ImplicitStyleManager`, 239–241
mixing styling and skinning, 443–444
overriding set styles, 222–223
overview of, 212–213
setters, 219
setting at application level, 223–224
setting at page level, 219–222
specifying in a central location, 218–219
summary, 242
visual styles connected to button state, 445–447
stylus, input devices, 256
`StylusDevice` **property, 256**

`svcutil.exe`**, 294**
symbol files, 567–568
Synchronized Multimedia Integration Language (SMIL), 516
syndication feeds
classes, 335–337
overview of, 332
RSS and ATOM syndication feeds, 333–335
syndication services, 22
`SyndicationFeed`
data-processing options, 289
RSS and ATOM syndication feeds and, 335
`SyndicationItem`**, 335**
syntax
property elements, 37
XAML, 33
`System.Core.dll`**, 23**
`System.Data`**, 17**
`System.Deployment.*`**, 17**
`System.Diagnostic`**, 587**
`system.dll`**, 24**
`System.Net`
Silverlight installed files, 24
`Sockets`, 338, 340
WebClient, 114–115
`System.Object`**, 19**
`System.Runtime`
`InteropServices.*`, 18
`Remoting`, 18
`Serialization`, 24
`Serialization.Json`, 328
`System.Security`
ASP.NET elements omitted from Silverlight 2, 18
CAS functionality, 464
Cryptography, 479
`System.ServiceModel.dll`**, 24**
`System.Windows.Application` **class, 66–69**
`System.Windows.Automation`**, 586**
`System.Windows.Browser` **namespace, 105**
`HTMLPage`, 281
`HtmlPage` class, 255, 281
`System.Windows.Browser.dll`**, 24**
`System.Windows.Controls`
`Button`, 21
`Calendar` and `DatePicker` controls in, 186
`ContentControl`, 20–21
`Control`, 20
`Data`, 403
`Image`, 540–542
`Primitives.ButtonBase`, 21
`System.Windows.DependencyObject` **, 19**
`System.Windows.dll`**, 24**
`System.Windows.FrameworkElement`**, 20**

System.Windows.Media.Geometry, **521**

System.Windows.Shapes.Shape, **517**

System.Windows.Thickness, **151**

System.Windows.Threading, **100–102**

System.Windows.Threading.Dispatcher, **100–102**

System.Windows.UIElement, **20**

System.Xml.dll, **24**

System.Xml.Serialization, **320**

T

TabControl control, **152–154**

tables, HTML

Grid layout object compared with, 143

overview of, 131

TabPanel control, **136, 152**

tags, use of short cut tags, 169

target object, data-binding architecture, 368

target property, data-binding architecture, 368

TargetType **property**

conversions and, 383

custom controls, 452

Style object, 218

styles and, 437

TCP

client access policy for socket server, 343–347

sockets for communicating over, 337–338

TcpClient, **338–340**

TcpListener, **338–340**

TDD (Test Driven Development)

overview of, 576

UI testing, 581–586

unit testing, 576–581

TemplateBinding **syntax, 232–234, 441–442**

templates

data templates, 402–403

ListBox control, 189–190

summary, 242

tools for working with XAML, 57

TemplateVisualState, **458**

templating

ControlTemplate class, 224

customzing with skins, 440–443

generic.xaml, 227–232

lookless cotnrol, 224

overview of, 224

TemplateBinding syntax, 232–234

using, 225–227

VisualState objects, 224–225

terminology, XAML, 33

text animation, performance and, 597–598

TextBlock

adding to Expression Blend design surface, 126

adding to page, 58–59

ASP.NET, 173

creating user control with, 271

layout process in Silverlight, 133–134

overview of, 173–174

placing in Grid, 145

scaling contents to take advantage of screen modes, 157–161

TextBox

applying inline styles to, 214–215

keyboard input and, 257

multiple Style objects and, 222

overview of, 174–176

themes

ASP.NET, 214

Microsoft.Windows.Controls, 239–241

Thickness, System.Windows, **151**

threading model, 95–105

BackgroundWorker, 95–100

DispatcherTimer, 102–105

overview of, 95

performance and, 607

System.Windows.Threading, 100

System.Windows.Threading.Dispatcher, 100–102

threat modeling, 462

timeline

animations and, 547

creating new, 59

timeline markers

Expression Encoder, 504–506

overview of, 503

via code, 506–510

Windows Media File editor, 503–504

timers, DispatcherTimer, **102–105**

ToggleButton **base class, 178, 179**

Toolbox, Visual Studio 2008, 205

toolkit, for troubleshooting, 562

Fiddler, 573–574

Firebug, 575

HTTP tracers, 570–571

Red Gate's Reflector tool, 575–576

Visual Studio 2008 as debugger, 563–566

Web Development Helper, 571–573

toolkit controls

AutoCompleteBox control, 206–207

Chart control, 210–212

list of, 205–206

TreeView control, 208–210

WrapPanel control, 207–208

tools, XAML, 56–57

ToolTip **control, 187–188**

touch screens, 256

Transform
overview of, 535
`RotateTransform`, 535–536
`ScaleTransform`, 537–538
`SkewTransform`, 536–537
`TranslateTransform`, 539–540
TranslateTransform, 539–540
transparent backgrounds, 601–602
TreeView control, 208–210
troubleshooting, 559–587
debugging applications, 566–570
exception handling, 586–587
Fiddler, 573–574
Firebug, 575
HTTP tracers, 570–571
instrumentation of code, 587
overview of, 559–560
Red Gate's Reflector tool, 575–576
summary, 587
toolkit for, 562
types of problems, 560–562
UI testing, 581–586
unit testing, 576–581
Visual Studio 2008 as debugger, 563–566
Web Development Helper, 571–573
truecolor, Image control, 199
TwoWay binding mode
conversions and, 382
data flow and, 369
data-binding example, 381
type converters, XAML, 37–38
Type Library, 16

U

UI (user interface)
animation and graphics and, 516
`Canvas` control, 136–143
challenge of creating rich user interface, 3–4
customization scenario, 436
display modes, 154
Embedded display mode, 154
Expression Blend, 123–129
Expression Design, 129
Expression Encoder, 130
Expression Media, 129–130
Expression Studio, 130
Expression Suite compared with Visual Studio, 121–122
Expression Web, 122
Full-screen display mode, 154–161
`Grid` layout object, 143–149
hosting plug-in and, 134–136

layout controls, 136
layout option in ASP.NET, 130–131
layout option in Silverlight, 131–132
layout process in Silverlight, 133–134
localization, 161–164
`Margin` property, 151–152
overview of, 121
resolution-independent rendering, 132
`StackPanel`, 150–151
summary, 165–166
`TabControl`, 152–154
unresponsive due to bottleneck, 591
vector graphics, 132–133
UI Core, 13
UI testing, 581–586
UI Virtualization, 616
UIElement
handling user interaction, 244–245
layout of child elements and, 613
`MediaElement` deriving from, 498–500
mouse and, 250
overview of, 244
`Shape` class inheriting from, 517
Silverlight Object Model, 84
styles, 436
`System.Windows`, 20
Uniform Resource Indicators (URIs), 483
Uniform Resource Locators (URLs), 33
unit testing, 576–581
updates, Silverlight, 28–29
URIs (Uniform Resource Identifiers), 483
REST and, 287
URLs (Uniform Resource Locators), 33
REST and, 287
supported by Silverlight, 286
user controls. *see also* **user interaction**
adding to project, 429–430
basic Silverlight page, 72
benefits of, 425
creating, 429
customizing, 431–434
deploying, 427
loading at runtime, 48
loading screens on demand from server, 276–280
overview of, 423–424
scenarios for use of, 428
in Silverlight, 426–427
transitioning for navigation, 268–273
XAML root element, 33–34
user input controls
`Button` control, 176–177
`Calendar` control, 183–185
`CheckBox` control, 178–179

user input controls *(continued)*
  `DatePicker` control, 186–187
  `HyperlinkButton` control, 177–178
  list of, 172–173
  `PasswordBox` control, 176
  `RadioButton` control, 179–180
  `RepeatButton` control, 180–182
  Silverlight control categories, 168
  `Slider` control, 182–183
  `TextBlock` control, 173–174
  `TextBox` control, 174–176
  `ToolTip` control, 187–188
user interaction, 243–283
  AJAX and, 249–250
  consuming properties, 245–246
  dependency properties, 247
  drag-and-drop, 263–266
  effects for enhancing user navigation, 273–275
  handling, 244–245
  Ink feature, 258–263
  with input devices, 250
  integration with ASP.NET, 280–282
  keyboard, 257–258
  mouse, 250–256
  multiple plug-in navigation, 280
  navigation in ASP.NET environment, 266–267
  overview of, 243
  screens on demand from server, 276–280
  scripts for interacting with properties, 247–248
  services for, 282–283
  Silverlight interaction context, 243–244
  simulation of modal screens, 275–276
  single plug-in navigation, 267–268
  stylus and touch screens, 256
  summary, 282–283
  `UIElements` events, 244
  user control transition for navigation, 268–273
user interface. *see* **UI (user interface)**
`UserControl.` *see* **user controls**

V

validation
  data-binding validation, 419–420
  dynamic languages and, 418–419
  input validation, 416–418
  overview of, 416
  standards validation in Expression Web, 122
`value` **parameter, 383**
`var` **keyword, 78**
variables, JavaScript, 78
vector graphics
  drawing objects with, 129
  Expression Blend and, 56

  raster graphics compared with, 132–133
  XAML vs. images, 606–607
video formats, 201, 482. *see also* **audio/video**
`VideoBrush, 533–534`
viewport, scrolling area, 193
`Visibility` **property, 602–603, 605**
visual customization, 435–436
visual state management, 445–447
Visual State Manager, 454, 459
visual states parts, parts model, 458–459
Visual Studio 2008
  `Add Service References` tool, 308–309
  configuring WCF service, 298–299
  creating new Silverlight project, 58
  creating proxy object for Web Service calls, 286
  as debugger, 563–566
  debugging applications with, 566–570
  editing code and, 56–57
  Expression Suite compared with, 121–122
  as IDE for Silverlight, 7–8
  interoperability with Expression Blend, 56, 59
  project explorer, 424
  support for creating ASP.NET Web Services, 301
  tools for working with XAML, 56–57
Visual Studio Test Edition (Web Testing), 581
`VisualState` **objects, 224–225**
`VisualStateManager`, **445**
`Volume` **property,** `MediaElement` **control, 488–490**

W

W3C (World Wide Web Consortium)
  animation standards, 516
  Expression Web compliance with, 122
  HTML standards, 10–11
WCF (Windows Communication Foundation)
  authentication and, 474–475
  .NET Framework and, 17
  networking and, 21
  overview of, 292–293
  service for consuming remote data, 397
  traditional data handling and, 408
WCF duplex service for Silverlight
  contracts for, 347–348
  creating receiver class, 352–357
  creating service, 348–349
  creating service factory, 350–352
  overview of, 347
  processing data using `XmlSerializer` class, 357–359
WCF service
  calling with Silverlight, 304–305
  configuring, 298–299
  creating, 295–298

creating WCF proxy, 305
data contract, 293–294
making asynchronous calls with WCF proxy, 305–308
overview of, 293
self-hosted, 299–301
service contract, 294–295
Web Development Helper, 571–573
Web reach, 4
Web Reference support, 57
Web Service Description Language (WSDL), 286, 301
Web Services
ASP.NET. *see* ASP.NET Web Services
consuming remote data, 397
networking and, 21
options for calls between Silverlight applications and
    data repository, 286
options for data exchange, 287–288
overview of, 292
REST and, 310
WCF duplex service for Silverlight, 348–349
WCF service. *see* WCF service
web tracing tools. *see* **HTTP tracers**
web user controls, 424
`WebClient` **class, 311–313**
`WebClient` **class,** `System.Net`**, 114–115**
`WebGetAttribute` **class, 299**
`WebMethods`**, ASP.NET Web Services, 302–303**
WF (Windows Workflow Foundation), 17
white space handling, XAML, 34–36
`Width` **property**
drawing in XAML, 41
`MediaElement` control, 487
performance and, 605–606
Windowless controls, 600–601
Windows Communication Foundation. *see* **WCF**
    (Windows Communication Foundation)
Windows Forms, 202
Windows Media Audio. *see* **WMA (Windows Media**
    Audio) format
Windows Media Digital Rights Management
    (WMDRM), 14–15
Windows Media File editor, 503–504
Windows Media Metafiles, 482
Windows Media Video. *see* **WMV (Windows Media**
    Video) format
Windows Presentation Foundation. *see* **WPF (Windows**
    Presentation Foundation)
Windows Workflow Foundation (WF), 17
WinForms, 95
WMA (Windows Media Audio) format
audio/video formats, 482
`MediaElement` control, 200–201
Silverlight support for, 6

WMDRM (Windows Media Digital Rights
    Management), 14–15
WMV (Windows Media Video) format
audio/video formats, 482
DRM and, 14
`MediaElement` control, 200–201
Silverlight support for, 6
World Wide Web Consortium. *see* **W3C (World Wide**
    Web Consortium)
WPF (Windows Presentation Foundation)
customization and, 437
data binding and, 386
`ImplicitStyleManager`, 239–241
navigation services, 267
.NET Framework and, 17
overview of, 18–21
routed events and, 92
runtime performance and, 617
styles, 440
threading model, 95
WPF-like graphics in Silverlight, 5
XAML at heart of, 32
XAML parser and, 13
`WrapPanel` **control, 207–208**
WSDL (Web Service Description Language), 286, 301

X

X and Y coordinates
drawing in XAML, 45
`GetPosition` method, 253–254
positioning elements with, 136
x objects, LINQ to XML, 413
XAML (eXtensible Application Markup Language),
    31–62
applying inline styles, 214–215
attached properties, 40–41
child objects in, 269
code behind and, 46–49
data-binding, 375–377
defining controls, 169–170
developers knowing basics of, 31–32
drawing basics, 41
dynamic XAML with LINQ, 414–415
dynamically generating, 26
dynamically loading, 49–50, 87–89
element reuse and, 611
`Ellipse` object, 41–43
example, 57–62
function of XAML parser, 13
vs. images, 606–607
`Line` object, 45–46
local resources, 389
markup extensions, 38–40

XAML (eXtensible Application Markup Language)
    (continued)
  namespaces, 33–34
  object and property elements, 36–37
  overview of, 31
  parser, 618–619
  as programming language, 32
  `Rectangle` object, 43–45
  referencing server-side page that dynamically creates
      XAML, 50–55
  Silverlight user interface defined in, 6
  syntax and terminology, 33
  tools for working with, 56–57
  type converters, 37–38
  white space, 34–36
.xaml file, 72–76
XAP files
  caching, 401
  local data and, 388
  on-demand XAP loading, 114
  retrieving images from, 199
`x:class` attribute, 72
`XDocument` object, 325–326, 413
XHTML+SMIL, 516
`x:Key`
  applying unique key to `Style` object, 218–219
  multiple styles and, 222
  styles and, 439
XML (Extensible Markup Language)
  ASP.NET Web Services and, 301
  binding from, 415
  LINQ to XML features, 22, 412–414
  namespaces, 363–364
  processing XML data, 314
  types of data Silverlight can access and process, 286
  XML visualization tools in Expression Web, 122
  `XmlReader` class, 314–318
  `XmlSerializer` class, 318–325
XML Paper Specification (XPS), 31
XML schemas, 294
`XmlHttpRequest` object, 289
`Xml.Linq`, 363
`xmlns` attribute, 33

`xmlns` command, 375
`XmlPreloadedResolver`, 364
`XmlReader` class
  data-processing options, 288–289
  processing XML data and, 314–318
  Silverlight data classes, 22
`XmlReaderSettings`, 363
`XmlResolver`, 363
`XmlSerializer` class
  data-processing options, 288–289
  processing data using, 357–359
  server communication of XML data, 318–325
`XmlWriter` class, 288
`XmlXapResolver`, 364
`x:Name`
  defining control names, 169
  `MediaElement` control and, 483
  property, 74
`XNamespace`, 413
XPS (XML Paper Specification), 31
`xsd.exe`, 320, 358
XSLT (Extensible Stylesheet Language
    Transformation)
  LINQ and, 364
  real-time standarads validation in Expression Web,
    122

Y

y coordinates. *see* **X and Y coordinates**

Z

ZIP packages, 64
zooming
  Deep Zoom, 203–204, 542–546
  `MultiScaleImage` control, 203$>, 413
XPS (XML Paper Specification), 31
`xsd.exe`, **320, 358**
XSLT (Extensible Stylesheet Language
    Transformation)
  LINQ and, 364
  real-time standards validation in Expression Web, 122